Springer Series in Cognitive Development

Series Editor
Charles J. Brainerd

Springer Series in Cognitive Development

Series Editor: Charles J. Brainerd
(recent titles)

Adult Cognition: An Experimental Psychology of Human Aging
Timothy A. Salthouse

Recent Advances in Cognitive-Developmental Theory: Progress in Cognitive
Development Research
Charles J. Brainerd (Ed.)

Learning in Children: Progress in Cognitive Development Research
Jeffrey Bisanz/Gay L. Bisanz/Robert Kail (Eds.)

Cognitive Strategy Research: Psychological Foundations
Michael Pressley/Joel R. Levin (Eds.)

Cognitive Strategy Research: Educational Applications
Michael Pressley/Joel R. Levin (Eds.)

Equilibrium in the Balance: A Study of Psychological Explanation
Sophie Haroutunian

Crib Speech and Language Play
Stan A. Kuczaj, II

Discourse Development: Progress in Cognitive Development Research
Stan A. Kuczaj, II (Ed.)

Cognitive Development in Atypical Children: Progress in Cognitive Development
Research
Linda S. Siegel/Frederick J. Morrison (Eds.)

Basic Processes in Memory Development: Progress in Cognitive Development Research
Charles J. Brainerd/Michael Pressley (Eds.)

Cognitive Learning and Memory in Children: Progress in Cognitive Development
Research
Michael Pressley/Charles J. Brainerd (Eds.)

The Development of Word Meaning
Stan A. Kuczaj, II/Martyn D. Barrett (Eds.)

Formal Methods in Developmental Psychology: Progress in Cognitive Development
Research
Jeffrey Bisanz/Charles J. Brainerd/Robert Kail (Eds.)

Children's Counting and Concepts of Number
Karen C. Fuson

Karen C. Fuson

Children's Counting and Concepts of Number

Springer-Verlag
New York Berlin Heidelberg
London Paris Tokyo

Karen C. Fuson
School of Education and Social Policy
Northwestern University
Evanston, Illinois 60208
USA

Series Editor
Charles J. Brainerd
Program in Educational Psychology
University of Arizona
Tuscon, Arizona 85715
USA

With 7 Illustrations

Library of Congress Cataloging-in-Publication Data
Fuson, Karen C.
  Children's counting and concepts of number.
  (Springer series in cognitive development)
  Bibliography: p.
  Includes index.
  1. Counting 2. Number concepts. I. Title
II. Series.
QA113.F87 1987   513'.2   87-16460
ISBN 0-387-96566-1

Typeset by Best-set Typesetter, Ltd., Hong Kong.
Printed and bound by R.R. Donnelley and Sons, Harrisonburg, Virginia.
Printed in the United States of America.

9 8 7 6 5 4 3 2 1
ISBN 0-387-96566-1 Springer-Verlag New York Berlin Heidelberg
ISBN 3-540-96566-1 Springer-Verlag Berlin Heidelberg New York

To my family

Series Preface

For some time now, the study of cognitive development has been far and away the most active discipline within developmental psychology. Although there would be much disagreement as to the exact proportion of papers published in developmental journals that could be considered cognitive, 50% seems like a conservative estimate. Hence, a series of scholary books to be devoted to work in cognitive development is especially appropriate at this time.

The *Springer Series in Cognitive Development* contains two basic types of books, namely, edited collections of original chapters by several authors, and original volumes written by one author or a small group of authors. The flagship for the Springer Series is a serial publication of the "advances" type, carrying the subtitle *Progress in Cognitive Development Research*. Volumes in the *Progress* sequence are strongly thematic, in that each is limited to some well-defined domain of cognitive-developmental research (e.g., logical and mathematical development, semantic development). All *Progress* volumes are edited collections. Editors of such books, upon consultation with the Series Editor, may elect to have their works published either as contributions to the *Progress* sequence or as separate volumes. All books written by one author or a small group of authors will be published as separate volumes within the series.

A fairly broad definition of cognitive development is being used in the selection of books for this series. The classic topics of concept development, children's thinking and reasoning, the development of learning, language development, and memory development will, of course be included. So, however, will newer areas such as social-cognitive development, educational applications, formal modeling, and philosophical implications of cognitive-developmental theory. Although it is anticipated that most books in the series will be empirical in orientation, theoretical and philosophical works are also welcome. With books of the latter sort, heterogeneity of theoretical perspective is encouraged, and no attempt will be made to foster some specific theoretical perspective at the expense of others (e.g., Piagetian versus behavioral or behavioral versus information processing).

C.J. Brainerd

Preface

My earliest number research focused on the activity of counting objects by preschoolers and on the more efficient and sophisticated counting procedures primary school children spontaneously invent and use to solve addition problems. It quickly became clear that children's use of the sequence of number words changed radically over this age span. The sequence changed from being a rote list of words paired with objects to being a representational tool used in flexible and generative ways to solve addition and subtraction situations. This change depended upon changes in children's ability to relate counting and concepts of cardinality. Counting and cardinality first had to become related for children so that counting produced cardinal knowledge. Counting of objects was then used for a considerable period of time to solve addition and subtraction problems. Gradually, however, this object counting became abbreviated and abstracted from the objects so that the number words themselves became the "objects" that represented the addition or subtraction situation. Thus, over this age span, the sequence, counting, and cardinal meanings of number words became increasingly closely related and eventually became integrated.

A primary purpose of this book is to trace these changes across the age span of 2 through 8. My work has necessarily concentrated in certain areas, so parts of this age span can be described only sketchily. Work by others is similarly concentrated in some areas, so the reviews of related literature can only fill in certain spots. An attempt is made nevertheless to describe changes in children's number-word sequences and in relationships between counting and cardinal meanings from single set situations through fairly complex cardinal operations (multidigit addition and subtraction) and cardinal relations (Piagetian operational equivalence and order relations). These developmental frameworks hopefully will provide a working context within which research on the sketchier parts can proceed but be easily related to past results and to concurrent efforts by other investigators. I hope that readers will leave the book both understanding a considerable amount about some specific aspects of children's counting and numerical thinking and with some notion of the overall kinds of changes children's thinking and performance undergo over the years 2 through 8.

Number concepts from age 2 through 8 provide a very interesting research arena. The mathematical concepts and behaviors are fairly well-defined, so one can concentrate on trying to understand how children are thinking in these numerical situations. The concepts are important, for they are formative concepts in mathematical thinking. The educational centrality of these concepts is widely accepted, so research results may lead fairly readily to instructional research. Development of these concepts is related both to linguistic development and to several aspects of general cognitive development. This book then may be of interest to readers from a wide range of backgrounds: cognitive development, education, and linguistics. Chapter summaries have been written to enable readers with varying backgrounds to obtain an overview of each chapter. Because the book was already so long, discussions of extensions to instruction and to many cognitive developmental issues have had to be curtailed. However, many readers will be able to make these extensions fairly readily.

This book was written with the intellectual, practical, and psychological support of many individuals. I feel fortunate that this area has had and continues to have such competent and professional people working in it. My own thinking and writing has benefited enormously over the years from the work of, and conversations with, many other researchers in this area. Some of these graciously agreed to react to earlier versions of one or more chapters of this book: Arthur Baroody, Charles Brainerd, Diane Briars, Tom Carpenter, Paul Cobb, Douglas Frye, Herbert Ginsburg, James Hall, Kevin Miller, John Richards, Walter Secada, Robert Siegler, and James Stigler. The book was improved in major ways by revisions stemming from their comments. Several graduate students have stimulated and contributed to my thinking over the years: Diane Briars, Birch Burghardt, Youngshim Kwon, Barb Lyons, Gerry Pergament, and Walter Secada. Many analyses reported here were carefully and intelligently carried out by Diane Briars, Walter Secada, and Gordon Willis. Work-study students for many years carefully scored, coded, and entered data of various kinds with meticulous care and continuing enthusiasm for the various projects in which we were engaged; these included Richard Ames, Tom Ciaglo, Thue Hoang, Fred Karr, Tracy Klein, Lloyd Kohler, Norman Lao, Krista Peterson, Arlene Siavelis, and Luann Troxel. Many undergraduates collected data from children and/or coded videotaped data, taking independent studies and being rewarded only by their learning about children: Kathy Amoroso, Holly Arnowitz, Patty Bloom, Steve Cieslewicz, Chris Daley, Del Flaherty, Sue Ivanov, Pui Ling Lee, Lisa Montgomery, Steven Myers, Joanne Murabito, Virginia Neal, Sharon Nussbaum, Debbie Rubins, Karen Simon, Sherri Weinstein, and Toya Wyatt. Pat Gaul, Joan LeBuhn, and Pat Terando patiently and capably typed tables, typed revisions, and checked references. And of course, special thanks to my cheerful Macintosh, who allowed me to type in all sorts of positions and places (even outdoors) and always greeted me with a smile no matter how early or how late work began.

Many schools and preschools in Chicago, Evanston, Glenview, Wilmette, and Highland Park have participated over the years in the studies reported or summarized here; understanding preschool directors and school principals, patient and supportive teachers, and children willing to share their mathematical thinking with us have made most of this research productive and enjoyable. Special thanks go to Betty Weeks and the National College of Education Demonstration School for continual interest and support of our efforts, to the Walt Disney Magnet School for supporting counting, conservation, and addition research over two years, and to the wonderful teachers on the primary teams at Lincoln and Orrington Schools in Evanston for three years of intensive involvement in addition and subtraction research. The school-based research could not have been carried out without the sensitive and organized field liaison work of Maureen Hanrahan and the intelligent and careful interviewing and data analysis of Gordon Willis.

Financial support for some of the research reported here was provided by the National Science Foundation and the National Institute of Education under Grant No. SED 78-22048 and Grant No. SED 78-17365, the AMOCO Foundation, a Spencer Foundation grant, and a Spencer National Academy of Education Fellowship. Any opinions, findings, and conclusions or recommendations expressed in this publication are those of the author and do not necessarily reflect the views of the National Science Foundation, the National Institute of Education, the AMOCO Foundation, or the Spencer Foundation.

Finally, I could not have completed the research, let alone write this book, without the continual understanding of my family over the years. My daughters Adrienne and Erica revealed many aspects of children's thinking to me and have consistently provided warm and interesting interactions, enabling me to return to my work renewed. Their childhoods have enriched my life and provided some sense of balance when work threatened to become all. The research on which the book is based and the writing of the book benefited enormously from the intellectual and psychological support of my husband, James Hall. He forced me to struggle for clarity of design, thought, and expression; patiently put up with very long hours of work on my part; and cooked at least 4,000 meals to keep all of us going. His humor has lightened our days, helping the six of us to become a 70s "blended" family (his two, my two, we two): the older sisters Julie and Adrienne, the blonde youngers Dan and Erica, and los padres. Of course ultimate thanks go to my own parents, for I would not have been prepared to tackle these issues without their early direction and support. My father encouraged my mathematical interests and helped me apply to and attend National Science Foundation summer institutes for high school students, my mother found Oberlin for me, and together they provided a wonderful supportive home.

Evanston, Illinois   Karen C. Fuson

Contents

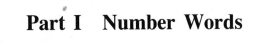

Part I   Number Words

1. Introduction and Overview of Different Uses of Number Words

1.1. Introduction

Number words are special kinds of words. The aspect of a situation described by a number word is not obvious. Understanding the many uses of number words requires many different conceptual structures. These conceptual structures are built over a number of years and move from quite simple to quite complex. Children's increasing ability to use number words correctly provides an interesting domain of study in which cognitive development, language, and procedural activity overlap.

Partly for this reason there has been a considerable amount of research in the past 15 years on children's understanding of numerical concepts and on their ability to carry out numerical procedures such as counting. This research has been conducted by people from different fields: cognitive science, developmental psychology, educational psychology, experimental psychology, and mathematics education. Many talented people have worked in this area, and there is now a considerable accumulation of information. However, the literature presently suffers from two limitations. First, the different kinds of literature remain somewhat separate, with increasing but still incomplete cross-referencing among them. Second, some terms are used in mathematically incorrect ways, particularly the terms "ordinal," "ordering," and "order relations." These differing uses of terms add quite unnecessary confusion to this area, limiting the extent to which studies can build upon one another. One goal of this book is to alleviate these limitations. First, throughout the book, the literature reviewed is drawn from all areas and findings from these areas are integrated. Also, new data and new conceptual analyses are presented, and these reflect a range of methodologies drawn from these areas: experiments, interviews, task analyses, and brief instructional intervention studies. Second, much of this chapter is devoted to providing a framework of possible uses of number words within which future research can function. Mathematically different number-word situations are identified, and the attributes of these situations are discussed. This framework will then allow research results to build on one another and provide cumulative and related knowledge.

The ultimate aim of my own work in this area is to improve the numerical learning experiences of young children in the home, preschools, and schools. However, in order to do this, I believe that we must understand the ordinary developmental sequence of concepts and procedures children come to use in different number-word situations. Once this is known we can then try to provide experiences that will maximize the opportunity of children to learn this sequence. Toward this aim this book traces developmental sequences in several different number-word situations. Such a sequential emphasis necessarily must isolate what younger children do not understand and/or cannot do while demonstrating that older children have such competencies. Therefore, it seems important to emphasize that reflection on my own data and on the data available elsewhere indicates that young children throughout the age range covered in this book, from age 2 to 8, demonstrate very considerable competence in the numerical domain. Numerical concepts are very abstract and become quite complex; children of these ages who have reasonable opportunities to learn these concepts show really quite amazing competence in their use of number words.

1.2. Number-Word Situations: Different Uses of Number Words

Number words are used in a variety of mathematically different situations with a concomitant variety of different external referents accompanied by different internal meanings. Children must come to learn both the number words themselves and these various situational uses of number words. Assessing children's understanding of these different uses is complicated by the fact that in English the same number word is used to refer to several different meanings. Adults understand all of these meanings and can shift among them with ease. However, a child may use a number word with only one of its meanings and may not know other meanings of that word or may not be able to shift easily among various meanings of that word. An important development throughout the age range traced by this book (age 2 to 8) is the inceasing ability to shift among meanings and, finally, to integrate several of these meanings. Adults shift so easily and have such integrated meanings that it is difficult for adults even to comprehend how separate these meanings are for young children.

In order to understand the learning task that faces the young English-speaking child in the domain of number words, it is necessary to ascertain what these various uses of number words are. These uses, the nature of the object situation in which each use occurs, and relations or operations for each use are presented in Table 1-1; the uses are not listed in the order in which they are learned. The first three uses of number words given in Table 1-1 are numerical uses: the meaning of the number word is a cardinal number, an ordinal number, or a measure number. The next two uses require the utterance of the conventional sequence of number words, either without (sequence situations) or with correspondences with entities (counting situations). Another kind of use is for reading symbols (numerals); these symbols may refer to any of the first five uses. Finally, number words are also used as labels in nonnumerical or quasi-numerical situations. Each of these uses are discussed in this chapter.

1.2.1. Cardinal, Ordinal, and Measure Uses

The entities in a cardinal situation are discrete. The cardinal number word refers to the whole set of entities and tells how many entities there are, that is, describes the manyness of the set. In an ordinal situation the entities are discrete and ordered (a linear ordering exists on the entities); the ordinal number word tells the relative position of one entity with respect to the other ordered entities. In a measure situation the entity to be measured is a continuous quantity (e.g., length, area, volume, time). A unit for that kind of quantity must be selected (e.g., a centimeter, a square mile, a cubic decimeter, a swing of a pendulum 1 m in length) and repeatedly applied to the particular

Table 1-1. Uses of Number Words

Uses of number words	Object situation	Ordering already exist?	Units exist?	Referent	Describes	Equivalence relation	Order relations	Operations[a]
Cardinal	Discrete entities	No	Perceptual unit items[b]	Whole set of entities	The manyness of the set	Same number as	More than, fewer than	+, − of whole numbers
Ordinal	Discrete entities	Yes	Perceptual unit items[b]	One entity within a set	The relative position of that entity[c]	Same relative position[d]	Ahead of, behind in the ordering[d]	+, − of ordinal numbers[e]
Measure	A continuous quantity	No	Unit of that continuous quantity	The continuous quantity	The manyness of the units that cover (fill) the quantity	Same amount	More than, less than	+, − of whole numbers, decimals, fractions
Sequence	None	Yes	Developmental changes in these (see chapter 2)	No reference	Nothing	The same word	After/before just after/just before	Sequence words taken as the sets for +, − of whole numbers
Counting	Discrete entities[f]	No[g]	Perceptual unit items[h]	Each entity	Nothing	None[i]	None[i]	None

Symbolic (numeral)	A symbol	No	No	That symbol; may also refer to one of the other uses	That symbol; whatever the use of the symbol is[j]	Only if interpreted as cardinal or measure	Only if interpreted as cardinal or measure	Only if interpreted as cardinal or measure
Nonnumerical labels or series	A single entity	No[k]	No	That entity	Various attributes of an entity	No[k]	No[k]	No[k]

[a] We deal here only with the two simplest operations, addition and subtraction.

[b] Perceptual unit items are the first unit items used in this situation. Children eventually come to use other unit items in this situation (see chapters 8, 9, and 11).

[c] An ordinal number word describes the position of a given entity with respect to the other entities in the set; this relative position is derived from the ordering on the set.

[d] The particular words used to describe the relation will depend on the kind of ordering on the entities.

[e] See text for explanations.

[f] These can be the units used in a measure situation.

[g] An ordering must be established by the counter during the activity of counting, but this ordering may be established over time and may not be able to be reconstructed at the end of counting.

[h] An early "precounting" may occur in which objects are not taken as perceptual unit items, but the number words do refer in a general unspecified way to the objects.

[i] Equivalence and order relations could be established, based on the ordering of the objects, but such relations are rarely established. The relations on cardinal, ordinal, measure, or sequence number words are used instead.

[j] For example, if the symbol has a cardinal use, the symbol will describe the manyness of the cardinal set.

[k] An ordering, relation, or operation may exist, but it is not crucial to the nonnumerical use (see text).

continuous quantity until the quantity is used up. The measure number word tells how many units are required to cover (fill) the continuous quantity.

Units also are required in cardinal and ordinal situations, although they are less obvious than in a measure situation. In a given cardinal or ordinal situation, one must decide which discrete entities are to be taken as part of that situation. These entities can be quite heterogeneous. For example one can consider a container of yogurt, a plastic spoon, an orange, a napkin, and two peanut butter cookies to be the entities and ask a question about those entities as a cardinal situation (e.g., "How many things did I put in the lunch sack?") or as an ordinal situation (e.g., "Which thing did I put in third?"). To convert the quite different entities in the lunch sack to a cardinal or an ordinal situation, one has to consider each entity as a separate and equivalent item, ignoring their different characteristics and focusing only on their characteristic of being a discrete unity. Steffe, von Glasersfeld, Richards, and Cobb (1983) have made this distinction for entities that are counted and call such a conceptual discrete unit taken from a perceived entity a "perceptual unit item." We will adopt this term and use it for cardinal and ordinal situations also. This discussion about units in cardinal and ordinal situations makes clear the fact that, although the units in a measure situation may have to be used to cover (or fill up) the actual quantity, these units must also be mentally considered as units by a perceiver in order for that situation to be a measure situation for that perceiver.

The cardinal and measure situations each also require another conceptual operation in order to be considered a cardinal or measure situation. In a cardinal situation the separate entities (the perceptual unit items) in the situation must be conceptually unified into a single whole in order for the cardinal number word to refer to that single whole. We will call this conceptual operation "cardinal integration."[1] Likewise, a measure situation requires a conceptual unifying of all the measure units into a single continuous quantity; we will call this conceptual operation "measure integration."

Any two cardinal situations, two ordinal situations, or two measure situations can be related by an equivalence relation or by one of two order relations. The equivalence and order relations differ for each of these situations (although most of the words used for the cardinal and measure order relations are the same). For any two cardinal situations, one situation has the same number as, more than, or fewer than the other situation. For any two measure situations, one situation has the same amount as, more than, or less than the other situation. The actual words used to describe the relation in an ordinal situation will depend on the nature of the ordering on that situation. Equivalence and order relations are not used very frequently to compare ordinal situations in ordinary life, and the words are sometimes a bit awk-

---

[1] Steffe et al. (1983) used the term "integration" for a cardinal unifying in a more complex addition situation discussed in chapter 8. We have adopted this term but use it with prefixes throughout the book in order to differentiate it from the original special use.

ward. For example, if the ordinal situations were the order in which two children put entities into their lunch sacks, a child could say, "We put our yogurts in our sacks at the same place in our orders" or "I put my yogurt in my sack earlier [in my order] than you did [in your order]," or "I put my yogurt in my sack later [in my order] than you did [in your order]." These uses "earlier than" and "later than" do not, of course, refer to the actual time at which the yogurt was put in the sack, because time is a continuous quantity and a comparison of times thus involves an order relation on two measures situations. If the ordinal situations involve two older siblings, each standing in a different line of people at the grocery store, one sibling could compare their relative positions in the two lines by saying. "We're in the same places in our lines," or, "I am closer to the front of my line than you are to the front of your line," or "I am farther behind in my line than you are in your line." Many different kinds of orderings are used in real life (e.g., shortest to tallest in a graduating class, highest to lowest grade-point average, first arrival to last arrival at a fish counter), so there are many different possible wordings for equivalence and order relations on ordinal situations. However, the rather forced nature of the examples given indicates how relatively infrequently we use equivalence or order relations on ordinal situations in real life. Of course, as with the situations themselves, the relations on two cardinal, measure, or ordinal situations must be established and understood by a given user of such relational terms. How this understanding is gradually obtained by children for cardinal situations is the focus of chapter 9.

Mathematical operations of various kinds can be performed on cardinal situations, measure situations, and ordinal situations (although, as with relations, the last are not usual and are quite awkward). Mathematically, cardinal situations are those to which the natural numbers, or the positive whole numbers, refer. Measure situations can be described by natural or whole numbers, decimals, and fractions. The latter two are used when a given until does not cover (or fill up) all of the continuous quantity; then a smaller unit is used to cover the part of the quantity not covered by the original units. There are several mathematical operations that can be defined on cardinal, measure, and ordinal situations. In this book we discuss only the two simplest such operations: addition and subtraction. Addition and subtraction of cardinal and measure situations are the familiar addition and subtraction of whole numbers that are taught in school arithmetic (see chapter 8). Addition of ordinal numbers (or addition in ordinal situations) must involve some notion of, to use a specific example, "sixth plus third equals what?" To return to the lunch sack example, if I put in the yogurt, orange, two cookies, plastic spoon, napkin, and then was interrupted, and then returned to put in two dimes and a nickel and another dime for milk money, I could (although my family would undoubtedly eye me warily) announce, "I put the napkin in sixth and then put the nickel in third, so overall the nickel was put in ninth." The artificiality of this example demonstrates how rarely we use addition of two ordinal situations, and we probably use subtraction of ordinal situations even less often.

How are number words assigned to cardinal, ordinal, and measure situations? Counting is a very important way of doing so; it is discussed in the next section. There are two other ways in which number words are assigned to cardinal and measure situations; it is possible that these methods can also be used in ordinal situations, but this seems not to have been investigated. For very small numbers (two, three, and possibly four and five), people seem to be able to apprehend directly the appropriate cardinal or measure word, that is, to *subitize* it. How this is done is still a matter of dispute (e.g., Cooper, 1984; Kaufman, Lord, Reese, & Volkmann, 1949; Klahr & Wallace, 1973, 1976; Mandler & Shebo, 1982; von Glasersfeld, 1982). Subitizing seems to be used by very young children and may even be used by infants (e.g., Cooper, 1984; Starkey & Cooper, 1980; Strauss & Curtis, 1984). However, there still is disagreement concerning the developmental relationship between labeling a subitized situation with the correct number word and counting in order to label that situation (see Chapters 7 and 9 for further discussion of this debate). The other way in which a number word is chosen for a given cardinal or measure situation is by estimation (e.g., Gelman, 1972; Klahr & Wallace, 1973, 1976). The bases for making numerical estimates are not clear, and the term is used to describe different kinds of behavior ranging from a very rapid appraisal of a situation to a more systematic use of a bench mark as a comparison or unit of measure (e.g., Siegel, Goldsmith, & Madsen, 1982). In short there are few data on children's use of estimation in either cardinal or measure situations.

1.2.2. Sequence and Counting Uses

The sequence and counting uses of number words are differentiated by whether or not the number words refer to objects. If number words are just said aloud (or later, silently) in their usual English sequence with no reference to objects, they are being used in a sequence situation. In this case an ordering exists on the number words (the standard English ordering of these words), and the words have no referents and describe nothing. If the number words are said in an entity situation and each number word refers to an entity,[2] then the situation is a counting situation. The counting words have reference to the objects to which they are attached by the activity of counting, but these words do not describe the objects. As in cardinal and ordinal situations previously discussed, in a counting situation involving physically present entities, the person counting must unitize the entities to be counted. Each of them must be taken as a single countable unit to which one word will be applied regardless of whether that entity is actually much larger than (or is in some other way different from) other entities to be counted, that is, each

---

[2] For simplicity this description assumes that no counting errors are made. Of course, an error can be made in which one word refers to more than one object or a word refers to no object (see chapters 3 through 6), but we would still wish to call this a counting situation.

must be taken as a "perceptual unit item" (Steffe et al., 1983). Counting in cardinal situations involves a developmental sequence of conceptual unit items that become more abstract and complex (chapters 8 and 9; Steffe et al., 1983).

For a number word to take on a numerical meaning, counting must occur within a situation that also can be thought of as a cardinal, ordinal, or measure situation. In this case the situation is first considered by the person counting to be a counting situation, and the counting is done. Then the situation is thought of as a cardinal, ordinal, or measure situation rather than as a counting situation. For this shift to occur in a cardinal situation, the counter, after counting, must make a cardinal integration of the counted entities and then think of the last counted word as referring to the manyness of this whole set of counted entities. Similarly, a measure situation requires a measure integration and a shift of the last counted word from its counting reference to the last counted entity to its measure reference to the manyness of the units covering (filling) the continuous quantity. An ordinal situation does not require an integration of the counted entities, but it does require a shift from the count reference to an entity during counting to the ordinal reference to the relative position of that entity with respect to the other entities in the situation; this ordinal reference is a much more complex one in which the entity must be considered in relation to all of the other entities. Counting is thus a method of deciding which number word should be used to describe a particular cardinal, ordinal, or measure situation. The use of counting in these situations requires the person doing the counting to consider the situation in two different ways: first as a counting situation and then, after the counting is completed, as a cardinal, measure, or ordinal situation in which the last counted word then describes the cardinal, measure, or ordinal number of that situation. Thus, the counter must make a count-to-cardinal, a count-to-ordinal, or a count-to-measure shift in conceptualization of the same situation.[3]

There is a standard ordering on the number words in the number-word sequence of every language. Children appreciate this ordering in English at a very young age (see chapters 2 and 10). This ordering permits equivalence and order relations to be established on sequence number words. The equivalence relation is just the trivial relation "is the same word as." Two pairs of order relations can be derived from the sequence ordering: After/Before and Just After/Just Before.[4] It is easier to see how these relations come only from the sequence ordering by considering the example of the alphabet or of an

---

[3] We called these count-cardinal, count-ordinal, and count-measure shifts in Fuson and Hall (1983). We have added the *to* here because we want to discuss shifts in both directions, and the "to" makes the directionality more explicit and easier to process.

[4] The After/Before relations were called Comes After/Comes Before in Fuson, Richards, and Briars (1982) and were simplified here to After and Before. The relations Just After and Just Before were called And Then and And Then Before in Fuson et al. (1982). The reason for the latter change is discussed in chapter 2.

unfamiliar number-word sequence: il ee sam sa o yuk chil pal koo.[5] Examples of the first pair of relations are the following: *G* is before *P*, *sam* is before *yuk*, *D* is after *A*, *koo* is after *ee*. Examples of the second pair of relations are the following: *X* is just before *Y*, *chil* is just before *pal*, *T* is just after *S*, *sa* is just after *sam*. Children who learn to say the English sequence of number words cannot immediately use the relations on the sequence. They go through a fairly long period of saying the sequence alone and of using the words in counting before these relations can be used. Changes in the internal representation of the sequence accompany the ability to construct these relations on sequence words. These changes are outlined in Fuson, Richards, and Briars (1982) and are summarized here in chapter 2. These sequence relations for larger number words (ten and higher) come to be used to make the order relations on cardinal and measure situations (see chapter 2). Changes in the sequence reflect changes in the units represented by the sequence number words. Children finally arrive at a level in which the sequence words themselves are taken as the entities, that is, as sequence unit items, for the addition and subtraction of whole numbers. When this occurs but not before, one can consider operations to occur with sequence number words. The uses of sequence words in this way are discussed briefly in chapter 2 and in more detail in chapter 8.

When the sequence words are used in counting objects, the standard sequence ordering is used. However, this ordering is a property of the sequence rather than of the counting (the ordering exists when the sequence is said alone). During the activity of counting, an ordering is also established on the objects. However, this ordering may only unfold over time as each object is moved from an uncounted to a counted set or as each object is indicated in turn; the ordering may be neither established before the counting begins nor able to be reconstructed after the counting ends. This is in contrast to an ordering such as the spatial ordering involved in objects arranged in a row; here the ordering is evident before counting starts, although one still must choose between the two orderings beginning at each end of the row. Because such a preexisting ordering does not have to exist in a counting situation, a "no" is entered in the ordering column of Table 1-1 for the counting use of number words.

1.2.3. Symbolic Uses

Reading numerals (written symbols such as 8, 2, or 16) is another use of number words. Initially, for young children this is just a simple associative learning task: See the numeral and recall its number word. However, sometimes numerals are intended to have cardinal, ordinal, or measure meanings. In these cases the fact that a child says the correct number word does not en-

---

[5] These are Korean number words. The spellings are those of a graduate student native Korean speaker, Youngshim Kwon, and myself and may not be the standard English transliterations.

sure that the child has understood or is using the cardinal, ordinal, or measure numerical reference of the symbol.

In schools concrete embodiments (physical materials) are sometimes used to give meaning to symbols, especially to operations on symbols. Such embodiments may be cardinal situations, such as poker chips, or measure situations, such as Cuisenaire rods (ten different lengths of rods, each length colored a different color). Young children who must use perceptual unit items in order to give meaning to cardinal and measure number words require some such embodiment that provides them with perceptual until items.

1.2.4. Nonnumerical Uses

A final use of number words is as a label, an identifying attribute of an object. These uses are quite common in the lives of adults, for example, the two-o-one bus (meaning the bus with 201 on the front, not the bus that arrives at 2:01), flight number six-ninety-seven, social security numbers, telephone numbers, house numbers, office numbers, area codes, and zip codes. These uses primarily involve the use of numerals, of symbols; number words are used to read these symbols. Because the nonnumerical uses of number words are not cardinal or measure uses, the whole English system of number words is not used (e.g., the telephone number 475-0386 is not read as four million seven hundred fifty thousand three hundred eighty six). Rather, each numeral is read as a separate number word, or sometimes pairs of symbols are used as number words under one hundred (e.g., the house address 1918 will often be said as nineteen eighteen rather than as one nine one eight).

Some of the nonnumerical uses are actually quasinumerical; parts of them have some simple numerical interpretation but parts do not. For example the first two numbers for a street address often tell the number of blocks that house is from some starting point; however, in many places the system for assigning the last two numbers is more mysterious (why is 1918 just next to 1924 and to 1914?). Some of these nonnumerical uses may also have had some numerical basis when they were first invented. For example the area code is a sort of roughly derived measure of the population of the area: The greater the population the smaller the numbers (considered as cardinal numbers) in the area code. With pushbutton phones rather than dial phones, this reason for the assignment of area codes no longer holds; it does not take longer to push the larger numbers, and pushing the larger numbers is not more subject to error. Similarly, other nonnumerical uses may be nonnumerical only to people who are not privy to the underlying system or may become nonnumerical to everyone once the reason for the underlying system no longer holds.

1.2.5. Which Number Words Are Used When?

In English the same number words are used in sequence, counting, cardinal, measure, and nonnumerical situations, although the use in measure situations does involve saying the word for the measure unit after saying the number word (e.g., eight centimeters, fifteen seconds). The uses are differentiated only by the referents of the number word. These same number words are used for symbols (numerals) up to 10. Beyond that, the number words used depend on the referent of the symbols (numerals). The conventional English system of number words is used for sequence, counting, cardinal, and measure referents of the symbols, and specific examples may be said as single or double digits for nonnumerical referents, as discussed previously. In ordinal situations there are special number words. Some of these are irregular (first, second, third, fifth), but most are constructed by adding *th* to the regular English number words (fourth, sixth, seventh, etc.). These number words do then differentiate the ordinal use from the other uses of number words.

1.2.6. Distinctions Among Ordinal, Order Relations, and an Ordering

We would like to emphasize some distinctions we have made here that are often confused in the literature on children's concepts of number and of counting. These are the differentiation of ordinal, order relations, and an ordering. An *ordinal situation* is very easy to distinguish. It is one to which an ordinal number word (first, second, third, etc.) will apply. An ordinal situation concerns the relative position of one entity with respect to all the other entities in an ordered situation. *Order relations* can be established on cardinal, ordinal, measure, and sequence uses of number words (see Table 1-1). Order relations involve a comparison between two nonequivalent cardinal, ordinal, measure, or sequence situations. The use of order relations on cardinal, measure, or sequence situations (e.g., seven cookies are more than five cookies or seven comes after five in the sequence) are not "ordinal" situations; they are still cardinal, measure, or sequence situations in which *an order relation* is being applied. Repeated use of a given order relation on all the elements of a given finite set results in *an ordering*. An ordering can be defined in a cardinal or a measure situation, but these situations do not require an ordering. An ordering *must* be defined on a situation for it to be an ordinal situation, because otherwise one could not use the ordinal number words to refer to the relative position of one item with respect to the ordering. However, the existence of an ordering in a situation does not ensure that the situation is ordinal. For example, asking how many people are in the ticket line requires that situation to be considered as a cardinal, not an ordinal, situation. This confusion is particularly acute with the ordering present in the sequence of number words. The existence of this ordering on the number words does not mean that saying the number words or using the number words in counting implies an ordinal situation. Because the number words and counting are both used in cardinal, ordinal, and measure situations, it seems particularly important to refrain from considering the number words and counting to be ordinal situations. If sequence and counting situations actually were ordinal situations, one would use the sequence of ordinal words for counting. We do not do so, because in sequence and counting situations we are not interested in the relative position of every entity with respect to every other entity. We only wish to say the sequence of words or to make a correspondence of the words with entities using the usual ordering on the sequence of number words.

1.3. Learning Number Words in the Home: Children's Early Experiences With Number Words

1.3.1. Results From Three Studies

There is little research on the kind and range of experiences young children have with number words. However, recently three studies provided some information about this. The results of these studies are briefly summarized here.

Because the same number words are used in cardinal, measure, sequence, counting, symbolic, and nonnumerical situations, a young English-speaking child will hear the same number words used in many different kinds of situations. Some research results indicate that this early experience may be heavily weighted toward the words *two* and *three* and that the spontaneous use of number words by young children is similarly weighted. The results of a longitudinal study of mothers interacting in a standard setting with their child over the age range from 9 to 36 months indicate that both mothers and children use the word *two* much more frequently than the word *three* and use *three* much more frequently than *four* (Durkin, Shire, Riem, Crowther, & Rutter, 1986). This result was also reported for a longitudinal study of nine children from their first birthday until they entered school (Wagner & Walters, 1982; Walters & Wagner, 1981). These latter observations were made in the home and involved both free play and structured tasks focused on number. Between the ages of 1–9 (one year nine months) and 3–9, the children used *two* 158 times, *three* 47 times, *four* 18 times, and *five* only 4 times (the type of situation was not specified). The use of counting was strongly and inversely related to the size of the number word. In a sample of cardinal situations that could be evaluated with respect to whether counting did or did not occur, counting occurred for 9%, 53%, 71%, and 100% of the situations in which the words *two*, *three*, *four*, and *five* through *twelve* were used, respectively. Thus, even for *four*, and certainly for words above that in the sequence, uses of number words are strongly connected to counting and sequence uses of the number words. Many of the uses of the word *two* seem to be in cardinal situations without the use of counting.

Mothers evidently provide experiences with number words that range over almost all of the uses listed in Table 1-1. For example in the simple structured situation studied longitudinally by Durkin et al. (1986), about 60% of mothers' uses of number words consisted of routine and/or pedagogical behavior that included nursery rhymes, stories, songs, saying the sequence of number words with the child, and counting objects (i.e., sequence and counting uses). The remaining 40% of mothers' uses of number words consisted of spontaneous incidental descriptions of quantifiable aspects of the environment (presumably labeling cardinal, ordinal, or measure situations). These uses also included order relations and addition and subtraction operations, at least for cardinal situations. Saxe, Guberman, and Gearhart (in press) found that mothers of 2- and of 4-year-olds reported using certain situations (e.g., playing a board game or a card game) to teach different uses of number and that over time the mothers structured the activity of the child in more complex ways. This restructuring of an activity as the child got older and learned certain numerical skills or concepts ranged over the four levels of complexity into which Saxe et al. divided the number domain: use of number words without correspondences (e.g., saying the sequence or nursery rhymes, reading numerals); single-array correspondences (e.g., counting in a cardinal situation, giving a cardinal estimate without counting); relating summations of correspondences (e.g., reproducing a cardinal situation or comparing two cardinal situations—what we have identified as establishing equivalence or order relations on cardinal situations; some examples were also given of sequence order relations); and relating and manipulating summations of correspondences in arithmetical reasonings (what we have called the addition and subtraction operations on cardinal situations). Although more data are needed on the kinds of experiences young children have with number words, these pioneering studies indicate that the experiences do range over sequence, counting, and cardinal situations and extend to order relations and addition and subtraction operations for these uses of number words.

Several aspects of the experiences with number words provided to children by mothers fall within a Vygotskiian framework of a common goal-directed activity structured by the mother with age-appropriate support for the child (e.g., Rogoff & Wertsch, 1984; Saxe et al., in press; Vygotsky, 1962; 1978; 1986). First, mothers seem to use number words more with very young children and then decrease their use as the children begin to use number words more frequently. Durkin et al. (1986) found that in mother–child interactions mothers used number words in the observed situation more frequently than did children from 9 to 33 months but that children's use increased considerably with age and surpassed that of mothers from 33 to 36 months. Second, mothers in both the Durkin et al. and the Saxe et al. studies frequently structured a given situation by the use of questions, directions, and gestures into one of the uses in Table 1-1. That is, they did not always just use the number word, but rather directed the child's attention to the appropriate attributes of a situation. Third, after such an initial structuring, the mother might then continue to restructure the same situation into other uses in a sequential goal-directed fashion (Saxe et al., in press). For example in order to help a child make a set equivalent to a given set, the mother might ask a 4-year-old to count the given set, then ask how many are in that set, then tell the child to go over to the chips and count out the same number of chips (or say the explicit number of chips: e.g., count out seven chips), and then check that there are the same number of chips by matching the two sets (the original and the one obtained by the child). Mothers made judgments about what steps their child could carry out and then structured the steps into greater or lesser difficulty accordingly. Thus, for a large set with a 2-year-old, they might carry out each step themselves but have the child count with the mother for each of the counting steps.

Saxe et al. reported some social class differences in which middle-class mothers structured a given situation so as to require more advanced numerical activities by the child than did working-class mothers, but in many aspects mothers did not differ across social class. Ginsburg and Russell (1981) also reported that social class and race affected few aspects of early mathematical thinking. However, their data pooled over kindergarten and preschool did indicate that children from middle-class intact families produced significantly longer accurate number-word sequences than did children from middle-class nonintact families or from lower class families and that middle-class preschool children produced significantly longer accurate number-word sequences than did lower-class preschool children.[6]

The Durkin et al. (1986) study did indicate that, with young children (up to age 3), parents often oversimplify number word situations and that such situations are replete with ambiguities, conflicts, and contradictions. In one example the mother cued the child to consider a situation in a given way (e.g., "How many eyes?") but then also used a cue that is often used to cue the saying of the number-word sequence ("one"). The child responded as in a sequence situation ("Doo fwee"), to the consternation of the mother. Another source of ambiguity is that the word *one* is often used by mothers both as a pronoun and as a number word, sometimes very close together: "The other one—look, one...two" (p. 283). The function words *to, too,* and *for* also are sources of confusion, conflicting with *two* and *four*. Durkin et al. speculate that the conflicts and contractions promote development, but it also seems possible that clearer differentiation of different uses of number words might accelerate children's understanding of these different uses.

1.3.2. Examples From a Mother's Diary

Table 1-1 provides a frame of reference for thinking about and carrying out research concerning children's increasing understanding of different uses of number words. However, neither it nor the research summarized in 1.3.1 indicate the richness and even precocity of the numerical thinking of which

---

[6] The data from the kindergarten children probably suffer from a ceiling effect because children were stopped at 50, and many kindergarten children have accurate sequences above that. Thus, there may also be effects of class or of family intactness at this age.

young children are capable when small number words are involved. Nor does it reveal how very dependent such learning is on specific experiences provided in the daily life of the young child. It seems very useful to give some flavor of each of these vital aspects of young children's uses of number words. Tables 1-2 and 1-3 are included for this purpose. They consist of all entries concerning number words in the diaries I wrote for my two children when they were young. During much of the diary period, I was not engaged in research on young children's number concepts. Thus, the entries were not systematic or even focused on what I might consider crucial if I were keeping such diaries now. However, having majored in mathematics as an undergraduate and having (or, initially, getting) a doctorate with graduate work in mathematics and in mathematics education, I did have an interest in these areas. The diaries were written to each child and consisted of descriptions of accomplishments, activities, and characteristics that I thought interesting, amusing, or noteworthy. They were intended to provide each child with some sense of herself when she was little and to capture that irreproducible charm and inadvertent wit exhibited by each young child as she constructs (and delightfully at times misconstructs) in her own way the human cultural mileu into which she is born. The second table is noticeably shorter than the first only because the amount of time available to the diary keeper unfortunately did not double with the birth of the second child; this second table does indicate some ways in which the experiences of a second child may be influenced by an older sibling.

Table 1-2. Mother's Diary Entries of Adrienne's Uses of Number Words

Age[a]	Diary entry	Use
1–8	You walking up the stairs: "A B C four five six."	S
	My phrases, your responses: "A–A, B–B, C-three."	S
	Five is by far your favorite number.	?
	You know *two* and use it correctly in new situations; *two* means one in each hand.	Cd
1–10	You were petting Sam (cat) and said "Sam tape [tail]." Then "Tshad tape". (Tshad, the dog, was not in the room). Then "Two tapes [tails]." Before now you had frequently said two cups, two cookies, but always when they were both physically present.	Cd / Cd
1–11	"I got two shobels [shovels]."	Cd
	You occasionally count things, especially pictures. You say one number each time you lift your finger and point it down again, but you count some things several times and others not at all. Typical counting series: "one, four, five, eight, four, five, two, six."	Ct
	Tonight we counted steps going up to bed (we usually do). We were on nine and you said, "One two fee four five six." First time so many correct.	Ct

2–0 You can count three things correctly. That is, you point to objects   Ct
and say "one two three." You also say three correctly when asked   Cd
"how many" (without counting).
    "One two three eight jump." (You are into counting and   S
jumping off the hassock or even the couch.)

2–1 You counting on your muffin (a toy): "One two three eight seven   Ct
three."
    Several times today: "I two years old."   M
    "Make a *B*. Do it again. Two *B*'s."   Cd +

2–4 You fixed my fingers for "two years old" (the pointing and index   M
fingers up and the thumb holding down the third and fourth
fingers).

2–6 Two tomatoes were on the table. You said and acted out the
following: "One tomato from two tomatoes leaves one. Two   Cd −
tomatoes from two tomatoes leaves no." I asked you what no   Cd −
tomatoes from two tomatoes was: "Two tomatoes." "Sesame   Cd −
Street" does things similar to the first two sentences.

2–7 Putting prunes back into a box, you correctly counted them up to   Ct
nine. When asked how many prunes: "three" (your standard   No
"how many" answer at this point: three eyes, etc.)   Ct–Cd

2–8 "Three of us are sitting down. You, Erica, and me [pointing to   Cd +
each]. If Daddy sits down, there will be four of us."

2–9 You to father: "Do you want to have a picnic?" Father: "Not
this time. I'll go next time." You: "We'll have two picnics. You'll
go to the second picnic."   Cd, O
    Father, asking you how you want to be swung around: "Do you
want one and one?" You: "No, I want two and two [two arms and
two legs held]."   Cd

2–10 I cut your peanut butter sandwich in half and then into half again.
You watched and said, "Two and two make four."   Cd +
    You just asked for four olives (you love olives!). Your father   Cd
gave them to you, and you said, "Two and two make four."   Cd +

2–11 "Daddy, I hear three cracker-fires." (It was the fourth of July.)   Cd

3–0 You were quite excited at your birthday party and immediately   M
understood and remembered that you were three years old.
    You count correctly putting fingers up (index first, then big   Ct
finger, then ring finger, then pinky finger) up to four.
    Several times you have said things like: "I can open the door   M
from the outside now. When I was two and a half I couldn't open
it, but now I am three years old and I can open the door."

3–2 "Eight nine ten eleventeen twelveteen thirteen." Later, raising   S
the correct number of (unit) fingers and concentrating very hard: Ct
"twenty-one, twenty-two, twenty-three, twenty-four, twenty-
five." Each *twen* was very long. You count everything. You love
to count.

Table 1-2. *Continued*

Age[a]	Diary entry	Use
3–4	There is a bit on "Sesame Street" in which a child counts backward from ten. Lately you have said (to me and your father), "I can count backwards. Ten nine eight seven six four" and then needed questions to finish off. Me: "What comes before four?" You: "Three." "What comes before three?" You: "Two." I didn't know if it was a rote thing or not. Later you got the clock and said: "I can count backwards: twelve eleven ten nine eight seven six five four three two one [pointing to each number in turn]."	S bk, S rel, S bk, Num
	You love to type. You ask me to spell words, and you type them. After we had done GO, you said, "Why is go a two word?"	Cd
	You were bothering your father while he was trying to tie a bow on a Christmas present. Father: "I can't do two things at once; I can only do *one* thing at a time." You, in a pout: "I can't do *nothing* at a time." (You had been trying to tie a bow and had been unsuccessful.)	Cd, Zero
3–5	You were typing and saying as you typed: "one, two, three, four, five, six, seven, eight, nine [pause]. I need a ten."	S, Num
3–6	You were counting pictures. Got (with a couple of omissions) to twenty. I said, "Twenty-one, twenty-two." You said, "No, this one [pointing to the second picture] was two." Evidently you thought twenty-two was the same as two. I explained that twenty-two meant twenty and two more. Later you counted hangings on the wall: "Twenty-one, twenty-two, twenty-three, twenty-four [there are four hangings]."	Ct, S, Cd, S, Cd, Ct
3–8	Pretending to water and feed the plants: "In the morning they get two amounts of food and in the evening they get three amounts of food."	M
	You frequently ask us: "Do you know how old Heather [your imaginary older sister] is?" The answer ranges from 5 to 16.	M
3–9	"Heather is 16. She goes to high school."	M
	"Mom. Three-quarters orange juice plus three-quarters orange juice equals what?" (I have been giving you "three quarters" of a glass of juice in the mornings and saying so). I asked you what would happen if we poured three quarters and then another three quarters in the glass. You: "Splat!" Then you asked: "What would sixteen three-quarters make?" I asked you, but you wanted me to answer. I said: "A very messy kitchen." You grinned and agreed.	M+
3–10	"White and yellow make light yellow. pause. White makes any color light."	Principle[b], Cd+
	"What's four and four?" I said to count on your fingers. "One, two, three, four. One, two, three, four. One, two, three, four, five, six, seven, eight. Four and four make eight."	Ct–Cd

3–11   "When Erica [younger sister] is four and I am four, we'll be   M
twins." At other times you say things like: "When I'm five, Erica   M+
will be two." (The arithmetic is not always accurate.)

4–0   You noticed the string from my tampon and asked me about it.
I said that "every month a tiny egg comes to the uterus (you have
known about babies growing in the uterus and used the word for
1½ years—since Erica was noticeable). If no baby is made, the
walls of the uterus wash off to make a nice clean place for a baby
to grow the next time. A baby is made if an egg from the mother
and a sperm from the daddy come together." You said, "And
that happened two times?" I said, "Yes. One time and the baby   Cd
was you, and another time and the baby was Erica." You had a   Cd+
funny look on your face when I mentioned the egg. I asked if you
thought it was funny that people came from eggs. You smiled in a
relieved way and said yes. I explained that they were different
from regular eggs.

4–4   "seventy sixty"   S
         "eighty zero"   S

4–6   You have learned about zero and infinity from Leslie (in carpool)   Zero
and use them a lot. One very cold morning I said to you, "Today   ∞
is very cold. The temperature outside is zero." You said, "That   M
means there is *no* temperature." I explained about the
thermometer and showed you the 0 and the numbers below zero.   Integers
A couple of days later I heard you say in an animated voice to a
neighbor boy "Did you know that there are numbers underneath
zero? Minus one, minus two, minus three...minus ten." (I had
not listed all of those; just some of them.)

4–7   "How many puppies does a dog have? How many kittens does a   Cd
cat have?"
        "Mommy, I can count backwards. Ten, nine, eight...three,   S bkwd
two, one, zero, minus one, minus two, minus three, minus   Integers
four...minus ten." I was floored. "Sesame Street" does ten to
zero and you had done zero to minus ten before but you had
never put them together before.

4–9   To Erica (younger sister): "No, you can't have it. It has my germs   Ct
on it. See [pointing] one, two, three, four, five."
        When we were preparing bags of popcorn and peanuts for your
(early) school birthday, you counted kernals of colored popcorn.   Ct–Cd
In great excitement and wonder: "Ooh! I counted up to one
hundred and two!" You refused to make piles of ten. You finally
quit at 150.
        You played this game with Erica (then 2–4): You put colored
beads or other objects out on a cloth and then asked her
questions. "Erica, what does it make adding one and one?" Erica   Cd+
(without looking at the beads): "Two." You would put out the
correct number of objects. Erica answered somewhat randomly,
rarely looking at the objects.

Table 1-2. *Continued*

Age[a]	Diary entry	Use
5–1	I asked you how many pieces I had been cutting apples into. You said: "Six." I asked you how you knew. You said: "Because upstairs we had 3 and 3" (you,. Erica, and friend each had two pieces).	Cd+ mental represen- tation
	To someone who asked when your birthday was: "Summer the ninth" (it is August the ninth; we have been doing seasons and months lately).	M, O
5–7	Conversation with you with in the bathtub: You: "How much is seven and seven?" I held up seven fingers and had you hold up seven fingers. You counted. You still usually will not count on from the first number; you need to count the fingers for the first number. You asked and we did nine and nine, four and four, six and six, five and five, and then ten and ten (you did that with your fingers and toes). You said twenty. I said it was called that because it was twin tens—two tens. You said, "I know" and thought for a bit. Then you said, "There's a zero to make the ten and the 2 to make the [pause] two tens." You asked what twenty and twenty were. We used all our fingers and toes. You counted on from twenty. Got forty. I asked you how many tens were in forty (pointing to our fingers and toes—took a bit of focusing for you to see the tens). You said, "Oh, the zero for ten and the 4 for four tens."	Cd+ Cd S Num Base ten num Cd–Ct Base ten num
	You drew a 2 in the air and asked, "Is it this way or the other way [backwards]?" You still do many of your numbers backward—but not letters. I asked you how you knew where to move your arm to draw a 2. "I don't know." "Do you see a picture of the 2?" "Yes, I see an invisible 2, and I just draw it."	Num
	One night before school (Montessori preschool) was out, I was getting you both ready for bed. Erica was crying at every little thing. We went into your room where you could see your digital clock and you said, "No wonder Erica has been acting like a baby. It's 8:00." (We usually get ready at 7:30). You and Erica both have digital clocks, and you are really getting good at telling time. You tell me that 7:50 is ten minutes before 8:00, etc. You know all the ten minutes that way. I asked, "Eight oh eight," the other day and you said, "Eight minutes after eight?"	M M M
	You brought home a Montessori numeral sheet today. It was divided into 1-inch squares and was ten squares by eight squares. The teacher had written the symbols in order from 1 through 10 across the top row. You then wrote seven more rows of numerals under them. Your 1, 3, 4, 5, and 7s were mostly quite good. You were struggling with 2s; they turned more and more into Zs as they went down the page. You had trouble with the loop in the 6. The reverse direction cross overs in the 8 were really difficult for you, so you tried different strategies on the 8s. You tried partial	Num

cross overs and overlapping loops and then settled for a circular
top and a U fastened to the bottom of the loop. Your 10s were
too scrunched because you started the zero too close to the 1; you
went to the right and then when you looped back to the left you
ran into the 1. You also started the zero at the bottom. But
overall quite a good job; everything was recognizable.

6–0	You know most of the double sums (3 + 3, 7 + 7, etc.). I asked	Cd+
	you some tonight and then asked nine plus nine. You closed your	
	eyes and scrunched up your face and thought and then said,	
	"Eighteen." I asked how you had figured it out. "Well, I knew	
	eight plus eight was sixteen, and I knew there had to be one in the	Thinking
	middle, so it was eighteen." (i.e., you knew the double sums went	Strategies
	up skipping every other number). I then asked you five plus	
	seven. You thought for a while and then said, "Now don't ask me	
	to describe it because it is very difficult." You closed eyes, etc.,	
	and after a while said. "Twelve." I was surprised. "Could you	
	give me a clue?" "Well, I had one five and there was another five	
	in seven with two left over, so that made one was eleven and two	
	was twelve." Big smile. Me too.	
6–7	You were doing a sheet of two-digit addition of numbers without	
	any trading (carrying) for first-grade homework. I said, "Look,	
	You can do problems with more digits in the same way," and	
	started to show you three-digit and four-digit problems. You got	Base ten
	almost hysterical, "I have to do it the way the teacher said. She	
	will get really mad if I do bigger problems. I can't do anything	
	else until she shows me. Don't make me do it, she'll get mad." I	
	had never seen you have this attitude toward anything.	

Cd, cardinal; Cd+, cardinal addition; Cd−, cardinal subtraction; Ct, count; M, measure; O,
ordinal; Num, numerals; S, sequence; S bkwd, sequence backwards; S rel, sequence relations;
Ct–Cd, Count-to-cardinal transition; Cd–Ct, cardinal-to-count transition; ∞, infinity.
[a] 1–8 is 1 year 8 months, 1–10 is 1 year 10 months, and so on.
[b] See chapter 10 for discussion of principles.

Table 1-3. Mother's Diary Entries of Erica's Uses of Number Words

Age[a]	Diary Entry	Use
1–11	"Eight, nine, come." (Hide-and-go-seek. It's a challenge to hide before you say come!)	S
	Building with blocks "Three, four, five, six, seven, eight, nine, ten." (I was astounded; you must have been counting with	Ct
	babysitter and son same age as you.) Also later "ten, eleven, twelve."	Ct
	"Adi home six o'clock" said half an hour after Adrienne went to a friend's house. I had told Adrienne she must be home at six o'clock, and she and her friend left chanting it.	M
2–0	"Mommy read for a little couple minutes."	M

Table 1-3. *Continued*

Age[a]	Diary Entry	Use
2–4	"I don't got some lots of milk" in a hurt tone when I gave you a small amount of milk. You wanted a lot and couldn't have it because you had diarrhea.	M
	Adrienne played this game with you several times: She put colored beads or other objects out on a cloth and then asked questions. "Erica, what does it make adding one and one?" You (without looking at the beads): "Two," Adrienne would put out the correct number of objects. You answered somewhat randomly, rarely looking at the objects. (This game obviously stemmed from "Sesame Street.")	Cd+
2–6	You took 2 crackers. I asked, "Do you want 4?" You said, "Yes. Two more."	Cd+
2–8	"Mommy. A lady gave us three pieces of candy [for you and two friends]. I ate mine, and I didn't get *any* cavities."	Cd
2–11	"When I was 4 years old, I went to first grade in California."	M, O
	"Mickey Mouse is the same age as I am." "How do you know?" "They said it on TV."	M =
	"Grandma lives very far away. She lives four months away." (We have been saying your birthday is one month away.)	M
	"I want manier than five."	Cd >
3–6	"Children can have babies. I had two babies. These babies were in my uterus."	Cd
	"I am 3 and a quarter and a penny." (We have been saying that you are 3 and a quarter, but you will soon be 3 and a half. Lovely confusion between fraction and money meanings of "quarter.")	M
	"I am 8 and 9 quarters." (In a pretend game.)	M
3–8	You brought home a Montessori number sheet today. It had a 9 by 6 array of 2-cm squares touching each other. The teacher had written the numerals 1 through 9 in the top row, and you were supposed to write numerals in the five rows below. You did reasonable 1s, 4s, and 7s. Your 8s were two overlapping or sometimes just touching circles: pretty good. All of the 9s were a circle with a stick at the bottom—just like a lollipop. You had a great deal of trouble with the 2, 3, 5, and 6. One or two of these at the top were fairly good—I imagine you had your usual group of 5-year-old boys helping/showing you (you go to the math corner with them and they go to the messy kichen stuff with you). There were some curvy squiggles in the other squares, except that in some of the 6 boxes you had written 7s and 4s (you could make those well!). All in all, very impressive. It must have taken you a very long time to do all of these.	Num
4–2	Walking to my office with you, I asked you how many chairs were in my office. You said, "Four." (This was the use of mental	

representation; you said you counted the chairs in your head.   Ct–Cd
There were four chairs in my office, one at my desk and three at a
table.)

5–10   At a conference with your first-grade teacher, I asked to see your
work when I was told that you were making a lot of mistakes and
were in the low group. Every problem was correct, but you were   Cd+
reversing many of your numbers in writing. These problems were   Num
all marked wrong. I pointed out this distinction between the
correct answer and writing the symbols correctly (barely able to
contain my anger and incredulity at this teacher's incompetence)
and further observed that it is quite common for children to
reverse numbers or letters in the primary grades. And this is
supposed to be a good school system!

6–2   You had been doing some two-digit problems without trading
(carrying) in first grade. I wrote down the problem 42 + 35 (with
the 35 under the 42) and asked you to do it. You wrote 77. I asked
you, "How does this work?" You said, "I don't know. The
teacher just told us how to do it." "But why does it work?"
"Mom. I don't. . . Oh, because you are adding the tens and   Base
adding the ones." You drew a 1 with a circle around it above the   ten
ones column and a 10 with a circle around it above the tens
column. You then said, "I can carry on over. Adri taught me how
to do it. Give me a problem." So I wrote down 46 + 38 (in   Base
vertical form). You crossed out the 6 in the 46 and wrote it above   ten+
the tens column and added the 6, 4, and 3 to get 138; you
obviously remembered that you had to carry something on
over—you just did not remember what. I wrote the problem
again and said that you should try again. I asked how much six
and eight were. You decided that 6 + 8 was 14, and you wrote the
14 at the side of the problem. You then said, "Oh, yes, I am
supposed to carry the ten on over." You then did that, writing   Base
down the 4 and carrying the 1 ten over. You wanted me to give   ten+
you more problems. I gave you three more problems and you
"carried on over" correctly on all of them. You wrote the sum of
the ones out to the side every time, and then carried the ten over
and wrote down the ones in the ones column. You still wrote your
3s and 5s backward. You were quite proud of being able to do
these difficult problems.

Cd, cardinal; Cd+, cardinal addition; Ct, count; Ct–Cd, count-to-cardinal transition; M,
measure; Num, numeral; O, ordinal; S, sequence.
" 1–11 is 1 year 11 months, 2–0 is 2 years 0 months, and so on.

The effect of specific experiences, that is, of opportunity to learn, is quite
clear from these diary entries. The influence of "Sesame Street" number activities was quite strong and clearly led to "seeing" and talking about addition
and subtraction of small numbers in many situations at quite a young age.
Some understanding of fractions (a half, one quarter, three quarters) and of

integers (the thermometer example) seems possible even before school age, and this understanding might have been extended more than it was (e.g., a demonstration of a three-quarter glass of juice plus a three-quarter glass of juice would have fairly easily led to the conclusion "a glass and a half of juice"). The availability of number symbols in the home (TV dials, clock faces with numerals, typewriter or computer, playing cards) and of adults or older siblings who will read these number symbols to a child obviously can influence enormously the age at which a child relates number words and number symbols.

Some other aspects of early number-word learning also are evident. First, the interest in and enthusiasm about knowing numerical concepts is reflected in many entries, including conversations between children. Second, the effect of living in a house containing an older sibling would seem to be to accelerate the exposure to number words, because the younger child will hear uses directed by the adult to the older child (e.g., in Table 1-3 "six o'clock") and will hear and be involved in games and fantasy play with the older sibling that involve number words (e.g., in Table 1-3 hide-and-go-seek at age 1–11, the adding game at 2–4, the statement about being 4 years old and being in first grade at age 2–11). This may or may not be accompanied by a decrease in the amount of adult use of number words to the second or later child (similar to the decrease in amount of reading to a later child). The accelerated exposure also may or may not be useful to the younger child. A particular experience may or may not be within the zone of proximal development of the child (Vygotsky, 1978), that is it may or may not be learnable even with the help of the older sibling, whose sensitivity to what may be understood and how to help with this understanding undoubtedly varies considerably. Third, it is quite evident that number-word situations include mental representations of entities not physically present (e.g., the comment "two tapes (tails)" in Table 1-2 at age 1–10 when the owner of one tail was not in the room and the counting of chairs in a mental representation of my office in Table 1-3 at age 4–2) and include imaginary entities (counting germs in Table 1-2 at age 4–9, presumably to keep the younger sibling from eating some desirable food). Fourth, the words used for different kinds of measures can be confusing. For example time and distance were confused in Table 1-3: "Grandma...lives four months away."; seasons and months were confused in Table 1-2: My birthday is "summer the ninth." Finally, the stress in school on doing things the way the teacher said to do it regardless of comprehension is evident in the later entries in both tables; neither thinking about nor extending what has been taught is perceived as necessary, and the latter even sometimes evokes almost terror. The contrast between the two interactions in Table 1-2 at ages 5–7 and 6–7 is very striking and clearly is not a recommendation for American elementary school mathematics instruction (in a "very good" school district).

The pervasive influence of the nature of the experiences young children have in different kinds of number-word situations and the rather considerable difference one might expect to find in the situations emphasized or provided in different home environments suggest that there may be considerable individual differences in children's ability to use number words in different situations. Thus, one child might have a very well-developed symbol domain by age 4 while another child may be able to recognize and write few symbols. One child may frequently play with cards or with dominoes and thus recognize figural patterns for the number words up to ten, while another child might have no such experiences and thus recognize few or no such patterns. In fact in much of the data we report in this book, there is a very considerable range in the age at which children respond correctly to most number-word situations. A considerable amount of this range would seem to result from differences in children's opportunity to learn about these number-word situations.

1.4. The Precocity of Use of Small Numbers

Infants and young children demonstrate considerable precocity in situations involving very small numbers (e.g., Table 1-2 and 1-3; Cooper, 1984; Starkey, 1987; Starkey, Spelke, & Gelman, 1983; Strauss & Curtis, 1984). Older preschool and school-aged children continue to show competence in more difficult situations that involve very small numbers (1, 2, 3) considerably before they do so with larger numbers. For example children can solve problems such as 7 + 1 or 7 + 2 before solving 7 + 6, and children establish equivalence or order relations on very small sets before doing so on large sets (see chapters 7, 8, and 9 for details of these examples and for other examples). Gelman and Gallistel (1978) argued that preschoolers showed competencies with small numbers before larger numbers because they can reason about specific numerosities but not about unspecified general "algebraic" numerosities.[7] Gelman and Gallistel furthermore argued that counting provides young children with specific numerosities for small but not larger numbers (because the counting of larger numbers is not accurate), and thus counting ability is responsible for this ability to deal with small but not larger numbers. We agree with the first part of this position (that concerning children's competence with specific numerosities) and in later chapters provide and discuss evidence that supports this argument. Our position, however, differs with the second part of the Gelman and Gallistel position in at least three ways. First, the evidence presented in this book indicates that even 3-year-olds show considerable competence in counting numbers above 3 and that by age 4½, most children can count large numbers of objects in rows (up to 20) with consi-

---

[7] This position was later modified in Gelman (1982a) to include young children's ability to use one-to-one correspondence (matching) without ascertaining specific numerosities. This position is consistent with that outlined in this book (e.g., data are provided here concerning children's use of correspondence in equivalence and order situations) and is not one of the three differences discussed later.

derable accuracy. Second, 4-year-olds show some ability to use counting of numbers larger than 3 to establish equivalence and order relations on cardinal situations and to add and subtract cardinal situations and 5-year-olds show considerable such ability. Third, children's precocious competence with very small numbers (i.e., that which outruns competence with larger numbers by a year or more) depends not on counting but on special perceptual methods of obtaining or representing specific numerosities in these situations. These special perceptual methods include subitizing and the use of auditory, visual, or kinesthetic figural patterns[8] (see examples and evidence in chapters 7 through 10). Thus, our position suggests that preschool children have both more and less competence than indicated by the Gelman and Gallistel position: they have more because they do have considerable competence even with larger numbers when they obtain or use specific numerosities from counting, and they have less because their competence with very small numbers derives from special nongeneralizable processes that will not extend to larger numbers.

The special perceptual processes used by infants and young children with very small numbers may be similar to those used by animals in numerical tasks. Primates, birds, rate, mice, cats, and raccoons have demonstrated competence in various kinds of numerical situations (e.g., see reviews in Davis & Memmott, 1982, and in Davis & Perusse, 1987; see also Matsuzawa, 1985; Pepperberg, in press; Thomas, Fowlkes, & Vickery, 1980). Some authors have claimed that such competence suggests counting competence in that given species. However, Davis and Perusse (1987) argued convincingly that such claims exceeded the presented evidence. Most such studies provide evidence only of use of relative numerousness judgments (which involve order relations on cardinal situations) and of subitizing or of figural patterns. Most of this literature concerns cardinal situations, but some recent work concerns ordinal situations (e.g., Davis & Bradford, 1986). Competence has been demonstrated with both simultaneous and sequential visual entities and with sequential auditory, tactile, and kinesthetic entities (Davis & Perusse, 1987). In contrast, in the literature on humans, there has been relatively little work with infants or young preschoolers with sequential entities. Almost all the evidence reviewed in this book, including the new evidence presented here, concerns entities that are all simultaneously physically present. This animal literature is similar to that on human infants because most of the animals and all of the infants have not been taught number words. Thus, subitizing used with respect to this literature refers only to the perceptual process underlying discriminations among very small numbers and does not include the ability to label these small number situations with distinctive "words." Human 1- and

---

[8] Because the debate concerning whether subitizing involves figural patterns is not resolved, we will include the use of figural patterns as a possible separate procedure.

2-year-olds do possess such abilities, as evidently do some primates[9] and the grey parrot trained by Pepperberg (in press).

The extent to which competence with small numbers facilitates later competence with larger numbers is not clear. This may even vary across kinds of number-word situations. However, as will become clear from chapters 7 through 9, competence in cardinal situations involving larger numbers frequently requires procedures and understandings that are not required in situations involving very small numbers. Thus, to understand children's developing competence in numerical situations from age 2 through 8, one must study children's ability in situations involving larger numbers. Matching, establishing a one-to-one correspondence between pairs of elements in two sets, is one procedure that is useful and comes to be used in situations with larger numbers (see chapter 9). Counting to establish specific numerosity is useful in even more situations. Thus, if one wants to understand the general development of children's understanding of concepts of number from age 2 through 8, one must study children's use of matching and especially of counting in numerical situations.

1.5. Focus and Outline of the Book

This book focuses on the very considerable increase in children's competence in cardinal, counting, and sequence situations from age 2 through 8. The increase in competence that occurs over this age span is quite impressive, with children moving from very little understanding of any of these situations to an ability to add, subtract, and compare (establish equivalence and order relations on) very large whole numbers. This increase is marked by changes in children's conceptions of the cardinal, counting, and sequence situations and of the relations that exist between and among them. This book traces these changes.

Measure and ordinal situations are not treated for three reasons. First, they are both more complex and begin to be understood later than are the other three situations. Measure situations involve continuous quantities and thus the repeated use of a unit. Because repeated use of a unit is more complex than just using a perceptual unit item (e.g., Carpenter, 1975; K. Miller, 1984), measure situations are more difficult for children than are cardinal situations (see Fuson & Hall, 1983, for a review). The necessity to learn special ordinal number words complicates performance in ordinal situations, and this learn-

---

[9] A friend's initial experience with Koko, the gorilla trained to sign, was a request by Koko, "Koko two flowers." My friend complied, picking two small flowers and handing them to Koko. Koko took one in each hand, as small children do, sniffed each of them delicately, and then ate each in turn.

ing clearly lags behind the learning of the sequence/counting/cardinal number words by several years (Beilin, 1975). For the first five ordinal words and the first eight cardinal words, 2-, 3-, and 5-year-olds were correct on 4% versus 48%, 0% versus 69%, and 57% versus 95% of the ordinal versus the cardinal number words, respectively. For words up through the first 23 words, the 5-, 6-, and 7-year-olds were correct on 2% versus 82%, 10% versus 90%, and 46% versus 100% of the ordinal versus the cardinal number words, respectively. Thus, even at age 7 many children either do not know the rule by which ordinal words are generated or cannot successfully use that rule. Second, there is relatively little literature on measure and ordinal situations compared to the other three situations. Third, the pattern of relationships among sequence, counting, and cardinal uses of number words would seem to extend fairly readily to both ordinal and measure uses. Thus, it seems sensible to obtain some understanding of this pattern of relationships and then to explore how the relationships might extend to ordinal and measure uses of number words.

This book sketches the development of children's competence in cardinal, counting, and sequence situations from age 2 through 8. New data concerning these areas are presented, and data from other investigators are reviewed. Chapter 2 briefly summarizes research on children's learning of the English sequence of number words and on later useful advances in children's representation of this sequence of number words. Chapters 3 through 6 focus on the kinds of correspondence errors children make when counting and on variables that affect these different kinds of errors. Chapter 3 contains an analysis of the activity of counting that generates a category system of possible errors in the correspondences among the words used in counting, the points used in counting, and the objects being counted (i.e., the perceptual unit items "seen" by the counter in the counting situation). Data are presented on age-related changes in different kinds of errors for counting objects arranged in a row and on the effects of location of object, effort, sex of counter, and number of objects counted. Chapter 4 reports on correspondence errors made when objects are presented in different spatial arrangements (rows, disorganized arrays, circles) and when indicating acts other than pointing are used. Chapter 5 returns to objects in rows and presents three studies in which the effects of certain variables on the occurrence of counting correspondence errors are examined; the variables include homogeneity of the objects, distance between the objects, location of the objects at the beginning, middle, or end of the row as well as within the first or second half of the row, number of objects counted, and age of counter. The results across the studies presented in chapters 3, 4, and 5 are summarized and discussed in chapter 6.

Chapters 7, 8, and 9 concentrate on relationships between counting and concepts of cardinal number that children learn over the age range 2 through 8. Chapter 7 focuses on the early relationships constructed between the ages of 2 and 5. Chapter 8 discusses the later, more complex relationships that underlie children's understanding of and ability to carry out the operations of addition and subtraction with whole (cardinal) numbers. Developmental progressions are proposed for children's representations of addition and subtraction situations, their addition and subtraction solution procedures, and their concepts of cardinal number and conceptual relationships between counting and cardinal number. Chapter 9 presents data on children's use of counting and of matching in establishing equivalence and order relations on cardinal number situations (i.e., the same number as, more than, fewer than relations) and then outlines a developmental sequence of strategies children use in equivalence and order situations that culminates in Piaget's conservation of cardinal equivalence and a postconservation stage of truly numerical counting. In all three of these chapters, the emphasis is on changes in children's concepts and representations of number words, counting activity, and cardinality. Together these chapters indicate how sequence, counting, and cardinal situations move from being separate situations to becoming integrated as the number-word sequence itself becomes a cardinalized unitized seriated embedded conceptual structure.

Chapter 10 relates chapters 2, 6, and 7 to each other by reporting data on sequence, correspondence, and cardinal aspects of counting within the same children. Developmental relationships among Gelman and Gallistel's (1978) three how-to-count principles are considered, and these principles are discussed in some detail. Because so much is covered in each chapter of this book, the final chapter does not attempt a final overall summary of results. Such a summary overview of the conceptual and empirical results can be obtained by reading the present chapter, chapter 6 (in which chapters 3, 4, and 5 are summarized and discussed), and the chapter summaries for chapters 2 and 7 through 10. The final chapter provides an overview of changes in children's number word concepts, over the age span age 2 to 8, including the increasing integration of sequence, count, and cardinal meanings of number words.

2. The Number-Word Sequence: An Overview of Its Acquisition and Elaboration

This chapter briefly reviews children's learning about the English sequence of number words. We find it helpful to separate such learning into two distinct, although overlapping, phases: a first acquisition phase, in which children learn to say the conventional sequence correctly, and a later elaboration phase, in which equivalence and order relations and operations on sequence words[1] are constructed and the sequence can be produced in more sophisticated and complex ways (Fuson, Richards, & Briars, 1982). These phases are overlapping because the early part of the sequence may be undergoing elaboration while later parts are still being acquired (i.e., cannot yet be said correctly). While children are still learning the sequence, the incorrect sequences they produce have certain characteristics. These are outlined in 2.1. The more advanced sequence skills, which come to be learned during the elaborative phase, are discussed in 2.2. A much more thorough discussion and presentation of data about each of these phases is given in Fuson et al. (1982). We draw heavily on the data in that paper in the following summary; where data are not otherwise identified, they are from that paper.

2.1. Learning the Sequence of Number Words

2.1.1. The Structure of the English Sequence of Number Words

The English number words below one hundred have an underlying base-ten place-value structure that is very obvious in our number symbols to 100. The symbols begin a pattern after the first nine arbitrary symbols by reusing the first symbol (1) but placing it in a different position than the initial position; a new symbol (0) is then used to demonstrate that the 1 is in the new position. This yields the symbol 10, which means one ten and zero ones and might be read as "one zero." The pattern then involves the symbols 11 (one one), 12 (one two), 13 (one three), 14 (one four), up through 19 (one nine). Then follows the "two-ten cycle" 20 (two zero), 21 (two one), 22 (two two), 23 (two three), up through 29 (two nine). The ten-cycles then follow in order: the three-ten-cycle (three zero through three nine: 30 through 39), the four-ten-cycle (four zero through four nine: 40 through 49), up through the nine-ten-cycle (nine zero through nine nine: 90 through 99). Reading the number symbols in this base-ten place-value way makes clear that in the symbols the value of the places are implicitly indicated by the relative position of the symbols (as in three four six eight: 3468) rather than named explicitly. In contrast the system of English number words does explicitly name the values of the places (e.g., three *thousand* four *hundred* sixty eight).

Because the values of the places are named, the English system of number words is potentially easier to understand than is the very implicit symbolic system. Unfortunately, the irregularities in the early number-word sequence and phonetic changes in certain terms obfuscate the underlying structure of the English sequence of number words. First, the words for the first decade mask its structure. It is not obvious that *teen* means *ten*, and the teen and the unit are reversed with respect to the symbols: seventeen (seven ten) sounds

---

[1] See chapter 1 and Table 1-1 for a preliminary discussion of these.

like it should be written as 71. *Eleven* and *twelve* give no hint that they mean *ten one* and *ten two*, and the irregular *thirteen* and *fifteen* (rather than "three-teen" and "fiveteen") make it quite difficult to see the teen pattern. Second, it is also not obvious that *ty* means ten, so even the regular decade names like *sixty* and *seventy* do not convey the underlying tens structure as meaning six tens or seven tens. Then the irregular *twenty*, *thirty*, and *fifty* mask the pattern in the decade names that might become patent if *two-ten*, *three-ten*, and *five-ten*, or even *twoty*, *threety*, or *fivety*, were used instead. The decade pattern itself (the x-ty, x-ty one,...x-ty nine repetition) is clear enough, but the decade names, the order of these names, and their derivation as multiples of ten is masked by these irregularities. Thus, one of the first experiences English-speaking children have with a mathematical structure is that it is complex, irregular, and must be memorized laboriously rather than that it has a clear and obvious *pattern* that is easy to learn. We will see what the implications of these characteristics of English number words are for children's learning of this sequence.

2.1.2. Distinguishing Number and Nonnumber Words

Children seem to learn very early the distinction between words that are in the number-word sequence and words that are not in the sequence. In our experiments through the years with 3-, 4-, and 5-year-olds, not one of the more than 500 subjects has ever used anything but number words when asked to say the sequence or to count entities. With more than 40 2-year-olds, three children have used letters from the alphabet (either alone or mixed in with number words) on one trial each. Gelman and Gallistel (1978) also reported very infrequent use of nonnumber words in counting by 2- to 5-year-olds. Baroody (1986b) reported for a large sample of moderately and mildly retarded children aged 6 to 14 that only one ever used nonnumber words when counting (the alphabet was used).

2.1.3. Structure of Incorrect Sequences

The incorrect sequences produced by children before they have learned the standard sequence have a characteristic structure. Gelman and Gallistel (1978) first identified a crucial aspect of this structure. The incorrect sequence produced by many children is *stable* in that the same incorrect sequence is produced repeatedly over trials. This finding led to one of the three principles that Gelman and Gallistel suggested underlie children's counting; this stable-order principle asserts that "Numerons used in counting must be used in the same order in any one count as in any other count (p. 94)." Fuson et al. (1982) also found considerable stability in children's incorrect sequences, but this stability was less than seemed to be implied by the stable-order principle. Children rarely produced the same whole incorrect sequence over repeated trials. Rather, for sequences up to 30, the sequence consisted of parts, one of which was a stable incorrect portion produced consistently over trials. Thus, the characteristic form of most sequences produced by children was a first portion consisting of *an accurate number-word sequence* followed by *a stable incorrect portion* of from two to five or six words that was produced with some consistency over repeated trials followed by *a final nonstable incorrect portion* that varied over trials and might have consisted of many words. The first portion simply consists of the first *x* words in the conventional sequence of number words. The stable and the nonstable incorrect portions each have characteristic features that are described in 2.1.3.2. and 2.1.3.3. Four examples of sequences with these different three portions are given in Table 2-1. These examples demonstrate the fact that there is variability in the production of the accurate and the stable portions. These portions are not necessarily produced consistently on *every* trial. Different criterion levels for the production of these portions were analyzed and discussed in Fuson et al. (1982); the overall pattern of results did not vary much for different criterion levels.

Table 2-1. Examples of Sequences with Accurate Portions, Stable Incorrect Portions, and Nonstable Incorrect Portions

---

Case L: Age 3 years 10 months
    $1 \rightarrow$ 12 14 18 19 15 19
    $1 \rightarrow$ 12 14 18 19 16 17 18
    $1 \rightarrow$ 12 14 18 19 15 17 18 19 17
    $1 \rightarrow$ 12 14 18 19 15 16 17 18 19 15 17
    $1 \rightarrow$ 12 14 18 19 16 17 12 14 18 19
    $1 \rightarrow$ 12 14 18 19 16 17 18 19 17 14 18
    $1 \rightarrow$ 12 14 18 19 16 17 18 19 16 17 18 19 16
    $1 \rightarrow$ 12 14 18 19 16 17 18 19 16 17 18 19 17 18
B^a $1 \rightarrow$ 12 14 18 19 13
R^b $1 \rightarrow$ 12 14 18 19 17 15

Case M: Age 3 years 6 months
    $1 \rightarrow$ 13 19 16 13 19
    $1 \rightarrow$ 13 16 19
    $1 \rightarrow$ 13 16 14 16 19
    $1 \rightarrow$ 13 16 19 16 13 14 19 16 19
    $1 \rightarrow$ 13 19 16 14
 B $1 \rightarrow$ 13 19 16 14 19 16 19 16
 R $1 \rightarrow$ 13 19 14 16 14
 R $1 \rightarrow$ 13 19 16 14 19

Case N: Age 4 years 2 months
    $1 \rightarrow$ 14 16 $\rightarrow$ 19 30 1
    $1 \rightarrow$ 14 16 $\rightarrow$ 19 30 40 60
    $1 \rightarrow$ 14 16 $\rightarrow$ 19 30 31 35 38 37 39
    $1 \rightarrow$ 14 16 $\rightarrow$ 19 30 40 60 800
    $1 \rightarrow$ 14 16 $\rightarrow$ 19 40 60 70 80 90 10 11 10 30

B 1→ 14 16→ 19 60 30 800
B 1→ 14 60 30 800 80 90 30 ten-eighty 60 31 38 39 32 31 34 35 thirty-ten 31
R 1→ 14 16→ 19 30 800 60
R 1→ 14 16→ 19 30 1 80 90 60 30 90 80 30

Case P: Age 4 years 4 months
    1→ 11 13 16 18 40 5 6
    1→ 11 13 16 18 40 5→ 8
    1→ 11 13 16 18 14 5→ 13
    1→ 11 13 16 18 14 5→ 13 16 18
    1→ 11 13 16 18 14 15 16 18 19 23 26 11 13 16 18
    1→ 11 13 16 18 40 16 18 10 11 13 16 18 24 26 28 24
    1→ 11 13 16 18 14 6 9 10 11 13 16 18 24 28 26 23
    1→ 11 13 16 18 24 28 22 3→ 11 13 16 18
    1→ 11 13 16 18 20 1→ 11 13 16 18 16 18
    1→ 11 13 16 18 20 21 26 24 28 1→ 5
    1→ 12 10 11 13 16 18 21 22 17 16 18 21 22 26 24 26 23 28 16 14 12 13 16
B 1→ 11 13 16 18
R 1→ 11 13 16 18

Note. From "The Acquisition and Elaboration of the Number Word Sequence" by K.C. Fuson, J. Richards, and D.J. Briars. In *Progress in Cognitive Development Research: Children's Logical and Mathematical Cognition* (Vol. 1) (pp. 50–51), edited by C. Brainerd, New York: Springer-Verlag. Copyright 1982 by Springer-Verlag. Reprinted by permission.
[a] B = Blocks trials: while counting a pile of 50 movable blocks.
[b] R = Rote trials: no objects.

2.1.3.1. Accurate Portions. Saxe, Guberman, and Gearhart (in press) reported that the mean accurate portion produced by their sample of middle- and working-class children aged 2–6 (two years six months) to 3–2 was the sequence up through five. Percentages of older children ranging from age 3½ through third grade who produce accurate sequences of various lengths are given in Table 2-2. These results are based on two different sets of data. The data for the children aged 3½ to 6 are from the heterogeneous sample of 86 children described in chapter 3 (these sequence data were also reported in Fuson et al., 1982). Each child was asked to "Count as high as you can" on two trials given at the beginning and at the end of a counting interview in which the children also counted a pile of 50 blocks and rows of blocks that increased in size from 4 to 34; number-word sequence data were taken from all these tasks. The data for the kindergarten through third-grade children are from a study by Bell and Burns (1981a, 1981b) with children from a small city bordering Chicago. The children first were asked to count to thirty. Then their sequence production was checked at certain key points (63 to 72, 98 to 101, 196 to 201, and even higher). The data in Table 2-2 indicate that most children between 3½ and 4½ were working on learning the sequence of number words between ten and twenty and that a substantial proportion of children between 4½ and 6 were still learning the upper teens part of the sequence (that between fourteen and twenty) but that many children in this

Table 2-2. Percentage of Age Groups Producing Accurate Sequences of Various Lengths

Age/grade[a]	$n < 10$	$10 \leqslant n < 14$	$14 \leqslant n < 20$	$20 \leqslant n < 30$	$30 \leqslant n < 72$	$72 \leqslant n < 101$	$101 \leqslant n < 201$	$201 \leqslant n$
3 years 6 months to 3 years 11 months	17	44	22	17	0	0	0	0
4 years to 4 years 5 months	0	41	35	12	12	0	0	0
4 years 6 months to 4 years 11 months	0	12	47	18	12	12	0	0
5 years to 5 years 5 months	0	6	25	13	44	13	0	0
5 years 6 months to 5 years 11 months	0	6	22	17	44	11	0	0
Kindergarten	0	7	11	30	26	4	22	0
First grade	0	0	3	14	7	21	48	7
Second grade	0	0	0	0	8	3	31	58
Third grade	0	0	0	0	0	4	25	71

Note. From "The Acquisition and Elaboration of the Number Word Sequence" by K.C. Fuson, J. Richards, and D.J. Briars. In *Progress in Cognitive Development Research: Children's Logical and Mathematical Cognition* (Vol. 1) (p. 38), edited by C. Brainerd, New York: Springer-Verlag. Copyright 1982 by Springer-Verlag. Reprinted by permission.
[a] The first five groups are from our cross-sectional sample. The last four are from Bell and Burns beginning of the year interviews.

age range were working on the decades from twenty through seventy. Most kindergarten children were learning the decades between twenty and seventy, but a substantial number of them were working on the sequence between one hundred and two hundred. Half the first graders and almost all the second and third graders knew the sequence to one hundred and were working on the sequence above one hundred. There was moderate variability in the correct sequence produced by a given child across trials. The difference between the mean correct sequence produced on every trial and the mean single best correct sequence for half-year age groups from 3½ to 6 ranged from two to seven words.

2.1.3.2. Stable Incorrect Portions. Learning the first part of the English sequence of number words is a serial recall task. The nature of the stable incorrect portions produced by children is exactly what one would expect in any serial recall task: Almost all of the stable incorrect portions have the words in the conventional order but they contain omissions. Of the stable incorrect portions in the sequences of the sample of children aged 3½ to 6, 88% contained omissions, 3% contained repetitions, and 9% contained reversals. How many times each number word between four and twenty was omitted in a stable incorrect portion and the few examples of reversals and repetitions in a stable incorrect portion are given in Table 2-3. A stable incorrect portion consists of the last word in the accurate sequence portion and all words in the incorrect stable portion. Table 2-3 indicates that by far the most common two-word stable incorrect portion omitted the word *fifteen*, that is, *fourteen, sixteen*. For stable portions of more than two words, most of the teen words were omitted by some children, although *fifteen* was still omitted by more children than was any other word. Why *fifteen* should be omitted the most and whether this high rate of omission is connected with its irregular formation (fifteen and not fiveteen) or with its phonetic qualities ("fif" is difficult to say) is not clear. The only repetitions were of fourteen and of sixteen, each of which was used by a single child to fill in the space where fifteen should have been. Gelman and Gallistel (1978), K. Miller and Stigler (1987), Pollio and Whitacre (1970), and Siegler and Robinson (1982) all reported that omissions were common errors in children's sequences; data were not provided on the relative frequency with which given words were omitted.

There is some controversy in the literature concerning whether children learn the teen structure of number words (in spite of the irregularities previously reviewed) and produce the sequence by using this structure or whether the irregularities mask the structure so much that the teens words are learned as separate new words just as the words from one through ten are learned Evidence of various kinds indicates that, except possibly for 18 and 19, the latter is the case for most children. First, the data in Table 2-3 on the omissions in stable portions of three or more words show that the words between twelve and nineteen are each consistently omitted by a good number of children. If children were guided by the repetitive structure in the teens, they

Table 2-3. Number of Occurrences of Particular Errors in Stable Incorrect Portions

Omissions

	Consistency level (%)	Word omitted																
		4	5	6	7	8	9	10	11	12	13	14	15	16	17	18	19	20
Two-word portions	40[b]		1		1				1	3	10	10	16	3	1	5	3	1
	100								1				13	2	1	2	1	1
Three or more-word portions	40[b]		3	2	2	1	0	2	2		3	5	16	9	10	2	1	5
	100								1				8	4	6			2

Reversals

Portion	Consistency level (%)
..., 15, 17, 19, 18	67
..., 4, 9, 10, 11, 8	71
..., 12, 14, 18, 19, 16, 17	83
..., 14, 18, 19, 17	62
..., 4, 8, 9, 6, 7	53
..., 16, 18, 19, 15	75

Repetitions

Portion	Consistency level (%)
..., 12, 14, 14, 16, ..., ..., 29	100
..., 14, 16, 16, 17	60

Note. From "The Acquisition and Elaboration of the Number Word Sequence" by K.C. Fuson, J. Richards, and D.J. Briars. In *Progress in Cognitive Development Research: Children's Logical and Mathematical Cognition* (Vol. 1) (p. 44), edited by C. Brainerd, New York: Springer-Verlag. Copyright 1982 by Springer-Verlag. Reprinted by permission.
a Percentage of child's trials on which error was produced.
b Between 40% and 100%.

might occasionally omit a word, but why would they do so consistently? The pattern of consistent omissions fits much more with the conclusion that children are learning the teens words as new words. Second, the invented words of children rarely reflected a regular structure in the teens. Few children substituted the words "threeteen" or "fiveteen" for thirteen and fifteen, as they would have done if the teens structure was obvious to them. Only one child on a single trial said "eleventeen, twelveteen" as an awareness of the teen structure might have suggested.[2] Third, the few reversals in the stable portions that did occur for the teens words (Table 2-3) indicate that these children were not following a pattern of generating the teens words in order. Fourth, for the age groups in which most children were working on learning the sequence in the teens, Fuson et al. (1982) reported a considerable difference between the mean best trial produced on every trial and the single best trial. This suggests that children did not at some point "see the teens pattern" and then produce that pattern consistently. Fifth, Siegler and Robinson (1982) concluded that their stopping point data supported the view that children were learning the sequence to twenty without understanding the teens structure. Sixth, Miller and Stigler (1987) interpreted their cross-cultural comparison of the counting of American and Chinese children as supporting the view that American children learn the words to twenty by rote. If this view is correct for most children, then English-speaking children have a much more difficult task in learning the sequence of number words than do children for the many languages (such as Chinese) in which the words above ten follow a regular and obvious pattern.

Stable incorrect portions can have different lengths (i.e., contain a different number of words), and the gaps in them can be of different sizes (e.g., "twelve, fourteen" is a one-word gap, whereas "twelve eighteen" is a five-word gap). For stable portions below twenty that were produced 100% of the time, the mean length was 3.6 words, the range of lengths was 2 to 10 words, 71% of the omissions involved a one-word gap (e.g., fourteen sixteen), and 21% of the omissions involved gaps of four or more words (e.g., twelve, eighteen, nineteen).

Many stable incorrect portions above twenty seem to reflect partial knowledge of the decade structure between twenty and one hundred but also indicate that children are still struggling with what we called the "decade problem" (Fuson & Mierkiewicz, 1980; Fuson & Richards, 1980; Fuson et al., 1982). The decade problem reflects the fact that, although children recognize the decade structure "x-ty, x-ty-one, x-ty-two,...x-ty-nine" followed by a different "x-ty to x-ty-nine" chunk, children have not yet learned the order of the x-ty words, that is, the order of the multiples of ten. In the unstable incorrect portions, children sometimes went on and on producing number

---

[2] My daughter at age 3–2 said these terms but only when she was working on the decade structure of the twenties (see Table 1-2). The pattern thus may become obvious to some children only after they have learned the teens by rote.

words in "x-ty to x-ty-nine" chunks but not in the correct order; twenties might be followed by fifties followed by thirties followed by seventies followed by fifties followed by twenties, and so on. Siegler and Robinson (1982) also reported such patterns for their sample of 3- through 5-year-olds, and their model for sequences between twenty and one hundred reflected knowledge of the "x-ty to x-ty nine" chunks.

Stable incorrect portions above twenty are of three kinds (Fuson et al., 1982). One group (38%) ended in twenty-nine and then jumped past the thirties to another decade (e.g., twenty-nine, fifty, fifty-one, fifty-two, fifty-three"). Another 25% of the stable portions above twenty began with the word "twenty" and then jumped back into the teens words and produced several of them. Another 38% ended in a word between ten and twenty and then jumped to a decade word (e.g., "eighteen, forty" or "seventeen, thirty") or to a decade-one word (e.g., "fourteen, forty-one" or "eighteen, eighty-one"). These latter confusions may stem from a misunderstanding of the decade structure or from acoustic confusion of "-ty" and "-teen." As further evidence that children had partial but incomplete knowledge of the decade structure, children in the Fuson et al. (1982) and Siegler and Robinson (1982) samples sometimes produced invented number words that were incorrect extensions of the decade pattern: twenty-ten, twenty-eleven, twenty-twelve; thirty-ten; sixty-ten.

It is not clear how children solve the decade problem, that is, learn the correct order of the decade chunks. We suggested in Fuson et al. (1982) three different methods that could be used to teach the order of the decades. Each of these could also be used by children in their learning. One method is linking the first member of a cycle to the last member of the preceding cycle (e.g., learning "twenty-nine thirty" or "thirty-nine forty"). Another method would involve learning the list of decade words (twenty, thirty, forty, fifty,... ninety) as a new rote sequence and using this rote sequence to select the correct next cycle. The third method would require children to see the pattern between the decade words and the words below ten, for example, two and twenty, three and thirty, four and forty, and so on, and then use the words below ten to generate the decade words. This method obviously is easy to use with numerical symbols, but how much difficulty the irregularities in the English decade words create in its use is not clear. Baroody (1986b) suggests that many mentally handicapped children seem to use the first method for the first new decade (twenty-nine, thirty). Baroody and Ginsburg (1984) report the use of the third method by a mildly retarded girl. It does seem probable that children might use the first method for the first couple of decades and then use either the second or third method to generate the remaining decades. However, the fact that the length of children's correct sequence between twenty and one hundred seems to increase gradually rather than showing a sharp increase between forty (or fifty) and one hundred does support the notion that children extend their sequence by a decade or two at a time and do not learn a single generative rule that they then use successfully over the whole range. This, of course requires more research and does not necessarily imply that children could not learn such a rule if they were helped to do so. The data to date do not reflect systematic efforts at teaching children to learn the sequence to one hundred but only uncontrolled "normal" opportunity to learn this sequence. Some kindergarten teachers do stress learning the sequence to one hundred and are successful in helping all their children to do so by the end of the year. Some school districts also stress such learning with parents and include counting to one hundred as one of the abilities children should have when they enter kindergarten.

Do all children produce stable incorrect portions? The sequences of a few children had an accurate portion that was followed by a portion better characterized as a "troublespot" than as a stable portion. The sequences of a few other children had only an accurate portion followed by inconsistent inaccurate words, that is, they contained no stable portion. However, overall our data (Fuson et al., 1982) indicated that stable incorrect portions are typical of sequences below thirty.

The data on stable portions previously reported all were gathered within a single session. One would expect the stability of sequences to be maximal under this condition and would certainly wish to see data concerning the stability of sequences across different sessions. Unfortunately, few such data exist. Fuson et al. (1982) did report that a follow-up of a small sample of children after 5 months revealed that about half the children produced sequences that were accurate at the old stable portion. The other half still produced stable portions that were related to their old stable portions. A third of these said the same stable portion, a third had filled in all but one of the omissions in their old stable portion, and a third now produced a word that had been omitted in the old stable portion but also now omitted a word next to it that had been said in the old portion (e.g., a change from "five, six, eight" to "five, seven, eight"). Baroody and Price (1983) reported that the portions of some children in their sample remained stable over periods ranging up to 10 weeks. Thus, not all stable portions are only temporary stabilities. Rather the stable portions for some children reflect ways in which the sequence is stored, remembered, and produced over fairly long periods of time. The extent of such stability and the length of time over which such stability is exhibited are important issues for further research.

2.1.3.3. Nonstable Incorrect Final Portions. Nonstable final incorrect portions are by definition irregular over repeated trials. However, they do possess some structure and some regularities. Four examples of such nonstable final incorrect portions are given in Table 2-1, and they show some of these patterns. The nonstable portions are composed largely of three different types of elements: (1) forward runs: from two to five words contiguous in the conventional sequence (e.g., "sixteen, seventeen, eighteen" or "twenty-one, twenty-two, twenty-three"); (2) forward runs with omissions: from two to five words in the conventional order but containing omissions (e.g., "twelve, fourteen, seventeen"); and (3) single, unrelated words. The runs and runs with omissions are all forward directed (i.e., they are in sequence order), and these runs, runs with omissions, and the separate words are concatenated in a generally forward direction. The average nonstable portion went toward four or five words, fell back to an earlier word, and then went forward another four or five words. Some words in the nonstable portions were favorites with children: thirteen, fourteen, sixteen, eighteen, nineteen, twenty, and twenty-nine occurred with considerable frequency (in the longest nonstable portion of at least 20 of the 86 children). Occasionally, children repeated a word within the unstable portion, a mean of about 1.4 words were repeated in this way. About a fourth of the nonstable portions contained words from early in the accurate sequence portion, about a half contained words from later in the accurate sequence or the stable incorrect portion, and about a fourth did not contain words from the accurate or the stable incorrect portion.

2.1.4. Structure of a Number-Word Sequence and Errors in Learning It

Studies of errors made in producing number-word sequences in languages other than English indicate that the structure of the sequence itself dictates the kinds of errors children make while learning that sequence. The American Sign Language (ASL) sequence of number signs to one hundred has few rote elements. Rather, most of the sequence can be characterized by various production rules that link a sign to the sign preceding it and/or to earlier signs. Separate production rules apply to 1 through 5, 6 through 9, 11 through 15, 16 through 19, and to the decades. Secada (1984) found that deaf, signing children of an ASL parent made errors that were related to incompletely learned production rules and to those signs that are difficult to form manually (Secada, 1984). The Chinese sequence is regular from ten up (ten, ten one, ten two, ten three, ten four,..., two ten, two ten one, two ten two, etc.). Chinese 4-, 5-, and 6-year-old children made many fewer errors in counting to 19 than did American children, who have to learn the irregular English teens words (K. Miller & Stigler, 1987). However, Chinese children were somewhat more likely to confuse decades and units and count on by tens instead of ones. Thus, after saying "two-ten" [twenty], some Chinese children said "three-ten [thirty], four-ten [forty], five-ten [fifty]," rather than "two-ten, two-ten one, two-ten two, etc." For both countries, errors in counting were most likely to occur at the decades. A "...38, 39" would be followed by "20, 21,..." rather than by the correct decade. Thus, even though the formation of the decades is regular in Chinese, applying this decade rule evidently is somewhat difficult. However, American 5-year-olds did demonstrate more difficulty with this decade problem than did Chinese 5-year-olds, so perhaps that regularity does give an advantage to Chinese children.

2.2. Elaboration of the Number-Word Sequence

Number-word sequence learning continues long after the child first is able to produce the number words correctly. Children's uses of the number-word sequence after they can produce it display an orderly succession of new abilities. We have characterized groups of these abilities as occurring at the same level because the abilities in that group seem to require a representation of the number-word sequence that differs qualitatively from the representation of the sequence at other levels. We have called the learning of these new sequence abilities "the elaboration of the sequence." This elaboration is a lengthy process ranging at least from age 4 to 7 or 8. The elaboration occurs first at the beginning of the sequence. Different parts of the sequence can be at different elaborative levels at the same time.

The five levels of elaboration (Fuson et al., 1982) follow:

1. String level. The words are a forward-directed, connected, undifferentiated whole.
2. Unbreakable list level. The words are separated, but the sequence exists in a forward-directed recitation form and can only be produced by starting at the beginning.
3. Breakable chain level. Parts of the chain can be produced starting from arbitrary entry points rather than always starting at the beginning.
4. Numerable chain level. The words are abstracted still further and become units in the numerical sense; thus sets of sequence words can themselves represent a numerical situation and can be counted or matched.
5. Bidirectional chain level. Words can be produced easily and flexibly in either direction.

These different levels are marked by performance differences in more complex aspects of sequence production (we called these "forward sequence skills" and "backward sequence skills"), in the ability to comprehend and produce relations on the words in the sequence, and in uses of the sequence of words in counting, cardinal, ordinal, and measure situations. The abilities at each level are briefly described in Table 2-4. Producing relations on the sequence words and using the number-word sequence in counting, cardinal, ordinal, and measure contexts require knowledge in addition to the sequence skills themselves. Placement of sequence relations or of uses on the same horizontal line in Table 2-4 implies that the sequence skill is required for that relation or use. The counting and cardinal uses of the number-word sequence listed in the right-most column of Table 2-4 are discussed in later chapters of this book. Counting correspondences are discussed in chapters 3 through 6 and 10. The cardinality rule is reviewed in chapter 7, and making a set of numerosity a (Table 2-4) is discussed in chapter 9. The more sophisticated

Table 2-4. Sequence Production Levels

Sequence levels	Forward sequence skills	Backward sequence skills	Sequence relations	Counting, cardinal, ordinal, measure context uses
String 1 2 3 4 5 →	Produce word sequence from one; words may be undifferentiated			Count: no intentional one-to-one correspondences can be established
Unbreakable list 1-2-3-4-5 →	Produce word sequence from one; words differentiated			Count: intentional one-to-one correspondences can be established Card: cardinality rule can be acquired (can count to find out "How many?") Ord.: ordinality rule can be acquired (can count to find out "What position?") Meas.: measure rule can be acquired (can count to find out "How many units?")

Card. Op.ᵃ: simple addition problems if objects for the sum just need to be counted

Card.: make a set of numerosity "*a*"

Ord.: find the "*a*th" entity

Meas.: make (find) a quantity made up of *n* units

Card. Op.: Count-all and count-part procedures for addition and subtraction

Card. Op.: Count on without keeping track (addition)

Just After, Just Before: The list can be used to find these relations

After, Before: The list can be used to find these relations

Just After, Just Before: These relations can be produced immediately

After, Before: These relations can be produced immediately

Count up from one to *a*

Start counting up from *a*

Breakable chain
1 2 3 4 5 →

Table 2-4. *Continued*

Sequence levels	Forward sequence skills	Backward sequence skills	Sequence relations	Counting, cardinal, ordinal, measure context uses
			Between: Partially correct solutions may be given by using Just After or Just Before relations	Card. Op.: Count on from a to b without keeping track (subtraction)
	Count up from a to b		Between: Can produce all words between a and b going forward	Card. Op.: Count back from b without keeping track (subtraction)
		Count down from b		
		Count down from b to a	Between: can produce all words between a and b going backward	Card. Op.: Count back from b to a without keeping track (subtraction)
Numerable chain ① ② ③ ④ ⑤ →	Count up n from a; give b as answer 1. $n = 1$ (Just After) 2. $n = 2, 3$ (4) 3. $n > 4$			Card. Op.: Count on with keeping track (addition)

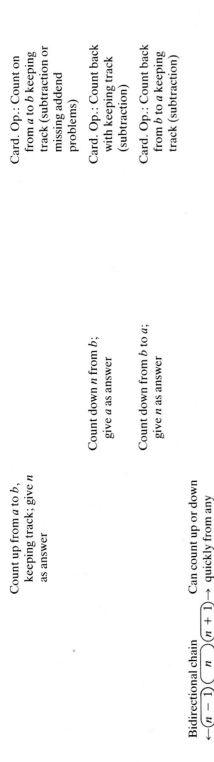

Bidirectional chain

$\leftarrow \boxed{n-1}\ \boxed{n}\ \boxed{n+1} \rightarrow$

Can count up or down quickly from any word; can shift directions easily

Count up from a to b, keeping track; give n as answer

Card. Op.: Count on from a to b keeping track (subtraction or missing addend problems)

Count down n from b; give a as answer

Card. Op.: Count back with keeping track (subtraction)

Count down from b to a; give n as answer

Card. Op.: Count back from b to a keeping track (subtraction)

Note. From "The Acquisition and Elaboration of the Number Word Sequence" by K.C. Fuson, J. Richards, and D.J. Briars. In *Progress in Cognitive Development Research: Children's Logical and Mathematical Cognition* (Vol. 1) (pp. 58–60), edited by C. Brainerd, New York: Springer-Verlag. Copyright 1982 by Springer-Verlag. Reprinted by permission.

[a] Card. Op.: Cardinal Operation—an operation on cardinal number words. We include the two earliest operations—addition and subtraction—here.

uses of sequence skills for the cardinal operations addition and subtraction and the relationships between counting knowledge and cardinality knowledge required for using these sequence skills are discussed in considerable detail in chapter 8. We therefore here only briefly review the sequence skills and the relations on sequence words that are outlined in Table 2-4.

2.2.1. String Level

When the number-word sequence is first learned, it functions as a unidirectional whole structure. The number words can be produced only by reciting the whole sequence. The sequence then may begin to become differentiated into separated words, but clusters of unseparated words may still remain. This phenomenon is common in the initial learning of other sequential material like the alphabet, poems, and songs. Early in learning, clusters like "LMNOP" or "sweet 'landaliberty'" may remain undifferentiated. This level occurs very early with respect to the number-word sequence. Walters and Wagner (1981), for example, report one child aged 1–11 who used the undifferentiated phrase one-two-three in counting. Nesher (personal communication, February, 1980; April, 1981) has described difficulties very young Hebrew-speaking children have in counting with the first multisyllabic Hebrew number words; they use each syllable to correspond with an object rather than each word. However, this level may be a very brief one and may not occur for all children.

2.2.2. Unbreakable List Level

At this level the separate words are differentiated from each other. However, children still must start saying the sequence from one. They cannot start saying the sequence from an arbitrary word in the sequence. This level seems to result from a relatively low level of learning of a sequence rather than only from developmental limitations of children. We have found, for example, that many adults cannot begin saying the sequence of musical "words" (*do re mi fa so la ti do*) from an arbitrary word; rather they must start at the beginning and get to that word from within the sequence. At this level the number-word sequence exists in a *recitation form*, as a forward-directed recited sequence, rather than as an associative chain of separable linked elements (as at the next level). If this recitation form is induced in children by saying two or three words in order from the sequence, they can give the correct next word more frequently than if only a single word is said (Fuson et al., 1982). Mothers seem to have some awareness of this feature of early sequence learning, because they sometimes give children such a "running start" within the sequence in attempts to elicit the next words (Saxe et al., in press). In Fuson et al. (1982) we called this level the "unbreakable chain" level. However, because each word cannot yet reliably elicit the next word, the word *chain* does not seem appropriate. The term *unbreakable list* seems preferable, and so we will use this term instead (and have replaced the original *chain* with *list* in Table 2-4).

Later in this level a child can demonstrate the sequence skill of counting up from one to a given number word, that is, can stop the count at a specified word. This, of course, requires that the child be able to remember the word while saying the sequence and be able to use this word within a feedback loop to check whether that word has yet been reached. With this sequence skill a child can establish two pairs of relations on sequence words, the Just After/Just Before[3] relations and the more general After/Before relations (see Table 2–4). The Just After and Just Before relations derive from words contiguous in the sequence to a given word. For example, 8 is just after 7, and 6 is just before 7. At the unbreakable list level, however, a child cannot begin from seven and move up or down the sequence. The child must use the sequence skill of counting up from one to seven to find Just After and Just Before relations. The After and Before relations are the more general successor and predecessor relations. For example, 9, 4, and 12 all are after 2 and they all are before 14. The After and Before relations are defined on any two words: For any word a and any different word b, either a is after b or b is after a. Although all four of these sequence relations can be found by using the sequence skill counting up from one to a, children at this level only sometimes find these sequence relations in this way. More frequently they just produce an incorrect answer (Fuson et al., 1982). The sequence skill of counting up from one to a also enables children to use the sequence in the counting, cardinal, ordinal, and measure ways specified in Table 2-4.

2.2.3. Breakable Chain Level

At the breakable chain level, children can start counting up from an arbitrary number in the sequence. They can break into the sequence of number words and can continue to say it without the running start of having multiple words said or of saying the sequence from one themselves. The representation of the sequence is also in the more flexible form of separated words, each with an association to the word following it and to the word preceding it. The term *chain* was adopted to portray this feature, and the term *breakable* was chosen to indicate the new sequence skill counting up from an arbitrary word.

Greeno, Riley, and Gelman (1984) noted the distinction between the unbreakable list and breakable chain levels in their counting model. They modeled the more primitive level by stipulating that the whole accumulated series of previously used words serves as the cue for retrieving the next word

---

[3] In Fuson et al. (1982), we called these relations *And Then* and *And Then Before* in order to preserve in the name of the relation the direction of the sequence and the actual process one goes through in using these relations. To answer "What is just after seven?" one thinks, "seven (and then is) eight" moving in the forward direction of the sequence from seven. To answer "What is just after seven?" one thinks, "seven (and then before is) six" moving backward from seven. However, these terms do not make the meaning of the relation as the immediate successor or predecessor as clear as do Just After/Just Before, and these latter terms also have a clearer parallelism with their related cardinal relations and with the After/Before sequence relations. For these reasons we have changed here to the use of the terms Just After/Just Before.

in the sequence. So the cue for producing "seven" is not "six," but is "one two three four five six." A developmentally later version of the model could then allow a single word to cue the production of the next word; this would then be a model of counting at the breakable chain level.

The ability to enter the sequence at an arbitrary word means that the Just After and Just Before relations can be produced immediately by saying the given number word and then proceeding to the next forward or to the next backward word. The After and Before relations also come to be able to be produced immediately at this level, although how children accomplish this is not clear (see Fuson et al., 1982, for more discussion of this point). In addition to counting up from a, three other sequence skills are learned at this level. One of these is the forward sequence skill counting up from a to b. The two others are backward sequence skills: counting down from a and counting down from b to a. In Fuson and Secada (1983), cross-sectional data indicated that the production of backward sequences lagged behind the production of forward sequences by about 2 years (i.e., the mean age of children who produced a forward sequence to x was 2 years younger than the mean age of children who produced a backward sequence from x). Children sometimes learn a backward sequence of numbers as a separate learning task (e.g., ten, nine, eight, ..., three, two, one, blast off!). But above ten, most children count down by generating a backward sequence from the familiar forward sequence. Producing such backward sequences from the forward sequence is a very difficult task for young children. It is so difficult that it seems possible that the sequence might be at the numerable chain level with respect to forward sequence skills while still being only at the breakable chain level with respect to backward sequence skills.

Evidence supporting the distinctions between the unbreakable list and breakable chain levels was described in Fuson et al. (1982). Fuson and Secada (1983) reported additional evidence supporting this distinction. For a sample of 60 middle-class children between 3½ and 6, counting up from one to a specified number a, a sequence skill at the unbreakable list level, was significantly easier than starting to count up from a specified number a, a sequence skill at the breakable chain level. The transition to the breakable chain level for words below ten seemed to be accomplished by about age 4 for most of these children. The count up from a sequence skill was well established by age 4½, while the Just After relation for words below ten was still being learned by a good portion of children aged 4½ and 5 (i.e., they could not yet immediately give the word that came right after a given word). Children began the elaboration of the early part of their sequence (they possessed the sequence skill of counting up to a for words eight and ten) while they were still learning a later portion of the sequence (e.g., they might not yet know the word "sixteen").

In languages in which successive number words are linked in each other in some meaningful way, the Just After and Just Before relations may be easier to derive than in English, where contiguous words are only connected by their rote linkage within the sequence. For example in ASL successive words within the chunks for 1 through 5, 6 through 9, 11 through 15, and 16 through 19 are linked in meaningful ways (by raising one more finger or by touching a finger next to a given finger). Secada (1984) matched ASL children to English-speaking children by the length of their accurate number-word sequences and found that the ASL children performed considerably better than did the English-speaking children on questions involving the Just After and Just Before relations.

In Table 1-1 in chapter 1, order relations on two cardinal situations (the relations More Than and Fewer Than) and order relations on two sequence words (the relations After and Before) are described. The same number words are used in sequence and in cardinal situations, and the order relations on two cardinal number words (number words said with intended cardinal reference) are related to the order relations on two sequence number words (number words said only with reference to their existence within the sequence of number words). If b is after a in the sequence, then b is more than a and vice versa. If b is before a in the sequence, then b is fewer than a and vice versa. Thus, either order relation can be derived from the other. In Fuson et al. (1982) and in Fuson and Hall (1983), we explored the nature of the relationships between these sequence and cardinal order relations.[4] Our data supported several conclusions. For number words of ten and less, the cardinal order relations are understood earlier than (or at least are more accurate than) the sequence order relations. Performance on the sequence order relations did not differ greatly for words below ten and for words between ten and twenty, suggesting that a single process for deriving the sequence order relations is used over the whole range of sequence words from one to twenty. For number words between ten and twenty, performance on sequence order relations was better than that on cardinal order relations, indicating that sequence order relations may then be used to derive cardinal order relations for words of this size. This is a sensible conclusion, because as number words get large, it would seem that cardinal order relations must be derived from sequence order relations. For example, in order to decide whether 83 is more than 79, we do not make a pile of 83 objects and another of 79 objects and compare the pile; that is, we do not use cardinal order relations. Nor is it likely that we have in the past had experience with this particular cardinal situation so that we have already learned the order relation on these two sets. Rather, we use the sequence of number words to decide that 83 comes after 79, and we then conclude that 83 is more than 79. Our data thus indicate that this use of sequence words probably begins for the words above ten. In spite

---

[4] The terms used with the children were "come earlier/come later" for sequence relations and "is bigger/smaller" for cardinal relations. Of course, one difficulty with such research is that results may reflect differential familiarity with the words for the order relations rather than differential ability to establish such order relations. This factor does not apply to the set size effects, but does affect the comparisons between the two kinds of order relations.

of a considerable amount of research by various people on More Than/Fewer Than relations on cardinal words below ten, the process used in producing these relations is still not clear. Nor is it clear whether the After/Before order relations on sequence words below ten are derived from those on cardinal words or whether the sequence order relations involve a different (although possibly similar) representation and an independent processing of this sequence representation.

The Just After and Just Before sequence relations also have analogous cardinal relations. If 7 is the word just after 6 (sequence relation), then 7 is one bigger than 6 (cardinal relation) and vice versa. If 6 is the word just before 7 (sequence relation), then 6 is one smaller than 7 (cardinal relation) and vice versa. In Fuson et al. (1982), we reported a study in which the relationship between these sequence and cardinal relations was explored. That study indicated that children are better at the sequence than the cardinal relations. Therefore, if one of these is derived from the other, the cardinal relations seem to be derived from the sequence relations rather than vice versa. This generalization may not be true, however, for languages such as ASL in which successive number words in at least part of the sequence are linked to each other by cardinal notions of "one bigger than."

The sequence After and Before relations can be used to determine words that are between two given words as in the question, "Tell me two numbers that come after three and before seven when you are counting." Likewise, the cardinal More Than and Fewer Than relations can be used to determine words that are between two given words as in the question, "Tell me two numbers that are bigger than three and smaller than seven." Both for pairs of numbers below ten and for pairs between ten and twenty, kindergarten children did much worse in the cardinal condition than in the sequence condition (Fuson et al., 1982). They seemed to have much more difficulty coordinating the directionality of the order relations in the cardinal condition than in the sequence condition, frequently answering one cardinal question correctly and then answering the other question in the same (and thus wrong) direction. For example, they might respond to the above cardinal question with six and eight (six is bigger than three but eight is not smaller than seven). They also responded in the sequence condition with the sequence strategies of counting up or down two successive words; for example, for the sequence question above, some children would respond "four, five" or "six, five." Children used such an integrated strategy much less often to the cardinal question; instead they responded to each separate part of the question. These problems in the cardinal condition disappeared in the first grade.

2.2.4. Numerable Chain Level

At the numerable chain level, each word in the sequence can be taken as an equivalent single word, that is, as a unit. Steffe et al. (1983) called such units "verbal unit items" or "abstract unit items," depending on the uses a child makes of these words. At this level children use these verbal unit items to represent cardinal addition and subtraction operations. For example, to add eight and five, a child will say the first eight sequence words (forming a set of eight words to represent the cardinal eight) and will then say five more sequence words (forming a set of five words to represent the cardinal five added to the cardinal eight). The final sequence word thirteen then tells the sum of eight and five. When the second number is greater than two or three, some method of keeping track of the words counted on must be used. The sequence skills and the understanding of relationships among sequence, counting, and cardinal number words required at this level are quite complex. These are described in some detail in chapter 8 and are not reviewed here. Data concerning the age and relative difficulty of various sequence skills are presented in Fuson et al. (1982). We will only emphasize here that, not surprisingly, counting down is much more difficult than is counting up and that the size of n in counting on n words from a is very important. For example, it is considerably easier to keep track of two than of five words counted up and of five than of eight words counted up. The ability to count down seems to develop fairly rapidly from early to late in the seventh year (within 6-year-olds), and children aged 6 to 6½ are working on, but have not yet mastered, ways to keep accurate track of the number words counted up or down.

2.2.5. Bidirectional Chain Level

At the bidirectional chain level, the difference in difficulty between proceeding forward in the sequence and backward in the sequence is greatly reduced. Children can count up or count down quickly from any word. They can shift directions easily and without intrusions from the opposite direction. These abilities then lead to relating counting up and counting down. This relationship can provide a basis for understanding the inverse relationship of certain aspects of addition and subtraction. Few data on this level exist, although Steffe and his colleagues (e.g., Steffe et al., 1983) have begun to explore some of these issues. Some aspects of these relationships are discussed in chapter 8 with respect to the most advanced solution procedures for the most complex addition and subtraction problems.

2.2.6. More Advanced Levels

There are even more advanced sequence skills than are listed in Table 2-4. For example, the decade portion of the number-word sequence also comes to be elaborated. Children can then count up or down by tens as well as by ones. Thus, children can think of a problem such as 48 + 36 by first counting up three tens from one number and then counting up six ones: 48, 58, 68, 78, 79, 80, 81, 82, 83, 84. They can also count three tens from one whole decade and then count up six ones: 40, 50, 60, 70, 78, 79, 80, 81, 82, 83, 84. Multiplication and division can be supported by learning multiplication strings for each number, for example, the string for eight—8, 16, 24, 32, 40, 48, 56, 64—and then running up or down the string to find a particular combination. Very little research has been done on these advanced sequence skills.

2.2.7. Changing From Level to Level

How children learn the sequence skills at each level and what enables them to move on to a new level is not at all clear at present. The approach of Case (1985a, 1985b) would seem to be very helpful in attacking these issues. The sequence skills seem fairly readily analyzed in terms of executive control structures, and measures of operational efficiency of sequence skills seem fairly easy to obtain. Both of Case's change factors, maturation and practice, may be involved in level changes. Maturation may enable the sequence to be said more rapidly, thus freeing sufficient processing space for the additional processing required by a given sequence skill. Those skills that show an improvement within a fairly short age span seem most likely to stem from maturational effects. The fact that even adults have difficulty in low-level sequence skills with sequences such as the alphabet and the musical scale suggests that practice is also required for the sequence skills, i.e., saying a sequence must reach a certain minimum level of automaticity in order for there to be sufficient processing space left to carry out even the early sequence skills. The rather wide age spans for certain sequence skills also suggests that practice (and the resulting automaticity of the sequence) is important.

2.2.8. Application of Levels to Other Languages

With respect to the acquisition or to the elaboration of the sequence, the extent to which these results apply to number-word sequences in other languages is not clear. Because the structure of the particular number-word sequence seems to affect the kinds of errors children make in learning that sequence (see 2.1.4), the results with respect to the acquisition of the English sequence of number words would seem to apply only to sequences that shared its features. The developmental levels involved in the elaboration of the number-word sequence would seem to depend less on particular features of the sequence and consequently would apply more widely. Some evidence does suggest that this is true. We noted previously the observation of the string level in Hebrew-speaking children. Saxe (1982) reported that New Guinea Oksapmin children and adults demonstrated sequence skills at the breakable chain and at the numerable chain levels. Younger children and adults less familiar with currency interactions counted up from *a* to *b* without keeping track (breakable chain level); older schooled children and adults with experience with currency and trade stores counted up from *a* to *b* with keeping track (numerable chain level). Davydov and Andronov (1981) reported that children in the Soviet Union demonstrated sequence skills at the numerable chain level and used these skills as outlined in chapter 8 of this book.

There also is evidence that the extent to which children elaborate their sequences as far as the numerable chain level may depend on the extent to which they are taught a particular method of addition and subtraction in school that does not require counting up and counting down. Hatano (1982) reported that Japanese children count up or down much less frequently than do American children in order to solve addition or subtraction problems. Japanese children are taught a particular method of addition and subtraction (using complements to ten and going up over ten or down over ten by using convenient subsets of numbers) that does not require counting up or down (Fuson, Stigler, & Bartsch, in press; Hatano, 1982). In contrast American children do not seem to be systematically taught any particular method (Fuson, et al., in press) and thus most of them invent counting up and counting down for themselves. However, the extent to which Japanese children can count up or down is not clear. They may have elaborated sequences even if the use of these sequence skills is not their method of choice for solving addition and subtraction problems.

2.3. Summary

Data on children's production of the English sequence of number words indicate that most middle-class children below age 3½ are working on learning the sequence to ten, most children between 3½ and 4½ are working on learning the sequence of number words between ten and twenty, and a substantial proportion of children between 4½ and 6 are still imperfect on the upper teens part of the sequence (that between fourteen and twenty) but many are working on the decades from twenty through seventy. Most kindergarten children are learning the decades between twenty and seventy, but a substantial number of them are working on the sequence between one hundred and two hundred. Half the first graders and almost all second and third graders know the sequence to one hundred and are working on the sequence above one hundred. Of course, children's ability to say the correct sequence of number words is very strongly affected by the opportunity to learn and to practice this sequence. Children within a given age group show considerable variability in the length of the correct sequence that they can produce. Frequent exposure to "Sesame Street" or to parents, older siblings, or teachers who provide frequent counting practice undoubtedly enables a child to say longer accurate sequences at a younger age.

The incorrect sequences produced by children before they have learned the standard sequence have a characteristic structure (Fuson et al., 1982). For sequences up to thirty, the characteristic form of most sequences produced by children is a first portion consisting of *an accurate number-word sequence*, followed by *a stable incorrect portion* of from 2 to 5 or 6 words that are produced with some consistency over repeated trials, followed by *a final nonstable incorrect portion* that varies over trials and may consist of many words. The first portion simply consists of the first *x* words in the conventional sequence of number words and varies with age as previously outlined. Almost all of the stable incorrect portions have words in the conventional order but words are omitted (e.g., fourteen, sixteen or twelve, fourteen, eighteen, nineteen). The patterns of these omissions and other data indicate that most children learn the words to twenty as a rote sequence of new words (except possibly for "eighteen, nineteen") rather than observing and using the somewhat irregular pattern of the teen words, whereas most children learn the decade pattern of repeated cycles of words from x-ty to x-ty-nine. However, the decade problem of learning the English decade names and their conventional order takes a long time to solve (as much as a year and a half), and it is not yet clear how children do learn these decade names in the correct order. Children very early (almost all 3-year-olds and most 2-year-olds) do learn to differentiate number words from nonnumber words and use only the former when saying the sequence; unstable incorrect portions almost always contain only number words. Nonstable, final incorrect portions for children 3½ and older are composed largely of three different types of elements (1) forward runs, from two to five words contiguous in the conventional sequence (e.g., sixteen, seventeen, eighteen or twenty-one, twenty-two, twenty-three); (2) forward runs with omissions: from two to five words in the conventional order but containing omissions (e.g., twelve, fourteen, seventeen); and (3) single, unrelated words.

This characteristic form of incorrect sequences while they are being learned seems to result from the irregularities in the English system of number words for the words between ten and twenty and for the decade words. These irregularities also suggest that one of the first experiences of English-speaking children with a mathematical structure (the English sequence of number words) is that it is complex, irregular, and must be memorized laboriously rather than that it has a clear and obvious *pattern* that is easy to learn.

Number-word sequence learning continues long after the child first is able to produce the number words correctly. Children's uses of the number-word sequence after they can produce it display an orderly succession of new abilities. We have characterized groups of these abilities as occurring at the same level because the abilities in that group seem to require a representation of the number-word sequence that differs qualitatively from the representation of the sequence at other levels. We have called the learning of these new sequence abilities "the elaboration of the sequence." This elaboration is a lengthy process ranging at least from age 4 to age 7 or 8. The elaboration occurs first at the beginning of the sequence. Different parts of the sequence can be at different elaborative levels at the same time.

The five levels of elaboration are (1) string level: the words are a forward-directed, connected, undifferentiated whole; (2) unbreakable list level: the words are separated, but the sequence exists in a forward-directed recitation form and can only be produced by starting at the beginning; (3) breakable chain level: parts of the chain can be produced starting from arbitrary entry points rather than always starting at the beginning; (4) numerable chain level: the words are abstracted still further and become units in the numerical sense; thus sets of sequence words can themselves represent a numerical situation and can be counted or matched; (5) bidirectional chain level: words can be produced easily and flexibly in either direction (Fuson et al., 1982; also see Table 2-4 in this chapter). These different levels are marked by increasingly complex sequence abilities: becoming able to start and to stop counting at arbitrary number words; to count up a given number of words; and to count backward starting and stopping at arbitrary number words and counting down a given number of words. Children also increase their ability across these levels to comprehend and to produce order relations on the words in the sequence. Two such order relations are the Just After and Just Before relations; these relations refer to the words just after and just before a given word: 6 is just before 7 and 7 is just after 6. The two other order relations are the After and Before relations. These terms relate any two sequence words; either a is after b or a is before b.

Both of these kinds of sequence relations have analogous order relations on cardinal situations (see Table 1-1 in chapter 1). For number words of ten and less, children seem to be more accurate on the cardinal order relations More Than/Fewer Than than they are on the analogous sequence order relations After/Before. However, for words between ten and twenty, children are more accurate with the sequence order relations. For words both below and above ten, children are more accurate with the sequence relations Just After and Just Before than on the analogous cardinal relations One More Than/One Fewer Than. The latter patterns suggest that, except for the cardinal relations More Than/Fewer Than on number words less than ten, children may derive the cardinal relations from the sequence relations.

How children learn the sequence skills at each level and what enables the representation of the sequence to change is not at all clear at present. The approach of Case (1985a, 1985b) would seem to be very helpful in attacking these issues. Both of Case's change factors, maturation and practice, may be involved in level changes. Maturation may enable the sequence to be said more rapidly, thus freeing sufficient processing space for the additional processing required by a given sequence skill. Practice increases the automaticity of the sequence, with the same result.

The extent to which these results with respect to the acquisition or to the elaboration of the sequence apply to number-word sequences in other languages is not clear. Because the structure of the particular number-word sequence seems to affect the kinds of errors children make in learning that sequence (see 2.1.4), the results with respect to the acquisition of the English sequence of number words would seem to apply only to sequences that share its features. The developmental levels involved in the elaboration of the number-word sequence would seem to depend less on particular features of the sequence and consequently would apply more widely. Some evidence does suggest that this is true (Davydov & Andronov, 1981; Nesher, personal communication, February, 1980; April, 1981; Saxe, 1982).

Part II   Correspondence Errors in
Counting Objects

3. Correspondence Errors in Children's Counting

With Diane J. Briars and Walter G. Secada

3.1. Introduction and Background

This chapter presents (1) an analysis of counting in which the indicating function of the act of pointing is made explicit, (2) a category system of correspondence errors in counting based on that analysis, and (3) a developmental description of correspondence errors in terms of that category system. The data are from observations of a large sample of children from 3½ to 6 years of age. The analysis of counting and the empirical results are pertinent both for those who may be interested in the more theoretical cognitive developmental issues raised by certain aspects of counting and for those who may be interested in the practical issues of improving counting skill. Counting is a complex activity, and this chapter deals only with one of its simpler variants—counting objects that are fixed but arranged in a single row. Counting objects that are movable and counting fixed objects arranged in disorganized arrays and in circular arrays are discussed in chapter 4. The effects of several variables on correspondence errors for objects in rows are reported in chapter 5. The results from all three chapters are then summarized and discussed in chapter 6.

3.1.1. A Definition of Counting and a Category System of Correspondence Errors in Counting

Counting immovable objects requires the person counting to establish a one-to-one correspondence between words and objects. Because words are located temporally and objects are located spatially, some sort of intermediary is needed to connect the two. The counter establishes this correspondence by using an indicating act, often the act of pointing, which has both a temporal and a spatial location. The indicating act thus serves as a mediator and involves two correspondences: the correspondence in time between a word and the indicating act and the correspondence in space between the indicating act and an object. The word–object correspondence then derives from the separate temporal and spatial correspondences involving the indicating act.

This use of the indicating act as a mediator requires the person counting to coordinate the production of two continuous sequences of actions (pointing and saying words[1]) and concurrently to coordinate spatially the sequence of points with the spatially distributed set of objects. Therefore, children can make a correspondence error that violates the word–point correspondence, or one that violates the point–object correspondence, or one that violates

---

[1] We shall find in this chapter that almost all 3- and 4-year-olds use pointing as their indicating act when counting objects in rows. To simplify the discussion throughout most of the chapter, we henceforth use the word "pointing" rather than the more general term "indicating act." The internalization of pointing to eye fixation among 5-year-olds is discussed in 3.3.11. Indicating acts other than pointing are discussed in chapter 4.

both correspondences. These different kinds of correspondence errors form the major categories within our proposed category system of correspondence errors in counting: word–point errors (W–P), point–object errors (P–O), and dual errors. A fourth error category plays a small role when counting objects fixed in rows but figures more heavily in the studies reported in chapter 4; this error category is returning to and recounting objects that have already been counted. Such errors stem from violating another requirement of accurate counting: One must remember which objects have already been counted. This memory demand is simple for objects fixed in rows, so discussion of it is postponed to chapter 4, in which the object arrays place more stress on memory.

To identify specific kinds of errors within the three broad categories (W–P, P–O, and dual) and to identify any additional kinds of correspondence errors young children might make in counting, we videotaped thirty 3-, 4-, and 5-year-old children[2] counting both linear and disorganized arrays, and we generated an exhaustive list of the error subtypes actually made by children (preliminary analyses and error subtypes were reported in Fuson & Mierkiewicz, 1980). The analysis of those errors led to the classification scheme shown in Table 3-1. A primary function of the present study was to test the adequacy of that scheme with a much larger sample of preschool children.

3.1.2. Goals of the Study

Because this was our first large-scale study of counting, our goals were many and varied. Our general questions included the following: What correspondence errors are commonly made by children and how do those errors change with age? How does the frequency of particular error types vary with the number of objects, their location, the sex of the counter, and the effort expended by the counter? What is the relative difficulty of coordinating the two counting activity sequences (pointing and saying words) versus coordinating spatially the points with the objects? Are children more likely to omit a word or a point? Are children more likely to do too much or too little when counting? Internalization of counting activity (cf. Vygotsky, 1962, 1978, 1986) also became of interest, though data on this aspect were not collected systematically. Several of these issues are discussed in more detail later.

A major objective was to ascertain whether the specific error subtypes given in Table 3-1 provide an exhaustive description of the correspondence errors commonly made by young children and, if necessary, to expand the subtypes to include new errors. The goal was to provide a validated category system of correspondence errors that could be used by other investigators. There has been considerable research on kinds of errors that children make in

---

[2] Six children were in each half-year age group.

Table 3-1. Categories of Correspondence Errors

Word–point errors: Violations of the temporal word–point correspondence

---

The temporal one-to-one correspondence between a number word and a point is violated, but the spatial one-to-one correspondence between a point and an object is maintained

---

Point–no word
    No word, one point, one object:
    point to an object without saying a
    number word

$$\begin{array}{c} \downarrow \\ \square \end{array}$$

Multiple words–one point
    Two words, one point, one object:
    point to an object once and say two
    number words; also three or four
    words, one point, one object

$$\begin{array}{cc} 5,\ 6 & 5,\ 6,\ 7 \\ \downarrow & \downarrow \\ \square & \square \end{array}$$

Part word–one point
    Part word, one point, one object: a
    word is stretched out over two or
    more objects

$$\begin{array}{ccccc} \text{sev-} & \text{en} & & \text{ni-} & \text{ii-} & \text{ine} \\ \downarrow & \downarrow & \text{or} & \downarrow & \downarrow & \downarrow \\ \square & \square & & \square & \square & \square \end{array}$$

Word between objects
    One word, no point, no object: a
    number word is said with no point
    and when the finger is over no object

$$\begin{array}{ccccc} 6 & 7 & 8 & 1 & 2 \\ \downarrow & & \downarrow & & \downarrow \\ \square & & \square & \text{or} & \square \end{array}$$

Point–object errors: Violations of the spatial point–object correspondence

---

The spatial one-to-one correspondence between point and object is violated, but the temporal one-to-one correspondence between word and point is maintained

---

Object skipped
    No word, no point, one object:
    finger passes over object but no word
    is said and no point is given to the
    object

$$\begin{array}{ccc} 5 & & 6 \\ \downarrow & & \downarrow \\ \square & \square & \square \end{array}$$

Multiple count
    Two words, two points, one object: a
    word and a point and then another
    word and a point are given to the
    same object; also three words, three
    points, one object; 4, 4, 1

$$\begin{array}{cc} 3\ \ 4 & 7\ \ 8\ \ 9 \\ \downarrow\downarrow & \downarrow\downarrow\downarrow \\ \square & \square \end{array}$$

Word and point–no object
    One word, one point, no object: a
    word and a point between objects

$$\begin{array}{ccc} 5 & 6 & 7 \\ \downarrow & \downarrow & \downarrow \\ \square & & \square \end{array}$$

Table 3-1. *Continued*

Dual errors: Violations of both the word–point and point-object correspondence

---

Both the temporal one-to-one correspondence between a number word and a point and the spatial one-to-one correspondence between point and object are violated

---

Multiple points–one word
    one word, two points, one object: 8
    one word and two points are given to   ↓ ↓
    an object   □

Multiple points–no word
    No word, two points, one object: no   ↓ ↓
    word is said and two points are given   □

Word–no point
    One word, no point, one object: 16   17   18
    word is said while the finger is over   ↓ – – – – – – – ↓
    the object but the point is omitted   □   □   □

Skim
    Finger skims over the array with no specific points, and words are produced in a stream having no apparent connection with the objects

Flurry
    Many points directed generally toward the array (rather than specific points directed at specific objects), and many words not in correspondence with the points are produced quite rapidly

---

Recount errors

A count of an object a second time after a different object has been counted

---

Reversing to recount a counted object
    A child returns and counts again an   5   6 8   7 9
    object already counted; the object   ↓   ↓ ↓   ↓ ↓
    returned from may also be counted   □   □   □
    again: 8 and 9 are such errors

Recount after counting an object skipped
    A child returns to a skipped object   5   7   6 8
    and counts it but then counts again   ↓   ↓   ↓ ↓
    the object returned from: 8 is this   □   □   □
    error

Note. The dual: multiple points–one word and word–no point categories are correspondence errors (there is a violation of the one-to-one correspondences) but nevertheless give the correct cardinality.

counting (Beckwith & Restle, 1966; Gelman & Gallistel, 1978; Ginsburg 1977; Ginsburg & Russell, 1981; Potter & Levy, 1968; Saxe, 1977; Schaeffer, Eggleston, & Scott, 1974; Wagner & Walters, 1982; Wilkinson, 1984). However, this body of research has suffered considerably because different error categories have been used for different studies, making comparisons across studies problematic (e.g., Kwon, 1986). The categories in some studies have not differentiated errors children make in saying the sequence of number words (e.g., omitting a number word or repeating a number word) from those correspondence errors in which an object does not receive a number word at all or receives more than one word. In fact, such a distinction seems likely to be fruitful. Children may consistently omit the same words in the sequence, and they rarely repeat number words (Chapter 2). In contrast the relative frequency of omissions and repetitions for correspondence errors is not clear. For this reason the analysis of errors in the sequence was done here independently of the analysis of correspondence errors: The correspondence errors in Table 3-1 are independent of the specific number words used. The categories used in some studies also have not explicitly considered the role of pointing, and thus quite different kinds of errors have been collapsed together. The category system presented and tested here includes both errors that have been identified in earlier studies and errors not described in other research but commonly made by the preschool children whom we studied.

Another purpose of the study was to examine the difficulty for young children of coordinating in time the production of two different sequences of actions (pointing and saying words) versus coordinating spatially the location of the points with the objects distributed in space. Given the difficulty young children have in coordinating two activities (e.g., Luria, 1959, 1961, and literature reviewed in Fuson, 1979b), one might expect children to make many errors when trying to coordinate the action of producing a word with that of producing a point. Such a coordination of two action sequences (speaking and pointing) seems likely to present more difficulties than simply coordinating successive acts of pointing with the spatial location of objects in a row. The relative difficulties of these two kinds of coordinations could be easily assessed with our category system by constrasting word–point errors with point–object errors.

A third focus of the present study concerns the extent to which counting displays the particular difficulty that young children seem to have in starting and in stopping activities (Luria, 1959, 1961). Gelman and Gallistel (1978) pointed out that the beginning and the end of the activity of counting involve the initial establishment of and the simultaneous ending of the correspondences involved in counting. They concluded from their counting studies that the ends of the activity of counting present special difficulty with respect to establishing accurate correspondences:

> Difficulty occurs to some extent at the starting of a count and to a larger extent at the stopping of a count. A child may start to point before he starts to recite tags, or vice versa; and if he does he may take some time to get beyond the first item. But

then things proceed smoothly. Trouble reappears only when he nears the end of a count. He may run over or under by one item—but not two, three, four or more items. (p. 205)

In some of the preliminary work for this study we observed just the opposite: that the probability of making an error per object in the middle of a count was higher than the probability at the beginning or end of a count. Therefore, the location of correspondence errors within the total activity of counting was of particular interest here.

The effect on different correspondence' errors of the effort expended by children in counting was another concern of the study. In the videotaped pilot work from which the error subtypes were generated, it appeared that many children put forth varying amounts of effort over the course of the interview and performance varied correspondingly. That is, some children counted fairly consistently over several trials, making roughly the same rate of errors over these trials and then began to make markedly more mistakes. If asked to "try hard" or "count really carefully," those children generally returned to the original lower rate of errors. It seemed possible that some types of errors were more affected than others by these attentional lapses. Therefore, in the present study on any trial in which a child made markedly more errors than before, experimenters gave that row length again with instructions to "try really hard." Kinds of errors made on those repetitions were then contrasted with those made on the previous trial.

This discussion has been phrased as if the objects were "out there." Of course, as discussed in chapter 1, in any given counting situation *the child* must decide what to consider as the "countables." When individual objects are considered as countables, the child is said to be using perceptual unit items (see chapter 1 and Steffe, von Glasersfeld, Richards, & Cobb, 1983). In the videotaped study we had found only two error types in which children did not seem to be using perceptual unit items. Whether new such error types would be found and the age at which children seemed to be using perceptual unit items was of interest with this larger sample. Once children begin to use perceptual unit items, the point–object correspondence is of course really a "point–perceptual unit item" correspondence. For simplicity we will continue to use point–object correspondence throughout the book.

A few words concerning our metrics for summarizing error data are necessary. Measures commonly used in earlier research were the percentage of trials on which the first error was of a certain type or the number or percentage of trials on which a particular type of error was made. Because larger sets provide more opportunities for making a correspondence error, both of those measures are highly correlated with set size, that is, with the number of objects counted. Thus, meaningful comparisons across different set sizes become problematic. Because different studies generally used different set sizes, meaningful comparisons across studies also are problematic. A measure that controls for the different number of objects is the number of errors per some standard number of objects, that is, an error *rate* measure. We found that using 100 as the standard number of objects for the calculation of the error rate produced numbers that were neither too large nor too small; this error rate measure is actually then the percentage of errors made. However, because we found that neither the use of "error rate" nor "percentage of errors" communicated clearly and consistently what this measure was, we will use the somewhat more awkward but more specific description "errors per 100 objects" in describing our analyses and results. Note that this measure only controls for set size, that is, it ensures that a higher number of errors on a larger set is not just an artifact of the measure itself. Whether the probability of making an error is actually higher per object in a larger set is an empirical question that this measure enables us to address. A second measure that seems important in understanding the development of accurate counting over the age span studied is how widespread a particular error is in the population of a certain age. Thus, the percentage of children of a given age who make a particular kind of error was also examined in this study. Unlike the errors per 100 objects measure, this measure does not control for set size. That is, one would expect more children to make an error in counting a very large set than in counting a very small set, because there are so many more opportunities for making errors on the very large set. However, this measure is useful in comparing the extent to which children make different kinds of errors in counting sets of the same size or in comparing error differences in children of different ages when they count sets of the same size.

3.2. Method

3.2.1. Subjects

The sample consisted of 86 children distributed over five half-year age groups: the 3½ to 4 group ranged in age from 3 years 6 months through 3 years 11 months, the 4 to 4½ group ranged in age from 4 years 0 months through 4 years 5 months, and so forth up through the 5½ to 6 group. The number of children in each age group was 18, 17, 17, 16, and 18, respectively, from the youngest to oldest age group. Sixty of these children—12 children balanced by sex in each half-year age group—were randomly selected from a Chicago public school whose population racially and economically matched the population of the city. The remaining 26 children were middle- to upper-middle-class children attending a private educational demonstration school. Initial analyses were done separately for each subpopulation. The analyses did not reveal any striking differences across the populations. Therefore, the analyses reported here are from the pooled sample.

3.2.2. Tasks and Procedure

A row of either four or five 1-inch blocks was presented, and the child was asked, "How many blocks are there?" On subsequent trials the row was systematically increased by alternately adding one or two blocks to the row, after which the experimenter said, "I put down one (or two) more block(s). How many blocks are there now?" Trials continued until a child either counted a row of 33 (or 34) blocks, refused to go on, or gave some indication over several trials of no longer attending to the task. Blocks in the row were placed approximately ¼ inch apart, and the children were not allowed to move the blocks. Sessions took from 10 to 30 minutes to complete. We used this procedure because it had been very effective in eliciting a considerable amount of counting in the pilot videotaped study. It did have the disadvantage that some of the oldest children counted on (added the 1 or 2 more objects to the previous result); such children were asked to count specific rows.

The effort manipulation was based on experimenter judgment. On any trial on which a child showed a marked increase in correspondence errors, the experimenter asked the child to count that row length again and to "try really hard" on that trial. A trial was given a third time with the same instruction if the counting was not more consistent with the error rate on earlier trials. Thus, repeated counts of the same set at different levels of experimenter-judged effort were obtained for those children who seemed to exhibit decreased effort during the task. All analyses reported, except the analysis of effort, are based on all count trials for a given child. The effort analysis contrasted only the high effort and the low effort trials and thus was restricted to those children judged by the experimenters to be showing considerably different amounts of effort across trials.

Three pairs of undergraduate students served as three experimenter teams; they were selected on the bases of a high grade-point average and considerable experience with young children. One member of each team recorded on a prepared sheet each point the subject made by making a mark on the row layout at the location for each point (defined as a pause at the end of a downward arc of the finger). The other coder on the team recorded the number words said by the subject by writing each number at the location on the row layout to which the subject's finger was directed when the number word was said (this location did not have to coincide with an actual point—the finger could be in an upward arc or still resting from an earlier point); this procedure thus transferred the stream of words said in time to a spatial record that could be compared to the spatial record of the points. Coders were trained to a criterion of at least 95% accuracy.[3] A check of the coding teams midway through the data collection indicated that accuracy was above 95%. After each data collection session, one of the coders compared the verbal and pointing records to ascertain the counting errors for each trial for each subject. A random 10% of the records was examined by a second coder, and agreement on error classification was high (98%).

---

[3] Accuracy was determined by having each team code adult counters making prescribed errors. These errors ranged over all of the error types in Table 3-1. These adult counters adopted the range of counting speeds we had observed in the videotaped study.

3.3. Results and Discussion

3.3.1. Amount of Counting in the Task

The basic counting situation proved to be quite involving for many children. They enjoyed seeing the row get longer and longer and stuck with the repeated counting for quite some time. However, not all children counted all row lengths. Some of the younger children would not complete the task and thus did not count some of the longer rows. Some of the older children counted on rather than counting the shorter rows; for example, for the row of 6 they said "4, 5, 6" if the first row was 4 and two more blocks were added. Children who were counting on were specifically asked to count four rows in the upper teens and twenties so that some sample of their counting was obtained; almost all of these children counted perfectly. The number of children in each half-year age group (beginning with 3½ to 4) who continued the counting at least into rows of 20 or more blocks was 11, 11, 16, 15, and 18, respectively. For each age group the mean longest row counted was 22, 23, 31, 29, and 31, respectively, and the mean number of rows counted was 16, 16, 19, 13, and 10, respectively. Thus, at all ages children did count a considerable number of blocks.

3.3.2. Kinds of Errors Made

The children in this larger sample made all of the errors identified in the smaller videotaped sample and listed in Table 3-1. They did not make any new errors, that is, errors that had not been identified in the smaller sample. Three errors that violate both correspondences were found very occasionally in the first videotaped sample but not in this larger sample; these are not listed in Table 3-1 because of their infrequency but are described in 4.2.3.3.6.

3.3.3. Word–Point and Point–Object Errors

There was a considerable drop in the rate of correspondence errors over this age range (Table 3–2), and there were considerably more point–object errors than word–point errors, 4.4 versus 2.3 per 100 objects counted. Furthermore, chi-square versions of McNemar's test indicated that significantly more children made at least one point–object error (83%) than made at least one word–point error (61%), $X^2(1, N = 86) = 13.37, p < .01$. The error rate effects were confirmed by a 2(error type) × 5(age) analysis of variance (ANOVA)[4] with error type as a repeated measure conducted on the rate of errors per 100 objects counted for word–point and for point–object errors.

---

[4] There was a considerable amount of variability in the error rates. The standard deviations for many error main types and subtypes were quite large, sometimes being as great as the rate (e.g., a rate of 5.2 might have a standard deviation of 5.4). The usual ANOVA assumptions concerning the distribution of the error rates and homogeneity of the variances involved in the analy-

Table 3-2. Error Rates and Percentage of Children Making an Error by Age for Word–Point and Point–Object Errors

Error categories	Age (years)					Mean
	3½ to 4	4 to 4½	4½ to 5	5 to 5½	5½ to 6	
Word–point total						
% Children	89%	76%	59%	38%	39%	61%
Error rate	5.0	2.5	2.3	1.1	0.3	2.3
Point–no word						
% Children	89%	71%	53%	38%	39%	58%
Error rate	4.0	1.5	1.6	0.9	0.3	1.7
Point–object total						
% Children	94%	100%	82%	75%	61%	83%
Error rate	10.6	6.5	2.0	1.7	0.8	4.4
Object skipped						
% Children	83%	82%	76%	56%	33%	66%
Error rate	8.6	4.4	1.2	0.8	0.2	3.1
Multiple count						
% Children	83%	88%	65%	69%	50%	71%
Error rate	1.7	2.1	0.7	0.8	0.6	1.2

Note. Error rates are the number of errors made per 100 objects counted. Two age groups whose rates are underlined by the same line had Newman-Keuls values indicating no significant differences between those rates. Two age groups whose percentage are underlined by the same line had a chi-square value indicating no significant difference between those percentages.

There was a significant main effect of age, $F(4, 81) = 11.79$, $p < .001$, and there was a significant main effect of error type, $F(1, 81) = 6.83$, $p < .01$.

The error type by age interaction was marginally significant, $F(4, 81) = 2.12$, $p < .09$. This interaction reflected the fact that the word–point error rate dropped significantly only at age 4 (Table 3–2), but the rate of point–object errors (which was much higher than the word-point rate at 3½) dropped significantly at age 4 and then again at 4½ but still ended at rates similar to the word–point rate for the three oldest groups. Word–point errors dropped out of children's repertoires before point-object errors did: the percentage of children making a word–point error dropped more rapidly than did the percentage of children making a point–object error.

ses were frequently violated. Therefore, we also did most of the analyses reported in this chapter on transformed versions of the data; the results were similar to those reported here. For this reason, and because ANOVA is known to be robust with respect to such violations, we continued to use ANOVA for all analyses here and in chapters 4 and 5.

Thus, contrary to our expectation, it proved to be more difficult for children to carry out one spatially distributed action sequence (pointing once and only once at each object) than to coordinate two continuous sequences of actions (pointing and saying words). Significantly more children (especially at the four oldest age groups) made point–object errors than word–point errors, and the point–object errors were made at a much higher rate (especially by the children aged 3½ to 4½). The children in fact were fairly good at coordinating the sequence of points with the sequence of words. On the average over this age range, they produced exactly one word with each point on more than 97 out of each 100 objects counted. Coordinating these two action sequences thus seems to be an exception to the reported difficulty young children have in coordinating two different action sequences (e.g., Fuson, 1979b; Luria, 1961). Perhaps internal motor organizational mechanisms exist that support the production in synchrony of these two special repetitive sequences of action. It is also possible that spreading out the objects or using objects of different colors might reduce the number of point–object errors and therefore also reduce (or even reverse) the difference in difficulty between these two kinds of correspondences. The effects of such variables are explored in chapter 5. Even though more point–object errors were made, children were also rather good at pointing once and only once at each object. Even the youngest children did this correctly for almost 9 out of every 10 objects.

3.3.3.1. The Most Prevalent Error Subtypes. The counting errors made by the most children at every age level were the point–object multiple count and object skipped errors and the word–point point–no word errors. Table 3-2 shows a breakdown by age level of both the percentages of children displaying each of these error subtypes and the mean frequency of errors per 100 objects for each subtype. Chi-square versions of McNemar's test indicated that significantly more children made each of these three kinds of errors than made any of the other subtypes of errors, the minimum value of these tests was $X^2(1, N = 86) = 10.13, p < .01$. The rates at which these three error subtypes were made also were much higher than were the rates for all other error subtypes except skims (discussed in 3.3.4. Dual Errors).

The rate of the object skipped errors (a mean of 3.1 over all ages) was higher than that for the other two frequently made errors (1.7 and 1.2) partly because of a particular aspect of the object skipped errors. Children could make several contiguous object skipped errors in one motion by skipping over two or more adjacent objects in one single skipping arc. Most such skipping arcs skipped over one to four objects, but there were arcs that skipped over as many as 15 objects. The mean number of objects skipped in a single arc was 1.5, and the mean number of skipping arcs per 100 objects was 2.0. This rate of 2.0 skipping actions per 100 objects counted is considerably closer to the rates of 1.7 for point–no word and of 1.2 for multiple count errors.

As would be expected, for all three of these prevalent errors, both the percentages of children making an error and the rates at which errors were made declined markedly with age (Table 3-2). The percentages showed a slower decline with age, with at least one third of the oldest children continuing to make these kinds of errors occasionally. The rates (errors per 100 objects counted) showed a much earlier and sharper decline, with the point–no word and object skipped errors showing a large significant drop at age 4 and the multiple count errors showing a significant drop at age 4½. The rates of all three of these errors were low for the 5-year-olds.

Interestingly enough, it was not the two point–object error subtypes (object skipped and multiple count) that were the most alike in their age-related changes. Rather the object skipped (a point–object error) and point–no word (a word–point error) errors were both quite high for the youngest children and showed a large significant drop at age 4. The other point–object error, multiple count, was not particularly high for the youngest children and did not drop at age 4. The object skipped and point–no word errors do share a common aspect. They both involve omitting some part of correct counting, while the multiple count error involves doing something extra. Thus, it seems that children younger than age 4 are more likely to omit some aspect of counting than to do extra counting, at least when counting long rows.

3.3.3.2. Other Word–Point Error Subtypes. The last three word–point errors in Table 3–1, multiple words–one point, part word–one point, and word between objects were made by few children: by 20%, 9%, and 2% of the children, respectively. They also were made at very low rates, 0.36, 0.20, and 0.02 per 100 objects counted, respectively.

When a child pointed but said no word, an examination of the sequence of number words said by the child indicated that the word was delayed rather than suppressed permanently. Such a judgment, of course, could only be made for that portion of the count in which a child produced the correct sequence of number words. However, within this part of the counting, almost all of the point–no word errors were of the form "...point–say 6, point–say nothing, point–say 7..." rather than of the form, "...point–say 6, point–say nothing, point–say 8." Thus, of the two action sequences involved in counting, the sequence of points seems to be produced more consistently than does the sequence of words. That is, if one of the sequences is to be temporarily ignored, that is, interrupted by a delay, this sequence is much more likely to be the sequence of words than the sequence of points. This is especially true of the younger children (where the number of point–no word errors was so high), but this inconsistency does persist. Many of the older children also occasionally did not say any word when they pointed at an object.

The low incidence of the part word–one point and multiple words–one point errors indicates that children have learned to segment the sequence of number words properly so that they produce a number word with each point, regardless of how many syllables that word may contain. It also indicates that they also rarely produce together two or more words with a single point. These results support the contention of Fuson et al. (1982) that the unbreakable list level of development in children's number-word sequences (the level at which they have properly segmented the words in the sequence) occurs quite early (see also chapter 2).

3.3.3.3. Other Point–Object Error Subtypes. The point–object error, word and point–no object, was made by only 17% of the children and at the low rate of 0.1 errors per 100 objects counted. The rate of such errors might rise somewhat if objects were placed farther apart than in this study, but the very low rate indicates that when children in this age range point while counting, they almost always point at an object to be counted.

For the point–object errors, children did fairly frequently make both of the possible simple kinds of errors—they skipped over some objects and did not count them at all and they remained "stuck" on some objects, counting them two or more times. The percentage of children making each of these kinds of errors was roughly similar, but the rate of making object skipped errors was much higher than the rate of making multiple count errors for the children aged 3½ to 4½ (3.1 versus 1.2, respectively) and remained higher even when the rate of making a skipping arc motion rather than the number of blocks skipped was considered (2.0 versus 1.2, respectively). This difference was particularly high for the 3½-year-olds. This pattern of results does not seem just to be due to children's knowledge about whether these two kinds of errors are errors. Briars and Siegler (1984) used our error categories and reported that most 3-year-olds were more likely to say that a puppet made a mistake when the puppet made an object skipped error than a multiple count error.[5] This is the reverse of the pattern of actual errors. Furthermore, it is not obvious why so many children made multiple count errors. Pointing serves not only to form the word–point and point–object correspondences from which the word–object correspondence can be derived; it also serves as a record of which object has just been counted. When objects are arranged in a row, the selection of the next object to receive a point does not involve making a complex choice as it does when the objects are disorganized. In a row the pointing finger must just move forward to the next object. Because the point records which object has just been counted, it is not clear why children so frequently fail to move the pointing finger on to the next object and thus make a multiple count error.

3.3.4. Dual Errors

The dual skim and flurry errors (see Table 3-1) are different from all other errors because they are highly concentrated on certain trials. When a child

---

[5] Of course, this difference might be a result both of children's knowledge about what is a counting error and of the salience of different counting errors, that is, the ability of children to detect different counting errors. More of these 3-year-olds might have noticed an object skipped error than noticed the multiple count error. The difficulty of assessing what children know about counting, as opposed to what they do in counting, is discussed further in chapter 10.

made a skim or a flurry, most of the objects in the row would be involved. Thus, the error rates for skims, especially, became comparatively high. The rate of skim errors per 100 objects counted was 3.9 for children aged 3½ to 4, rose to 9.4 for children aged 4 to 4½, came back to 4.4 for the 4½ to 5-year-olds, and then fell to 1.2 and 0.3 for the two oldest groups. About half the children aged 3½ to 4½ and a fourth of the children aged 4½ to 5½ sometimes made skim errors. Skims were made on only 5% of the trials, but on such trials a skim error was made on an average of 12% of the first objects, 67% of the middle objects, and 61% of the final objects.

Every child who made skim errors pointed at distinct objects on at least one other trial. Thus, skim errors in this age range do not seem to be an early developmental stage in which children do not yet point to distinct objects, as suggested by Saxe (1977), but rather are a degenerate form of counting in which some children engage at some times. This interpretation is also supported by the fact that the rate of making skim errors peaked not in the youngest age group, where one would expect a peak if some of these young children were just emerging from such an early developmental stage, but in the 4- to 4½-year-olds (9.4 vs. 3.9 and 4.4 in the contiguous earlier and later age groups).

Only the youngest children made flurry errors—produced a frenetic burst of points and words unrelated to each other or to specific objects. Flurries were made by the youngest children at a rate of 3.8 per 100 objects counted for a mean flurry rate over all ages of 0.8; 39% of the youngest children made flurry errors. Flurries were produced on only 1% of the trials, and on such trials were made on an average of 25%, 80% and 79% of the first, middle, and last objects, respectively. Every child who made flurry errors also on at least one other trial pointed at specific objects and said words in some correspondence to the points. Thus, by age 3½ flurry errors are a degenerate form of counting rather than the only form of counting available to a child.

The first three dual errors in Table 3-1 (multiple points–one word, multiple points–no word, word–no point errors) were produced by few children, 27%, 6% and 14%, respectively, and at low rates, 0.54, 0.01, and 0.09 per 100 objects counted, respectively. This low incidence indicates that, except for occasional trials with skims or flurries, counting objects in long rows from age 3½ on is really quite organized—most errors violate only the point–object correspondence or the word–point correspondence but not both. This pattern suggests that children attend both to the point–object correspondence and to the word–point correspondence but occasionally do not have sufficient resources to allocate to both of these correspondences. When this happens, they continue to attend to one of these correspondences and do accomplish it correctly, but then make some error in the other correspondence. Only occasionally do they abandon attention to both correspondences and violate them both (thus making a dual error).

The multiple points-one word and word–no point errors are correspondence errors because both the word–point and the point–object correspondences are violated. However, they are not counting errors, because in each case one word is attached to one object, as required for correct counting. It is not clear whether children realize that such correspondence errors are not counting errors or whether the cardinal correctness of these errors is merely serendipitous. The fact that 5-year-olds judged that a puppet making a multiple points–one word error made a mistake on 42% of such trials (Briars & Siegler, 1984) indicates that the latter is at least possible. Therefore, both such correspondence errors are included as errors in Table 3-1.

3.3.5. Recount Errors

Only 15% of the children made a recount error, and these errors were made at the low rate of 0.6 errors per 100 objects counted. Most of the children making recount errors were in the age group 3½ to 4; half of such children made a recount error. By age 4 most children counted objects in rows by moving from one end to the other without any reversal in direction. Almost all of the recount errors were of the two types illustrated in Table 3-1.

3.3.6. Relative Number of Words, Points, and Objects

When children count they point and they say words. The data on the word–point and the dual errors enable us to answer the question: Are children more likely to point without saying a word or say a word without pointing? The mean rate of all errors in which a point was made without an accompanying word was 2.2.[6] The mean rate of all errors in which a word was said without an accompanying point was 0.5.[7] Thus, when children for some reason do not produce both a point and a word, they are much more likely to point and not say a word than vice versa. This finding again underscores the central importance of pointing in the counting act.

The mean rate of all errors in which more than one point was given to an object (or a point was given to no object) was 2.2,[8] and the mean rate of all errors in which an object never received a point was 3.2.[9] Thus, for objects arranged in long rows, it is more likely that an object will fail to be pointed to than that it will receive more than one point.

The word–point and the point–object correspondences together create the word–object correspondence that is the result of counting. The specific error subtypes permit a comparison to be made between all those errors in which the number of words said exceeds the number of objects present and all those errors in which the number of objects exceeds the number of words said. The

---

[6] These were point–no word, part word–one point, multiple points–no word, and multiple points–one word errors.

[7] These were word between objects, multiple words–one point, and word–no point errors.

[8] These were multiple count, word and point–no object, multiple points–no word, multiple points–one word, and recount errors.

[9] These were object skipped and word–no point errors.

mean rate of all errors in which there are more words than objects is 2.3,[10] and the mean rate of all errors in which there are more objects than words is 5.0.[11] Thus, in counting entities in fairly long rows, it is considerably more likely that an object will not receive a word than that it will receive more than one word. This does not necessarily mean, however, that the last word actually said by the child when counting has a cardinal value less than the number of objects counted; the relationship between the correct cardinality of a group of objects and the last word produced by a child in counting those objects depends on both the correspondence errors and the errors in the number-word sequence.

Finally, the specific error types can be collapsed in order to determine whether errors of surplus (i.e., errors that have extra points, extra words, or both) or errors of deficit (omissions of a point, a word, or both) are more frequent. The mean rate of all errors of surplus was 2.6, and the mean rate of all errors of deficit was 5.1. Thus, children counting the long rows in this study were considerably more likely to omit some part of counting than to do extra.

3.3.7. Error Location: Beginning, Middle, or End of the Row

Errors were identified as falling at the beginning (on either of the first two objects), at the end (on either of the last two objects), or in the middle (on any object between the first two and last two) of the row. Analyses were done separately for the single-object errors (word–point, point–object, and the first three dual errors) and for the errors involving more than one object (skim, flurry, and recount errors). For most of the rows counted, there were more than two objects in the middle and thus more objects in the middle than at the beginning or at the end. These differences were controlled by using for each location the rate of errors at that location per 100 objects counted at that location. Thus, the beginning rate per 100 objects was calculated by dividing the number of errors made on the first two objects by the total number of beginning objects counted and multiplying by 100. The middle rate per 100 objects counted was calculated by dividing the number of middle errors (the errors made on all objects except the first two and the last two objects in each row) by the total number of middle objects counted (all objects except the first and last two of each row) and multiplying by 100. The end error rate was calculated in the same way as the beginning rate, except that the last two instead of the first two objects were used.

A 3(location) × 5(age) analysis of variance with location as a repeated measure was carried out on the error rates per 100 objects for the sum of all single-object errors (all errors in Table 3-1 except skim, flurry, and recount

---

[10] These were multiple words–one point, word between objects, multiple count, word and point–no object, and recount errors.
[11] These were point–no word, part word–one point, object skipped, and multiple points–no word errors.

errors). This analysis revealed significant main effects of location and of age and a significant location by age interaction, $F(2, 162) = 45.53, p < .001; F(4, 81) = 13.26, p < .001$; and $F(8, 162) = 8.53, p < .0001$, respectively. The error rate per 100 for a middle object was significantly and considerably higher than either the error rate per 100 for a beginning or for an end object: 9.5 errors per 100 middle objects counted versus 1.2 and 2.0 errors per 100 beginning and end objects counted, respectively (Newman-Keuls, $p < .01$). This pattern of a much higher error rate per 100 for a middle than for a beginning or an end object was consistent across age groups (Table 3-3); end error rates were higher than beginning error rates at all ages (although the difference was small in some cases). The interaction stemmed from age differences in the ratios of middle/end and of end/beginning errors per 100 objects. Many more children also made errors on a middle than on a beginning or end object (Table 3-4); this much higher percentage of children making errors on middle than on end or beginning objects is particularly striking in the four oldest age groups. These percentage data are not particularly surprising, because on long rows there are so many more opportunities to make middle than beginning or end errors. But they do indicate that the characterization by Gelman and Gallistel (1978) of the beginning and the ends of counting as the least accurate parts of that activity (see 3.1.2) is not accurate.

Individual 3(location) × 5(age) analyses of variance with location as a repeated measure were conducted on the word–point total errors per 100, on the point–object total errors per 100, on the total single-object dual errors per 100, and on the errors per 100 for each of the error subtypes within the point–object and the word–point categories.[12] These analyses revealed a significant effect of location in all cases and significant location by age interactions for word–point and point–object total errors and for the point–no word, object skipped, and word and point–no object error subtypes. In all cases the rate of middle errors per 100 middle objects counted was considerably higher than the rate of beginning or end errors per 100 beginning or end objects counted. Children made more object skipped errors on a beginning than on an end object; for all other error subtypes, more errors were made on an end than on a beginning object. The interactions were due to variations across age groups in the ratios of middle/end and of end/beginning error rates.

In the preceding analyses errors on the first and second objects were combined as beginning errors, and errors on the next-to-last and last objects were combined as end errors. A comparison of the rate of errors on the first with that on the second object and a comparison of the rate of errors on the next-to-last with the rate on the last object indicated that there were fewer errors on the first than on the second object (38% of the beginning errors were on the first object) and fewer errors on the last object than on the next-to-last

---

[12] The last three word–point subtypes were pooled for a single analysis because individual rates were so low.

Table 3-3. Error Rates by Location and Age

Location	3½ to 4	4 to 4½	4½ to 5	5 to 5½	5½ to 6	Mean
			Age (years)			
Beginning	3.7	.4	.7	1.0	—	1.2
Middle	23.0	14.0	5.5	3.5	1.4	9.5
End	4.0	1.9	2.5	1.3	.2	2.0

Note. Beginning error rates are the number of beginning errors made per 100 beginning objects counted; middle error rates are the number of middle errors made per 100 middle objects counted; end error rates are the number of end errors made per 100 end objects counted. Two age groups underlined by the same line had Newman-Keuls values indicating no significant differences between the rates for those groups. These error rates are the sum of all single-object errors (all errors except skim, flurry, and recount errors).

Table 3-4. Percentage of Children Making an Error by Age and Location

Location	3½ to 4	4 to 4½	4½ to 5	5 to 5½	5½ to 6	Mean
			Age (years)			
Beginning	50	18	18	6	0	19
Middle	94	100	94	81	78	90
End	72	41	35	13	6	34

Note. Lines indicate for which age groups pairwise χ^2 analyses indicated no significant differences. These are the percentage of children making at least one single-object error (all errors except skim, flurry, and recount errors).

object (37% of the end errors were on the last object). That is, considerably more errors occur on the inner object. Thus, using a definition of location identical to that of Gelman and Gallistel (1978) would have reduced the rate of errors reported here previously on a beginning or an end object by almost two–thirds, giving an even higher probability than reported above that any given error will fall on an object not at either end of the row.

The skim, flurry, and recount errors also showed more errors on a middle than on a beginning or end object, although for each kind of error, either the first or the last object had an error rate close to that for a middle object. For trials on which there was a skim, there were skims on 12% of the first objects, 67% of the middle objects, and 61% of the last objects. For flurries these figures were 25%, 80%, and 79%, respectively. Recounts showed a different pattern, with errors of 19%, 28%, and 8% for the first, middle, and last objects, respectively.

Our data indicate a different relationship than that reported by Gelman and Gallistel (1978) between errors at the beginning and end of a count and those in the middle. We find that the very beginning and the very end of the counting act are the most accurate parts of that act. This result is not really so surprising for objects in rows, because the ends of the rows are visually the least confusing parts of the display. That is, it would seem to be easier to focus attention on the first and the last object, framed as they are on one side by empty space, than on any middle object, framed by two other objects. This visual advantage seems to outweigh the difficulties pointed out by Luria (1959, 1961) that young children ordinarily have in coordinating the starting and stopping of two separate streams of activity.

The reasons for the difference between Gelman and Gallistel's (1978) findings and our own are not immediately evident. The difference does not seem likely to be due to the slight age difference in the samples (their sample included children aged 3 to 3½); Gelman and Gallistel did not limit their location finding to children aged 3 to 3½. Our result may be partly related to set size: although more than half of our counted rows were in the set size range of 4 to 19 used by Gelman and Gallistel, we did have rows in the twenties and low thirties for some children. Another possibility is that our data do not differ from the Gelman and Gallistel data as much as their discussion of their location results would indicate. Their data in tables on their two main error types in fact show for the most part more middle than beginning or end errors. However, the amount of actual location difference is difficult to tell from these data, because they are error rates per trial, and thus there are more chances to get a trial wrong by making an error on a middle object than on a beginning or an end object. A third possibility is that the difference stems from the fact that the Gelman and Gallistel data were pooled across objects arranged in rows and objects arranged in disorganized arrays. The latter arrays present considerable difficulties in coding location errors. (E.g., in a scattered array are all the objects that never get counted middle or end objects? Where is the end of a scattered array?) Different solutions to these difficulties would create differing amounts of middle and end errors and thus differing error rates at a particular location.

3.3.8. Effects of Sex of the Counter

For that part of the sample that was blocked evenly by sex within each age group (the urban sample, $n = 60$), all of the above analyses on error rates (main error types, error subtypes, location) were also done with the variable of sex added to each analysis. These analyses revealed no main effect of sex and no interaction with this variable.

3.3.9. Effects of Effort

The effects of effort were measured by comparing performance on the first trial in which an experimenter judged there to be a "high" error rate to performance on the lowest error trial of the repeated trials for that row length given with the directions to "try really hard this time." The analysis was carried out on the urban school subsample ($n = 60$). The number of children who had repeated trials was 11, 8, 4, 4, and 2 (out of 12) for the youngest through oldest age groups, respectively. A 2(effort) × 3(error type) × 5(age) ANOVA with effort and error type as repeated measures was conducted on the errors per 100 objects counted for each of the three main error types (word–point, point–object, and dual). The main effects of age and effort were significant, $F(4, 24) = 2.77$, $p < .05$, and $F(1, 24) = 10.31$, $p < .004$. Every main error type decreased with age and with effort (Table 3-5). Most error subtypes also were reduced by effort at least somewhat within every age group. The prevalent error subtypes are given in Table 3-5. Particularly large decreases due to effort occurred in the object skipped (from 6.6 to 2.8), skim (from 8.2 to 4.8), and flurry (from 2.2 to 0) error subtypes. One age by error subtype cell did show a rise of 1.0 (from 0.6 to 1.6) with increased effort: the 4- to 4½-year-olds produced with high effort somewhat more multiple counts, perhaps as a result of decreasing the rate of their object skipped errors so considerably (from 8.2 to 1.8).

3.3.10. Effects of the Number of Objects in a Row

For the analysis on the number of objects in a row, the following groupings of number of objects were used: 5 through 9, 10 through 14, 15 through 19, 20 through 24, 25 through 29. Because an analysis across these five groups required a repeated measures design, only those subjects who had at least one trial in each group could be included in this analysis. Many of the younger children refused to count the largest rows, so this analysis was confined to the first three set-size groups only. A 5(age) × 3(number of objects) × 3(main error type) ANOVA with number of objects and main error type as repeated measures was performed on the errors per 100 for the urban part of the sample ($n = 12, 11, 9, 5$, and 4 out of 12 for the youngest to oldest age groups, respectively; the small ns for the oldest groups reflect the counting-on behavior of these children on the small rows). Because errors per 100 objects counted controls for set size (it can be thought of as the probability of making an error on an object in a given size of set), any increase in the errors per 100 objects counted would not just be due to a greater opportunity to make errors on the larger sets.

This analysis revealed main effects of age, $F(4, 36) = 4.86$, $p < .003$, and of number of objects, $F(2, 72) = 3.36$, $p < .04$, and an age by number of objects interaction, $F(8, 72) = 2.19$, $p < .04$. The interaction was the result of a floor effect across all three set sizes for the three oldest age groups (i.e., their errors per 100 were very low for all three set sizes), which contrasted with large increases in errors per 100 as the rows got larger for the two youngest groups. These increases in the two youngest groups were entirely due to increases in the point–object and the dual errors: Point–object errors increased from 4.2 to 6.4 and 7.9 errors per 100 objects counted and dual rates

Table 3-5. Error Rates by Effort and Age

Error type	3½ to 4		4 to 4½		4½ to 5		5 to 5½		5½ to 6		Mean[a]	
	Low effort	High effort	Low effort	High effort	Low effort	High effort	Low effort	High effort	Low effort	High effort	Low effort	High effort
Word–point total	7.7	5.3	2.1	1.3	4.9	2.2	1.3	—	—	—	4.3	2.7
Point–no word	5.4	3.9	1.2	1.0	1.8	2.2	—	—	—	—	2.6	2.0
Point–object total	11.6	8.0	8.9	3.4	7.0	0.8	4.2	0.8	4.5	—	8.7	4.2
Object skipped	7.7	6.1	8.2	1.8	5.5	—	2.7	—	4.5	—	6.6	2.8
Multiple count	2.3	1.8	.6	1.6	1.5	—	1.5	0.8	—	—	1.5	1.2
Dual total	17.8	6.1	16.7	10.6	—	0.8	—	—	—	—	11.4	5.0
Skim	11.2	5.7	14.4	9.5	—	—	—	—	—	—	8.2	4.8
Flurry	5.7	—	—	—	—	—	—	—	—	—	2.2	—

Note. Error rates are the number of errors per 100 blocks counted with low effort or with high effort.
[a] Every subject was weighted equally in this calculation.

increased from 0.1 to 3.5 and 14.0 per 100 for the sets of 5 through 9, 10 through 14, and 15 through 19, respectively. The point–object increases were entirely due to increases in object skipped errors (from 1.9 to 4.7 and 6.2 per 100); multiple count and word and point–no object errors per 100 did not increase on the larger rows. The dual increases resulted from small increases with set size for errors per 100 for the first three (see Table 3-1) dual errors combined (0.1, 0.4, and 1.7 per 100) and larger increases for flurries (0.0, 2.9, 6.7 per 100) and for skims (0, 1.7, 8.9 per 100). Thus, increasing the number of objects in the row to be counted from 5 through 9 to 10 through 14 and to 15 through 19 substantially increased the object skipped, skim, and flurry errors made per 100 objects counted. One explanation of this effect of set size is motivational. Because these are precisely the kinds of errors that showed the greatest increases with decreased effort, it may be that a major effect of increasing the number of objects to be counted, especially for the younger children who make the most object skipped, skim, and flurry errors, is to decrease the amount of effort they expend on counting the larger rows.

An analysis like that above was also done on the three largest set size groups both across all ages ($n = 5, 7, 10, 5, 8$ from youngest to oldest) and for the three oldest groups. The only main type or subtype that showed a significant effect of number of objects was skims for the analysis across all five ages, $F(2, 60) = 3.13, p < .05$; the skim errors per 100 increased as the size of rows increased. The fact that the three oldest groups did not show any significant increase in the rate of making any kind of correspondence error as the rows increased from 15 through 19 to 25 through 29 seems to indicate that these children are less susceptible to effects of increasing set size than are the younger children.

Of course, a major limitation of the design of this task is that set size is confounded with order: The rows got larger as the task continued. Therefore, the above findings may be due to time of occurrence within the interview rather than to set size per se. A study in which set size is counterbalanced across trials is clearly required for a definitive determination. These results also may have been affected by the need to drop children who did not count rows within each set size grouping. Studies in which all children count rows of all sizes are also clearly needed. Studies in which set size is counterbalanced and in which children count all set sizes are reported in chapter 5.

3.3.11. Internalization of Counting

Both action parts of counting immovable objects—pointing and saying number words—undergo progressive internalization with age. Pointing may move from touching to pointing near objects to pointing from a distance to using eye fixation. Saying number words moves from saying audible words to making readable lip movements to making abbreviated and unreadable lip movements to silent mental production of number words. Across the age range studied here (3½ to 6), children already showed this internalization.

All of the youngest children pointed and counted out loud. A considerable number of 5-year-olds first counted silently and had to be asked to "count so I can see and hear you count." Ginsburg and Russell (1981) reported that when counting sets between 10 and 20, preschoolers pointed on almost all trials but kindergarteners did so on only 75% of the trials. The kindergarteners used eye fixation on the remaining 25% of the trials.

This first internalization of counting may result in less accurate counting. In the study reported later in chapter 9 (9.2.1), children aged 5½ to 6 made more errors in counting two rows to judge their cardinal equivalence than did children aged 5 to 5½ because the latter predominantly pointed and said words out loud while the former said words silently and used eye fixation as the indicating act. Internalized counting does evidently become as accurate as external counting, however, because Saxe and Kaplan (1981) reported that 6-year-olds were as accurate in counting an array that required an internal indicating act as in counting one for which pointing could be used.

The internalization of counting is an interesting example of the internalization of a cognitive procedure as discussed for speech in general by Vygotsky (1962, 1978, 1986). This example even follows his proposal of re-externalization of the cognitive procedure when the task is difficult (see for example, Fuson, 1979b; Zivin, 1979). Briars and Fuson (1979) found that when high school students counted large disorganized arrays, they often first counted without pointing (i.e., used eye fixation) but then either began pointing spontaneously or began to do so when the experimenter said something like "This is really hard counting. You don't have to do it in your head."

3.3.12. Perceptual Unit Items

Saxe and Kaplan (1981) argued that there is a developmental change in the function of pointing from age 2 to age 4 in which children shift from using pointing as in referential naming activities (e.g., pointing at a dog and saying "dog") to deploying gesture to aid in relating the standard set of number words to objects. If this means that when first counting children may only direct pointing in a rather vague way toward the objects to be counted rather than attempting to point at each object while saying a number word, then we concur with this view. Counting requires that the counter take each entity to be counted as a perceptual unit item, that is, takes it as a single equivalent unit regardless of whether the entity is larger than or otherwise different from the other entities to be counted. One would expect that very young children might exhibit some countinglike behavior and direct pointing in a general way toward a set of entities while saying number words before taking each entity as a perceptual unit item and using pointing to link words to the entities taken as perceptual unit items. Whether there is a shift in the function of pointing from its earliest vague nonunit use to its use with entities taken as perceptual unit items seems to us to depend on whether the first counting of a child consists of several points and words (albeit directed only in a general way at the entities to be counted) or whether there is only a single point toward the objects while words are said. The latter does seem to be the naming use of pointing. The former, the use of more than one point directed at the same situation, seems to indicate already some differentiation of the situation as a counting situation in which multiple points are given, i.e., some awareness that counting is a special situation that requires multiple pointing. We have rarely seen children who did not give multiple points when counting on at least some trials, but we have rarely studied children younger than 2½. All of the children, even the 2-year-olds and 3-year-olds, in studies reported in later sections of this book pointed multiple times and said more than one number word when they counted. The fact that all children in our sample here who displayed skim or flurry errors also pointed at individual objects on some trials indicates that by age 3½ children are able to construct and use perceptual unit items in a counting situation.

3.4. Summary

Counting immovable objects requires the counter to establish a one-to-one correspondence between words in time (i.e., said serially) but having no spatial location and objects located in space but having no differentiable location in time (i.e., they are all continuously present). In our view the counter establishes this correspondence by using an indicating act, usually the act of pointing, which has a location in time and also isolates a location in space. Each indicating act connects a word said in time to an object located in space by producing a time–space (word–object) correspondence that is derived from the two correspondences made with the indicating act: the word–indicating act correspondence made in time and the indicating act–object correspondence made in space. A counting correspondence error can be made in the temporal word–point correspondence, in the spatial point–object correspondence, or in both.

A category system of counting correspondence errors based on the preceding differentiations was developed from watching videotapes of children counting objects in rows and in disorganized arrays. This category system was then used to analyze counting correspondence errors made by a larger sample of children aged 3½ to 6 when counting rows containing from 4 to 34 objects. Children were found to make only the kinds of errors identified in the category system. Three kinds of errors were made especially frequently: object skipped (in which an object receives neither a word nor a point), multiple count (in which an object receives a word and a point and then another word and point), and point–no word (in which an object receives a point but not a word). Skim errors (those in which a finger traces across a row without definite points while words are said in no definite pattern) also were made at a high rate, but these were made by a smaller proportion of children than the above three errors and were confined to a small number of trials. Every child who made a skim error pointed at distinct objects on at least one other trial. Therefore, skim errors in this age range do not seem to be an early developmental stage in which children do not yet point to distinct objects but rather are a degenerate form of counting in which some children engage at some times. Other errors made less frequently were also identified (Table 3-1).

Particular errors showed different age patterns in the number of children making such an error and in the rate of making such errors. In general the rate of making a given error dropped earlier than did the number of children making that error. This is consistent with a picture of learning that involves a gradual improvement rather than one in which the child has sudden insight regarding these matters. A sudden-insight notion would predict that a given child would move abruptly from error-filled to error-free performance and thus the error rate pattern would parallel the pattern for the number of children making an error.

Point–no word and object skipped error rates dropped significantly at age 4 (from 4.0 to 1.5 errors per 100 objects counted and from 8.6 to 4.4 errors per 100 objects counted, respectively), and the multiple count error rate dropped at age 4½ (from an error rate of 2.1 to .7). These three most pervasive errors were made by most of the youngest children (these aged 3½ to 4), and by between a third and a half of the 5-year-olds. Skim errors were highest for the children aged 4 to 4½ (9.4 such errors per 100 objects counted), were considerably lower for the children just younger and just older than this (3.9 for children aged 3½ to 4 and 4.4 for children aged 4½ to 5), and were quite low for both groups of 5-year-olds (1.2 and .3). Only the youngest children made flurry errors in which a rapid burst of words and points was randomly generated along the row (made at a rate of 3.8 per 100 objects counted). Very few recount errors (in which an object was returned to and counted after another object had been counted) were made by any age group. Most of the children making these few recount errors were aged 3½ to 4. Half of the children in this age range made such an error, but they were made only very occasionally (i.e., at a very low rate). Therefore, by age 4, most children counted objects in rows by moving from one end to the other without any reversal in direction. There were no effects of sex and no age by sex interactions on any error main type or subtype. The fact that all children who made skim or flurry errors also pointed at individual objects on some trials indicates that children by age 3½ are able to "see" and use perceptual unit items in counting situations.

The definition of counting and the resulting category system enabled certain errors to be differentiated that are not differentiated when only the derived word–object correspondence is considered. The quite different error rates and percentages of children in different age groups making these errors indicate that these errors are in fact different and should not be collapsed. Thus, for example the object skipped and point–no word errors both result in no word corresponding to an object, but the error rates and percentages of children making these errors differ across age groups (Table 3-2).

The error rate measure of errors per 100 objects counted used in this study permits us to determine how good children at various ages are at creating the necessary word–point and point–object correspondences. In fact children turned out to be quite good at achieving these correspondences when counting. There was, of course, a very considerable improvement over the age range studied in the ability to make such correspondences. But even the youngest children were fairly good at making such correspondences. When all types of errors were added together, the youngest children (aged 3½ to 4) still made a correct word–point and correct point–object correspondence on about three out of every four blocks counted,[13] and the children aged 4 to 4½ made both correct correspondences on about four out of every five blocks counted. These ratios were correct correspondences on 9 out of 10, 24 out of 25, and 49 out of 50 blocks counted for the children aged 4½ to 5, 5 to 5½, and 5½ to 6, respectively. These rates are based on the counting of quite long rows and include some trials with low effort expended. Both of these factors increase the rate of errors. Thus, one might expect that children counting shorter rows and trying hard to count accurately would make even fewer correspondence errors.

It proved to be more difficult to children to carry out one spatially distributed action sequence (pointing once and only once at each object) than to coordinate two continuous sequences of actions (pointing and saying words): more errors violated the spatial point–object correspondence than the temporal point–word correspondence. Therefore, counting seems to be an exception to the finding that preschool children have difficulty coordinating two concurrent streams of activity (Fuson, 1979b; Luria, 1959, 1961).

Children were much less likely to make a correspondence error at the beginning and at the end of a row than on any given object in the middle of a row. The errors made per 100 objects counted were considerably higher for a middle object than for a last or a first object. The mean over all age groups was 9.5 errors per 100 middle objects counted versus 2.0 errors per 100 last objects counted and 1.2 errors per 100 first objects counted.[14] Thus, counting was much more accurate at the ends than in the middle of a count. This was true for all ages and for all error subtypes. For all error subtypes except object skipped errors, more errors were made on the last objects than on the first objects. Because this finding was based on the number of errors per 100 blocks counted at each location, the finding of more errors per middle object was not just due to the fact that most long rows have more middle than first or

---

[13] The sum of the mean error rates of all types of errors was about 25 errors per every 100 objects counted (it was 24.7).

[14] These means are actually based on beginning errors defined as the first two blocks and end errors defined as the last two errors. Because a second analysis indicated that there were considerably fewer errors on the first than on the second block and also considerably fewer errors on the last than on the next-to-last block, the rate of middle object errors compared to the errors on the first and last object is actually considerably higher than the figures here (i.e., counting at the very ends of the row was even more accurate than these figures indicate).

last objects. Thus, it may be that, at least for objects in the long rows used in this study, the special visual salience of the objects at each end of a row seems to outweigh the difficulties that young children ordinarily have in coordinating the starting and stopping of two separate streams of activity. This result contrasts sharply with the conclusion of Gelman and Gallistel (1978) that the most difficulty occurs at the beginning and end of a count.

Increased effort by a child reduced errors of all kinds but particularly reduced object skipped and skim errors. The fact that errors are so variable across trials for some children seems to indicate that counting activity is not really automatized yet. This variability and lack of consistent effort is also a potential experimental problem in counting research. Fortunately, it does seem to be easy to increase children's attention to or effort at counting.

Increasing the number of objects in a row particularly increased the rates of skim and object skipped errors made by the 3½ to 4½-year-olds. Because these are the error types that are increased by decreased effort, it may be that increasing the number of objects to be counted increases the rate of errors by decreasing the effort children are willing to expend in counting those larger rows.

Both pointing and saying words undergo internalization from age 3 to 6, and counting is externalized by adolescents under difficult circumstances. Counting thus is an excellent example of the kinds of cognitive activities with these features discussed by Vygotsky (1962, 1978, 1986).

Our results raise the possibility that the relationship between what children *know* about accurate counting and what they *do* in counting may not be simple, and it may vary with particular types of correspondence errors. The Briars and Siegler (1984) data indicate that most 3-, 4-, and 5-year-olds know that skipping an object is an error. However, such errors were made in the present study at a relatively high rate and by a significant proportion of all ages. These two findings thus are consistent with the position of Gelman and Gallistel (1978) and Gelman and Meck (1983) that children often understand the nature of correct counting but make execution errors when counting. However, the multiple count and point–no word errors indicate that the relationship between knowing and doing is not always so simple and does vary across error types. Within each age group (age 3, 4, and 5) the proportions of trials on which children in the Briars and Siegler (1984) study identified counts having these two errors as errors were very close, that is, within each age group the children demonstrated the same amount of knowledge about these two error types. However, in our study children showed a significant drop in point–no word errors before they showed such a drop in multiple count errors, that is, performance on these two errors was not the same. Therefore, children's knowledge about whether these two error types are errors seems to be the same, but they nevertheless make more errors of one type than of the other. Further aspects of what children know about counting and what they do in counting are discussed in chapter 10.

There may be limitations to the generalizability of the results summarized here. Two thirds of the sample consisted of a very heterogeneous range of children who varied in ethnicity and socioeconomic level, but one third of the sample was predominantly from middle- and upper-middle-class homes. Thus, the counting of this sample might have been somewhat above average. Children counted only blocks of the same color placed close together in increasingly long rows. Effects of different arrangements of objects are explored in the next chapter, and effects of variables such as color of and distance between objects counted in rows are explored in chapter 5. However, although these variables might affect the rate of different kinds of errors at different ages, the considerable heterogeneity of the sample would seem to indicate that the category system of errors proposed here accurately describes the errors made by children aged 3½ to 6.

4. Effects of Object Arrangement on Counting Correspondence Errors and on the Indicating Act

In this chapter the effects of two different nonlinear array shapes on correspondence errors in children's counting are reported. Unlike a row in which the pointing finger separates the uncounted from the counted objects, both of these array shapes require children to remember which objects they have counted. One study contrasts the kinds of correspondence errors children make when counting objects in a maximally disorganized array with those made when counting objects in a row. The correspondence errors are those outlined in Table 3-1 and discussed in chapter 3. Two studies focus on children's ability to use a stop-rule when counting objects arranged in a circular loop. In the maximally disorganized array, children must remember for all the objects which ones have been counted, while the linearly ordered circular arrays require only remembering with which object one started counted. Children's use of two indicating acts other than pointing are also explored. One is moving objects from an uncounted to a counted pile, and the other is a microcomputer pen.

4.1. Methods of Remembering Which Objects Have Been Counted

Counting objects distributed in space requires an indicating act to mediate between the words said in time and the objects distributed in space. Such indicating acts seem to fall within two categories: (a) moving objects from a pile of uncounted objects to a pile of counted objects and (b) some variation of pointing at unmoved objects, including the later internalization of pointing as eye fixation (see 3.3.11). Potter and Levy (1968) focused on this aspect of counting and defined it as "the ability to take (or point to, or look at) each item in the array, one at a time, until all have been taken exactly once (p. 265)." This definition (or any definition of correct indicating act–object correspondence) includes four requirements, the violation of which leads to the class of error listed:

1. each indicating act must be directed toward an object: one indicating act—less than one object
2. each indicating act must not be directed toward more than one object: one indicating act—more than one object
3. every object is indicated: less than one indicating act—one object
4. no object is indicated more than once: more than one indicating act—one object.

The first two requirements are accomplished locally during counting by setting limits on each separate indicating act: Each act must be directed toward an object, and it must not be directed toward more than one object. We can see that the two different classes of indicating acts differ with respect to these two requirements. A point could easily be directed at an empty space (i.e., not directed at any object), but it is quite difficult to direct a point toward more than one object. In contrast, it seems unlikely that one would move one's empty hand from the uncounted to the counted pile of objects (i.e., not direct the indicating act "moving objects" at an object), but one could easily take two or more objects with each move. In chapter 3 we found that children rarely pointed at an empty space, that is, pointed but not at an object. In this chapter we explore whether children do move more than one object at a time.

How the last two requirements for correct indicating act–object correspondence are met depends on the method of remembering which objects have been counted. Four such methods are listed in Table 4-1. Two of them involve the "marking" of individual counted objects in some way so that it is clear that the object has been counted. The first method uses the indicating act of moving objects from an uncounted to a counted pile; membership in the counted pile thus "marks" each counted object. In the second method the indicating act is pointing, but each object is physically or mentally "marked" in some way as it is counted. Such methods would include putting a sticker or a check-mark on each object as it is counted (such marks might be considered to be the record of a touching indicating act) and spatial memory strategies such as mentally "shading" the objects counted in a disorganized array to differentiate them from the to-be-counted objects. With the latter such strategies, each "next" object selected is probably near to the last object counted, but with the former strategies and with moving objects, any uncounted object can be selected at random. Both of these methods of remembering create successive partitions of the objects into counted and to-be-counted sets (Beckwith & Restle, 1966). These successive partitions are obvious to any viewer with moving objects and with physically marked objects; they are not obvious with mentally marked objects. With these methods of remembering, one does not have to make a linear ordering on the objects. Such a linear ordering is accomplished in the course of counting by the successive choices of the next object, but this linear ordering need neither be noticed or remembered before, during, or after counting. Moving objects clearly is the easier of the two methods, for with it one does not have to remember just which objects have been counted; the procedure keeps track of this for the counter. Thus, moving objects is the optimal strategy when objects can be moved.

The other two methods in Table 4-1 use a linear ordering on the objects. Such a linear ordering can be already established and obvious in the situation, such as in a row, or the situation can require an individually established nonevident linear ordering, such as in a disorganized array. The key difference between these two situations then is the spatial arrangement of the objects. Pointing at objects in an established linear ordering creates successive partitions of the objects into counted and to-be-counted sets: each object pointed to partitions the objects into those earlier in the ordering (the counted objects) and those still to come in the ordering (the to-be-counted objects). However, only if the linear ordering is obvious to the onlooker, as in a row, can this partitioning be evident to an observer.

Therefore, successive partitions of the objects are only obvious to the onlooker when the counter is moving objects, physically marking the counted objects, or pointing to objects with an obvious linear ordering. However, it is not at all clear that a child pointing to objects in a row realizes that the objects are being successively partitioned, and it may not really be obvious for the first two cases either. That is, in all of these cases, it seems more likely that the child is merely carrying out the culturally learned method for remember-

Table 4-1. Attributes of Methods of Remembering Which Objects Have Been Counted

Methods of remembering	Successive partitions of uncounted/counted objects observable?	Linear ordering observable?	Need to make a linear ordering?	How select "the next" object
"Mark" each counted object				
Move objects from an uncounted to a counted pile	Yes	No	No	At random from the uncounted
Point and physically or mentally mark each counted object	Yes if physical No if mental	No	No	At random or may be near last uncounted
Use a linear ordering on the objects				
Point at an already established evident linear ordering	Yes	Yes	Yes	The next in the linear ordering
Point at an individually established nonevident linear ordering	No	No	Yes	The next in the linear ordering

Note. "Observable" for the first two columns means that any observer can tell at any time during the activity of counting either the partitioning into the uncounted/counted objects (column 1) or the linear ordering on the objects (column 2).

ing which objects have been counted without realizing that these methods depend on either successive partitioning or linear ordering. Both for this reason, and because partitioning is observable only in some cases of counting, it does not seem wise to consider counting *in general* as consisting of tagging and of partitioning, as is done by Gelman and Gallistel (1978) and then by others following this terminology. It seems more accurate to recognize that the method of remembering which objects have been counted depends heavily on both the object situation and the indicating act used in that situation. With movable objects and with objects in rows, the usual indicating acts (moving objects and pointing) are sufficient methods for remembering the counted objects. With immovable objects and most nonrow arrangements, some method of remembering must be adopted and used with the indicating act of pointing. This method may involve partitioning or it may involve establishing a linear ordering; either is sufficient. Thus, it seems more accurate and more general to consider counting as consisting of the word–indicating act correspondence, the indicating act–object correspondence, and a method of remembering which objects have been counted. With pointing in rows and with moving movable objects, the third aspect (remembering) is already subsumed in the indicating act.

These different methods of remembering have implications for how models of counting select the next object to be counted (see the last column in Table 4-1). Greeno et al. (1984) have included the potential for several of these remembering methods in their model of counting. The schemata *pick-up*, *put-down*, and *add-to* accomplish the method of moving objects. *Add-mark* places a physical mark on an object as in the second method; the model uses this schema is used in conjunction with *pick-up* and *put-down* is the model, but it might better be used with a schema *point*, because marking makes it unnecessary to move the object. There are also two schemata for retrieving items from linear orderings, *retrieve-first* and *retrieve-next*. These would seem to be sufficient for using an established linear ordering on the objects, such as in a row, although an indicating act to link the words said in time to each object in space still would be necessary. However, for many other object arrangements, the model would need the ability to establish a linear ordering on the objects, not just to use an already established ordering. The model when functioning often uses two other schemata, *initialize* and *increment*, to create successive segments of word sequences and of ordered objects that stem from successive partitionings of the set into the subset that has been counted and the subset that has not been counted. However, we see these two schemata as unnecessary for counting. The methods of remembering require *either* marking (and thus successive partitioning) *or* linear ordering *and not both*. The model uses these segments when a cardinal number is assigned to the counted set by the schema *count*, but segments are not necessary to assign a cardinal number. One could just use the schema *assign* to give a cardinal number when *retrieve-next* or *add-to* or *add-mark* have used up all the objects. The segment schemata do seem useful for later addition problems, where they could be used to create embedded subsets of the sequence of number words in a sequence model of an addition or subtraction situation (see chapter 8 for further discussion). Thus, this counting model has potential for covering a developmental span of uses of counting as well as a range of different counting situations.

The first two requirements for correct indicating act–object correspondence are determined locally (with each indicating act) and the last two requirements are determined overall (the whole record of local indicating act–object correspondences must be examined). However, with some methods of remembering, the last two requirements can also be determined locally. Violation of the local indicating act–object correspondence creates a different kind of error than violation of the overall correspondence. When a linear ordering is used to remember, an object in the ordering can be skipped over (a local violation of requirement 3) or an object can be counted and immediately counted again (a local violation of requirement 4). These object skipped and multiple count errors occur frequently for objects in rows (chapter 3) and are different from the overall errors of uncounted objects (stopping counting before the end of the row) and recount errors (returning to objects earlier in the order and counting them again). When objects are marked to remember them and pointing is the indicating act, local multiple count errors (violations of requirement 4) can also occur. Such errors would seem to be nonexistent with moving objects because one would have to move an object back to the uncounted pile in order to count it again.

4.2. Effects of Array Shape: Rows Versus Disorganized Immovable Arrays

4.2.1. Remembering Which Objects Have Been Counted in Disorganized Immovable Arrays

In a disorganized array of immovable objects, two general methods of re-membering which objects have been counted are available. One method is to physically or mentally "mark" each object as one counts it, thus designating it as a counted object. Physical marks reduce the load on memory very consid-erably, but this method may not be usable very often. With mental marking it seems more likely that some sort of spatial strategy is used in which objects near each other are counted successively and one "shades," draws a mental boundary line, or otherwise differentiates the area of the counted objects from the area of the uncounted objects.

The other method is to establish a linear ordering on the objects and then point to the objects in this linear ordering. There seem to be several general approaches one can take to this task. First, one can plan the linear ordering before beginning. However, with a large disorganized array, this places considerable demands on memory. Second, one can adopt a general strategy for the linear ordering and then sketch out the details while one is counting. For example one can "chunk" disorganized arrays into groups and count those groups in a particular order; one might then construct a linear ordering on each group only when one is actually counting that group. In this case each linear ordering of the smaller group is easier to construct and use, and one need only remember the order and membership of the smaller groups. Such a strategy is made simpler if perceptual subgroupings exist (e.g., Schaeffer et al., 1974). Third, one can construct no linear ordering in advance but construct it as one is counting, that is, make a path through the disorganized array as one counts.

Regardless of whether one establishes a linear ordering or mentally marks individual counted objects, using these remembering methods may be expected to make much heavier demands on processing resources than does simply using the linear ordering already available for objects arranged in a row. Therefore, certain kinds of errors seem much more likely to be made in disorganized arrays than in rows. First, unless the methods for remembering exactly which objects one has already counted work very well, one would expect many more objects to be recounted (counted again after at least one different object had been counted) in the disorganized than in the row condition. Similarly, it may be possible that more objects never get counted than in rows. It is not quite so obvious what effects one might expect the disorganized array to have on word–point, point–object, and dual errors. This prediction depends on two kinds of assumptions about counting. The first is whether one considers the remembering method to be part of establishing the point–object spatial correspondence or whether this method is a separate component of counting. The question here is "In what functional part of counting is the choice of the next object made during counting?" The second assumption concerns whether or not a constant ratio of processing resources is allotted to various counting components. Suppose the remembering demands are part of the point–object processing and that a constant ratio of processing resources is allotted to various components of counting. Then one would predict a considerable rise in point–object correspondence errors for disorganized arrays, because the construction and use of the remembering method is so demanding. Alternatively, one might postulate no constant ratio allotted to components but rather that the least well-organized or least well-automatized aspects of counting will be the most disrupted by the additional remembering demands in a disorganized array. However, because we do not know what aspects of counting are the least well organized, this position does not easily lead to the prediction of an increase in particular error types.

The present study is an investigation of differences in the kinds of correspondence errors children make when counting immovable objects arranged in rows and in disorganized arrays. In order to maximize the difference between the conditions, the disorganized arrays used in the present study were constructed so that no obvious subgroupings existed (although of course, it is always possible that subjects constructed such subgroupings mentally). Strategies used to remember the disorganized arrays were also explored.

4.2.2. Method

4.2.2.1. Sample. Children in the videotaped sample referred to in chapter 3 (the sample originally used to construct the error categories in Table 3-1) counted objects in a row and objects in a disorganized display. The sample consisted of 36 children, with 6 children in each half-year age group from age 3–0 (3 years 0 months) through 5–11 (5 years 11 months). One child in the 4½ to 5-year-old age group did not count any disorganized arrays, so the sample used in the following analyses consists of the remaining 35 children. The children lived in a northern suburb of Chicago and were from middle- and upper-middle-class homes.

4.2.2.2. Procedure and Materials. The procedure was the same in the row and in the disorganized conditions. A row (or disorganized array) of either four or five 1-inch blocks was presented, and the child was asked, "How many blocks are there?" On subsequent trials the row (or disorganized array) was systematically increased by alternately adding one or two blocks, after which the experimenter said, "I put down one (or two) more block(s). How many blocks are there now?" Trials continued until a child either counted a row (or disorganized array) of 33 (or 34) blocks, refused to go on, or gave some indication over several trials of no longer attending to the task. If a child moved the blocks when counting, the counting was interrupted, and the child was told that the blocks could not be moved. The blocks were replaced, and that trial was begun again. The two array shapes (rows and disorganized arrays) were given in counterbalanced order; half the children within each age group counted each type of array first. The blocks for a given condition were all of the same color. All counting took place on a carpeted floor in a room near the children's classrooms. Sessions took from 10 to 30 minutes to complete.

Blocks in the row were placed approximately ¼ inch apart, and new blocks were added to the end of the row on the child's right. Each disorganized display was determined in advance, designed to be as patternless as possible, and identical across children. The disorganized arrays were made by the experimenter on a large cardboard base containing 34 faint dots. To ensure uniformity of the arrays, the experimenter used a smaller facsimile of this dot pattern on which the dots were numbered in order. Blocks were added to the array in the numbered order. The centers of the 1-inch blocks were approximately 2 inches apart, and the overall shape covered by each disorganized display was roughly that of a circle. The diameters of these "circles" became larger as additional blocks were added around the circumference of the smaller arrays.

4.2.2.3. Error Analysis of the Videotapes. Coding for the rows trials was
done on special forms containing for each trial a long rectangle divided verti-
cally into as many small rectangles as there were blocks in that trial. Each
long rectangle was also divided horizontally into two rows of these small
rectangles. Each rectangle represented a block that was to be counted. A
coder watched a particular videotaped trial and wrote in the bottom row a
numeral for each number word said by the child; each numeral was written on
the form in the location to which the child's finger was directed at the time the
child said that number word. This procedure transferred the words said in
time to a spatial location relative to the counted blocks. The coder then
watched the videotape again, and this time recorded in the top row of rectangles a check-mark at the location of each point the child made. These
records permitted errors to be classified into the correspondence error categories in Table 3-1. Because this was our initial work with counting errors, all
trials were viewed and coded by two coders. Agreement on recorded behavior was greater than 97% for both the top and the bottom rows. Disagreements were viewed and resolved by a third coder.

The coding of the disorganized arrays was much more complicated, time-
consuming, and tedious. First, although the experimenter oriented the cardboard foundation for the disorganized displays in the same way for each child
so that each child would have the same viewpoint for the disorganized arrays,
our camera-person (unfortunately) was not so meticulous. The camera was
placed in somewhat different positions on different days, and the children and
experimenter sometimes sat in somewhat different places with respect to the
camera. Consequently, the viewpoint of the coder seeing the disorganized
displays on the videotape varied slightly from child to child, and no one
coding form of the disorganized displays could be used for all children. Therefore, for each trial, a layout of that trial as it appeared to the coder on the
videotape had to be made by stamping rectangles on a sheet of paper with a
small square stamp. The coder then wrote on this layout a number (beginning
with 1 and continuing up the sequence) for each successive point made by the
child while counting. This number was written at the location on the layout to
which the child's point was directed. A double row of connected rectangles
like those used for the row trials appeared at the bottom of each layout. The
top row contained numbers from 1 to n (the number of points made by the
child on that trial); this formed a time sequence made by the succession of
points. In the bottom row a check was made for each number word said by the
child; the location of this check was related to the time sequence of the points
made by the child. For example, if a word was said at the same time a point
was made, one check was made in the rectangle below the number of that
point. If two words were said, two checks were made. If no word was said,
the rectangle was left blank. If a word was said in between two points, the
check was made at the common side of the rectangles for those points. These
records permitted errors to be classified into the correspondence error

categories given in Table 3-1. Two coders coded each trial. Agreement on the location of the points was 95%, and agreement on the location of the words within the point–time sequence was 96%. A third coder resolved all disagreements. Some trials were fairly easy to code, but some of the disorganized trials required repeated stop-action viewing by the coder.

The coding of both row and disorganized arrays was done over a period of several months by 10 Northwestern University undergraduate students. The data for each subject were coded by a different pair of coders so as to avoid any possible systematic bias stemming from a single pair of coders. All resolution of disagreements was done by the graduate student project assistant director.

4.2.3. Results

4.2.3.1. Recount Errors. A 2(organization of objects) × 6(age) analysis of variance (ANOVA) with organization as a repeated measure was carried out on the number of recount errors per 100 objects counted. This analysis revealed a significant effect of organization, $F(1, 29) = 29.97$, $p < .0001$, no significant effect of age, and no significant age by organization interaction. Far more recount errors were made in the disorganized than in the rows condition: a mean rate of 17.6 versus 0.7 errors per 100 objects counted (Table 4-2). Thus, when blocks were not arranged nicely in a row, over all ages almost 20% of the blocks were returned to and recounted later. All 35 children made at least one recount error in the disorganized condition, and only four children made a recount error in the row condition. This difference in the number of children making a recount error was significant by McNemar's test, $\chi^2(1, N = 35) = 31.0$, $p < .01$.

4.2.3.2. Three Main Error Categories. The analysis of counting presented in chapter 3 yielded three main categories of correspondence errors: violations of word–point errors, of point–object errors, and of both (dual errors) (Table 4-2). Individual 2(organization) × 6(age) ANOVAs with organization as a repeated measure were conducted on the number of errors per 100 objects counted for each of these three main error categories. More word–point and point–object errors were made in the disorganized than in the rows condition: error rates of 8.3 versus 3.6 for word–point errors and of 16.7 versus 12.0 for point–object errors (Table 4-2). The dual errors did not differ in any systematic way over the two different organizations. Younger children make more errors than did older children for all three major kinds of errors (see Table 4-2 for age means). These relationships were confirmed by the results of the ANOVAs. These revealed significant main effects of organization for the word–point and for the point–object categories, $F(1, 29) = 13.88$, $p < .001$, and $F(1, 29) = 4.97$, $p < .03$, but not for the dual category. There was a significant main effect of age in all three of these analyses, and

Table 4-2. Error Rates by Object Organization and Age

Error type	3 to 3½		3½ to 4		4 to 4½		4½ to 5		5 to 5½		5½ to 6		Mean	
	Rows	Dis[a]	Rows	Dis	Rows	Dis	Rows	Dis	Rows	Dis	Rows	Dis	Rows	Dis
Word–point total[b]	8.8	22.4	4.1	8.8	5.5	9.1	1.3	2.9	1.0	4.4	0.7	4.4	3.6	< 8.3
Point–no word	8.2	7.2	1.7	1.3	4.5	4.2	1.0	1.1	0.6	2.5	0.6	3.0	2.8	3.2
Part word–one point	—	8.3	—	3.0	0.1	3.2	0.1	1.5	—	1.8	—	1.4	0.0	< 3.2
Multiple words–one point	0.6	4.8	2.4	4.5	0.8	1.5	0.2	0.3	0.4	0.1	0.1	—	0.8	1.9
Point–object total[c]	26.8	27.5	20.2	22.1	9.2	22.3	4.6	5.1	3.9	11.1	7.1	12.0	12.0	< 16.7
Object skipped/uncounted	22.2	20.5	16.4	17.7	7.1	18.7	3.4	4.8	2.1	9.1	6.6	10.3	9.7	< 13.5
Multiple count	3.8	6.8	3.2	4.3	2.0	1.6	1.0	0.3	1.5	0.8	0.4	0.3	2.0	2.4
Dual total[d]	7.1	9.0	10.8	3.3	14.0	8.3	14.6	29.6	1.5	0.5	2.2	0.9	8.4	8.6
Multiple points–one word	3.3	2.3	2.8	3.3	2.4	2.2	0.7	0.2	1.5	0.5	1.3	0.9	2.0	1.6
Skim	3.3	1.8	6.4	—	10.5	6.0	13.9	29.1	—	—	—	—	5.7	6.2
Recount	1.7	25.2	1.2	13.1	0.6	19.0	—	17.3	0.1	10.8	0.6	20.3	0.7	< 17.6
Total errors[e]	44.4	84.1	36.3	47.3	29.3	58.7	20.5	54.9	6.5	26.8	10.6	37.6	24.7	< 51.2

< is a main effect of organization with $p < .05$.

[a] Disorganized array.

[b] This total includes word between objects errors that are not given separately in the table because their incidence was so low.

[c] This total includes word and point–no object errors that are not given separately in the table because their incidence was so low.

[d] This total includes multiple points–no word, word–no point, and flurry errors that are not given separately in the table because their incidence was so low.

[e] The error rate is the number of errors made on 100 objects given for counting. For all errors except recount errors, only one type of error can be made per object. However, it is possible that an object could receive one type of error when it is first counted and then receive a recount error. Objects in the disorganized condition also occasionally received more than one recount error.

none of the interactions between age and organization was even close to significant.

The number of children making an error in a given error category did not differ by organization for any of the three main error categories. Almost all children made at least one point–object error in both the row and disorganized conditions, and the number of children making at least one error ranged between 60% and 80% for the word–point and dual categories in each organization condition.

In order to examine whether the difference in block arrangement affected the relationship between the number of errors violating the word–point correspondence and the number violating the point–object correspondence, a 2(organization) × 2(error type: word–point versus point–object) × 6(age) ANOVA was conducted with organization and error type as repeated measures. The main effects of organization, error type, and age were all significant, $F(1, 29) = 15.03$, $F(1, 29) = 21.06$, $F(5, 29) = 7.96$, $p < .001$, respectively. Children made more errors of both types counting disorganized arrays than rows, children made considerably more point–object than word–point errors, and younger children made many more errors than did older children (see Table 4-2 for details of these effects). No interactions even approached significance, indicating among other things that the finding in chapter 3 that children made considerably more point–object than word–point errors extended to objects in a disorganized array.

4.2.3.3. Error Subtypes. The number of errors per 100 objects counted are given in Table 4-2 by organization and age for each of the seven error subtypes in which a considerable number of errors was made. Individual 2(organization) × 6(age) ANOVAs with organization as a repeated measure were carried out on the number of errors per 100 objects counted for each of the 12 error subtypes (see Table 3-1 for descriptions of these error subtypes). These analyses revealed significant effects of age for point–no word and object skipped/uncounted errors and a marginally significant effect for multiple words–one point errors ($p < .08$). Organization was a significant main effect for four error subtypes: word between objects, part word–one point, object skipped/uncounted, and word–no point, the $F(1, 29)$s ranged between 4.70 and 6.12, $p < .04$. Each of the first three types had significantly more errors in the disorganized than in the rows condition: 0.4 versus 0.01, 3.2 versus 0.03, and 13.5 versus 9.7. There were more word–no point errors in the rows than in the disorganized condition: 0.6 versus 0. Each of these organization findings are discussed in turn.

4.2.3.3.1. Word Between Objects Errors. The significantly higher rate of word between objects errors in the disorganized condition was entirely due to the rates of the youngest children (age 3 to 3½). Four of the six youngest children said a word while the finger was raised between points made at contiguous objects (so the finger was between objects but was not pointing at any object) at a rate of 2.1 such errors per 100 objects counted in the disorganized condition; these children made no such errors in the rows condition. Only two other children made such errors, one in each shape condition. Thus, by age 3½, most children seem to have learned to say number words only when they are pointing to an object, even in a very disorganized array.

4.2.3.3.2. Part Word–One Point Errors. When counting objects in a row, only two children occasionally said part of a word while pointing to one object and the rest of the word while pointing to the next object, that is, made a part word–one point error as in "siii"-point, "iiix"-point. In sharp contrast, in the disorganized arrays 60% of the children (including half or more in each age group) made such an error, and the mean overall rate was 3.2 such errors (see Table 4-2 for the different age group means). Both the error rate and the number of children making such errors was significantly higher in the disorganized condition. The ANOVA was discussed previously, and the Mc-Nemar's test was χ^2 (1, $N = 35$) = 16.9, $p < .01$. Because the number of syllables in a counting word would seem to affect this particular error, the number words uttered when committing this error were compared to the number words said in the rest of the counting. Approximately half of such errors were made while saying a number word of a single syllable; the other half were made while saying number words of two, three, or four syllables (e.g., seven, thirteen, seventeen, twenty-one, thirty-five). Of all the number words said by this sample, 60% were single-syllable words. Thus, there was some tendency for the number words said during a part word–one point error to be disproportionately multisyllabic, but this tendency was not strong. Therefore this error was *not* just due to a momentary failure to distinguish syllables from words. This error seems rather to occur because a child while in the process of saying a number word shifts attention from saying a word to making the next point (or to choosing the block that will be pointed to next). That next point is initiated, and attention shifts back to the word production part of the act. That production has stopped in midword, so the production of the word is finished or occasionally even interrupted by the next pointing act as one word is stretched out over three blocks (with three points).

Several aspects of this error are interesting. First, this error is a violation of the word–point correspondence. This makes it clear that the additional processing demand for remembering which objects have been counted in disorganized arrays does disrupt the word–point correspondence. However, this disruption seems limited to this increase in the part word–one point errors. The most common type of word–point error in the rows condition (point–no word) is not more frequent in the disorganized condition, nor is the multiple words–one point error made significantly more often in the disorganized condition. Thus, it seems that the pressure of choosing the next object for disorganized arrays is sometimes sufficient to interrupt the production of a word before its completion but is not so overwhelming that the word component of counting is totally ignored (as it is with point–no word errors). This error also makes it clear that children at least sometimes choose and point to the next object while they are saying a number word rather than beginning this next point after they have finished saying a number word.

4.2.3.3.3. Object Skipped/Uncounted Errors. The finding of a significantly higher rate of object skipped/uncounted errors in the disorganized condition is difficult to interpret because of a methodological problem inherent in such disorganized displays, a problem that led to the use of the name "object skipped/uncounted" rather than the simpler "object skipped" for these errors. We initially tried to differentiate object skipped errors and uncounted object errors (those objects not skipped over during counting but which by the end of counting had received neither a word nor a point) in order to permit a comparison between the rows and disorganized arrays in the rate of actual skipped object errors. However, this proved impossible in most cases. Because the blocks were so disorganized, when a finger moved from one block to another, it was rare for any block to be directly under the path of the moving finger. There were fairly frequently blocks that were "close to" the path, but because the viewer of the videotapes was seeing the disorganized display from a different angle than did the counter, it was not clear whether such blocks were skipped over or were simply not in the path of the linear ordering the child was constructing. We finally abandoned the attempt to make this discrimination and placed all object skipped and uncounted object errors in one category. Almost all such errors in the rows condition are object skipped errors. The most conservative description of these errors in the disorganized condition is that they are uncounted object errors. However, the general impression generated from watching the tapes is that more than just a few of such errors in the disorganized condition were similar in genesis (whatever this is) to the object skipped errors in the rows condition. This was particularly evident when a child got tired or stopped trying hard to count and skipped around just counting a few of the blocks in the disorganized array. There was not a significant difference in the number of children making at least one object skipped/uncounted object error in the row and in the disorganized conditions. Almost all the children in the sample made at least one such error in each condition.

4.2.3.3.4. Other Point–Object Errors. The higher rate of point–object errors in the disorganized condition was confined to the object skipped/uncounted errors. There was no significant difference between the rows and disorganized conditions in the error rates of the multiple count or of the word and point–no object error subtypes. There were even significantly *fewer* children making multiple count errors in the disorganized than in the rows condition by McNemar's test, $\chi^2 = 6.23$, df $= 1$, $p < .02$; 11 children made a multiple count error in the rows condition and not in the disorganized condition, whereas only two children made such an error in the disorganized and not in the rows condition. The slightly higher multiple count rate present in

Table 4-2 for disorganized arrays was due to a very few children with extremely high rates of multiple count errors. There were very few children in either condition who made word and point–no object errors, and such errors were made at low rates (0.3 and 0.8 in the row and disorganized conditions, respectively).

4.2.3.3.5. Word–No Point Errors. Seven children spread across four of the six age groups when counting blocks in a row occasionally did not point at a block but did say a number word while the finger was passing over the block, that is, made a word–no point error, at an overall error rate of 0.6. Such errors violate both the word–point and the point–object correspondences, because no point is given to the object at all. However, such errors are not counting errors, because the object does receive a number word even if no indicating act is used. As mentioned in chapter 3, it is not clear whether children know that such errors are correspondence but not counting errors. Because six of the seven children making such errors were in the three youngest age groups, it seems rather likely that many children do not know this. No child made a word–no point error in the disorganized condition. This difference in the number of children making such errors was significant by McNemar's test, $\chi^2 = 7.0$, $p < .01$. This was the only error subtype made more frequently in the rows than in the disorganized condition.

4.2.3.3.6. Other Dual Errors. Finally, three kinds of dual errors not shown in the error subtypes in Table 4-2 or in Table 3-1 were made on the videotaped trials very occasionally (from one to five times each). Three children pointed more than once to an object while saying more than one number word, but the number of points was not the same as the number of words (i.e., multiple points–different multiple words: x words, y points, 1 object, and $x \neq y$). Several children pointed between objects and said no word (i.e., point between objects: no words, one point, no objects). One child pointed at no object and said two words (multiple words–one point–no object: two words, one point, no object). Thus, errors other than those listed in Table 3-1 may be observed, but they can easily be described by a number triplet telling the number of words, points, and objects involved in the error.

4.2.3.4. Relative Number of Words, Points, and Objects. In the large increasing rows sample of chapter 3, children were found to make considerably more errors in which the number of points exceeded the number of words[1] than in which the number of words exceeded the points[2] (a mean rate of 2.2 vs. 0.5). The relationship in the present sample was the same for both the rows, mean rates of 4.8 versus 1.4, and the disorganized arrays, mean rates of

---

[1] These were point–no word, part word–one point, multiple points–no word, and multiple points–one word errors.

[2] These were word between objects, multiple words–one point, and word–no point errors.

8.1 versus 2.3, respectively. For all three cases (the rows in chapter 3 and the rows and disorganized arrays here), a point was about four times more likely to be produced without a word than a word to be produced without a point. This finding may not be surprising given that pointing has a spatial function with respect to the objects as well as a function in time, but the finding does again underscore the central importance of pointing in young children's counting.

In chapter 3 children counting objects in rows made more errors in which an object received no point[3] than in which an object received more than one point or a point was given to no object[4] (3.2 vs. 2.2). When counting objects in rows, the errors for the present sample showed a similar relationship: a mean rate of 10.3 compared to a mean rate of 5.0. However, for the disorganized arrays, a very strong reversal of this pattern was found: the mean rate of errors in which an object received no point was 13.5, and the mean rate for errors in which an object received more than one point was 22.5. This difference was the result of the much higher rate of recount errors in the disorganized arrays than in the rows.

In the larger sample of chapter 3, children were about twice as likely to give no word or a part word to an object[5] than to give more than one word to an object or say a word without indicating an object[6] (mean rate of 5.0 vs. 2.3). The direction of this relationship held for the counting of objects in rows by the present sample, although the relative number of objects never receiving a word was considerably greater (12.5 vs. 3.8). In contrast for the disorganized arrays the number of objects receiving no word was roughly the same as the number of words given to no object or the number of objects receiving more than one word (20.0 vs. 23.1). Again, this difference for the rows and disorganized arrays was largely due to the large number of recount errors, in which an object received more than one word.

The same pattern was evident when errors of surplus (errors in which something extra was done) were compared to errors of deficit (errors in which some part of the counting act was omitted). When counting objects in rows, the present sample was similar to the larger sample in chapter 3: They made about twice as many errors of deficit as errors of surplus (13.1 vs. 5.8). However, when counting objects in a disorganized array, roughly equal numbers of errors of surplus and errors of deficit were made (24.4 vs. 20.4). Again, this result was largely the result of the large number of recount errors, which are errors of surplus.

---

[3] These were object skipped and word–no point errors.

[4] These were multiple count, word and point–no object, multiple points–no word, multiple points–one word, and recount errors.

[5] These were point–no word, part word–one point, object skipped, and multiple points–no word errors.

[6] These were multiple words–one point, word between objects, multiple count, word and point–no object, and recount errors.

4.2.3.5. Strategies for Remembering Counted Objects in Disorganized Immovable Arrays. The quite high rate of recounted and of uncounted blocks indicated that many children were not able to generate effective strategies to remember which objects they had already counted. Many children when counting these large disorganized arrays used the same general spatial approach. They started at a block on the edge of the array and began to move around the circumference of the solid "circle" formed by the blocks in the array, moving toward the center and back out to the edge counting a wide swath of blocks around the circumference of the circle. About a fourth of the children, two in each of the four youngest age groups (children aged 3–0 through 4–11) and one aged 5–6 to 5–11, demonstrated a particular difficulty with this approach. They counted several blocks deep around the edge of the disorganized display until one complete revolution had been made and then continued on and on around the disorganized array. It appeared that these children either did not know that with such a circular strategy counting should stop at the starting point or they did not remember even roughly their starting point. Another third of the sample also counted using this "edge" strategy, but they stopped at approximately the place they had started.

The undergraduates working on these data noticed this strategy and commented that they would not have used this "circumference" approach. To explore this issue Diane Briars and I ran a small comparison group to see if there was an age-related difference in the spatial strategies for counting such arrays (Briars & Fuson, 1979). Sixteen high school students were given disorganized arrays in the same way as were the young children. The number of blocks was gradually increased by 1 or 2 blocks from 4 to 33 objects, and the students were not permitted to move the blocks. None of these high school students used the circumference approach. Instead, they used one of two other approaches. They either mentally divided up the array into several compact subgroups (even though the arrays were designed to make such a separation nontrivial) and then counted each subgroup in turn, or they counted along (usually inevitably somewhat curving) "lines" that went clear across the solid "circle" but that together covered the whole array. The accuracy of our descriptions of these strategies and their intentional use in remembering which entities had been counted were confirmed by questions asked after the counting was finished. Both of these strategies ease the load of remembering just which entities one has counted. One only has to remember the edge entities in the subgroup approach (and one can forget certain earlier edges as one counts contiguous subgroups) and only has to remember each last "line" in the line approach (because the next "line" will involve entities close to this last line). This limited evidence suggests that there may indeed be an age difference in the general spatial strategies used to count large disorganized arrays. Furthermore, at least for the older counters, these spatial strategies are intentionally used to remember which entities have been counted. Further work with young children is needed in order to determine the extent to which their "circumference" strategy functions intentionally as a memory aid. It also is not totally clear for any of these strategies whether a given user was trying to establish a linear ordering on the array or trying mentally to mark the spatial location of the counted objects, that is, whether the second or fourth remembering method in Table 4-2 was being used. It may be that for large disorganized arrays aspects of each of these two methods may be part of a given strategy.

4.2.4. Summary

The major changes in the kinds of correspondence errors made in counting immovable objects in a disorganized rather than in a linear array are a very large increase over all ages (from age 3 through 5 years 11 months) in the rate of objects recounted (from almost no objects recounted in rows to a mean of about one in five objects recounted in disorganized arrays), a considerable increase in the rate of objects never counted (object skipped/uncounted errors), and a considerable increase in stretching a number word out over two or more objects. The actual change in the rate of object skipped errors (objects skipped over by the indicating act) as opposed to uncounted errors (objects never counted) is not clear because of the difficulty of isolating these two kinds of errors in a disorganized array. There also may be a developmental difference in the spatial strategies used in counting large disorganized arrays, with a shift from many young children counting around a wide swath of blocks on the edge of the array (using the "circumference" strategy) to high school students counting either compact subgroups or longer "lines" of entities that go across the circle.

4.3. Counting Entities in a Circular Loop: Use of a Stop-Rule

In the disorganized arrays just discussed, children sometimes counted around the "edge" of the array but instead of stopping when they returned to their starting point, they continued on and on around the circular path. We noticed a similar phenomenon when we piloted the tasks for the cardinality study reported in chapter 7. This piloting was done with children aged 2½ to 3½. They counted entities arranged in a row and entities arranged in a circular loop.[7] When counting the circles some children continued around two or even three times before stopping, in some cases on every circle trial. They did not seem to know that one stopped counting where one had started, that is, that one counted each entity only once. Other children only counted on and on for some circle trials, but for other trials they stopped fairly near their starting point. These children thus seemed to understand at least a general version of

---

[7] The objects were arranged in a circular loop, that is, around the circumference of a circle. For ease of reference we will call such arrays "circles" or "circular arrays."

a stop-rule but did not use it consistently. When children's counting of circular arrays begins to reflect use of such a stop-rule and when this use becomes consistent became of interest to us. We also wondered how accurate young children would be in remembering exactly where they had started counting in a circular array. At this time we were exploring the use of the graphics tablet in counting research (see 4.4.2 for more details), so half of the arrays in that study were made circular. Wilkinson (1984) identified such stopping as one of his components of counting, but because only the first error a child made in counting was recorded in his study, his data on stopping only pertain to children who were good enough counters to have counted accurately up to the stopping point. Our method of recording correspondence errors permitted us to observe violations of the stop-rule as well as correspondence errors.

4.3.1. Circle Study 1: Children Aged 3½ to 6

4.3.1.1. Method. The subjects were 46 middle- and upper-middle-class children age 3½ to 6 years from a preschool in a northern suburb of Chicago. The children were separated into half-year age groups as follows: 3–6 (3 years 6 months) through 3–11, 4–0 through 4–5, 4–6 through 4–11, 5–0 through 5–5, and 5–6 through 5–11. The number of children in each group was 10, 10, 10, 9, and 7, respectively.

The procedure involved placing a large sheet of paper containing colored sticker dots on the graphics tablet used in conjunction with an Apple IIe microcomputer; further details are given in section 4.4.2 and in Fuson and Darling (1984). For half the counting trials, the dots were arranged in a row, and for half they were arranged in a circle (in a linearly ordered loop with a constant diameter). Half of the trials for each arrangement were counted in the usual manner by pointing with a finger, and half were counted by pointing to dots with the graphics tablet pen, which permitted the time and location of each point to be entered into the microcomputer. The data reported here are from the trials in which dots were arranged in a circle. There were three trials of 16, 18, and 19 dots in both the finger condition and the pen condition. The dots for a given array were all the same color; colors varied across the arrays. The two experimenters recorded on a prepared sheet containing drawings of 16, 18, and 19 dots the number words said by the child at the location to which the child's finger (or the pen) was directed when the word was said. Other special codings were used to permit coding of errors in the error categories described in chapter 3 (Table 3-1). Children were not told where to start counting in the circular array; each child picked the starting dot for each trial.

Recount errors for each trial were classified into two groups: those in which the child recounted one, two, or three dots and those in which the counting on around the circle continued for four or more dots. On all of the circles, the fourth recounted dot really was in a noticeably different location than the starting dot, subtending a central angle between 57° and 68° past the starting point. It thus seemed that even a fairly diffuse spatial memory of the location of the starting dot should enable a child to stop within three recount errors. Therefore, we inferred that a child making one, two, or three recount errors on a given trial was trying to use a stop-rule (i.e., knew to stop counting where the counting had started) but that a child making four or more errors either did not know a stop-rule or had forgotten the location of the start of the count. This was only a first rough attempt at such a distinction. Later evidence might indicate that other angles (and thus other numbers of dots) are better choices.

4.3.1.2. Results. The only recount errors observed in the circle trials were those in which children continued on around the circle and recounted (counted again) dots they had counted at the beginning of their count. The experimenter records agreed on more than 98% of the recount errors discussed here. Almost all of the children counting these large circles showed evidence of knowing the stop-rule: On at least two of the six trials, they stopped within three objects of their starting point. However, eleven children demonstrated the stop-rule inconsistently: on one or two trials they had four or more recount errors. These children were distributed across all age groups: 4, 3, 2, 1, and 1 from the youngest to the oldest age group, respectively. The number of such children did not differ significantly for the pointing with the finger and the pointing with the pen. Two children had such trials of four or more recounts in both conditions, three children had such trials with the finger but not with the pen, and six children had such trials with the pen but not with the finger. If the criterion of five or more recounts is used instead of four or more, only five children (all in the three youngest age groups) displayed the stop-rule inconsistently, showing one or more trials with five or more recounts (these trials ranged from 5 to 10 recounts).

Although most children showed evidence of trying to stop about where they started, few were able to do so accurately with any consistency. Most of the children, 41 of the 46, counted on past the last dot on at least one trial (i.e., had at least one recount error), and 20 children stopped short of the last dot (i.e., had one or more object skipped errors on the dots just before the starting dot) on at least one trial. Only four children (one in all age groups except those aged 4 to 4½) correctly stopped their counting on the last dot (the dot just before the dot at which they had started counting) on as many as four trials; seven more did so on half the trials. Children aged 4 and older were more likely to count past the last dot than to stop short of the last dot: They had more than three times as many trials with a recount error as trials with an object skipped error at the end. The youngest children (aged 3½ to 4) were about equally likely to overcount (recount) and to stop short. Most of the object skipped error trials only involved one to three dots uncounted at the end, but in about a fourth of them, children left from four to eight dots uncounted at the end.

Although children were not consistently accurate in their stopping place, overall performance was really not too bad. Children stopped counting on the last dot (i.e., stopped correctly) on 22% of the trials, recounted only one dot on 22% of the trials, and recounted two dots on 17% of the trials. They also stopped short of counting just the last dot on 9% of the trials and stopped short of the last two dots on 4% of the trials.

Only one child was observed to use a visible strategy to remember which dot was counted first. This 5½-year-old kept her finger on the first dot while she pointed for counting with her other finger. However, she was not able to use this strategy completely correctly, for she still made object skipped errors at the end of two trials. How the other children were able to remember as well as they did where they had started counting is not clear.

Thus, most children aged 3½ to 6 do seem to know to use a stop-rule for counting entities in circular arrays and do seem usually to use such a stop-rule, even though they may occasionally show a lapse in such use. The most pervasive problem is in remembering the exact starting (stopping) point. Only one child used an observable strategy for remembering the starting dot.

4.3.2. Circle Study 2: Children Aged 2½ to 3½

Circle study 1 indicated that by age 3½ most children counting objects in a circle know a stop-rule, although they may have trouble employing it exactly when the only cue is spatial location, and they may occasionally forget to use the rule. This naturally raised the question of when children begin to use a stop-rule. To examine whether younger children would use a stop-rule even in an easy situation in which the starting dot was differentiated from other dots, children aged 2½ to 3½ were asked to count dots arranged in a circle in which one dot was a different color from the other dots. Children were asked to start counting with that dot, so their starting dot was clearly identifiable. In order to try to separate the issue of knowing that one should stop from being able to do so even with the memory aid of the colored dot, children were shown examples in which recounting extended halfway or more around the circle, in which the starting dot was recounted, and in which counting was correct. They were asked to judge these counts as correct or incorrect. In order to assess whether children who did not know to use a stop-rule (or at least did not evidence such knowledge on either of the first two tasks) could use a stop-rule, children were then told the stop-rule and asked to count dots in a circle again.

4.3.2.1. Method. The sample consisted of 19 children aged 2½ to 3½. Four children were aged 2–6 through 2–11, six were aged 3–1 through 3–3, and nine were aged 3–4 through 3–6. They all attended a preschool in a small city on the northern border of Chicago and were from middle- and upper-middle-class homes. Nine other children within this age range were intended to be in the sample. However, three 3-year-olds and one 2-year-old refused to leave their classroom to do the task, and one 3-year-old and four 2-year-olds came with the experimenters but would not or could not count.

In the first task children were given three trials in which they were asked to count colored dots arranged in a circular path (i.e., equally spaced along the circumference of a circle) on a piece of white cardboard. The dot at the top of the card was red, and the other dots on each card were the same color (yellow, green, and blue each on one trial). There were 6, 7, and 8 dots on the three trials (6 was the smallest number of dots that really looked like a circle). The child was directed, "Count these dots. Start at the red dot" (the experimenter pointed to it). After the child counted, she or he was asked, "How many dots are there?" Each of the two experimenters recorded on a prepared sheet containing drawings of the circular arrays each number word at the location to which the child's finger was directed when the word was said. Points without words were recorded as Ps, and words without points were recorded as a numeral with a stroke through it.

For the second task one experimenter said to the child, "Now it's Sue's turn to count. Sometimes she will count right and sometimes she will count wrong. You watch her and tell me if she counted wrong or right." The second experimenter (Sue) counted as specified below. If the child said the count was wrong, the child was asked to tell "What did she do wrong?" The same stimulus materials were used as in the first task. Two trials demonstrated each of three kinds of counting: *correct counting* in which the count stopped at the last dot before the red dot, *wrong counting* in which the *counting stopped on the red dot* (i.e., the red dot was recounted), and *wrong counting* in which the *counting went on around past the red dot to halfway or more around the circle* (i.e., the number of recounted dots was 4 or 5, depending on the number of dots in the circle). One trial of each of these three kinds of counting was done first. All possible orders of these three were used across children. For each child the second three trials were given in the same order as the first three trials. The three sizes of dot circles (6, 7, 8) were given in the same order to all children so that, across children, set size and color would vary across the kinds of counting errors made.

The purpose of the third task was to see if a verbal statement of the stop-rule and a short demonstration of its use would be sufficient to enable children to use it. This third task was identical to the first task except that it was preceded by a short verbalization and demonstration of the stop-rule. The child was told, "You know, when you count you are only supposed to count each dot *once*. So you should stop when you get around to the first dot [experimenter points to red dot]. Like this" The experimenter counted the green circle twice, saying after each count, "See, I already counted this dot, so I don't want to count it again." Then, for each of the three trials of this task, the child was directed, "Count these dots. Start at the red dot [experimenter points to it] and stop when you get back to the red dot. Don't count the red dot again."

4.3.2.2. Results. Each trial was classified as to whether the counting correctly stopped on the last dot (the dot just before the red dot), stopped x dots before this last dot, or stopped x dots after the last dot (i.e., had x recounted dots). On 96% of the trials, the records of the two experimenters agreed on the dot at which counting had stopped.

Contrary to our expectations, almost all the children gave evidence of knowing the stop-rule. Marking the starting point permitted most of them to stop their counting accurately, but some execution problems remained for a few of the children. On the first task, 17 of the 19 children correctly stopped on the last dot on at least one trial, 13 stopped at the last dot on 2 of the 3 trials, and 11 of the 19 did so on all three trials. The incorrect trials were evenly balanced between stopping before the last dot and recounting on past the last dot.

Performance on the second task, designed to assess children's knowledge of the stop-rule, was extremely poor. Most children did give both possible responses (wrong and right) across trials, but these responses often seemed to follow a pattern across trials (e.g., WWWRRR or RWRWRW) rather than to reflect judgments about the counting observed. Only five children (on 11 trials) correctly described what was wrong after a judgment that the counting was wrong; seven of these descriptions were of the recounted red dot and four were of the counting halfway or more around the circle. Judgments were in the right direction for the correct trials (72% of the judgments were of correct counting), but 9 of the 19 children said that one or both correct trials were wrong. Judgments for the two kinds of incorrect counting were at chance. Half of the judgments for each kind of violation of the stop-rule were that the counting was correct. Twelve children made one or two such judgments for each kind of incorrect counting.

This poor performance was particularly striking because children's use of the stop-rule in the first task had been relatively good. This counting-judgment task was included in the study on the assumption that some children might know the stop-rule (i.e., know that they are not supposed to count on around the circle) even though they might have trouble actually using it (e.g., they might forget the stop-rule by the time they got back around to the starting dot). Thus, we expected that some children might do better on this second task than on the first task. To the contrary few children who used a stop-rule correctly were able to judge its use in this task. Whether these children did not understand the task, could not attend adequately to the counting, or could not access their stop-rule in order to make judgments about correct and incorrect counting is not clear. Clearly, obtaining evidence concerning children's understanding of aspects of counting through counting-judgment tasks is a tricky matter.

Because performance on the first task demonstrated such widespread use of a stop-rule, there was not much room for improvement on task 3. Of the 11 children who stopped correctly on every trial on task 1, 7 did so on task 3.

Four stopped early or late on one of the three trials; for these children, trying to be conscious of stopping correctly seemed to make stopping correctly more difficult. Of the 16 trials on which improvement could take place (i.e., on which children had not stopped correctly in task 1), children stopped correctly on 12. Thus, every child stopped correctly on at least one trial of task 3, 18 stopped correctly on two of the three trials, and 12 stopped correctly on all three trials. Thus, every child was able to demonstrate the stop-rule at least once after a short statement and demonstration of its use.

Some caveats are clearly in order here. The red dot was very salient and might even have conveyed a stop meaning. One would certainly want to repeat this study using a different color of dot for the starting dot. Some children would not participate in the study, and thus we might have been studying the best counters in this age span. The ability to use a stop-rule may not be as widespread in this age span as our data indicate. However, these data do suggest that young children may in fact know that they should stop when they come around to their starting point, but may have trouble remembering this when they are caught up in the actual throes of counting, especially when counting a large circle or a disorganized display such as in 4.2.

4.4. Indicating Acts Other Than Pointing With a Finger

Pointing at objects with an extended index finger seems to be by far the most common indicating act used by preschool children when counting. Gelman and Gallistel (1978) reported that 98% of their sample of 3- through 5-year-olds pointed when counting (p. 112). Most of our sample of 3- through 5-year-olds in the study reported in chapter 3 pointed, although some of the 5-year-olds had internalized counting and did initially use eye fixation as the indicating act (see the discussion of the internalization of counting in 3.3.11). A few children also tried to move the blocks, one counted on one trial with his toe, and one counted on some trials with the first two fingers in "Itsy-bitsy-spider fashion" (each finger walking along touching every other object). Secada (1984) reported that young native-signing children when counting using American Sign Language (ASL) sometimes point with one hand and sign with the other hand and sometimes point at objects with the signing hand, changing the sign between each point. Children also sometimes shift between these two methods even within a single counting trial. Saxe, Guberman, and Gearhart (in press) described mothers' reports of children's counting in the home that included pointing at objects and moving objects (e.g., counting while picking up coins and putting them in a paper cup). Thus, indicating acts seem either to be variations of pointing (including the later internalized eye fixation) or to involve moving objects from one spatial location to the other.

Neither variations of pointing nor moving objects have been studied very much. We report below one exploratory study focused on each of these.

4.4.1. Counting Movable Blocks

An initial exploration of children's use of the indicating act of moving objects was included in our first large-scale study of counting. We assessed children's spontaneous use of moving objects rather than asking them to move objects. The task selected was one in which moving objects was by far the easiest and most accurate indicating act. This task was ascertaining how many blocks were in a large pile of blocks in which some blocks are hidden by other blocks. The only accurate way to answer this question is to move at least some of the blocks so that all are visible. One can first unpile the blocks into a one-dimensional array and then count them in place by using pointing or a variation of pointing. However, a much easier and more accurate way to count them is to move the blocks one at a time from an "uncounted blocks" to a "counted blocks" pile while counting each block. The advantage of this strategy is that one does not then have to remember exactly which blocks have been counted: the piles keep track of this. Such a successive partitioning of the set of objects to be counted is the type of counting discussed by Beckwith and Restle (1966). In this type of counting, the physical relocation of an object rather than pointing is the indicating act. The same main categories of correspondence errors are still possible: word–indicating act errors, indicating act–object errors, and dual errors. However, some new error subtypes (discussed below) also become possible with this new indicating act.

4.4.1.1. Method. The sample was the same as the sample in chapter 3. It consisted of 86 children distributed among five half-year age groups: 3½ to 4 (3–6 through 3–11), 4 to 4½, 4½ to 5, 5 to 5½, and 5½ to 6 years. From the youngest to oldest age group, there were 18, 17, 17, 16, and 18 children in the age groups. Sixty of these children—12 children balanced by sex in each half-year age group—were randomly selected from a Chicago public school whose population racially and economically matched the population of the city. The remaining 26 children were middle- to upper-middle-class children attending a private educational demonstration school.

This task was given first so as not to bias the indicating act chosen by the child. A pile of 50 blocks all of the same color was pushed in front of the child. Much of the pile was two blocks deep, and a few blocks in the middle were three deep; many blocks were therefore partially or completely hidden. The child was asked, "How many blocks are there?" If the how-many question did not elicit counting, the child was told to count the blocks. The observers made notes concerning the indicating act chosen by each child, the general finger path used by those pointing at unmoved objects, errors made by children who moved objects as their indicating act, and any other behavior of the child that seemed pertinent. More detailed analyses of the errors made in counting (comparable to the analyses done in chapter 3) were not possible because of the complexity of this task of counting 50 blocks. Videotaping would be necessary for a fully detailed analysis of such counting.

4.4.1.2. Results. About half of the children in the youngest four age groups (half-year age groups ranging from 3½ to 5½) and most of the oldest children (age 5½ to 6) spontaneously moved blocks in this task. A few of these moved the blocks so that all were visible and then pointed while counting; most of the spontaneous movers used the movement of blocks as an indicating act. Some of these children who moved blocks simply placed the counted blocks into one pile; others built towers, rows, or designs with the counted blocks, adding each new counted block to the construction. Children who did not move blocks pointed to the blocks as they counted them. A small number of these "pointers" produced behaviors showing that they were aware that there were hidden blocks to be counted (e.g., tried to count the hidden blocks or said, "I counted all the blocks I could see"), but most did not. Thus, a substantial portion (almost half) of the children aged 3½ to 5½ did not think about how, did not know how, or did not choose to make all of the objects to be counted visible (a prerequisite for accurate counting) or to use the most efficient indicating act in this situation (moving blocks). Herscovics, Bergeron, and Bergeron (1986) reported a similar finding on the use of moving objects with a set of 15 cubes for French-speaking kindergarten children in Montreal. Only half of them moved cubes spread out in front of them to a counted pile; most of the others pointed, and a few used eye fixation as the indicating act.

Some differences in indicating act–object correspondence errors were observed for pointing and moving a block. First, errors with more than one indicting act per one object were replaced by errors with one indicating act per more than one object. When these same children pointed to objects in rows (see chapter 3), multiple count errors (two successive indicating acts given to one object) were frequent. Such errors never occurred with moving blocks; a block was never moved and then immediately moved again. However, with blocks children sometimes moved more than one object at a time (sometimes handfuls at a time) but treated each hand movement as a single indicating act: Each hand movement of from two to five blocks was accompanied by one word. In contrast, when pointing instead of moving objects is the indicating act, it is difficult and unusual to give one point to more than one object. Thus, it may be that the indicating act of pointing constrains the kinds of errors children can make (virtually eliminating errors in which one indicating act is given to more than one object) and thus inadvertantly makes the counting activity more accurate than is warranted by the conceptions of the child. Using a different indicating act such as moving objects would be one way to test whether children in fact know that one indicating act does not include more than one object.

An error that was almost nonexistent with pointing to objects in a row occurred with moving blocks. Children stopped counting before getting to all the objects. In the row task children almost never stopped counting before they had counted the whole row; they might skip over many blocks toward the end of a row, but they would count the last block. When moving blocks, several children stopped before all of the blocks were moved. This task did have a larger number of blocks (50) than did the row task (maximum of 34), so it is possible that the size of the set was responsible for many of these early stopping errors. However, an additional new problem with the movable pile of blocks was that some children began to focus less on the uncounted pile of blocks and much more on the pile or design they were making with the moved counted blocks. They then began to move blocks according to the requirements of their design and stopped when it was "finished" rather than stopping when the uncounted pile of blocks was gone. It is not clear whether some young children do not understand that they do not stop counting until all objects have been counted or whether they simply become distracted from this requirement when they are moving objects instead of pointing.

For pointing at objects in rows, point–no word errors (pointing without saying a word) were always interspersed among correct word–point correspondences, that is, such points without words were almost always preceded and followed by points with words. Such interspersed point–no word errors also occurred when moving blocks, but several of these errors also sometimes occurred together. A few children began by producing a word as they moved each block but then became so engrossed in what they were building as they moved blocks that they stopped saying words at all and just moved and built. In these cases moving a block ceased to be an indicating act and took on another function, a building function. Using blocks may have increased such occurrences. This possibility might be examined in future research.

Two additional "new" errors occurred with moving objects as the indicating act. The first was in a way the reverse of a counting error described by Saxe (1977). Saxe reported that when told to count two sets of objects to compare their cardinality, some children counted the first set and then continued on counting the second set rather than beginning to count it starting from one. In our task the child sometimes turned the counting of one large set into the counting of several smaller subsets of this set. Even though the child was asked to tell how many blocks were in the whole pile, a child sometimes would make a row or tower of blocks, counting as the row or tower was built, and would then begin to make another row or tower, counting the blocks in this row or tower by starting the counting over and beginning with the number word "one." The cardinality of each such row or tower was reported by the child as the child finished it. Thus, moving the blocks led some children to change their definition of their counting task. This never occurred with pointing to blocks in rows. A second "new" error with moving objects was a failure to keep the pile of counted blocks separate from the pile of uncounted blocks. Several children did not begin their pile of counted blocks far away enough from their original pile of counted blocks. The piles of blocks then got somewhat mixed up, with some blocks being recounted and some blocks never getting counted.

4.4.2. A Microcomputer Pen: A Variation of Pointing

In an effort to develop a method for collecting data on counting that would eliminate the time-consuming and laborious separate steps of coding correspondence errors, entering them into computer files, and then analyzing the data, we explored the use of a graphics tablet connected to an Apple lle (Apple, Cupertino, CA) microcomputer to record children's counting. The graphics tablet has the capability to record the location of a point made on its surface by using a specially wired pen. In conjunction with the Appleclock, both the location and the time of each point on the surface could be recorded to the millisecond. Such time records would permit microanalyses of irregularities in children's counting. The procedure that was originally envisioned also involved the use of the Supertalker (Mountain Hardware, Scotts Valley, CA), by which the timing of children's number words could be recorded. Programs were written to determine from the location of the points and of the counting stimuli the nature of the counting errors made by children, and the graphics tablet part of the package was tested. Unfortunately, the graphics tablet pen was not a reliable enough instrument. The pen had a small tip that had to be depressed in order to make the record of the point, and not all children consistently depressed the pen when pointing with it. Furthermore, there were some significant differences in the rates of certain types of errors made when pointing with the pen and when counting as usual by pointing with the finger. These problems are reported in some detail in Fuson and Darling (1984). For present purposes, the graphics tablet pen offers an interesting contrast to the usual indicating act of pointing with a finger. Observations using that approach with preschool children are summarized in the following section.

4.4.2.1. Method. The subjects were the same subjects for the study reported in 4.3.1: 46 middle and upper-middle-class children aged 3½ to 6 years from a preschool in a northern suburb of Chicago. Children were separated into half-year age groups as follows: 3–6 (3 years 6 months) through 3–11, 4–0 through 4–5, 4–6 through 4–11, 5–0 through 5–5, and 5–6 through 5–11. The number of children in each group was 10, 10, 10, 9, and 7.

The procedure involved placing a large sheet of paper containing colored sticker dots on the graphics tablet used in conjunction with an Apple lle microcomputer; further details are given in Fuson and Darling (1984). Half of the trials for each arrangement were counted in the usual manner by pointing to the dots with a finger, and half were counted by pointing to dots with the graphics tablet pen. Within each indicating–act condition, half of the trials had dots arranged in a row and half had the dots arranged in a circle. These array shapes were blocked and counterbalanced within each age group. There were three trials of 16, 18, and 19 dots for both the row and the circular arrays in the finger condition and in the pen condition (for a total of 12 counting trials). The dots for a given array were all the same color; colors varied across the arrays. The two experimenters recorded on a prepared sheet containing drawings of 16, 18, and 19 dots in rows and in circles the number words said by the child at the location to which the child's finger (or the pen) was directed when the word was said. Other special codings were used to permit coding of errors in the error categories used in Table 3-1.

4.4.2.2. Results. The indicating act had no effect on the number of trials on which a child made completely accurate correspondences, produced an accurate sequence of number words, or counted accurately. However, 2(indicating act: finger vs. pen) × 2(array shape: row vs. circle) × 5(age) ANOVAs with indicating act and array shape as repeated measures were conducted on the errors per 100 objects counted for each of the error types and subtypes in Table 3-1. These revealed that the indicating act did affect the production of three kinds of correspondence errors: point–no word, multiple points–one word, and skim errors. Children made significantly more point–no word errors when pointing with the pen than with the finger, an error rate of 0.22 versus 0.06, $F(1, 41) = 4.96$, $p < .03$, and significantly more children made such errors when pointing with the pen: five children made such errors with the pen and not with the finger versus 0 with the reverse, McNemar's test $\chi^2 = 5.0$, $p < .05$. Children also made significantly more multiple points–one word errors when pointing with the pen than with the finger: 0.3 versus 0.0, $F(1, 41) = 6.56$, $p < .01$, and significantly more children made these errors with the pen than with their finger: seven children made them with the pen and not with their finger while no child did the reverse, McNemar's test $\chi^2 = 7.0$, $p < .01$. Children made significantly fewer skim errors when pointing with the pen than when pointing with the finger, the error rate per 100 objects counted was 0.8 versus 4.3, $F(1, 41) = 4.14$, $p < .05$, and significantly fewer children made a skim error with the pen: no child made a skim error with the pen and not with their finger and seven children made skim errors with a finger and not with the pen, McNemar's test $\chi^2 = 7.0$, $p < .01$.

One interpretation of these results is that pointing with the pen rather than with the finger made the pointing act more salient to some children, leading them occasionally to focus only on that pointing (and produce the two kinds of errors with a point but no word) and almost never to neglect to point at all (and thus they rarely skimmed). Other manipulations that increase the salience of the indicating act might have similar effects. This particular manipulation affected only a few children in the sample. Furthermore, the error rates for the first two kinds of errors were low, and the skim errors were concentrated on a few trials. For these reasons the pen significantly affected these three kinds of errors but did not affect the overall rate of accurate correspondence trials. Whether other manipulations that affect the salience of the indicating act would be so limited is not so clear. In particular, asking children to touch objects so that they receive kinesthetic as well as visual information might have a much larger effect on correspondence errors and might be examined in future research.

4.5. Summary

Counting objects distributed in space requires an indicating act to mediate between the words said in time and the objects distributed in space. Such indicating acts fall within two categories: (a) moving objects from a pile of uncounted objects to a pile of counted objects and (b) some variation of pointing at unmoved objects, including the later internalization of pointing as eye fixation (see 3.3.11). Correct indicating act–object correspondence includes four requirements, the violation of which leads to the class of error listed:

1. each indicating act must be directed toward an object: one indicating act—less than one object
2. each indicating act must not be directed toward more than one object: one indicating act—more than one object
3. every object is indicated: less than one indicating act—one object
4. no object is indicated more than once: more than one indicating act—one object.

Whether the indicting act–object correspondence is correct is determined in some cases locally (as each spatial correspondence is made) and in some cases over all the correspondences. The latter requires a method of remembering which objects have been counted. Thus, accurate counting requires accurate local word-indicating act correspondences, accurate local indicating act–object correspondences, and an overall method of remembering the objects counted.

The first two requirements for correct indicating act–object correspondences are accomplished locally during counting by setting limits on each separate indicating act: Each act must be directed toward an object, and it must not be directed toward more than one object. Both moving objects and pointing usually meet this requirement. In chapter 3 we found that children rarely pointed at an empty space (i.e., pointed but not at an object), and it is not really possible to point to more than one object at a time.[8] In this chapter we found that moving objects was always directed toward at least one object and that, although some children do move more than one object at a time (even handfuls), this behavior was infrequent.

---

[8] One can gesture toward more than one object with sweeping gestures, but a point requires a downward motion that is then directed toward only a single spatial location. This location will not certain more than one object unless the objects are exceptionally small.

How the last two requirements for correct indicating act-object correspondence are met depends on the method of remembering which objects
have been counted. Four such methods are listed in Table 4-1. Two of them
involve the "marking" of individual counted objects in some way so that it is
clear that the object has been counted. The first method uses the indicating
act of moving objects from an uncounted to a counted pile; membership in
the counted pile thus "marks" each counted object. In the second method the
indicating act is pointing, but each object is physically or mentally "marked"
in some way as the object is counted. Both of these methods of remembering
create successive partitions of the objects into counted and to-be-counted sets
(Beckwith & Restle, 1966). These successive partitions are obvious to any
viewer with moving objects and with physically marked objects; they are not
obvious with mentally marked objects. With these methods of remembering,
one does not have to make a linear ordering on the objects. Such a linear
ordering is accomplished in the course of counting by the successive choices of
the next object, but this linear ordering need neither be noticed or remembered before, during, or after counting. Moving objects clearly is the easier of
the two methods, for with it one does not have to remember just which
objects have been counted; the procedure keeps track of this for the counter.
Thus, moving objects is the optimal strategy when objects can be moved.

The other two methods in Table 4-1 use a linear ordering on the objects.
Such a linear ordering can be already established and obvious in the situation,
such as in a row, or the situation can require an individually established
nonevident linear ordering, such as in a disorganized array. The key difference between these two situations then is the spatial arrangement of the
objects. Pointing at objects in an already established linear ordering also
creates successive partitions of the objects into counted and to-be-counted
sets: Each object pointed to partitions the objects into those earlier in the
ordering (the counted objects) and those still to come in the ordering (the to-
be-counted objects). However, only if the linear ordering is obvious to the
onlooker, as in a row, can this partitioning be evident to an observer, and it is
not clear in any of these cases that the counter is aware that the objects are
being successively partitioned. Therefore, it does not seem wise to consider
counting *in general* as consisting of tagging and of partitioning, as is done by
Gelman and Gallistel (1978) and then by others following this terminology.

The method of remembering which objects have been counted depends
heavily on both the object situation and the indicating act used in that
situation. With movable objects and with objects in rows, the usual indicating
acts (moving objects and pointing) are sufficient methods for remembering
the counted objects. With immovable objects and most nonrow arrangements, some method of remembering must be adopted and used with the
indicating act of pointing. This method may involve partitioning or it may
involve establishing a linear ordering; either is sufficient. Thus, it seems both
more accurate and more general to consider counting as consisting of the
local word-indicating act correspondences, the local indicating act–object
correspondences, and a method of remembering which objects have been

counted. With pointing in rows and with moving movable objects, the third aspect (remembering) is already subsumed in the local indicating acts.

In the first study the kinds of correspondence errors made by children aged 3–0 to 6–11 when counting immovable objects arranged in maximally disorganized arrays were compared to those made when counting objects arranged in a row. Objects in a row already have an established linear ordering that permits the last two requirements for indicating act–object correspondences to be satisfied by the local point–object correspondences, while objects in a disorganized array do not already have such an ordering. Children must then satisfy those requirements either by establishing a linear ordering or by remembering for each object which objects have been counted. Children were not very successful in doing either. They had a considerably higher rate for the disorganized than for the linear arrays of both kinds of errors which violated the last two requirements for overall point–object correspondence. Recounted objects rose from almost no objects recounted in rows to a mean of about one in six objects recounted in disorganized arrays. The large number of recounted objects was partly due to some children continuing to count on and on around a disorganized array, not even stopping approximately where they had started counting. Many children used this "circumference" strategy, counting a wide swath of blocks on around the edge of the array. In contrast, high school students counted either compact subgroups or longer "lines" of entities that went across the array. Thus, there may be a developmental difference in the spatial strategies used in counting large disorganized arrays. Objects never counted rose from almost no such errors in rows to many such errors in disorganized arrays. However, in disorganized arrays errors that violate requirement 3 overall (objects never counted) cannot readily be differentiated from local violation errors (objects skipped over). Therefore these two kinds of errors had to be pooled for disorganized arrays. The change for this pooled category was from about one in ten objects skipped or never counted in rows to about one in seven such objects in disorganized arrays.

The rate of making other correspondence errors did not differ very much by array shape except for a considerable increase in part word–one point errors (stretching a number word out over two or more objects) in the disorganized arrays. Half or more children in each age group made such an error in the disorganized arrays, whereas almost no one made such an error in rows. Why the increased processing demands of meeting the last two requirements for the point–object correspondence should increase part word–one point errors rather than, for example, point–no word errors in which no word is said, is not clear. This is an interesting issue for future research.

Two studies explored the extent to which young children know and use a stop-rule when counting objects arranged in a circular loop, that is, know that they should stop counting at the object just before their first counted object instead of counting on and on around the circle. Most children aged 2½ to 6 demonstrated knowledge of such a stop-rule (i.e., they did not consistently go counting on and on around the circle), although many of them had some problems in executing the stop-rule exactly or consistently. When spatial location was the only cue for the starting object, and the sets counted were large (circles consisting of 16, 17, or 18 homogeneous dots), children aged 3½ to 6 were not able to stop exactly on the last dot very often (on only about 1 in 5 trials). They did stop within two dots before or after the last dot on about half of the trials. Therefore, their memory for the location of their starting dot seems to be a reasonable but not exact estimate. When the starting object was made very obviously different (a different color) from the other objects counted and the circles were small (6, 7, 8 dots), most children aged 2½ to 3½ used a stop-rule at least once, and about half of these children consistently stopped correctly on the object just before the starting dot. Most of these children then did very poorly on a counting-judgment task in which they were to identify as right or wrong counting trials of correct counting, of recounting the first dot counted, and of recounting halfway on around the circle. Whether these children did not understand the task, could not attend adequately to the counting, or could not access their stop-rule in order to make judgments about right and wrong counting is not clear. After a short explanation and demonstration of the stop-rule, all children used it on at least one trial, and all but one child stopped correctly on at least two of the three trials. These results are limited by the use of the color red for the starting object, which might have conveyed a stop meaning to some children, and by the fact that some children in the original sample refused to participate in the study, and thus the sample might have been weighted toward the better counters in this age span. The extent to which children this young can execute the stop-rule without a salient cue such as the different colored dot was also not established.

Another study explored the extent to which children spontaneously will use the indicating act of moving blocks from an uncounted to a counted pile in a task in which moving blocks is by far the most efficient indicating act. Children were asked how many blocks were in a pile of 50 blocks; many blocks in the pile were hidden from view by other blocks. Only about half the children aged 3½ to 5½ moved blocks; the others pointed. Most of the children aged 5½ to 6 did move the blocks while counting them, so perhaps there is an increased tendency with age to move objects when possible. Whether the failure to move blocks reflects a view of counting as necessarily involving pointing or only an assumption that moving the blocks was not acceptable to the experimenter is not clear but might be explored in the future by trying to eliminate the latter possibility.

Four new kinds of errors were observed when moving objects rather than pointing was the indicating act. Three of these seemed to result at least partly from the tendency of children to make something with the blocks they moved into the "counted blocks" pile. Some children made towers, rows, and other constructions with the counted blocks. In some cases their attention came to be focused more on these constructions and on the counted blocks than on the uncounted blocks. Thus, some children stopped saying number words while moving blocks to the counted blocks pile (i.e., made many successive point–no word errors), some stopped counting when a particular construction was completed rather than when all the uncounted blocks were counted (thus making many uncounted errors), and some counted parts of the whole pile of 50 blocks, starting with the number–word "one" as they started each new construction with counted blocks. These errors might have been increased by the use of blocks as the objects counted; the frequency of such errors with other objects might be explored in future research. A fourth new error was an indicating act–multiple objects error: Children sometimes moved whole handfuls of blocks to the counted blocks pile while saying only one number word. The fact that such an error is very difficult to make with pointing suggests that sometimes we may infer more understanding about correct counting than children actually possess when they use pointing as the indicating act because pointing constrains the kinds of errors children can make. Children also sometimes failed to carry out correctly a fundamental requirement of the moving objects strategy. They did not keep the pile of counted blocks separate from the pile of uncounted blocks, resulting in some blocks being recounted and some blocks never getting counted.

Thus, when the indicating act was moving objects, children usually met all four requirements of indicating act–object correspondence, but they did sometimes violate each of the last three requirements. In contrast the evidence from chapter 3 and from the study in this chapter with disorganized objects indicates that with pointing, children rarely violate the first requirement either for rows or disorganized arrays and never violate the second requirement (unless one wishes to consider skim errors such a violation). For objects in rows they somewhat frequently violate the third and fourth requirements locally by skipping over objects and by counting them again immediately. When pointing at objects in disorganized arrays, children violate the third and fourth requirements locally by skipping over objects and counting them again immediately and also violate these overall by failing to establish a linear ordering or another adequate strategy for remembering which objects have been counted and thus recounting many objects and leaving many objects uncounted.

In the final study, when pointing at objects with a microcomputer pen rather than with their finger, children made significantly more point–no word errors (pointing at an object but not saying a number word) and multiple points–one word errors (pointing two or more times at an object while saying only one number word) and made significantly fewer skim errors (in which the finger moves along the row without making any definite points and words are said in a haphazard manner). Pointing with the pen rather than with the finger thus may have made the pointing act more salient to some children, leading them occasionally to focus only on that pointing (and produce the two kinds of errors with a point but no word) and almost never to neglect to point at all (and thus to skim). Other manipulations that increase the salience of the indicating act might have similar effects. In particular asking children to touch objects so that they receive kinesthetic as well as visual information might have a considerable effect on correspondence errors and might be examined in future research.

5. Effects of Object Variables and Age of Counter on Correspondence Errors Made When Counting Objects in Rows

The results of the study reported in chapter 3 in which children counted objects in a row left several issues unresolved. In the three studies in this chapter, certain of these issues are explored. One study will be presented at a time, but the discussion for each will be cumulative over all of the previous studies in the book in which children counted objects in rows. To facilitate comparisons across studies, each study has been given a name that reflects an important aspect of the study. The study described in chapter 3 is called the Increasing Row study, and the study in chapter 4 in which correspondence errors on rows and on disorganized arrays were contrasted is called the Disorganized study (unless otherwise noted, however, only the data from the rows are discussed in this chapter). Important variables in these two studies and in the three studies reported in this chapter are summarized in Table 5-1. This chapter is quite long and detailed. Many readers may want to read only the summary of results across all the correspondence studies that is presented in chapter 6 and then perhaps dip into this chapter at specific points in order to pursue particular points.

Table 5-1. Variables in the Five Studies with Rows of Objects

Study name	Chapter	n	Ages[a]	Type of counted objects	Number of objects	Variables examined[b]
Increasing Row	3	86	3–6 through 5–11	1-inch blocks, close,[c] same color	4 through 34	Effort, Sex Number: 5 to 9, 10 to 15, 16 to 19, 20 to 24, 25 to 29 Location[d]
Disorganized	4	36	3–0 through 5–11	1-inch blocks, close, same color	4 through 34	Object arrangement: row vs. disorganized
Color Homogeneity	5	24	3–0 through 4–11	1-inch blocks, close, same and different color	7, 9 12, 14 17, 19	Object color: same vs. different Number: Small (3s 7, 9; 4s 12, 14) Large (3s 12, 14; 4s 17, 19) First half vs. second half of the row Location
Toy Homogeneity	5	43	3–2 through 4–5	Toys, far,[c] homogeneous and heterogeneous	4, 5, 6, 9, 12, 14	Object homogeneity: same vs. different Number: 4 to 6 vs. 9 to 14 Verbal label: class vs. collection term Location
Proximity	5	36	3–0 through 4–5	cars, chips, blocks, close and far, different color	4, 5, 6 9, 12, 14	Distance between objects: close vs. far Number: 4 to 6 vs. 9 to 14 Location

[a] 3–6 through 5–11 represents 3 years 6 months through 5 years 11 months; other ages are represented similarly.

[b] Age was also examined in each study.

[c] Objects close together were about ¼ inch apart; objects far apart were separated by a space greater than the width of the subject.

[d] Location compared errors at the beginning, within the middle, and at the end of a row.

In the Increasing Row study, the effect of the number of objects in a row was confounded with practice and fatigue because children in that study counted longer and longer rows as the session continued. In two studies in this chapter, the order in which children counted rows with a different number of objects was counterbalanced across children, and in the third the different rows were given over two sessions separated by several days. Increasing Row and Disorganized used very long rows. Rows of more moderate length were used in all three studies in this chapter, and the last two studies compared errors on such rows with errors made on rows with only a few objects (4, 5, 6 objects). The error rate measure described in chapter 3 (the number of errors per 100 objects counted) controls for differing numbers of objects in a row and thus permits errors meaningfully to be compared over rows.

Another feature of Increasing Row was that all of the blocks in the counted row were the same color. On the one hand it seems possible that it is more difficult to count a row of blocks of the same color than of different colors because a child might get confused as to whether a given block had already been counted. However, it also seems possible that the use of different colors might be somewhat distracting, diverting attention from counting and causing errors to increase. The first study in this chapter (Color Homogeneity) was undertaken to examine the effect of the homogeneity of the color of the counted objects. Correspondence errors made when counting rows of blocks all of the same color were contrasted with errors made when counting rows of blocks of different colors. Examination of the effect of homogeneity of the objects counted was extended to the second study, Toy Homogeneity, in which the kind or the size of the objects counted was varied.

Several other aspects of the objects themselves or of their placement were examined. In Increasing Row, Disorganized, and Color Homogeneity, the objects counted by the children were blocks. It seemed important to extend the objects counted to different kinds of objects. Therefore, in both the second and the third studies, children counted several different kinds of small toys. Effects of the verbal label used to describe the objects (class vs. collection terms, Markman, 1979) were examined in Toy Homogeneity. Because the blocks were placed quite close together in Increasing Row, Disorganized, and Color Homogeneity, the effect of proximity of objects was assessed. The distance between objects was manipulated in one study (Proximity), and the toys were placed far apart in another (Toy Homogeneity).

Because children aged 3 to 3½ years had made such a high rate of errors on the rows in Disorganized, all three studies in this chapter included children between 3 and 3½. The samples did not include 5-year-olds because they had made relatively few counting errors even on the large rows of Increasing Row and Disorganized.

The issue of whether the beginning and the end of counting present particular difficulties in counting was also examined in all three studies in this chapter. Errors made on the first, last, and middle objects were compared. Raw errors were converted to the number of errors made per 100 objects counted at each location in order to control for the greater number of middle objects. Analyses were also carried out on the individual trial data to ascertain how many trials conformed to the pattern of counting described by Gelman and Gallistel (1978, p. 205) in which trouble appeared at the beginning and end of counting but proceeded smoothly in between.

For each study following, a table summarizes the results by error type and variable. The results will be discussed by error type in order to attempt to understand the nature of the errors children make in counting and the ways in which certain variables affect a given type of error. The effect of a given variable can be ascertained by reading down the column for that variable in the summary table.

The next chapter summarizes the results from chapters 3 and 4 and the present chapter. For this reason and because the discussion of the results of each study in this chapter is cumulative across all of the previous row studies, the summary for this chapter will be quite brief and limited to a discussion of specific error subtypes.

5.1. Effects of Homogeneity of Color and Number of Objects: Color Homogeneity Study

5.1.1. Method

Twelve 3-year-olds and twelve 4-year-olds in a nursery school in a small city on the northern border of Chicago served as subjects. The children were from middle- and upper-middle-class home. The 3-year-olds counted rows of 7, 9, 12, and 14 blocks; the 4-year-olds counted rows of 12, 14, 17, and 19 blocks. These different row lengths were given in an attempt to control the difficulty of the task, that is, to give each age group a counting task that seemed likely to be of moderate difficulty. Color homogeneity was varied within subjects. At each age level half of the children received the same-color blocks first and half the different-color blocks first. Within those conditions half of the children counted the rows in ascending order of number of blocks (i.e., 7, 9, 12, 14 for the 3-year-olds and 12, 14, 17, 19 for the 4-year-olds), and half counted them in descending order. Each row was counted twice in succession by each child. The various colors used in the different-color-condition (e.g., red, green, orange) were also used in the same color condition; they were rotated across rows and subjects so that no bias could result from the disproportionate use of a particular color in that condition.

The children were interviewed individually by two undergraduates in a room near their classroom. The blocks were 1 inch on each edge and were placed about ¼ inch apart. They were glued to a cardboard strip so that each row could quickly be placed in front of the child. The rows of blocks were each covered by another larger strip of cardboard so that the child could not see what kind of rows were to be counted. Giving 16 counting trials proved to be fairly demanding, especially for some of the 3-year-olds. In these cases it helped to have all the rows laid out so that the number of rows to be counted could be seen, because the experimenters could just gesture at the rows not counted yet and say, "We only have to count these rows. It won't take very long." Children were offered the chance to stand up and stretch between the eighth and ninth trials (the switch to the opposite color condition). When asked to count a row the second time, children were asked to "count this row one more time. Count very carefully."

Two experimenters recorded counting behavior as in the live coding in chapter 3. Using the coding sheets described in chapter 3, one experimenter recorded the number words while the other experimenter recorded the location of the points. One of the experimenters and another coder separately went over the coding sheets and classified the errors made by each child into the error categories in Table 3-1. These coders agreed on the classification of 97% of the errors. One experimenter had gathered data for the study reported in chapter 3; the other experimenter was trained as those experimenters were trained.

5.1.2. Results and Discussion

5.1.2.1. Analyses of the Data. As in chapter 3 the raw number of errors within each error subtype and main type was converted to an error rate measure (the number of errors made per 100 objects counted) in order to facilitate comparisons across studies. A preliminary analysis showed that the order (ascending vs. descending number of objects) in which the rows were given was not a significant main effect and did not interact with any variable. A 2(color) × 2(number of objects) analysis of variance with repeated measures for color and number of objects was conducted on the error rates for each error main type and subtype for each age group separately. Also, a 2(age) × 2(color) analysis of variance with repeated measures for color was conducted for each error subtype and main type for the rows counted by both ages (the rows of 12 and 14). Because the studies in this chapter were conducted as much to generate as to test hypotheses, we have reported marginally significant results for the analyses of variance ($.05 < p < .10$) but will discuss such results only when they occur across more than one study. Pearson correlation coefficients were calculated for each pair of the five most common error subtypes. McNemar's test was used to ascertain whether the percentage of children differed for the smaller and larger rows.

To pursue the issue of whether the beginning and end of counting are particularly difficult, errors were further classified with respect to the location of the error in the row (first object, last object, and all middle objects), and the raw errors at each location were converted to the number of errors per 100 objects counted at that location[1] in order to control for the fact that there were many more middle objects than first or last objects (i.e., one would expect the number of raw middle errors to exceed the number of raw first or raw last errors). For each error type and subtype at each age, a 2(color) × 2(number of objects) × 3(location) analysis of variance (ANOVA) with repeated measures for all three variables was carried out on the errors made per 100 objects counted at each location. For error types for which there was a main effect of location, correlated t tests were conducted to locate the differences within these kinds of errors.[2] To ascertain whether there might be effects of the location of an object within the middle of a row, errors of each type were separated according to whether they occurred in the first or the second half of the row. The percentage of errors in each half was calculated both with and without the first and last objects.

The overall pattern of the results by specific error subtype and by each of these variables is given in Table 5-2. The errors per 100 objects counted are given by number of objects and by age in Table 5-3; this measure controls for the different number of objects in the larger and smaller rows. The percentage of children making at least one error of a given type is given by age and by number of objects in Table 5-4. Because this measure does not control for the number of objects in a row, the results for the number of objects in Table 5-4 are not discussed. The percentage of each type of error occurring in the first and second half of a row appears in Table 5-5. The effects of a given variable can be seen by reading down the column for that variable in Table 5-2. In the following discussion the results are discussed across variables for each error subtype separately, and then some comments are made about some of the variables. (See Table 3-1 for descriptions of each type of error.)

5.1.2.2. Correlation Results. For the 4-year-olds, the correlations between each pair of error subtypes discussed in sections 5.1.2.3 through 5.1.2.8 below were significant and high; they ranged between $r = .66$ and $.96$. Thus, for the 4-year-olds the children who made errors tended to make all kinds of errors. For the 3-year-olds most of the correlations were quite low and not significant. Therefore, different children tended to make different kinds of errors. The significant correlations are reported in the error type sections following.

---

[1] The number of errors made on first blocks was divided by the number of first blocks counted and multiplied by 100, the number of errors made on the middle blocks (all those not first or last) was divided by the number of middle blocks counted and multiplied by 100, and the number of errors made on the last block in a row was divided by the number of last blocks counted and multiplied by 100.

[2] The Bonferroni test would control for these multiple tests by using a p level of .017 for significance. Because the studies reported in this chapter are early hypothesis-generating studies in this topic area, we have reported marginally significant results for the analyses of variance ($p <$ .10). For the same reason, we will here use $p < .05$ instead of the more conservative $p < .017$ for the t tests. For ease of reading we will not report specific t values.

Table 5-2. Overall Pattern of Results by Error Type and by Variable (Color Homogeneity)

Error type	Color	Number of objects	Age	First or second half of row	Location: first object, middle objects, last object
Word–point	None	None	3s > 4s		3s 0 < 2.5 11.5 4s 0 < 0.8 2.1
Point–no word	None	None	None	4s second > first half	None

Multiple words–one point	color × location
	         M L
	3s: Same 1.4 7.3
	    Different 1.8 12.5
	Also different > same
		None	None	3s second > first half
				4s second > first half
					4s 0 < .6 1.6

Point–object	None	Large > small (3s) Small > large (4s)	None		None
Object skipped	None	None	None	No difference	None
Multiple count	3s: different > same 83% > 58%	Large > small (3s)	None	3s second > first half 4s second > first half	None
Dual	None	Large > small (3s)	None		3s 0.5 4.1 5.2
Multiple points–one word	3s: same > different 58% > 17%	Large > small (3s)	3s > 4s	3s second > first half	3s 0 0.6 3.6 4s 0 < 0.4 > 0
Skim	None	Large > small (3s)	3s > 4s	3s second > first half 4s second > first half	None
All	None	Large > small (3s) Small > large (4s)	None		3s 1.0 < 11.3 < 20.8

Note. M is the error rate per 100 middle objects and L is the error rate per 100 last objects counted. Two underlined location error rates or two location error rates connected by > or < differed significantly (correlated t-tests).

Table 5-3. Error Rate by Number of Objects and Age (Color Homogeneity)

Error type	3-year-olds			4-year-olds		
	Smaller[a]		Larger[b]	Smaller[a]		Larger[b]
Word–point total[c]	3.9		2.6	0.8		0.9
Point–no word	0.9		1.0	0.2		0.1
Multiple words– one point	3.0		1.6	0.6		0.8
Point–object total[d]	2.9	<	5.4	3.7	⩾	0.9
Object skipped	1.8		2.9	0.9		0.6
Multiple count	1.0	<	2.5	2.6		0.3
Dual total	2.0	<	6.4	0.5		1.5
Multiple points– one word	0.4	⩽	1.2	0.3		0.4
Skim	1.3	<	4.9	0.2		1.1
Recount	0.3		0.1	0.2		0.2
Total	9.1	<	14.5	5.2	>	3.5

Note. Error rate is the rate of errors per 100 blocks counted.

$> <$ indicate significant differences, $p < .05$.

$⩾ ⩽$ indicate marginally significant differences, $p < .09$.

[a] Smaller rows for 3-year-olds were 7 and 9 and for 4-year-olds were 12 and 14.

[b] Larger rows for 3-year-olds were 12 and 14 and for 4-year-olds were 17 and 19.

[c] Children of both ages made only the two listed kinds of word–point errors.

[d] Point–object total for 4-year-olds includes word and point–no object errors that are not given separately in the table because their incidence was so low.

[e] Dual total for 3-year-olds includes multiple words–different multiple points errors and word–no point errors that are not given separately in the table because their incidence was so low.

5.1.2.3. Point–No Word Errors. Half of the 3-year-olds pointed at a block without saying a number word on an average of 1 in every 100 objects counted.[3] Only a fourth of the 4-year-olds made such an error, and they did so at the very low rate of only about 0.2 per 100. Only one of the variables had any effect on the number of point–no word errors made or on the percentage of children making such an error. The 4-year-olds made more point–no word errors (all of the few such errors) on the second than on the first half of a row. For the 3-year-olds these errors were distributed evenly across the

---

[3] All errors per 100 objects counted are reported averaged across the two sizes of sets. That is, the number of errors per 100 objects counted for sets of 4, 5, and 6 was added to the number of errors per 100 objects counted for sets of 9, 12, and 14 and divided by 2 for the 3-year-olds; this average was calculated similarly for the 4-year-olds.

Table 5-4. Percentage of Children Making Errors by Number of Objects and Age (Color Homogeneity)

Error type	3-year-olds		4-year-olds	
	Smaller[a]	Larger[b]	Smaller[a]	Larger[b]
Word–point total[c]	58 <	92	42	42
Point–no word	25	25	25	17
Multiple words– one point	50	67	42	42
Point–object total[d]	42 <	83	83 >	33
Object skipped	42	25	42	17
Multiple count	33 <	83	50	33
Dual total[e]	25 <	92	42	33
Multiple points– one word	25 <	58	33	33
Skim	8 <	42	8	8
Recount	8	8	8	17
Total errors	75	100	75	50

Note. There are more opportunities to make an error on a larger than on a smaller row.
> < indicate proportions significantly different by McNemar's test, $p < .05$.
[a] Smaller rows for 3-year-olds were 7 and 9 and for 4-year-olds were 12 and 14.
[b] Larger rows for 3-year-olds were 12 and 14 and for 4-year-olds were 17 and 19.
[c] Children of both ages made only the two listed kinds of word–point errors.
[d] Point–object total for 4-year-olds includes word and point–no object errors that are not given separately in the table because their incidence was so low.
[e] Dual total for 3-year-olds includes multiple words–different multiple points errors and word–no point errors that are not given separately in the table because their incidence was so low.

first and second half of the row. Because children learn the first words in the sequence before the later words, it should be more difficult for children to think of the words when counting objects in the second half than in the first half of the row. This suggests that, at least for the 3-year-olds, point–no word errors are not primarily caused by difficulty in thinking of the next word.

5.1.2.4. Multiple Words–One Point Errors. Most (83%) of the 3-year-olds and half of the 4-year-olds pointed at a block and said two or more number words at least once. These errors were made at more than twice the rate of the point–no word errors: 2.3 for the 3s and 0.7 for the 4s. For the 3-year-olds, these errors were significantly correlated with object skipped errors ($r = .73$) and with multiple count errors ($r = .85$) but not with point–no word errors.

Table 5-5. Percentage of Errors Occurring in the First and Second Half of a Row (Color Homogeneity)

Error type	3-year-olds				4-year-olds			
	All blocks		Not first and last[a]		All blocks		Not first and last[a]	
	FH	SH	FH	SH	FH	SH	FH	SH
Word–point errors								
Point–no word	47	53	56	44	0	100	0	100
Multiple words–one point	12	88	22	78	17	83	20	80
Point–object errors								
Object skipped	40	60	49	51	45	55	45	55
Multiple count	21	79	27	73	33	67	36	64
Dual errors								
Multiple points–one word	19	81	27	73	60	40	60	40
Skim	32	68	34	66	27	73	29	71

Note. FH, first half; SH, second half of the row.

[a] Because many 3-year-olds made considerably more errors on the last than on the first block, percentages were also calculated for all blocks except the first and last block in order to assess the effect of first half/second half separate from the effect of the first and last blocks.

There were no main effects of color in the nonlocation analyses nor any interactions with color. For the 3-year-olds, there was a significant color by location interaction, $F(2, 22) = 4.01$, $p < .03$. No such errors were made on any first objects; the middle-object error rates were fairly similar for the different colored and for the same colored blocks (1.8 and 1.4, respectively); and the last-object error rates were considerably higher for the different colored than for the same colored objects (12.5 and 7.3, respectively). The main effect of color was also significant in the location analysis, $F(1, 11) = 5.13$, $p < .04$; the errors per 100 objects were higher for different colored rows than for the same colored rows on both the middle and the last objects. The number of objects had no effect on the number of multiple words–one point errors or on the percentage of children making such an error, and the two ages did not differ in the error rate on the rows they both counted (12 and 14).

Location of both kinds affected such errors. The 4-year-olds made marginally significantly fewer errors per 100 first objects than per 100 middle or 100 last objects counted (0 vs. 0.6 and 1.6, respectively), the main effect $F(2, 22) = 3.02$, $p < .07$; the errors per 100 middle and per 100 last objects did not differ significantly, because the variability for the last block errors was so high. As noted previously in discussing the color by location interaction for the 3-year-olds, they showed a considerably higher number of errors per 100 last objects than errors per 100 middle objects (9.9 vs. 1.6); this difference was not significant because the variability of such errors was so high. Both 3- and 4-year-olds had about four times as many of these errors in the second than in the first half of a row, even when the errors on the last block were disregarded.

The particular number words said on the last object were examined for the five 3-year-old children making a multiple words–one point error on a last object. One child made more than half these errors, and almost all of his errors consisted of saying three, four, or five number words in sequence that ended in ten (e.g., 7, 8, 9, 10 or 8, 9, 10). One other child showed a similar pattern (although with many fewer such errors), with all such errors being "9, 10" said on the last block. This seems to be a modified version of the "list exhaustion scheme" mentioned by Wagner and Walters (1982) in which a child shows a compulsion to finish saying the number words she knows. Our findings modify the more general predication of Wagner and Walters because we found this tendency only for a couple of children and only for the list to ten (a common stopping point for counting aloud when not counting objects). The inclusion of a few such children in a sample could increase the last word error rate for multiple words–one point errors quite considerably. Using sets larger than ten, as in the Increasing Row study, would decrease the opportunities to use such a scheme and thus mask this behavior by children.

In this study children made many more multiple words–one point errors than were made in the Increasing Row study; this was especially true for the 3-year-olds. Three factors seem to be related to this higher rate here: younger children, smaller sets, and different-colored blocks. Multiple words–one point errors were made at a high rate by the young children here (the 3-year-olds), about half of whom were younger than the youngest age group in the earlier study. These errors were also made at a much higher rate on the smaller than on the larger rows. The Increasing Row study had only four rows as small as the smaller rows the 3-year-olds counted here, and the mean longest rows counted there ranged from 22 to 31 across age groups. If the multiple words–one point errors continued to drop with increasing numbers of objects, very few such errors might be made on many of the large rows counted in the Increasing Row study. Part of the effect of the small rows was that they enabled two children to use a "list exhaustion scheme" to ten, increasing the rate of such errors considerably. But many other of the 3-year-olds also made multiple words–one point errors on the small rows without continuing on to ten, so small sets seems to elicit such errors independently of a list exhaustion effect. Finally, the 3-year-olds produced a particularly high rate of such errors on the rows of different colored blocks, and especially on the last block of such rows. All of the blocks in Increasing Rows were the same color.

5.1.2.5. Object Skipped Errors. About half the children of both ages sometimes skipped over one or more objects without counting them. The 3-year-olds made such errors on an average of 2.3 per 100 objects counted, and the 4-year-olds made them much less frequently at an average of 0.8 per 100. These were much lower than the rates at which object skipped errors were made in the Increasing Row and Disorganized studies. For the 3-year-olds object skipped errors were significantly correlated with multiple words–one point errors ($r = .73$) and with multiple count errors ($r = .61$). Object skipped errors were not affected by color homogeneity, number of objects, age, location in the first or second half of a row, or location as first, last, or middle object in a row. It does seem a bit surprising that color homogeneity does not affect such errors, for one would think that it might be easier to keep track of just where one is in a row with different-colored objects.

5.1.2.6. Multiple Count Errors. Most (83%) of the 3-year-olds and half of the 4-year-olds sometimes counted an object (pointed and said a number word) and then immediately counted it again (pointed again and said another number word). Such multiple count errors were made at about the same rate for both ages, at 1.8 for the 3s and 1.5 for the 4s. For the 3-year-olds, multiple count errors were significantly correlated with multiple words–one point errors ($r = .85$) and with object skipped errors ($r = .61$). For the 3-year-olds, chi-square versions of McNemar's test indicated that marginally significantly more children made a multiple count error when the blocks were different colors than when they were the same color, 83% versus 58%, $\chi^2(1, N = 12) = 3.0$, $p < .10$. Thus, either having blocks of different colors did not seem to make it easier to keep track of just which block had been counted, or any such advantage was more than offset by some other consequence of the different-colored objects. What this consequence might be is explored after other results on heterogeneity are reported, in section 5.3.2.5. Turning to the effect of row numerosity, the 3-year-olds had a significantly higher error rate in the larger rows (12, 14) than in the smaller rows (7, 9), $F(1, 11) = 5.90$, $p < .03$; the difference for 4-year-olds was not significant. Both 3- and 4-year-olds made more multiple count errors on the second than on the first half of a row, even when the first and last object are disregarded.

5.1.2.7. Word–Point Versus Point–Object Errors. For the 3-year-olds on the larger rows and for the 4-year-olds on the smaller rows, the relationship was the same as in the Increasing Row and Disorganized studies: The point–object error rate was much higher than the word–point rate. Relatively high rates of multiple words–one point errors for 3-year-olds on the smaller rows and for the 4-year-olds on the larger rows led to word–point rates that were greater than and equivalent to, respectively, the point–object errors. These results for the 3-year-olds were confirmed by the statistical analyses. For the 3-year-olds, a 2(color) × 2(number of objects) × 2(error type: word–point vs. point–object) ANOVA with repeated measures for all variables revealed a significant interaction between number of objects and error type, $F(1, 11) = 8.19$, $p < .02$. The word–point error rate exceeded the point–object error rate on the smaller rows (3.9 vs. 2.9), and the point–object error rate exceeded the word–point error rate on the larger rows (5.4 vs. 2.6). For the 4-year-olds, a similar analysis revealed only a marginal effect of number of objects, $F(1, 11) = 4.13$, $p < .07$. The overall rate of errors was higher for the smaller than for the larger rows (although this was actually only true for the point–object errors, see Table 5-3).

5.1.2.8. Multiple Points–One Word Errors. About half the children of each age sometimes pointed two or more times at a given object while saying only one number word. Such errors were made quite infrequently, however, at average rates of 0.8 for the 3-year-olds and 0.4 for the 4-year-olds. Chi-square versions of McNemar's test for correlated proportions indicated that significantly more 3-year-olds made a multiple points–one word error when the blocks were all the same color than when they were different colors, 58% versus 17%, $\chi^2(1, N = 12) = 5.0$, $p < .05$). The 3-year-olds also made marginally significantly more such errors per 100 blocks counted in larger rows than in smaller rows, 1.2 versus 0.4, $F(1, 11) = 3.67$, $p < .08$. For the rows counted by both ages (12 and 14 objects), 3-year-olds made marginally significantly more such errors than did the 4-year-olds, 1.2 versus 0.3, $F(1, 22) = 3.37$, $p < .08$. The 3-year-olds, but not the 4-year-olds, made more multiple points–one word errors on the second than on the first half of a row, even when the first and last objects were disregarded. The 3-year-olds made more such errors per 100 last objects counted than per 100 first objects counted, 3.6 versus 0, the main effect $F(2, 22) = 4.38$, $p < .03$. The 4-year-olds made more such errors per 100 middle objects counted than per 100 first objects or per 100 last objects counted, 0.4 versus 0 and 0, $F(2, 22) = 5.32$, $p < .01$.

5.1.2.9. Skim Errors. Half of the 3-year-olds but only a sixth of the 4-year-olds sometimes skimmed their finger along a row, saying number words in a haphazard way and not pointing at any objects. The 3-year-olds made such errors on an average of 3.1 per 100 objects counted, while the 4-year-olds made them more rarely, on 0.7 per 100. Color did not affect the rate at which such errors were made or the percentage of children making them. The 3-year-olds made significantly more errors per 100 objects counted in larger rows than in smaller rows, 4.9 versus 1.3, $F(1, 11) = 4.99$, $p < .05$. On the analysis by age on the rows counted by both ages (12 and 14 objects), 3-year-olds made marginally significantly more errors than did the 4-year-olds, 4.9 versus 0.2, $F(1, 22) = 3.52$, $p < .07$. Both age groups made about twice as many skim errors on objects in the second half of a row as in the first half of a row, even when the first and last objects were disregarded.

5.1.2.10. The Sum of All Errors. Every 3-year-old and all but one 4-year-old made at least one correspondence error of some type. There was no effect of color homogeneity on the sum of all errors. Number of objects had opposite effects for the two age groups. The 3-year-olds made significantly more errors per 100 objects counted in larger rows than in smaller rows, 14.5 versus 9.1, $F(1, 11) = 8.05$, $p < .01$; this effect was due to the similar higher rate for larger than smaller rows for point–object and for dual errors. The 4-year-olds made significantly more errors per 100 objects counted in smaller rows than in larger rows, 5.2 versus 3.5, $F(1, 11) = 8.48$, $p < .01$; this effect was primarily due to their similar higher rate for smaller than for larger rows for multiple count errors. The 3-year-olds made significantly more errors per 100 last objects counted than per 100 middle objects counted (20.8 vs. 11.3) and significantly more errors per 100 middle objects counted than 100 first objects counted (11.3 vs. 1.0), $F(2, 22) = 8.60$, $p < .002$; this effect was primarily due to the location pattern of multiple words–one point errors.

5.1.2.11. Location of an Error: First, Middle, or Last Object. The 3-year-olds here made more errors per 100 last objects than per 100 middle objects on multiple words–one point and on multiple points–one word errors, though neither of these effects was signficant due to the high variability of last-object errors. That the factors of younger children, smaller number of objects to count, and different-colored objects contributed to the high rate of multiple words–one point last-object errors has already been discussed. Another variable that might be related to a higher last-object error rate is whether a given row of entities is counted more than once. In this study each row was counted twice. For 3-year-olds, there were far more last-object errors on the second count of a row than on the first count of a row. In the Gelman and Gallistel (1978) study, each row was counted six times, perhaps leading to a higher rate of errors on the last object than if each row had only been counted once. The effect of this variable on the rate of last-object errors might be examined in future research.

Although for 3-year-olds the error rates for some error types were higher for the last object than for a middle object, these results do not support the Gelman and Gallistel (1978) description of counting as presenting some difficulty at the starting of a count, proceeding smoothly in the middle, and then presenting even more difficulty at the stopping of a count (p. 205). First, by far the lowest error rate for every error type occurred on the first object, so the beginning of a count is the most accurate part of counting. Second, an analysis of each trial counted indicated that very few trials met this description of more errors at the end and the beginning than in the middle. For the 3-year-olds, of the 91 trials on which an error was made, only 12 (15%) had more beginning or more end errors than middle errors (i.e., trials in which there were more errors on the first object or on the last object than on the intervening middle objects). For the 4-year-olds, not a single trial met this description. Thus, on any given count of a set of objects, a child was much more likely to make an error in the middle of counting than at the beginning or at the end of counting.

5.1.2.12. More Errors: First or Second Half of a Row? There seemed to be a tendency to spread out across the rows the errors of neglect (those in which not enough was done) and to concentrate in the second half of a row the errors of surplus (giving extra points or words or both). Both age groups distributed object skipped errors evenly across the first and second half of a row, and the 3-year-olds did so for point–no word errors. Other errors were more frequent in the second half, even when the first and last objects were disregarded.

An analysis on location in the first or second half of a row was also done separated by the smaller and larger rows. For both age groups and for all error subtypes, the percentage of errors made in the second half of a row was larger for the smaller than for the larger rows.[4] Over all error types combined, the percentage of errors made on the second half of a row was 82% for the smaller and 66% for the larger rows for 3-year-olds and was 75% for the smaller and 61% for the larger rows for 4-year-olds. This pattern seems almost as if both age groups can count a certain number of objects fairly accurately but then begin making errors. This "error-point" occurs in the second half of the objects on the smaller rows but within the first half for the larger rows. This possibility might be examined in future research.

5.1.2.13. Relative Number of Words, Points, and Objects. The relationships among the number of words, points, and objects was somewhat different here than with the much larger rows in Increasing Row and in Disorganized. The mean rate of all errors in which a point was made without an accompanying word[5] was 1.3 for the smaller rows and 2.2 for the larger rows for the 3-year-olds and 0.5 for both sizes of rows for 4-year-olds. The mean rate of all errors in which a word was said without an accompanying point[6] was 3.0 for the smaller rows and 1.6 for the larger rows for the 3-year-olds and 0.6 and 0.8, respectively, for the 4-year-olds. Thus, the results for the larger rows for the younger children replicated the finding on the very large rows in Increasing Row and Disorganized: Children were more likely to make a point without a word than vice versa, although the ratio here of the former to the latter was much less than the 4:1 ratio in the other two studies. However, this relationship did not hold here for the smaller rows for the younger children, where the rate of words without points was much higher than the rate of points without words, or for the 4-year-olds in both conditions, whose rates were roughly similar. This difference is largely due to the lower rate of point–

---

[4] This was true except for point–no word errors for 4-year-olds in which no errors were made in the first half of the row for either shorter or longer rows and the second half percentages were therefore both 100%.

[5] These were point–no word, part word–one point, multiple points–no word, and multiple points–one word errors.

[6] These were word between objects, multiple words–one point, and word–no point errors.

no word errors and the higher rate of multiple words–one point errors in this study.

The mean rate of all errors in which more than one point is given to an object[7] was 1.7 and 3.8 for the smaller and larger rows for the 3-year-olds and 3.3 and 0.9 for the 4-year-olds. Mean rates of errors in which objects never received a point[8] were 1.8 and 2.9 for 3-year-olds and 0.9 and 0.6 for 4-year-olds. Thus, the younger children were more likely to give extra points than to skip an object on the larger rows and about equally likely to do these on the smaller rows. The 4-year-olds showed the reverse pattern. They were much more likely to give extra points than to skip an object for the smaller rows and about equally likely to do each of these on the larger rows. These relationships held because the children here made multiple count errors at an equivalent or higher rate than the rate for skipped objects. In disorganized arrays, objects also were more likely to receive an extra point than to be skipped, but this was because so many objects were recounted. In the very large rows of Increasing Row, an object was more likely to be skipped than to receive extra points by all age groups.

When the relative number of words and objects are compared, the results again differ somewhat from those in Increasing Row, where there were many more objects not receiving any word than objects receiving more than one word. For errors in which an object received more than one word or a word was said to no object,[9] 3-year-olds had mean rates of 4.3 and 4.2 for the smaller and larger rows, and 4-year-olds had mean rates of 3.6 and 1.3, respectively. The mean rates for all errors in which an object received no word or a part word[10] were 2.7 and 3.9 for 3-year-olds and 1.1 and 0.7 for 4-year-olds for the smaller and larger rows, respectively. Thus, for the smaller rows for both ages, an object was considerably more likely to receive more than one word than to be skipped and receive no word. For the larger rows this difference was in the same direction but was much smaller. This finding was due to the higher rates here of both multiple words–no points errors and multiple count errors as well as to the relatively lower rate of object skipped and point–no word errors.

The three counting studies discussed so far do make it clear that over a range of different counting situations, no single relationship will hold between the number of points produced without words and the number of words produced without points, or between the number of extra points given to objects and the number of objects given no point, or between the number of objects

---

[7] These were multiple count, word and point–no object, multiple points–no words, multiple points–one word, and recount errors.

[8] These were object skipped and word–no point errors.

[9] These were multiple words–one point, word between objects, multiple count, word and point–no object, and recount errors.

[10] These were point–no word, part word–one point, object skipped, and multiple points–no word errors.

receiving more than one word and the number of objects not receiving any word. Instead, the variables of object arrangement, object color homogeneity, repeated counting of the same set, age of children counting, and size of set affect all of these relationships.

5.2. Effects of Homogeneity, Number, and Verbal Label of Objects: Toy Homogeneity Study

In all studies reported so far, children counted blocks. When the blocks were arranged in rows, they were placed fairly close together. It seemed possible that some attribute of blocks themselves or of their placement close together might influence the kinds and rates of errors made. The effect of the distance between objects (close, far) is examined in 5.3. In the present study several different kinds of toys (instead of blocks) were used as the objects to be counted in order to see whether children made the same kind and distribution of errors as they did when counting blocks as in the earlier studies. Effects of homogeneity of the objects, number of objects, and verbal label used to describe the objects were also examined. Younger children than those in chapter 3 also participated in this study, which focused on children from age 3 to age 4½.

This study was designed primarily to test whether Markman's (1979) finding of the positive effect of collection terms (e.g., the words *army*, *family*, and *pile* rather than the words *soldiers*, *pigs*, *blocks*) on children's use of the cardinality rule (answering the question "How many X's are there?" with the last word said in counting) would extend to larger sets and whether homogeneity of the objects affected the use of the cardinality rule. A secondary purpose was to study the effects of these three variables (number of objects, homogeneity of objects, and verbal label describing the objects) on counting accuracy and on particular kinds of counting errors. The effects on the use of the cardinality rule and on accuracy of counting (but not effects on particular errors) are reported as experiment 1 in Fuson, Pergament, and Lyons (1985), and the cardinality-rule results are summarized here in chapter 7.

5.2.1. Method

Forty-eight middle- to upper-middle-class children ranging in age from 3-2 (3 years 2 months) to 4-7 (4 years 7 months) and attending preschools in a northern suburb of Chicago served as subjects for the study. Children were ordered by age and then one of each successive pair in this order was randomly assigned to the class condition and the other to the collection condition. The mean age for each condition was 4.0. For the analyses on specific types of counting errors, the five children older than 4½ were dropped, and the remaining 43 children aged 3–2 through 4–5 were divided into three 6-

month age groups: 3 to 3½ (3–0 through 3–5), 3½ to 4 (3–6 through 3–11), and 4 to 4½. There were 11, 12, and 20 children in these three age groups, respectively.

Two trials were given for each of the three smaller set sizes (4, 5, 6) and for each of the three larger set sizes (9, 12, 14). For each set size, one of the two trials involved homogeneous objects and one involved heterogeneous objects. The homogeneous sets were small dolls, toy soldiers, and 1-inch red wooden blocks. The heterogeneous sets were different toy animals, different-sized and different-colored small pigs, and 1-inch blocks of different colors. The same kinds of objects were used for both sizes of arrays.

Markman (1979) used four homogeneous dolls, five heterogeneous animals, five heterogeneous pigs, and six heterogeneous blocks. Two modifications of this were required in order to balance the homogeneous and heterogeneous items within each set size. Five homogeneous soldiers were used instead of five heterogeneous animals, and four (rather than five) heterogeneous animals were used. Soldiers were chosen to be added as stimulus items because "soldiers in the army" was a collection term that Markman discussed with respect to the cardinality-rule result.

For each trial a board containing the objects was placed on a table in front of the child. The objects were placed about 1½ inches apart. The objects ranged in width from ½ to 1½ inches; therefore the ratio of the space between objects to the width of an object varied according to the type of object from about 3:1 to 1:1. The procedure described by Markman (1979) was used. Children in the collection condition were told, "Here is a nursery school class [or pig family/pile of blocks/animal party/army]. Count the children in the class. How many children are in the class?" Children in the class condition heard, "Here are some nursery school children [or pigs/blocks/animals/soldiers]. Count the children. How many children are there?" If a child did not answer with the last count word when asked the how-many question, the question was repeated once. As the child counted, the experimenter recorded on a prepared array the number words said by the child; each word was recorded at the location to which the child's finger was directed when the word was said. Points without words were also recorded, and words said with no accompanying point were marked with a dot. Children were given the six trials with the smaller rows, and 7 (sometimes 10) days later, each child received the six trials with the larger rows. Half of the children received a row of homogeneous objects first and half received a heterogeneous row first; each half was distributed across the whole age span. Counting correspondence errors were categorized from the recording sheets into the counting errors in Table 3-1.

5.2.2. Results and Discussion

5.2.2.1. Statistical Analyses. The results of all analyses are summarized by error type and by variable in Table 5-6. A 3(age) × 2(number of objects) ×

Table 5-6. Overall Pattern of Results by Error Type and Variable (Toy Homogeneity)

Error type	Toy Homogeneity	Number of objects 4, 5, 6 vs. 9, 12, 14	Age 3 to 3½, 3½ to 4, 4 to 4½	Verbal label class/collection	Location: first object, middle object, last object Main effects	Location Interactions
Word–point	None	None	Y3 > O3 > <u>Y4</u>	Number × VL Number × VL × age Large class Y3 highest	L > M > F	Loc × age
Point–no word Multiple words–one point	None None	None None	None Y3 > O3 > <u>Y4</u>	None Number × VL Number × VL × Age Large class Y3 highest	M, L > F L > M > F	 Loc × age
Point–object	Hom: 4,5,6 = 4.8; 9,12,14 = 8.3 Het: 4,5,6 = 3.6; 9,12,14 = 10.6	Large > small	Y3 > O3 > <u>Y4</u>	Number × VL Small coll = class Large coll > class	M > L > F	None
Object Skipped	None	Large > small	None	Number × VL × age Large coll Y3 highest	M > L, F	Loc × number
Multiple Count	Hom: 4,5,6 = 2.9; 9,12,14 = 2.6 Het: 4,5,6 = 1.0; 9,12,14 = 3.9	None	Y3 > O3 > <u>Y4</u>	None	M, L > F	Loc × age
Dual	Hom > het	Large > small	Marginal	Number × VL Small coll = class Large class > coll	M > L, F	Loc × age Loc × number
Skim	Hom > het	Large > small	Marginal	Hom × number × VL	M > L, F	Loc × age Loc × number
All	None	Large > small (also number of objects × age interaction)	Y3 > O3 > <u>Y4</u> Y3 O3 Y4 4, 5, 6: 13 6 3 9, 12, 14: 28 22 4	Class Coll Hom 13 10 Het 10 10	M, L > F	Loc × age Loc × number

Note. Two ages underlined or connected by a > differed significantly; Y3 is young three (3 to 3½), O3 is old three (3½ to 4), Y4 is young four (4 to 4½). Coll. collection; hom, homogeneous; het, heterogeneous; loc, location; VL, verbal label.

2(verbal label) × 2(homogeneity) ANOVA with repeated measures for number and for homogeneity was applied to the errors per 100 objects counted for each of the error subtypes and for the main error types.[11] These error rates are given by age and number of objects in Table 5-7 for each error subtype on which the rate was at least 1.0; significant main effects of age and of number are indicated in the table. Pearson correlation coefficients were calculated separately for each age group for each pair of error subtypes made from the first four frequent error subtypes given in Table 5-7. The percentage of children making an error of a given type is given by age and by number of objects in Table 5-8; McNemar's tests were used to test whether these percentages differed significantly. Errors were categorized according to whether they were made on a first object, last object, or middle object (any object not first or last), and the raw errors at each location were converted to the errors per 100 objects counted at that location to control for the fact that there were considerably more middle than first or last objects (see Footnote 1, p. 134). A 3(location: first, middle, last) × 3(age) × 2(verbal label) × 2(homogeneity) × 2(number of objects) ANOVA with repeated measures for location, homogeneity, and number was applied to the errors per 100 objects counted at each location for each of the frequent error subtypes and for the error main types. Location was a significant main effect for each of these analyses; correlated *t* tests were then used to test the significance of the individual location comparisons.[12] The location means and the results of all analyses are summarized in Table 5-9. There were several significant interactions in the preceding ANOVAs; these are discussed in the sections on each type of error. Results are discussed for each specific error type. The effect of each variable across all error types can be understood by reading down each column in Table 5-6.

5.2.2.2. Point–No Word Errors.

Between a fourth and two-fifths of the children in each age group sometimes pointed at an object without saying a num-

---

[11] The number of children aged 4 to 4½ was considerably larger than the number in either of the 3-year-old age groups. The means for all variables that collapsed across all children in the sample are given in all tables and in the text as if there were the same number of children in each age group (i.e., each sample mean for a given variable was calculated by adding the relevant means for the three age groups and dividing by three). Therefore, the given means are more generalizable; they reflect the three age groups sampled and not just the particular number of children in each age group. All results were examined to see whether these unequal *n*s affected the findings. In general there were few interactions with age, and the few such interactions had other characteristics that minimized the effect of the unequal age groups.

[12] These correlated *t* tests treat each subject equally. Because there were more children in the group aged 4 to 4½, they receive more emphasis in this test than would be true if the age groups had equal numbers of children. The location means actually used in this test were checked with the location means calculated by weighting each age group equally (these are the means given in Table 5-9). In all cases the latter location differences were larger than the differences used in the *t* tests. Therefore, these tests are a conservative measure of actual differences, and all differences found in these tests would be even stronger if conducted on the means given in Table 5-9. See footnote 2 for the use of *p* < .05 here.

ber word. Such point–no word errors were made at relatively low rates, ranging between 0.4 and 1.0 such errors per 100 objects counted. Point–no word errors were negatively correlated with multiple words–one point errors for the 3-year-olds, but positively correlated for the 4-year-olds. Point–no word errors were significantly correlated with object skipped errors for the youngest and oldest children, $r = .58$ and $.60$. There was no effect of toy homogeneity, number of objects, age, or verbal label on the rate of such errors. Significantly more such errors were made per 100 middle objects counted and per 100 last objects counted than per 100 first objects counted, 0.7 and 1.5 versus 0.0, $F(2, 74) = 4.03$, $p < .02$.

5.2.2.3. Multiple Words–One Point Errors. More than half of the youngest children (3 to 3½) sometimes pointed to an object and said two or more number words, a third of the children aged 3½ to 4 did so, and a fifth of the oldest children (4 to 4½) did so. The rate of such errors per 100 objects counted was quite high for the youngest age group (3 to 3½) and fell significantly to a very low rate for the two older groups, from 4.8 to 0.4 and 0.3, $F(2, 37) = 8.07$, $p < .001$. Multiple words–one point errors were significantly correlated with multiple count errors for children aged 3 to 3½, $r = .57$. There was no effect of toy homogeneity or number of objects on such errors.

Both the number by verbal label interaction and the number by verbal label by age interactions were significant, $F(1, 37) = 5.22$ and $F(2, 37) = 4.06$, $p < .03$. The means for the three-way interaction are given in Table 5-10. The youngest children in the collection condition had a much higher error rate on the smaller than on the larger rows, while the reverse was true for the youngest children in the class condition. The error rates for both groups of older children were quite low, but the older children in the class condition did make somewhat more such errors than did the older children in the collection condition. Because the number of children in each of the verbal-label conditions in the two youngest age groups was quite small ($n = 5, 6, 6, 6$), these results definitely require replication. It is quite possible that these results stem from error patterns in individual children who just happened to be assigned to certain verbal-label conditions rather than from the use of the verbal labels themselves. For this reason we will not discuss these verbal label results in any detail.

There were significantly fewer errors per 100 first objects counted than 100 middle or last objects counted, and significantly fewer errors per 100 middle objects counted than last objects counted, 0.3 versus 1.7 versus 4.4, respectively, $F(2, 74) = 12.87$, $p < .001$. However, a significant location by age interaction indicated that this effect was limited to the two youngest age groups, $F(2, 74) = 6.30$, $p < .001$ (see Table 5-11 for means). The multiple words–one point errors on the last object were examined to see which number words were said for these errors. About 30% of the children making such errors sometimes said two or more words ending in ten (especially "nine ten"). So here, as in Color Homogeneity, there was a tendency for some

Table 5-7. Error Rates by Age and Number of Objects (Toy Homogeneity)

Error type	Age				Number	
	3 to 3½	3½ to 4	4 to 4½	Sig?	4, 5, 6	9, 12, 14
Word–point errors[a]	5.8 >	1.4	0.8	*	2.4	2.8
Point–no word	0.8	1.0	0.4		0.7	0.6
Multiple words– one point	4.8 >	.4	0.3	*	1.5	2.0
Point–object errors[b]	9.5	7.9	2.7	*	4.2 <	9.2
Object skipped	6.6	3.7	1.9		2.3 <	5.9
Multiple count	2.9	4.2 >	0.7	*	1.9	3.3
Dual errors[c]	4.9	4.8	0.1	√	0.6 <	6.0
Skim	4.9	4.8	0.0	√	0.6 <	6.0
All errors[d]	20.4	14.1 >	3.6	*	7.3 <	18.1

Note. Two underlined numbers or two numbers connected by a > differed significantly, Newman-Keuls $p < .05$.

* and $<: p < .05$. $\sqrt{}: .05 < p < .10$.

[a] This total includes word between objects and part word–one point errors that are not given separately in the table because their incidence was so low.

[b] This sample made no word and point–no object errors.

[c] This total includes word–no point errors that are not given separately in the table because their incidence was so low.

[d] This total includes recount errors that are not given separately in the table because their incidence was so low.

children at some times (no child did this on more than three trials) to count on to ten regardless of the number of objects, and this tendency did contribute to these last object errors. However, here this factor certainly does not compose the bulk of such errors. As in Color Homogeneity, the youngest children made most of these errors, but the differentiation here between young and old 3-year-olds indicated that such errors were largely limited to the young 3-year-olds, those aged 3 to 3½. As in Color Homogeneity, these young children made these errors at a higher rate on the last object than on middle objects. However, there was no indication that the heterogeneity of toys affected these errors in any location, as did heterogeneity of color.

5.2.2.4. Object Skipped Errors. Three-fourths of the 3-year-olds and half of the children aged 4 to 4½ sometimes skipped over an object without giving it a point or a word. These errors were made at a fairly high rate and dropped very considerably with age, from 6.6 to 3.7 to 1.9; this age effect was not significant because the variability of these errors was so very high. Object

Table 5-8. Percentage of Children Making Errors by Age and Number of Objects (Toy Homogeneity)

Error type	Age			Number	
	3 to 3½	3½ to 4	4 to 4½	4, 5, 6	9, 12, 14
Word–point errors[a]	91 >	50	30	21 <	47
Point–no word	27	42	25	12	23
Multiple words– one point	64	33	20	12 <	33
Point–object errors[b]	100	100 >	65	44 <	74
Object skipped	73	75	50	26 <	56
Multiple count	100	92 >	55	28 <	58
Dual errors[c]	45	25 >	5	5 <	19
Skim	45	25 >	0	5 <	19
All[d]	100	100 >	65	49 <	77

Note. There are more opportunities to make an error on a larger than on a smaller row.
Two percentages underlined by different lines or connected by > or < differed significantly, McNemar's test $p < .05$.

[a] This total includes word between objects and part word–one point errors that are not given separately in the table because their incidence was so low.
[b] This sample made no word and point–no object errors.
[c] This total includes word–no point errors that are not given separately in the table because their incidence was so low.
[d] This total includes recount errors that are not given separately in the table because their incidence was so low.

skipped errors were significantly correlated with point–no word errors for the youngest and oldest children, $r = .58$ and $.60$. With respect to the number of objects, the object skipped error rate was fairly high for the smaller rows, but still almost tripled for the larger rows, 2.3 versus 5.9, $F(1, 37) = 8.60$, $p < .006$. There was a significant number of objects by verbal label by age interaction, $F(2, 37) = 3.46$, $p < .04$. The youngest children in the collection condition made a very high rate of object skipped errors, especially on the large rows (see Table 5-10). As discussed previously, however, the number of children in each age by verbal label cell was quite small, so this may reflect particular predispositions of these children rather than the effects of the verbal labels. Turning to the location results, children made significantly more object skipped errors per 100 middle objects counted than either per 100 first or last objects counted, 5.4 versus 0.3 and 0.5, $F(2, 74) = 13.12$, $p < .001$. This effect was particularly strong for the large rows (Table 5-12), the location by number of objects $F(2, 74) = 5.81$, $p < .005$.

Table 5-9. Error Rates by Location (Toy Homogeneity)

Error type	First object		Middle object[a]		Last object	Sig?
Word–point errors[b]	<u>0.3</u>	<	2.6	<	<u>5.9</u>	*
Point–no word	<u>0.0</u>	<	0.7		<u>1.5</u>	*
Multiple words–one point	<u>0.3</u>	<	1.7	<	<u>4.4</u>	*
Point–object errors[c]	<u>1.2</u>	<	7.9	>	<u>4.6</u>	*
Object skipped	0.3	<	5.3	>	0.5	*
Multiple count	<u>1.0</u>	<	2.7		<u>4.1</u>	*
Dual errors[d]	0.7	<	3.8	>	1.6	*
Skim	0.7	<	3.7	>	1.6	*
All[e]	<u>2.2</u>	<	14.3		<u>12.0</u>	*

$<$, $>$, and underlined first and last object entries indicate correlated t tests significant at $p < .05$.
* Indicates a significant main effect of location, $p < .05$.
[a] Error rate for an object not first or last in the row.
[b] This total includes word between objects and part word–one point errors that are not given separately in the table because their incidence was so low.
[c] This sample made no word and point–no object errors.
[d] This total includes word–no point errors that are not given separately in the table because their incidence was so low.
[e] This total includes recount errors that are not given separately in the table because their incidence was so low.

Table 5-10. Multiple Words–One Point and Object Skipped Error Rates by Age, Number of Objects, and Verbal Label (Toy Homogeneity)

	Collection terms		Class terms	
Age	4, 5, 6	9, 12, 14	4, 5, 6	9, 12, 14
	Multiple words–one point errors			
3 to 3½	5.3	1.7	3.3	8.2
3½ to 4	0.0	0.5	0.0	1.0
4 to 4½	0.0	0.0	0.6	0.6
	Object skipped errors			
3 to 3½	6.0	18.3	2.8	1.2
3½ to 4	1.7	7.1	1.1	5.0
4 to 4½	1.1	1.4	0.9	3.9

Table 5-11. Error Rates by Location and Age (Toy Homogeneity)

Age	First object	Middle object[a]	Last object	First object	Middle object	Last object
	Multiple words–one point			Word–point		
3 to 3½	0.8	4.5	10.6	0.8	5.7	12.1
3½ to 4	—	0.2	2.1	—	1.2	4.2
4 to 4½	—	0.5	0.5	—	0.9	1.3
	Multiple count					
3 to 3½	2.2	2.5	5.8			
3½ to 4	0.7	4.7	4.9			
4 to 4½	—	0.8	1.2			
	Skim			Dual		
3 to 3½	—	5.7	.7	—	5.9	.8
3½ to 4	2.1	5.2	4.2	2.1	5.2	4.2
4 to 4½	—	—	—	—	0.1	—
				All		
3 to 3½				3.8	22.9	19.7
3½ to 4				2.8	15.7	13.9
4 to 4½				—	4.4	2.5

[a] Error rate for an object not first or last in the row.

5.2.2.5. Multiple Count Errors. Almost all of the 3-year-olds and half of the children aged 4 to 4½ sometimes pointed to an object and said a number word and then pointed and said another number word to the same object. Such multiple count errors were made at fairly high rates by the children aged 3 to 3½ and 3½ to 4 (2.9 and 4.2) and at a significantly lower rate by the children aged 4 to 4½ (0.7), $F(2, 37) = 6.06$, $p < .005$. Multiple count errors were significantly correlated with multiple words–one point errors for children aged 3 to 3½, $r = .57$. The rate of such errors did not differ by number of objects, but there was a significant number by homogeneity interaction, $F(1, 37) = 6.56$, $p < .01$. Number had no effect on the error rate for rows of homogeneous objects (2.9 for smaller and 2.6 for larger) but had a large effect on rows of heterogeneous objects (1.0 for smaller and 3.9 for larger). Another way of phrasing part of this finding is that for the rows of 9, 12, and 14, there were more multiple count errors on the heterogeneous rows than on the homogeneous rows. This finding is consistent with the finding in the Color Homogeneity sample that significantly more 3-year-olds made a multiple

Table 5-12. Error Rates by Location and Number of Objects (Toy Homogeneity)

Number of objects	First object	Middle object[a]	Last object
		Object skipped	
4, 5, 6	.0	3.4	1.0
9, 12, 14	.6	7.4	.0
		Skim/dual[b]	
4, 5, 6	.5	.6	.5
9, 12, 14	.9	6.7	2.8
		All	
4, 5, 6	1.0	8.7	9.2
9, 12, 14	3.4	19.9	14.9

[a] Error rate for an object not first or last in the row.
[b] Skim and dual error rates are identical for first and last objects. The dual middle object error rate is 0.1 higher than the values in the table because it includes a few word–no point errors.

count error on different-colored rows than on same-colored rows (because most of the rows there were of length 9, 12, or 14, and the majority of children here were aged 3). Thus, objects that differ in color, size, or kind seem to elicit more multiple count errors. This result is discussed in 5.3.2.5 after the report on the third experiment.

There was a marginally significant location by age interaction for multiple count errors, $F(2, 74) = 2.22, p < .07$. The youngest children had more last-object errors than first or middle-object errors, while the two older age groups had higher middle- and last- than first-object errors (see Table 5-11 for means). At all ages, however, the means did conform to the results of the main effect of location over all the ages, $F(2, 74) = 9.52, p < .001$: the errors per 100 middle and per 100 last-objects counted were higher than the errors per 100 first-objects counted (2.7 and 4.1 versus 1.0).

5.2.2.6. Word–Point Versus Point–Object Errors. As did the Increasing Row sample, this sample showed much higher rates of point–object errors than of word–point errors. This effect was considerably more marked for the larger than for the smaller rows: a mean error rate of 9.2 for point-object and of 2.8 for word–point for the larger rows and of 4.2 versus 2.4 for the smaller rows. This relationship was confirmed statistically by a significant error type by number of objects interaction in a 3(age) × 2(number of objects) × 2(verbal label) × 2(homogeneity) × 2(error type: word–point vs. point–

object) ANOVA with repeated measures for number, homogeneity, and error type applied to the errors per 100 objects counted, $F(1, 37) = 8.26, p <$ .007. Because several different kinds of objects were used and because these objects were not placed close together as were the blocks in Increasing Row, the earlier finding of more point–object than word–point errors clearly is not just a result of the objects being blocks and/or of being placed quite close together and thus increasing the rate of point–object errors vis-a-vis word–point errors. That both studies in this chapter yielded error type by number interactions suggests that one can expect a higher rate of point–object errors than of word–point errors on rows with a larger number of objects.

There was a significant number by verbal label by error type by age inter-action and a significant number by verbal label by error type interaction, $F(2, 37) = 4.97, p < .01$, and $F(1, 37) = 6.48, p < .02$. The second interaction reflected the fact that the word–point and the point–object error categories had significant number by verbal label effects in the opposite directions. On the large rows children made more word–point errors when hearing class terms (see the means in Table 5-13), $F(1, 37) = 4.48, p < .04$, and they made marginally more point–object errors when hearing collection terms (see Table 5-13), $F(1, 37) = 3.29, p < .08$. The former pattern was due to multiple words–one point errors, especially by the youngest children; the word–point number by verbal label by age interaction was also significant, $F(2, 37) = 5.00, p < .01$. The point–object effect was due to object skipped errors, again especially by the youngest children (see 5.2.2.4, preceding). However, because there were so few children in the age by verbal label cells, it is not clear whether the verbal labels induced these effects or whether children having a tendency to make many multiple words–one point errors and few object skipped errors happened to be assigned to the class condition and children with the opposite tendency happened to be assigned to the col-lection condition. This issue certainly should be pursued in future research. The number by verbal label interaction was also marginally significant for dual errors, $F(1, 37) = 3.54, p < .07$ (see Table 5-13). The error rate for these errors, which were predominantly skim errors, was particularly high for the large rows and class terms, as were the word–point errors. Thus, perhaps skimming is done by the same children who make many multiple words–one point errors.

The number by homogeneity by error type interaction was significant, $F(1, 37) = 5.67, p < .03$. This interaction resulted because there was no effect of homogeneity on word–point errors, but there was a significant number by homogeneity interaction for point–object errors, $F(1, 37) = 7.02, p < .01$. The point–object error rates for the rows of heterogeneous objects were somewhat more extreme than those for the rows of homogeneous objects: 3.6 and 10.6 for the smaller and larger heterogeneous rows and 4.8 and 8.3 for the smaller and larger homogeneous rows. These means are what one would ex-pect when the multiple count means with their number by homogeneity inter-action are combined with the object skipped means with their significant effect of number of objects (see Table 5-6).

Table 5-13. Word–Point, Point–Object, and Dual Error Rates by Number of Objects and Verbal Label (Toy Homogeneity)

Number of objects	Collection terms	Class terms
	Word–point errors	
4, 5, 6	2.8	2.0
9, 12, 14	1.7	3.9
	Point–object errors	
4, 5, 6	4.0	4.4
9, 12, 14	12.0	6.9
	Dual errors	
4, 5, 6	1.1	.1
9, 12, 14	2.3	9.4

5.2.2.7. Skim Errors. About half of the youngest children and a fourth of the children aged 3½ to 4 sometimes skimmed their finger along a row saying number words haphazardly and not pointing at specific objects. These errors were made at a similar rate by these two age groups, 4.9 and 4.8. Significantly more skim errors were made per 100 objects counted in large rows than per 100 objects counted in small rows, 6.0 versus 0.6, $F(1, 37) = 6.02$, $p < .02$. There was a significant homogeneity by number by verbal label interaction, $F(1, 37) = 6.43$, $p < .02$; the relevant means are given in Table 5-14. Children in the class condition had a very high error rate for both kinds of large arrays, although the homogeneous rate was more than twice the heterogeneous rate; children in the collection condition had much lower error rates, and these errors were distributed evenly over both large conditions and the small homogeneous condition. That heterogeneous arrays would reduce skims relative to homogeneous arrays seems sensible, but it is not obvious why collection terms should do so relative to class terms. The main effect of homogeneity was also significant: an error rate of 4.4 on homogeneous rows and of 2.0 on heterogeneous rows, $F(1, 37) = 4.47$, $p < .04$.

The youngest children made almost all their skim errors on middle objects, while the children aged 3½ to 4 distributed them more evenly across the first, middle, and last objects (see Table 5-11 for means). Skim errors were distributed evenly across the small rows and were concentrated most heavily on the middle objects in large rows (see Table 5-12). Both these location by age, $F(2, 74) = 3.94$, $p < .006$, and location by number of objects interactions, $F(2, 74) = 8.90$, $p < .001$, were significant.

Table 5-14. Skim Error Rates by Homogeneity, Number of Objects, and Verbal Label (Toy Homogeneity)

Type of objects	Collection terms		Class terms	
	4, 5, 6	9, 12, 14	4, 5, 6	9, 12, 14
Homogeneous objects	2.2	2.3	0	13.0
Heterogeneous objects	0	2.3	0	5.7

5.2.2.8. The Sum of All Errors. Every 3-year-old made an error and two thirds of the children aged 4 to 4½ did so. The youngest children made an error on 20% of the objects counted, the children aged 3½ to 4 did so on 14% of the objects, and the children aged 4 to 4½ did so on only 4% of the objects counted. A significant number of objects by age interaction (Table 5-15) indicated that for small rows, the number of errors dropped very considerably at 3½ while the number of errors on large rows dropped only at age 4, $F(2, 37) = 5.58$, $p < .008$. There was a significant interaction between homogeneity and verbal label, $F(1, 37) = 3.97$, $p < .05$. There were more errors made when class terms were used for the rows of homogeneous objects (13.3) than for the other three conditions (9.9 for heterogeneous rows with class terms and 10.1 and 9.7 for the heterogeneous and homogeneous rows with collection terms). Much of this effect is due to the triple interaction for skims in which a very high rate of skim errors is made on the large homogeneous arrays described bv class terms. A significant location by number of objects interaction revealed a higher rate on middle objects than on last objects on the larger rows and the reverse on the small rows, see Table 5-12, $F(2, 74) = 4.50$, $p < .01$. This finding is consistent with the finding of much higher middle- than last-object rates in Increasing Row, where the rows got considerably larger than 9, 12, and 14. A significant location by age interaction indicated that all age groups had a middle object rate slightly above the last object rate but that both these rates were very considerably above the rate of errors per 100 first objects counted, see Table 5-11, $F(4, 74) = 3.80$, $p < .007$. This is also consistent with the findings of all previous studies: Children make the least errors on the first object in a row.

5.2.2.9. Location of an Error: First, Middle, or Last Object. Even though for three error subtypes the number of errors per 100 middle objects counted was not significantly greater than the number of errors per 100 last objects counted, the counting of this sample did not conform to the Gelman and Gallistel (1978) description of counting difficulty occurring to some extent at the starting of a count and to a larger extent at the stopping of a count but proceeding smoothly in between. Only 16 of the 516 counting trials (3%) in this study fit that description: the first object errors or the last object errors

Table 5-15. Error Rates for the Sum of All Errors by Number of Objects and Age (Toy Homogeneity)

Number of objects	Age		
	3 to 3½	3½ to 4	4 to 4½
4, 5, 6	<u>13.0</u>	6.1	<u>2.7</u>
9, 12, 14	<u>27.8</u>	22.0 >	<u>4.4</u>

Two underlined numbers or two numbers connected by > differed significantly, Newman-Keuls $p < .05$.

exceeding the middle object errors. This proportion did not differ for the small and the large rows (3% for each). The proportion of trials matching this description remains small even when only trials on which an error was made are considered: only 16 of the 190 trials on which an error was made (8%) fit this description. Because children made an error on many fewer small than large rows, the percent of trials fitting this description out of the trials on which an error was made was considerably larger for the small than for the larger rows (21% vs. 5%). Thus, for rows of four to six objects, children had more trouble at the end of the row than in the middle on about one in five rows on which they made any error. For rows of 9 to 14 objects, children had more trouble at the end of a row than in the middle on only about 1 in 20 rows on which they made any error.

5.3. Effects of the Distance Between Objects: Proximity Study

The distance between objects in rows was manipulated across various studies reported thus far but was not manipulated within the same study. This study was designed to contrast the effect of placing objects very close together and placing them fairly far apart. We could not place objects too far apart, because placing objects extremely far apart makes rows very long and introduces errors made when a child changes position to count a very long row. Therefore, the far distance between objects was chosen to be greater than the width of the object itself; this choice meant that the spaces between objects were very noticeable, but the rows did not get too long. Number of objects counted (4, 5, 6 and 9, 12, 14) and age (3 to 3½, 3½ to 4, 4 to 4½) were also included as variables in this study. Including color or homogeneity of objects as another variable would have required too many counting trials for the 3-year-olds, so all rows were composed of different-colored objects in order to relate more closely to the Gelman and Gallistel (1978) counting situation.

5.3.1. Method

The sample consisted of 36 middle- and upper-middle-class children attending a preschool in a city just north of Chicago. Twelve children were in each of three age groups: 3 to 3½ (3–0 through 3–5), 3½ to 4 (3–6 through 3–11), and 4 to 4½.

Small (4, 5, 6) and large (9, 12, 14) rows were given within each distance condition (objects close, objects far). In the close distance condition, objects were spaced ¼ inch apart. In the far distance condition, the distance between objects was 1.2 times the width of the object. The counting stimuli were 1-inch blocks, 2-cm plastic poker chips, and small plastic toy cars 2 cm wide. The stimuli were glued to cardboard strips. Each kind of object was used on one trial in each of the four number-by-distance cells. Each strip contained objects of several colors alternated so that objects of the same color were never contiguous.

Trials were blocked by distance so that a child received all six of the close (or far) trials consecutively. Half of the children within each age group received the close trials first and half received the far trials first. Within each of the distance conditions, trials were also blocked by number of objects (i.e., all three small trials were consecutive and were either preceded by or followed by all three large trials). Number of objects was counterbalanced within each distance condition so that half of the children within each age group within each distance condition received the large trials first and half received the small trials first. Within each group of three number-by-distance trials, the objects were given in the same order (cars, blocks, and poker chips).

Children were interviewed individually in a small room near the classroom by two experimenters trained in the coding of counting behavior. Both coders recorded each number word said by the child at the location on the prepared coding sheet to which the child's finger was directed when the word was said. A word said without an accompanying point (i.e., without a downward motion of the finger) was recorded at the location to which the finger was directed, and a line was drawn through the word to differentiate it from a word having an accompanying point. Points without accompanying words were recorded as a P in the location to which the point was directed. Two coders were used to increase the probability that an error would be recorded and to permit an assessment of the reliability of this method of coding (a form of which was used by a single coder in the Toy Homogeneity study).

The records of errors made by the two experimenters agreed on 95% of the errors. Evidently, for rows of up to 14 objects, this method of recording is adequate, and one very bright experimenter quite experienced with small children would be sufficient to collect reliable data.

5.3.2. Results and Discussion

5.3.2.1. Statistical Analyses. The overall pattern of results is given by error type and variable in Table 5-16. For each analysis the raw errors for each

Table 5-16. Overall Pattern of Results by Error Type and Variable (Proximity)

Error type	Proximity	Number of objects 4, 5, 6 vs. 9, 12, 14	Age 3 to 3½, 3½ to 4, 4 to 4½			Location: first object, middle objects, last object	
			Y3	O3	Y4	Main effects	Interactions
Word–point	None	None	<u>Y3</u>			M > L, F	Loc × proximity × age M > L for all except O3 L > M for Far O3
Point–no word	None	Large > small	<u>Y3</u> Age × number	O3	<u>Y4</u>	M > L, F	Loc × age, loc M > F, L all ages
Multiple words– one point	None	None	None			None	None
Point–object	Close > far error rate	Large > small	None			M, L > F	Loc × proximity × age Close: M > L Y3 Far: L > M Y3 O3 L ≥ M Y4 M > L

Error					
Object skipped	None	None	None		M > L, F	None
Multiple count	None	None	None		M, L > F	None
Dual	Close > far % Children	Large > small	Y3 > O3	Y4	None	Loc × age
Multiple points— one word	None	None	None		None	None
Skim	None	Large > small	Y3 > O3	Y4	M > F	Loc × age
All	Close > far error rate	Large > small	Y3 > O3	Y4	M > L > F	Loc × age Loc × proximity Close: M very > L Far: M little > L Loc × number

Note. Two ages underlined or connected by a > differed significantly; Y3 is young three (3 to 3½), O3 is old 3 (3½ to 4), Y4 is young four (4 to 4½); F is the error rate per 100 first objects counted, L is the error rate per 100 last objects counted, M is the error rate per 100 middle objects counted; Loc, location.

Table 5-17. Error Rates by Age and Number of Objects (Proximity)

Error type	Age				Number of objects		
	3 to 3½	3½ to 4	4 to 4½	Sig?[a]	4, 5, 6	9, 12, 14	Sig?[a]
Word–point errors[b]	<u>5.3</u>	2.8	<u>0.4</u>	√	2.8	2.9	
Point–no word	<u>2.7</u>	1.0	<u>0.3</u>	*	0.9 <	1.7	√
Multiple words–one point	2.3	1.7	0.1		1.7	1.1	
Point–object errors[c]	4.8	2.0	1.8		1.9 <	3.8	√
Object skipped	2.0	0.7	0.9		0.7	1.6	
Multiple count	2.6	1.2	0.5		1.1	1.8	
Dual errors	<u>5.8</u> >	0.8	<u>0.7</u>	√	1.6 <	3.3	*
Multiple points–one word	2.1	0.5	0.2		1.1	0.8	
Skim	<u>3.6</u> >	0.2	<u>0.5</u>	√	0.5 <	2.3	*
Recount errors	0.3	0.1	0.0		0.1	0.2	
All Errors	<u>16.2</u> >	5.5	<u>2.9</u>	*	6.4 <	10.0	*

* $p < .05$; √ $.05 < p < .10$.
> and two underlined numbers indicate significant differences, Newman-Keuls $p < .05$.
[a] Significance level of the analysis of variance.
[b] A few word between objects and part word–one point errors were made and are not reported separately in the table because the incidence was so low.
[c] Some word and point–no object errors were made and are not reported separately in the table because the incidence was so low.

error type were converted to an error rate measure, the errors per 100 objects counted. Within each age group there were four different number-by-distance orders of counterbalancing (far/small first, far/large first, close/small first, close/large first). Preliminary analyses indicated that there was no main effect of order and no interactions with order. A 2(proximity: close/far) × 2(number of objects: small/large) × 3(age) ANOVA with proximity and number as repeated measures was applied to the error rates for each error subtype and main type. The error rates for each error type are given by age and number of objects in Table 5-17. Pearson correlation coefficients were calculated for each pair of the first five error subtypes in Table 5-17. The percentage of children making each type of error by age is given in Table 5-18; McNemar's tests were used to determine whether these percentages differed significantly. For the location analyses errors were categorized according to whether they were made on a first object, a last object, or a middle object (any object not first or last); the raw errors at each location were converted to the errors per 100 objects counted at that location to control for the fact that there were considerably more middle than first or last objects. A 3(location: first, middle,

Table 5-18. Percentage of Children Making an Error by Age and Number of Objects (Proximity)

Error type	Age			Number of objects	
	3 to 3½	3½ to 4	4 to 4½	4, 5, 6	9, 12, 14
Word–point errors[a]	67	50	33	31	42
Point–no word	67 >	25	17	25	28
Multiple words– one point	33	33	8	14	17
Point–object errors[b]	<u>100</u>	75	<u>58</u>	33 <	67
Object skipped	58	42	42	17 <	42
Multiple count	<u>92</u>	58	<u>33</u>	25	47
Dual errors	58	50	25	17 <	42
Multiple points– one word	42	33	17	14	25
Skim	33	8	8	3	17
Recount	25	8	0	3	8
All errors	100	92	75	53 <	86

Note that there are more opportunities to make an error on a larger than on a smaller row.
$<, >: p < .05$.
Two underlined percentages differ significantly, $p < .05$.
[a] A few word between objects and part word–one point errors were made and are not reported separately in the table because the incidence was so low.
[b] A few word and point–no object errors were made and are not reported separately in the table because the incidence was so low.

last) × 2(proximity) × 2(number of objects) × 3(age) ANOVA with all variables except age as repeated measures was applied to the errors per 100 objects counted at each location for each of the frequent error subtypes and the error main types. For those error types on which location was a significant main effect, correlated t tests were then used to test the significance of the individual location comparisons (see Footnote 2, p. 134). The location means and main effects are presented in Table 5-19. There were some significant interactions in the preceding ANOVAs; these are discussed in the sections on each type of error. Results of all analyses are discussed for each specific error type. The effect of each variable across all error types can be understood by reading down each column in Table 5-16.

5.3.2.2. Point–No Word Errors. Two-thirds of the youngest children, a fourth of the children aged 3½ to 4, and a sixth of the children aged 4 to 4½ sometimes pointed at an object without saying a number word. The youngest children made such point–no word errors at a fairly high rate of 2.7, and the

Table 5-19. Error Rates by Location (Proximity)

Error type	First object		Middle object[a]		Last object	Sig?
Word–point errors[b]	0.7	<	3.5	≥	1.9	*
Point-no word	0.0	<	1.8	>	0.5	*
Multiple words-one point	0.7		1.6		1.2	
Point–object errors[c]	0.5	<	3.3		3.0	*
Object skipped	0.2	<	1.4	≥	0.7	*
Multiple count	0.2	<	1.6		2.1	*
Dual errors	0.9		2.8		1.6	
Multiple points–one word	0.7		1.2		0.2	
Skim	0.2	≤	1.6		1.2	√
Recount	0.0		.2		0.0	
All Errors	2.1	<	9.7	>	6.5	*

$* \ p < .05; \sqrt{} \ .05 < p < .10.$

$>, <,$ and underlined first and last object entries indicate correlated t–tests significant at $p <$ .05. $≥, ≤$ indicate $.05 < p < .10.$

[a] Error rate for an object not first or last in a row.

[b] A few word between objects and part word-one point errors were made and are not reported separately in the table because the incidence was so low.

[c] A few word and point–no object errors were made and are not reported separately in the table because the incidence was so low.

rate dropped significantly over the next two age groups to 1.0 and 0.3, $F(2, 33) = 3.56, p < .04$. Children made marginally more point–no word errors per 100 objects counted in large rows than per 100 objects counted in small rows, 1.7 versus 0.9, $F(1, 33) = 3.80, p < .06$. The age by number of objects interaction was also significant for these errors, $F(2, 33) = 3.47, p < .04$; the age differences were much greater for the larger rows than for the smaller. These results are consistent with the very large drop in the rate of point–no word errors at age 4 in Increasing Row and with the generally higher rate of point–no word errors there and in Disorganized than in the three studies in this chapter. Both Increasing Rows and Disorganized had many very long rows of objects, which might then have increased the rate of point–no word errors even more than in this study. There was no effect of proximity on point–no word errors. Children made significantly more point–no word errors per 100 middle objects counted than per 100 last or first objects counted, 1.8 versus 0.5 and 0.0, $F(2, 66) = 7.81, p < .001$. A marginally significant location by age interaction, $F(4, 66) = 2.39, p < .06$, reflected a considerably higher error rate for the youngest children and ratios across location that varied somewhat by location, but the relationship at all ages was the main effect just described: more middle than first or last object errors per 100 objects counted.

5.3.2.3. Multiple Words–One Point Errors. A third of both groups of 3-year olds but only one child aged 4 to 4½ sometimes pointed once at an object but said two or more number words. This low number of children making multiple words–one point errors and the high variability with which such errors were made by these children resulted in no significant effects for any variable for these errors. However, the pattern of differences for some variables were similar to those in Color Homogeneity or Toy Homogeneity and are revealing with respect to the quite considerable differences in multiple words–one point errors across the five studies with objects in rows. As in Color Homogeneity and Toy Homogeneity, multiple words–one point errors were made here at a much higher rate by the youngest children and at quite a low rate by the oldest children; the rate of such errors decreased from 2.3 to 1.7 to 0.1 from the youngest to the oldest children. Children made somewhat fewer multiple words–one point errors when objects were close than when objects were far, 1.2 versus 1.6, and they made more errors on small than on large rows, 1.7 versus 1.1. Thus, multiple words–one point errors seem to be maximized for very young (age 3 to 3½) children, on small rows, and when objects are placed far apart. Increasing Row had very low rates of multiple words-one point errors; it also had no children aged 3 to 3½, very long rows, and objects placed close together. Disorganized also had low rates of multiple words–one point errors on the row trials except for the children aged 3½ to 4; it also had very long rows and objects placed close together.

As in the two other studies in this chapter, multiple words–one point errors were significantly correlated with multiple count errors for the children aged 3 to 3½, $r = .95$; this correlation was also significant for the sample as a whole, $r = .65$. This result is discussed in section 5.3.2.5, following.

In spite of the fact that all rows in this study contained different-colored objects, the rate of multiple words–one point last-object errors did not exceed the rate for middle objects, 1.2 versus 1.6. Thus, the finding in Color Homogeneity that more multiple words–one point errors, and especially more last-object errors, are made on different than on same colored rows does not necessarily imply that the last-object rate will always exceed the middle-object rate on different-colored rows. In this sample also only one child on one trial continued saying number words to ten (i.e., said "eight, nine, ten"). Why fewer children did so here than in Color Homogeneity or Toy Homogeneity is not clear to us.

5.3.2.4. Object Skipped Errors. About half the children in each age group sometimes skipped over an object without giving it a point or a word. These object skipped errors were made at rates ranging from 2.0 to 0.7 across the three age groups. Object skipped errors did not vary significantly by proximity, number of objects, or age. Children did make significantly more object skipped errors per 100 middle objects counted than per 100 first or last objects counted (1.4 versus 0.2 and 0.7), $F(2, 66) = 3.15$, $p < .05$.

5.3.2.5. Multiple Count Errors. Almost all the youngest children, half the children aged 3½ to 4, and a third of the children aged 4 to 4½ sometimes pointed to an object and said a number word and then pointed again at the same object and said another number word. The number of children making such a multiple count error did drop significantly from the youngest to the oldest children. These multiple count errors dropped across the increasingly older age groups from 2.6 to 1.2 to 0.5 errors per 100 objects counted, but this age difference was not significant. The rate of errors was higher for objects spaced close together than for objects spaced for apart, 1.9 versus 0.9, but this effect was significant only when these errors were pooled with object skipped errors as the point–object errors (see following). Multiple count errors were significantly correlated with multiple words–one point errors for the children aged 3 to 3½, $r = .95$, and for the total sample, $r = .65$.

It is not obvious why children should ever make a multiple count error. Any given point to an object always can tell the counter that the object has just been counted and thus should not be counted again. Over the three studies in this chapter, multiple count errors increased with object hetero-geneity, larger arrays, and objects spaced more closely together. These in-creases are perhaps more understandable if considered together with the effects of these same variables on multiple words–one point errors. These two error types, multiple count and multiple words–one point errors, were the only error types to be consistently correlated across all three studies, these correlations for the children aged 3 to 3½ were $r = .85, .57$, and .95. Multiple words–one point errors differ from multiple count errors only in that fewer points are given to an object; for both errors, an object receives more than one word. Multiple words–one point errors increase with object color heterogeneity, smaller arrays, and objects spaced farther apart. Therefore, perhaps heterogeneity of objects to be counted elicits more words from young children via some vague association between lots of "different features in an object situation" and lots of "talking" about that situation. For children aged 3 and older, we never had intrusions of nonnumber words into counting (e.g., children never used a color word even on the different-colored blocks), so any such association was clearly successfully limited by the constraint of using only number words in counting. If it is correct that somewhat more words are elicited by heterogeneity of objects, then whether children make multiple words–one point errors or multiple count errors depends on whether the features of the counting situation also tend strongly to elicit pointing. Objects close together or many objects would seem to attract pointing and thus result in more multiple count errors, which is the case in these conditions. Objects far apart or only a few objects would not seem to elicit pointing to the same extent and thus these situations result in more multiple words–one point errors.

5.3.2.6. Word–Point Versus Point–Object Errors. Proximity had no effect on word–point errors, but children made significantly more point–object errors per 100 objects counted when the objects were close together than when they were farther apart, 3.9 versus 1.9. This result was confirmed by a significant proximity by error type interaction found for a 2(proximity) $\times$ 2(number of objects) $\times$ 2 (error type: word–point versus point–object) $\times$ 3(age) ANOVA with repeated measures for the first three variables, $F(1, 33)$ = 4.66, $p < .04$. The effect of proximity was significant in an analysis just for the point–object main category, $F(1, 33) = 5.46$, $p < .03$. The means of both frequent subtypes within the point–object main category were higher for the close than for the far condition: object skipped, 1.6 versus 0.8, and multiple count, 1.9 versus 0.9. Number of objects affected the rate of point–object errors, with children making marginally significantly more errors in the larger rows than in the smaller rows, 3.8 versus 1.9, $F(1, 33) = 3.31$, $p < .07$. The rate of word–point errors did not differ on the two sizes of rows.

Thus, children make more point–object errors when objects are spaced close together and when the rows contain more objects, but neither of these variables consistently affects word–point errors. These results then clarify some aspects of the differing relationships between the rates of word–point and point–object errors across the five studies with objects in rows. The rows in Increasing Row and in the rows portion of Disorganized had many objects, and the blocks were close together, conditions that greatly increase point–object errors. The rate of point–object errors was much higher than that of word–point errors in both those studies. Here in the Proximity study, with smaller rows and half the objects spaced far apart, the error rates of these two major types were equivalent (both were 2.9 overall). However, the ratio of word–point to point–object errors evidently is not predictable solely from number of objects and proximity, because children in the Toy Homogeneity study had a much higher point–object rate than word–point rate, but the rows there contained the same number of objects as the present study and all objects were placed relatively far apart. Homogeneity of the objects had no main effect on error rates in that study, so the fact that all rows in the present study contained objects of different colors does not seem to be responsible for this difference. It is not obvious why children in Toy Homogeneity had much higher rates of object skipped errors and somewhat higher rates of multiple count errors than did the children in Color Homogeneity and Proximity. Perhaps a general motivational effect was present in Toy Homogeneity, with the children for some reason trying less hard to count accurately. This possibility is supported somewhat by the fact that skim errors were also a bit higher in Toy Homogeneity than in Color Homogeneity and Proximity and these error subtypes are both increased by less effort.

Proximity interacted with location of an error and age for both point–object and word–point errors. For point–object errors, with the youngest children (3 to 3½), closely spaced blocks generated a considerably higher error rate for a middle than for a last object, while blocks spaced farther apart had a higher last-object than middle-object error rate. Children aged 3½ to 4 had a slightly higher error rate for a last object than for a middle object, and the children aged 4 to 4½ had a considerably higher error rate for a middle than for a last object. For word–point errors, in all age-by-proximity cells except one, the error rate was higher for a middle than for a last object; the exception was that children aged 3½ to 4 had a higher error rate for a last object than for a middle object when the objects were spaced far apart. These effects were confirmed by significant location by proximity by age interactions for point–object and word–point errors, $F(4, 66) = 3.13$ and 2.69, $p < .04$. Thus, very young age and objects spaced farther apart increase the rate of errors on last objects relative to those on middle objects. These results thus provide a clue as to the source of some of the differences in location results in the studies reported thus far. Increasing Row contained blocks closely spaced and had no children aged 3 to 3½: there the point–object middle-object rate was much higher than the last-object rate. Toy Homogeneity had objects spaced far apart and children aged 3 to 3½. The multiple count error rates there did not differ for middle and last objects (although the object skipped error rates there also were much higher on the middle than on the last objects, even though the objects were far apart). Proximity had half the objects closely spaced and had point–object and multiple count error rates that did not differ for middle and last objects.

5.3.2.7. Multiple Points–One Word Errors.

Two-fifths, a third, and a sixth of the children in the youngest through oldest age groups sometimes pointed two or more times at an object while saying only one number word. These multiple points–one word errors were made at rates of 2.1, 0.5, and 0.2 from the youngest to oldest children, respectively; this age difference was not significant. Proximity, number of objects, and location of objects did not affect the rates of these errors.

5.3.2.8. Skim Errors.

A third of the youngest children and only one child in each of the other two age groups sometimes skimmed their finger along objects saying number words haphazardly and not pointing at distinct objects. The rate of such skim errors dropped marginally significantly from the youngest to both of the other age groups, from 3.6 to 0.2 and 0.5 errors per 100 objects counted, $F(2, 33) = 3.26$, $p < .05$. Children made significantly more of these skim errors per 100 objects counted in large rows than per 100 objects counted in small rows, 2.3 versus 0.5, $F(1, 33) = 4.09$, $p < .05$. Children made marginally significantly more skim errors per 100 middle objects counted than per 100 first objects counted, 1.6 versus 0.2, $F(2, 66) = 2.88$, $p < .06$. The rate of skim errors on middle objects did not differ from that on last objects, 1.6 versus 1.2. A significant location by age interaction reflected the much higher rate of skim errors by the youngest children, and ratios across location that varied somewhat by age but all of which reflected the main effect of higher middle than first-object rate and no difference between the middle and last-object rate.

5.3.2.9. The Sum of All Errors. Every child aged 3 to 3½, every child aged 3½ to 4 except one, and three fourths of the children aged 4 to 4½ made a correspondence error. The youngest children made errors at a significantly higher rate than did the two older age groups, on 16% of the objects counted compared to 6% and 3% of the objects counted, $F(1, 33) = 4.86, p < .01$. Children made more errors when objects were close together than when they were far apart, 9.5 versus 6.9, $F(1, 33) = 5.35, p < .02$. This result reflected a significantly higher rate of point–object errors for close than for far objects, a higher rate of skim errors when objects were close together than when they were far apart (2.0 vs. 0.8), and a significantly greater number of children making a dual error in the close than in the far condition, 55% versus 8%, McNemar's χ^2 (1, $N = 36$) = 5.0, $p < .05$.

Children made more errors per 100 middle objects counted than per 100 last objects counted, $F(2, 66) = 2.69, p < .04$. This difference was quite considerable when objects were close but was not great when they were far (Table 5-20); this location by proximity interaction was marginally significant, $F(2, 66) = 2.57, p < .08$. This result stemmed from the results for word–point and point–object errors previously discussed. Children also had a lower middle-object/last-object ratio for larger than for smaller rows, the location by number of objects interaction $F(2, 66) = 3.79, p < .03$ (see Table 5-20 for the means). This finding is not consistent with the location effect reported across the preceding studies, in which the highest such ratio was reported for the Increasing Row study that had the largest rows. The effect here seemed to be due to the fact that the multiple count errors, which were the only type in this study in which the last-object rate exceeded the middle-object rate, and the skim errors, in which the middle-object rate was not too much greater than the last-object rate, both were made at a much higher rate on the larger than on the smaller rows. There was also a significant location by age inter-

Table 5-20. All Error Rates by Location and Proximity and by Location and Number (Proximity)

Proximity/number	First object	Middle object[a]	Last object
	Location by proximity interaction		
Close	2.3	11.4	6.0
Far	1.9	8.0	6.9
	Location by number interaction		
4, 5, 6	2.8	8.3	4.2
9, 12, 14	1.4	11.1	8.8

[a] Error rate for an object not first or last in a row.

action, $F(4, 66) = 3.17, p < .02$, reflecting a considerably higher error rate for the youngest group than for the other age groups and somewhat differing ratios across location for the different age groups that varied by the error type. However, all of these variations conformed to the same overall pattern: Children made more errors per 100 middle objects counted than per 100 last objects counted than per 100 first objects counted.

5.3.2.10. Location of an Error: First, Middle, or Last Object. Those cases in Table 5-19 in which the error rate for the last object did not differ significantly from that for the middle objects resulted from a few children frequently making an error on the last object. For all error categories many more children made at least one error on a middle object than on a last object. These numbers for the errors listed in Table 5-19 are, in order: 18 to 5, 13 to 2, 10 to 3, 25 to 9, 17 to 2, 18 to 7, 14 to 5, 9 to 1, 6 to 4, 4 to 0, and 28 to 14.

Individual trials were examined to ascertain how many of them fit the Gelman and Gallistel (1978) description of counting difficulty occurring to some extent at the start of a count and to a larger extent at the stop of a count but proceeding smoothly in between. Only 8 of the 432 counting trials (2%) met this description of more errors on the first or the last object than on the middle objects. When only trials on which an error was made are considered, 11% of the small rows having at least one error and 3% of the large rows having at least one error matched this description. Thus, for most of the smaller rows and for almost all of the longer rows, children were much more likely to make an error in the middle of counting than at the ends.

5.4. Summary

Age and the number of objects in a row affect the rate at which children point to an object without saying a number word, that is, make a point–no word error. Younger children made these errors at a fairly high rate on the very large rows in the Increasing Rows and Disorganized studies, and there was a higher rate of such errors on the larger rows with 9, 12, and 14 objects than on the smaller rows of 4, 5, and 6 objects in the Proximity study. However, the number of objects did not have a significant effect in Toy Homogeneity. In that study the youngest children had very high rates of multiple words–one point errors and low rates of point–no word errors. Thus, it may be that some children produce or some situations particularly elicit the former at the cost of the latter. This possibility received some support from the correlational analyses; the correlations between these two kinds of errors were not significant, but they were almost always negative.

Five different factors seem to affect the rate of multiple words–one point errors: age, number of objects, proximity of objects, the homogeneity of the color of the objects, and the tendency of individual subjects to continue saying number words to ten. These errors are made at a particularly high rate by very young children (especially those aged 3 to 3½). They are made at higher rates on rows with few rather than many objects (4, 5, and 6 vs. 9, 12, and 14 and 7, 9 versus 12, 14), with objects far apart rather than close together (with spaces between objects wider than the objects rather than ¼ inch), and with blocks in a row being different colors rather than all the same color. In two studies the rate of multiple words–one point errors on the last object in the row was particularly high. In one of these studies children made more last-object errors when counting rows of different colored blocks than when counting rows of blocks all of the same color. However, in a second study homogeneity of the toys counted did not elicit a similar effect on last-object errors. In a third study in which each row contained objects of different colors, the last-object rate was (nonsignificantly) less than the middle-object rate. Thus, the effect of homogeneity on last-object errors is not clear at present. The rate of errors on the last object clearly is affected by the fifth factor, the tendency of some children to point to the last object once and continue saying number words to ten. The number of such children varied over the three studies in this chapter, and no paticular variable seemed to affect this distribution. Thus, it may be that certain children have this tendency to use what Wagner and Walters (1982) called a "list exhaustion scheme," and they sometimes finished saying words to ten.[13] If this is so, whatever, if any, variables that affect this individual difference in children will affect the rate of multiple words–one point errors made on the last object in a row, at least for sets with nine or fewer objects.

Only two variables seem to increase the rate at which children skip over an object without giving it a point or a word: a larger rather than smaller number of objects and location in the middle rather than at the beginning or end of a row. Children in almost all studies made more such object skipped errors per 100 middle objects counted than per 100 last or 100 first objects counted.[14] Children in Toy Homogeneity made more object skipped errors per 100 objects counted in larger rows than per 100 objects counted in smaller rows. This result is certainly consistent with the quite high rate of object skipped errors in Increasing Row and Disorganized. However, it does not explain why the rate of object skipped errors was higher in Toy Homogeneity than in Proximity or in Color Homogeneity, which had the same number and more

---

[13] The list exhaustion scheme was hypothesized to operate with whatever sequence the child had. We found little evidence of such a scheme except for counting on to ten, a very common stopping place in counting. However, such a list exhaustion scheme may operate with 2-year-olds.

[14] Object skipped errors on the last object are really uncounted errors. In all the row studies such errors were very rare; children almost never left the last object in a row uncounted. Therefore in the rows analyses we left those few uncounted errors as object skipped errors in order to be able to carry out location analyses.

(respectively) objects in a row. In Increasing Row effort was found to affect the rate of object skipped errors considerably, so perhaps the children in Toy Homogeneity for some reason counted with less consistent, high effort than did the children in Color Homogeneity or Proximity. This interpretation is consistent with the higher rate of skim errors found in Toy Homogeneity, because skim errors also increase with less effort. It is also notable that, for the three studies in this chapter, object skipped errors were the only error subtype to show no significant decrease with age either in the rate of such errors or in the percentage of children making such errors. The lack of a rate effect was partly due to the large variability of such errors, but also to the fact that the oldest children continued to make them at a rate higher than all or most other error subtypes. For the study in this chapter in which object skipped errors were made at a somewhat high rate (Toy Homogeneity), these errors were significantly correlated with point–no word errors for the youngest and oldest age groups. Thus, both of these errors may reflect a more general tendency to be sparing with words when counting.

Across the five row studies, the percentage of children who sometimes pointed to an object and said a number word and then pointed and said another number word to the same object was as high as or higher than all other errors. Such multiple count errors showed significant drops with age both in the rate of errors and in the percentage of children making such errors. Homogeneity of color and toys and number of objects affected such errors. Three-year-olds made more multiple count errors per 100 objects counted in larger rows than per 100 objects counted in smaller rows (Color Homogeneity). More 3-year-olds made multiple count errors when blocks in a row were different colors than when they were the same color (on rows of 7 to 14 objects in Color Homogeneity). The rate of such errors was similarly affected by heterogeneous toys for the longer rows of 9, 12, and 14 (a higher rate of multiple count errors with heterogeneous than with homogeneous toys), but for the small rows of 4, 5, and 6, the rate was lower for heterogeneous than for homogeneous toys (Toy Homogeneity). Thus, for very small sets objects that differ may reduce multiple count errors. But for rows of 7 or more objects, objects that differ in color, size, or kind seem to elicit more multiple count errors.

Over the three studies in this chapter, multiple count errors increased with object heterogeneity, larger arrays, and objects spaced more closely together. These increases are perhaps more understandable if considered together with the effects of these same variables on multiple words–one point errors. These two error types, multiple count and multiple words–one point errors, were the only error types to be consistently correlated across all three studies; these correlations for the children aged 3 to 3½ were $r = .85$, $.57$, and $.95$. Multiple words–one point errors differ from multiple count errors only in that fewer points are given to an object; for both errors, an object receives more than one word. Multiple words–one point errors increase with object color heterogeneity, smaller arrays, and objects spaced farther apart. Therefore, perhaps heterogeneity of objects to be counted elicits more words from young children via some vague association between lots of "different features in an object situation" and lots of "talking" about that situation. For children aged 3 and older, we never had intrusions of nonnumber words into counting (e.g., children never used a color word even on the different colored blocks), so any such association was clearly successfully limited by the constraint of using only number words in counting. If it is correct that somewhat more words are elicited by heterogeneity of objects, then whether children make multiple words–one point errors or multiple count errors depends on whether the features of the counting situation also tend strongly to elicit pointing. Objects close together or many objects would seem to attract pointing and thus result in more multiple count errors, which is the case in these conditions. Objects far apart or only a few objects would not seem to elicit pointing to the same extent, and thus these situations result in more multiple words–one point errors.

In a multiple point–one word error, a child points to an object two or more times but says only one number word. Such errors were not made very frequently except on both the rows and the disorganized arrays in Disorganized. Multiple points–one word errors were made more frequently when children pointed with a microcomputer pen than with their finger in the usual way (chapter 4), on larger than on smaller rows, and when the color of objects in a row was the same rather than different. However, these variables do not seem necessarily to predict more multiple points–one word errors, for children had fairly low rates of such errors when counting the long rows of same colored blocks in the Increasing Row study. There was some indication that more multiple points–one word errors are made by younger rather than by older children and by 3-year-olds on the last rather than on the first or on the middle objects in a row. Thus, when a counting situation does elicit more pointing, it may be especially difficult for young children to stop such extra pointing, resulting in higher rates for the last object counted. These errors do violate both the word–point and the point–object correspondences, but they do not create an error in the cardinality result because one word still corresponds to one object. However, because the rate of such errors decreases considerably for older children, it does not seem likely that younger children make such errors because they realize that they are not really errors. Further research concerning these errors seems to be required, including when children understand that these errors do not affect cardinality.

About half the youngest children in each study sometimes skimmed their finger along a row, saying number words in a haphazard fashion and not pointing at specific objects. Every such child spontaneously pointed at specific objects on at least one trial, so such skim errors are not a consistent form of behavior. Age and number of objects affected the rate of skim errors in all three studies in this chapter. Children made such skim errors at higher rates on larger than on smaller rows, and younger children made more such skim errors than did older children. Children made more skim errors when the toys counted were homogeneous (all the objects in a row were identical) than when they were heterogeneous.

In the Increasing Row and Disorganized studies, for both rows and disorganized arrays, the rate of point–object errors was between double and triple the rate of word–point errors. Thus, when counting closely spaced objects in increasingly long rows, children found it considerably easier to coordinate two continuous sequence of actions (pointing and saying words) than to carry out one spatially distributed action sequence (pointing once and only once at each object). In situations in which either of the frequent point–object errors (object skipped or multiple count) decrease or either of the frequent word–point errors (point–no word or multiple words–one point) increase, this relationship obviously will change. Situations that minimize point–object errors and maximize word–point errors were those with small rows counted by young children (3-year-olds) with high effort (or at least with low object skipped errors); the rate of word–point errors exceeded the rate of point–object errors in such a situation. Thus, no characterization of the relative difficulty of establishing the temporal word–point correspondence compared to the spatial point–object correspondence applies across all different counting situations.

6. Correspondence Errors in Children's Counting: A Summary

The results of chapters 3, 4, and 5 with respect to the nature of the correspondence errors children make in counting are briefly summarized in this chapter. These studies are obviously only a first step toward understanding the complexities of young children's counting. However, they do contribute a definition of counting that yields a comprehensive category system of correspondence errors. They provide an initial descriptive mapping of the kinds of correspondence errors children make most frequently and of variables that affect these errors. They suggest how frequently young children of different ages make different kinds of errors, although of course the figures reported are subject to the effects of the variables in the particular studies. For example these results make it clear that someone wanting to see many correspondence errors in counting must study 3-year-olds rather than 4-year-olds and that the number of objects in an array must be controlled because this variable affects different kinds of errors in different ways. The hope is that these results will provide a basis for future research that will be able to be related easily because all studies are using the same error categories and reporting the same measures.

The characteristics of the studies reported in chapters 3, 4, and 5 are summarized in Table 6-1. Five studies examined the errors children make in counting immovable objects arranged in a row. Three studies focused on immovable objects arranged in a disorganized array or in a circular loop. Two studies explored ways of indicating objects that differed from the usual pointing at objects with a finger.

6.1. A Definition of Counting and a Category System of Correspondence Errors in Counting

Counting objects distributed in space requires an indicating act to mediate between the words said in time and the objects distributed in space. Such indicating acts seem to fall within two categories: (a) moving objects from a pile of uncounted objects to a pile of counted objects and (b) some variation of pointing at unmoved objects, including the later internalization of pointing as eye fixation (see 3.3.11). The indicating act involves two correspondences: the correspondence in time between a word and the indicating act and the correspondence in space between the indicating act and an object. The word–object correspondence then derives from the separate temporal and spatial correspondences involving the indicating act. For counting to be correct, one word must correspond to one indicating act and that one indicating act must correspond to one object. The words must come from the standard number–word sequence; children's learning of the English sequence of number words is discussed in chapter 2.

Correct indicating act–object correspondence includes four requirements, the violation of which leads to the class of error listed:

1. each indicating act must be directed toward an object: one indicating act—less than one object
2. each indicating act must not be directed toward more than one object: one indicating act—more than one object
3. every object is indicated: less than one indicating act—one object
4. no object is indicated more than once: more than one indicating act—one object.

Whether the indicting act–object correspondence is wrong is determined in some cases locally (as each spatial correspondence is made) and is determined in some cases over all the correspondences. The latter requires a method of remembering which objects have been counted. Thus, accurate counting requires accurate local word-indicating act correspondences, accurate local indicating act–object correspondences, and an overall method of remembering the objects counted.

The first two requirements for correct indicating act–object correspondence are accomplished locally during counting by setting limits on each separate indicating act: Each act must be directed toward an object, and it must not be directed toward more than one object. Our studies indicated that children's use of both pointing and moving objects usually met these requirements. In all the studies with immovable objects, children's points almost always were directed at objects, and it is not really possible to point to more than one object at a time.[1] When moving objects, children always moved at least one object and they only occasionally moved more than one object at a time.

How the last two requirements for correct indicating act–object correspondence are met depends on the method of remembering which objects have been counted. Such methods fall into two general classes: (a) "marking" individual counted objects in some way so that it is clear that the object has been counted and (b) using a linear ordering on the objects. The indicating act of moving objects from an uncounted to a counted pile is in the first class; membership in the counted pile "marks" each counted object. Another method in the first class is pointing in which each object is physically or mentally "marked" in some way as the object is counted. Both of these methods

---

[1] Gestures can be made that include several objects, but these do not have the downward motion that defines a point. Any such downward motion is directed toward a single location that can contain only a single object, unless the objects are extraordinarily small.

Table 6-1. Summary of Features of the Studies in Chapters 3, 4, and 5

Study name	Chapter	n	Ages[a]	Type of counted objects	Number of objects	Variables[b]
				Studies with immovable objects in a row		
Increasing Row	3	86	3–6 through 5–11	1-inch blocks, close,[c] same color	4 to 34	Effort Number: 5 to 9, 10 to 15, 16 to 19, 20 to 24, 25 to 29 Sex Location[d]
Disorganized	4	36	3–0 through 5–11	1-inch blocks, close, same color	4 to 34	Object arrangement: row vs. disorganized
Color Homogeneity	5	24	3–0 through 4–11	1-inch blocks, close, same and different color	7, 9 12, 14 17, 19	Object color: same vs. different Number: Small (3s 7, 9; 4s 12, 14) Large (3s 12, 14; 4s 17, 19) First half vs. second half of the row Location
Toy Homogeneity	5	43	3–2 through 4–5	Toys, far[c]	4, 5, 6 9, 12, 14	Object homogeneity: same vs. different Number: 4 to 6 vs. 9 to 14 Verbal label: class vs. collection term Location
Proximity	5	36	3–0 through 4–5	cars, chips, blocks, close and far, different color	4, 5, 6 9, 12, 14	Distance between objects: close vs. far Number: 4 to 6 vs. 9 to 14 Location

Studies with immovable objects not in a row

Disorganized	4	36	3–0 through 5–11	1-inch blocks, close, same color	4 to 34	Objects in a row vs. objects in a disorganized array
Circle study 1	4	46	3–6 through 5–11	dots in a circular loop	16, 18, 19	Use of a stop-rule examined
Circle study 2	4	19	2–6 through 3–6	dots in a circular loop	6, 7, 8	Use of a stop-rule examined: starting dot different from other dots

Studies focused on the indicating act

Movable objects	4	86	3–6 through 5–11	pile of 1-inch blocks	50	Indicating act used by child: pointing or moving blocks
Microcomputer pen	4	46	3–6 through 5–11	dots in rows and in circular loops	16, 18, 19	Pointing with finger vs. pointing with a microcomputer pen

[a] 3-6 represents 3 years 6 months; other ages represented similarly.

[b] Age was also examined in each study.

[c] Objects close together were about ¼ inch apart; objects far apart were separated by a space greater than the width of the object.

[d] Location compared errors at the beginning, within the middle, and at the end of a row.

of remembering create successive partitions of the objects into counted and to-be-counted sets (Beckwith & Restle, 1966). These successive partitions are obvious to any viewer with moving objects and with physically marked objects but are not obvious with mentally marked objects.

A linear ordering can already be established and obvious in the situation, such as in a row, or the situation can require an individually established non-evident linear ordering, such as in a disorganized array. Pointing at objects in an already established linear ordering creates successive partitions of the objects into counted and to-be-counted sets. Each object pointed to partitions the objects into those earlier in the ordering (the counted objects) and those still to come in the ordering (the to-be-counted objects). However, only if the linear ordering is obvious to the onlooker, as in a row, can this partitioning be evident to an observer, and it is not clear in any of these cases that the counter is aware that the objects are being successively partitioned. For objects in rows it is not even clear that young children realize that they are using a linear ordering on the objects; they may just be counting from one end to the other as they have seen others do. Therefore, it does not seem wise to consider counting *in general* as consisting of tagging and of partitioning, as is done by Gelman and Gallistel (1978) and then by others following this terminology. Rather partitioning should be replaced by local indicating act–object correspondences and overall indicating act–object correspondences; the latter are determined by a method of remembering, some of which methods use partitioning.

The category system of correspondence errors was initially formulated for the indicating act of pointing. With pointing, children can make a correspondence error that violates the word–point correspondence, the local point–object correspondence established with each point, both of these correspondences, or the overall (remembering) point–object correspondence resulting after all of the counting activity. These different kinds of correspondence errors form the four major categories within our category system of correspondence errors in counting: word–point errors, point–object errors, dual errors, and overall (remembering) point–object errors. The subtypes of errors that children make within these major categories were established initially by viewing videotapes of children counting objects in rows and in disorganized arrays and were verified in the subsequent studies. The errors that children were found to make are listed in Table 6-2. For this analysis errors children make in saying the sequence of number words are considered to be sequence errors and not correspondence errors. The errors children make in saying the sequence and in creating correct correspondences are quite different. Such sequence errors are discussed in chapter 2. Relationships between correspondence errors and sequence errors are discussed in chapter 10.

When the indicating act is moving objects rather than pointing, the possible errors in Table 6-2 change somewhat. All of the word–point errors are possible word–moving object errors, so no change occurs in this category.

None of the local point–object errors in Table 6-2 seems likely or possible to be made with moving objects, but a new local error now becomes possible: children do sometimes move more than one object with a single indicating act, making a moving object–multiple objects error. No dual errors seem likely or possible, but children can make overall recount or uncounted errors if the counted and uncounted piles overlap or if counting ends before all objects are counted.

This discussion has been phrased as if the objects were "out there." Of course, in any given counting situation *the child* must decide what to consider as the "countables." When individual objects are considered as countables, the child is said to be using perceptual unit items (see chapter 1 and Steffe et al., 1983). When children begin to use perceptual unit items is discussed in 6.2.4.2. Once this occurs, the point–object correspondence is of course really a "point–perceptual unit item" correspondence. For ease of reference we will continue to use point–object correspondence throughout this chapter.

6.2. Specific Correspondence Errors Children Make in Counting

The kinds of correspondence errors children actually make in counting are described in Table 6-2.[2] Of the 14 types of errors listed in the table, only 6 are made very frequently for objects in rows. The rates at which children between age 3 and 5 made these six kinds of errors and the percentage of children making such errors are given by half-year age groups in Table 6-3; 5-year-olds are not included in the table, because their rates of errors were so low. The error rate measure used is the rate of errors per 100 objects counted; this measure enables fair comparisons to be made across circumstances in which different numbers of objects are counted.[3] A summary of the effects of

---

[2] Three other errors that children made very occasionally are described in 4.2.3.3.6 and are not listed in the table. It also seems likely that some other errors made rarely will be found in the future. The triad of word–point–object used in Table 6-2 gives an easy way to define any such new errors.

[3] Comparisons across two conditions with different numbers of objects (let us call them the "smaller array" and the "larger array" conditions) are made by dividing the number of errors made on the smaller arrays by the number of objects in the smaller arrays and by dividing the number of errors made on the larger arrays by the number of objects in the larger arrays; we then multiply both these numbers by 100 in order to report whole number measures. This measure controls for the greater chance of making errors in arrays with a larger number of objects that is not controlled by a measure such as errors per trial or the first error made on an array. However, this measure is not independent of the circumstances in which the counting occurred. As will be discussed, for some kinds of errors children do have higher error rates on arrays with more objects, that is, they make more errors per 100 objects counted in large arrays than per 100 objects counted in small arrays. Therefore, the error rates in Table 6-3 all depend on the array sizes in the particular experiments. For the three studies from chapter 5 in which the number of objects was manipulated, these rates are all simple averages of the error rates from the two different number-of-object conditions in each study.

Table 6-2. Categories of Correspondence Errors

Word–point errors: Violations of the temporal word–point correspondence

---

The temporal one-to-one correspondence between a number word and a point is violated but the spatial one-to-one correspondence between a point and a block is maintained

---

Point–no word
  No word, one point, one object:
  point to an object without saying a
  number word

$$\downarrow$$
$$\square$$

Multiple words–one point
  Two words, one point, one object:
  point to an object once and say two
  number words.
  Also three or four words, one point,
  one object

5, 6   5, 6, 7
↓   ↓
□   □

Part word–one point
  part word, one point, one object: a
  word is stretched out over two or
  more objects

sev-   en   ni-   ii-   ine
↓   ↓   or   ↓   ↓   ↓
□   □   □   □   □

Word between objects
  One word, no point, no object: a
  number word is said with no point
  and when the finger is over no object

6   7   8   1   2
↓   ↓   or   ↓
□   □   □

Point–object errors: Violations of the local spatial point–object correspondence

---

The local spatial one-to-one correspondence between point and object is violated but the temporal one-to-one correspondence between word and point is maintained

---

Object skipped
  No word, no point, one object:
  finger passes over object but no word
  is said and no point is given to the
  object

5   6
↓   ↓
□   □   □

Multiple count
  Two words, two points, one object: a
  word and a point and then another
  word and a point are given to the
  same object.
  Also three words, three points, one
  object; 4, 4, 1

3 4   7 8 9
↓↓   ↓↓↓
□   □

Word and point—no object
  One word, one point, no object: a
  word and a point between objects

5   6   7
↓   ↓   ↓
□   □

Table 6-2. *Continued*

Dual errors: Violations of both the word–point and local point–object correspondence

---

Both the temporal one-to-one correspondence between a number word and a point and the local spatial one-to-one correspondence between point and object are violated

---

Multiple points–one word
    One word, two points, one object: 8
    one word and two points are given to   ↓↓
    an object   □

Multiple points–no word
    No word, two points, one object: no   ↓↓
    word is said and two points are given   □

Word–no point
    One word, no point, one object: 16   17   18
    word is said while the finger is over ↓_ _ _ _ _ _ _ _ _↓
    the object but the point is omitted   □   □   □

Skim
    Finger skims over the array with no specific points, and words are produced in a stream having no apparent connection with the objects

Flurry
    Many points directed generally toward the array (rather than specific points directed at specific objects), and many words not in correspondence with the points are produced quite rapidly

---

Overall point–object correspondence errors

Recount errors
    An object receives a point a second time after a different object has been counted
Uncounted errors
    An object never receives a point

Note. The dual: multiple points–one word and word–no point categories are correspondence errors (there is a violation of the one-to-one correspondences) but nevertheless give the correct cardinality.

variables other than age in the four studies involving only rows of objects is given in Table 6-4.

Two of the six errors violated the word–point correspondence: children sometimes pointed without saying a word and sometimes said two or more words while pointing once at an object. Two violated the point–object correspondence: Children sometimes skipped over an object without counting it, and they sometimes counted an object and immediately counted it again. The

Table 6-3. Effects of Age on the Error Rate and on the Percentage of Children Making Prevalent Subtypes of Errors

Study name	Point–no word				Multiple words–one point				Object skipped				Multiple count				Multiple points–one word				Skim			
	Y3	O3	Y4	O4	Y3	O3	Y4	O4	Y3	O3	Y4	O4	Y3	O3	Y4	O4	Y3	O3	Y4	O4	Y3	O3	Y4	O4
Increasing Row	4.0	>1.5		1.6	1.0	0.3		0.4	8.6	>4.4		1.2	1.7	2.1		>0.7	1.6	0.7		0.3	3.9	9.4		4.4
	89	71		53	39	18		29	83	82		76	83	88		65	44	35		41	50	47		24
Disorganized (objects in rows)	8.2	>1.7	4.5	1.0	0.6	2.4	0.8	0.2	22.2	16.4	>7.1	3.4	3.8	3.2	2.0	1.0	3.3	2.8	2.4	0.7	3.3	6.4	10.5	13.9
	100	83	83	50	33	67	67	17	100	100	83	67	83	100	100	50	50	83	67	50	17	17	17	33
Color Homogeneity		(1.0		0.2)		(2.3		0.7)		(2.4		0.8)		(1.8		1.5)		(0.8		0.4)		(3.1		0.7)
		(50		25)		(83		50)		(50		58)		(83		50)		(58		50)		(50		17)
Toy Homogeneity	0.8	1.0		0.4	4.8	>0.4		0.3	6.6	3.7		1.9	2.9	4.2		>0.7	—			—	4.9	4.8		0.0
	27	42		25	64	33		20	73	75		50	100	92		55					45	25		>0
Proximity	2.7	1.0		0.3	2.3	1.7		0.1	2.0	0.7		0.9	2.6	1.2		0.5	2.1	0.5		0.2	3.6	>0.2		0.5
	67 >	25		17	33	33		8	58	42		42	92	58		33	42	33		17	33	8		8
Disorganized (objects in disorganized arrays)	7.2	>1.3	4.2	1.1	4.8	4.5	1.5	0.3	20.5	17.7	18.7	>4.8	6.8	4.3	1.6	0.3	2.3	3.3	2.2	0.2	1.8	—	6.0	29.1
	83	33	100	67	50	67	50	17	100	100	100	67	100	50	67	33	50	67	67	17	17	0	33	33

Note. Y3 is young three (3 to 3½), O3 is old three (3½ to 4), Y4 is young four (4 to 4½), O4 is old four (4½ to 5). The sample for Color Homogeneity was not divided into half-year age groups; the left figures are for 3-year-olds and the right figures are for 4-year-olds. The top row for each study is the rate of errors per 100 objects counted and the bottom row is the percentage of children who made at least one error of the given type. Two rates or percentages underlined or connected by > differed significantly.

Table 6-4. Summary of Effects of Number, Homogeneity, Proximity, Verbal Label, and Location of Objects in a Row

Study name	Point–no word	Multiple words–one point	Object skipped	Multiple count	Multiple points–one word	Skim
Increasing Row	Loc: M > L > F		Number: large > small Loc: M > F > L Effort: low > high	Loc: M > L > F		Number: large > small Effort: low > high
Color Homogeneity		Color hom Dif > same (3s rate) Color × loc (3s) Last > middle Dif > same last dif esp. high Location 4s: M, L > F		Number: large > small (3s) Color hom dif > same (% 3s make)	Number: large > small (3s) Color hom same > dif (% 3s make) Location 3s: L > F 4s: M > F, L	Number: large > small (3s)
Toy Homogeneity	Loc: M, L > F	Loc: L > M > F	Number: large > small Loc: M > L, F	Hom × number large het > large hom = small hom > small het Loc: M, L > F		Number: large > small Hom: hom > het Hom × number × verbal label: Hom class large esp. high Loc: M > L, F
Proximity	Number: large > small Loc: M > L, F	Proximity: close > far Loc: M > L, F	Proximity: close > far Loc: M > L, F	Proximity: close > far Loc: M, L > F	Number: large > small	Number: large > small Loc: M > F

Dif, different colored blocks; F, first; het, heterogeneous; hom, homogeneous; L, last; loc, location; M, middle (not first or last); same, same colored blocks.

fifth violated both correspondences: Children sometimes pointed twice at an object while saying one word. Only two errors, skim and flurry errors, involved more than single isolated errors. These both were found to be degenerate forms of counting; all children exhibiting them also counted with reasonable word–point and point–object correspondences on other trials. These results lead to an important conclusion about young children's counting. By age 3 counting is already very organized and exhibits the general structure of mature, effective counting: It has a recognizable structure of word–point and point–object correspondences, and most of the frequent errors violate only one of these correspondences. Each of the frequent errors is briefly discussed in the following sections.

The correlational analyses for the three studies in chapter 5 revealed age differences in the patterns of correlations among the frequent kinds of errors. In two of these studies, the correlations among the first five kinds of errors in Table 6-3 were generally higher and more similar for the 4-year-olds than for the 3-year-olds. For the 3-year-olds, many correlations were small and some were negative. This suggests that, for the 3-year-olds, different children tend to make different kinds of errors, but that for 4-year-olds, children who are still making a considerable number of errors tend to make most of the common kinds of errors. We report only the results for the 3-year-olds in the sections below, as these are the results that provide insights concerning specific relationships between particular kinds of errors.

6.2.1. Types of Word–Point Errors

6.2.1.1. Point–No Word Errors. In a point–no word error, a child points to an object but does not say a number word. In the studies in which children counted very long rows or large disorganized arrays, such errors were by far the most common violation of the word–point correspondence. Most 3-year-olds made such errors, which were made at higher rates than other errors except object skipped and skim errors (Table 6-3). A lower rate of such errors were made in the three studies in chapter 5 in which children counted smaller arrays. The rate of making such errors seems to be especially large for the youngest children (3-year-olds) and for the rows with a larger number of objects. When children make these point–no word errors, they do not omit a word from the sequence; they merely delay it until the next object. Thus, for such an error on the third object a child would count, "one" (point to first object), "two" (point to second object), silence (point to third object), "three" (point to fourth object). Three-year-olds distribute these errors equally over the objects in the first and second half of rows ranging from 7 to 14 objects, rendering it less likely that these errors are caused just by difficulty in thinking of the next number word (if this were so, the errors would occur more frequently in the second half on the later less-well learned words in the number-word sequence). The rate of such errors did not differ between the rows and the disorganized arrays. These errors were made more frequently when children pointed with a microcomputer pen than with their finger in the usual way. Because pointing with the pen would seem to have made the pointing act more salient to some children, leading them occasionally to focus only on that pointing, this suggests that any variable that increases the salience of pointing may increase the rate of point–no word errors. Point–no word errors tended to be negatively correlated with multiple words–one word errors, although these correlations were never significant. Thus, there seemed to be some tendency for children who omitted a word with a point not also to say extra words with a point, and vice versa. In the study in chapter 5 in which children made a fairly considerable number of object skipped errors, such errors were significantly correlated with point–no word errors for the children between 3 and 3½ and between 4 and 4½; this suggests that some children have a common tendency toward errors of omission.

6.2.1.2. Multiple Words–One Point Errors. In a multiple words–one point error, a child points once at an object and says two or more number words. The rate of multiple words–one point errors varies with age, number of objects, proximity of objects, and the homogeneity of the color of the objects. These multiple words–one point errors are made at a particularly high rate by very young children (especially those aged 3 to 3½). They are made at higher rates on rows with few rather than many objects (4, 5, and 6 vs. 9, 12, and 14 and 7 and 9 vs. 12 and 14), with objects far apart rather than close together (with spaces between objects wider than the objects vs. ¼-inch spaces), and with blocks in a row being different colors rather than all the same color. It is somewhat curious that these errors are made more frequently by the youngest children, who know fewer number words than older children and consequently might be expected to use them more sparingly. That more such errors are made on rows with fewer and with more widely spaced objects suggests that these very young children may have a conception of counting that involves saying a certain number of words at a certain rate. When objects are spaced more widely, the rate of pointing just may not always keep pace with the rate of saying words. The concern with saying a certain number of words might be connected to the pride young children feel in "knowing their number words": *more* is definitely better when one is just saying the sequence of words. It may take some time to learn that *more* is not necessarily better when one is counting objects. In all three studies of chapter 5, multiple words–one point errors were significantly correlated with multiple count errors for children aged 3 to 3½; this result in discussed in section 6.2.2.2.

In two studies the rate of multiple words–one point errors on the last object in the row was particularly high. Such last-object errors may be increased by different- rather than same-colored objects, but findings across studies are conflicting with respect to this issue. As discussed in 6.2.2.2., different (rather than identical) objects seem to elicit more counting activity, here the saying of more words. Therefore, with different objects it may be particularly difficult for children to stop this heightened activity, leading to a higher rate of such "over-active" errors on the last object in a row. The rate of errors on the last object also clearly is affected by the tendency of some children to point to the last object once and continue saying number words up to ten. The number of such children varied considerably over the studies, and no variable seemed to affect this variation (except of course giving arrays larger than ten, which decreased this behavior). Thus, it may be that certain children have a tendency to use what Wagner and Walters (1982) called a "list exhaustion scheme" so that they finish the sequence words to ten.[4] If this is so, whatever, if any, variables that affect this individual difference in children will affect the rate of multiple words–one point errors made on the last object in a row.

6.2.1.3. Part Word–One Point Errors. In a part word–one point error, a child points once to an object and says part of a number word and then points once to a different object and says the rest of the number word. In some cases the child may distribute the number word over three or four objects, with each object receiving one point. These errors are very rare when counting objects in rows. However, this error was one of only three error types affected by arranging objects in disorganized arrays rather than in rows. Children aged 3 to 4½ made more such errors than did the children aged 4½ to 6, but some children within each half-year age group made such errors when counting objects in large, disorganized arrays.

Approximately half of such errors were made while saying a number word of a single syllable, so this error was *not* just due to a momentary failure to distinguish syllables from words. It is interesting that the increased point–object processing demand for remembering which words have been counted in disorganized arrays does disrupt the word–point correspondence for this one kind of error: The pressure of choosing the next object for disorganized arrays is sometimes sufficient to interrupt the production of a word before its completion but is not so overwhelming that the word component of counting is totally ignored. This error also indicates that children at least sometimes choose and point to the next object *while* they are saying a number word rather than beginning this next point after they have finished saying a number word.

6.2.2. Types of Point–Object Errors

6.2.2.1. Object Skipped Errors. An object skipped error is one in which a pointing finger skips over an object without giving it either a point or a word. Many children make such errors when counting objects in rows, and these

---

[4] The list exhaustion scheme was hypothesized to operate with whatever sequence the child had. We found little evidence of such a scheme except for counting on to ten, a very common stopping place in counting. However, such a list exhaustion scheme may operate with 2-year-olds.

errors are made at fairly high rates (Table 6-3). Five variables are associated with higher rates of such errors when counting objects in a row: younger rather than older age (for large arrays there may be considerable drops in such errors at 4 and 4½), a larger rather than smaller number of objects, location in the middle rather than at the beginning or end of a row,[5] objects spaced close together rather than far apart, and counting with less effort or attention. Children aged 4½ to 6 eliminated such errors entirely when they were asked to "try really hard," whereas those aged 3½ to 4 only reduced such errors a little bit. These errors indicate that children have some difficulty in choosing the next object in the linear ordering on a row. The variables affecting these errors suggest that these choices of the next object initially may be partly driven by the arcs made by the moving pointing finger of the child, and only by age 4½ or so do these arcs come consistently under the control of the objects to be counted even when these objects are spaced closely together in a long row. At an earlier age each object is more likely to "pull" a point to itself if each object is salient, as when spaced far apart or located at the end of a row. The considerable effect of effort on object skipped errors indicates that these errors are also obviously affected by the child's motivation to count accurately; on some trials the goal "finish counting the row" seems to replace the goal "count the objects correctly." This motivational effect may contribute to the increase in such errors on rows with a large number of objects.

With disorganized arrays it proved to be impossible to differentiate those objects that were skipped over (i.e., object skipped errors that locally violated the point–object correspondence) from those objects that were never counted (uncounted errors that violated the overall point–object correspondence), because the linear ordering (or partitioning with mental marking of objects) was not evident to the observer. For children aged 3 to 4½, the rate of object skipped/uncounted errors in disorganized arrays was very high— about one in five objects was never counted. Children aged 4½ to 6 also still had fairly high rates of such errors—a mean of one in twelve objects was never counted by children in this age range. Thus, children at age 6 still have not devised effective methods of remembering which objects have been counted in large disorganized arrays, and their counting violates the third requirement of point–object correspondence.

6.2.2.2. Multiple Count Errors. In a multiple count error, a child points to an object while saying a number word and then points to that same object again while saying another number word.[6] Across the row studies the percentage of

---

[5] Object skipped errors on the last object are really uncounted errors. However, children almost never left the last object in a row uncounted. In the rows analyses the few uncounted errors were classified as object skipped errors in order to carry out location analyses.

[6] In almost every case the second number word is different from the first number word. If the error occurs while the child is using her correct portion, the two words are two successive words from the sequence.

children making such multiple count errors was usually as high as or higher than the percentage making any other error, although the rate was not as high as that for some other errors (Table 6-3). Such multiple count errors showed significant drops with age both in the rate of errors and in the percentage of children making such errors; the drops occurred at age 4 for sets up to 14 and at age 4½ for larger sets. Homogeneity of toys and the number of objects counted interacted to affect such errors. For very small sets (4 to 6 objects), objects that differ reduced multiple count errors. But for rows of 7 or more objects, objects that differ in color, size, or kind elicited more multiple count errors. Three-year-olds made more multiple count errors on larger than on smaller rows, and objects spaced close together rather than far apart increased multiple count errors.

It is not obvious why children should ever make a multiple count error. Any given point to an object always can tell the counter that the object has just been counted. The increase of multiple count errors with object heterogeneity, larger arrays, and objects spaced more closely together is perhaps more understandable if considered together with the effects of these same variables on multiple words–one point errors. Such a common approach is suggested by the fact that in all three studies in chapter 5, multiple count errors were significantly correlated with multiple words–one point errors for children aged 3 to 3½ ($r = .85, .57$, and $.95$), the age group at which children commonly made multiple words–one point errors. Multiple words–one point errors differ from multiple count errors only in that fewer points are given to an object; for both errors, an object receives more than one word. Multiple words–one point errors increase with object color heterogeneity, smaller arrays, and objects spaced farther apart. Therefore, perhaps heterogeneity of objects to be counted elicits more words from young children via some vague association between lots of different features in an object situation and lots of "talking" about that situation. For children aged 3 and older, we never had intrusions of nonnumber words into counting (e.g., children never used a color word even on the different colored blocks), so any such association was clearly successfully limited by the constraint of using only number words in counting. If it is correct that somewhat more words are elicited by heterogeneity of objects, then whether children make multiple words–one point errors or multiple count errors depends on whether the features of the counting situation tend also strongly to elicit pointing. Objects close together or many objects would seem to attract pointing and thus result in multiple count errors, which is the case in these conditions. Objects far apart or only a few objects would not seem to elicit pointing to the same extent, and thus these situations result in multiple words–one point errors.

6.2.3. Relative Number of Word–Point and Point–Object Errors

In Increasing Row and Disorganized studies for both rows and disorganized arrays, the rate of point–object errors was between double and triple the rate of word–point errors. Thus, when counting closely spaced objects in increasingly long rows or in counting large, disorganized arrays, children found it considerably easier to coordinate two continuous sequences of actions (pointing and saying words) than to carry out one spatially distributed action sequence (pointing once and only once at each object). In situations in which either of the frequent point–object errors (object skipped or multiple count) decrease or either of the frequent word–point errors (point–no word or multiple words–one point) increase, this relationship obviously will change. Situations in which the word–point errors were maximized and the point–object errors were minimized were those in which small rows were counted by young children (3-year-olds) with high effort (or at least with low object skipped errors); in such situations the rate of word–point errors exceeded the rate of point–object errors. Thus, no characterization of the relative difficulty of establishing the temporal word–point correspondence compared to the spatial local point–object correspondence applies across all different counting situations.

6.2.4. Types of Dual Errors

6.2.4.1. Multiple Points–One Word Errors. In a multiple points–one word error, a child points to an object two or more times but says only one number word. Such errors were not made very frequently except on both the rows and the disorganized arrays in the Disorganized study. Multiple points–one word errors were made more frequently when children pointed with a microcomputer pen than with their finger in the usual way, on larger than on smaller rows, and when the color of objects in a row was the same rather than different. However, these variables do not seem necessarily to predict more multiple points–one word errors, for children had a fairly low rate of such errors when counting the long rows of same colored blocks in Increasing Row. There was some indication that more multiple points–one word errors are made by younger rather than by older children and by 3-year-olds on the last rather than on the first or on the middle objects in a row. Thus, when a counting situation does elicit more pointing, it may be especially difficult for young children to stop such extra pointing, resulting in higher rates for the last object counted. These errors do violate both the word–point and the point–object correspondences, but they do not create an error in the cardinality result, because one word still corresponds to one object. However, because the rate of such errors decreases considerably for older children, it does not seem likely that younger children make such errors because they realize that they are not really errors. Further research concerning these errors seems to be required, including when children understand that these errors do not affect cardinality.

6.2.4.2. Skim Errors. About half the youngest children in each study except the Disorganized study sometimes skimmed their finger along a row, saying number words in a haphazard fashion and not pointing at specific objects. Every such child spontaneously pointed at specific objects on at least one trial, so such skim errors are not a consistent form of behavior. This indicates that by age 3 children are able to construct and use perceptual unit items in counting. Children made skim errors at higher rates on larger than on smaller rows, and younger children made more skim errors than did older children. Children made more skim errors when the toys counted were homogeneous (all the objects in a row were identical) than when they were heterogeneous. Increasing counting effort decreased skim errors considerably. Skim errors are highly concentrated on a few trials; when a child skimmed, most of the objects in an array would be involved. Thus, skim errors seem to be primarily a degenerate form of counting in which some children engage on trials on which they lose interest (e.g., in homogeneous arrays) or get discouraged (larger arrays).

6.2.5. Recount Errors

Recount errors were made quite infrequently when counting objects in rows. Thus, even by age 3, most children most of the time begin counting at one end of a row and move consistently down the row in one direction. In a disorganized array, avoiding recount errors requires one to remember just which objects one has already counted. The rate of recount errors rose very dramatically when children counted large disorganized arrays. Every child aged 3 to 6 made at least one such error, and children in the half-year age groups between 3 and 5 had recount means ranging between one of every four and one of every eight objects recounted. This large number of recounted objects was partly due to the use by some children of a "circumference" strategy in which they counted a wide swath of blocks on around the edge of the array. Some children continued to count on and on around a disorganized array, not even stopping approximately where they had started counting.

6.3. Effects of Variables on Correspondence Errors

6.3.1. Age

Children aged 3 to 3½ make a considerable number of errors of the six kinds listed in Table 6-3 and also make flurry errors in which they rapidly direct a burst of points and of words along a row or around a disorganized array without the points being directed at specific objects or the words accompanying specific points. All children who made flurry errors also pointed and said words in reasonable correspondence on other trials, so this seems to be a degenerate form of counting for children aged 3 and older, perhaps reflecting frustration or impatience to complete the session. The rate of most errors drops at least somewhat at age 3½ and continues to drop at every half year after that. Five-year-olds have quite low rates of correspondence errors, except for errors that violate the overall point–object correspondence in disorganized arrays and thus require remembering just which objects one has already counted (object skipped/uncounted and recount errors). Age had a significant effect in at least one study on five of the six prevalent error types (see Table 6-3 for a summary of these age effects). In at least one study, point–no word and multiple words–one point errors showed a sharp drop at age 3½, point–no word and object skipped and multiple count errors showed a sharp drop at age 4, and multiple count errors and object skipped/uncounted errors (in disorganized arrays) showed a sharp drop at age 4½. There was no effect of age on recount errors.

Over all the studies the percentage of children making at least one error of a given type generally dropped more slowly than did the rate of making that error. This pattern indicates that learning to count primarily involves gradual improvement rather than sudden insights in which a given error type drops entirely out of a child's repertoire, for the latter case requires the age effects on the percentage measures to parallel those on the rate measures.

One obvious feature of counting that is strongly associated with age is the internalization of counting around age 5 or 6. Both action parts of counting immovable objects—pointing and saying number words—undergo progressive internalization with age. Pointing may move from touching to pointing near objects to pointing from a distance to using eye fixation. Saying number words moves from saying audible words to making readable lip movements to making abbreviated and unreadable lip movements to silent mental production of number words. This first internalization of counting may result in less accurate counting, although internalized counting does evidently become as accurate as external counting in many situations. The internalization of counting is an interesting example of the internalization of a cognitive procedure as discussed for speech in general by Vygotsky (1962, 1978, 1986) and even follows his proposal of reexternalization of the cognitive procedure when the task is difficult (see 3.3.11).

Clearly, there are developmental changes from age 3 to age 6 in some fundamental cognitive abilities of young children, for example in attention, memory, motor organization, and spatial strategies for ordering objects. There also seem to be developmental changes in specific knowledge about counting, for example knowledge of the sequence of number words (chapter 2) and knowledge of what constitutes accurate counting (chapter 10). At the moment we know very little about how these developmental changes affect specific counting errors except to note that most errors decrease linearly and considerably with age.

6.3.2. Sex of the Counter

The effect of the sex of the counter was examined in the large Increasing Row sample for children between 3½ and 6. No significant effect of sex and no interaction of sex with age or with location was found for any error subtype or main type.

6.3.3. Number of Objects in a Row

Fairly consistently across studies, children aged 3 to 4½ made more object skipped, multiple count, and skim errors per 100 objects counted in rows with a large number of objects than per 100 objects counted in rows with a smaller number of objects.[7] The effect was in the same direction but not so consistent for point–no word and multiple points–one word errors; these each had higher error rates on rows with a larger number than on rows with a smaller number of objects in one study but had equivalent rates in the other studies. Multiple words–one point error rates were higher in small rows in two studies and higher in large rows in another study; none of these differences was significant because the variability of these errors was so great. Children aged 4½ to 6 did not show effects of number of objects across the sets 15 to 19, 20 to 24, and 25 to 29, so the effect of number of objects in a row may be limited to younger children.

6.3.4. Proximity of Objects in a Row

The proximity of objects (¼ inch apart vs. farther than the width of the object apart) did not significantly affect the rate of any specific error subtype. However, both kinds of frequent point–object errors (object skipped and multiple count errors) had higher rates when objects were close than when they were farther apart, and this effect was significant when these errors were pooled as point–object errors. Proximity also interacted with location of error for point–object errors. When objects were close, children made a higher rate of errors on objects in the middle than on the last object; when objects were farther apart, the error rate on the last object was greater than the error rate on a middle object.

6.3.5. Homogeneity of Objects

Heterogeneity rather than homogeneity of objects seems to increase multiple count and multiple words–one point errors. These results are discussed in 6.2.2.2 with respect to a hypothesis about heterogeneity increasing the number of words said.

Heterogeneity of objects also seems to decrease the rate of skim errors relative to homogeneous objects. This was especially true for children hearing

---

[7] Recall that this error rate measure controls for the different number of objects in larger and in smaller arrays. A finding of a higher error rate in a larger than in a smaller row means that it is more likely that an error will be made *on each object* in the larger array than *on each object* in the smaller array. See footnote 3 for further clarification.

class terms (e.g., animals, pigs, blocks, soliders) for the larger (9, 12, and 14) arrays; children hearing collection terms (e.g., animal party, pig family, pile, army) had much lower rates of skim errors for both homogeneous and heterogeneous arrays. These results might be accounted for by differences in effort (see 6.3.7, following). Identical objects or objects described in the usual class rather than the less usual collection terms might seem less different and interesting; children might then make less effort in counting them and thus make more skim errors.

6.3.6. Verbal Label: Class or Collection Terms

The verbal label (class terms—animals, pigs, blocks, soldiers—vs. collection terms—animal party, pig family, pile, army) used to describe objects was involved in the interaction with homogeneity and number of objects for skim errors described in 6.2.4.2 and was involved in other interactions with age and with number of objects. For larger sets (9, 12, and 14) but not for smaller sets (4, 5, and 6), children hearing collection terms had lower rates of word–point and dual errors and higher rates of point–object errors than did children hearing class terms. These patterns are partly dependent on triple interactions with age reported in 5.2.2.3 for multiple words–one point errors and in 5.2.2.4 for object skipped errors; these are not summarized here, because the number of children involved is so small. These results require replication.

6.3.7. Effects of Effort

In the Increasing Row study, errors made on trials in which experimenters judged that children were not trying hard were contrasted with errors made on immediately following trials in which experimenters told the children to "try really hard." The error raates of most error subtypes were reduced at least somewhat by increased effort. Particularly large decreases due to effort occurred for the object skipped, skim, and flurry subtypes. The amount of such effort and attention expended on a given counting trial can affect performance quite considerably. Controlling effort and attention across studies and across manipulated variables therefore is a challenge. For example, it may be that some of the increased rates of errors when counting arrays with a large number of objects stem from discouragement and from a resulting lower effort expended in counting these larger arrays.

6.3.8. Location of Objects: First Objects, Middle Objects, or Last Objects

One general cognitive development issue pertinent to counting is the extent to which counting displays the particular difficulty that young children seem to have in starting and in stopping activities (Fuson, 1979b; Luria, 1959, 1961; Zivin, 1979). Gelman and Gallistel (1978) discussed this issue and concluded that the ends of the activity of counting present special difficulty with respect to establishing accurate correspondences:

> Difficulty occurs to some extent at the starting of a count and to a larger extent at the stopping of a count. A child may start to point before he starts to recite tags, or vice versa; and if he does he may take some time to get beyond the first item. But then things proceed smoothly. Trouble reappears only when he nears the end of a count. He may run over or under by one item—but not two, three, four or more items. (p. 205)

We pursued this issue with two kinds of analyses. One type compared the rate at which children made an error on the first, the last, and all middle objects (all those not first or last in the row). An error rate measure of the number of errors made in counting 100 first objects, 100 middle objects, and 100 last objects was used in order to control for the fact that in all rows with more than three objects there are more middle than first or last objects.[8] The error types in Table 6-2 were completely crossed with location: each kind of error was coded over all three locations. In the coding system used in Gelman and Gallistel (1978), some kinds of errors changed categories depending on whether the error was made at the ends or in the middle of counting; this made it quite difficult to understand the effects of location on particular kinds of errors.

All studies were similar in one respect: the very *first* object in a row was the object on which it was *least* likely that children would make an error. On the very long rows of the Increasing Row study, children had higher error rates for a middle than for a last object for every kind of error. For other studies with smaller rows, the relationship between the last- and middle-object error rates varied. In at least one study, point–no word, object skipped, multiple points–one word, and skim errors had significantly higher error rates for a middle than for a last object. In the other studies, error rates were also non-significantly higher for a middle than for a last object for object skipped and skim errors. For one study the point–no word last-object error rate was non-significantly higher than the middle-object rate, and this was also true for 3-year-olds in one study for multiple points–one word errors. Multiple words–one point errors and multiple count errors showed a different pattern. In two studies the multiple words–one point error rate was significantly higher on last than on middle objects, and in two studies the multiple count error rate was nonsignificantly higher on last than on middle objects. Objects being spaced apart rather than close together may increase multiple count errors on the last object, and objects being different colors rather than the same color may increase multiple words–one point errors on the last object.

---

[8] These rates were calculated by dividing the number of errors on a first object by the number of first objects counted and multiplying by 100, dividing the number of errors on a last object by the number of last objects counted and multiplying by 100, and dividing the number of errors on all objects not first or last by the number of such objects counted and multiplying by 100. Each rate was multiplied by 100 to avoid dealing with small decimal numbers.

One variable that might affect the relationship between the rate of middle- and last-object errors more generally is whether a given row is counted over again. In the Color Homogeneity study, each row was counted twice: counted once and immediately recounted. Twice as many last-object errors occurred on the second count of a row as on the first count. Thus, recounting a row over and over may, for some reason, increase the rate of errors made on the last object in the row. Because each row was recounted five times in Gelman and Gallistel (1978), this factor might have contributed to a high last-object error rate in that study.

A second type of analysis was done for the three studies with smaller rows of objects on which the middle-object error rate did not always exceed the last-object error rate. Each counting trial was examined to determine whether it met the description of more errors at the end or at the beginning than in the middle of counting (i.e., more errors on the first or on the last than on a middle object). Few trials met this description. The description that fit most of the counting trials on which an error occurred for children aged 3 and older and that fit nearly all of the counting of larger rows is that counting begins smoothly, difficulty occurs to some extent in the middle of the count, and accuracy then reappears at the end of a count, although children do have considerably more difficulty at the end than at the beginning of a count.

6.3.9. Location of Objects in the First or Second Half of the Row

For both 3- and 4-year-olds, many more errors in which an extra word or extra point or both were produced (multiple words–one point, multiple count, and multiple point–one word errors) occurred on the second than on the first half of a row, even when errors on the first and last object were disregarded.[9] Skim errors also occurred more frequently on objects in the second half of a row. Errors in which a point or a word or both were omitted (point–no word and object skipped errors) tended to be distributed fairly equally over the first and second half of a row. The reason for this pattern is not evident.

6.4. Effects of Object Arrangement

6.4.1. Counting Disorganized Arrays Versus Rows

There were increases in three kinds of errors children aged 3 through 5 made in counting large disorganized arrays compared to counting large rows. Recount errors (counting an object again after at least one other object has been counted) were rarely made in rows but were made on a mean of about one in

---

[9] The analysis was also done excluding the first and the last object because error rates were usually higher on the last than on the first object.

every six objects in disorganized arrays. Object skipped/uncounted errors increased from about one in ten objects in rows to about one in seven objects in disorganized arrays; in the disorganized arrays this category included many objects never counted (i.e., not necessarily skipped over by a finger) while virtually all the row errors were objects skipped over by the pointing finger. Part word–one point errors in which one number word was stretched out over two or more objects (each receiving one point) were quite rare in rows but increased quite considerably in the disorganized arrays. The first two errors clearly increased because of the increased demand in disorganized arrays to remember just which objects have already been counted; children were not very successful in meeting this demand. It is interesting that this point–object memory demand also affected the production of number words and increased the part word–one point errors.

6.4.2. Use of a Stop-Rule in Counting Circular Arrays

Most children aged 2½ to 6 demonstrated knowledge of a stop-rule when counting objects arranged in a circular loop; that is, they did not consistently go counting on and on around the circle, although many of them had some problems in executing the stop-rule consistently or exactly. When spatial location was the only cue for the starting object and the sets counted were large (circular loops consisting of 16, 17, or 18 homogeneous dots), children aged 3½ to 6 were not able to stop exactly on the last dot very often (on only about one in five trials). They did stop within two dots before or after the last dot on about half of the trials. Therefore, their memory for the location of their starting dot seems to be a reasonable but not exact estimate. When the starting object was made very obviously different (a different color) from the other objects counted and the circles were small (6, 7, and 8 dots), most children aged 2½ to 3½ used a stop-rule at least once, and about half of these children consistently stopped correctly on the object just before the starting dot. After a short explanation and demonstration of the stop-rule, all children used it on at least one trial, and all but one child stopped correctly on at least two of the three trials. These results are limited by the use of the color red for the starting object, which might have conveyed a stop meaning to some children, and by the fact that some children in the original sample refused to participate in the study, and thus the sample might have been weighted toward the better counters in this age span. The extent to which children this young can execute the stop-rule without a salient cue such as the different-colored dot is also, of course, not established by this study.

6.4.3. Errors Made When Moving Objects as the Indicating Act

When asked how many blocks were in a pile of 50 blocks, only about half the children aged 3½ to 5½ moved blocks from an uncounted to a counted pile while counting them; the others pointed at the blocks without moving them. Most of the children aged 5½ to 6 did move the blocks while counting them, so perhaps there is an increased tendency with age to move objects when possible; this, of course, is the easiest and most accurate indicating act for movable objects. Four new kinds of errors were observed when moving objects rather than pointing was the indicating act. Three of these seemed to result at least partly from the tendency of children to make something with the blocks they moved into the "counted blocks" pile. Some children made towers, rows, and other constructions with the counted blocks. In some cases their attention came to be focused more on these constructions and on the counted blocks than on the uncounted blocks. Thus, some children stopped saying number words while moving blocks to the counted blocks pile (i.e., made many successive moving object–no word errors), some stopped counting when a particular construction was completed rather than when all the uncounted blocks were counted (and thus had many uncounted errors), and some counted parts of the whole pile of 50 blocks, starting with the number word "one" as they started each new construction with counted blocks. All of these errors might have been increased by the use of blocks as the objects to count. A fourth new error was an indicating act–multiple objects error: Children sometimes moved whole handfuls of blocks to the counted blocks pile while saying only one number word. The fact that such an error is very difficult to make with pointing suggests that sometimes we may infer more understanding about correct counting than children actually possess when they use pointing as the indicating act because pointing constrains the kinds of errors children can make. Some children also were not successful in keeping the pile of counted blocks separated from the pile of uncounted blocks, resulting in some blocks being recounted and some blocks remaining uncounted. Therefore, for children less than 5½, several problems are associated with moving objects as the indicating act, including the seeming reluctance of many children to use this act.

When the indicating act was moving objects, children usually met all four requirements of indicating act–object correspondence (see 6.1), but they did sometimes violate each of the last three requirements. In contrast, children when pointing rarely violate the first requirement either for rows or disorganized arrays and never violate the second requirement (unless one wishes to consider skim errors such a violation). For objects in rows children somewhat frequently violate the third and fourth requirements locally by skipping over objects and by counting them again immediately but rarely violate these requirements overall. When pointing at objects in disorganized arrays, children violate the third and fourth requirements locally by skipping over objects and counting them again immediately and also violate these overall by failing to establish a linear ordering or another adequate strategy for remembering which objects have been counted and thus recounting many objects and leaving many objects uncounted.

6.5. The Accuracy of Children's Correspondences in Counting

For four chapters, we have been discussing the correspondence errors children make in counting. The many kinds of errors that can be and are made emphasize how difficult it is consistently to coordinate the indicating act with the number words and with the objects to be counted. However, perhaps even more striking is how very good young children are at this complex act when the objects are arranged in a row. This is reflected by the fact that we had to multiply raw errors by 100 to get an error rate measure that consisted of whole numbers. The sum of all correspondence errors made when counting objects in rows varied considerably across studies because of the effects of the variables previously discussed. In the easiest study (Proximity, with rows from 4 to 14), children aged 3 to 3½, 3½ to 4, and 4 to 4½ had correct correspondences on 84%, 94%, 97% of the objects, respectively. In the most difficult study (the long rows of Disorganized), these age groups still had correct correspondences on 56%, 64%, and 71% of the objects, and children aged 4½ to 5, 5 to 5½, and 5½ to 6 had correct correspondences on these long rows on 80%, 93%, and 89% of the objects. Of course, these figures do not guarantee that the *counting* is as accurate as the correspondences. Accurate counting also depends on producing an accurate sequence of number words. The accuracy of young children's counting, including both correct correspondences and correct number-word sequences, is discussed in chapter 10.

6.6. Remaining Questions

These studies clearly established the fact that correspondence errors are subject to the influence of many variables. Consequently, counting research will have to pay careful attention to such variables. These studies clarified which errors are made most frequently but made little progess in ascertaining why children make these errors rather than others. They did not begin to address fundamental issues such as whether correspondence errors for a given child are relatively stable over repeated counting in similar situations and whether stable individual differences exist among children. The latter possibility suggests interesting relationships such as that children with high verbal ability might make more errors that involve extra words (multiple words–one point and multiple count errors). The studies did not examine the extent to which the decrease in errors with age is due to increased understanding of what constitutes correct counting, to increased skill in counting that comes with practice, and to improvements in underlying motor-organizational and visuo-spatial abilities. Future research might profitably be addressed toward all of these issues. Another area of needed research is how children's counting might be improved. Training studies that test different approaches might also illuminate some of these issues. Finally, two kinds of counting situations have received little attention. Counting movable objects using the indicating act of moving objects was only explored in one study, and counting objects existing only in time (e.g., clock chimes, flashing lights) was not even explored.

Part III   Concepts of Cardinality

7. Children's Early Knowledge About Relationships Between Counting and Cardinality

With James W. Hall

7.1. Introduction

Counting and cardinal situations are at first separate and different situations for children. A given situation is either a cardinal situation (to which a single number word is applied, as in "I have five people in my family.") or it is a counting situation (in which counting is carried out but with no end result). A very important step is taken when children first begin to connect counting and cardinal meanings, when children first indicate that they understand that counting has a result instead of just being an isolated activity. The nature of these first relationships between counting and cardinality, and how these relationships come to be established by children, is the focus of this chapter. The following three chapters continue the exploration of relationships children establish between counting and cardinal meanings of number words. The more complex relationships between counting and cardinality that are established after the first simple ones and that enable children to devise increasingly sophisticated solution procedures for addition and subtraction are discussed in chapter 8. Chapter 9 outlines the roles counting plays in children's construction of equivalence and order relations on cardinal situations. Chapter 10 presents data on relationships between aspects of children's ability to say number words, count objects, and relate counting to cardinal meanings. These chapters permit us to follow young children from age 2, when they understand only very small numerosities, to age 8, when they have constructed a general and abstract notion of cardinal number.

One task has been used in the literature to assess children's first understanding of the relationship between counting and cardinality. This task is to have a child count some objects (e.g., pennies) and then answer the question "How many pennies are there?" Of interest is whether the child answers with the last word the child said in counting. Note that the last word does not have to be the correct cardinality of the pennies, that is, understanding that the last counted word has a special significance may be independent of the ability to count accurately. Answering this question with the last counted word was called use of the "cardinality rule" by Schaeffer, Eggleston, and Scott (1974) and the "cardinal principle" by Gelman and Gallistel (1978). There are different positions on how children come to this first connection between counting and cardinality and even on what understanding this first connection entails. Five different positions are outlined. Then, because the data to be presented in this chapter are somewhat complex, we briefly summarize our results so that they can guide the reader through the presentation and discussion of the data. The studies undertaken in this area are then described, and the results are presented organized with respect to their support or lack of support for each of the five positions. To facilitate a neutral discussion of these positions, we call accurate responding to the how-many question task "last-word responding." The chapter closes with a summary of the results concerning how children establish the first relationships between counting and cardinality.

7.2. Five Positions Concerning the Origins of Last-Word Responding

Schaeffer et al. (1974) hypothesized that last-word responding is learned by children as they subitize (immediately apprehend the numerosity of) a very small set (2, 3, or 4), count that same set, and then notice that the last word said in counting is the same as the subitized word for that set. Klahr and Wallace (1976) also noted the possible importance of children being able to verify their counting result for very small sets by subitizing those sets. Schaeffer et al. suggested that children then later generalize last-word responding to somewhat larger sets when the counting of these somewhat larger sets is accurate; otherwise this extension would be contradicted by other people. Schaeffer et al. did not specify how long after the initial discovery of last-word responding it took to make the generalization to somewhat larger sets or when a generalization to much larger sets might occur.

Gelman and Gallistel (1978) proposed a different account in which the initial development of last-word responding (the cardinality principle[1])—as well as its generalization to larger sets—is tied to accurate counting. In this view preschool children have implicit understanding of three "how-to-count" principles, and their knowledge about counting and their ability to count does not depend on subitizing. The first two counting principles concern accurate counting, and the third principle (the cardinality principle) is marked by last-word responding. Gelman and Gallistel found that last-word responding decreased markedly with increasing set size, as did accurate counting. They posited that children monitor their counting and when the counting is no longer accurate, children stop giving last-word responses. The cardinality principle thus seems to entail considerable understanding both of counting (so as to be able to assess one's accuracy) and of the relationships between counting and cardinality (knowing that a counting error will affect the cardinality). This dependence of the cardinality principle on accurate counting was reiterated in a later discussion (Gelman, 1982b): "And because their application of the cardinality principle depends on applying the one-one and

---

[1] Gelman used the term *cardinality principle* in the more recent paper Greeno, Riley, and Gelman (1983). We use *cardinality principle* rather than the original term *cardinal principle* because of its consistency with the term *cardinality rule* and because of its lack of ambiguity (*cardinal principle* could be the first or most important principle).

the stable-order principle,[2] they obviously must be using these as well" (p. 189). In this later discussion (Gelman, 1982b), a reason other than monitoring the counting is also suggested for the decrease in use of the cardinality principle with increasing set size: "Gelman and Gallistel concluded that the performance demands of counting larger and larger set sizes became too great. Thus, a child forgot to repeat the last tag." (p. 186). This approach does not really explicate how children learn last-word responding, but it does specify that this learning does not depend on subitizing and does depend on accurate counting.

Fuson and Hall (1983) suggested that there are at least two levels of understanding involved in correct last-word responding. The first level involves learning a simple relationship: Count and then give the last count word when asked "How many Xs are there?" This rule involves a cardinal meaning only in that the number word is given as the answer to the how-many question and the question refers to a set of entities; however, the final count word given as the answer to the question may not *for the child* involve any reference to the set of entities as a whole or to the cardinality of the set. Such last-word responses are nevertheless an important step, for they are the first *use* of counting. A higher level of understanding involves what Fuson and Hall termed a "count-to-cardinal[3] transition" in word meaning in which the child actually means the answer given to the question to refer to the set as a whole and, more specifically, to the cardinality of the set. The term "count-to-cardinal transition" was used because Fuson and Hall postulated that in this higher level of last-word responding, the child actually makes a shift (a *transition*) from the *counting meaning* elicited when the word is said in counting (i.e., its meaning as referring to the object with which it is paired in the act of counting) to a *cardinal meaning* of the word when it is given as the response to the how-many question. That is, when asked "How-many Xs are there?," a child first thinks of the how-many question as a count directive and therefore considers the object situation as a counting situation; the child counts, with each number word having as a referent a single object. At the end of counting, a mental reconstruction of the situation (what we called in chapter 1 a "cardinal integration of perceptual unit items") must occur in which the child no longer considers the situation as a counting situation of separate entities (in which each number word refers to a single entity) but as a cardinal situation in which a number word refers to *all* of the entities. At this higher level the final reference of the word given as the answer to the how-many question is a cardinal reference (it refers to the manyness of the set as a whole) and is not just a referentless response to the how-many question. The terms "cardinality rule" as used by Schaeffer et al. (1974) and "cardinality principle" as

---

[2] These two principles underlie accurate counting.

[3] The term *count-cardinal* transition was used in Fuson and Hall (1983). We use *count-to-cardinal* transition to clarify the direction of the shift because we wish to discuss shifts in the opposite direction in the next chapter.

used by Gelman and Gallistel (1978) seem to imply knowledge at this second level, that is, knowledge that the last counted word refers to the set as a whole and to the cardinality of that set. The first two positions thus also entail assumptions that children move directly to this second higher level. Fuson and Hall did not hypothesize how children might move from their first to their second level nor did they specify whether all children go through the first level.

A fourth possibility, the role of memory, was raised by Pergament and Fuson (1982) and by Fuson and Hall (1983). We would place this role of memory within the general cognitive developmental framework of Case (1985b) and suggest that very young preschoolers may simply not have enough processing space both to count and to remember the last word said in counting. Wilkinson (1984) presented a related analysis of counting in which accurate counting and last-word responding might compete for processing space, with accurate counting being produced on certain trials and last-word responding being produced on different trials. Wilkinson also proposed that accurate counting appeared before last-word responding in very small sets but that children were able to give last-word responses for very large sets while being unable to count such sets accurately. Both of these accounts implicate the general cognitive developmental level of a child and the level of automaticity of the counting procedure, for these two factors interact to predict performance in these working memory approaches.

A fifth possibility for the origin of last-word responding was also suggested by Fuson and Hall (1983), although their focus was on the reliability of counting rather than only on last-word responding. This possibility is that children may be taught last-word responding by parents, siblings, peers, teachers, and so on. It seems possible that an emphasis on cardinality in such teaching might move a child straight to a count-to-cardinal transition or that a lack of such emphasis would result only in last-word responding with no cardinal reference to the situation as a whole.

7.3. Origins of Last-Word Responding: An Overview of the Results of This Chapter

Some aspects of each of the positions were supported by the data presented in this chapter, although some positions had to be modified considerably. No position fit all children. Rather, children seem to follow different routes to last-word responding. Some children fit a modified version of the Schaeffer et al. (1974) subitize and count description: they first gave a last-word response on a set they could subitize. However, they immediately generalized last-word responding to nonsubitizable sets, and they did not have to count accurately to make this generalization. Furthermore, children varied in the sets they could subitize, with many unable to subitize sets of 3 and most unable to subitize sets of 4. There was also little evidence of subitizing during the how-many question task, even of those sets which a child could subitize.

There was no evidence of the precipitous decline in last-word responding reported by Gelman and Gallistel (1978). Nor did last-word responding require accurate counting. There was some evidence of performance demands interfering with last-word responding. Also as proposed, neither last-word responding nor accurate counting required subitizing.

Many children do seem at first to learn only the first Fuson and Hall (1983) level of last-word responding, where the last word does not seem to refer to the set as a whole or to its cardinality. Children clearly also do move on to the count-to-cardinal transition, probably sometime during age 4. At both levels, children give last-word responses consistently across set sizes; thus, the words "rule" or "principle" do seem appropriate at either level, although "cardinality" may be appropriate only at the second level. The strong recency bias of young children, that is, the tendency to give the last stated answer, and the echoic salience of the last counted word may be the source of children's first last-word responses.

Memory does not seem to be a major limiting factor in last-word responding; many children who did not give last-word responses were able to recall the word they had said when counting the last object in the row. Nor did there seem to be a competition for cognitive resources between counting and last-word responding, as suggested by Wilkinson (1984); few children showed a pattern of production of each of these across different trials. Accurate counting and last-word responding did show the relationship across set size (and thus the derived developmental relationship) proposed by Wilkinson: children counted very small sets accurately before they gave last-word responses on them but they began to give last-word responses consistently even for very large sets before they could count them accurately.

The success of a minimal training session indicates that children may learn last-word responding through brief instruction from parents, siblings, and so on. Developmental and performance data on incorrect last-word responses indicate that older children not yet giving last-word responses and children easily taught last-word responding seem to be "searching around" for the correct answer to the how-many question: They recount on some trials and give a single number word or a sequence of number words on other trials.

7.4. The Origins Study: The Origins of Last-Word Responding

7.4.1. A Description of the Study

The subitize and count position was examined by obtaining separate measures of last-wording responding and of subitizing. Last-word responding was measured for very small subitizable sets (2, 3, 4) and for small sets just beyond the subitizing range (5, 6, 7). Children who gave last-word responses for these sets were also given the last-word response task for very large sets (19, 23, 26). Accuracy of counting was assessed on all last-word response trials. For the last-word response trials, children were first directed to count and were asked "How many Xs are there?" after their counting was completed so that last-word responding would not depend on their remembering while they were counting that they were to tell how many objects there were.

The preceding measures permitted an assessment of the Gelman and Gallistel (1978) position. The possibility that performance demands might interfere with last-word responding was evaluated by giving a second trial for all very large sets (19, 23, 26) to try to differentiate a momentary inability from a consistent inability to give last-word responses for such sets. Any task on which a child failed to perform adequately was also followed by a version of the task in which the experimenter did the counting to ascertain whether the performance demand of counting interfered with last-word responding.

The Fuson and Hall (1983) rule-learning position was assessed by determining the consistency of last-word responding across varied set sizes, the independence of last-word responding and accurate counting, the lack of dependence of last-word responding on subitizing, the nature of the reference of last-word responses, and the extent to which last-word responses were generally consistent with the cardinality of the given set.

The feasibility of children's learning last-word responding by being taught it by parents, siblings, etc. was explored by giving a short period of instruction to all children who did not spontaneously give last-word responses. A demonstration that such instruction is successful does not, of course, substitute for data indicating that children actually do receive such instruction in daily life, but it does indicate that this is a reasonable position and such instruction could be successful.

The present study explored the role of memory in two ways. First, answering the how-many question requires that the child recall the last word said in counting. It seems possible that, as with other phenomena, a child might be capable of recognizing the correct answer but not of recalling it, that is, of retrieving it from memory. Therefore, in the present study a failure to respond correctly to the how-many question was always followed by a forced-choice recognition how-many question. Likewise, whether children who did not demonstrate the last-word rule could remember the last word they said in counting was assessed first with a recall question and then with a recognition question, if a child did not recall the last counted word. However, recalling the last word one said in counting requires both an adequate memory of that word and the prerequisite ability to separate the last part of the counting activity (indicating the last object and saying a word) from the rest of the whole counting act. This in turn requires that the child be able to separate the last word from the whole sequence of words said in counting. Fuson et al. (1982) hypothesized that when children first learn to say the sequence of number words, that sequence is in the form of an undifferentiated "string" of words (like *LMNO* in early alphabet learning). It was not obvious to us how to distinguish behaviorally a child's ability to recall the last word from the ability to separate that last word (or the last part of the counting activity) from the other words (or other previous counting activity). Therefore, we regard this memory task as an assessment of a child's ability "to separate and to recall" the last word rather than just as an assessment of recall.

7.4.2. Subjects

The subjects were 42 middle-class and upper-middle-class 2- and 3-year-old children from a nursery school in Madison, Wisconsin. The 23 boys and 19 girls ranged in age from 2 years 4 months (2-4) through 3 years 11 months (3-11).

7.4.3. Tasks and Materials

7.4.3.1. How-Many Task With Objects. To motivate continued participation by the very young children in this study, each child was allowed to select the objects to be counted for each of the six trials in this task. Eleven piles of small objects (e.g., blocks, animals, dolls, trucks, pennies) were placed on the carpet in view of the child. Five piles contained identical objects, and six piles contained objects that differed in some way. Choice among these alternatives was permitted because Pergament and Fuson (1982) reported no differences in last-word responses or in counting accuracy between sets of homogeneous and of heterogeneous entities. After a child chose a groups of objects, the child closed his or her eyes (or turned away), and the experimenter placed the required number of objects in a straight line on an 11½ by 18-inch black "counting tray" on the floor between the child and the experimenter. The child was then instructed to open her eyes (or to turn around) and to "Count the *X*s (dolls, trucks, etc.)." Correspondence errors made in counting and errors in the number-word sequence were recorded as the child counted. The child was then asked, "How many *X*s are there?" If the child failed to respond to this question with the last word said in counting, the child was again told to count the objects and was then given a forced-choice how-many question; "Are there *a*, *b*, or *c X*s?" The last word that the child had actually used on that trial was always in the middle (i.e., was *b*) because Siegel and Goldstein (1969) reported a strong response bias by very young children toward the last item in a three-choice question. Values *a* and *c* were always the numbers one less than and one more than *b*; half the time *a* was the number one less than *b*, and half the time *a* was one more than *b*. Three of the six trials were of subitizable sets (two, three, and four), and three were of nonsubitizable small sets (five, six, and seven). Subitizable and nonsubitizable sets were alternated, with half the children receiving a subitizable set first.

7.4.3.2. How-Many Task With Stickers. This task was just like the how-many task with objects except that the stimuli were stickers such as stars, animals, and smiling faces, and three sizes of sets were used: subitizable (2, 3, 4), non-subitizable small (5, 6, 7), and very large (19, 23, 26). For each trial the child was shown a strip of while cardboard containing a row of one kind of stickers. The nine trials alternated in turn through the three sizes, and the order of this alternation was counterbalanced across children. For the very large sets, a failure to give a last-word response was followed by the instruction, "Count the Xs again, and tell me how many there are." This was done to distinguish those cases in which a failure was a momentary forgetting that a how-many question had been asked from those cases in which a child could not give a last-word response for such a large set.

On each of the last three trials, the how-many question was followed by a *count-reference question*: "Show me the star (face, duck) where you said n (the child's last counted word)" and by a *cardinality-reference question*: "Show me the n (child's last counted word) stars (faces, ducks)." If a child did not answer a question or answered a question in an ambiguous manner, a forced-choice version of the question was asked in which the child was forced to choose between the count and the cardinality references. "Is this the star where you said n (experimenter gesture *to the last counted star*) or is this the star where you said n (experimenter gesture to *the whole set*)?" was the forced-choice count-reference question. "Are these the n stars (gesture to *the last counted star*) or are these the n stars (gesture to *the whole set*)?" was the forced-choice cardinality-reference question. The order of pointing to the last counted object and to the whole set was counterbalanced across children. Half of the children always had the count-reference question first (followed if necessary by the forced-choice count-reference question) and then the cardinality-reference question (followed if necessary by the forced-choice cardinality question), and half had these questions in the opposite order.

7.4.3.3. Subitizing Task. Twelve 3 by 5-inch cards were used in this task. Two cards each displayed one star, two stars, a line of three stars, three non-linear stars, a line of four stars, and four nonlinear stars. The star cards were hidden behind a brightly colored "busy" postcard that served as a mask. In the "word" subitizing task, a star card was shown above the postcard for a very brief period and then hidden again by covering it with the masking card (the masking card moved up to the location of the star card). The child was asked to report how many stars there were. This continued until each of the 12 star cards had been shown to the child. In the "finger" subitizing task, the cards were presented in the same manner, but the child was asked to show the number of stars by raising the appropriate number of fingers. This version was used because in piloting the various tasks in the study, some children had responded with fingers rather than with words when asked how many stars were on the card. The word- and finger-subitizing tasks were given in counter-balanced order across children. Children were reminded to look at the postcard and to get ready for the next card; a card was shown only if the child was attending to the area where the star card would be shown. The cards were shuffled after each use so that the order differed across children.

7.4.3.4. Last-Word Memory Task. For each of the three trials in this task, the child selected the objects to count from the objects available for the first how-many task. While the child's eyes were hidden, the experimenter placed five, six, or seven objects in a straight line on the counting tray. After the child counted the objects, the experimenter directed, "Tell me what you said for this (experimenter pointed to the last object the child counted)." If the child did not respond correctly, the child was instructed to count the objects again and say what number had been said for this (experimenter pointed to last object). If the response was incorrect again, the child was told to count the objects once more and was given a forced-choice question about the number of objects: "Did you say *a*, *b*, or *c* for this (experimenter pointed to last object counted)," where *a*, *b*, and *c* were as in the how-many task with objects. Each child was given the trials in the order six, five, and then seven objects. Children who did not recall the last counted word were given the last-word memory task again with the experimenter doing the counting.

7.4.3.5. Last-Word Response Teaching. The last-word response teaching consisted of two verbal statements of the rule (one at the beginning and one at the end of instruction) and three demonstrations of its use. The experimenter put out a line of six blocks on the counting tray and said, "When you count, the last word you say tells you how many things there are. Watch me, one, two, three, four, five, six (experimenter counts blocks). *Six.* There are *six* blocks (experimenter gestures in a narrow ellipse over the set of six blocks). Watch again." The demonstration was repeated for five pigs and for seven pennies. The experimenter then said, "So the *last* word you say in counting tells you how many things you have."

7.4.3.6. How-Many Task on Five, Six, and Seven Objects. After the last-word response teaching, three trials of a how-many question were given to see if children had learned to give last-word responses. The procedure was identical to that for the how-many task with objects, except that only set sizes five, six, and seven were used. The very small sets were not used to ensure that children were not answering the how-many question merely by subitizing the very small sets.

7.4.3.7. How-Many Task on Five, Six, and Seven Objects With Experimenter Counting. If a child did not give a last-word response on the how-many task on five, six, and seven objects, that task was given again, except that here the experimenter did the counting and then asked the how-many question. This task was given because it was thought possible that some children who did not give last-word responses when they counted might be able to give last-word responses when attention and operational capacity were freed by having the experimenter do the counting.

7.4.4. Procedure

Children were tested individually in a small room in their nursery school. Testing was completed in anywhere from one to four sessions. Testing was interrupted when children refused to continue or were not attending to tasks (or asked to have their diapers changed). Testing resumed on a different day by repeating the last trial that had been given on the earlier day. All children were given a colored 3 by 5-inch file card of a color of their choice and were allowed to select from a range of choices three small colorful stickers to put on *their* card. This reward proved to be extremely effective in motivating children to return to complete the testing and to stick with testing on a given day. The three stickers were given out at different times for different children in ways that would support attention and effort at the tasks. Total testing time ranged from 15 to 35 minutes.

The how-many task with objects was given first to all children. Subsequent tasks depended on a child's performance and were given following the flow chart in Figure 7-1. Recording sheets for the various task and the flow chart

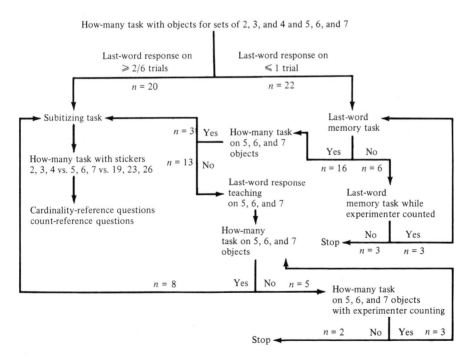

Figure 7-1. Flowchart showing the order of tasks (Origin study) and the number of children completing each task successfully.

used by the experimenter were color coded to permit rapid and accurate execution at decision points. This was a very complex experiment to run and required a very intelligent experimenter who was also excellent with small children.[4]

7.5. The Forced-Choice Count-Cardinality Reference Study

7.5.1. Description of the Study

Some children in the Origins study who were asked to demonstrate a counting reference and a cardinality reference for a number word gave more ambiguous demonstrations for cardinality than for counting. It seemed possible that the children were less familiar with a way to demonstrate a cardinality reference to a whole set than with a way to demonstrate a counting reference to a single entity. To control for this possible difference, another study was undertaken in which children were asked three-part forced-choice questions for both references. These questions were added to one of the last-word response studies we reported in Fuson, Pergament, and Lyons (1985, Experiment 3).[5]

7.5.2. Method

Twenty-six middle- and upper-middle-class children ranging in age from 3 years 2 months through 4 years 9 months and attending a preschool in Evanston, IL, served as subjects.

Four dolls, five animals, five pigs, and six blocks were the objects to be counted in last-word response trials. Children were directed to count and were then asked "How many Xs are there?" If a child did not give the last counted word when asked the how-many question, the question was repeated once. The order of the objects was counterbalanced across children.

Forced-choice count-reference and cardinality-reference questions were asked at the end of the fourth trial, and two additional trials containing such

---

[4] I was very fortunate to find a psychology major at the University of Wisconsin-Madison who met this description. Thanks, Ginny Neal.

[5] Three studies examined the finding of Markman (1979) that collection terms (army, pig family, pile) induced more last-word responding than did the usual class terms (soldiers, pigs, blocks). Our results are discussed in 7.6.2.4. There seemed to be some possibility that the verbal label might affect the responses to the counting-reference and cardinality-reference questions; for example, the collection terms might make the conceptual aggregate more salient and thus improve performance on the cardinality-reference questions. Therefore, the results were analyzed separately by verbal-label condition. No significant effect of verbal label and no interaction with verbal label was found. Therefore, the results in the text are pooled across the verbal-label conditions.

questions were given. The objects for these two trials were soldiers and plastic colored chips. Thus, there were three initial trials to assess last-word responding and then three trials on which both last-word responding and responses to count and cardinality reference questions were obtained.

The *count-reference question* was "Is this the soldier (chip) where you said *n*?", where *n* was the last number said by the child. The experimenter asked this question three times (the questions were connected by "or") and pointed to the last item, the next-to-last item, and all the items in the row. The *cardinality-reference question* was "Are these the *n* soldiers (chips)?", where *n* was the last number word the child had said when counting the row. The experimenter asked this question three times (the questions were connected by "or") and pointed to all of the items, all but the last item, and the last item. Both questions were of forced-choice form, with the child being forced to select one of the three choices. The correct choice was always in the middle, as Siegel and Goldstein (1969) reported a strong bias toward choosing the last alternative in children this age, and we had found such a bias in the Origins study. The two incorrect choices were counterbalanced (first and last) across children, and half the children always received the count-reference question first (the two types of counterbalancing were crossed).

We realized that even though the questions followed immediately the child's how-many response, the child's response to them did not necessarily reflect the child's construction of the context at the time of the last-word response but only at the time of the questions. Children's ability to answer such questions nevertheless seemed to be of interest. If a child could not choose the correct cardinality reference from the three choices, it seemed unlikely that the child was spontaneously making a count-to-cardinal transition.

7.6. Results of the Two Studies and Other Recent Literature Related to Each Position

7.6.1. The Subitize-and-Count Position

7.6.1.1. Do Children Subitize and Count to Give Last-Word Responses? In the Origins study 20 of the 42 children gave last-word responses on two or more of the six trials of the first how-many task with objects. Twelve children gave last-word responses from the first trial onward; their age ranged from 2-4 to 3-10, with a mean age of 3-3. Eight children seemed to discover last-word responding during the task, beginning to give such responses between the second and fifth trials, and giving them consistently thereafter; they ranged in age from 2-7 to 3-11, with a mean age of 3-2. The response patterns of three of these eight "discoverers" fit a subitize and count pattern: they gave their first last-word response on a set which they later (on the subitizing task) showed they could subitize (on a set of two, two, and three), respectively. One of these three children clearly subitized the set of two before counting; the other two did not clearly subitize, but they could have done so, as indicated by their later subitizing task performance. However, all three children *immediately* generalized last-word responding—they used it on the very next trial on a nonsubitizable set and on all trials thereafter. The behavior of two of these three children on the subsequent how-many task with stickers was also consistent with a subitize and count account. They either gave last-word responses on all nine trials (i.e., the generalization was immediately also made to the very large sets and was applied consistently) or last-word responses were not given on initial trials (the intervening subitizing task seemingly having made the child forget the discovery) but were again first given on a set subitizable by that child (i.e., it was "rediscovered" on such a set). The third child began to give last-word responses on a set of 19. Thus, some children do seem to follow a subitize and count approach, but they immediately generalize last-word responding both to sets just larger than subitizable sets and to very large sets.

The response patterns on the original task for the remaining five "discoverers" did not fit a subitize and count account on either the how-many task with objects or with stickers: the first trial on which the how-many question was answered with the last counted word was not a set subitizable by that child. These set sizes and the last words actually said by the child in counting the set (and also then in answering the how-many question) were five and nine, six and five, seven and eight, four and eight, and four and four (four was not subitized on the subitizing task by either of the last two children). Three of these five children then showed additional evidence that they were not using a subitize-and-count approach. On one or more trials after they began giving last-word responses, they failed to count accurately the only set they could subitize (as indicated by the subitizing task—a set of two) but gave their incorrect last counted word as their response to the how-many question. Of course, these five children might not have been "discoverers" of last-word responding. They might at an earlier time have learned to give last-word responses by subitizing a counted set. But in this case one would expect them to subitize in this situation and to give last-word responses for those subitizable sets. Therefore, the subitize-and-count path does not seem to be a universal path followed by all children.

Furthermore, the 22 children who were neither discoverers nor original consistent last-word responders gave little evidence of the use of subitizing in the how-many task with objects. Children were asked the how-many question after they had counted a set. Those who could subitize sets of two, three, or four could have ignored their counting and answered the how-many question by subitizing the set, because the objects were visible in front of them when the question was asked. However, only three children showed response patterns that could possibly have reflected such subitizing. They each gave a last-word response on one very small set and no such responses on the sets of five, six, and seven. Thus, either children who did not give last-word responses could not subitize sets or they did not subitize in a context that had been defined as a counting context by the experimenter's request to count. Both of these conclusions undermine the subitize-and-count position. Many children do not seem to be able to or do not spontaneously use subitizing in a counting task.

Even for the last-word responders, last-word responding seemed to be stronger than subitizing. When very small sets were counted inaccurately, children gave the incorrect last counted word as the answer to the how-many question rather than the correct subitized answer, even when they could subitize that set. Five of the 12 original last-word responders on eight trials of the very small sets (two, three, and four) counted inaccurately and answered the how-many question with their incorrect last word; two of these trials were on set sizes the child had subitized on the subitizing task. The discoverers had five such trials on the very small sets; three of these were on sets that the child had subitized on the subitizing task.

Finally, on the how-many task with stickers, the 2-year-olds among the discoverers and original last-word responders gave significantly fewer last-word responses on the very small (53%) than on the small and very large sets (80% and 93%), $F(2, 8) = 6.59$, $p < .02$. This result is based on a very small number of children ($n = 5$), so it should be regarded as quite tentative. There was no apparent reason for the low rate of last-word responding on the very small sets, but these results clearly do run counter to the Schaeffer et al. (1974) hypothesis of last-word responses appearing for very small sets first. A possible reason that these children did not show a decrease in last-word responding on the very large sets is that they did not produce long number-word sequences when counting these sets; they skipped over many objects and said a mean of only seven counting words for each very large set.

7.6.1.2. Can Last-Word Responders Subitize? The results of the subitizing task for both the original last-word responders and the discoverers were similar. Almost all children subitized two, only some children subitized three, and few children subitized four (see Table 7-1). The mean trials subitized was significantly higher for the original last-word responders than for the discoverers for the set size three nonlinear sets, $t(18) = 2.24$, $p < .05$, but for no other arrangements. Every child answered correctly for both cards containing one star, and the answers given for other cards were close to the displayed set; thus, the children seem to have understood the task. The cards with one and with two items were scattered throughout the sequence of subitizing cards, so the lower subitizing performance on sets of three and four is not due to attenuated attention on later trials. One also cannot explain away this lower performance by arguing that children need more time to subitize sets of three and four: the definition of subitizing is a constant time (or almost constant— certainly constant within the limits of our procedure) to apprehend numerosities greater than one.

Table 7-1. Percentage of Subitizers and Mean Trials Subitized by Last-Word Responding and Set Size

Type of last-word response	Measure	2^a	3			4		
			Linear[a]	Nonlinear[a]	L + NL[b]	Linear[a]	Nonlinear[a]	L + NL[b]
Original last word responders (n = 12)	Percentage of subitizers[c]	83%	33%	50%	33%	8%	25%	8%
	Mean trials subitized (SD)	3.3 (1.4)	2.1 (1.7)	2.2 (1.2)	4.3 (2.7)	0.7 (1.0)	1.1 (1.5)	1.8 (2.1)
Discoverers (n = 8)	Percentage of subitizers[c]	88%	38%	25%	25%	13%	13%	0%
	Mean trials subitized (SD)	3.5 (1.1)	1.5 (1.4)	0.9 (1.4)	2.4 (2.6)	0.9 (1.1)	1.0 (1.2)	1.9 (2.1)

L + NL, linear plus nonlinear.
[a] Out of 4.
[b] Out of 8 (L + NL trials).
[c] A subitizer had at least 75% of the subitizing trials correct.

The subitizing results are similar if one considers only the traditional word form of the task (in which a child had to say "one" or "two" or "three" or "four") and disregards the trials on which the children had to show fingers instead of saying a number word. Most children could subitize two, about half sometimes subitized three, and almost no children consistently subitized four, although about a third sometimes did. Eighty percent of the children subitized the set of two on both trials of two, and 90% subitized two correctly on at least one of the two trials. For the sets of three, 40% subitized the linear sets on both trials, 30% subitized the nonlinear sets on both trials, and 20% subitized three on all four trials; these figures increase to 50%, 60%, and 50% for correct subitizing performance on half the trials of a given type. For the sets of four, 0% subitized the linear sets on both trials, 15% subitized the nonlinear sets on both trials, and 0% subitized correctly on all four trials; these figures increase to 35%, 40% and 30% for correct subitizing performance on half the trials of a given type.

There was no significant last-word responding group difference between performance on the word form and on the finger form of the subitizing task. However, individual children showed preferences for one form over the other. One child was not able to do the task with fingers, and seven children always said the word on the finger task and then showed fingers. Two children, both discoverers, always showed fingers first on the word trials and often had to be prompted to say the word.

Thus, many last-word responders in the age range 2-4 through 3-11 do not seem to be able to subitize sets of 3 and 4, and some do not even consistently subitize sets of 2. It is not clear whether these failures result from an inability to discriminate sets of two, three, and four objects or from an inability to label the discriminated sets with the proper word or both. These results clearly indicate that, for this age range, sets cannot be characterized as subitizable or nonsubitizable across all children. Rather, sets need to be characterized as subitizable *by particular children*. Because all of these children gave last-word responses, subitizing sets of two, three and four clearly does not precede last-word responding.

7.6.1.3. Does Last-Word Responding Require Accurate Counting? The relationship between last-word responding and counting accurately is given by set size in Table 7-2 for the how-many task with stickers. The original last-word responders gave last-word responses on every trial across the three set sizes. The discoverers did not consistently give last-word responses, but across all discoverers last-word responding did not vary with set size. The discoverers failed to give a last-word response on from three to five trials of each set size. Both groups of children counted inaccurately about a fourth of the very small sets, between half and two-thirds of the small sets, and all of the very large sets. Thus, accurate counting was not required for the generalization of last-word responding either to sets just beyond the subitizing range or to very large sets.

Table 7-2. Last-Word Responding and Counting Accuracy on Each Trial of the How-Many Task With Stickers by Set Size

	Set size					
	Very small 2, 3, 4		Small 5, 6, 7		Very large[a] 19, 23, 26	
	Count not accurate	Count accurate	Count not accurate	Count accurate	Count not accurate	Count accurate
Original last-word responders						
No last-word response	0	0	0	0	0	0
Last-word response	8	28	16	20	36	0
Discoverers						
No last-word response	2	2	2	1	5	0
Last-word response	5	15	14	7	19	0

[a] Last-word response trials include those trials in which a child did not respond with the last word on the first trial of that very large set but did so respond when that set size was immediately given again. So as not to give more opportunities for last-word responding on the very large sets, performance on the how-many task with objects was used as a second trial for any very small or small sets on which a child did not give a last-word response. The numbers of last-word responses added by these adjustments were six, one, and eight for the very small, small, and very large sets, respectively.

7.6.2. The Subitize-Independence Count-Dependence Performance-Demand Position

7.6.2.1. The Independence of Counting and Last-Word Responding From Subitizing. Many of the results presented and discussed with respect to the subitize-and-count position obviously are pertinent here. Because subitizing may trigger some children into last-word responding, the position that last-word responding never depends on subitizing seems untenable. However, all of the evidence indicating that few children use subitizing in the how-many situation is supportive of a position that argues that last-word responding does not require subitizing.

Furthermore, Gelman and Gallistel's (1978) position that children's ability to count does not depend on subitizing was supported. When counting performance on the two how-many tasks was compared to subitizing performance, counting and subitizing seemed to be independent for sets of two, and counting was better than subitizing for sets of three and four. Most children both subitized and counted accurately all the sets of two. However, three children were better at subitizing than at counting, and five children were better at counting than at subitizing. For the sets of three, six children counted both sets of three accurately but subitized three on less than half of the subitizing trials, while no child who subitized fairly well (on half or more of the subitizing trials) made any counting errors. The sets of four showed a similar pattern, except that eight rather than six children counted both sets of four accurately but subitized four on less than half of the subitizing trials. Thus, children's ability to count very small sets clearly does not depend on and is not necessarily preceded by the ability to subitize those sets.

7.6.2.2. Set Size and Last-Word Responding. We did not find on the sticker task the precipitous drop with set size for last-word responding that was reported by Gelman and Gallistel (1978). When performance on the second how-many question for the very large sets (19 to 26 stickers) is included, there was no effect of set size on last-word responding. The original last-word responders gave last-word responses on *all* trials for sets ranging from 2 to 26. The discoverers did not give last-word responses on all trials across this set range (see Table 7-2), but such failures were distributed equally across the sets of size 2 to 4, 5 to 7, and 19 to 26.

The performance demand of the very large sets (19 to 26 stickers) did affect last-word responding for our 3-year-olds when only the first how-many question for such sets was considered. The 3-year-old discoverers and original last-word responders gave significantly fewer last-word responses on the first how-many question for the very large sets than on the very small or small sets (73% versus 93% and 98% last-word responding, respectively), $F(2, 28) = 5.30$, $p < .01$. However, most of these children *could and did* give last-word responses for the very large sets. Last-word responses rose to 89% (and did not differ significantly from last-word responses on the other set sizes) when performance on the second how-many question for the very large sets was included. Some of these momentary failures to give last-word responses seem to have resulted from difficulty in remembering just what the last counted word was; on half of the failures, children gave the next-to-last instead of the last counted word in response to the how-many question. These memory difficulties might have been exacerbated by the similarity of the words children were producing at the end of their counts—these words were either in the late teens or in the twenties. These words are less differentiable by their form, and they are less familiar than words coming earlier in the sequence (Fuson, et al., 1982).

As discussed previously, 2-year-olds did not show any drop in last-word responding on the very large sets, even on the first how-many question for these sets. A possible reason for this age difference is that these very young children did not produce long number-word sequences when counting these sets; they skipped over many objects and said only a mean of 7 counting words for each very large set. The 3-year-olds, in contrast, said a mean of 18 words when counting the very large sets. Thus, the momentary failures to give last-word responses on very large sets seem to be limited to children who say long number-word sequences when counting those sets.

Additional data concerning the consistency of last-word responding across various set sizes were presented in Fuson, Pergament, Lyons, and Hall (1985). There we reported data for three samples. One sample was the Origins sample (plus three 4-year-olds who had been run in the original study but were dropped here to simplify the discussion by age). In this sample of 45 children, there was no effect of set size on last-word responding on the first how-many object task. Two-year-olds gave last-word responses on 19% of the trials with two, three, or four objects and on 16% of the trials with five, six or seven objects. Three- and 4-year-olds gave last-word responses on 65% of the sets of two, three, or four objects and on 63% of the sets of five, six, or seven objects. Another sample of 48 middle-class children ranging in age from 3-2 to 4-7 (mean 4-0) also showed no effect of set size on last-word responding. These children gave last-word responses on 70% of the trials with four, five, or six objects and on 67% of the trials with 9, 12, or 14 objects. A third sample of 24 middle- to upper-middle-class children between the ages of 3-6 and 4-5 also showed no effect of set size on last-word responding. These children gave last-word responses on 92% of the trials of seven, eight, or nine objects and on 92% of the trials of 16, 18, or 19 objects. Thus, in three samples of children between the age of 2-4 and 4-7, size of set showed no effect on last-word responding for sets ranging from 2 to 19 objects. Ginsburg and Russell (1981) also observed that last-word responding did not vary with set sizes ranging from 3 to 11, and Wilkinson (1984) reported no decrease in last-word responding between set sizes of 6 and 12.

The children in the three Fuson, Pergament, Lyons, and Hall samples (1985) were also fairly consistent in their last-word responding. Children tended either to give last-word responses on all trials or on no trials (Table 7-3). Of 3- and 4-year-olds in the Fuson et al. experiment 1, 73% gave a last-word response on all 12 trials or on no trial, even though these responses were given in two sessions a week apart. Most (85%) of this sample either consistently gave a last-word response on 11 of the 12 trials or consistently failed to give a last-word response on 11 of the 12 trials. The 2-year-olds in the Fuson et al. Experiment 2 showed a similar consistency, with 68% never giving a last-word response and 84% consistently giving or not giving a last-word response on 5 out of the 6 trials. Somewhat fewer (62%) of the 3- and young 4-year-olds in this sample were totally consistent, but a similar high percentage (88%) consistently gave or did not give last-word responses on 5 out of the 6 trials. The 3½ to 4½-year-olds in the Fuson et al. Experiment 3 were perfectly consistent. All 24 either gave a last-word response on all 6 trials or did not give a last-word response on any trial. Thus, not only does set size not seem to affect last-word responding across a sample of children, but also individual children are quite consistent in such responses: They either almost always or instead almost never give last-word responses.

These data are quite at variance with the very strong effect of size of set on children's use of the cardinality principle (i.e., last-word responding) reported by Gelman and Gallistel (1978): Last-word responding fell by 30% and 55% from sets of 2 to sets of 7 and 19 for 4-year-olds and by 46% and 66% for these sets for 3-year-olds (percentages from p. 124). However, three aspects of the procedure used there might have decreased considerably the amount of last-word responding by their sample. First, several different directions were given to the children over different trials. Sometimes children were told to

Table 7-3. Number of Children Giving Last-Word Responses Across Trials

Exp[a]	n	Age	Set size	Number of trials in which last-word response is given												
				12	11	10	9	8	7	6	5	4	3	2	1	0
1	48	3-2 through 4-7	4 to 14	24	5	1	2	0	1	1	1	1	0	0	1	11

				Number of trials						
				6	5	4	3	2	1	0
2	19	2-4 through 2-11	2 to 7	0	2	1	1	1	1	13
2	26	3-0 through 4-3	2 to 7	12	2	2	0	1	5	4
3	24	3-6 through 4-5	7 to 19	22	0	0	0	0	0	2

[a] Data are from experiments 1, 2, and 3 of Fuson, Pergament, Lyons, and Hall (1985).

"Count them" or to "Go ahead" rather than being asked "How many Xs are there?" On these trials the child's volunteering of the last-word response was assessed rather than the child's ability to give a last-word response when asked. Second, children had six trials for each set size. The plate on which the object lay was spun after each trial, and the child was given one of the directives. It seems possible that, as the interview progressed to the larger and larger sets and as "Count them" and "Go ahead" continued to be used as directives, many children interpreted the task as primarily a counting task and stopped volunteering the result of the count (i.e., stopped volunteering a last-word response). Third, even when a how-many question was asked, it was asked only before counting began. Thus, it seems possible that a child might forget during the course of counting that a last-word question had been asked. This seems especially likely with larger sets, which would require more time and effort for counting than would small sets. This third possibility has recently been supported in a study by Frye, Braisby, Lowe, Maroudas, and Nicholls (1986). They reported that when the how-many question was asked before the counting, last-word responding for large (12 to 14) sets was significantly lower than for small (4 and 5) sets (i.e., they got the Gelman and Gallistel drop with set size). However, when the how-many question was asked after the counting, size of set had no effect on last-word responding (i.e., they found the pattern reported in our data). This finding and the consistency of our set size data across several studies suggest that the Gelman and Gallistel data and procedure considerably underestimated the ability of their sample to give last-word responses.

7.6.2.3. Counting Accurately and Last-Word Responding. As discussed in 7.6.1.3. (see Table 7-2), last-word responding in the Origins study did not require accurate counting at any set size. On the trials on which last-word responses were given, children counted accurately on 77% of the sets of 2 to 4, on 47% of the sets of 5 to 7, and on 0% of the sets of 19 to 26. Thus, children did not seem to monitor their counting accuracy and stop giving last-word responses when their counting was inaccurate.

A more complete developmental picture of the relationship between accurate counting and last-word responding is provided by data we reported in Fuson, Pergament, Lyons, and Hall (1985). The results from three samples indicate that the relationship between giving last-word responses and counting accurately varies with set size. For very small sets of 2, 3, and 4, significantly more children counted accurately and did not give last-word responses than gave last-word responses but did not count accurately (16 children versus 1 child when performance on all three trials was considered and 8 versus 2 when performance on two out of three trials was used). For sets just beyond the subitizable range (from 4 through 7), results from two samples indicated that accurate counting and last-word responding are independent. In both samples the number of children who gave last-word responses and did not count accurately did not differ significantly from the number of children who counted accurately and did not give last-word responses. For larger sets (9 to 14 and 16 to 19) in two samples, significantly more children gave last-word responses and did not count accurately than counted accurately but did not give last-word responses. Thus, for sets larger than 7, last-word responding seems developmentally to precede rather than to follow accurate counting.

7.6.2.4. Performance Demands and Last-Word Responding. There were three kinds of data in the Origins study that indicated that performance demands limited children's ability to demonstrate some aspect of last-word responding. The first has been discussed in 7.6.2.2: on the very large sets of 19 to 26, 3-year-olds gave somewhat fewer last-word responses on the first than on a repeated how-many question. Evidently, the difficulty of counting a very large set or of distinguishing number words in the late teens or twenties (or both) interfered initially with the ability to give a last-word response. The other two kinds of data concern children who could do a task when the experimenter did the counting of objects but not when they did the counting (either before or after they had succeeded with the experimenter counting). Three children aged 2-9 or 2-10 who were given the brief instruction on last-word responding did not give last-word responses following instruction when they counted but did subsequently give such responses when the experimenter did the counting; they still did not give last-word responses when they counted after this. Three other children aged 2-6 through 2-10 did not recall the word they said in counting the last object, but when the experimenter did the counting they were able to recall the last counted word on at least one trial or answer the forced-choice recognition question on at least two trials. Their spontaneous and forced-choice memory responses were all still wrong when they subsequently did the counting. These results suggest that in many studies, for any task in which the child counts but fails some related task, it may be useful to branch to a parallel form in which the experimenter does the counting. Such a method may be one way to distinguish between conceptual and procedural competence (Greeno et al., 1984).

One other attribute of how-many situations that has been used as an example of performance demands limiting last-word responses is the use of class rather than collection terms to label a set of objects (Gelman, 1982b; Gelman & Baillargeon, 1983). Markman (1979) reported that children who were asked a how-many question about sets described in collection terms (e.g., army, pig family, pile) gave more last-word responses than did children hearing the same sets described in the more usual class terms (e.g., soldiers, pigs, blocks). Markman hypothesized that collections have greater psychological coherence than do classes, and thus collection terms help children form the conceptual aggregate necessary to consider the cardinality of a set. Gelman (1982) and Gelman and Baillargeon (1983) discussed this finding with respect to the cardinality principle and proposed that class terms are an example of performance demands interfering with children's demonstration of the cardinality principle. The reasoning here is that because children can demonstrate the cardinality principle with collection terms, they must have some understanding of it that is masked by the use of class terms. However, in three experiments involving 122 subjects, Fuson, Pergament, and Lyons (1985) reported finding no effect of collection terms on last-word responding. We argued there that this result does not necessarily indicate that collection terms do not help children form a conceptual aggregate. Rather, if last-word responses for many children reflect last-word responding with little cardinal reference, one would not expect last-word responding to be affected by collection terms. Collection terms would help only the later count-to-cardinal transition. Because of these limitations of questionable replicability and of interpretation, collection terms do not seem to be a good example of performance demands affecting children's last-word responding.

7.6.3. The Rule-Learning and Count-to-Cardinal Transition Position

7.6.3.1. Are There Last-Word Responses With No Cardinal Reference? Some data discussed previously are consistent with the conclusion that children give last-word responses that have no reference to the set as a whole or to the cardinality of the set. More than half of the "discoverers" spontaneously began to give last-word responses on a nonsubitizable set and continued to give them on sets of all sizes up to 26 objects. Last-word responding did not depend on accurate counting. Last-word responses are given consistently by a given child across quite different sizes of sets.

Other data from the Origins study are also consistent with this position. Experience with a situation that increases the salience of the last counted word evidently is enough to induce last-word responding in some children. Three children (aged 2-7 through 3-5) who gave no last-word responses on the six how-many trials with objects began spontaneously to give last-word responses after the last-word memory task in which they were asked what word they had said for the last counted object. Most of the children given the short instructional intervention began to give last-word responses (see 7.6.5. for more details), indicating that it is very easy for children to learn such responses.

More direct evidence concerning the lack of cardinal reference for some last-word responders comes from three sources: the count-reference and cardinality-reference questions in Origins; the forced-choice count/cardinality reference study, and responses from these two studies and others we have done in which children's last-word responses indicated little understanding of the cardinality of the set. Each of these are discussed in turn.

7.6.3.1.1. The Count- and Cardinality-Reference Questions in Origins. Correct responses to the count-reference and the cardinality-reference questions grouped by last-word response performance are in Table 7-4. Over all these groups, the mean response to the count-reference question ("Show me the star where you said n") was significantly higher than the mean response to the cardinality-reference question ("Show me the n stars."), 1.8 versus 1.1 out of 3, $t(30) = 2.88$, $p < .05$.

This difference occurred partly because it seemed more difficult for some children to give an unambiguous demonstration for the cardinality-reference than for the count-reference question: 23 of the 31 children given these questions gave an ambiguous response on a cardinality-reference trial and had to be given at least one forced-choice question (choosing between the experimenter-demonstrated cardinal reference—pointing to the whole set—and the counting reference—pointing to the last object counted), while no ambiguous responses were given on a counting-reference trial. Nine of these 23 children then demonstrated the cardinality reference correctly on 14 of the 43 given forced-choice demonstration trials. These correct demonstrations did not follow a pattern of chance choice of the correct meaning: 12 of the 14 correct demonstrations were made by seven children who unambiguously demonstrated the correct cardinal reference on every other trial or who correctly demonstrated the cardinality reference on a forced-choice demonstration on every trial. These 12 demonstrations thus seem to demonstrate understanding of the cardinal reference, and scores modified by these trials are also given in Table 7-4 in the lenient scoring column. A different factor that somewhat decreased the counting-reference scores was that some children seem to have forgotten in which direction they had counted the row, for in their counting-reference response they pointed to the first rather than to the last object they had counted. Counting-reference scores adjusted to include pointing to the first object are also given in Table 7-4 in the lenient scoring column.

A comparison of the lenient counting-reference and the lenient cardinality-reference scores over all groups indicates that children were still significantly better able to demonstrate the counting reference than the cardinality reference, 2.1 versus 1.5 out of 3, $t(30) = 2.04$, $p < .05$. The original last-word responders had a significantly higher total mean score on the strict scoring than did children in the other groups pooled, $t(29) = 2.10$, $p < .05$, but this difference was not significant on the lenient scoring.

Count- and cardinality-reference responses of the 20 children who spontaneously gave last-word responses on the first task were analyzed by age. Two-year-olds gave correct demonstrations (i.e., they somehow indicated the last counted object) to 27% of the count-reference questions, and the 3-year-olds gave correct demonstrations to 76% of the count-reference questions. Thus, the 3-year-olds were considerably better than were the younger children at remembering and reflecting on their counting activity and isolating the last part of that activity.

The 2-year-olds gave correct demonstrations to 20% of the cardinality reference questions (i.e., they somehow indicated all n objects), and the 3-year-olds gave correct demonstrations to 53% of the cardinality reference

Table 7-4. Responses to Count-Reference and Cardinality-Reference Questions by Group (Origins Study)

n	Description	Strict scoring			Lenient scoring		
		Count reference mean	Cardinality reference mean	Total mean	Count reference mean	Cardinality reference mean	Total mean
12	Original last-word responders	2.3	1.4	3.8	2.4	1.8	4.2
8	Discoverers	1.4	1.0	2.4	1.6	1.3	2.9
3	Recalled last word, then last-word responders	2.0	.0	2.0	2.7	1.0	3.7
8	Recalled last word, taught last-word responding and then gave last-word responses	1.5	1.3	2.8	1.9	1.6	3.5

Note. The strict score gave credit only for an unambiguous pointing to the last object (count reference) or to all the objects (cardinality reference). In the lenient scoring count reference credit was given for pointing to the first object counted as well as pointing to the last object counted, and cardinality reference credit was given for a correct forced-choice cardinality response if a child unambiguously demonstrated the cardinality reference on every other trial or chose the correct forced-choice response on every trial. The count and cardinality reference means are out of a possible 3 and the total means are out of a possible 6.

questions. Only one 2-year-old and four 3-year-olds indicated all of the objects in a set on all three trials of the cardinality-reference questions; four other 3-year-olds indicated all of the objects on two of the three cardinal trials. The remaining eleven children (those who correctly indicated the whole set to only one or to none of the three cardinality directives) showed little awareness of any reference of the how-many answer to the set as a whole. They chose the last counted object rather than the whole set as the answer to the question "Are these the n stars" on 80% of the forced-choice cardinality-reference questions contrasting these two choices, in spite of the 50% score obtainable by chance and the plural linguistic cues in the question that supported the cardinality choice. Thus, in half of the spontaneous last-word responders, there seemed to be little understanding of the cardinality reference of this last word to the set as a whole. These children seemed to have learned only a level-one last-word response. The cardinal references of the other nine children did show evidence of having learned to make counting-to-cardinal transitions when giving last-word responses.

If the lenient scoring is used, one of the three children who began to give last-word responses after responding to the last-word memory task and three of the eight children who began to give last-word responses after the last-word response teaching showed understanding of the cardinal reference of the last word. Thus, it may be that some children can move directly to count-to-cardinal transitions. This possiblity would seem to be increased when there is considerable focus on the cardinal reference of the last word.

7.6.3.1.2. Forced-Choice Count-Cardinality Reference Study. Only two children chose the last item instead of the next-to-last or all items for all three count-reference questions ("Is this the soldier where you said n?") and chose all the items instead of all but the last item or the last item for all three cardinality-reference questions ("Are these the n soldiers?"). Two other children answered five out of the six questions correctly. More children indicated understanding of one of the two kinds of questions; 10 additional children got all three of one type of question correct while getting none or only one of the other type correct. Seven of these demonstrated an understanding of the count-reference questions while three demonstrated an understanding of the cardinality-reference questions. Most of the children (19 out of the 23 children giving a last-word response) demonstrated some confusion between the count and cardinal meanings, 14 of them doing so fairly consistently (on two or three of the three possible opportunities to do so). Over the whole sample of last-word responders, the counting meaning seemed to dominate the cardinal meaning more than the reverse. Seven children chose or otherwise demonstrated the cardinality-reference for the count-reference question while 13 children demonstrated or chose the count-reference for the cardinality-reference question (one child did both). However, the difference in the number of correct choices to the count-reference (1.6 out of 3) and the cardinality-reference questions (1.2 out of 3) was not significant.

The 20 children who gave last-word responses on three or four of the four trials were not able in general to answer the cardinality-reference questions ("Are these the n soldiers?") correctly. Only 5 of these children chose the correct answer on all three trials, with an additional two choosing the correct answer on two out of the three trials. The mean correct number of choices was 1.3 out of 3. Of the 15 imperfect responders to the cardinality-reference questions, 11 chose the last object counted rather than $n-1$ objects as the answer. This choice of a single object was made in spite of the plural linguistic cues in the cardinality-reference question ("Are these the n soldiers?"). Thus, again the last-word responses of many children seemed not to reflect a count-to-cardinal transition. Many chose the last item rather than all the items as the reference for the question "Are these the n soldiers?"

A rather serious concern before we ran the study was the extent to which the inevitable form of the question (singular or plural words) would provide usable cues that would enable performance to overestimate children's understanding. However, the strong linguistic cues of singular and plural in the question forms (singular in the count question and plural in the cardinality question) did not seem particularly helpful. In fact most of the children (16 of the 23) used singular and plural forms incorrectly when answering the questions. Children did not have to answer the forced-choice questions verbally; they could just repeat the gesture of the adult. However, most children spontaneously gave some verbal response; the response was scored only for the correctness of the choice it conveyed and not for correct use of quantitative terms. Five of the 16 children with verbal errors simply misused "these" (used it when pointing to a single entity) or "this" (used it when pointing to all the entities). The remaining 11 children misused singular or plural words in a sentence containing a number word. These mistakes are quite illustrative of the kinds of confusions that arise and the complexities in correct number-word usage that children must learn. Some examples are the following:

Response to cardinality question: "Those are five soldiers" as child points to the last soldier.

Response to cardinality question: "This one's the five chips" as child points to the last chip.

Response to cardinality question: "This is the six soldiers" as child points to each soldier (said six times).

Response to cardinality question: "This is the four chips" as child points to the last chip.

Response to cardinality question: "This is where I said chip four" as child's hands gesture to all of the chips.

Response to count question: "All of these animals I said five."

There are obvious limitations to the use of verbal questions with young children. However, the issues involved here are linguistic as well as conceptual. These examples illustrate how much linguistic as well as numerical knowledge is involved in a child's being able to answer correctly the seemingly rather simple questions we posed and especially in their being able to use correctly the words in these questions. This needed additional knowledge indicates clearly that even the count-to-cardinal transition is an important, but still quite primitive, milestone in children's construction of numerical understandings.

It is a bit puzzling to us that the children here and those in the Origins study did not do better on the count reference questions. These questions were just the opposite of the task in Origins that assessed children's ability to recall the last counted word. In that task the experimenter indicated the last item counted and asked the child what word had been said for that item. In contrast in the count reference questions, the child was told the last counted word and was asked to indicate the item (or choose the correct indication) where the last word had been said. All last-word responders obviously remember their last counted word, and many children not yet giving last-word responses also remembered the word said for the last counted item (see 7.6.4.). However, a substantial number of children giving last-word responses were not able to indicate the last item as the place where they had said the last counted word. Thus, children's memory for the location to which the last word was paired seems to be much worse than their memory for a word said for a given item (or at least for the last item).

The use of these cardinality-reference and count-reference questions was obviously only a small first step toward understanding what meanings accompany a child's last-word responses. There are obvious difficulties in using verbal questioning with very young children, and learning the meaning of such a question as "Are these the n stars?" clearly goes beyond the knowledge necessary to give last-word responses. However, being able to indicate all the set just counted as "the n items" or at least being able to choose the whole set rather than the last object counted as "the n items" does seem to be a fairly minimal criterion for inferring that the child's last-word response has some reference to the set as a whole, that is, has some minimal cardinal meaning. Clearly, it would be very useful to devise methods for ascertaining whether a child intends each of the aspects of cardinality involved in the count-to-cardinal transition: reference to the set as a whole and reference to the numerosity of the set. Tracing the ability of the child to use the singular and plural nouns, verbs, and special quantity terms involved in counting and in cardinality number-word meanings would also seem to be important for understanding children's developing knowledge of number.

7.6.3.1.3. Last-Word Responses Demonstrating Little Understanding of Cardinality. Some children seem to give last-word responses in a nonreflective pattern fashion—they simply answer the how-many question with whatever last word they happen to produce. The nature of some last-word responses given in these cases provides additional support for the notion that this last word does not have a cardinal reference because the last-word responses obviously violate notions of cardinality. The following are examples of ways in which some last-word responses of children are inconsistent with the actual cardinality of the set counted; these examples were taken from last-word responses given in Origins and in the three experiments reported in Fuson, Pergament, Lyons, and Hall (1985).

Children sometimes miscount a set that they can subitize but nevertheless stick with their incorrect last word based on the inaccurate counting:

Counting a set of 2: "1, 2, 3. There are 3."

Children sometimes give a very small number as the how-many response for a very large set:

Counting a set of 26: "1, 2, 3, 6, 7, 8, 9, 1, 2." "How many?" "2."
Counting a set of 26: "1, 2, 3." "How many?" "3."
Counting a set of 26: "1, 2, 3, 4," "How many?" "4."

Large numbers would sometimes be given as the how-many response for much smaller sets:

Counting a set of 16: "1, 2, 3, 4, 5, 6, 7, 8, 9, 16, 17, 18, 19, 20, 30, 40, 50, 70. 70 dots!"

Made-up numbers used in counting might be given as the how-many response:

Counting a set of 18: "1, 2, 3, 4, 5, 6, 7, 8, 9, 10, 9, 10, 11, 12, 13, 14, 16, 17, 18, 19, 20, 2-teens, 3-teens, 4-teens." "How many?" "4-teens."
Counting a set of 23: "1, 2, 3, 4, 5, 6, 7, 8, 9, 10, 14, 16, 11-teen, 18, 19, 16, 11-teen, 18, 19, 17, 14, 16, 11-teen." How many? "11-teen"

Children would also sometimes reuse a number over again within a fairly short space but still give that number as the cardinality:

Counting a set of 18: "1, 2, 3, 4, 5, 6, 7, 8, 9, 10, 11, 12, 13, 18, 19, 20, 19, 16, 18, 19." "How many?" "19."
Counting a set of 23: "1, 2, 3, 4, 5, 6, 7, 8, 9, 10, 11, 12, 16, 14, 15, 16, 14, 16, 15, 15, 16, 11-teen, 15." "How many?" "15."
Counting a set of 19: "1, 2, 3, 4, 5, 6, 7, 8, 9, 10, 12, 15, 8, 9, 10." "How many?" "10."

Examples such as these would seem to stem from last-word responding that is not connected to cardinal referents for the answer to the how-many question.

7.6.3.2. Do All Children First Give Last-Word Responses With No Cardinal Reference? Whether all children initially give last-word responses with no cardinal reference and later come to understand the cardinality reference of the last counted word or whether some children immediately understand the cardinality reference is not clear. Two of the eight discoverers in the Origins study answered all three of the cardinality-reference questions correctly, but it is of course possible that they were "rediscoverers" who had given last-word responses without any cardinality meaning at an earlier time. Two of the eight instructed children answered all three cardinality-reference questions correctly and a third so answered two of the three, so these children seem to have moved from no last-word responding to making count-to-cardinal transitions. It does seem possible for a child to move immediately to count-to-cardinal transitions, especially if last-word responding is learned in a context in which the cardinal aspect of the set is particularly salient or is made salient. However, it is also quite clear that many children do at first learn only last-word responses with little reference to cardinality.

A definitive answer to this question depends on devising satisfactory ways to measure children's understanding of the cardinal reference of the last-word response, of both the reference to the set as a whole and to the cardinality of the set. Gelman, Meck, and Merkin (1986) have suggested that one way to assess whether children are obtaining a cardinal value of a set is to have children judge whether a puppet who makes a correspondence error in counting and gives the obtained (incorrect) last word was right or wrong. The argument here is that children having no cardinal referent for the last-word response should say the puppet was right because the puppet did use the last counted word to tell how many there were. Gelman et al. reported that 3- and 4-year-olds were correct on 81% of such trials, that is, they said that the puppet was wrong. Of the 4-year-olds, 78% made "explicit reference at least once to the fact that the resulting count sequence and/or the consequent cardinal number was wrong on such trials" (p. 14), and 65% of the 3-year-olds "corrected the puppet's cardinal answer and/or set of count words" (p. 16).

This procedure certainly does assess understanding beyond mere last-word responding and is a step forward for this reason. However, the procedure seems as likely to assess the understanding that inaccurate counting will affect the last-word response, that is, the word said for the last object, as assess the understanding that inaccurate counting will affect the cardinal value of the set as a whole. If the puppet skips an object or counts an object twice, the last word said would be wrong because the puppet should have said one more or one fewer words. For both the 3- and 4-year-olds, some children evidently did in fact point out the correct "count sequence" as what the puppet should have said. Because this count sequence contains the last counted word, its use seems to point more directly to the last counted word than to the cardinality of the set (unless, of course, the child makes some other comments directly about the cardinality). Undoubtedly, some of the children did in fact know a relationship between accurate counting and the cardinality of the set; for example, one child may have been indicating such knowledge when saying, "No. He had to go 1, 2, 3, 4, 5, 6, 7. And that's 7 [pointing to the display] because all these animals are out [here on the table]." (p. 14). However, even here, whether the point at the display was indicating the whole set or the last object is crucial to interpreting this example. Thus, the 80% of the children who judged the puppets counting to be wrong did demonstrate some under-standing beyond just last-word responding. Whether this understanding in-cluded the cardinal reference of the last word, rather than an understanding of the effect of certain counting errors on the last-word response, is not clear from the data presented.

Frye et al. (1986) carried out a similar study using Moore's (Moore & Frye, 1986b) trick game paradigm in order to avoid false-positives as well as false-negatives due to context effects. The experimenter counted (either correctly or incorrectly) and then said, "I think I have counted right/wrong." On other trials the experimenter counted (either correctly or incorrectly) and then said, "I think there are X. Are there?" X was either the last counted word or one less than the stickers in the array. The child's task was to "catch the experi-menter out" and tell when the experimenter was "playing a trick," i.e., making a mistake. The child's understanding of this task was established by an initial procedure. The 3½ to 4½-year-old children were better at identi-fying sequence and correspondence errors in counting than in assessing the implications of counting errors for the accuracy of the last-word response. Analyses of response patterns of individual children[6] revealed that some children could derive a last-word implication from information about the accuracy of counting for the small sets of four and five: The last-word answers were called correct if and only if the counting was correct. However, just as many children followed a last-word strategy in which the information about the accuracy of counting was disregarded, and an answer was judged to be correct if and only if it was the last counting word said by the experimenter. Thus, some children did not even use counting accuracy to determine the accuracy of the last counted word, let alone relate counting accuracy to a cardinal meaning of the last counted word.

These studies have thus raised at least two interesting questions about what children understand about relationships between counting and cardinality. When do children understand that a given kind of correspondence error or a given kind of number-word sequence error will affect the last word said in counting? How is this understanding related to children's understanding that a last-word response to a how-many question has a cardinality reference, that is, refers to the set as a whole and to the cardinality of that set? This second question obviously requires an adequate way to measure a child's understand-ing of such cardinality reference.

7.6.3.3. How Do Children Learn Last-Word Responding? This rule-learning account raises the question: "In the normal course of events, what might lead to a child's discovery of last-word responding?" Two kinds of evidence from the Origins study and other studies are pertinent to this question. The first concerns age differences in the wrong responses children give to a how-many

---

[6] These analyses were reported in a paper by C. Maroudas and summarized in a personal communication from D. Frye, January 1987.

question, and the second is the evidence of a recency bias in young children's responses to questions. Each of these is discussed in turn.

7.6.3.3.1. Performance and Age Differences in Incorrect Responses to the How-Many Question. The 22 children in the Origins study who did not spontaneously give last-word responses in the first how-many task with objects exhibited four different kinds of responses on that task:

1. Sixteen children on 42% of the trials recounted when asked the how-many question (and did not give a last-word response after the recount).
2. Seventeen children on 33% of the trials gave a single word answer (or showed a group of fingers) that was not the last word said in counting (there was no obvious pattern in these responses except that a few children gave the same word on all six trials).
3. Ten children on 15% of the trials responded with a string of number words (usually not a repetition of the words just said in counting).
4. Five children on 9% of the trials gave no answer or said "I don't know."

Children who later showed some evidence of last-word responding (either spontaneously after the last-word memory task or after the last-word response teaching) showed more evidence of "searching around" for the correct response to the how-many question than did those who showed no last-word evidence. Significantly more of the former children than of the latter children gave two or more different kinds of wrong responses (1 to 3 above): 13 of 14 versus 3 of 8, $\chi^2 = 7.87$, $p < .01$. Most of these 13 children gave responses 1 and either 2 or 3. Thus, interpreting the how-many question both as an instruction to count and as a request for a single number word or a string of number words may facilitate learning a last-word response.

Age effects on the kinds of incorrect responses given to the how-many question were explored in two samples. One sample was the subset of the Origins sample consisting of the 33 children (19 two-year-olds and 14 three-year-olds) who gave on the first how-many task with objects any response other than a last-word response.[7] The other sample consisted of the 24 children (17 three-year-olds and 7 four-year-olds) from Experiment 1 in Fuson et al. (1985) who gave on any trial a response other than the last counted word. The size of the set (2 to 4 versus 5 to 7 in the first sample and 4 to 6 versus 9 to 14 in the second sample) did not affect the incorrect last-word responses, so these were pooled over the different set sizes.

These responses fell into two frequent and three less-frequent categories. When asked the how-many question, children recounted the set and did not give that last counted word as the answer, gave a single number word that was not the last word they had used in counting, gave a sequence of number words

---

[7] This includes three original last-word responders who gave a response other than a last-word response and then spontaneously self-corrected by counting again and then giving a last-word response.

(often different from the sequence they had used in counting the set), gave no answer or said they did not know, or did something else (showed some fingers, said some variation of "I already did it," etc.). There was an interesting age difference in these incorrect how-many responses. The 3-year-olds in both samples had a very similar distribution of responses, while the responses of the 2-year-olds and of the 4-year-olds differed from these and were similar to each other in one way (see Table 7-5). The predominant incorrect response of the 2-year-olds was to give a single number word that was different from the last word said in counting. The numbers given were small numbers: the numbers 1, 2, 3, 4, 5, 6, and 7 were given 4, 6, 10, 5, 1, 1, and 1 times, respectively. Of these, only 4 numbers were the correct numerosity of the set (and of course none of them was the last counted word said by the child). The other 2-year-old responses were distributed fairly evenly over three other categories. The responses of the 3-year-olds in both samples were heavily concentrated in the recounted category, although more than 40% of these children occasionally responded with one number. The responses of the 4-year-olds were evenly split between recounts and giving one number.

These results suggest that for 2-year-olds, a how-many question functions predominantly as a directive to say a number word (though not the last counted word). The how-many question changes to functioning as a directive to count for 3-year-olds, and then shifts back for 4-year-olds to an even split between these two responses. This age pattern suggests that it is important for children to learn both of these responses to the how-many question. Last-

Table 7-5. Incorrect How-Many Question Responses by Age

	Recounted	Said one number	Said a sequence of numbers	No answer or "I don't know"	Other
Origins sample					
2-year-olds	23%	40%	18%	14%	4%
3-year-olds	67%	16%	10%	3%	5%
Experiment 1 Sample					
3-year-olds	73%	11%	8%	1%	6%
4-year-olds	45%	43%	5%	0%	8%

Note. Entries in the table are the percentage of trials that fell into that category out of all trials on which a last-word response was not given. A single line under an entry indicates that 40% or more of the children who failed to give a last-word response on at least one trial gave one or more responses in that category. A double line indicates that 60% or more of such children gave one or more responses in that category. The Origins sample consists of the 33 children who failed to give a last-word response on one or more trials, and the experiment 1 Sample consists of the 24 children from Experiment 1 (Fuson, Pergament, Lyons, and Hall, 1985) who met the same criterion.

word responding then may begin when the count-directive meaning of the how-many question is linked to the single number-word meaning of the question but with a focus on a special single number-word—the last word said in counting. A how-many question then elicits counting followed by the single number-word response of the particular last word said in counting. How this last word may come to be selected is discussed in the next section.

7.6.3.3.2. A Recency Bias in Responding to Questions. One part of an answer to the question of how children might first come to hazard the last counted word as the answer to the how-many question seems to us to rest in the nature of the how-many situation. What a child is counting, the last word said in counting is quite salient, because it is not followed by another distracting word. This salience is underscored by the fact that most children who did not give last-word responses nevertheless could remember the last word they had said in counting (see 7.6.4). Another part of the answer comes from previous findings of a recency bias in young children's answers to questions, that is, a bias toward choosing the last alternative mentioned (e.g., Siegel & Goldstein, 1969). If this bias were demonstrated to extend to the how-many situation, such a bias might itself be sufficient to prompt a child to give a last-word response at some point.

Therefore, the responses to the forced-choice how-many questions given in the Origins study were examined for a recency bias. Each time a child failed to give a last-word response in the first how-many task with objects, the child's incorrect answer was followed by a forced-choice how-many question, such as, "Were there six, five, or four trucks?" where the last word the child had said in counting was always in the middle and the order of numbers given was sometimes increasing and sometimes decreasing. The forced-choice responses given by the 22 children who were not last-word responders or "discoverers" were marked by a strong recency bias, that is, a bias toward choosing the last number in the forced-choice question. All 22 children answered with the last choice on at least one of the six trials, while only 10 children ever chose the first number, and only 10 ever chose the correct middle number. The last choice was selected on 73% of the trials on which the forced-choice question was answered, while the first number and the correct middle number were chosen on 11% and 16% of the trials, respectively. Thus, even though most of these children could recall their last counted word (see 7.6.4), they did not choose it as the answer to this forced-choice last-word question. Instead, they answered the question with the last choice stated in the question.

7.6.4. Memory and Processing Constraints on Last-Word Responding

In the Origins study 17 children did not ever give a last-word response on the first how-many task with objects, and 5 children gave a last-word response on one early trial and then failed to give it again. These 5 children could not be classified either as consistent last-word responders or as "discoverers" of last-word responding, for they did not continue to give last-word responses after this one trial. Three children gave last-word responses of "two" on the set of two, and the other two children gave a last-word response of "seven" (one on a set of six and the other on a set of seven). The first three children later subitized sets of two on the subitizing task, so their answer to the how-many question might have been subitized. Given the propensity of some children to give a single number word as the answer to the how-many question (see 7.6.3.3.1), one would expect occasional congruence of this single number word with the last counted word. The correct responses of "seven" might have been such chance congruences, or they might have been early tentative choices of the last counted word as the single number-word answer to the how-many question.

On the last-word memory task, 11 of these 22 children correctly recalled the word they had said for the last counted object on all three trials, and 5 children did so on one trial. The 6 children who did not recall their last counted word when they counted all perseverated on a single number-word response across all three last-word memory questions. Three of these children then gave some evidence of being able to separate and recall the last counted word when the experimenter counted; they gave the experimenter's last counted word on one or more trials or chose the correct last word on two or three forced-choice trials (but were not able to give any correct spontaneous or forced-choice responses when they counted subsequently). The perseverated words initially used by these three children were five, four, and two. All three of the children who never gave any evidence of separating and recalling the last counted word gave one as their response to all trials of the last-word memory task. It therefore seems possible that they misunderstood the task and were replying with the word they said on the first, rather than the last, counted object even though the experimenter did try to clarify this issue when these children continued to give "one" as the answer. In summary the ability to separate and recall the last word said in counting does not seem to be the major obstacle to learning last-word responding. Half of the children who did not give last-word responses on the first how-many task consistently recalled their last counted word, another fourth did so occasionally, and another eighth gave some evidence of remembering the last counted word when the experimenter counted. Thus, many children seem to be able to remember their last counted word but still do not give last-word responses.

With respect to the hypothesis advanced by Wilkinson (1984) that accurate counting and last-word responding might compete for processing space, there was little evidence in our data reported in Fuson, Pergament, Lyons, and Hall (1985) of children having trouble coordinating accurate counting and last-word responding. Very few children in any of the three samples showed only one of these abilities on one trial and the other on a different trial. However, these data did support Wilkinson's proposal that accurate counting emerged before last-word responding and that the latter reached functional maturity sooner (see 7.6.2.3).

7.6.5. Can Children Learn Last-Word Responding From Brief Instruction?

The 22 children in Origins who were not last-word responders or "discoverers" were given the last-word memory task. Sixteen of these recalled the last word said in counting and were given three trials of the how-many task on 5, 6, and 7 objects. Three of these gave last-word responses on this task. The remaining 13 were given the last-word response teaching on sets of 5, 6, 7 and were then given three trials of the how-many task again. Eight of these 13 gave last-word responses on a mean of 2.4 of these three trials and then, after the subitizing task, gave last-word responses on a mean of 6.8 of the nine trials of the how-many task with stickers (the range of last-word responding was from four to nine trials). This mean and range is identical to the mean and range of last-word responding on this task by the eight discoverers. Mean last-word responding for these instructed children was identical across the very small (2, 3, and 4), small (5, 6, and 7), and very large (19, 23, 26) sets. An additional 3 of the 13 instructed children did not give last-word responses when they counted but did so when the experimenter counted. The remaining two instructed children did not give last-word responses either when they or when the experimenter counted; on the last-word memory task, these two children had recalled the last word on only one trial. Thus, this very brief instruction in last-word responding was effective in inducing last-word responding in a majority of the children who could recall the last counted word, and only two children showed no evidence of any learning concerning last-word responding.

  If a young child is asked a how-many question and does not answer it correctly, it seems quite likely that the questioner (a parent, sibling, or nursery-school teacher) might then try to teach the last-word rule by stating or demonstrating it, much as our experimenter did. The Origins study indicates that very brief teaching may be quite effective. Whether this teaching then leads to last-word responding with little reference to cardinality or to count-to-cardinal transitions would seem to depend on how much the teacher focused on the cardinal reference of the last-word response and on how much knowledge about cardinality the child already possessed. Three of the eight instructed children who gave last-word responses when they did the counting did demonstrate the whole set on the cardinality-reference questions, so they seem to have moved directly to making count-to-cardinal transitions. The likelihood that a child receives such instruction may vary by social class; Hodges and French (1987) reported that not a single lower-class 3-year-old gave last-word responses on as many as three of four trials.

7.7. Summary and Conclusion

Some aspects of the proposals of various authors concerning early relationships between counting and cardinality are supported by the data presented in this chapter. The results also suggest that children follow different routes to these early relationships.

The results do not support the subitize and count account as originally proposed by Schaeffer et al. (1974). There was no effect of set size on last-word responding: Children therefore do not first discover last-word responses on subitizable sets and then later generalize such responding to larger sets. There was little evidence of subitizing in the how-many counting situation. Children who did not give last-word responses rarely answered the how-many question by subitizing even though the objects were always visible, and last-word responding children who incorrectly counted sets they could subitize held to their incorrect counted last-word response rather than subitizing the set. Children between 2-4 and 3-11 who gave last-word responses did not all consistently subitize sets of two, many did not subitize sets of three, and almost all did not consistently subitize sets of four. Counting accurately is not required for the generalization of last-word responding to sets just beyond the subitizing range or to very large sets. Many children gave last-word responses for sets of size five to seven but did not count them accurately, and all children who gave last-word responses on very large sets counted them inaccurately.

However, the results do support the following radically revised version of the subitize and count description: *Some* children first give last-word responses on a set that *they* can subitize and then *immediately* (on the very next trial) generalize such responses to sets that they cannot subitize. The main points of revision are italicized. First, the subitize- and-count account is now seen to apply only to some and not to all children. Second, the results of the subitizing task indicate that one cannot characterize *sets* of a particular size as subitizable but only as subitizable by a *particular child* (and thus this must be determined for each child). Third, it does not seem necessary for a child to have many separate subitize-and-count experiences before giving last-word responses consistently. Rather, one experience may be (and for the children in this study, was) sufficient. This implies that the subitize and count approach is really much more closely linked to the rule-learning approach—one subitize-and-count experience seems to be enough to *trigger* the rule, which is then applied immediately to larger sets.

There was some evidence of performance demands of counting interfering with last-word responses, as suggested by Gelman (1982b), Gelman and Meck (1983), and Greeno et al. (1984), though this interference did not operate exactly as suggested by these authors. Children who counted very large sets of 19 to 26 using number words in the teens and twenties sometimes gave the wrong word (often the next-to-last word) in response to the how-many question. However, almost all such children gave the correct last-word response when the question was repeated. Some children also gave last-word responses or recalled the word said for the last object when the experimenter counted but not when they counted themselves.

There was no evidence of the precipitous decline in last-word responding with set size reported by Gelman and Gallistel (1978); last-word responding was constant for sets of 2 through 19. Results of Frye et al. (1986) indicate that the decline found by Gelman and Gallistel is at least partly due to the how-many question being asked before rather than after the child counted. There was also little indication that children monitored their counting accuracy and stopped giving last-word responses when they stopped counting accurately. Accurate counting did drop precipitously with set size, but last-word responding stayed almost constant across set size, with many children giving last-word responses but counting inaccurately on larger sets. More children counted very small sets (2, 3, and 4) accurately than gave last-word responses on such sets, accurate counting and last-word responding were independent for sets between 4 and 7 with some children doing each without doing the other, and for sets larger than seven more children gave last-word responses and did not count accurately than vice versa. Thus, Wilkinson's (1984) proposal that accurate counting emerges before last-word responding but that last-word responding reaches functional maturity sooner seems to be true. However, contrary to Wilkinson's suggestion, there was little evidence that children had trouble coordinating accurate counting and last-word responding; rather, for sets of certain sizes, individual children did one consistently without doing the other.

Several aspects of the Fuson and Hall (1983) proposal were supported. Children who give last-word responses do seem to be using a *last-word rule* or *principle*. Last-word responses are given fairly uniformly across sets sizes from 2 to 26 (i.e., they do not vary with set size), and the distribution of children according to the number of trials on which last-word responses are given is bimodal rather than normal. Most children either give a last-word response on every (or almost every) trial or never (or almost never) give a last-word response. These last-word responses seem for many children at first to reflect only a *how-many-question rule* in which the answer to the how-many question does not refer to the cardinality of the set. More than half the "discoverers" in the Origins study first gave a last-word response on a nonsubitizable set, children did not have to count accurately to give a last-word response, children sometimes gave last-word responses that strongly violated concepts of cardinality, many children could not demonstrate that the answer to the how-many question referred to the whole set, and many could not even choose the whole set as the referent of the last-word response in preference to the last counted object. Children also clearly advance on to making count-to-cardinal transitions in which the last-word response does refer to the set as a whole. Some children consistently chose the whole set as the reference for "the six ducks," and some children could consistently indicate that whole set when asked to "show the six ducks." In summary the early terms *cardinality rule* and *cardinality principle* were accurate in that children really do behave as if they are using a rule or a principle, but the terms were inaccurate in that "cardinality" implies understanding of various aspects of cardinality that last-word responders may not really understand. Last word responding nevertheless is an important step forward, for it is the child's first use of counting.

Difficulty in remembering the word said for the last counted object does not seem to be the major obstacle to children's giving of last-word responses. Many children who did not give last-word responses were able to recall the word they had said for the last object in a row. Evidently, some event or events must occur to suggest to the child that this last counted word might be the answer to the how-many question.

Data from the Origins study suggest three possible ways (other than the subitizing previously discussed) in which this link might be made. First, some event might make the last counted word especially salient to the child. Some children spontaneously gave last-word responses after the task in which they were asked to recall the word said for the last counted object; this task obviously increased the salience of that last counted word. The salience of this last word might also be increased if it is a large number word (and therefore less common in the child's experience) or if one hears another person emphasize the last word. The latter is evidently a fairly common occurrence, for Gelman and Gallistel (1978) reported that some of their children emphasized the last word rather than giving it again in response to the how-many question, and we have observed children emphasizing the last counted word. Second, children might be taught by a parent or sibling that the last counted word tells how many there are. The success of our very brief teaching intervention (two statements of the rule and three demonstrations of it by the experimenter) indicates that it does not take much teaching for children to learn the last-word rule. Most children so instructed did then give last-word responses, although only three-fifths did so when they themselves counted. Such teaching may even seem exciting and important to a child. One girl given the last-word response instruction excitedly said to herself at the end of the teaching, "And that tells you how many things there are!" Third, young children's tendency to answer a question with the last mentioned alternative (their recency bias) may move them to hazard the last counted word as a guessed response to the how-many question, a guess that then may be followed by feedback and reinforcement.

The kinds of incorrect responses given to the how-many question also suggest a developmental pattern that may support any of these routes to last-word responding. Many very young children (2-year-olds) give a single number word as the answer to a how-many question; this may occur because parents and others are labeling groups of objects with a number word either without counting ("Oh look. There are three little kittens.") or with counting ("Look. Three kittens. One, two, three. Three kittens.") However, children initially do not give their last counted word as this number word response;

they say some other word. As children get a bit older and parents begin deliberately to model counting more often, children seem to learn to count in response to a how-many question, that is, they interpret the how-many question as a directive to count. For most 3-year-olds who did not give last-word responses, the act of counting itself was regarded as a sufficient response to the how-many question, and they usually recounted if asked the how-many question again. Some of these children even complained when their counting was followed by another how-many question, "But I already did it." or "I already said it." At some point then the child may put together these two different responses to a how-many question (giving a single number word and counting the set) and give a last-word response. The 4-year-olds not giving last-word responses split their responses to the how-many question about equally between these two different responses: giving a single number word (not the last counted word) and recounting the set. Many of them seemed to be alternating between these two kinds of responses, thus facilitating the eventual relationship to be established between them. Giving each of these responses on different trials also seems to characterize children who are "ready" to give last-word responses. Children who did not give last-word responses on the first how-many task in Origins but later did give last-word responses (after the last-word memory task or the last-word response instruction) initially gave more different kinds of incorrect responses to the how-many question than did children who never gave last-word responses; these "ready" children recounted on some trials and either said a single number-word or a sequence of number words on other trials. Social class may affect progress toward last-word responses. Hodges and French (1987) reported worse last-word responding for working-class 3-year-olds than for suburban middle-class 3-year-olds, and Ginsburg and Russell (1981) reported poorer last-word performance by their lower-class than by their middle-class preschoolers (mean age 4-8).

In summary, then, how do children first begin to use a how-many-question rule or a count-to-cardinal transition? This final connection between counting and the how-many question may be made in several ways. The child may connect a subitized numerosity and the last counted word for that set. A recency bias or an auditory "echoing" of the last word may prompt the child to hazard the last counted word as a guess to the how-many question. The child may notice someone else giving the last counted word as the how-many answer. The child may be told that the last counted word tells how many there are. In all of these cases the generalization to sets of other sizes apparently occurs quite rapidly. These routes to last-word responding would seem to vary in the extent to which they are likely to induce a how-many-question rule or a count-to-cardinal transition. The subitizing path is connected to numerosity at the beginning, but the rapid generalization of the rule to larger sets may not be accompanied by a generalization of the cardinal meaning of the last-word response to these larger sets. Learning the last-word rule by observation or from a recency bias or auditory "echoing" seem to be the least likely to result in a count-to-cardinal transition. Learning by being told might sometimes result in a count-to-cardinal transition (if the "teacher" attends well to this aspect and the child can assimilate it) and might sometimes result only in a how-many-question rule (depending on both the teacher and the learner).

Furthermore, although the evidence seems quite clear that at least two levels exist in last-word responding, at present we know very little about what moves children from using only a how-many-question rule to making the cardinal integration of perceptual unit items involved in the count-to-cardinal transition or about what may enable other children to make such a cardinal integration, and therefore a count-to-cardinal transition, with their first last-word response. Exploring these issues will require adequate measures of children's understanding of the cardinal reference of a last-word response. The heavily verbal methods we used here do not seem entirely satisfactory, for they introduce aspects of language that may not be necessary for understanding cardinal reference. However, understanding and learning to use correctly the linguistic quantitative terms differentiating counting and cardinal reference is surely an important developmental task for the preschooler. The many confusions in children's use of such terms illustrated in 7.6.3.1.2. indicate that this task has many complicated components.

8. Later Conceptual Relationships Between Counting and Cardinality: Addition and Subtraction of Cardinal Numbers

8.1. Introduction

The focus of this chapter is the developmental progression of relationships between count meanings and cardinality meanings of number words that extends from the earliest and simplest situations of addition and subtraction through the solution of the most complex addition and subtraction situations with large multidigit whole numbers.[1] Articulating this progression requires us to consider changes in children's representations of three differentiable aspects of addition and subtraction operations: (1) the addition or subtraction situation, (2) the solution procedure used to carry out the addition or subtraction operation, and (3) the relationships between count and cardinal meanings that are required by the solution procedure used. We hypothesize that each of these moves through a developmental sequence determined by the representational ability of the child. This representational ability shifts from a dependence on perceptually available entities to progressive internalization and abstraction of these entities. The key representational change at each developmental level involves either a change in the kind of unit item the child is able to conceptualize or in the complexity of the structure that the unit item can represent (an addend, a sum, or both simultaneously).

The focus on a developmental change in the kinds of unit items a child is able to conceptualize stems from the work of Steffe et al. (1983).[2] They proposed that children when counting pair a number word with a conceptual unit item. Initially, children can only count when entities are physically present. Each entity is taken by the child as a "countable" by a conceptual isolation of each entity as a perceptual unit item. Steffe et al. identified figural, motoric, verbal, and abstract unit items as progressively less concrete unit items that

---

[1] We use the term *whole number* rather than *natural number* because the addition and subtraction situations we describe could involve 0 as an addend.

[2] This viewpoint is extended in Steffe, Cobb and von Glasersfeld (in press). This manuscript was not available to me, so my discussion here does not reflect their most recent position.

children become able to use when counting in addition and subtraction object situations. Steffe et al. also used the term "integration" to refer to the conceptual uniting operation that permits a child to focus on a group of unit items as a single entity. They used this term to refer to a fairly advanced addition situation, but it seems to be an excellent term to describe the conceptual operation one must use to consider a situation as a cardinal situation. A cardinal number word then refers to the result of such a conceptual integration. We therefore use this term but attach prefixes to all of our uses to differentiate our uses from the special Steffe use. Our treatment therefore specifies for each developmental level the kind of conceptual units used by a child in counting and the kind of uniting conceptual operation used to create a cardinal situation out of these conceptual units. The cardinal conceptual structures available to a child also are specified for each level. Because our treatment spans such a long period, we omit the level of specificity in the Steffe figural, motor, and verbal items and include all of these within perceptual unit items, as they all require some perceptual support. Our treatment is similar in focus and intent to the Steffe et al. work, but our levels and terminology stem from our own work with children's counting in addition and subtraction situations.

Three hypothesized developmental sequences are outlined, one for relationships between count and cardinal meanings, one for addition and subtraction solution procedures, and one for addition and subtraction situations. The first is a detailed specification of the understandings required for the various solution procedures in the second. The third draws on the very considerable body of literature concerning addition and subtraction school word problems. School word problems are special decontextualized forms of real world addition and subtraction situations. These problems preserve the characteristics crucial to the mathematical structure of the relations among the cardinal numbers in the problem, but omit details irrelevant to this structure (and sometimes information useful to naive solvers, e.g., see Nesher, 1980, and De Corte & Verschaffel, 1985a). Children can only represent the relations among the cardinal numbers in such problems with the conceptual unit items they have available. The developmental progression in unit items thus constrains the addition and subtraction situations a particular child can represent. Initially, the limited unit items available to a child do not even permit a differentiation between the representation of the addition or subtraction situation and the solution procedure used in that situation. Later more abstract and flexible unit items do permit a separate representation of the problem situation and of solution procedures that can be used in that situation.

Because some development occurs in the relationships between counting and cardinal meanings before there are changes in the other two aspects of addition and subtraction (solution procedures and problem situations), these relationships are discussed first. To stress the inverse relationship between addition and subtraction operations and to avoid the unfamiliar terms used for the three numbers in a subtraction problem (*minuend*, *subtrahend*, and *difference*), the terms *addend* and *sum* are used for both addition and subtraction situations. The developmental levels of word problem representation and of solution procedures draw heavily on the work of Briars and Larkin (1984), Carpenter and Moser (e.g., 1983a, 1984), Cobb (1985, 1986, 1987), and Riley and Greeno (e.g., Riley, Greeno, & Heller, 1983).

It is important to stress that the focus of this chapter is on children's construction of conceptions that enable them to solve addition and subtraction problems with cardinal (whole) numbers of any size. Very young children (even 2-year-olds) can solve addition and subtraction problems with very small numbers up to sums of four (Starkey & Gelman, 1982; Starkey, 1987; Tables 1-2 and 1-3 in this book). However, these solutions are based on special perceptual processes that are not available for larger numbers. Children continue to use these perceptual processes (subitizing and visual and auditory patterns) at every level of addition and subtraction performance we outline. These processes permit precocious performance that drops back one or two levels as soon as larger numbers are used. For example children can count on one or two (e.g., $6 + 2$ is "6, 7, 8") long before they can count on more than four. It is not clear how or whether this precocious performance with small numbers contributes to the construction of the later more general solution procedures based on counting. This is an important question for future research. Whenever ages are given in this chapter, they refer to the more general counting solution procedures and not to the earlier more limited procedures involving small numbers.

8.2. Relationships Between Counting and Cardinality in Single-Set Situations

8.2.1. The How-Many Question Rule and Count-to-Cardinal Transitions

The earliest relationship between counting references and cardinality references is the how-many-question rule. This rule is demonstrated by answering the question "How many Xs are there?" with the last word said in counting the Xs but failing to demonstrate any understanding that the answer refers to the set as a whole or to the cardinality of the set. The count-to-cardinal transition is a more meaningful relationship in which the child also gives the last counted word as the answer to a how-many question but does demonstrate some understanding that this last word refers to the set as a whole and/or to the cardinality of the counted set. This transition requires that a child shift from thinking of the counting reference of the last counted word to the last object to thinking of the cardinal reference of this word to the numerosity of the set as a whole. Various proposals about how these early relationships are learned are discussed in chapter 7.

8.2.2. The Cardinal-to-Count Transition

A cardinal-to-count transition is required to count out a certain number of objects. To count out six buttons, for example, one must shift from the cardinal reference "six buttons" to knowing that one must count out buttons until one says "six," i.e., that the last counted word will be "six." One must also use a feedback loop to remember how many objects one is trying to count out. It seems likely that the cardinal-to-count transition follows the count-to-cardinal transition developmentally because the former seems to require that a child reflect on the count-to-cardinal transition or anticipate his or her counting with such a transition in order to determine what the last count word would be. Because the task of counting out *n* objects also requires the use of a feedback loop to remember *n* while counting, we tried to devise a task that would tap a cardinal-to-count transition more directly. Such a transition would be required if one were, for example, shown a row of butterflies, told that there were seven butterflies, and then asked what one would say when counting the last butterfly. We began an exploration of this cardinal-to-count transition with the subjects from the origin study reported in 7.4 who gave last-word responses (answered the question "How many *X*s are there?" with the last word said in counting). We wondered how many of the young subjects in that study who gave last-word responses also would be able to make cardinal-to-count transitions.

8.2.2.1. Method. The subject pool for the study consisted of the 31 children (aged 2 years 4 months [2-4] through 3 years 11 months [3-11]) from the study described in 7.4 who gave last-word responses plus 3 children aged 4-2 and 4-3 who were dropped from the analysis in 7.4 to simplify the reporting by age. A few of these 34 children were not given the task for the present study, because they were very tired by the time they reached this point in the interview; this was particularly true for the children who were taught to give last-word responses, because they had already had so many tasks. The number of children actually used in the present study was 28. They fell into four different groups differentiated by when they first started giving last-word responses: 14 were original last-word responders (gave last-word responses consistently from the very first trial); 8 were discoverers (began to give last-word responses sometime during the first task and gave them consistently for the rest of that task); 2 gave last-word responses after a memory task in which they were asked to recall what they had said for the last counted object; and 4 were instructed last-word responders (they were successfully taught to give last-word responses in a short teaching session).

After the tasks described in 7.4.3 were completed, the 28 children were given a task to assess the use of a cardinal-to-count transition in a single-set situation. For each of three trials, a row of stickers pasted to a strip of cardboard was placed in front of the child. The child was told, "Here are seven [five, six] stars [butterflies, faces]. If you count the stars [butterflies, faces] like this [experimenter gestures from the child's left-most sticker along the row to the right-most sticker], what will you say for this [experimenter points to the last right-most sticker] star [butterfly, face]?" For each of the first two trials on which the child did not answer correctly, the sticker rows were given again after the third trial. Thus, each child had up to five trials for this task.

Half the children in each of the four last-word response groups were given this task first, and half were given the task described in 8.3.1. first. Order of tasks did not seem to affect performance.

8.2.2.2. Results. Only three immediate last-word responders (the three 4-year-olds) and one discoverer (aged 2-10) correctly said the given number word for all three trials, that is, consistently demonstrated cardinal-to-count transitions. The three immediate last-word responders were classified as making count-to-cardinal transitions (rather than just using a how-many-question rule) on the basis of their consistently correct responses to the cardinality-reference questions (see 7.6.3.1.1). Two other children, one immediate last-word responder (aged 3-2) and one discoverer (aged 2-10), gave a correct answer to the cardinality-to-count task on a single trial.

All of the other 22 children failed to give a correct answer on a single trial. These children gave a single number word other than the given cardinal word, counted to find the answer, or said "I don't know." Seven children (distributed across all four groups) said "one" as the answer for all trials. For these children on trials following the first trial on which they said "one," the experimenter particularly emphasized the gestural direction of counting and made sure that the child was watching that gesture in order to minimize the possibility that this response was due to the child's misunderstanding the direction of counting (i.e., thinking that the question was asking what would be said for the first sticker instead of what would be said for the last sticker). Nevertheless, it is not clear whether some children were still confused about the direction of counting or whether they did not know the answer and were giving the best reasonable response they could give (i.e., they knew they could count and say "one" for that sticker even if the counting was different from that indicated by the experimenter). It might be helpful in the future to change the question to "...what will you say for this last star?" (Art Baroody, personal communication, December 1986).

Before giving the task we had been concerned that the task might overestimate children's understanding. It seemed possible that children would not know the answer to the question but would nevertheless respond with the given number word out of a lack of anything better to say. This clearly was not a problem. Most children simply did not connect the given cardinal word for the stickers to the activity of counting the stickers. Evidently, it takes some time for children to be able to represent their counting activity to themselves in order to make a cardinal-to-count transition.

8.2.3. Uses of Single-Set Transitions in Addition and Subtraction Situations

The single-set count-to-cardinal and cardinal-to-count transitions are very powerful conceptual tools. They enable children to solve a number of different kinds of elementary addition and subtraction problems. Children use these transitions from age 4 to age 6 or so in a variety of addition and subtraction solution procedures (e.g., Baroody, 1987b; Carpenter & Moser, 1984; Houlihan & Ginsburg, 1981; Siegler, in press; Siegler & Shrager, 1984; Steffe et al., 1983). However, before describing how these transitions are used in particular solution procedures, we discuss the kinds of addition and subtraction situations within which these solution procedures are used. This background will then permit us to discuss all three aspects of children's representations using perceptual unit items for single items: representations of the situation, the solution procedure, and the relationships between counting and cardinality meanings.

8.2.3.1. Classification of Addition and Subtraction Word Problems. There are many different real-world situations that lead to addition and subtraction operations on whole numbers. These situations can be described in the special decontextualized form of school word problems, which preserve the essential mathematical relationships but strip the situation of most other characteristics. Addition and subtraction word problems have been classified by many researchers (e.g., Briars & Larkin, 1984; Carpenter & Moser, 1983a; Riley, Greeno, & Heller, 1983). These classifications are basically similar, although they do differ in some details. Our modification of the Riley et al. classification is given in Table 8-1; the modifications stemmed from efforts to teach this classification to teachers so that it could be used in teaching word problems to children. The classification in Table 8-1 evidently has some validity outside this country, where most of the classifications have been made. Stigler, Fuson, Ham, and Kim (1986) reported that the addition and subtraction word problems in the Soviet mathematics textbook series fit such a classification and that the problems were distributed almost evenly across all the categories, as if the textbook constructors had used a similar classification.

The problem types on the left of each part of Table 8-1 use addition and subtraction as unary operations. In these situations there is an initial state that is operated on by a $(+x)$ or $(-x)$ to yield a changed final state. The problem types in the right columns of Table 8-1 involve addition and subtraction as binary operations: two givens are inputs for the operation $+$ or $-$ and yield a new third output. Problem types on page 254 of Table 8-1 (Change-Get-More and Put-Together) are basic addition situations: An initial state gets more or two parts are put together to make all. The problem types on page 255 of the table (Change-Get-Less and Compare) are basic subtraction situations: An initial state is decreased or a big and small quantity are compared to find the difference.[3] The relative difficulty of these different word problems and the procedures children use to solve them have been studied by many researchers

---

[3] We are not arguing that a given individual child or adult always considers each of the left six problems to be additive or the right six problems to be subtractive. Rather, the Change-Get-More and the Put-Together situations define two common meanings of addition, and Change-Get-Less and Compare situations define two common meanings of subtraction.

Table 8-1. Classification of Addition and Subtraction Word Problems

Unary operations	Binary operations

Basic addition situations

Change-get-more	Put-together
Change-get-more: missing End	Put-together: missing All
(Change 1: Result unknown)	(Combine 1: Combine value unknown)
Joe had 3 marbles.	Joe has 3 marbles.
Then Tom gave him 5 more marbles.	Tom has 5 marbles.
How many marbles does Joe have	How many marbles do they have
now?	altogether?
* Change-get-more: missing Change	* Put-together: missing Second Part
(Change 3: Change unknown)	(Combine 2: Subset unknown)
Joe had 3 marbles.	Joe and Tom have 8 marbles
Then Tom gave him some more	altogether.
marbles.	Joe has 3 marbles.
Now Joe has 8 marbles.	How many marbles does Joe have?
How many marbles did Tom give him?	
* Change-get-more: missing Start	* Put-together: missing First Part
(Change 5: Result unknown)	(Combine 2: Subset unknown)
Joe had some marbles.	Joe and Tom have 8 marbles
Then Tom gave him 5 more marbles.	altogether.
Now Joe has 8 marbles.	Tom has 3 marbles.
How many marbles did Joe have in the	How many marbles does Tom have?
beginning?	

(see Carpenter & Moser, 1983a; Riley et al., 1983, for reviews of this literature), and computer models that simulate children's solution patterns have been constructed (Briars & Larkin, 1984; Riley et al., 1983). Many variations in wording and in situational aspects of each subtype exist and exert considerable influence over children's performance. Particularly strong variations are those that cue or facilitate a solution procedure or are more specific with respect to the problem structure (e.g., De Corte, Verschaffel, & De Win, 1985).

Each problem type involves three entities (see Figure 8-1 for schematic drawings of each problem type). Each of these entities can be unknown, leading to three subtype variations within each problem type. Because these problem types are all additive/subtractive structures, they all have the same "addend + addend = sum" structure: one entity is the sum and the other two are addends, which together equal the sum. Therefore, in each problem type there is one problem that requires addition for its solution (the problem where the two addends are known) and two problems that require subtraction

Table 8-1. *Continued*

Unary operations	Binary operations

Basic subtraction situations

Change-get-less	Compare
* Change-get-less: missing End (Change 2: Result unknown) Joe had 8 marbles. Then he gave 5 marbles to Tom. How many marbles does Joe have now?	* Compare: missing Difference (Compare 1: Difference unknown) Joe has 8 marbles. Tom has 5 marbles. How many more marbles does Joe have than Tom?
* Change-get-less: missing Change (Change 4: Change unknown) Joe had 8 marbles. Then he gave some marbles to Tom. Now Joe has 3 marbles. How many marbles did he give to Tom?	Compare: missing Big (Compare 3: Compared quality unknown) Joe has 3 marbles. Tom has 5 more marbles than Joe. How many marbles does Tom have?
Change-get-less: missing Start (Change 6: Start unknown) Joe had some marbles. Then he gave 5 marbles to Tom. Now Joe has 3 marbles. How many marbles did Joe have in the beginning?	* Compare: missing Small (Compare 5: Referent unknown) Joe has 8 marbles. He has 5 more marbles than Tom. How many marbles does Tom have?

Note. These examples are adopted from the Riley, Greeno, and Heller (1983) example problems. Our terms are on the first line and the Riley et al. (1983) designations are contained below these in parentheses.

Asterisks mark problems that require subtraction. Compare problems also can ask the question using less rather than more and by using equalize questions containing either less or more (How many more marbles does Joe have to get to have as many as Tom?).

for their solution (the problems where an addend and the sum are known). The fact that there are variations of each problem type, which are solved by each operation, leads to an important distinction: the semantic structure of the underlying problem type as basically additive or subtractive versus the solution procedure (addition or subtraction) that is required to solve the given specific problem type variation. In the simplest instances of each problem type (the first instance given in Table 8-1), the semantic structure of the basic problem type and the necessary solution procedure are the same. These problems are the easiest for children to solve. However, in half the problem subtypes, there is a conflict between the basic semantic structure of the problem

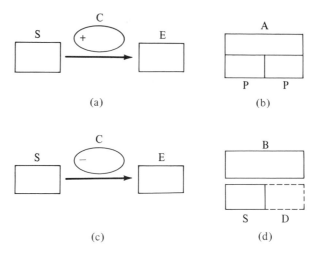

Figure 8-1. Schematic drawings for word problems. (a) Change-Get-More (S is start, C is change, E is end). (b) Put-Together (A is all, P is part). (c) Change-Get-Less (S is start, C is change, E is end). (d) Compare (B is big, S is small, D is difference).

type and the necessary solution procedure. These problems are considerably more difficult for children to solve.

8.2.3.2. Solution Procedures With Single-Representation Perceptual Unit Items. Children's earliest attempts to solve the word problem subtypes involve the direct modeling of the situation by objects (e.g., Briars & Larkin, 1984; Carpenter & Moser, 1983a; Riley et al., 1983). At this level children's representation of the problem situation is the same as their representation of the solution procedure used to solve the problem; both involve the acting out of the problem situation with objects. However, objects themselves are not numbers. Rather, some attribute of the objects must be abstracted to form the numbers in the problem. For perceptually available objects, the "entity-ness" of each object is conceptually isolated by the child as a perceptual unit item. These perceptual unit items can be counted, and the conceptual operation of "cardinal integration" can group unit items into a referent for a cardinal number word. Thus, at the earliest level of representation of addition and subtraction situations and at the earliest level of solution procedures for such problems, children's representations consist of perceptual unit terms. Furthermore, children at the earliest level seem to be able to use perceptual unit items only to represent one given set at a given moment. Thus, a given group of objects may at one time represent Mary's cookies and at a later time may be used together with some other objects to represent all of the cookies, but these objects (or, rather, the perceptual unit items the child forms from the objects) cannot at the same time represent *both* the addend and the sum.

The problem situations that can be solved only with perceptual unit items that represent a single set are given in level 1 of Table 8-2, and the direct modeling solution procedures that use such unit items are listed in level 1 of Table 8-3. Four solution procedures are listed at Level 1 in Table 8-3. The procedures in the left column, "count all" and "add on up to *s*," are additive (forward) solution procedures; the procedures in the right column, "take-away *a*" and "separate to *a*," are subtractive (backward) solution procedures. The top row of procedures, "count all" and "take-away *a*" are inverse operations characterized as "addend + addend = [*s*]" and "sum − addend = [*a*]". The bottom row of procedures, "add on up to *s*" and "separate to *a*," are inverse operations characterized as "addend + [*a*] = sum" and "sum − [*a*] = addend." Specific word problem variations that can be solved with level 1 conceptual units are listed in Table 8-2 in the level 1 quadrant (top/left, top/right, bottom/left and bottom/right) according to the same four basic underlying addend-addend-sum structures (see the top of the table). The relationships between counting and cardinality that are required to carry out the level 1 solution procedures are those discussed in 8.2.1. and 8.2.2. These are listed and described pictorially in Table 8-4 under level O, Single-set situation.

The four level 1 solution procedures require only count-to-cardinal transitions, cardinal-to-count transitions, and feedback loops to stop counting objects at a specified number. Problems requiring only the first would seem to be able to be solved first, those requiring only the first and second would seem to be solved next, and those requiring all three would seem to be solved last. Of course, these differences could be masked by variations in problem wording that affect children's understanding of the problem situation and by differences in children's understanding of basic problem subtypes. Children's ability to use these solution procedures is also considerably affected by three conditions of object availability. A problem can be presented already accompanied by objects arranged to model the problem, objects can be available with which a child can do the modeling, or no objects can be made available to the child. The first is, of course, the easiest, both for comprehension of the problem situation and for the solution. Whenever the child must count out objects herself, a cardinal-to-count transition and a feedback loop must be used, so such situations are more demanding. The third situation is of course the most demanding. This situation is especially prone to errors with numbers greater than five, for children cannot then simply use the fingers of each hand for one addend. Each of the level 1 solution procedures are now briefly described.

8.2.3.2.1. Count All. Count all is used to solve the simple Change-Get-More: missing End and Put-Together: missing All problems (see Table 8-1). If objects[4] representing each addend are presented with the problem, then

---

[4] In this chapter we use the term *object* to mean any entity that has materiality that can provide perceptual input and thus can be taken as a perceptual unit item. An object can be a picture, a dot on a piece of paper, and so on.

Table 8-2. Developmental Levels of Word Problem Representation

Level	Representational units	Additive situation	Subtractive situation
		addend + addend = [s] addend + [a] = sum	sum − addend = [a] sum − [a] = addend
I	Perceptual unit items single representation of the addend *or* sum	Ch⁺: Start + Change = [End] PT: Part + Part = [All] Ch⁺: Start + [Change] = End	Ch⁻: Start − Change = [End] PT: All − Part = [Part] Cm: Big − Small = [Difference] Ch⁻: Start − [Change] = End
II	Perceptual unit items simultaneous representation of the addend *within* the sum	Ch⁺: Start + Change = [End] PT: Part + Part = [All] [a] Cm^m: Small + Diff = [Big] Ch⁺: Start + [Change] = End [a] PT: Part + [Part] = All [a] Cm: Small + [Diff] = Big [a] Cm^l: Diff + [Small] = Big	Ch⁻: Start − Change = [End] PT: All − Part = [Part] Cm: Big − Small = [Diff] [a] Cm^l: Big − Diff = [Small] Ch⁻: Start − [Change] = End

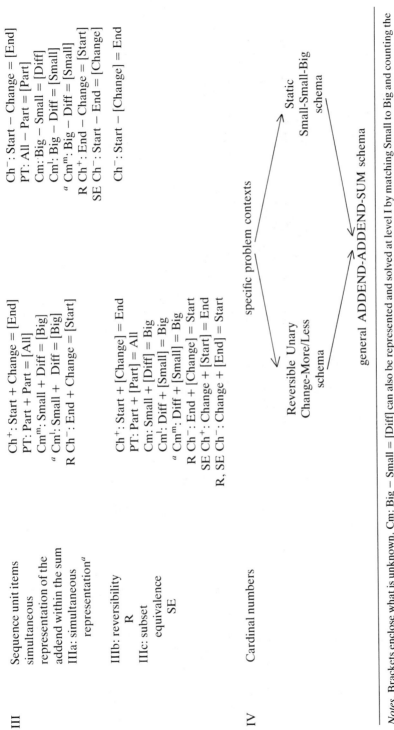

III — Sequence unit items simultaneous representation of the addend within the sum
IIIa: simultaneous representation[a]

Ch+: Start + Change = [End]
PT: Part + Part = [All]
Cm^m: Small + Diff = [Big]
[a] Cm^l: Small + Diff = [Big]
R Ch-: End + Change = [Start]

Ch-: Start - Change = [End]
PT: All - Part = [Part]
Cm: Big - Small = [Diff]
Cm^l: Big - Diff = [Small]
[a] Cm^m: Big - Diff = [Small]
R Ch+: End - Change = [Start]
SE Ch-: Start - End = [Change]

IIIb: reversibility R
IIIc: subset equivalence SE

Ch+: Start + [Change] = End
PT: Part + [Part] = All
Cm: Small + [Diff] = Big
Cm^l: Diff + [Small] = Big
[a] Cm^m: Diff + [Small] = Big
R Ch-: End + [Change] = Start
SE Ch+: Change + [Start] = End
R, SE Ch-: Change + [End] = Start

Ch-: Start - [Change] = End

IV — Cardinal numbers

specific problem contexts

Reversible Unary Change-More/Less schema   Static Small-Small-Big schema

general ADDEND-ADDEND-SUM schema

Notes. Brackets enclose what is unknown. Cm: Big − Small = [Diff] can also be represented and solved at level I by matching Small to Big and counting the extra (the Diff). Ch+, Change-Get-More; Ch−, Change-Get-Less; Cm^m a Compare problem using the word "more" in the question; Cm^l a Compare problem using the word "less" or "fewer" in the question; Cm, Compare; PT, Put Together; R, reversibility; SE, subset equivalence.
[a] A new problem at this level.

Table 8-3. Developmental Levels of Solution Procedures

Level	Cardinal conceptual operation	Conceptual units	Cardinal conceptual structures[a]	Additive (forward) solutions	Subtractive (backward) solutions
I	Cardinal integration	Perceptual unit items single representation addend *or* sum	[sketch]	addend + addend = [s] addend + [a] = sum Count all Add on up to s	sum − addend = [a] sum − [a] = addend Take-away a Separate to a
II	Embedded integration	Perceptual unit items simultaneous representation addend *within* sum	[sketch]	Count on a with objects Count up to s with objects	Count down a with objects Count down to a with objects
III	Embedded integration	Sequence unit items simultaneous representation addend *within* sum	[sketch: PI]	Sequence count on a Sequence count up to s	Sequence count down a Sequence count down to a
IV	Numerical equivalence	Cardinal numbers can be decomposed into ideal unit items[b]	[sketch: s, s]	Add (also thinking strategy[c]) Subtract (also thinking strategy)	Subtract (also thinking strategy) Subtract (also thinking strategy)
V	Base-ten integration	Base-ten numbers Perceptual ten-unit, hundred-unit, thousand-unit items	[sketch]	Multidigit addition Multidigit subtraction	Multidigit subtraction Multidigit subtraction

Note. Brackets enclose what is unknown. PI is paired integrations: the pairing of the embedded integration of the second addend with the integration of the keeping-track method. In the cardinal conceptual structures for levels II and III, a dotted line represents the unknown set and a solid line represents a known set; the top sketch in each level is the conceptual structure for the solution procedures in the top row and the bottom sketch is the structure for the solution procedures in the bottom row.

[a] See Table 8-4 for more details of the cardinal conceptual structures.

[b] At this level a child may solve a problem using an object or a sequence procedure, but the procedure will not necessarily directly model the problem representation. Children at this level also can use derived facts and strategies such as the over-ten method.

[c] Thinking strategies operate on cardinal numbers and relate the sum of two numbers to the sum of two related numbers.

counting all requires only a count-to-cardinal transition. All of the objects are considered as the single sum set, they are counted, and the last counted word is reported as the cardinal value of the sum, that is, as how many there are in all. When objects are not present and a child has to generate objects for each addend, more knowledge is needed. When the addends are small, the child may know figural patterns for each addend and generate these (e.g., Steffe et al., 1983). For example, for $4 + 3$, a child might put up four fingers on one hand and three fingers on the other hand and then count all of these fingers. Because these fingers can be counted all together, counting them to find the sum may require only a count-to-cardinal transition (or even only a how-many-question rule). If figural patterns are not known for a given problem, a set of objects must be generated for each addend. Counting out n entities requires a cardinal-to-count transition, that is, it requires that a child know that when making a set of n entities, the last counted word will be n. The child must also be able to use a feed-back loop to monitor the counting—be able to maintain the number n in memory while checking each counted word against it to see whether the counting should stop. Once sets for both addends have been counted out, all the objects can just be counted and a count-to-cardinal transition can be used to find the sum. Thus, the kinds of relationships between count and cardinal meanings that are required by counting all vary from a count-to-cardinal transition (when objects already represent the problem) to that transition plus a cardinal-to-count transition plus use of a feed-back loop to monitor counting (when children count out entities to model the problem).

8.2.3.2.2. Take Away a. Children solve Change-Get-Less: missing End problems by taking away a: making a set of (for example) *eight*, counting a set of *five* from these eight objects and taking them away from the eight objects, and then counting the remaining set for the answer (*three*). This procedure requires cardinal-to-count transitions and feedback loops monitoring the count in order to count out the sets for the sum and the addend, and a count-to-cardinal transition to find the remaining addend. If the problem is already modeled for a child with pictures or objects (the latter is a bit difficult to do because the five objects have to be modeled both as belonging to the initial sum state and then as the addend taken away), the child only has to use a count-to-cardinal transition to find the answer.

The Put-Together: missing First Part or missing Second Part problems can be solved by direct modeling if the child makes the set for all the objects first. Carpenter and Moser (1984) reported that a considerable proportion of first graders solved such a problem ("There are 12 children on the playground. 7 are boys and the rest are girls. How many girls are on the playground?) by taking-away a (Carpenter and Moser termed this solution procedure "separating from"): counting out 12 objects, counting 7 objects and removing them from the 12, and counting the objects left. This procedure requires the count-to-cardinal and cardinal-to-count transitions and a feedback loop for remembering 12 and 7 while counting out those sets.

Table 8-4. Developmental Levels in Relationships Between Counting and Cardinality

Level 0: Single-set situation Perceptual unit items Single representation	Level 1: Subset situation Perceptual unit items Single representation as an object in a subset

How-many-question rule ⟶ **Subset how-many-question rule**

000000
123456   How many? 6

0000000000
123456   How many? 6

Count-to-cardinal transition ⟶ **Subset count-to-cardinal transition**

000000
123456   How many?

six   (Cardinal
(000000)   integration)

0000000000
123456   How many?

six   (Subset
(000000)0000   integration)

Cardinal-to-count transition – – – – – – – ⟶ **Subset cardinal-to-count transition**

(000000)   What do you say for
six   this (last) dot?

6
000000

(000000)0000   What do you say for
six   this (last) dot?

6
0000000000

Level 2: Object embedded situation
Perceptual unit items: Simultaneous representation of the addends within the sum

---

Forward counting transitions	**Backward counting transitions**

Object-embedded count-to-cardinal transition of first addend within the sum count

Count down *a* with objects

Object-embedded cardinal-to-count transition of the sum

notice
same
     8 ⟵   5
[0 0 0 0 0 0 0 0][0 0 0 0 0]
1 2 3 4 5 6 7 8 9 10 11 12 13

     ?   5   = 13
[0 0 0 0 0 0 0 0][0 0 0 0 0]
                 13 ⟵

Count on *a* with objects

Object-embedded cardinal-to-count transition of first addend within the sum count (Embedded integration of first addend)

Object-embedded count extension to first addend within the backward sum count

     8   5
[0 0 0 0 0 0 0 0][0 0 0 0 0]
     ?

     ?   5   = 13
[0 0 0 0 0 0 0 0][0 0 0 0 0]
                 ? 9 10 11 12 13

If I counted all these dots, what would I say for this (?) dot?

Counting all these dots backward, what would I say for this dot?

Table 8-4. *Continued*

Object-embedded count extention to second addend within the sum count

$$\overset{8}{\boxed{0\ 0\ 0\ 0\ 0\ 0\ 0\ 0}}\ \overset{5}{\boxed{0\ \ \ 0\ \ \ 0\ \ \ 0}}$$
$$?$$

f I counted all these dots, what would I say or this (?) dot?

Object-embedded count-to-cardinal transition of the sum
(Embedded integration of the sum entities)

$$\overset{8}{\boxed{}}\ \overset{5}{\boxed{0\ \ \ 0\ \ \ 0\ \ \ 0\ \ \ 0}}\ \ = 13$$
$$8\quad 9\ 10\ 11\ 12\ 13$$

How many dots are there?

Object-embedded count-to-cardinal transition of first addend within the backward sum count
(Embedded integration of first addend)

$$\overset{?}{\boxed{0\ 0\ 0\ 0\ 0\ 0\ 0}}\overset{5}{\boxed{0\ \ \ 0\ \ \ 0\ \ \ 0\ \ \ 0}}\ \ = 13$$
$$8\quad 9\ 10\ 11\ 12\ 13$$

If I count this dot as 8, how many dots are in the first addend?

Level 3: Number-word sequence-embedded situation
Sequence unit items: Simultaneous representation of the addends within the sum

Forward-counting transitions	Backward-counting transitions
Sequence-embedded count-to-cardinal transition of first addend within the sum count **Sequence count on** a **Sequence-embedded cardinal-to-count transition of first addend within the sum count (Embedded integration of first addend)** **Sequence-embedded extension to second addend within the forward sum count** **and** **Method of keeping track of second addend coordinated with forward count of second addend (Pairing of integrations of second addend)** **Feedback Loop: Have counted on** a **and** **Sequence count-to-cardinal transition of the sum (Embedded integration of the sum)**	**Sequence count down** a **Sequence embedded cardinal-to-count transition of the sum** **and** **Method of keeping track of second addend coordinated with backward count of second addend (Pairing of integrations of the second addend)** **Feedback Loop: Have counted down** a **and** **Sequence-embedded extension to first addend within the backward sum count** **Sequence-embedded count-to-cardinal transition of first addend within the backward sum count (Embedded integration of first addend)**

Notes. An object may be a picture, a dot on a piece of paper, etc. Solid arrows denote developmental relationships that are supported by data. Broken arrows denote hypothesized developmental relationships. In tasks for children, the dots should all be equidistant apart; space did not allow that here.

A direct modeling of the simple Compare problem (the missing Difference form) is usually carried out by matching the small set to the large and then counting the extra unmatched objects (Carpenter & Moser, 1984; Fuson & Willis, 1986). We did not include this matching procedure in Tables 8-2 and 8-3 because the tables were already so complicated. The matching procedure requires understanding the compare situation and being able to represent it by making the Big and the Small sets of objects, being able to match the objects in the Small set to the objects in the Big set, and making a count-to-cardinal transition for the counted difference. There seems to be wide variation in the extent to which children in various settings use matching; this leads to differences in performance on this problem type across studies (e.g., see Carpenter & Moser, 1983a; Riley et al., 1983). Some children also seem to represent this kind of Compare problem by a "sum − addend = [a]" structure and find the difference by using a take-away a counting procedure: Count the small set, count that many and take them away from the big set, and count the remaining objects (Carpenter & Moser, 1984; Fuson & Willis, in press).

8.2.3.2.3. Separate to a. There is some evidence (Hiebert, 1981; Riley et al., 1983; Tamburino, 1980) that children successfully directly model the Change-Get-Less: missing Change problem with objects. They make a set of eight objects, count three of the eight to make the End state, separate the rest of the objects from these three, and count the separated objects to find how many were given away. This separate to a procedure differs from the take-away a procedure, because an unknown rather than a known number of objects is taken away (separated). Separate to a requires a cardinal-to-count transition and a feedback loop to make the sum set and the addend set and a count-to-cardinal transition to find the missing addend.

8.2.3.2.4. Add on up to s. Children also seem to be able to model the Change-Get-More: missing Change problem directly if the final question gives a clue to a solution procedure (for example, "Kathy has nine pencils. How many more pencils does she have to put with them so she has 15 pencils altogether?"). Carpenter and Moser (1984) reported that a substantial proportion of first graders solved this problem by adding on: Making a set of 9 objects, adding on objects until there were 15 objects, and then counting the objects added on. This solution procedure requires a count-to-cardinal transition for the final count, a cardinal-to-count transition and a feedback loop to count out 9 objects, and a cardinal-to-count transition and a feedback loop to count out 15 objects if the 9 objects are at that time considered as part of the sum and the counting of them begins at one. This procedure also can only succeed at this level if the new objects added on are placed in such a way that they are differentiable from the original 9 objects. It is not clear whether children in the Carpenter and Moser study followed this procedure or the more complex procedure (with the counting starting at 9) discussed in section 8.4.1.3.

8.2.3.3. Symbolic Addition and Subtraction Problems. Children in the United States spend a considerable amount of time in first and second grade solving symbolic addition and subtraction problems like $3 + 2 = ?$ and $15 - 8 = ?$ (see almost any first or second grade textbook). For these activities, the $+$ and the $-$ symbols must be given meanings by relating them to specific addition and subtraction situations. Tables 8-1, 8-2, and 8-3 indicate quite clearly how many different addition and subtraction situations exist, that is, how many potential meanings there are for $+$ and $-$. Children cannot be introduced to all of these situations at the same time. But at present the extreme alternative is followed in the United States. For at least the first three grades, the symbols $+$ and $-$ are given very limited meanings, and children do not even see many of the addition and subtraction situations in Tables 8-1 and 8-2 (Stigler et al., 1986). In contrast first-grade textbooks in the Soviet Union present all of the problems in Table 8-1 (Stigler et al., 1986) and even begin to present many kinds of two-step problems involving various combinations of two different problems from Table 8-1. We would suggest that *at least* the simplest problem types from each of the four main kinds of problems (Table 8-1) be used initially to given meanings to the $+$ and $-$ symbols.[5] Problem wordings that facilitate understanding of the problems (such as Equalize forms[6] of the Compare problems) should probably be used initially.

Children also need to have varied experiences to help them learn different interpretations of the equals sign ($=$) in symbolic addition and subtraction problems. In both Tables 8-2 and 8-3 a single symbol for equals was used throughout. In actuality there are several different interpretations for the $=$ sign in the various entries in these tables. These interpretations are especially clear for the simplest kind of word problem of each type (the first entry for each type in Table 8-1) (Fuson, 1979a). In Change problems the $=$ means "becomes" or "results in" and might best be represented by an arrow; the left-hand side of the Change "equations" in Table 8-2 disappear when the right-hand sides appear. In the Put Together problem the $=$ means "is identical to" or "consists of exactly the same entities"; the part and the part *are*

---

[5] We are not suggesting that children be taught a particular way to view a given word problem situation. In fact at later levels, a given word problem subtype can come to be viewed in several different ways. Different people seem to develop their own favorite ways of looking at certain problem subtypes, and we would certainly want to protect such individual choosing by children. What we are suggesting is the reverse: that the different problem situations be used to provide children with different interpretations of the $+$ and $-$ symbols so that children are not restricted to thinking of these symbols in only one way, as they are by present teaching methods in which $-$ means only take-away.

[6] The Equalize problems use a change to relate the two compared sets; the change for any of the three possible missing numbers (the Big, the Small, or the Difference) can be an increase or a decrease. Thus, for example, the simple Compare: missing Difference problem in Table 8-1 can be stated as an Equalize problem by substituting for the compare question either "How many marbles does Tom have to get to have as many as Joe?" or "How many marbles does Joe have to lose to have as many as Tom?"

the all. In the Compare problems the = means "is equivalent to" or "has the same number as"; the Big is equivalent to the Small and the Difference. The interpretation of the = sign for the other subtypes of each problem type is less clear, for these frequently are assimilated into a solution procedure representation with a different interpretation of the = than provided by the underlying problem type. For symbolic problems such as 8 + 6 = ? or 14 − 8 = ?, the equal sign means an arrow; the left side is operated on to "become" the right-hand side. Given the large number of symbolic problems children do in school, it is no surprise that their interpretations of the = sign is "results in" rather than either of the other interpretations (Baroody & Ginsburg, 1983; Behr, Erlwanger, & Nichols, 1980). The "is equivalent to" interpretation is the closest to the mature algebraic interpretation of the = sign. Research might explore the possible flexibility in interpretation of = that could be achieved by helping children interpret the = in the context of different word problems.

8.3. Relationships Between Counting and Cardinality in Subset Situations

At a later level a child becomes able to consider perceptual unit items as simultaneously representing elements of an addend and of a sum. An intermediary between that level and the first single-set level is one in which a subset is included within a larger set but the perceptual unit items represent only that subset within the larger set (see the level 1 pictures in Table 8-4). Thus, at this subset level (level 1), the child needs only to focus at a given moment on the subset and can ignore the rest of the items in the larger set. Data about relationships between counting and cardinality in such subset situations are reported in this section. Some data concerning developmental relationships between knowledge at level 0 (single-set situations) and knowledge at this level 1 (subset situations) are also discussed. Where there is evidence that some children know one entry in Table 8-4 but not another (i.e., evidence exists for developmental precedence), a solid arrow has been drawn connecting the entries. Broken arrows designate hypothesized developmental sequences that are suggested by task analysis but for which no empirical evidence is presently available.

8.3.1. The Subset How-Many-Question Rule and Count-to-Cardinal Transitions

The subset count-to-cardinal transition requires that a child be able to make the transition from a counting meaning attached to a single counted object to a cardinal meaning attached to a set as a whole *for any entity* within a counted set (see level 1 in Table 8-4). For example, if a person counting a set of 10 objects is stopped after saying "six," knowing that the cardinal number of entities counted up to that point is six would demonstrate a subset count-to-cardinal transition. We began an exploration of this more advanced transition with the Origin subjects (see 7.4) who gave last-word responses.

8.3.1.1. Method. The subjects were the same as those used in the study reported in 8.2.2. Half the children were given the task for that study first, and half were given the task for this study first. Order of tasks did not seem to affect performance. Both of these tasks were given after the tasks described in 7.4.3 were completed. All of these children had given last-word responses on at least some of those tasks.

For each of three trials, a row of stickers pasted to a strip of cardboard was placed in front of the child. The child was told to count the bears (stars, pigs). For each row the child was stopped at a predetermined number word (six, five, and seven) and asked, "How many bears [stars, pigs] are here?" while the experimenter gestured to all counted stickers. For each of the first two trials on which the child did not answer correctly, the sticker rows were given again after the third trial. Thus, each child had up to five trials for this task.

8.3.1.2. Results. Children were given one point for each row of stickers for which they answered the how-many question with the number word at which their counting had been stopped. The mean correct responses out of the possible 3 were 1.6 (immediate last-word responders), 1.3 (discoverers), 2.0 (last-word responders after the last-word memory task), and 0.8 (last-word responders after brief last-word responding instruction). The percentages of each group with a correct response on at least one trial were 64%, 63%, 100%, and 50%, respectively. A few children made large jumps, skipping many stickers when they counted and thus did not get up to the count words five, six, and seven. For these children the trials were redone with the experimenter doing the pointing and the child saying the number words. With this procedure four more children (two in each of the first two groups) responded correctly on a mean of 2.0 trials for each group. On the trials for which a correct answer was not given, children either recounted the indicated subset and gave the last counted word as the answer to the how-many question, gave a single number word different from the word at which they had stopped counting, or said, "I don't know." It was actually somewhat of a surprise to us that any children answered incorrectly, for we had feared that the task would overestimate children's understanding because many children might just say their last counted word as a guess. It is, of course, possible that some responses were just that, but the substantial number of children who gave other responses is somewhat reassuring that the task does not vastly overestimate children's knowledge.

We gave this task in an attempt to distinguish those children who could make subset count-to-cardinal transitions. However, the task itself required only a response to a how-many question. Thus, it seemed possible that the task might not require any cardinal meaning for the entities counted but might only be distinguishing children who could use a how-many-question rule in a subset situation. Because in chapter 7 we had used these children's responses to the cardinality reference questions (see 7.6.3.1.1 and Table 7-4) to differentiate use of a how-many-question rule from use of a count-to-cardinal transition, we compared children's performance on the cardinality reference questions to their performance on the present task. Seven children (one or more from each group) responded correctly on two or more trials of the subset count-to-cardinal task and did not respond correctly on two or more cardinality reference questions, even when the more lenient forced-choice scoring was used. Four of these children did not give a single correct response to a cardinality reference question. Therefore, it seems likely that some children can give a last-word response in a subset situation before they learn the cardinal aspects of the last counted word and begin to make even single-set count-to-cardinal transitions; that is, some children seem to be able to use a subset how-many-question rule.

There also seems to be for some children a time gap between the use of a single-set count-to-cardinal transition and the use of a subset count-to-cardinal transition. Of the 10 children not answering a single subset count-to-cardinal question correctly, 6 answered all three cardinality reference questions correctly (if forced-choice responses are included). These 6 children thus demonstrated a single-set count-to-cardinal transition but not a subset count-to cardinal transition. Therefore, the subset count-to-cardinal transition does seem to be a separate and more complex kind of understanding.

Of course, these two developmental conclusions are only as good as the tasks we used to measure these transitions. These tasks are admitedly quite verbal and complex and so are potentially confusing to children. We certainly think that more work is needed to develop good measures for these relationships between counting and cardinality meanings of number words. We also wish to underscore the fact that this level does *not* assess children's ability to include the subset within the larger set while they are counting, for this would require a perceptual unit item to represent an element of the smaller and the larger set simultaneously. This level only involves the ability to make a subset integration of perceptual unit items that *ignores* the remaining objects. Finally, we note that the subset level may be important for other kinds of situations. A subset count-to-ordinal transition is required to determine the ordinal word for every entity except the last in the ordering.

8.3.2. The Subset Cardinal-to-Count Transition

A subset cardinal-to-count transition is the ability to make a transition from a cardinal meaning to a count meaning for a subset within a larger set (see level 1 in Table 8-4). Again, perceptual unit items at this level represent only one object at a time, so such a transition does not imply that the child can represent the subset as included in the whole set; when the child is focusing on the subset, the extra objects are just ignored. We have not yet given a task like this so have no evidence about how much more difficult this transition might be than a single-set cardinal-to-count transition. This task would seem to be more difficult than either the subset count-to-cardinal transition or the single-set cardinal-to-count transition. These assumptions are reflected in Table 8-4 by broken arrows.

8.3.3. Use of the Subset Transitions in Addition and Subtraction Situations

A counting solution procedure that requires a subset transition may be used to solve Compare: missing Difference problems if picture displays that are difficult to match are provided with the compare problem. In this case children may count the small set, count out the same number within the big set, and then count the extra uncounted objects in the big set (Hudson, 1983). This procedure is like take-away *a* except that the addend set cannot be taken away because it is composed of pictures. The count of the small set requires only a single-set count-to-cardinal transition. However, when that set is counted out from within the large set, a subset cardinal-to-count transition and a feedback loop to remember the cardinality of the small set are required. A subset count-to-cardinal transition is then required at the end of counting the extra set.

Both take-away *a* and separate to *a* may also be done requiring subset transitions rather than single-set transitions. If objects for the known addend are taken away one by one while they are counted so that they form a new set, only single-set transitions are needed. However, the child may instead count the addend set while it still is part of the sum set, and then separate it from the sum set. In this case subset transitions are required. A similar distinction holds for separate to *a*.

8.4. Relationships Between Counting and Cardinality in Object-Embedded Situations

8.4.1. Solution Procedures and Relationships Between Count and Cardinality Meanings

At the next developmental level (level II), children still require perceptual unit items for representing and solving addition and subtraction problems. However, now a given perceptual unit item can simultaneously represent an object in an addend and in the sum. This distinction was termed using "double-role counters" in the word problem model proposed by Briars and Larkin (1984). The cardinal conceptual operation available with these simultaneous perceptual unit items is embedded integration: A given set of objects is integrated to form an addend embedded within a sum (see the sketch in Table 8-3). That is, the child can think of the addend and can simultaneously think of the whole sum as containing that addend. This simultaneous representation permits children to carry out count-to-cardinal and cardinal-to-count transitions for the addend within the counting of the sum. Such transitions enable children to use the more efficient counting procedures listed in Table 8-3: count on a, count up to s, count down a, and count down to a. At this level the child still requires perceptual support for the rest of the objects in the sum; objects must still be available for the second addend.[7]

8.4.1.1. Counting On a With Objects. Counting on with objects present for one or both addends is a major conceptual advance (Fuson, 1982a, 1982b; Fuson & Secada, 1986; Secada, Fuson, & Hall, 1983; Steffe et al., 1983). In counting on, the child does not count the objects for the first addend. The number for the first addend is stated,[8] and the counting of the sum continues on through the objects for the second addend: For example, for 8 + 5, the child says, "eight, nine, ten, eleven, twelve, thirteen" rather than counting from one to thirteen. In Secada et al. (1983), we suggested that three abilities are required for counting on with objects. The first is the number-word sequence skill of being able to start counting up from an arbitrary word in the number-word sequence; most kindergarten children possess this skill (see chapter 2 and Fuson et al., 1982). The second and third abilities are relationships between count and cardinality meanings: a cardinal-to-count transition within an object embedded situation and an object embedded count extension to the second addend within the sum count.[9] The tasks used to assess these abilities are the middle two pictures on the left in level 2 of Table 8-4. The embedded cardinal-to-count transition requires a shift from the given cardinal meaning of the first addend number word to its count reference to the last counted object of the first addend *within the final sum count of all the objects*; this requires the child to consider each perceptual unit item for the first addend as simultaneously representing the first addend and the sum. The object-embedded count extension to the second addend within the sum count requires the ability to continue the count initiated by the cardinal-to-count transition (saying a) by counting the first entity in the second addend as $a + 1$. We now add a third conceptual ability to these: a count-to-cardinal transition

---

[7] The first addend may be the first addend in an addition or subtraction situation given to the child, or the first addend may be the addend chosen to be first by the child. There is considerable debate in the literature as to the timing of counting on from the given first addend compared to counting on from the larger (i.e., chosen first) addend. We do not deal with this literature here, because the developmental patterns are not yet clear. In this chapter "first addend" means either the first addend given to the child or the addend (usually the larger) chosen to be first by the child. Similarly, then, "second addend" means either that given to the child or chosen by the child to be second.

[8] Some children seem later on to omit saying the word for the first addend and just continue the count by beginning with the next number word.

[9] We used somewhat different terms in that paper. Steffe et al. (1983) use the word "extension" to describe the third ability, and we have adopted that word here for both levels 2 and 3.

for the sum that must be made at the end of counting. This transition requires an embedded integration of the sum perceptual unit items and is pictured as the last sketch on the left in level 2 of Table 8-4.

In Secada et al. (1983), we found that children who counted on could demonstrate all three of the identified abilities and children who could not count on could not demonstrate one or more of these abilities. Children who failed to continue the count on to the second addend often gave the answer "one" or gave the cardinality of the second addend. Thus, these children seemed to be unable to consider that first entity of the second addend as *both* an entity in the addend and as an entity within the total sum set. However, both the embedded cardinal-to-count transition and the embedded count extension proved to be fairly easy to teach to first graders. Such teaching was successful in individual interviews and resulted in spontaneous counting on by most children so taught (Secada et al., 1983). Such teaching followed by the teaching of counting on in an object situation was also successfully carried out by teachers of first- and second-grade children of all ability levels (this instruction thus included work on the embedded integration of the sum entities); this instruction resulted in counting on by most children (Fuson & Secada, 1986). Thus, this analysis of understandings required for counting on does seem to be accurate and has resulted in successful classroom instructional interventions.

How might counting on come about? The fundamental required insight would seem to be an object embedded count-to-cardinal transition (see the top left drawing in level 2 of Table 8-4). Eventually, as the child counts all of the entities for the final sum count, the child will notice that the counting word n said for the last entity in the first addend is the same number word as the word n that tells the cardinality of that addend. This embedded count-to-cardinal transition will then enable the child to carry out the reverse embedded cardinal-to-count transition required for object counting on. We know little about how a child ordinarily moves on to counting on with objects, but it would seem possible that such a move might be precipitated by a peer, parent, or teacher. Baroody and Ginsburg (1986) argue that the move is motivated by considerations of efficiency: it is much faster to omit the counting of the first addend. The move to counting on does not occur instantaneously in all children, for one can see children who are in transition to such counting on. Such children say the counting words for the first addend very rapidly and without looking at the first addend objects and then begin to count on the objects for the second addend (A. Baroody, personal communication, April, 1987; Fuson, 1982b; L. Steffe, personal communication, August, 1980). The ease with which we have been able to induce first- and second-grade children to begin to count on with objects when we have followed the conceptual steps in Table 8-4 (it takes from one to four class periods) suggests that most first graders already have the conceptual understanding required and that the instruction is merely permitting them to reflect on and organize their knowledge to bring about this conceptual advance of counting on. However, without instructional support it evidently takes some children until third grade to begin to count on spontaneously (Carpenter & Moser, 1983a, 1983b).

8.4.1.2. Counting Down a With Objects. There is little research at present on relationships between counting and cardinality that are required to count down *a* in an object-embedded situation. Counting down *a* requires a child to count backward (count down) rather than forward and would seem to require the reverse of the counting/cardinal transitions used in the forward counting on. These reverse transitions are described and illustrated in level 2 of Table 8-4. The last picture on the right illustrates the end of counting down 5 from 13 to get 8. Because making the backward transitions would seem to require considerable experience with the forward transitions and because just counting backward is much more difficult for children than is counting forward (Fuson et al., 1982), it would seem that children would learn the backward-counting transitions considerably later than the forward transitions. Secada (1982) found that counting on preceded all forms of counting for subtraction, and Baroody (1984) and Fuson (1984) discussed how much more difficult counting down is than counting on. If a set of *a* objects is available or made, counting down can also be done by the second method described in 8.5.1.4.

8.4.1.3. Counting Up To s and Counting Down To a With Objects. The two procedures in the bottom row of level II of Table 8-3, counting up to *s* and counting down to *a*, are similar to the procedures just above (counting on *a* and counting down *a*) except that they each require an auditory feedback loop during the counting of the second addend. The feedback loop for count up to *s* is controlled by the known sum. To count up from 8 to 13, the count of the second addend begins at 9 and stops at 13, the known sum. The objects that have been counted up beyond the first addend 8 are then counted to find the missing addend; deciding to carry out this count requires an embedded integration of the perceptual unit items for that second addend within the sum. The feedback loop for count down to *a* is controlled by the known addend. To count down from 13 to 8, the count of the unknown second addend begins at 13 and ends just before the first addend word, 8 is said. The objects that have been counted down in the second addend are then counted to find the missing addend; deciding to count these objects also requires an embedded integration of the perceptual unit items for this second addend. Counting down to *a* also can be carried out by the second method described in 8.5.1.4. Because of the requirement for auditory feedback loops (rather than a visible set of objects) to control the counting, counting up to *s* and counting down to *a* might be slower to appear than are counting on *a* and counting down *a*. Cobb (1985) places both of these at a conceptual level that is two levels higher than counting down *a*. However, this finding may be limited to children whose only interpretation of subtraction is "take-away," for counting down *a* seems to be their first standard solution procedure for subtraction problems; in this case, the other solution procedures need to be derived from a counting down (sum − addend) structure.

8.4.2. Solution Procedures and Representations of Word Problems: Solving Word Problems

Word problems at level II can now also be represented by perceptual unit items that simultaneously represent the addend within the sum. The problem types that could be represented at level I with single sets can now be represented in the simultaneous form, and this simultaneous representation enables the level II solution procedures just discussed to be used to solve these level I problem subtypes. The availability of simultaneous representation of the addend and the sum now also enables new problem types to be represented and solved. These types are the problems in level II that did not appear in level I (they are marked with an *a* in Table 8-2).

The Put-Together: missing Part problem does not now have to be solved by counting out the sum objects first. It can now be represented by "addend + [a] = sum" and solved by counting up to *s*. This distinction between the two methods of solving this problem was also made in the word problem model proposed by Briars and Larkin (1984).

Carpenter and Moser (1984) reported that a substantial proportion of first graders solved the Change-Get-More: missing Change problem by adding on up to *s* when the final question gave a clue to a solution procedure (for example, "Kathy has 9 pencils. How many more pencils does she have to put with them so she has 15 pencils altogether?"). The children made a set of 9 objects, added on objects until there were 15 objects, and then counted the objects added on. We placed this problem at level I for those cases in which a child started the counting up from nine by starting at one. However, the more efficient count up to *s* procedure in which one starts counting at nine and then continues the count from nine to fifteen objects is a level II procedure. This analysis is consistent with the models of Riley (Riley et al., 1983) and of Briars and Larkin (1984), which put the solution of this kind of Change-Get-More problem at the same second level. Carpenter and Moser (1984) found that almost all children used adding on with objects before they used counting on as a number-word sequence procedure (see 8.5.1.2.). Two possible reasons for this finding might be explored. The first is that, as described in 8.2.3.2.4., children in fact might have done adding on by counting all. They might have begun making the final sum of 15 objects by starting to count the 9 objects already there at the first object and then just added on more objects when needed. Such counting all obviously would precede counting on as a sequence procedure. Second, Carpenter and Moser did not seem to isolate counting on with objects as a separate solution procedure. Thus, their adding on with objects might have been our level II counting up to *s* procedure, and it thus might well follow counting on *a* with objects but precede sequence counting on *a* (see Table 8-3).

At level II the missing Difference form of the Compare problem can be

· represented as an "addend + [a] = sum" structure: Small + [Difference] = Big. This representation enables the missing Difference form to be solved by counting up to s with objects. Children who interpreted such problems as sum − addend = [a] at level I can keep that interpretation but can now use counting down a to solve such problems. However, we found such problems to be solved much more frequently (10 solutions versus 1 solution) by counting up to s with objects than by counting down a with objects (Fuson & Willis, in press). This was especially true for the Equalize form of the problem (the final question being "How many more marbles does Tom have to get to have as many as Joe?"), where the wording of the problem gave an addition cue (17 count up solutions versus 2 count down solutions). These children had learned to count on to solve symbolic addition problems, so this may have made counting up easier for them to conceptualize. Carpenter and Moser (1984) found in their longitudinal study that most children who did not use matching could not solve the regular Compare form until they could use count up to s. However, they did not make a distinction between counting up with objects (Level II) and counting up as a sequence procedure (level III), so the extent to which their children used count up to s with objects is not clear.

Two new forms of Compare problems are able to be represented at level II: missing Big using "more than" (Small + Difference = [Big]) and missing Small using "less than" (Big − Difference = [Small]). These representations are possible because the Difference comparison has-more-than (has-less-than) terms happen to be consistent with the action interpretations of these terms: the gets-more Difference is added and the gets-less Difference is subtracted. Thus, the comparison terms may cue the action terms, suggesting a representation and solution procedure at the same time. The missing Big problem (Joe has 3 marbles (Small). Tom has 5 more marbles than Joe (Difference). How many marbles does Tom have [Big]?) can be represented by addend + addend = [s] (Small + Difference = [Big]) and can be solved by counting on a. The missing Small problem (Joe has 8 marbles (Big). Tom has 5 less marbles than Joe (Difference). How many marbles does Tom have [Small]?) can be represented by sum − addend = [a] (Big − Difference = [Small]) and solved by counting down a. This problem can also be represented by addend + [a] = sum (Difference + [Small] = Big) and solved by counting up to s.

8.5. Relationships Between Counting and Cardinality in Number-Word Sequence-Embedded Situations

8.5.1. Solution Procedures and Relationships Between Count and Cardinality Meanings

Eventually, counting becomes abstracted from the objects being counted and the words in the number-word sequence are taken as the entities, or the units, representing the addends and the sum (Fuson et al., 1982; Steffe et al. 1983). It is the number words themselves that are counted as the number words are said. Each number word is taken as an equivalent unit regardless of the cardinal value of that word, that is, a sequence unit item is formed for each word in the sequence. Fuson et al. (1982) proposed that this use of the number-word sequence required that the words in the sequence be at the representational level of a "numerable chain"; that is, the words could be taken as units to form sets that could have cardinal numbers. Steffe et al. (1983) described the equivalent unit items of this kind as "verbal unit items" or "abstract unit items" (depending on the sophistication of the use of the second addend). The conceptual operation of embedded integration forms these sequence unit items into cardinal situations and permits these sequence unit items to represent cardinal addition and subtraction.

When the second addend (or the addend taken as the second addend by the child) is very large, all the sequence procedures in level III of Table 8-3 require some method of keeping track of the number of words said for the second addend. At level II objects represented the second addend and were counted in the final sum count (either forward or backward). For counting on *a* and counting down *a* with objects, the objects governed the amount of counting (counting stopped when the second addend objects were counted). For counting up to *s* and counting down to *a* with objects, the perceptual unit items for the second addend objects underwent an embedded integration to give the unknown second addend. However, for the level III sequence procedures, objects are not used, so some other means must be used to govern the number of words said (for sequence counting on *a* and counting down *a*) or to record the number of second addend words said (for sequence counting up to *s* and counting down to *a*). Three ways in which children keep track of the second addend (Fuson, 1982a, 1982b; Steffe et al., 1983) are by saying the second addend words in an auditory pattern (for example, an auditory pattern for 6: "8, 9, 10, 11, 12, 13, 14"), by using known finger patterns (e.g., 1 hand plus 1 finger is 6) and matching each second addend word to a finger extended as the word is said, and by double counting ("8, 9 is 1, 10 is 2, 11 is 3, 12 is 4, 13 is 5, 14 is 6").

The sequence counting procedures require new relationships among sequence, counting, and cardinal number-word meanings in which the conceptual unit items are sequence unit items. These new relationships are listed in level 3 of Table 8-4. Most of these relationships are the sequence analogies of the relationships in object-embedded situations in level 2 of Table 8-4. However, a major new requirement of level 3, as mentioned previously, is the use of an effective keeping-track method for the second addend and the coordination of this keeping-track method with the (forward or backward) count of the second addend. The use of these keeping-track methods requires that the embedded integration of the sequence unit items for the second addend be paired with an integration of the unit items that are used in the keeping-track method. The latter may be figural (for a pattern method), motoric, or sequence until items, depending on the method of keeping track. Thus, a major new conceptual achievement at this level is the pairing of unit items from the two different integrations for the second addend; this pairing permits the keeping-track methods to function accurately.

8.5.1.1. Sequence Counting All. The first forward sequence transition is the sequence embedded count-to-cardinal transition of the first addend within the sum count. This transition, in which a child notices that the final word for the first addend is the cardinal word for that addend, can occur when a child is carrying out a primitive sequence procedure called count-all. For example, to add 8 + 6 by counting all as a sequence procedure, a child might say: "1, 2, 3, 4, 5, 6, 7, 8 [pause] 9, 10, 11 [pause] 12, 13, 14." The first eight number words represent the addend 8 and the second six number words represent the addend 6 (Baroody, 1987b; Fuson, 1982a; Stefÿe et al., 1983). The first eight words may be said very rapidly and almost cursorily as though the child is ready for the next transition (the sequence cardinal-to-count transition and sequence counting on) but just cannot quite trust it yet. The evidence is clear that with sums above ten children count on with objects (level II) but do not sequence count on (level III), that is, that count on with objects does precede sequence count on (Fuson & Secada, 1986). However, how sequence counting all fits into the developmental sequence and whether all children sequence count all at some time is not yet clear. This issue is particularly cloudy because most evidence concerning sequence counting all is for problems with small second addends. Because children are able to keep track of small second addends by special perceptual processes that do not work for larger addends, such problems are considerably easier to solve. They thus may be solved considerably earlier than sequence counting all can be used more generally. It is not at present clear what moves children from sequence counting all to sequence counting on; Baroody and Ginsburg (1986) and Resnick and Neches (1984) argue that considerations of procedural efficiency are the most likely source of this shift.

8.5.1.2. Sequence Counting On a. For counting on as a sequence procedure, the initial cardinal-to-count transition is within a number-word sequence situation and so is the counting word bridge, the extension, to the second addend. When a count-to-cardinal transition occurs at the end of the final sum count, the cardinal reference is then to the set of number words just produced. Thus, this is a count-to-cardinal transition within a number-word sequence situation. If an auditory pattern or successive finger extension is used as the method of keeping track of the second addend, the sequence words are entities to be matched to the auditory or finger pattern. For keeping track by double counting, the sequence words are entities to be counted. In all cases the use of the keeping-track method must be coordinated with the forward count of the second addend, and the auditory or finger pattern or the double counted number must function within a feedback loop, that is, it must be checked with each forward count so that the forward count can stop correctly.

8.5.1.3. Sequence Counting Up To s. Sequence counting up to s uses the same transitions as does counting on a. However, the keeping-track method functions differently. The feedback loop is controlled by the forward counting (each word must be monitored to see if s has been said yet), and the keeping-track method (the auditory or finger pattern or the double count) records the second addend. The answer is obtained by focusing on the cardinality of the pattern or double count, that is, by making an embedded integration of the keeping-track unit items.

8.5.1.4. Sequence Counting Down a and Counting Down To a. The backward counting transitions necessary for sequence counting down a are given in level 3 of Table 8-4. These transitions are the reverse of the forward counting transitions required for counting on a. For sequence counting down a, a words (the words representing the second addend in the backward sum count) are generated in reverse order (from the sum down to the first addend), and the next word down is the cardinality of the first addend (the remainder in a take-away situation). This procedure requires the reverse of the embedded extension. The child must recognize that the ath word counted down is the last word for the second addend and that the next word counted down is the first word of the first unknown addend [a]. However, the child must then also understand that this first word for the first addend (first word said when counting down) would be the *last* word for the first addend if the counting were being done in the usual forward way. Thus, a child must make a sequence embedded count-to-cardinal transition for the first addend within the backward sum count. Therefore, this counting down a requires both backward number-word sequence skill (the ability to count backward from a given word) and a reversible understanding of counting on as a sequence procedure.

However, children actually use two different counting-down procedures (Fuson, 1984). The other counting-down procedure may not be linked so well to cardinal understandings. It is the procedural backward analogue[10] to the counting-on procedure. For $14 - 6$, this would be: say a word (14), say 6 more words (13, 12, 11, 10, 9, 8), and the last word said is the answer (8). A possible meaningful interpretation of this procedure is given in Baroody (1984): 14 (words in all), 13 (1 word taken away), 12 (2 words taken away), 11 (3 words taken), 10 (4 words taken), 9 (5 words taken), 8 (6 words taken). The parentheses represent the keeping-track method, and the counting down stops when 6 (the known a) is reached. In this case at each backward count the word is also the cardinality for the remainder set left by taking away

---

[10] As acknowledged in Fuson, 1984, this possibility was pointed out to me by both Jim Moser and Ruth Steinberg.

objects. Thus, a sequence embedded count-to-cardinal transition is required at the end of the counting down. Most reports of counting down have not differentiated these two procedures, so their relative prevalence is not clear. However, children sometimes confuse these two procedures, and make both kinds of possible mistaken combinations of them (Steinberg, 1984). This indicates that some children may use counting down in a procedural way without close ties to cardinality.

Counting down to a requires the same backward counting transitions as does counting down a. The difference is that the backward counting is monitored in order to stop the counting at a, and the keeping-track method accumulates the second addend and must be checked to find the answer when counting stops at a. Counting down to a can also be done by the second method described above for sequence counting down a.

8.5.1.5. Relationships Among the Sequence Counting Procedures. Counting on may precede the use of the other three sequence procedures. Secada (1982) found that all children who used a sequence procedure for subtraction also counted on, and Fuson and Secada (1986) reported that it was quite easy for teachers to teach counting up as a sequence procedure after teaching counting on as a sequence procedure. However, Carpenter & Moser (1984) reported that 17% of their children used counting up before using counting on for Change-Get-More word problems, while 30% used counting on in an interview before they used counting up. Therefore the timing of the first uses of counting on a and of counting up to s might be examined in future research.

The backward counting-down procedures are much more difficult for children than are the forward procedures (Baroody, 1984; Fuson, 1984; Steffe et al., 1983). This led us to suggest (Fuson, 1984) that children be taught to subtract symbolic problems by sequence counting up to s. We then carried out such instruction by introducing the minus sign as having three meanings: a take-away, compare, and equalize meaning (Fuson, 1986b). First- and second-grade teachers were very successful in teaching subtraction as sequence counting up after they had taught children counting on a with objects and sequence counting on a (Fuson, 1986b; Fuson & Willis, in press). Even below-average first graders were able to solve all subtraction fact problems (those with single-digit addends and sums through 18) by counting up. Because the usual two-handed method of keeping track can be slow and cumbersome (children often put down their pencil to use both hands or even to use one hand), a special, efficient one-handed method of keeping track of the words counted on or counted up was taught (Figure 8-2). This method proved to be so efficient that children were able to count on with these finger patterns to solve large multidigit addition problems and to count up to solve large multidigit subtraction problems (Fuson, 1986a). Teaching subtraction as counting up did not interfere with children's understanding of take-away problems (Fuson & Willis, in press), and children were able to solve compare and equalize problems as well as they solved take-away problems (Fuson, 1986b; Fuson & Willis, in press).

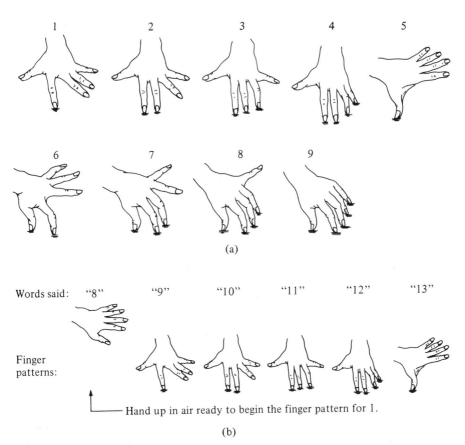

Figure 8-2. Counting on and counting up with finger patterns. (a) The finger patterns for 1 through 9 are made by touching certain fingers and/or the thumb to some surface such as a table. Thus, there is kinesthetic as well as visual feedback for the finger patterns. The finger patterns use a subbase of 5. The thumb is 5, and 6 is the thumb plus the 1 finger (6 = 5 + 1), 7 is the thumb plus the two fingers (7 = 5 + 2), etc. The motion from 4 to 5 is a very strong and definite motion—the fingers all go up and the thumb goes down, all in one sharp motion with the wrist twisting. The finger patterns in (a) are the patterns used in Chisanbop (Lieberthal, 1979). We use the finger patterns differently from the way in which they are used in Chisanbop. We use them (b) in the way that children spontaneously use fingers on both hands to keep track—the fingers just match the counting words that are counting on through the second addend (or counting up to the sum in subtraction).

Addition	*Subtraction*
8 + 5 = ?	13 − 8 = ?

The counting-on procedure:
1. Count on 5 more words from 8.
2. Stop when finger pattern for 5 is made.
3. Answer is last *word* said (13).

The counting-up procedure:
1. Count up from 8 to 13.
2. Stop when say 13.
3. Answer is what the *hand* says—the finger pattern for 5.

8.5.2. Solution Procedures and Representations of Word Problems: Solving Word Problems

We suggest that at level III (see Table 8-2), three different sublevels of word problem representations may occur. At the first sublevel, IIIa, problems are represented by sequence unit items with simultaneous representation of the addends within the sum. This permits all of the old problems from level II to be represented and solved by sequence counting solution procedures as well as the new level III problems now to be so represented and solved. The old entries at level III (those repeated from level II and not marked with *a*) are consistent with sequence solution procedures reported for those specific problem types by Carpenter and Moser (1984). The new Compare problem entries in level III are based on our own observational data (Fuson & Willis, 1986 and 1987).

At sublevels IIIb and IIIc, children use reversibility (R) and subset equivalence (SE), respectively, to solve change problems. Briars and Larkin (1984) describe these as operations that are carried out on problem representations, and they specify how reversibility and subset equivalence can be used to solve the Change-Get-More and Change-Get-Less missing Start problems. For example, to solve a Change-Get-More: missing Start problem (see Table 8-1) by reversibility, a child would think of beginning with the sum (the marbles Joe has at the end), giving back the marbles that were given (taking away the change marbles), and ending up with the marbles Joe had at the start (the End − Change = [Start] marbles). To solve this problem by subset equivalence, the child considers the Start and Change amounts to be interchangeable, represents the problem as Change + [Start] = End, and solves it by sequence counting up. Briars and Larkin consider the use of reversibility or subset equivalence to require a rerepresentation of the problem. We place reversibility before subset equivalence because Cobb (1986) reported that reversibility seemed to precede the use of subset equivalence in change problems. Problem representations that result from reversibility or subset equivalence are marked in Table 8-2 with R or SE.

We are not so sure that children at this level actually first represent problems and then rerepresent them by reversibility or subset equivalence. Our observations of second graders asked to use dolls and objects to "show what is happening in the problem" for the most difficult Compare problems (missing Small using has-more and missing Big using has-less) suggest a different possibility (Fuson & Willis, 1986b). Children did not first set up the problem with objects (i.e., represent it) and then solve it. Rather they told or showed the answer or displayed the solution procedure with objects. They seemed to assimilate the problem directly into a representation that led to a solution; that is, as they read the problem, they constructed a coherent representation which then supported a solution procedure. For example, for the missing Small more problem ("Bob has 7 stickers. Bob has 3 more stickers than Joe. How many stickers does Joe have?"), some children counted up from 3 to 7 or just gave 4 objects to Joe and said they added. They seemed to have represented the problem as Diff + [Small] = Big and solved it by the isomorphic addend + [a] = sum procedure. Others gave Bob 7 and took away 3 of them. These children seemed to reinterpret the middle "3 more" sentence as a "3 less" sentence (Joe has 3 less than Bob), thus reducing this to the easier Compare less form, and then solving this form by Big − Difference = [Small]. This reinterpretation of a sentence containing "more" to an equivalent sentence containing "less" is a key part of this solution procedure, but it is not to us the same as first representing and then rerepresenting the entire problem.

Another aspect of these data that led us to the suggestion of assimilation into a representation consistent with a problem solution is that these children were first asked to retell each story. Some children did not retell the story correctly but solved it correctly nevertheless. One example for the preceding missing Small problem was a child who retold the story as "Bob had 7 stickers. Joe had 3 stickers. How many stickers did Bob have?" and put 7 objects with Bob, 3 with Joe, and said the answer was 4 "because I take away 3 from Bob." Thus, the take-away solution procedure and the explanation are correct and consistent but the original problem has been lost (or never was represented). In particular, this child had difficulty representing and stating the known difference.

The representation of problem situations and solution procedures by embedded sequence unit items in level IIIa might support the steps to reversibility and to subset equivalence. It seems possible that the very strong embedded integration of the second addend that is required by the pairing of the second addend unit items with those of the keeping-track method helps to make *both addends* quite salient within the sum and may then help lead children to be able to use reversibility and subset equivalence.

It may also be that the three sublevels within level III do show an increasing separation between the representation of the word problem and the solution procedure such that the word problem is initially modeled and then this representation undergoes reversibility or subset equivalence to yield the form of the problem listed in Table 8-2; this form then supports a sequence counting solution procedure. However, our argument is that at this level the initial representation of the problem is still with sequence unit items representing the specific numbers given in the problem, and this specific problem representation is then transformed. This is in contrast to an argument that a child possesses a general problem schemata on which reversibility or subset equivalence operate.

Riley et al. (1983) and Kintsch & Greeno (1985) also propose models that use rerepresentation at the highest level. However, these models do not just change around the parts of a specific problem. Rather, one problem main type is changed into another main type. For example, these models solve the Change: missing Start problems by rerepresenting these problems as Put-Together problems. However, De Corte & Verschaffel (1985b) found a sizable number of children who could solve Change-Get-Less: missing Start problems but not the analogous supposedly required Put-Together: missing Part problems. Thus, initially at least, children seem to have some representation of Change-Get-Less: missing Start problems that enables them to solve this problem without rerepresenting it as a Put-Together problem. We suggest that they assimilate such problems into one of the interpretations in level III of Table 8-2.

8.5.3. Summary

All of the sequence procedures for both adding and subtracting require embedded count-to-cardinal or cardinal-to-count transitions within a number-word sequence situation, and the counting-down procedures may also require understanding of the forward counting procedures in reverse as well as the ability to count backward. These transitions within a number-word sequence situation require a child to consider sequence unit items as belonging simultaneously to an addend and to the sum (both of which are composed of number words). Thus, these transitions mark a new integration of number-word meanings: relationships now involve counting, cardinal, and sequence meanings. When second addends are very large, the sequence procedures require a method of keeping track of the words said for the second addend. Such keeping-track methods require the pairing of the unit items for two integrations of the second addend: the embedded integration of the sequence unit items and the integration of the unit items used in the keeping-track method. The availability at this level of sequence unit items for representing numbers seems to free children's problem representations from the concrete actions of the problem situation. This new flexibility enables many problems to be solved in different ways by different children (see Table 8-2).

8.6. Level IV: Addition and Subtraction of Cardinal Numbers

Our discussion of the remaining levels in Tables 8-2 and 8-3 is considerably more speculative than the earlier discussion. Few data exist concerning specific details of these levels, although some general patterns seem fairly clear. The major step forward in level IV is that the representational units are no longer single-unit items that must be integrated to represent a cardinal situation. The representational unit is now a cardinal number itself. The available cardinal conceptual structure relates three cardinal numbers by the operation of numerical equivalence so that two numbers together are equivalent to a third (see Table 8-3). These two numbers are now not embedded within the third, but can be represented separately and compared to the third number. The representations of word problem situations at this level become increasingly general and related to each other, culminating in a general ADDEND-ADDEND-SUM schema within which all addition and subtraction problems can be subsumed. At this level there may be a quite definite separation of and difference between the child's representation of the problem and of the solution procedure by which the problem will be solved.

8.6.1. Solution Procedures at Level IV

Children have by this point had so many experiences in school in working with specific numbers that a single-digit number has itself become a single concrete unit to the child. Moreover, the child has now had many experiences with specific triplets of numbers related in an additive/subtractive manner, for example, 5, 3, 8 and 6, 6, 12 and 7, 3, 10. For these triplets, the child can find any missing number if two are known. Experience with such triplets has now led to the construction of a cardinal triplet conceptual structure in which two cardinal numbers are together equivalent to a third cardinal number (see the sketch in Table 8-3). This conceptual structure does not require that the two smaller cardinal numbers be embedded within the larger numbers, as in the earlier additive structures composed of perceptual and sequence unit items. Rather, each of the three cardinal numbers in the triplet structure can be thought of separately. This separation enables this conceptual structure to operate very flexibly; any two numbers can be combined to give the third. With this conceptual structure, the child can also be conscious of wanting to add or to subtract and may carry out these procedures in ways that do not directly model the problem situation that requires an addition or subtraction. Thus, at this level there may be a definite separation of and difference between the child's representation of the problem and the solution procedure by which the problem will be solved. Finally, the structure also provides an eventual basis for relating all three of the possible missing number situations, and thus, of relating addition to subtraction.

A child at this point may not have learned all single-digit combinations and may need to add or subtract to find the missing triplet for a given problem. The conceptual cardinal numbers in this case can each be decomposed into what we will call "ideal unit items." The child may decide to use sequence unit items or even perceptual unit items, but these uses are not limited by the cardinal conceptual structures in levels I, II, and III. For a missing part Put-Together problem, for example, the child might now represent the known part and the known whole and compare them in the triplet structure rather than needing to have the known part embedded within (being part of) the known whole. The child may then carry out addition or subtraction in a certain favored way for all problems regardless of the problem structure. For example Carpenter and Moser (1984) found in a longitudinal study that sometime in second or third grade many children shifted to a consistent use of counting up to s to solve four problems with different situational subtraction structures: Change-Get-More: missing Change, Change-Get-Less: missing End, Put Together: missing Part, and Compare: missing Difference. Earlier, these children had solved each problem with a sequence solution that modeled the problem structure (e.g., Change-Get-Less: missing End by counting down a). Of course, these children might have just been assimilating each problem into the problem representation in the addend + [a] = sum cell of level III of Table 8-2. However, it would seem that at some point children would reflect on the similarity in their solution procedure for these problems and be able to identify it as a single operation, subtraction. Their consistency in solving *all* subtraction problems by counting up to s seems rather to suggest that they were deciding to subtract and then carrying out the subtraction operation by their perferred method of subtraction, counting up to s.

Another example of this kind of separation of problem and solution procedure comes from some bright first graders who solved Change-Get-Less: missing End, Compare: missing Difference, and Equalize: missing Difference problems by sequence counting up to s when objects were not available but later solved them all by take-away a when asked to solve them with objects (Fuson & Willis, in press). In all these cases the children could have assimilated each problem type into the counting up to s structure (addend + [a] = sum) in level III of Table 8-2. However, their use of take-away a when asked to solve the problems with objects seems to make this less likely. Did the availability of objects change their representation of each problem (into sum − addend = [a] in level III in Table 8-2)? These children were part of an instructional study. They had been taught object and then sequence counting on to solve symbolic addition problems. The − in symbolic subtraction problems had then been introduced as having at least three meanings: take away, compare, and how many more (equalize). That is, subtraction was initially introduced in the context of Change-Get-Less: missing End, Compare: missing Difference, and Equalize: missing Difference ("Joe has 8 marbles. Tom has 5 marbles. How many more marbles does Tom have to get to have as many as Joe?") problems. Children then practiced solving symbolic subtraction problems using counting up to s (using the Equalize interpretation) because it was so much easier than counting down a. Thus, the behavior of these children seems to be better explained by assuming that when they saw each problem, they made a decision to subtract. That is, their solution procedure did not derive directly from the representation of the problem, as at level III. Rather, their solution procedure was an arithmetic operation, subtraction. When objects were not available, they carried out the subtraction operation in their usual way—by counting up to s; when objects were to be used, they carried oiut the subtraction operation by one fundamental object interpretation of subtraction—take-away a.

The fact that so many children in Carpenter and Moser's (1984) sample chose counting up rather that counting down as their subtraction solution procedure seems to us to stem from at least two reasons. First, counting up is very much easier than is counting down both procedurally (it requires forward rather than backward counting) and conceptually (the forward counting/cardinal transitions are simpler than are the backward counting/cardinal transitions). Second, children at this time solve many subtraction problems by using the related addition fact (Carpenter & Moser, 1983a). Thinking of a related addition fact is an additive procedure (given $14 - 8$, to think "8 plus what is 14?") that has an underlying structure similar to that of counting up; the units here are just whole numbers rather than unit items. Thus, children might try to think of a related addition fact and then count up if they could not think of one to fit. Thus, the triplet cardinal conceptual structure pictured in Table 8-3 may actually support a counting up to s procedure for subtraction.

The availability of cardinal numbers as conceptual units enables children to use new methods of addition and subtraction. These methods have had different names, including, for example, thinking strategies, heuristic strategies, derived facts, indirect solutions (e.g., Baroody, Ginsburg, & Waxman, 1983; Carpenter & Moser, 1984; Houlihan & Ginsburg, 1981; Rathmell, 1978; Steinberg, 1985; Thornton, 1978). These methods all involve operating on numbers as numbers. For example, children now can use derived facts, deriving an answer from a known fact triplet by relating the addends in the known triplet to the addends in the unknown triplet and then relating their sums in the same way: "$6 + 7 = 13$ because I know $6 + 6 = 12$ and it is just one more." Doubles $(a + a)$ are often used as the basis for derived facts because they are learned so early. Children also can use strategies such as the "over ten method," in which one addend is divided into the part that will make ten when combined with the other addend and the remaining part that makes the teens number with the ten: $8 + 6 = 8 + 2 + 4 = 10 + 4 = 14$. These thinking strategies involve the decomposition of the cardinal numbers into various kinds of ideal unit items tailored for the relationship required by the strategy. It may be that certain of these thinking strategies are available at levels lower than IV, if the conceptual units available at that level will support the strategy. Cobb (1985) has reported the use of an addend increasing strategy at a level lower than this level IV, and Steinberg (1985) reported that children who did not regularly count on as a sequence procedure could be taught derived facts. At the moment, however, little is known about the conceptual structures required by various thinking strategies or about the relationships between the availability of these strategies and the sequence counting strategies. Children's inconsistency in solving the same kinds of problems even within the same session (e.g., Carpenter & Moser, 1984; Steinberg, 1984) promise to make these issues difficult ones to resolve.

Children begin learning small sums and differences quite early and continue to memorize sums and differences for a considerable period of time. However, there is considerable debate concerning the form in which such memorized facts are represented and even whether all facts are actually recalled as opposed to reconstructed or generated from a rule (e.g., Ashcraft & Fierman, 1982; Ashcraft & Stazyk, 1981; Baroody, 1983; Groen & Parkman, 1972; Hamann & Ashcraft, 1985; Kaye, Post, Hall, & Dineen, 1986; McCloskey, Sokol, & Goodman, 1986; Resnick, 1983; Siegler, in press; Siegler & Campbell, in press; Woods, Resnick, & Groen, 1975). At present these issues are not resolved for children or for adults.

8.6.2. Representations of Word Problems at Level IV

There is at present very little evidence about children's later representations of word problems. Because these comments about level IV in Table 8-2 are speculative, we put the IV in the table in parentheses. It seems to us that the next step in problem representations may be the building of explicit connections between different problem types. The most obvious links are between the two unary situations and between the two binary situations. Reversibility would seem to provide an important link between the unary Change-Get-More and Change-Get-Less problems. After some experience in using reversibility to solve particular problem situations, these two problem types might become integrated into a single Reversible Unary Change-More/Less problem representation that could facilitate the choice of addition or subtraction as a solution procedure. The similarities between the two binary situations, the Put-Together: All-Part-Part and the Compare: Big-Small-Difference situations, might also become obvious to children, leading to the integration of these two problem types within a Static Small-Small-Big representation.[11] Such a representation may be facilitated by experience with the more difficult Compare problems, because the role of the Small and the Difference as together being equivalent to the Big becomes clearer in these more difficult forms. The formation of such a static representation also would seem to draw fairly heavily on children's many addition and subtraction experiences with triplets of numbers related in the same way: 5, 3, 8; 9, 6, 15, etc. (Small-Small-Big).

After these two representations are formed and are available for use in choosing solution procedures for given word problems represented by these two schemata, relationships between these two may begin to be made. This then may culminate in the formation of a single, over-arching ADDEND-ADDEND-SUM schema within which all problem representations and all addition and subtraction solution procedures can be subsumed. This schema would easily generate, assimilate, and relate all four of the separate solution procedure structures: addend + addend = $[s]$, addend + $[a]$ = sum, sum − addend = $[a]$, and sum − $[a]$ = addend. Addition could then be seen generally as any situation in which two addends are known, and subtraction would be viewed as any situation in which the sum and one addend are known. In our view symbolic numbers (i.e., 1, 2, 3, 4, etc.) and written addition and subtraction problems would play an important role in the formation of this generalized addition/subtraction schema. Children in the first two grades of school have many, many experiences with symbolic addition and subtraction

---

[11] A common "error" of children who had been taught to make schematic drawings of Put-Together and Compare problems was in fact to put the numbers for a Put-Together: missing Part problem into a Compare drawing (Fuson & Willis, 1987). Children argued that the Put-Together: missing Part problem was asking them to compare the smaller part to the larger whole.

problems (e.g., 8 + 6 and 14 − 8). Eventually, *for many specific triplets of numbers*, they learn the basic relationship of addition and subtraction as derived from the same three numbers: a big number and two small numbers such that "small number + small number = big number" and "big number − small number = small number." Using this "complement principle" (Baroody & Ginsburg, 1986), children can go on to derive subtraction combinations from known addition facts. Children later on might also have many experiences in seeing that the same triplet can be used to solve several different problem types. This would provide an important way to see similarities between the structures of different problems. An ADDEND-ADDEND-SUM schema formed in this way would be based on (generalized from) many specific cardinal number triplet structures. This schema would be an equivalence class of interchangable aspects of addition/subtraction in which the Reversible Unary Change-More/Less schema, the Static Small-Small-Big schema, and the solution procedure conceptual structures (cardinal triplets, embedded simultaneous sequence unit items with keeping track, embedded perceptual unit item) were all related to each other. This schema would then provide enormous flexibility and creativity for solving addition and subtraction problems of all types.

Resnick (1983) made a proposal that is similar in some ways to this one. That proposal was that during early school arithmetic, a part-whole schema knowledge structure is used by children to relate triples of numbers and to interpret various kinds of word problems so that the problems can be solved by informal arithmetic methods or by more formal methods taught in school. We see the developmental process occurring in the opposite direction. Children first have many different experiences with different situations that are represented differently by children, even though many of the situations share a deep underlying common part-part-whole structure. For example, De Corte and Verschaffel (1985c) reported that an instructional attempt to use a single schematic Part-Part-Whole drawing (similar to the top right-hand drawing in Figure 8-1) was not successful. Children had difficulty filling numbers into this drawing for some of the difficult Change and Compare problems, but did not have such difficulty in filling numbers into three different kinds of drawings for Change, Put Together, and Compare problems. We also found that children found it easy to use different drawings for different problem types. Second graders learned quite successfully to fill three-digit numbers into the drawings in Figure 8-1 for even the most difficult problems (Willis & Fuson, 1985, 1986), and average and below-average first graders easily learned to fill numbers into the drawings for the four simplest word problems (Fuson & Secada, 1986). Thus, a general pervasive Part-Whole schema may be something that is salient to adult researchers in all aspects of addition and subtraction but is not salient to children until they have had many different experiences with addition and subtraction problem situations and with specific addition and subtraction number combinations.

8.7. Level V Solution Procedures: Base-Ten Numbers and Multidigit Algorithms

The addition and subtraction operations, and real addition and subtraction situations, are not limited to single-digit addends. However, children need new solution procedures for adding and subtracting multidigit numbers. These solution procedures are the multidigit addition and subtraction algorithms. These algorithms use various properties of our base-ten system of numeration. Therefore, in order to understand these algorithms, children need to understand our base-ten system. This leads to the usual school approach of teaching concepts of place value first and then teaching the algorithms. However, concepts of place value are notoriously difficult to teach and difficult to learn, and it is not clear that they are related in children's mind to the multidigit algorithms in the usual school teaching of these algorithms (e.g., Resnick, 1983). An alternative approach, which we used with second graders and above-average first graders, is to teach concepts of place-value and base-ten numeration at the same time as the multidigit algorithms (Fuson, 1986a). In this way the numeration concepts become more meaningful because they can be seen to be useful in adding and subtracting.

Base-ten numbers require new representational units. The perceptual, sequence, and ideal unit items used earlier were all single-unit items. Base-ten numbers require multiple-unit items: ten-unit items, hundred-unit items, thousand-unit items, and so on. A ten-unit item is a *single* unit item composed of ten single-unit items. Forming these multiple-unit conceptual items is a difficult task, and children initially need perceptual support in order to make the conceptual base-ten integration operations necessary to form a conceptual ten-unit, hundred-unit, and so on. Such perceptual support can be provided by any *size* embodiment in which a ten is a single entity easily seen to be composed of ten ones (i.e., it must be ten times larger than a one), a hundred is a single entity easily seen to be composed of ten ten-units, and a thousand is a single entity easily seen to be composed of ten hundred-units. Such a size embodiment thus can support the learning of the fundamental trade rules governing the base-ten system and the multidigit algorithms (the one-for-ten trades to the right and the ten-for-one trades to the left) as well as the formation of perceptual ten-unit, hundred-unit, and thousand-unit conceptual items. A major property of the multidigit addition and subtraction algorithms is that the procedure is identical in every column. In order to appreciate this property, children need to have experience with several places. In our experience four places provides enough of an example for children to see the general nature of the algorithm and the general nature of the base-ten system. They can make extensions of the system and of the algorithm beyond four places without the need for perceptual multiple unit items for the larger places. Thus, children first record work with the embodiment with symbols of up to four places. When they understand and can talk about the procedure, they can then practice doing the algorithm symbolically without the embodiment. After this, the extension to more places can be made, if desired.

The particular embodiment we used, base-ten wooden blocks, is shown in Figures 8-3 and 8-4; these figures illustrate how the blocks were used for the multidigit algorithms (see also Dienes, 1960). For subtraction, we used a simplified algorithm in which all the trading (borrowing, regrouping) is done first to avoid making children alternate between trading and subtracting. Because the embodiment provides the representational units for the symbols in the multidigit algorithms, every action on the embodiment must be *immediately* related to an action with the symbols (Bell, Fuson, & Lesh, 1976). Children can only relate the actions on the blocks to the operations on the

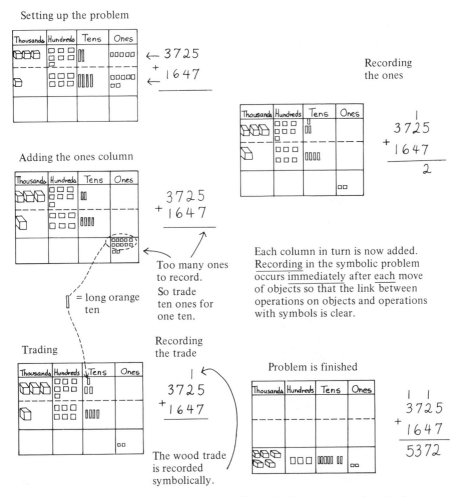

Figure 8-3. Multidigit adding and recording with base-ten wood embodiment.

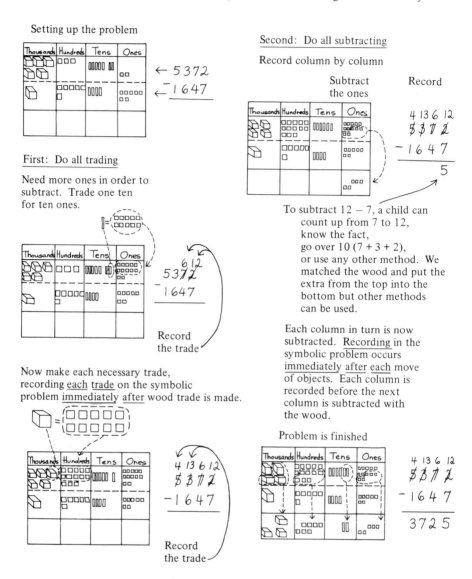

Figure 8-4. Multidigit subtracting and recording with base-ten wood embodiment.

symbols if the links are made very closely. Thus, each action with the blocks must be recorded *immediately* with symbols. This is shown in Figures 8-3 and 8-4.

Instruction providing perceptual multiple-unit items to support the learning of multidigit algorithms and concepts of place value was very successful (Fuson, 1986a, 1987). Second graders of all ability levels and above-average first graders learned the multidigit addition and subtraction algorithms (including problems with zeroes in the minuend) and generalized them to as many as 10 places. Children also learned all the place-value concepts that were in their first-, second- or third-grade textbooks, as well as a more conceptual test of place-value understanding such as "Write in base-ten symbols: six tens fourteen hundreds five ones three thousands" (Underhill, 1984, p. 114). Most children were able to form mental representations of the blocks that enabled them to self-correct their errors (Fuson, 1986a), and they gave meaningful base-ten rather than rote procedural explanations of why examples of "solved" written problems were correct or incorrect (Fuson, 1987). Children were able to carry out the algorithms symbolically without the embodiment at so early an age because they had also been taught to count on with one-handed finger patterns for single-digit addition and to count up for subtraction (Fuson, 1986b; Fuson & Secada, 1986). They used these sequence procedures to find the answer in any multidigit column for which they did not know the fact.

Evidence discussed in this chapter indicates that children initially require perceptual unit items in order to think about simple single-digit addition and subtraction situations. If this is so, it seems absolutely necessary that children require conceptual support from perceptual materials that embody the crucial aspects of the base-ten system for the formation of perceptual multiple-unit items in order to understand base-ten numbers and the multidigit addition and subtraction algorithms. This is particularly true in English where the English number words are structurally different from the base-ten system of numeration (see pp. 429–436 in Bell, Fuson, and Lesh, 1976) and the irregularities in the words below one hundred mask the similarities that do exist. This difference occurs as early as the number word "ten" and is illustrated by the diary example (see Table 1-2) of my daughter at age 3 years 5 months who was typing the numerals and said, "One, two, three, four, five, six, seven, eight, nine. I need a ten." There is nothing in the word to indicate that ten is symbolized by 10 (by one-zero). Our research indicates that such conceptual support by perceptual embodiments does make the base-ten system and the multidigit algorithms accessible to children at a surprisingly early age (second grade) if the children have some reliable method of obtaining single-digit sums and differences. Some evidence indicates that such conceptual support may be unnecessary for children who speak Japanese because the Japanese number words provide this support (Miura, 1987). These number words are entirely regular and explicitly name the larger places, for example, five-tens three (53), two-tens nine (29), and ten-three (13). Providing children in the United States with conceptual base-ten support enabled them to learn the multidigit concepts and procedures considerably earlier than they appear in textbooks in this country and as early as they are taught in mainland China, Japan, the Soviet Union, and Taiwan (Fuson et al., in press).

When children are given word problems containing multidigit numbers, it is very difficult for them to solve the problems by direct modeling. They are almost forced to make a decision about whether to add or to subtract, and they then must use the requisite multidigit procedure. This solution procedure is represented by level V in Table 8.3. Because it is so easy to model a problem situation directly with single-digit numbers, it seems possible that some children do not ever use level IV solution procedures when they are solving single-digit problems; that is, they may never consciously choose addition or subtraction for word problems containing single-digit numbers. They may only do this when forced to do so by word problems containing multidigit numbers. Thus, some children may move directly from level III to level V in Table 8-3. Deliberately deciding whether to add or subtract would seem to require a representation of the problem situation on which one could reflect. Thus, solving word problems with large multidigit numbers would seem to be easiest if the child can represent problems at level IV in Table 8-2.

In actually the relationships among levels III, IV, and V in Table 8-3 and levels IIIa, IIIb, IIIc, and IV in Table 8-2 are probably quite complicated. For example, children who have the conceptual ten-units and hundred-units of level V can decompose these into sequence unit items and carry out sequence counting solution procedures that may directly model a problem using level III sequence solution procedures and problem representations. For example, a child might solve a Change-Get-Less: missing End problem containing the numbers 48 and 73 by counting up from 48 to 73: "48, 58, 68, 69, 70, 71, 72, 73. That was two tens and five ones, 25 is the answer." Children may also try to form a specific representation of a word problem situation containing very large numbers rather than using more general conceptual "slots" for those large numbers. Thus, a child may struggle to picture 856 marbles compared to 475 marbles rather than just thinking about "some" marbles compared to "some other" marbles. However, because in general one cannot build a model of large number addition and subtraction situations from the conceptual units available to children at levels I, II, and III, solution of such problems in general would suggest the ability to generate a representation of the problem situation that is general enough to suggest addition or subtraction as the solution procedure. This in turn suggests that a general test for whether a child has directly modeled a problem situation with perceptual or sequence unit items that both model the problem situation and permit a direct solution is to give that same situation with much larger numbers. If a child can then say whether to add or subtract (even if unable to carry out the addition or subtraction operation), then the child is capable of separate representations of the problem situation and the solution procedure and is just choosing a sequence procedure as a way of adding or subtracting.

The representations of the solution procedures and the problem situations within each level of Tables 8-2 and 8-3 are yoked by the use of common conceptual units of levels I, II, and IIIa. Beginning at level IIIb in Table 8-2, the situation becomes more complex and flexible. The cardinal conceptual triplets (level IV of Table 8-3) may free the representations of the problem situations and support reversibility and subset equivalence (IIIb and IIIc of Table 8-2). Level V solution procedures may be carried out in level III problem representations. There may not even be universal relationships among these levels that hold for all children. Children instead may construct different connections, depending on their strengths and preferences as well as on their exposure to certain problem situations. The latter possibility implies that the kinds of addition and subtraction situations children meet in schools can affect quite considerably the addition and subtraction schemata they construct. We continue this discussion in the following section.

8.8. School Instruction and Children's Understanding of Addition and Subtraction

The evidence is clear that most children in kindergarten, before receiving any school arithmetic instruction, can solve the simpler level I types of word problems (e.g., Carpenter & Moser, 1983a; Riley et al., 1983). Children presently progress through levels I through IV of the solution procedures in Table 8-3 largely on their own, for the solution procedures in levels II through IV are well documented but are rarely taught in schools. Children also progress through the levels of representation of word problems (Table 8-2) virtually on their own, for with rare exceptions, only the simplest level I problems appear in American textbooks (Stigler et al., 1986). Furthermore, the effect of school instruction is to present very limited concepts of addition and of subtraction, concepts that limit flexible approaches and doom children to using the difficult count down *a* procedure for subtraction. Textbooks weight early subtraction teaching entirely or very heavily toward take-away as *the* interpretation of subtraction (Stigler et al., 1986, and unpublished data from the same analysis). Any other situation solved by subtraction (Compare, Equalize, Put Together: missing Part) is not presented at all, is presented considerably later, or is presented considerably less often, depending on the textbook series. This situation is changing somewhat in some new text series, which are giving earlier and more space to Compare problems. But even if this change becomes universal, teachers will still have to change their common reading aloud of the $-$ sign as "take-away." Children who interpret the word "subtract" or the $-$ symbol only as "take-away" are limited to the solution procedures in the "sum $-$ addend $= [a]$" cells in Table 8-3. This limited notion of subtraction will then interfere with their shifting to the easier forward solution procedures for subtraction (those in the addend $+ [a] =$ sum cells) and possibly with their ability to represent nontake-away problems in the take-away form in Table 8-2. Given that two-thirds of the addition/subtraction situations are in fact solved by subtraction and given the very rich array of such situations, we really limit children very considerably when we restrict the definition of subtraction, and the subtraction solution procedure, to one kind of situation and action.

The present treatment of word problems in American textbooks is a disaster (Stigler et al., 1986, and unpublished data from that analysis). By and large, only the problem subtypes that children can already solve in kindergarten are presented in the first- and second-grade texts. In many text series addition problems are grouped together, as are subtraction problems, so children do not even need to read any problem but the first on a page. Number size frequently predicts the operation reliably (add if the two numbers are less than 10 and subtract if one number is greater than 10). Hardly any two-step problems requiring more than one operation are given. In contrast the first-grade text in the Soviet Union gives many more word problems than do American texts, gives roughly equivalent numbers of all the problem subtypes in Table 8-1, gives about 25% of the addition and subtraction problems as two-step problems requiring two different problem subtypes from Table 8-1, and distributes all these different problems maximally across all the pages of the text.

We certainly do not know at this time how best to help children build the strongest and most flexible concepts of addition and subtraction. However, we certainly should expose children to more varied types of addition and subtraction situations, via word problems and more realistic context-rich situations. An understanding of the developmental progression of conceptual structures that children require in order to solve addition and subtraction problems would help teachers provide learning environments in which children could move through that developmental progression with facility. It seems worthwhile to help children build the flexible level III problem representations and the flexible level III and level IV solution procedures. Such flexibility and provision of individual choice would seem to convey important aspects of confident problem-solving attitudes in mathematics. However, because subtraction presents so many difficulties to slower children, it also seems quite sensible to help these children learn an efficient method of subtraction that is easy for them and on which they can fall back if other methods fail. Recent work of Siegler and Campbell (in press) suggests that it is particularly important for weaker students to possess a reliable fallback strategy if they are eventually to remember number triplets accurately. Counting up to s with one-handed finger patterns has been demonstrated to be easy and effective for such students (Fuson, 1986b) and might be considered for this purpose, particularly as it has also been demonstrated to be effective enough to be used by slower second graders in the multidigit subtraction algorithm (Fuson, 1987).

Because American children have had so little opportunity to solve the more difficult addition and subtraction problem subtypes, we know little about how to help them build the general related level IV problem representations that can lead to a mature understanding of addition and subtraction. This would seem to be a fruitful area for future research. Teaching the general multidigit addition and subtraction algorithms in a meaningful manner that supports the construction of base-ten conceptual units (perceptual ten-units, hundred-units, thousand-units) and moving this teaching down into the second grade would seem to support the development of more general problem representations at a younger age, because children could then work with a range of problem situations containing larger numbers.

It may be that although children do not initially possess a general ADDEND-ADDEND-SUM or Part-Part-Whole schema, such a schema in a verbal-question form nevertheless can be useful to them in instruction in symbolic addition and subtraction and in addition and subtraction word problems. Rathmell (1986) reported that asking children to answer the questions "What is the part" and "What is the whole?" in various addition and subtraction situations seemed to facilitate their performance. Most of these situations involved symbolic addition or subtraction (e.g., 8 + 3) rather than addition or subtraction word problems, but the technique was also used with some word problems. It seemed to be more difficult to use with Compare problems, underscoring again children's use initially of different problem representations. But the efficacy of helping children think of different problem situations as consisting of parts and wholes (or as addends and sums) might be explored.

Finally, we need to say at least a word about the use of equations in solving addition and subtraction word problems. There has been a fairly general finding that equations do not help children solve problems, and that if forced to write equations, children tend to get answers first and then write the equation. This finding has resulted partly from a failure to make a distinction between an equation that models the solution procedure and an equation that models the problem situation. Equations that model the solution procedure are totally unnecessary. For single-digit numbers it is easier just to find the answer, and for multidigit numbers it is easier to write the problem in vertical form for calculation. However, with respect to equations that model the problem situation, Carpenter, Bebout, and Moser (1985) and Bebout (1986) have reported that children can quite readily write equations that model Change problem situations and can then solve those equations. Because young children interpret the = in an equation as "results in" rather than as "is equivalent to" (e.g., Baroody & Ginsburg, 1983; Behr, Erlwanger, & Nichols, 1980), the equation does seem to be a good representation for Change problems, a representation that can support a common representation of the problem and a solution procedure. It is not clear how easily equations can be used to model Put-Together or Compare problems, however, so some other schematic support may be helpful for these problems. Nor is it clear whether one wants to support children's narrow interpretations of the = sign as only "results in" by using equations for change problems as well as for symbolic problems. A full understanding of equations and of interpretations of = other than "results in" requires fairly complex conceptual structures, especially when equations are used as they are in schools without any interpretation as a familiar situation (Kamii, 1985). The conceptual structures required by various interpretations of = and of equations might be explored further in future research.

8.9. Summary

Developmental progressions in three related areas were described: relationships between count and cardinality meanings of number words, representations of solution procedures for addition and subtraction situations, and representations of addition and subtraction word problems (see Tables 8-2, 8-3, and 8-4). Levels of successively more complex and abstract relationships between count and cardinal meanings of number words were described and related to the counting solution procedures that can be carried out if these relationships are understood. The early representations of word problems and of solution procedures used for word problems were hypothesized to rely on three successively more complex kinds of conceptual units: single representational perceptual unit items, simultaneous representational perceptual unit items, and simultaneous sequence unit items. The cardinal conceptual operations of cardinal integration and embedded integration unite these unit items to form a cardinal conceptual structure that serves as a common representation for a word problem and for the solution procedure used to solve the word problem. More problem subtypes are able to be solved by the more complex kinds of units, and problems are able to be represented more flexibly with these units. Children finally come to take cardinal numbers themselves as conceptual units and use a conceptual cardinal triplet structure in which two cardinal numbers together are numerically equivalent to a third cardinal number. This structure permits children to relate addition and subtraction combinations, to decide consciously to add or to subtract to solve a problem, and to use thinking strategies to derive an answer from a related known number combination. At this level the representation of a word problem may be separate from the representation for the procedure used to solve the problem, and this separation continues with the later solution procedures involving base-ten multidigit numbers. Experience with different specific problem contexts for addition and subtraction permits children eventually to build a Reversible Unary Change-More/Less schema and a Static Small-Small-Big schema, which then become integrated with the cardinal triplet conceptual structure into a general ADDEND-ADDEND-SUM schema for addition and subtraction.

The earliest relationships between count meanings and cardinality meanings of number words are formed within single-set situations. The first two, a how-many-question rule and a count-to-cardinal transition, were discussed in considerable detail in chapter 7. The ability to make count-to-cardinal transitions eventually leads to the third relationship at this level, cardinal-to-count transitions. Both of these simple transitions can be used by children in object addition or subtraction situations to solve simple kinds of addition and subtraction situations. Solution procedures available at this point are count all, add on up to s, take-away a, and separate to a.

More complex subset transitions with structures similar to the transitions at the first level can be learned for a subset within a larger set. These transitions enable somewhat different object solution procedures to be carried out and prepare the way for the more complex embedded transitions at the next level.

Certain more difficult addition and subtraction problems and certain solution procedures require more complex count-to-cardinal and cardinal-to-count transitions within an addition or subtraction object situation. For these transitions children must consider an object simultaneously as being in the addend and in the sum set. Forward counting transitions at this level are the object-embedded count-to-cardinal transition of the first addend within the sum count, a similar object-embedded cardinal-to-count transition, an object-embedded count extension to the second addend within the sum count, and a final object-embedded count-to-cardinal transition of the final sum count (an embedded integration of the sum entities). These object-embedded transitions enable children to carry out the solution procedures count on a with objects and count up to s with objects. Three backward object-embedded transitions that are the reverse of the forward transitions enable children to carry out the solution procedures count down a with objects and count down to a with objects. The availability of perceptual unit items that simultaneously represent the addend within the sum enables children to represent more difficult word problems and solve them with these solution procedures. Simpler problems solvable at the first level can also be represented at this higher level and solved by the new solution procedures.

Children eventually come to be able to use number words themselves to represent addition and subtraction situations. Sequence words are taken as the entities for the addends and sum. The conceptual transitions within a number-word sequence situation require a child to consider a word as belonging simultaneously to an addend and to the sum (both of which are composed of words). Thus, these transitions mark a new integration of number-word meanings. Relationships now involve count, cardinal, and sequence meanings and use the conceptual sequence unit items. In addition to the sequence-embedded count-to-cardinal and sequence-embedded cardinal-to-count transitions of the first addend within the sum count (each entailing an embedded integration of the first addend), the forward-counting transitions include a sequence-embedded extension to the second addend within the sum count, a method of keeping track of the second addend that must be coordinated with the forward counting of the second addend within the sum count, and a feedback loop that verifies when one has counted on a and then initiates a sequence count-to-cardinal transition of the sum count (an embedded integration of the sum). The coordinated use of a keeping-track method requires a pairing of the embedded sequence and keeping-track method integrations for the second addend. These transitions enable children to carry out the solution procedures sequence counting on a and sequence counting up to s. Backward counting/cardinal transitions that are the reverse of the forward transitions enable children to carry out the solution procedures sequence counting down a and sequence counting down to a. The more abstract sequence unit items enable children to use reversibility and subset equivalence to form specific problem representations that enable children to carry out the sequence counting solution procedures. All addition/subtraction situations involving whole numbers can be represented and solved at this level.

Two later levels of solution procedures also occur. Children become able to make a decision to add or subtract for a given problem situation and then may carry out the actual addition or subtraction in a way that does not model the structure of the problem situation. At this level a cardinal number has become a concrete conceptual unit for the child, and these cardinal numbers are related within a cardinal triplet conceptual structure in which two cardinal numbers together are numerically equivalent to a third number. Thus, at this level children can use thinking strategies to derive one sum from another related known combination and can derive a subtraction answer from a known addition fact. Children also learn the multidigit addition and subtraction algorithms and come to be able to use them in solving addition and subtraction situations. Solutions at this stage require a conscious decision to add or subtract rather than a direct modeling of the problem situation. Understanding the multidigit algorithms requires children to form and to use new multiple representational units: perceptual ten-unit items consisting of ten perceptual unit items, hundred-unit items consisting of ten ten-unit items, and thousand-unit items consisting of ten hundred-unit items.

At the highest level of problem representation, children come to relate separate addition and subtraction situations within specific problem types. Children may come to relate the unary Change-Get-More and Change-Get-Less problem situations into a single Reversible Unary Change-More/Less problem representation and relate the Put-Together: All-Part-Part and the Compare: Big-Small-Difference situations into a single Static Small-Small-Big representation. These two representations then may get related to form a single general and flexible ADDEND-ADDEND-SUM schema within which all addition and subtraction situations and numerical combinations can be represented.

9. Uses of Counting and Matching in Cardinal Equivalence Situations: Equivalence and Order Relations on Cardinal Numbers

$Ch^+ = change$
$gets\ more$

9.1. Introduction

Cardinal equivalence situations are those in which the issue is the nature of the *equivalence or order relation* on the two cardinal situations. Any two cardinal situations A and B are related either by equivalence or by one of two order relations: A has the same number as B ($A \cong B$) or A has more than B ($A > B$) or A has less than B ($A < B$).[1] How young children come to understand these equivalence and order relations on cardinal situations and when they become able to use various strategies for determining which relation applies to a given situation is the focus of this chapter. We discuss three different classes of cardinal relational situations: the static comparison of two cardinal situations, the dynamic transformation of a single cardinal situation, and the dynamic transformation of a cardinal situation within a static compare situation. The particular strategies by which the appropriate cardinal relation can be determined for each class of situations is described; for each class there is a range of possible strategies available. For each class a developmental sequence of strategy use from age 2 to 8 is proposed. Literature supporting these sequences is reviewed.

Our particular focus in tracing this development of cardinal relations is the roles played in this development by counting and matching (the behavioral activity of establishing a one-to-one correspondence between the elements of two cardinal situations). This focus stems from what we see as a major gap in the most well-known treatment of cardinal equivalence—Piaget's (1941/1965) analysis of number. Piaget focused on the development of logical operational mental structures that determine how a child thinks about cardinal equivalence situations. Piaget discounted the role of counting in conservation, arguing that the logical structures that determined children's thinking about equivalence also determined their thinking about counting (see 9.3.6 for further discussion of this point). Furthermore, although the concept of one-to-one correspondence was crucial to his notion of number, Piaget also did not explicitly discuss children's use of matching throughout his stages. However, some of my own recent work and that of others has convinced me that counting and matching do play very important roles in children's developing

---

[1] We use *less* rather than the grammatically correct *fewer* throughout because *less* is a more familiar word than *fewer* to young children.

ability to establish cardinal relations. This chapter is an attempt to articulate what we know at present about these roles and to suggest what we might attempt to discover about these roles in the future.

There is some recent literature on children's use of counting and matching in the conservation of number task. This task falls within the third class of cardinal relational situations just identified: a dynamic transformation of one cardinal situation within a static compare situation. There have been comparatively few data concerning the first class of situations: the static compare situation. Therefore, the first part of this chapter reports three experiments concerning children's use of counting and matching in the static compare situation. These experiments raise several general issues that are important in the later developmental sequences of strategy use. These general issues include differences between children's spontaneous use of a strategy and their ability to benefit from that strategy if it is imposed on them, conflict between the use of multiple available strategies, conflict between information obtained from the use of different strategies, and the quite striking differences in strategy use in different contexts. Some readers may prefer only to read the summary of the results of these experiments in 9.2.4 and move on to the more theoretical treatment in 9.3.

The literature concerning equivalence and order relations on cardinal situations is dominated by Piaget's conservation of number (discrete quantity) task. In this task an initial equivalence between two rows of objects is established or agreed on by the child, the experimenter then transforms one row by spreading out or pushing together the objects in that row, and the child is then queried concerning the cardinal equivalence of the two rows after this transformation has been made. Before the transformation, the objects in the two rows are in optical one-to-one correspondence with each other (being directly across from each other), and the rows are equal in length and density. After the transformation the correspondence between the objects in the rows is not obvious, and the rows are of different lengths and densities. Nonconserving children typically are drawn by the misleading attribute of length and judge the longer row as having more, although occasionally children instead focus on the density of the objects in the shorter row and assert that the denser row has more. Conserving children know that a transformation that only stretches or shrinks the length of a row of objects does not change the number of objects in the row, and they judge the rows still to be equivalent. This developmental pattern has been verified in many studies (see, for example, reviews by Siegel & Brainerd, 1978, and see Modgil & Modgil, 1976, for a compilation of abstracts). Because most literature concerning equivalence and order relations on cardinal situations has used some variation of this task, our review and analysis also largely concern this task.

Our treatment of equivalence and order relations on cardinal situations moves from early perceptual and quantitative strategies used to establish equivalence and order relations by children aged 2 through 5 through two levels of conservation of number to a postconservation stage characterizied by

Piaget as "truly numerical counting" and occurring at age 7½ to 8. The last three levels relate children's conceptual structures used in addition and subtraction cardinal situations (and discussed in chapter 8) to the conceptual structures available for establishing equivalence and order relations on cardinal situations. In the final level children have integrated count, sequence, and cardinal meanings within a cardinalized unitized number-word sequence. Within this sequence cardinal numbers can be conceptualized as both seriated and included within each other. At this level children for the first time have a concept of cardinal number, as distinct from their earlier conceptualizations of cardinal situations only as specific numerosities closely tied to sets of perceptually present entities.

9.2. Three Experiments on Children's Use of Counting and Matching in Static Compare Situations

The first experiment examines the extent to which children use the strategies of length, counting, and matching in three different cardinal relational situations: making a set of objects equivalent to a given set when a numerosity is specified but no objects are shown to represent that set, making a set of objects equivalent to a set that is presented by showing objects in a row and has no numerosity specified, and judging whether two cardinal situations are equivalent when they are presented by objects in rows with length a misleading cue (i.e., equivalent situations have one row longer than the other, and nonequivalent situations have the smaller situation as the longer row of objects). Changes in the use of and the accuracy of these strategies over the age range 3½ to 6 was of interest. In the second experiment children were asked to count before deciding the cardinal relation between two cardinal situations presented by objects in rows with length a misleading cue. Several aspects of children's ability to use count information to judge cardinal equivalence was then assessed: the ability to count both arrays accurately, the ability to remember the count information from both arrays, and the ability to use count information (obtained specific numerosities) to judge whether one set had more than, the same number as, or less than another set. Changes in these aspects of the counting strategy over the age range 3½ to 6 were examined. In the third experiment children's spontaneous use of matching and counting with and without misleading length information was contrasted, and their ability to distinguish between "more" as "looks like more" and "is really more" was explored.

9.2.1. Experiment 1: Children's Use of Counting and Matching in Producing Equivalent Sets and in Judging Cardinal Equivalence

This experiment focuses on differences in children's use of the strategies of counting, matching, and length in three different cardinal relational situations. Situations were chosen that seemed to favor each of these strategies. At what age during the preschool years children become able to carry out each of these strategies and the extent to which they use strategies differentially in the different situations was of interest. The first situation favored counting. When one is asked to make a set of *n* objects, the simplest approach is to count out objects while remembering the numerosity *n* so that one can stop when one has counted to *n*. The second situation seemed to favor matching. If one is asked to make a set containing as many objects as another given set whose objects are arranged in a row, it is simpler to generate the required equivalent set by matching objects to the given set than by counting twice (first the given set and then counting out the required set). The third situation was one that would elicit the length strategy in those children who had not yet identified the unreliability of length alone as a basis for cardinal equivalence: judging the cardinal relation on two sets for which length was always a misleading cue.

9.2.1.1. Method. 9.2.1.1.1. Subjects. The subjects were 60 middle- and upper-middle-class children aged 3½ to 6 years who attended a preschool in a northern suburb of Chicago.[2] Twelve children were in each of five half-year age groups: 3½ to 4 (3 years 6 months through 3 years 11 months), 4 to 4½ (4 years 0 months through 4 years 5 months), 4½ to 5, 5 to 5½, and 5½ to 6.

9.2.1.1.2. Tasks: *Judging Cardinal Equivalence task.* Two long, narrow strips of cardboard of equal length, each containing a row of circular stickers, were placed parallel to each other in front of the child. One strip contained red dots, and the other strip contained blue dots. For three trials the number of dots on the two strips was the same (seven and seven; eight and eight; nine and nine), and for three trials one strip contained one more dot than did the other strip (seven and eight; eight and nine; nine and ten). For each pair one row of dots was longer than the other. For the unequal sets, the longer row was always the smaller set. Thus, length was always a misleading cue. The stickers were not equidistant from each other; stickers in each row were randomly placed apart one of four different distances. The trials were given in two random orders, with half the children in each age group beginning with an equal row and half beginning with an unequal row.

The child was asked, "Are there more red dots, the same number of dots, or more blue dots?" The question was asked in this form because Siegel and Goldstein (1969) reported that preschoolers showed a bias toward responding with the last choice given in tripartite equivalence questions. For the equal rows the correct answer was thus always in the middle. For the unequal rows the first answer (red dots) was correct twice and the last answer (blue dots)

---

[2] These subjects formed the pool of hearing subjects for Walter Secada's dissertation comparing early numerical abilities of hearing children and of deaf children of ASL parents (Secada, 1984). The deaf children's performance on the tasks described here is reported in that dissertation.

was correct once. After an answer was given, the child was asked, "How did you figure that out?" Any behavior of the child from the time of the first question was recorded, as were the verbatim verbal responses.

Make an Equivalent Set task. For each trial a row of red poker chips glued to a strip of cardboard was placed in front of the child. The red chips were irregularly spaced, ranging from twice a chip's distance apart to almost touching. A pile of 20 blue poker chips was placed on the table, and the child was told, "Give me as many blue chips as there are red ones." (or "Give me as many blues as the reds," if the child did not react to the first question). Four trials were given; strips with 7, 9, 16, and 18 red chips were used. The sets below and above 10 were alternated, and half the children in each age group began with a set below 10.

Make a Set of n. A pile of 20 white poker chips was placed in front of the child. The child was told, "Give me *n* poker chips." There were four trials, and *n* was 7, 8, 17, and 19. The numbers below 10 and above 10 were alternated, and half the children in each age group began with a number below 10.

Number-Word Sequence task. The child was asked to "count as high as you can"; the child just said number words aloud and did not count objects. The child was stopped at 121 if the child counted that far. Three trials of this task were given; they were separated by other tasks.

Object Counting task. A strip of cardboard containing a row of black dots was placed in front of the child. The child was asked, "How many dots are there?" If the child did not count in response to this question, the child was told to "count these dots." Trials of 7, 8, 9, 16, 18, and 19 dots were given. Trials of sets below 10 alternated with trials of sets above 10; half the children in each age group received a set below 10 first. Children who counted covertly were asked to count out loud and to count so the experimenter could watch the counting.

9.2.1.1.3. Procedure. Children were interviewed individually in a room in their preschool by one of two undergraduate interviewers. The tasks were given in the order in which they are listed above. The first two tasks were given at the beginning of the interview so as not to bias the solution procedures chosen by the children. The tasks were spaced out over two different days. Tasks through the first trial of the Number-Word Sequence task were given in the first interview. Some number-word sequence tasks not reported here, the Object Counting task, and the other two trials of the Number-Word Sequence task were given in the second interview. Each interview took from 20 to 30 minutes to complete. Sessions were audio recorded so that verbal responses could be rechecked if necessary.

9.2.1.1.4. Scoring. Explanations for the Judging Cardinal Equivalence task were classified as Quantitative (using counting or matching), Perceptual (using length or density), or Other (e.g., saying "I don't know" or giving an ambiguous or irrelevant explanation). A trial was classified as Quantitative if the child exhibited either overt counting or matching behavior before the equivalence judgment or a counting or matching explanation was given that did not contradict observed behavior. A trial was classified as Perceptual if a child gave a length explanation (mentioned length or the extra dot[s] at the end[s] of the longer row) or a density explanation (mentioning "bunched up" or "closer" or the extra dot[s] in the middle of the denser row) or (for a few subjects) gave an incomplete explanation but whose answers on at least four consecutive trials reflected a length or density basis for judgments. These bases could be determined because length and density gave distinctive patterns of equivalence responses that varied by the color of the longer/denser row for the equal and unequal sets. Two judges independently classified all of the trials; they agreed on 95% of the trials. Children sometimes changed their equivalence judgment; only the last judgment given was scored. Children also occasionally gave more than one explanation for a judgment. Multiple explanations given for the child's last answer were included in the analyses.

Responses on the Make An Equivalent Set task were categorized by solution procedure as matching, counting while matching, counting, and ineffective. The matching procedures were further subclassified as Put Near-Match or Look Match as described in the results section. Children were given one point for each set below 10 and for each set above 10 for which they correctly made an equivalent set.

For the Make a Set of *n* task, children were given a point for each set below 10 and for each set above 10 for which they correctly made the set of *n*.

On the Number-Word Sequence task, children were given as a score the highest number word to which they counted correctly on *any* of the three trials.

For the Object Counting task, children were given one point for each set below 10 and one point for each set above 10 that they counted without making any correspondence errors, that is, for which each object received exactly one word and exactly one point. The correctness of the number-word sequence said by the child was ignored in this scoring.

9.2.1.2. Results. 9.2.1.2.1. Producing Equivalent Sets With and Without Specified Numerosities. Two different tasks were given that required a child to produce a set equivalent to a given set. In one task (Make An Equivalent Set), the numerosity of the given set was not given to the child but objects representing the set were visible, and in the other task (Make A Set of *n*), the numerosity was given but objects were not visible for the set. The percentages of correct performance on these two tasks is given in Table 9-1 by age and size of set (set size less than 10 and between 10 and 20). A 2 (Task) × 2 (Size: Small and Large) × 5 (Age) analysis of variance revealed no main effect of Task. As one would expect, performance increased as size of set decreased and as age increased; both the main effects of size and age were

Table 9-1. Percentage Correct Performance by Age When Producing Equivalent
Sets With and Without Specified Numerosities (Experiment 1)

Task	Age				
	3½ to 4	4 to 4½	4½ to 5	5 to 5½	5½ to 6
Make An Equivalent Set task	19	56	56	56	77
set < 10		17	71	54	71	83
10 < set < 20		21	42	58	42	71
Make a Set of n task	15	60	65	69	85
set < 10		25	92	75	79	92
10 < set < 20		4	29	54	58	79

Note. Two scores underlined by the same line do not differ significantly from each other,
Newman-Keuls $p < .05$.

significant, $F(1, 55) = 27.79$, $p < .001$, and $F(4, 55) = 10.25$, $p < .001$. The
size by age and task by size interactions also were significant, $F(4, 55) = 3.55$,
$p < .01$, and $F(1, 55) = 4.76$, $p < .001$. For the size by age interaction, each
task showed patterns of age differences that varied similarly with the size of
the set. Newman-Keuls tests ($p < .05$) indicated that, for the sets below 10
on both tasks, mean performance of the youngest children was significantly
poorer than that of all other age groups, whose performance did not differ
significantly. For sets above 10, performance improved more gradually across
age (see Table 9-1). The task by size interaction reflected the fact that performance was significantly higher on Make A Set of n than on Make An Equivalent Set for sets below 10, 73% versus 59% overall, $F(1, 55) = 6.37$, $p <$
.01, but not for sets larger than 10 (45% versus 47%). This task by size interaction was especially marked for the three youngest age groups, where performance for the larger sets was actually higher on Make An Equivalent Set
than on Make A Set of n. Making equivalent sets in these two ways were
somewhat independent, especially for the larger sets; correlations were significant but were not particularly high, .54 for sets below 10 and .36 for sets
above 10.

Children used quite different strategies to solve these two equivalence
tasks. On the task with a given specific numerosity, 23% used no classifiable
solution (they just pushed some chips toward the experimenter), and 82%
counted out (or tried to count out) a set of n chips (some children used both
kinds of solutions on different trials). All of the correct solutions were
achieved by counting. There was a big difference between the youngest children (those aged 3½ to 4) and all of the other children. Only a third of these
children counted or tried to count while almost all or all of the children in the
other age groups counted.

On the task with no specific numerosity, only 25% of the children ever counted. These children first counted the given row of red chips and then counted out a set of blue chips with the same numerosity. Most children (73%) used one of two matching procedures to produce the given set. In Put Near-Match, the child moved a blue chip near to (on top of or beside) each of the given red chips. In Look-Match, the child looked at the given red row of chips and moved blue chips one by one into a pile; the eye fixation of the child (or, occasionally, a pointing finger) moved along the red row as the child made the pile of blue chips larger. For each of these matching procedures, children sometimes counted as they made the blue set. The use of counting is different from counting to produce an equivalent set, because the given set is not counted first. In this use the count does give a specific numerosity to the produced set (and thus by equivalence to the original set), but it is the matching that actually produces the equivalent set. Some (20%) of the children sometimes used no effective solution procedure. They made a pile of chips one-by-one or by handfuls without looking at the given set of objects or, occasionally, made a row of chips at the edge of the table or at the edge of the card containing the given chips, but this row had no relationship to the objects in the given set (in particular there was no attempt to make the row of blue chips as long as the given row of red chips).

The number of children using a given strategy, the number of trials on which a strategy was used, and the percentage of trials on which an equivalent set was made are given by age in Table 9-2. Put Near-Match composed 49% of the strategy uses, Look-Match 20%, Counting (without matching) 14%, and no identifiable strategies 17%. In every age group except those aged 5 to 5½, more children used Put Near-Match than Look-Match, and Put Near-Match was used on many more trials than was Look Match. At every age group Put Near-Match was much more accurate than was Look-Match. Put Near-Match was accurate about half the time for the two youngest groups and was accurate most of the time for the three oldest groups, while Look-Match varied in accuracy from 0% to 36% accuracy. The exact sources of errors in the Look-Match procedure were not evident from observation. Errors in Put Near-Match were almost all of two kinds: One chip too few or too many was put in (usually in a part of the red row with three red chips close together), or the blue row was started by one-to-one matching but at some point blue chips were put down close together for the rest of the row instead of in correspondence to the red chips. Because some of the older children could count covertly, the figures in the table may underestimate the use of counting with the match strategies for the older children. Behavioral evidence of such counting (counting out loud, lip movement) was present for only a few of the trials classified as Count While Put Near-Matching but was present for about half of the trials classified as Count While Look-Matching; the trials without such behavioral evidence of such counting were classified as Count While Matching because children said that they had counted while they matched. There were no age differences in the use of the Count Only strategy; some children in each age group counted on a few trials to make the equivalent set.

Table 9-2. Strategies Used on the Make An Equivalent Set Task (Experiment 1)

Age	Match						Count while matching												No identifiable strategy		
	Put near			Look			Put near			Look			Count only					
	n	t	%C	n	t	%C	n	t	%C	n	t	%C	n	t	%C				n	t	%C
3½ to 4	4	16	44%	1	2	0%	1	4	50%	1	1	0%	2	8	13%				6	23	0%
4 to 4½	7	27	56%	3	4	25%	1	4	50%	1	2	50%	2	5	40%				4	12	0%
4½ to 5	7	26	96%	2	4	0%	3	9	100%	1	2	0%	3	9	44%				4	9	11%
5 to 5½	6	16	88%	7	22	36%	—	—	—	4	13	46%	5	11	55%				—	—	—
5½ to 6	9	34	94%	2	5	20%	1	2	100%	—	—	—	3	7	43%				2	4	25%

%C, percentage of trials on which procedure was used that resulted in an equivalent set being produced by the child; n, number of children using the procedure at least once; t, number of trials on which procedure was used.

The trials on which no identifiable strategy was used were concentrated in the youngest age group; half of such trials occurred there. With only two exceptions children never produced an equivalent set on these trials.

On both tasks children sometimes did not use the given set or given numerosity as a limit to their activity and just continued moving the blue chips until they had made a pile of all 20 blue chips for the experimenter. On the task with a specific numerosity, this seemed to happen because the children forgot the given numerosity and continued counting past it until they had counted out all 20 chips. Three of the youngest children did this on every trial, and four, five, two, zero, and two children in the youngest through oldest age groups, respectively, did this on some but not all of the trials. Almost all of the latter occurrences were on the sets above 10. On the task with visible objects, for most (68%) cases of giving all the chips the child did not even look at the objects in the given set (and thus did not know how to make an equivalent set or was not trying to do so on that trial). Inadequate matching techniques (9%), errors in an adequate matching technique (18%), and counting past the count word the child had already obtained for the given set (6%) contributed the remainder of these cases. Three of the youngest children and one child aged 4 to 4½ gave all the chips on every trial (only one of these youngest children also counted out 20 chips on every trial), and six, three, two, one, and zero children in the youngest through oldest age groups, respectively, did this on some but not all of the trials. Most of the latter were on the sets above 10. Thus, the behavior of putting out all 20 chips seemed to have different sources in these two tasks. With the given numerosity children began to carry out the correct strategy, but they either could not remember the given numerosity or could not maintain while counting the feedback loop to check whether they had yet reached that numerosity.[3] With no given numerosity, children who put out all 20 chips usually did not even begin to use an adequate strategy.

9.2.1.2.2. The Judging Cardinal Equivalence Task. When asked to judge the equivalence of a row of blue dots and a row of red dots, 58% of the children used length (on 42% of the trials), 38% used counting (on 30% of the trials), and only 10% used matching (on 4% of the trials); some children used more than one approach. These are the same children who immediately afterward when given a row of red chips and asked to give the experimenter as many blue chips as red chips (i.e., the Make an Equivalent Set task), never used length but used matching (69% of the strategies) or counting (14%). Thus, children seem much more likely to use matching (i.e., to make a one-to-one correspondence) when there is no misleading length information and they can move objects close to one another to make visually obvious pairs than when there is misleading length information and they have to match

---

[3] One could differentiate between these alternatives by asking a child who counted out all 20 chips what *n* had been; we did not think to do this until after we had run the study.

unmovable objects in more difficult ways (e.g., by drawing lines in the air, pairing them with fingers, etc).

The number of children using various strategies on the Judging Cardinal Equivalence task, the mean number of trials on which such children used these strategies, the overall percentage of trials on which the strategy was used, and the effectiveness (the percentage of correct trials) of these strategies are given by age in Table 9-3. Four of the oldest children used matching on some trials, and this use was always effective. Two other children used matching, with more variable results. Sixty-seven percent of the children used a perceptual solution method on 51% of the trials: 58% of the children on 42% of the trials made an equivalence judgment based on length, and 12% did so based on density on 9% of the trials. Nine or ten of the twelve children in each of the three middle age groups used a perceptual solution method[4]; somewhat fewer of the youngest children used them (more children in this age group used no discernible method) and somewhat fewer of the oldest children used them (more children in this age group used counting and matching). The perceptual methods were used by the four youngest age groups on between 51% and 71% of the given trials and by the oldest children on 31% of the trials. The effectiveness of these solution procedures was dictated by the design of the task. Length was a misleading cue on every trial, and density was a misleading cue on the equal trials (and thus equivalence judgments based on these cues were incorrect). About half of the children in the two youngest age groups used neither a quantitative nor a perceptual solution procedure for some trials; about one in four equivalence judgments made in this way were correct. These responses included guesses, refusals to make a judgment, and choosing on the basis of color (e.g., always choosing red or choosing alternating colors across trials). Such responses were given on 31% and 21% of the trials by the youngest children and the next-to-youngest children, respectively. Only one or two of the older children had trials classified in this way.

More detailed data concerning the children who counted are given by age in Table 9-4. Some children at each age counted, with no difference within the first four age groups in the number of children counting (from 3 to 5). The number of children counting in the oldest group (aged 5½ to 6) was significantly higher than the number counting in the youngest and next-to-oldest groups (8 versus 3), $\chi^2 = 4.20$, df $= 1, p < .05$, and marginally higher than the number of the older 4-year-olds, $\chi^2 = 2.89$, $p < .10$. Children in the first four age groups counted for between 21% and 29% of the trials given, and the oldest children counted for 60% of the trials. Children in all age groups except the next-to-youngest tended to count fairly consistently (i.e., count for most or all of the six trials) if they counted at all. The youngest children were much less accurate counters than were all the older groups. Only 17% of the counted trials by the youngest had both rows counted correctly versus accuracies ranging between 75% and 87% by the four older groups. The decrease

---

[4] Two children aged 5 to 5½ used both length and density.

Table 9-3. Strategies Used on the Judging Cardinal Equivalence Task by Age (Experiment 1)

Solution methods	Age																			
	3½ to 4				4 to 4½				4½ to 5				5 to 5½				5½ to 6			
	n^a	Mn^b	$\%T^c$	$\%C^d$	n	Mn	$\%T$	$\%C$	n	Mn	$\%T$	$\%C$	n	Mn	$\%T$	$\%C$	n	Mn	$\%T$	$\%C$
Quantitative																				
Counting	3	6.0	25	28	5	3.2	22	56	4	5.3	29	67	3	5.0	21	80	8	5.4	60	79
Matching	0	—	—	—	0	—	—	—	1	6.0	8	50	1	1.0	1	0	4	2.3	13	100
Perceptual																				
Length^e	6	5.3	44	0	10	4.5	63	0	5	3.8	26	0	9	4.9	61	0	5	4.4	31	0
Density^f	1	5.0	7	40	0	—	—	—	4	5.5	31	45	2	3.5	10	43	0	—	—	—
Other^g	6	3.7	31	23	5	3.0	21	27	2	4.5	13	44	1	6.0	8	0	2	2.5	7	40

^{a} n is the number of children using a method on ≥ 1 trial. As some children gave more than one explanation for a single equivalence judgment, and children used more than one type of explanation across trials, the n exceeds 12 for some ages.

^{b} Mn is the mean number of trials for which that explanation was given by the children giving that type of explanation.

^{c} %T is the percentage of total task trials on which that method was used.

^{d} %C is the percentage of trials solved by the method on which a correct equivalence judgment was made.

^{e} Includes trials on which a length explanation was given or on which an incomplete explanation was accompanied by answers on four consecutive trials that reflected a length basis for judgments.

^{f} Includes trials on which a density explanation was given or on which an incomplete explanation was accompanied by answers on four consecutive trials that reflected a density basis for judgments.

^{g} Includes no answers, ambiguous answers, and irrelevant answers for trials that did not fit the error patterns described in e and f. All but one of the correct equivalence judgments in this category were on unequal sets.

Table 9-4. Counting in the Judging Cardinal Equivalence Task by Age (Experiment 1)

	Age				
	3½ to 4	4 to 4½	4½ to 5	5 to 5½	5½ to 6
Number of children counting on ≥ trial	3	5	4	3	8
Mean number of trials counted by these children	6.0	3.2	5.3	5.0	5.4
Percentage of counting children who counted on every trial	100%	20%	75%	68%	88%
Percentage of task trials counted by age group	25%	22%	29%	21%	60%
Percentage of counted trials with both rows counted accurately	17%	75%	76%	87%	77%
Percentage of trials counted overtly[a]	100%	100%	95%	81%	17%
Percentage of counted trials with correct equivalence judgment	28%	56%	67%	80%	79%

[a] Overt counting used pointing as the indicating act; in covert counting, eye fixation was the indicating act.

in counting accuracy by the oldest children (77% compared to 87% for the next-to-oldest group) was probably due to the fact that most of the counting by these oldest children was done using eye fixation (covert counting) rather than pointing (overt counting) as the indicating act; only 17% of the trials counted by the oldest children were counted overtly, while 81% of the trials counted by the next-to-oldest group were counted overtly. The counting strategy was much less effective for the youngest children than for all other age groups. The youngest children who counted made accurate equivalence judgments on only 28% of the counted trials as opposed to accuracies between 56% and 80% for the older children. The counting strategy led to incorrect equivalence judgments for several different reasons. Children counted inaccurately, they counted but then based the equivalence judgment on length (their justifications indicated this basis), they counted accurately but nevertheless gave an incorrect equivalence judgment, and one child used "more" backward (counted correctly but always chose the smaller counted set as the one with more). Children also occasionally counted incorrectly but nevertheless made a correct equivalence judgment.[5]

---

[5] The 11% of such children aged 3½ to 4 represents only two responses because the total number of trials counted was so small (18).

Performance on various other tasks was compared for those children who spontaneously counted on two or more trials and those who did not. Spontaneous counters scored significantly higher ($p < .05$) on the Make a Set of n task (3.1 versus 2.0), the Number-Word Sequence task (63.7 versus 33.1), and the Object Counting task (4.6 versus 3.8 correct correspondence), but not on the Make An Equivalent Set task (2.5 versus 1.9). Thus, as might be expected, these children are better at various aspects of counting than are children who did not spontaneously count. However, they are not better at thinking of and using matching to make an equivalent set.

Returning to the data from all strategies, a one-way analysis of variance by age on the mean number of correct trials revealed a significant effect of age, $F(4, 55) = 3.49$, $p < .03$. For this analysis the few trials on which a density strategy was used were given a score of 0, because some density trials were correct only because of the design of the task. A Newman-Keuls test indicated that the children aged 5½ to 6 scored significantly higher than all other age groups except the children aged 4½ to 5. The means by age groups were 3.2, 1.0, 1.8, 1.1, and .9 for the oldest through youngest groups, respectively.

Set equality or inequality did not affect the choice of any strategy. For all strategies the number of trials on which a strategy was used for equal sets was close to the number of trials on which that strategy was used for unequal sets. Counting and matching were about equally effective on equal and unequal sets, except for the younger 4-year-olds, where one boy counted accurately but used "more" backward (and thus did worse on the unequal sets). The design of the task dictated the effectiveness of the length and density strategies on the equal and unequal sets, as discussed previously. Strategies classified as other were very considerably more effective for unequal than for equal sets; all but one of the correct equivalence judgments in this classification were made on unequal sets. However, this was largely due to the fact that children using a strategy classified as other almost always said one row had more than the other rather than that they had the same. Such responses had a 50% chance of being correct on the unequal trials. When trials were eliminated for which some basis other than guessing could be determined (e.g., alternating colors), the number of correct equivalence judgments for unequal sets was in fact just half the number of trials for unequal sets.

9.2.2. Experiment 2: Children's Ability to Count, Remember, and Use Count Information in a Misleading Length-Equivalence Situation

Effective use of counting to make equivalence judgments requires three kinds of abilities: accurate counting of both arrays, accurate memory of both counted numerosities when ready to make the equivalence judgment, and knowledge of the relationship between specific numerosities and equivalence for equal sets ("same counted word implies equivalent sets") and between specific numerosities and order relations for unequal sets ("for different counted numerosities, the larger numerosity belongs to the set with more"). The third ability obviously entails several different kinds of knowledge, for example, how to establish order relations on cardinal number words, the meaning of *more*, *less*, and *the same number as*. These aspects are discussed in more detail in 9.3.4. Furthermore, effective use of counting in the presence of misleading perceptual information requires one to know that perceptual information is not a reliable indicator of cardinal relations and requires that one be able to resist using the perceptual information.

On the spontaneous Judging Cardinal Equivalence task in experiment 1, 20 of the 23 children who counted made one or more correct equivalent judgments on counted trials (the 3 children who did not were in the two youngest age groups). Thus, these children seem to have had these abilities and were able to use them all together at least once. For 12 of these children, counting was used consistently, and this counting yielded an accurate equivalence judgment on at least four of the six trials. Half of these 12 were aged 5½ to 6; the others ranged from 3½ to 5½ (1, 2, 1, and 2 children in each half-year age group from 3½ to 5½). Thus, these abilities to count in equivalence situations *and* the selection of counting as the preferred strategy become fairly widespread by age 5½ but also characterize occasional children as young as age 3½. The focus of experiment 2 was to ascertain the extent to which the children who did not spontaneously choose the counting strategy nevertheless possessed the requisite abilities to use counting to make equivalence judgments in the presence of misleading length information.

9.2.2.1. Method. The subjects were the children from the sample in experiment 1 who did not count consistently and effectively (those who did not count to produce four or more correct trials) on the Judging Cardinal Equivalence task. A total of 48 children met this criterion; the numbers of children were 11, 10, 11, 10, and 6, from the youngest to the oldest age group, respectively.

This Forced-Count Equivalence task used the same stimulus materials that were used for the Judging Cardinal Equivalence task, and trials were given in the same order that they were given in that task. On each trial the strip with the red dots was placed in front of the child and the child was asked, "How many red dots are there?" If the child did not spontaneously count the dots, the child was told to count the dots and was then asked, "So how many dots are there?" If the answer was wrong, the experimenter then helped the child count the row accurately and ensured that the child could say correctly how many red dots there were. The same procedure was followed for the strip containing the blue dots. A memory question was then asked: "Do you remember how many red dots you counted?" The correct answer was given if the child did not remember or remembered incorrectly. The same memory procedure was then followed by the blue dots. Then the following memory prompt was given just before the equivalence question, as in Fuson, Secada, and Hall (1983), to ensure that the child knew both numerosities at the time of the equivalence question: "So remember, there are *a* red dots and *b* blue dots." The equivalence question asked in the Judging Cardinal Equivalence task was then asked. This task was given at the end of the first testing session, after the Judging Cardinal Equivalence task and after both tasks in which children made a set equivalent to another.

9.2.2.2. Results. Because some children made some correct equivalence judgments on the Judging Cardinal Equivalence task when using Density or Other strategies, the analysis of performance on this Forced-Count Equivalence task is somewhat problematic. One could argue that children who used Density or Other strategies in the earlier task would, when asked the equivalence question in this forced-count task, disregard the count information and just make their equivalence judgment on the same basis as in the earlier task. To control for this possibility, one would want to use the measure of "improvement" on the forced-count task (i.e., use the number of trials by which performance on the forced-count task exceeded performance on the spontaneous task). However, one could also argue that the forced-count task involved such a strong emphasis on counting that children would think of the task as a counting context and try to use the count information. In this case one could simply consider the number of trials that were correct on the forced-count task. The truth probably lies between these two arguments (i.e., they probably are each accurate about some children). Therefore data are reported in both ways in Table 9-5.

Most of the children in the four youngest age groups (10 or 11 from each group) and half of the oldest children were given the Forced-Count Equivalence task. About a fourth of the youngest children improved on this task, about two thirds of the three middle age groups improved, and all of the oldest children improved on this task (see Table 9-5). Thus, some children at each age group showed an ability to use specific numerosities obtained by counting to make equivalence judgments, and this number increased over the age range tested. The children showing any improvement did improve on between one third and two thirds of the trials on which improvement was possible. However, over the whole sample, the youngest children improved on only 10% of the trials on which they could show improvement, the oldest children improved on 70% of such trials, and the three middle age groups improved on between a third and a half of such trials. The incorrect equivalence judgments by children of all ages were almost all based on length.

The children in the two age groups between 4½ and 5½ showed a greater tendency to improve on the equal than on the unequal trials; in both these age groups, 70% of the children who could improve on equal trials did so, whereas only 22% of those who could improve on unequal trials did so. The children in these age groups had used the perceptual strategies of length and density very heavily on the earlier spontaneous task, whereas many of the younger children had used other strategies. Perhaps for the children between 4½ and 5½, it took the strong salience of getting *the same* count word (the same counted numerosity as in equal trials) to interfere with the use of the well-established perceptual strategies, while obtaining different counted nu-

Table 9-5. Performance on Forced-Count Equivalence Task by Age (Experiment 2)

	Age				
	3½ to 4	4 to 4½	4½ to 5	5 to 5½	5½ to 6
Number of children given FCT[a]	11	10	11	10	6
Data based on improvement					
Number (%) of children improving on FCT[b]	3 (27%)	6 (60%)	8 (73%)	7 (70%)	6 (100%)
Mean number of improved trials[c]	2.0	2.7	2.5	2.7	3.2
Improved trials/trials on which improvement was possible[c] (as a %)	33%	48%	69%	51%	70%
Improved trials/trials on which improvement was possible for the whole sample (as a %)	10%	29%	50%	35%	70%
Data based on performance					
Number (%) of children getting ≥ 1 trial correct	6 (55%)	6 (60%)	11 (100%)	7 (70%)	6 (100%)
Mean number of correct trials[d]	1.5	3.2	3.5	3.4	4.5
Mean number of correct trials/trials given for the whole sample (as a %)	14%	32%	58%	40%	75%

[a] FCT: Forced-count equivalence task.
[b] Number of children with correct trials on forced-count equivalence task minus correct trials on spontaneous equivalence task ≥ 1 (percent is out of those children given FCT).
[c] For those children showing an improvement.
[d] For those children getting ≥ 1 trial correct.

merosities for the two sets (as in the unequal trials) was not as arresting (because the two sets were different) and did not contradict the perceptual strategy as long as the child did not think carefully about *which* counted set was more.

Turning to the data based just on performance rather than on improvement, between half and all of the children in each age group made one or more correct equivalence judgments on this forced-count task (see Table 9-5). The youngest children had few correct trials, while in all of the older groups, children who got any trial correct got a mean of more than half of the trials correct. Over all the sample, the youngest children made few correct equivalence judgments (14% correct trials), and the next oldest group increased only to 32% correct judgments. The three oldest groups ranged between 40% and 75% correct equivalence judgments. Almost all incorrect equivalence judgments were based on length. There was not a big difference in any age group in the *number* of children getting at least one trial correct on the equal and on the unequal trials. However, in every age group, the mean number of equal trials correct (based on those children who got an equal trial correct) was higher than the mean number of unequal trials correct (based on those children who got an unequal trial correct): an overall mean of 2.6 versus 1.8 out of a possible 3. This difference is in spite of the fact that the undetected use of density or other strategies (rather than the use of the count information) would increase the number of correct unequal but not correct equal trials. Therefore, children who used the counted numerosities for equal sets used them more consistently than did children who used them for unequal sets.

Thus, with both analyses, children (especially those in the middle three age groups) used the counting information more on equal than on unequal sets. Two sources seem likely for this difference. First, when the count words are different, one has to be able to establish an order relation on these number words (decide which of them is more), while for count words that are the same, one only has to notice that they are the same. Siegler and Robinson (1982) found that 3-year-olds' knowledge of order relations on cardinal words was minimal. This may then be one reason why their performance was so poor on this task. Even when reminded of the two unequal words, most 3-year-olds could not establish an order relation on them. Second, as argued previously, two words that are the same conflict more directly with the perceptual information that the sets are different than do two words that are different. This conflict may then allow the child to reject the information obtained from the lengths and use the count information.

Parts of the Forced-Count Equivalence task directly measured two other abilities required to use counting to judge cardinal relations: counting both sets accurately and remembering both counted numerosities. For the youngest children, remembering both counts proved to be more difficult than obtaining the correct numerosity by counting. There were significantly more of the youngest children for whom the number of trials on which they counted correctly for both rows exceeded the number of trials on which they remembered the numerosities of both rows than children for whom the number of trials on which they remembered both numerosities exceeded the number of trials on which they counted both numerosities correctly, 9 versus 0 out of 11, $\chi^2 = 4.46$, $p < .05$. For all other age groups, memory and counting skill seemed to place more equal constraints on the ability to provide oneself with information necessary to make an equivalence judgment based on numerosities obtained by counting. Some children counted correctly for both rows on more trials than on which they remembered both numerosities and some children did the opposite, with no discernible pattern by age (see the two right-most columns in Table 9-6). All or almost all of the children in each age group were able to count both sets in a given trial accurately at least once, but the youngest children did so on fewer trials (52%) than did the older children (between 68% and 83%). Both the number of children who ever remembered both counted numerosities (4 of 11) and the percentage of trials on which both numerosities were remembered (20%) were considerably lower for the youngest children than for the children in the four older age groups. *All* the 4- and 5-year-olds did remember both numerosities at least once, and both numerosities were remembered between 67% and 81% of the time (see Table 9-6). The same age pattern occurred for being able to combine counting accuracy and remembering on the same trial. The youngest children were considerably worse than all of the older children (see Table 9-6). However, the older children did not always count accurately and remember accurately on the same trial; the percentage of trials on which they did both of these accurately ranged across the four age groups between 7% and 14% below the lesser of counting and remembering.

Because inaccurate counting was corrected and children who forgot counted numerosities of either set were told these numerosities, children possessed adequate information to make an equivalence judgment at the time the equivalence question was asked. However, this information could be self-obtained (if the child both counted and remembered correctly) or it could be provided by the experimenter (if the child had made a counting or remembering error). In the youngest age group, only one child made a correct equivalence judgment on a trial on which adequate information was self-obtained. Most of the correct equivalence judgments were on trials on which part or all of the information was supplied by the experimenter, and most trials with adequate self-obtained knowledge had incorrect equivalence judgments. For the next-to-youngest age group, half the correct equivalence judgments were made on trials with adequate self-obtained knowledge. There were also many trials (38% of the total) on which children obtained adequate information but did not make correct equivalence judgments. These statements also describe the performance of the next-to-oldest children. The middle age group and the oldest children had two-thirds and three-fourths, respectively, of the correct equivalence judgments made on trials with self-obtained knowledge, and they had only 17% and 11% of the total trials on which adequate information was self-obtained but incorrect equivalence judgments were made. These patterns are of course related to the fact that older children both obtained all the required information more frequently and used this information more frequently than did the younger children. But these figures do indicate that obtaining adequate information and using it remained somewhat separate throughout this age range. Neither of these seems to be a necessary prerequisite for the other.

Table 9-6. Counting Accuracy and Memory Accuracy on Forced-Count Equivalence Task (Experiment 2)

Age	n^a	Accurate on both arrays						Relationship between counting and memory accuracy	
		Counting		Memory		Counting and memory			
		$NAcc^b$	$\%Acc^c$	$NAcc^b$	$\%Acc^c$	$NAcc^b$	$\%Acc^c$	N counting $>$ Memory^d	N memory $>$ Counting^e
3½ to 4	11	10	52%	4	20%	4	18%	9	0
4 to 4½	10	10	75%	10	67%	10	53%	5	3
4½ to 5	11	10	71%	11	80%	9	64%	1	3
5 to 5½	10	9	68%	10	72%	9	55%	4	2
5½ to 6	6	6	83%	6	81%	6	69%	2	2

^{a} Number of children given this task.

^{b} NAcc is the number of children accurate on both arrays on at least one trial.

^{c} % Acc is the percentage of trials on which children of that age group were accurate on both arrays.

^{d} Number of children who had more trials with both arrays counted accurately than trials with both arrays remembered accurately.

^{e} Number of children who had more trials with both arrays remembered accurately than trials with both arrays counted accurately.

9.2.3. Experiment 3: Use of Counting and Matching With Misleading Length Information, Without Misleading Length Information, and When "Looks Like More" is Distinguished From "Is Really More"

In Experiment 1 the use of counting, matching, and length to make equivalent sets in different situations was contrasted with their use in judging cardinal equivalence. Children predominantly counted to make a set of a given specified numerosity, predominantly matched to make a set equivalent to one presented by objects in a row, and predominantly used length (or density) to judge cardinal equivalence when length was a misleading cue. The fairly competent use of counting and matching to generate sets equivalent to a given set raised the question of whether children would spontaneously use these effective strategies to judge cardinal equivalence if length was not a misleading cue. Therefore, in experiment 3, baseline data were first obtained concerning the strategies used to judge cardinal equivalence when length was a misleading cue, and then children were asked to judge the cardinal equivalence of sets of objects not arranged in a row. Because children had been found to use matching procedures in which objects were moved next to each other, real objects rather than pictures were used in this second task so that children could use these Put-Near matching procedures. To make matching a more accessible strategy in the first task also, the corresponding pairs of entities in each row were colored identically, and the nature of the objects was also varied by pairs in one trial (see following discussion).

Because a common criticism of Piaget's conservation of number task is that children are just confusing two different meanings of more (a length meaning and a number meaning), we also pursued in this static compare situation the issue of whether children would be able to make a distinction between these two meanings of more. We termed these "looks like more" for length and "is really more" for counting and matching. We told children that things can "look like more" but "really be the same" and then showed them stimuli materials like those in the first task (misleading length cues and support of matching by colors of the entities in the rows). Children were asked which row "looks like more" and then whether that row "was really more." The question was the extent to which this distinction would inhibit the usual use of length and density cues and enable children spontaneously to use counting or matching.

9.2.3.1. Method. 9.2.3.1.1. Subjects. The subjects were 40 middle- to upper-middle-class children attending an educational demonstration school. Half were 4-year-olds ranging in age from 4-0 (4 years 0 months) through 4-9 (4 years 9 months) (mean 4-5), and half were 5-year-olds ranging in age from 5-0 to 5-11 (mean 5-6).

9.2.3.1.2. Tasks, Materials, and Procedure. All children were given three tasks in which they were asked to make equivalence judgments. The first and third tasks were identical except for the manipulation described below. In these tasks two long strips of construction paper were placed one above the other about 8 cm apart on the table in front of the child. The strips each contained identical rows of pictures (line drawings), but the pictures on one strip were spaced farther apart than the pictures on the other strip. There were three trials for both the first and third tasks, and the pictures for these tasks were chosen so that the stimuli materials for the two tasks would be very similar. The pictures for the first task were identical pictures of boys, pictures of different animals, and identical pictures of football players. Those for the third task were identical pictures of girls, pictures of different kinds of fruit, and identical pictures of basketball players. The pictures were colored so as to make matching fairly easy to carry out: the leftmost picture on each strip was colored the same, the next pictures on each strip were colored the same (but different from the other pictures on the strip), etc. The pictures of the animals and fruit were colored their usual colors, and the shirts of the boys and girls and the uniforms of the football and basketball players were colored a different color in the same order on each strip.

After the experimenter placed the two strips parallel to each other in front of the child, she said, "I have some boys [gesturing along her row], and you have some boys [gesturing along the child's row]. Do *I* have more boys [gesturing along her row], or do we have the *same number* of boys, or do *you* have more boys [gesturing along the child's row]?" After the child's response, the child was asked, "How do you know?" This procedure was repeated for the next two trials (animals and then football players on task 1 and fruit and basketball players on task 3). Each trial alternated whether the strip with the longer row of pictures was the child's or the experimenter's row; half the children in each age group were given the longer row first. Each trial also alternated whether the question said "I" or "you" first. Half the children in each age group within each of the above counterbalancing conditions were asked the first question with "I" first.

In task 2 the objects were not presented with length as a misleading cue, and real objects rather than pictures were used so that children could carry out matching procedures in which objects were placed near each other. For each of the three trials, two groups of objects were placed beside each other about 15 cm apart. The objects in each group were close to each other and arranged randomly, except that an attempt was made to keep the two groups from looking quite different in size (i.e., to keep one from looking scattered over a larger area than the other). Children were presented six green and six yellow small toys cars, then eight orange and eight purple 1-inch wooden blocks, and then seven red and seven green small boats.

After the objects were placed in front of the child, the experimenter said, "Here are some green cars [gesture to them] and some yellow cars [gesture to them]. Are there more *green* cars [gesture], the *same number* of green and yellow cars, or more *yellow* cars [gesture]?" After the child responded the experimenter asked, "How do you know?" If the child just seemed to guess or did nothing with the cars, the experimenter said, "Do something with the cars to show me if they are the same or if one has more." The same procedure was repeated with the blocks and with the boats.

Prior to task 3 the experimenter said, "You know, sometimes I can make these rows of things so that it *looks like* one has more but really they have *the same number*. I'm going to show you some more cards. I'll ask you which *looks like* more. Then I'll ask you to tell me if it *really* is more. OK? Sometimes it will really be *more* and sometimes it will really be *the same* but just *look like* more. OK?"

After the strips of girls were placed in front of the child, the experimenter said, "I have some girls [gesture], and you have some girls [gesture]. Which girls *look like* more?" After the child responded the experimenter asked, "How do you know?" The child then was asked, "Do I *really* have more girls, or do we *really* have the same number of girls, or do you *really* have more girls?" If the child held to a length or density response, this prompt was given, "But that's how it just *looks like* more. What could you do to tell if it *really* is more or if they're the same?" Fruit and players had similar questions.

For all tasks both sets contained the same number of entities. Adding a condition of unequal sets within each task would have made the experiment too long. We chose equivalent sets because children had used counting information more on these than on unequal sets, and we wanted to assess children's earliest abilities to use counting and matching to judge cardinal equivalence. Results for equal sets would also relate to more of the literature on the Piagetian conservation of number task.

9.2.3.1.3. Scoring. Children sometimes changed their answer to the equivalence question; their last response was the response scored. One point was given for each correct equivalence judgment, for a possible score of 3 on each task. The strategies used on each trial of task 1 and task 3 were classified as Count/Number, Match, Length, and Density. Count/Number was chosen if the child was observed to count, said (s)he had counted, or used specific numerosities in responding to the equivalence question or to the "How do you know?" question. Matching was selected if the child exhibited matching behavior (e.g., pointed with thumb and forefinger to successive pairs of pictures on the two strips) or gave a matching justification (e.g., "These match. They have the same clothes on." "Because there are two browns, two blues, etc." "There's none different fruits on yours or mine."). Length was designated as the strategy if the child's justification focused on one strip's row of pictures being longer than the other (e.g., "Yours has this one out here." or "Mine is longer.") or (in three cases) the child did not justify the response, but all three equivalence choices were of the longer strip. Density was chosen if the justification focused on the space between pictures rather than on the length of a row. All but five trials fell into these categories for task 1, and all but four trials fell into them for task 3. The Count/Number and the Match strategies were classified as Quantitative, and the Length and Density strategies were classified as Perceptual.

For task 2, Shape was added as another kind of matching. Children sometimes made one group of objects into some shape and then formed the other
group into the same shape and size. The Shape strategy was considered to be
a type of one-to-one correspondence and thus was collapsed into Match for
this task. On Task 2 children also used general perceptual strategies. They
just looked at the two groups and said one had more or they rearranged one
or both groups (not making them the same shape and size as in Shape) and
then said one had more. There was no identified use of density and little
observed or self-described use of length (use on 9% of the trials). For most of
these few uses of length, the two rows constructed by the child were not
placed under each other, so the judgment of length was a general perceptual
one rather than one based on an adequate length strategy. Therefore, all the
uses of length were placed in the general category of Perceptual strategies.
Thus, the strategy categories for task 2 were Count/Number, Match, and
Perceptual. All but two trials fell into these categories.

Two scorers categorized the strategies used on each trial. Interrater agreement was 98%. The final categorization for the disagreements was arrived at
by discussion.

9.2.3.2. Results. A 2(task 1 versus task 2) × 2(age: 4-year-olds versus 5-year-
olds) analysis of variance with repeated measures for the first factor was
carried out on the equivalence judgment scores. This revealed a significant
main effect of task, $F(1, 38) = 42.04, p < .001$, no effect of age, and no interaction. An identical analysis comparing the equivalence judgment scores on
task 1 and task 3 revealed a similar pattern: a significant main effect of task,
$F(1, 38) = 53.38, p < .001$, no effect of age, and no interaction. Children of
both ages made considerably more correct equivalence judgments on both
tasks 2 and 3 than on task 1 (Table 9-7).

Consideration of the strategy data indicated that this difference resulted
because children of both ages shifted from a predominance of use of perceptual strategies on task 1 to a predominance of use of quantitative strategies
on tasks 2 and 3 (see Table 9-8). On task 1 children did use perceptual strategies significantly more often than they used quantitative strategies (use on
75% versus 50% of the trials), and on tasks 2 and 3 children did use quantitative strategies significantly more often than they used perceptual strategies
(91% versus 26% on task 2 and 90% versus 16% on task 3), the task $F(1, 38)$
$= 5.16, 58.8,$ and $78.71, p < .05$, from a 2(strategy: Quantitative versus Per-

Table 9-7. Percentage of Correct Performance by Task and Age (Experiment 3)

Task	4-Year-olds	5-Year-olds
1	33%	37%
2	70%	93%
3	73%	93%

Table 9-8. Use of Strategies by Task and Age (Experiment 3)

	4-Year-olds		5-Year-olds	
	Ever used[a]	Last used[b]	Ever used[a]	Last used[b]
Task 1				
Quantitative	53%	(30%)	47%	(40%)
Count/number	43%	(27%)	43%	(37%)
Match	13%	(10%)	10%	(10%)
Perceptual	80%	(70%)	70%	(60%)
Task 2				
Quantitative	83%	(83%)	98%	(93%)
Count/number	70%	(70%)	87%	(80%)
Match/shape	30%	(30%)	37%	(37%)
Perceptual	25%	(13%)	27%	(10%)
Task 3				
Quantitative	83%	(81%)	97%	(97%)
Count/number	63%	(63%)	60%	(60%)
Match	27%	(27%)	43%	(43%)
Perceptual	19%	(17%)	13%	(0%)

[a] Ever used means the strategy was used sometime during the trial.
[b] Last used means the strategy was the basis for the last equivalence judgment.
Note. The percentages are the percentage of trials on which a strategy was used. For both criteria these sometimes exceed the total because children sometimes used more than one strategy on a given trial, even to justify or obtain the last equivalence judgment.

ceptual) × 2(age: 4-year-olds versus 5-year-olds) analysis of variance carried out on the "ever-used" strategy scores for each task.[6] In all three analyses there was no effect of age and no interaction. Children counted on significantly more trials on tasks 2 and 3 than on task 1: 79% and 62% versus 43%, as indicated by significant main effects of task, $F(1, 38) = 25.87$ and 6.00, $p < .02$, in two 2(task) × 2(age) analyses of variance (there was no effect of age and no interaction in either analysis). Similar analyses of variance carried out on scores for matching revealed a similar pattern. Children

---

[6] The quantitative score was obtained by giving one point for each trial on which a child used a quantitative strategy, and the perceptual score was obtained by giving one point for each trial on which a child used a perceptual strategy.

matched on significantly more trials on both tasks 2 and 3 than on task 1: 34% and 35% versus 12%, task $F(1, 38) = 14.53$ and 16.97, $p < .001$ (there was no effect of age and no interaction in either analysis). Analyses using scores based on the "last used" column (the strategy on which the equivalence judgment was actually based) yielded the same results.

In task 1 on 11% of the trials, children first used the Count/Number strategy and then made their equivalence judgment using a Perceptual strategy (the difference in Table 9-8 in the Count/Number "ever-used" percentages and the "last-used" percentages). The 4-year-olds made such shifts more frequently than did the 5-year-olds (on 16% versus 6% of the trials). In task 2 the shifts away from counting were instead from an inaccurate count to the accurate use of Match/Shape. In task 1 children also sometimes first used a perceptual strategy and then shifted to use of Count/ Number strategy (on 10% of the trials). In the 4-year-olds, the shifts in this direction seemed to require forced reflection because all of such changes were made after the child was asked, "How do you know?" The 5-year-olds seemed more likely to make these shifts on their own because only 1 of the shifts occurred after this question. In the tasks 2 and 3, shifts from Perceptual to Quantitative strategies sometimes seemed to require reflection and/or questioning. In task 2 for the 4-year-olds, of the 7 such shifts from Perceptual to Quantitative strategies, 2 occurred spontaneously, 3 occurred after the "How do you know?" question, and 2 occurred after the child was prompted to do something to show whether there were more or the same. For the 5-year-olds, of the 10 such shifts, 6 occurred spontaneously and 4 occurred after the child was prompted to do something. In task 3, the one such shift by a 4-year-old was spontaneous, and the 6 such shifts by 5-year-olds were equally split between spontaneous shifts and shifts in response to the final prompt ("But that's how it just looks like more.").

Equivalence judgments based on a perceptual strategy were invariably wrong in tasks 1 and 3 because the rows were made so that length and density were misleading cues. In task 2 perceptually based judgments almost always were wrong, that is, one group was almost always indicated as more when such judgments were made. Matching strategies almost always led to correct equivalence judgments; in only 3% of its uses on any task was a matching strategy carried out incorrectly. Counting was carried out correctly (i.e., both rows were counted correctly) by the 4-year-olds and by the 5-year-olds on 77% and on 77% of its uses on task 1, on 74% and on 79% of its uses on task 2, and on 84% and on 86% of its uses on task 3. Thus, there was no age difference in the accuracy of counting and no drop in counting accuracy when more children counted (i.e., on tasks 2 and 3). There also was no change in counting accuracy when children could move the objects to count on task 2; most children in fact did not move objects on task 2 but instead pointed at the objects without moving them.

In tasks 1 and 3, almost all of the perceptual strategies used to justify an equivalence judgment involved the use of length and not density. Similarly, on the first question on task 3 in which children had to choose which row "looked like more," all children except one chose the longer row on at least one trial. The shorter row was chosen on only 3% of the trials, no choice was made on 7% of the trials, and the longer row was chosen on the remaining 90% of the trials. Children aged 4 to 5½ justified these choices much more on the basis of length (57% of the choices were justified by length) than on density (14% of the choices were justified by density), but the children aged 5½ to 6 justified more of these choices of the longer row by focusing on differences in the gaps between the pictures (the justifications for 47% of the choices were based on density) than by focusing on how one row was longer (the justifications for 30% of the choices were based on length). Thus, these oldest children seemed to be more aware than the younger children of the gaps between the objects. There was also an interesting age difference in the extent to which justifications referring to density explicitly referred to a transformation of spreading apart the entities. Of the 13 density justifications made by the children aged 4 to 5½, most (11) of them used language that described a transformation that moved the entities apart or closer together, for example, "These are spreaded out," "These are scooted over," "These are moved a little closer." Of the 14 density justifications by the children aged 5½ to 6, only 3 explicitly mentioned a transformation. Most instead used descriptions of the density difference that were similar to the length descriptions such as, "These are farther apart." "Those are closer," "These are wider apart." None of the length justifications by children of any age referred to a transformation of making one row longer or shorter; the justifications merely described the length (e.g., "Mine is shorter." "Yours is more long") or referred to extra or missing entities at one or both ends (e.g., "There isn't one out here," "This has one at the end"). Thus, it may be that the width of the space between objects is closely associated by young children with moving those objects apart or closer in a way that length is not so associated. Whether this is just true of the younger children or whether the descriptive nontransformational terms used by the children aged 5½ to 6 also are linked to transformational ideas is an interesting question to be addressed in the future.

On task 3, 16 of the 20 4-year-olds and all 20 5-year-olds made the distinction between "looks like more" and "is really more" on one or more trials, and these 36 children made this distinction on 87% of the trials. That is, they identified the longer row as "looks like more" but said that the two rows were "really the same." On all but four of these trials, children counted or matched to make or to justify their choice of "really the same;" on three of these remaining four trials, a transformation justification was given such as "These are just spreaded out and they still have the same." Thus, these choices of "really the same" were not just guesses in response to pressure from the experimenter. Only 2% of these uses of quantitative strategies to decide who "really had more" were in response to the final prompt in the procedure. (This prompt was said after a child's response that the longer row really had more, "But that's how it *looks like* more. What could you do to tell if it *really* is more or if they're the same?") Thus, when given the information that a distinction could be made between rows that looked like more and rows that really were more, these children could and did make the distinction that one of the two rows looked like more but the rows really were the same, and they spontaneously used counting or matching to decide if they really were the same.

However, because this task followed the second task in which the availability of movable objects and the lack of strong misleading perceptual information elicited high rates of use of the quantitative strategies counting and matching, these quantitative strategies may have been primed for use in task 3. One aspect of this possible influence that was especially striking was the increase from task 1 to task 3 in the use of matching by the 5-year-olds: from use on 10% to use on 43% of the trials. This increase occurred in spite of the fact that the matching strategies in task 2 (physically pairing objects by placing them near to each other and forming the objects into the same shapes) were not available for use in the pictures in task 3; nevertheless, children in task 3 did notice and use the matching cues available there (the colors) even though they had not used them in task 1. Because the "looks like more/really more" distinction in task 3 is confounded with following task 2, it is not clear whether the distinction made in task 3 would have been as successful if the quantitative strategies had not already been prompted by task 2. The combined treatment of eliciting the quantitative strategies by the task 2 setting and then making the "looks like more/really more" distinction[7] is, however, evidently a powerful one.

No effect of age even approached significance in any analysis. However, there was one puzzling anomolous characteristic of the data by age. The original intention was to analyze the data by half-year age groups; 10 children had been interviewed in each half-year age group. However, the 4-year-olds turned out to be heavily distributed in the middle of the age range: 10 of the 20 4-year-olds were within a 3-month age span. Thus, the use of the half-year splits did not seem sensible. Furthermore, for some reason the younger 4-year-olds (those from 4-0 through 4-5) used more quantitative strategies and made more correct equivalence judgments on task 1 than did the older 4-year-olds; the performance of these 10 youngest children on task 1 even exceeded that of the 5-year-olds. The 4-year-old half-year age data on tasks 2 and 3 looked more usual; performance by this youngest group was lower than or equivalent to that of the older children. It is not clear to us why these children used quantitative strategies so frequently on task 1. The performance of the

---

[7] Strictly speaking more children may also have used quantitative strategies in task 3 than in task 1 just because task 3 followed task 1. However, we found no difference in equivalence judgments across the three trials within task 1, 2, or 3. Thus, there was no evidence to support a hypothesis of learning within a task. This result therefore reduces the probability that much of the increase in performance on task 3 was due merely to its being the third task, that is, to learning over trials.

children age 4½ to 5 looked more typical on this task. Almost every equivalence response on task 1 was based on length. The 33% correct equivalence judgments and the relatively high use of quantitative strategies for the 4-year-olds on task 1 may therefore be an overestimate for this age group (i.e., the "usual" performance of 4-year-olds over the whole age range may be more like that of the older 4-year-olds here and thus demonstrate very little use of quantitative strategies). In this case one might ordinarily find a difference in correct equivalence judgments on static equivalence tasks between 4- and 5-year-olds. If the spontaneous use of quantitative strategies on task 1 by the 4-year-olds here is an overestimate, then the shift to quantitative strategies on tasks 2 and 3 would then ordinarily be even more striking than it was here, that is, any of our 4-year-olds who "untypically" used quantitative strategies on task 1 could not make such a shift on tasks 2 or 3 in the present study but might ordinarily be able to show such a shift.

A few children were not willing to make the distinction between "looks like more" and "is really more." One of these used quantitative strategies with the movable objects but articulated very clearly her insistence that the longer row in task 3 really had more, "If you taked them off and stacked them, you'd know they were the same but for now there are more because they are more spread out." Some other children were quite surprised by the conflict between the length result and their counting result. They spontaneously counted to find out which really had more but continued to be very surprised each time that the count numbers were the same. One child colorfully captured his reaction by showing surprise each time and exclaiming, "Oh my God! I'm wrong again. They're the same."

9.2.4. Summary of the Results of the Experiments

In Experiment 1 children aged 3½ to 6 used quite different strategies on the different equivalence tasks. To make a set of a specified numerosity (e.g., "Give me nine white chips"), they predominantly counted; no one matched or used length. To make as many blue chips as red chips arranged in a row, they predominantly matched; some counting was used, but length was almost never used. The most frequent matching technique was placing a blue chip near each red chip (49% of the strategies); the other matching technique was looking at the red row while pulling blue chips into a pile (20% use). Children sometimes counted while matching (13% of the strategies) and sometimes counted without matching (14%). To judge whether two sets of entities arranged in two parallel rows were equivalent, children predominantly used length (58% of the children judged the longer row to have more on 42% of the trials) or density (12% of the children judged the denser row to have more on 9% of the trials). Only 38% of the children ever counted (and they did so on 30% of the trials), and only 10% ever matched (and they did so on 4% of the trials). The predominance of perceptual strategies over counting and matching was limited to the four younger age groups, where it was quite strong (57% versus 23% and 2%, respectively, pooled over these four age groups). In contrast, two thirds of the children aged 5½ to 6 did count or match on at least one trial and more than half of them did so consistently. On all three tasks the youngest children (3½ to 4) showed no identifiable strategy or used some nonquantitative strategy (e.g., choosing the red row as having more) more than did the other children. In summary children use counting when a specific numerosity is given, use matching when there is no misleading length information and they can move objects to do the matching, and tend to use length when length information is available.

For sets below 10 and between 10 and 20, the youngest children (3½ to 4) were able to make a set equivalent to another set by matching on about a fifth of the trials. They were able to make a set of specified numerosity below 10 on a fourth of the trials but could do so on hardly any of the trials for the larger numerosities between 10 and 20. There was no age difference in the half-year age groups from age 4 to age 6 in the effectiveness of making a set of specified numerosity by counting for sets below 10 (ranging from 75% to 92% accuracy), but improvement did occur over the age range for numerosities between 10 and 20 (increasing from 29% to 79%). There was no age difference in this range for either set size for making a set equivalent to a set of unspecified numerosity (ranging from 42% to 83% accuracy). The majority of children in each age group matched by putting objects near each original object. This was a very accurate strategy for those aged 4½ and older (88% and above accuracy). Counting the original set and then counting out a set with the same numerosity was used by a few children and was effective only about half the time. Matching by looking at the original objects while moving new objects into a pile was used by a few children but was relatively ineffective (accurate only about 30% of the time).

The children who did not spontaneously use counting accurately on at least four of the six equivalence trials in the Judging Cardinal Equivalence task of experiment 1 were given the same task again but counted both sets before being asked the relational question. Inaccurate counting was corrected, and children were reminded of both counted numerosities before being asked the relational question. In this experiment 2, about a third of the children aged 3½ to 4 made more correct equivalence choices after counting than they had in experiment 1 using their chosen strategy, about two thirds of the children aged 4 to 5½ did better after counting, and all of the children aged 5½ to 6 did better after counting than they had originally. The youngest children improved on 10% of the trials on which they could show improvement, the middle children improved on between a third and a half of the trials, and the oldest children improved on 70% of the possible trials. Incorrect equivalence judgments were almost all based on length.

In experiment 1 whether the sets were equal or unequal did not affect the choice of any strategy when judging cardinal equivalence. However, when counting was imposed in experiment 2, children (especially those in the middle three age groups) used the counting information more on equal than on unequal sets. This is not surprising for two reaons. First, for different count words, one has to choose between the less than and greater than relation on these words and decide which of these applies, while only the equivalence relation can apply when the count words are the same. Second, two words that are the same conflict more directly with the perceptual information that the sets are different than do two words that are different. In the latter case children might only note that the words are different and the rows are different lengths and not process the directions of these differences. Children might then base their judgment on the length information, not realizing that it is the opposite of the order relation on the words.

Parts of the Forced-Count Equivalence task in experiment 2 directly measured two abilities required to use counting to judge cardinal relations; counting both sets accurately and remembering both counted numerosities. For the youngest children remembering both counts proved to be considerably more difficult than obtaining the correct numerosity by counting, 20% versus 52% accuracy. For all other half-year age groups, memory and counting skill seemed to place more equal constraints on the ability to provide oneself with information necessary to make an equivalence judgment based on numerosities obtained by counting. These 4- and 5-year-olds did so on between 67% and 83% of the trials. The youngest children were able to coordinate counting and remembering accurately on the same trial (and thus providing themselves will adequate count information) on 18% of the trials. This figure ranged from 53% to 69% for the half-year age groups from age 4 to age 6. Obtaining adequate counting information oneself (counting and remembering accurately) and using counting information provided by the experimenter (when counting or remembering was inadequate) remained somewhat separate throughout the age range studied. Children at each age group sometimes obtained adequate counting information but did not use it and sometimes did not obtain adequate counting information but used the information provided by the experimenter.

In experiment 3 presence of misleading length cues had a very strong effect on the strategies used by 4- and 5-year-old children. When length was a misleading cue (i.e., when one of the two equal rows was longer than the other), children predominantly used perceptual strategies (mostly length) to make their final cardinal equivalence judgment, doing so on 65% of the trials while using counting on 32% of the trials and matching on 10% of the trials (some children used both counting and matching on the same trial). In sharp contrast, when length was not a misleading cue and objects could be moved, children based 75% of their final equivalence judgments on counting (or number) and based 34% of their judgments on matching,[8] while basing only 12% of their final judgments on perceptual strategies. The strength of the misleading length cue manifested itself even for those children who spon-

---

[8] Again, some children used counting and matching on the same trial.

taneously counted or used number as their initial strategy on this task. On 16% of the trials the 4-year-olds who obtained count or number information nevertheless made their final equivalence judgment using length rather than the count or number information; this was true on 6% of the trials for the 5-year-olds. Some shifts occurred in the opposite direction, from perceptual to quantitative strategies, but some of these occurred only after reflection or questioning (e.g., after being asked "How do you know?").

Most (80%) of the 4-year-olds and all of the 5-year-olds did make a distinction between two meanings of "more," choosing the longer row as the row that "looks like more" and counting or matching to decide that the rows "really are the same." Children counted to decide "really more" on 62% of the trials and matched the colors or objects in the two rows on 35% of the trials. This was a considerable and significant increase in counting and in matching from the first task in which very similar stimulus materials were used. Because this task followed the task with no misleading length cues, it is not clear how much of the increased used of counting and matching is due to the reflection forced by the distinction between the two meanings of "more" and to the priming of counting and matching by the second condition. It is noteworthy, however, that the use of counting and matching as appropriate strategies to determine "is really more" was never suggested to the children; all who used counting and matching came to this decision on their own.

Almost all children chose the longer row as the one that "looks like more." However, children aged 4 to 5½ justified their choice more on the basis of length than of density, while children aged 5½ to 6 justified more of these choices of the longer row by focusing on differences in the gaps between the pictures, that is, by focusing on the density. Thus, these oldest children seemed to be more aware than the younger children of the gaps between the objects. Almost all of the younger children who did mention the gaps in their justifications used language that described a transformation that moved the entities apart or closer together, for example, "These are spread out," "These are scooted over," "These are moved a little closer." None of the length justifications by children of any age referred to a transformation of making one row longer or shorter; the justifications merely described the length (e.g., "Mine is shorter," "Yours is more long") or referred to extra or missing entities at one or both ends (e.g., "There isn't one out here," "This has one at the end"). Thus, it may be that the width of the space between objects is closely associated by young children with moving those objects apart or closer in a way in which length is not so associated.

9.3. Equivalence Situations and the Development of Equivalence Strategies: Equivalence and Order Relations on Cardinal Numbers

There are at least three different situations in which one might be asked to establish the equivalence or nonequivalence of two sets of discrete objects: a static compare situation in which the two sets are presented at the same time, a dynamic situation in which one set is presented and then a transformation is made on that set, and a dynamic situation within a compare situation in which a cardinal relation is first established on the two sets and then a transformation is made on one of the sets (see Table 9-9). The question in each case is the nature of the relation between the cardinal numbers represented by the two sets: is one set equivalent to, greater than or less than the other set? The two sets at issue are the two sets present in the static compare situation, the initial and the transformed set in the dynamic situation, and the nontransformed and the transformed set in the third situation. The transformations may change the cardinality of the sets (Ch$^+$: Change-Get-More or Ch$^-$: Change-Get-Less transformations) or they may only move the objects in the sets around so that the sets look different (Displace transformations). There

Table 9-9. Equivalence and Inequivalence Situations

Static compare situation: Set A and set B	
Compare A and B	Find specific numerosities of A and B and
If there is no extra, $A \cong B$	then compare the numerosities of A and B
If there is an extra, $A \not\cong B$	If $N_A = N_B$, then $A \cong B$
If extra is in A, then $A > B$	If $N_A \neq N_B$, then $A \not\cong B$
If extra is in B, then $A < B$	If $N_A < N_B$, then $A < B$
	If $N_A > N_B$, then $A > B$
Comparison Strategies	
Perceptual Length Density	**Specific Numerosity Strategies**
Matching	**Subitize Count**

Dynamic situation: Set A	
Change$^+$ and Change$^-$ transformations	Displacement Transformations
Ch$^+$ (A) $> A$ Ch$^-$ (A) $< A$	Displace $(A) \cong A$

Dynamic situation within a static compare situation: Set A and set B	
Change$^+$ and Change$^-$ transformations	Displacement transformations
if $A \cong B$, then Ch$^+$ (A) $> B$	if $A \cong B$, then Displace $(A) \cong B$
and Ch$^-$ (A) $< B$	
if $A > B$, then Ch$^+$ (A) $> B$	if $A > B$, then Displace $(A) > B$
and Ch$^-$ (A) ? B	
if $A < B$, then Ch$^+$ (A) ? B	if $A < B$, then Displace $(A) < B$
and Ch$^-$ (A) $< B$	

Note. Ch$^+$ is a Change-Get-More transformation and Ch$^-$ is a Change-Get-Less transformation of a single set in which one or more objects are added to (Ch$^+$) or subtracted from (Ch$^-$) a set. $>$: "is more than", $<$: "is less than", $\cong$ "is equivalent to" or "has the same number as." The comparison strategies may also focus on the "missing" rather than on the "extra."

are variations of each of these situations (e.g., the two sets in the static compare situation can be presented sequentially, a transformation or a set can be hidden), which may affect quite considerably the ability of children to establish the correct cardinal relation on the two sets, but these variations do not affect the underlying structure of the situation.

The structure of each situation determines the strategies that may be used to establish a cardinal relation on the two sets. These strategies and proposed developmental sequences in children's uses of these strategies within each situation are presented in Tables 9-9 and 9-10. Each situation will be discussed in turn. Because so much of the literature to date has concentrated on the limited situations in which the objects in the two sets are arranged in a row, the treatment here will also concentrate on such situations. The later sections will focus more specifically on counting and on matching in equivalence situations, on how the developmental transitions in Table 9-10 might ordinarily occur, and on Piaget and cardinal number.

9.3.1. Static Compare Situations

9.3.1.1. Static Comparison Strategies. In the static compare situation no information is provided concerning the cardinal relation on the two given sets; this relation must be established by some sort of comparison of the two sets. This comparison may be made directly, or specific numerosities may be found for each set[9] and then the numerosities compared to established the relation (see Table 9-9). The direct comparison strategies all share a common feature. The comparison of the two sets either results in or does not result in what we will call "the extra." If the two sets are compared, and there is no "extra" left over in either set after this comparison, then the sets are equivalent (they have the same number of objects). If there is an "extra," the set with the "extra" has more. The set without the "extra" instead has one or more objects "missing." The comparison may result in a focus on this missing instead of on the extra; in this case the set with the missing object(s) has less.

When objects in the two sets are arranged in a row, the child may compare the two sets by comparing the lengths of the two rows or by comparing the densities of the two rows (i.e., the size of the gaps between, the closeness of, the objects). Two row situations can vary only in length, only in density, or in both. A comparison based only on length will be correct if the densities of the two rows are the same, and a comparison based on density will be correct if the lengths of the two rows are the same. In these two special cases, number varies directly with length and density: number gets larger as the row gets longer and as the row gets more dense (the gaps get smaller). When both length and density vary in the same direction across two rows (one row is both

---

[9] Of course, a static compare situation can also be given in which specific numerosities are provided and are to be compared; objects for the sets may or may not also be provided in such a case.

Table 9-10. The Development of Strategy Use in Equivalence Situations

Static compare situations: Set A and set B

Strategies Used

Age (years)	Perceptual		Quantitative
3	P, L+D, L > D Nonquantitative		C, M
4	P, L+D, L, D	← Choose ← Use information	C, M
4	P, L+D, L, D	← Choose Use information →	C, M
5½	P, L+D, L, D	Choose → Use information →	C, M
7	L × D (Compensation) E (development continues)	Choose Use information	

Dynamic situation within a static compare situation: Set A and set B

Ignore displacement and compare postdisplacement situations   Focus on displacement

Strategies used

Age (years)	Perceptual	Quantitative
3	P, L+D, L > D Nonquantitative	Invariance of displacement if there is no conflicting source of equivalence information

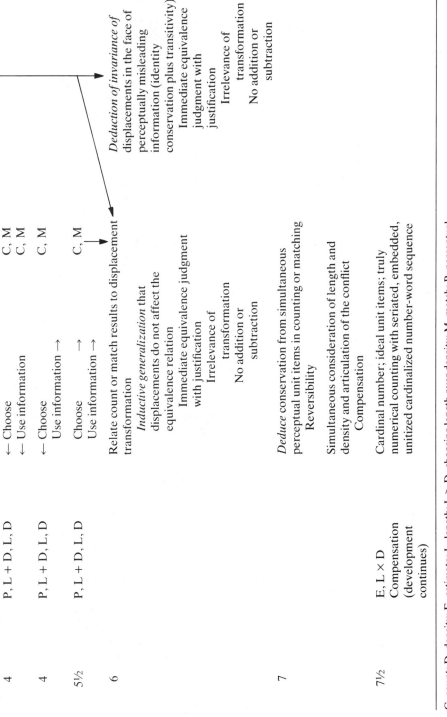

C, count; D, density; E, estimate; L, length; L > D, choosing length over density; M, match; P, perceptual.
Note. A ← or → indicates the kind of strategy that predominates at a given age (on the left is perceptual and on the right is quantitative)

longer and denser—has smaller gaps—than the other row), the comparison may accurately be based on either. When length and density vary in opposite directions (one row is longer and less dense than—has larger gaps than—the other row), one may have to quantify and compare the ratio of the increase in length across the two rows to the ratio of the decrease in density across the two rows to determine which row has more. If the two sets are not arranged in rows, a child can make a global perceptual comparison of the areas covered by the two sets. In all three of these kinds of comparisons (perceptual, length, and density), the comparison may not be a careful thorough one but rather a quick search for "the extra" or "the missing" such that the search (and the comparison) stops when an "extra" or a "missing" are found in either set. Thus, these strategies may result in an incorrect choice of a cardinal relation because the comparison may stop before other missing or extra parts are found.

Matching is a comparison strategy in which a one-to-one correspondence is established between the objects in two sets. There are many different ways to match two sets. One can move the objects in one set so that each object is near or on top of an object in the other set, connect each pair by strings or lines or a path drawn in space with the finger or the eye, use thumb and fore-finger to make successive pairs down each row, or use color or object differences to make pairs. Children in our studies have used all these ways of making what several children called making "partners." After partners have been created by some method of matching (after the one-to-one correspondence has been established), the sets are judged to be equivalent if there are no extra and no missing in either set, one set is judged to be more (than the other set) if it has any extra objects, and one set is judged to be less (than the other set) if it has any missing objects. Matching is an accurate comparison strategy. If the matching procedure is carried out correctly and the implications concerning the existence and location of the extra for the cardinal relation are known, matching will result in a correct equivalence judgment, that is, it will result in the choice of the correct cardinal relation between the two sets.

Two strategies are available to turn the static compare situation into one in which the specific numerosities of both sets are known: subitizing and counting. Subitizing is a rapid process for determining the specific numerosity of very small sets (from one to three in young children and perhaps also four or five in older children); the exact nature of this process is still not clear (see, for example, Chi & Klahr, 1975; Cooper, 1984; Jensen, Reese, & Reese, 1950; Klahr, 1984; Klahr & Wallace, 1976; Mandler & Shebo, 1982; Strauss & Curtis, 1984; Van Oeffelen & Vos, 1982). We have also observed in experiments 1 and 3 (see 9.2) and Fuson et al. (1983) the use of a related strategy, which we called "subitize and add." Here children for each row subitize two numbers whose sum they know and observe that the sums (and thus the rows) are the same, for example, "two and three here and here so they are the same" or "six here and six here because there is three and three." Subitizing is restricted to small numbers, but counting can be used for any size of sets that can be counted accurately. Counting yields a last counted word that, at some age (usually age 3 or 4), comes to refer to the numerosity of the counted set, that is, it takes on a cardinal reference (see chapter 7). We will refer in the following discussion to these number words obtained by counting as "specific numerosities," but it is possible that for some children these are only count words and not yet cardinal words with reference to the whole row.

With either subitizing or counting, after the specific numerosities for both sets have been determined, children need to know the relation on these two specific numerosities in order to determine the relation on the two sets; that is, they need to know whether $n_1 = n_2$, $n_1 > n_2$, or $n_1 < n_2$. Furthermore, they need to know the following connections between the relations on the specific number words and the relations on the sets: (1) if the counted (subitized) number words are the same, the sets are equivalent (have the same number of objects); (2) if the counted (subitized) number word for one set is greater than the counted (subitized) number word for the other set, then that set has more objects; and (3) if the counted (subitized) number word for one set is less than the counted (subitized) number word for the other set, then that set has fewer objects.

9.3.1.2. The Development of Static Comparison Strategies. In the static compare situation, a range of different strategies can be used. Children obviously have to learn to use each of these strategies, but once learned, these strategies then must compete for use in a given situation. Furthermore, if the child uses more than one strategy in a given situation, and if these strategies generate different cardinal relations, then the child must decide which strategy information to use. Our developmental hypothesis is that all of these strategies become available to children relatively early and that the main aspects of development concern changes in which strategy is chosen and changes in which information is given precedence when the information from different strategies conflicts. This developmental picture is often clouded, however, by the strong effects within a given static compare situation of contextual cues that influence the choice of a strategy or the use of strategy information. We will first describe the developmental picture outlined in the top of Table 9-10 and then discuss briefly some examples of contextual aspects that can influence the basis for the equivalence judgment. The ages given are fairly rough and are almost entirely based on work with middle-class and upper-middle-class children; research to date indicates that the age ranges for the use of a given kind of equivalence strategy can be quite large.

Three-year-olds can use length as a basis for making equivalence judgments in static compare situations (our experiment 1 in 9.2.1; Bryant, 1974; La-Pointe & O'Donnell, 1974; Lawson, Baron, & Siegel, 1974; McLaughlin, 1981; Siegel, 1978), and they can also use density (Cuneo, 1982; McLaughlin, 1981; LaPointe & O'Donnell, 1974; Siegel, 1977). They do seem to choose length rather than density as the basis for the equivalence judgment when either may be the basis for the choice (our experiment 1 above; LaPointe & O'Donnell, 1974); this tendency is expressed in Table 9-10 by L > D (choosing length over density). At this age (and for a long time) the length and the density strategies do not yield correct equivalence judgments when these conflict with cardinal number, for these attributes are not yet used in a co-ordinated way. Rather, children using length ignore density and children using density ignore length. However, when children are given a task in which they do not have to choose between length and density, their numerical judgments show the effects of both length and density (Cuneo, 1982). In this task, however, children coordinate these strategies by a general adding rule rather than by the multiplicative rule that characterizes the accurate relationship (see the discussion at the end of this section); we have represented this in Table 9-10 by Cuneo's expression L + D. Many 3-year-olds also use nonquantitative strategies, such as alternating answers from question to question, using the color of the objects, answering with the most recent part of the equivalence question (all these were used by children in our experiment 1) and answering all comparison questions with "Yes" (LaPointe & O'Donnell, 1974); they may also simply guess or use unidentifiable bases for responding on some trials (our experiment 1). Children may use these other strategies consistently, or they may be mixed in with the length or density strategies.

Four-year-olds make several developmental advances. Although Siegel (1982) indicates that some 4-year-olds will focus on color, size, shape of objects, and heterogeneity of objects rather than on number, the use of such noncomparison strategies is now much less frequent than at age 3. This is an important advance, for the comparison strategies at least focus on identifying "the extra" or "the missing." When length is available as a cue, most children now consistently use length to judge cardinal equivalence. Some 4-year-olds do now choose density rather than length (e.g., our experiment 1 in 9.2.1); this is indicated in the table by the expression L, D meaning some children choose each of these strategies. Children also use density when length is equal (e.g., Pufall & Shaw, 1972). Many children at this age can also now count to establish numerical equivalence or inequivalence (for sets from six to nine objects, and heterogeneity of objects rather than on number, the use of such 1984a, 1984b), and they can also use matching procedures (for sets with from six to nine objects in our experiments 1 and 3 in 9.2; for sets of six and seven in Avesar & Dickerson, in press).

Even though many children at this age can use count and match information to judge cardinal equivalence, most still choose to use length or density even when they can use counting or matching (our experiments 2 and 3; also Michie, 1984a, 1984b). If counting is imposed, some will still use the information from length or density rather than the information obtained from counting (our experiments 2 and 3; also Michie, 1984a, 1984b). Children may even appear to make a mistake in their counting of the second row in order to make their count result consistent with their length comparison (some children in task 1 of our experiment 3 seemed to do this) or fail to use counting information that they spontaneously obtained (our experiment 3). However, children at this level are quite likely to make correct equivalence judgments based on counting or matching when there is no misleading perceptual information. For example, the 4-year-olds in our experiment 3 spontaneously used counting or matching on 83% of the trials to make correct equivalent judgments for sets of six, seven, and eight when objects were not arranged in rows, and children counting six and eight objects into boxes made accurate equivalence judgments on 80% of the trials (Michie, 1984a). However, children still tend to make incorrect judgments when the rows are arranged so that a length-based or density-based judgment will be incorrect because they choose the length or density strategy and/or they use the information from this strategy rather than use information obtained from counting or matching. Finally, although length and density strategies are used if length or density cues are already available, children seem to use these strategies only when provided with these strategies, that is, when objects are already arranged in rows. Even 3½-year-old children in our experiment 1 hardly ever arranged objects in parallel rows under each other to make a set equivalent to another; children aged 3½ to 6 instead primarily used matching to make an equivalent set, and they especially used matching procedures in which the objects in a set were put near the objects in the other set.

Once children begin to count and match, they can begin to move on to considering the static compare situation as a setting for addition/subtraction cardinal operations and not just as a setting for cardinal relations. One can quantify "the extra" (the difference $|A - B|$ between the two sets) by matching the two sets and counting the extra or by counting the smaller set, counting out that amount from the larger set, and then counting the extra (Hudson, 1983). This static compare situation then has become the Compare subtraction situation discussed in chapter 8. How children's ability to use counting and matching in these Compare addition and subtraction situations has not yet been related to the developmental sequence in Table 9-10.

At the next level children still spontaneously choose the length or density strategies. However, if counting or matching is imposed on children, they will use the information obtained from counting or matching rather than the information from length or density (our Experiments 2 and 3; also Avesar & Dickerson, in press; Cowan, 1984; Michie, 1984a, 1984b). We did not find much difference in the number of children using counting information rather than length or density information between the ages 4 and 5½; about two thirds of the children in this age range used the count information after counting was imposed. However, larger samples may show some progression over this age range in the proportion of children who will use count information or match information[10] rather than length or density information.

The change in the next level (see Table 9-10) is that children spontaneously

---

[10] We have not done a forced-match condition nor found such a study in the literature in which failure to use the match information could be differentiated from failure to understand the use of the match procedure for cardinal equivalence. Therefore, it may be that matching information, whenever it is obtained, takes precedence over length or density information. This may be because the extra in the match procedure is as salient as the extra in the length or density procedure.

choose to count or match rather than to use length or density to establish cardinal relations on two sets (our experiments 1 and 3; also Saxe, 1977), and they then use the information obtained from counting or matching to decide the cardinal ralation on the two sets. Children in our experiment 1 showed an increase in the spontaneous use of counting and matching at age 5½, and all children of this age used the count information to make accurate equivalence judgments in experiment 2. Some children younger than this may enter this level. Some children aged 4 to 5½ spontaneously used counting and matching in Experiments 1 and 3 when length was a misleading cue. Some children may also exhibit a transition to this level in which they spontaneously obtain count or match information but cannot always use it in the face of the conflicting length information; some children, especially 4-year-olds, did this in experiments 1 and 3.

A final more adultlike level appears at least by age 7. At this level children use length and density information in their correct inverse relationship. A longer but less dense row is judged to be equivalent to a shorter but denser row (if the L1/L2 and D1/D2 ratios are inverses of each other). Cuneo (1982) symbolized this as $L \times D$ (i.e., length and density are logically multiplied), and we used this expression in Table 9-10. Now length and density information do not so often yield incorrect judgments, although Pringle and Hennessey (1987) indicate that even fourth graders still experience considerable difficulty in using length and density multiplicatively in a numerousness scaling task. We also at this level in Table 9-10 replaced the global perceptual (P) strategy used earlier for disorganized arrays with an estimating (E) strategy. This E might be a measurelike strategy of repeated application of a given unit, such as proposed by Klahr and Wallace (1976) for their Q_e, and/or some other more mature estimating process. Such estimating processes may become quite complex for large number situations, so one might expect considerable progress in both the use of estimating and of $L \times D$ to be made for some time past the age of 7; we are not concerned here with tracing such progress. At this final level in Table 9-10, no particular strategy has a necessary priority (none has an arrow beside it), but rather the choice may be dependent on speed, accuracy, and effort trade-offs or on idiosyncratic preferences.

We do want to make one final comment concerning length and density strategies. The adult use of denser (more dense) refers to entities that are more crowded, that is, which have a greater number of entities per some unit of length. However, this notion of density clearly is derived from length and from number and uses the notion of measure; it is a sophisticated derived measure. This is the measure of density that has been used implicitly in the research literature and that was followed above in the description of length and density as being inversely related to each other when number is held constant (as a row of n objects is made longer, it gets less dense). However, it is not at all clear to me that young children understand or use this concept of density as based on some number of entities per unit of length. The children in the experiments in this chapter who gave density justifications seemed rather to be focusing on two other aspects of density. The first is the "extra" entities in the middle of a denser row. These entities are "extra" because no entities are across from them in the opposite row. This focus on density "extras" is, of course, inversely related to a focus on length "extras" at the end of a row. If two rows are equal in number but differ in length and density, density "extras" in one row will always be compensated by length "extras" in the other row. A focus on extra entities then will lead to a necessity for compensating length and density, but this compensation would involve the density and length extra entities and not density and length measures as usually defined. The second focus children using density demonstrated was a concern with the size of the gap between entities, that is, their justifications talked about this gap. The size of the gap is a much more direct measure of density than is the number per unit length measure. It also varies directly with length (as a given row is made longer, the gaps get longer) and inversely with number (if two rows are the same length, the one with bigger gaps has fewer objects). Because children use some intuitive measure of length when comparing lengths, it seems sensible that they would also use a measure of length when comparing densities, that is, they would focus on the length of the gap. If so, then one reason young children may not initially prefer the density measure (and may not be able to use it as accurately as length) is that it varies *inversely* with number while length varies *directly*. To the extent that children continue to use a gap measure of density rather than a number of entities per unit length measure, the actual strategy by which they coordinate length and density information to yield number judgments may be affected. Thus, future research might well try to ascertain young children's functional measure of density.

We suggest that the general developmental pattern outlined interacts with particular static compare situational contexts to affect both the choice of strategy and the use of strategy information. Furthermore, these uses are subject to speed, effort, and accuracy decisions made by the child. Because the contextual factors that affect strategy choice and the experiences that might promote children to move from one level to the next are similar for the static compare situation and for the dynamic situation within a compare situation, discussion of these contextual factors and of level changes is postponed to 9.3.3.2.2.

9.3.2. Dynamic Situations

9.3.2.1. Transformations That Change Cardinal Number: Ch^+ and Ch^-. The transformations involved in a dynamic situation can change cardinal number or leave it unchanged. The transformations that change cardinal number involve new meanings of "more" and "less" that are different from the cardinal relational meanings. When one adds objects to a given set, that set "gets more." Similarly, when one subtracts objects from a given set, that set "gets less." Children understand this transformational meaning of more very early. When a child aged 1½ has a cookie in one hand and reaches for the cookie box saying, "More," the child does not mean the comparative "the box has more than I have" but rather means the dynamic "get more": "Give me some more cookies." The relationship between the meanings of more and less used by these dynamic Ch^+ (Change-Get-More) and Ch^- (Change-Get-Less) transformations and the meanings of the comparative cardinal relations "more" and "less" ($>$ and $<$) are very simple. A set that gets more has more, $Ch^+ (A) > A$, and a set that gets less has less, $Ch^- (A) < A$. Because in fact children learn the "get more" meaning so early, it may even be that they learn the "has more" cardinal relational meaning partly from the dynamic meaning. Cooper (1984) made this argument for infants. Other researchers have pointed out this distinction between the two meanings of more (e.g., Beilin, 1969; Weiner, 1974), and a similar distinction for liquid quantity was made by Moore and Frye (1986a) using the terms sequential (our "get more") and simultaneous (our "has more") taken from Hudson, Guthrie, and Santilli (1982). We have chosen our terms so that they will relate to terminology used in addition and subtraction situations (see chapter 8).

Very little work has been done with young children in this area of Ch^+ and Ch^- transformations on a single set; we therefore did not describe developmental levels in this area in Table 9-10. At the moment the major developmental progressions we see in this area are from (1) not understanding "get more" or "get less" to (2) understanding these but not understanding the comparative "have more" and "have less" meanings to (3) understanding both kinds of terms and relating them as in Table 9-9 (e.g., knowing that adding some objects to a set means that it now has more objects) to (4) being able to quantify the results of Ch^+ and Ch^- transformations. This last step involves being able to solve unary addition and subtraction situations by counting (e.g., Mary had five cookies and got three more. How many does she have now?). It is a step from dynamic situations involving cardinal *relations* on a set to dynamic situations involving *operations* on cardinal situations. Children can directly model with objects and solve such addition and subtraction stories involving numbers less than 10 by kindergarten (e.g., Carpenter & Moser, 1983a; Riley et al., 1983). Thus, the developmental transitions to this fourth state are completed quite early with respect to a single set.

9.3.2.2. Transformations That Leave Cardinal Number Unchanged: Displacement Transformations. Displacement transformations in a dynamic situation make the transformed set look different from its appearance before it was transformed. The objects in the set may be in a longer row or a denser row or be arranged in some disordered fashion. Nevertheless, such displacements do not affect the cardinality of the set; the set after such a displacement is equivalent to the set before the displacement, Displace $(A) \cong A$. The displacements most studied have been those that stretch out or push together the objects in a row. These transformations carried out on a set of objects in a row are a special form of the conservation task that has been called "identity conservation" (Elkind, 1967). In this identity conservation situation, and in any dynamic displacement situation, the judgment of the cardinal relation between the set before and after it is transformed can be made by focusing on the transformation alone (and using information about the effect of such transformations on cardinal relations) and/or by comparing the objects in the set before and after the transformation by one of the comparison strategies previously outlined (perceptual, length, density, matching, subitizing, counting). At present the literature is quite contradictory with respect to the ages at which children in the dynamic situation can use each of these, spontaneously choose to use each of these, and do use the information from these comparison strategies. We therefore can only make some rather general comments concerning this area. However, many of the points made in the next section on the dynamic situation within a static compare situation also apply to this situation; there is considerably more literature on dynamic situations within the static compare situation than within the single-set situation discussed here.

There is a considerable amount of literature on the question of whether identity conservation precedes equivalence conservation (the usual two-set conservation task involving a dynamic situation within a static compare situation discussed in the next section); this issue applies to conservation of all kinds of quantities, not just cardinal number. The argument that identity conservation precedes equivalence conservation is made on logical grounds by some (e.g., Elkind, 1967). The argument here is that equivalence conservation requires identity conservation [Displace $(A) \cong A$] and the use of transitivity of cardinal relations on the original equivalence and on the identity conservation: $B \cong A$ and $A \cong$ Displace (A) imply $B \cong$ Displace (A). Some problems with this position are discussed later. The argument that identity conservation appears first is also made on empirical grounds (e.g., see reviews by Acredolo, 1982; Brainerd & Hooper, 1975, 1978) but is refuted on this same basis by others (e.g., see the review by S.A. Miller, 1977).

This controversy is complicated in the area of cardinal number by the fact that researchers often report only correct equivalence judgments or report judgments with pooled explanations, so one cannot tell how a child arrived at the equivalence judgment. Thus, it is not clear whether a child ignored the transformation and just used a comparison strategy such as length or counting or whether the child used information about the transformation. Although the sequential nature of the dynamic situation would seem to make it difficult for children to use these comparison strategies, they evidently can do so. Cowan (1979a), for example, reported that 5-year-olds can covertly quantify sets of five objects and seem to do so in identity conservation situations, because if counting is prevented, their performance declines. However, we do not have much systematic data about the ability of children at various ages to use the comparison strategies in the identity situation or data about the relative difficulties of such uses compared to the static compare situation and to the equivalence conservation situation. Resolving issues concerning these relative difficulties would seem to be affected by two inversely related attributes of the identity situation: The sequential nature ought to make some comparison procedures more difficult to carry out (e.g., a comparison by density or by matching) and therefore perhaps decrease the use of some comparison strategies, but it also may decrease the salience of the misleading perceptual cues such as length and therefore increase the use of the reliable procedures such as counting.

A final difficulty with identity conservation (and with all displacement transformations in a dynamic situation) is ensuring that children are using "the same" or "the same number" to mean cardinal equivalence and not just identity of the objects (i.e., that the objects are still the same objects); this distinction in other areas of conservation has been termed the difference between quantitative and qualitative identity (e.g., Brainerd, 1977; Bruner, Olver, & Greenfield, 1966; Piaget, 1968a, 1968b). Though some studies have reported that children as young as age 4 judge a row of five pennies that was spread out to have the same number of pennies as it did before (e.g., Elkind & Schoenfeld, 1972), some recent evidence seems to indicate that even 6-year-olds may have trouble in a dynamic displacement task that eliminates the identity interpretation of "the same." Herscovics, Bergeron, and Bergeron (1986) had kindergarten children (aged 6-0 to 6-6) count a row of nine cubes and then asked "If we put them like this (stretching out the row), how many are there?" Only 6 of the 22 children answered nine; another 8 answered on the second trial with the specific numerosity of the second row after having counted again on the first trial; the remaining 8 children continued to count the row after the transformation on the last two trials. Herscovics et al. found performance on this task somewhat independent of performance on the standard equivalence conservation task. Five children correctly answered this identity task and did not conserve, whereas 3 children conserved but did not answer this identity task correctly.

9.3.3. Dynamic Situation Within a Static Compare Situation

The dynamic situation within a static compare situation obviously involves both a dynamic situation (a transformation of a single set) and two static compare situations: a static comparison of the two sets before any transformation and a static comparison of the two sets after the transformation of one of the sets. To find the cardinal relation applying to the two sets after one of them has been transformed, one can ignore the final compare situation and focus just on the transformation, one can ignore the transformation and use the static comparison strategies to compare the two sets after the transformation, or one can attend to both (and also perhaps try to relate the compare information to the kind of transformation made). If one attends to the transformation, one also needs to remember the cardinal relation between the two sets before the transformation, because the effect of the transformation is determined by this original relation in the ways outlined in Table 9-9. In this situation children thus have to choose from all of the strategies available in the static compare situation plus any available strategies focusing on transformations.

9.3.3.1. Transformations That Change Cardinal Number. The development for the Ch^+ and Ch^- transformations is not outlined in Table 9-10, because there is a great deal we do not know about how children decide cardinal relations after such transformations. We do know some things, however, mostly from the work of Cooper and colleagues (Cooper, 1984; Blevins, Mace, Cooper, Starkey, & Leitner, 1981) but also from Brush (1978). First, even many 2-year-olds make the connection between the Ch^+ "gets more" on the transformed set and the cardinal "has more" on the final comparison between the transformed and the untransformed sets and between the Ch^- "get less" on the transformed set and the cardinal "have less" on the final comparison (Cooper, 1984). However, these young children do not take into consideration the cardinal relation between the two sets in the initial state or the size of the change or the size of the original difference, and so their equivalence judgments are only serendipitously correct (in particular they are incorrect in the two question mark situations in Table 9-9 whenever the change is equal to or greater than the original difference between A and B). Some 3-year-olds then begin to consider the cardinal relation in the initial state but still do not consider the size of the difference, that is, they move from the first "primitive" rule to a "qualitative" rule (all terminology is taken from Cooper, 1984). Thus, if an object is added to the set that is less or is subtracted from the set that is more, the child will say that the resulting sets are equivalent. However, these judgments will only be correct when the difference between the original sets is one. Some children may then move on to use a "superqualitative" rule in which the size of the difference between the original sets is able to be considered correctly when it is one or two but not when it is three. These children thus will correctly say that two objects added to a set that was originally only one less than the other set makes that set now greater (rather than equivalent), but they will also say that two objects added to a set originally three less than the other set makes that set now equal to the other set. However, if the original difference between the two sets is very large, these children will use a comparison procedure and judge the effect of the change transformation correctly. Finally, about half of the 5-year-olds and 6-year-olds tested by Cooper used a "quantitative" rule. They were able to coordinate two successive additions of one object (i.e., a Ch^+ 2) and an original difference of three to say that the transformed (added to) set which was originally less was still less than the other set. Additional evidence is not yet available to ascertain when this quantitative rule will be used for all change transformations and all differences, that is, when a completely general solution to the question mark situations in Table 9-9 becomes available to children.

The ages given previously for this developmental sequence were those found for larger numerosities. For smaller numerosities the shifts to the more advanced rules occurred as much as 2 years earlier (Cooper, 1984). However, the shift to the use of these more advanced rules for small numerosities seems to depend on the use of static comparison strategies on the end states of the change transformations. When the end state of the change transformation on these small numerosities was not shown to children, performance dropped considerably below that when the end state was visible (Cooper, 1984). It also dropped to the level of performance on large numerosities, indicating that in such situations children use static comparison strategies for small numerosities before they use them for large numerosities. The shift to qualitative and quantitative rules for large numerosities also seems to depend on the use of static comparison strategies such as counting, because the performance of children just beginning to show qualitative or quantitative rules was considerably poorer on large numerosity arrays that were difficult to count than on large numerosity arrays that were not difficult to count (Blevins-Knabe, Cooper, Starkey, Mace, Leitner, 1987; Cooper, 1984). Children also evidently use static comparison strategies when a change transformation is made on originally equivalent sets. We found (Fuson, Pergament, Lyons, Hall, & Kwon, in press) that of children aged 4-0 to 5-6 asked to justify their equivalence judgment after an object had been added to or subtracted from one of two rows in optical correspondence (length and density the same for both rows), 36% mentioned the change transformation (e.g., "You added one.") while 52% mentioned the extra or missing object or used specific numerosities (i.e., used a static compare strategy). Markman (1979) found 50% and 25% use of transformation and static comparison justifications, respectively, in the same task.

Although children do eventually begin to use comparison strategies on the end states of change transformations, for a fairly considerable period of time, children in the posttransformation situation will use the information from the change transformation rather than the perceptual input from the posttransformation static compare situation. For example, although the length strategy is very strongly established for static compare situations by the age of 4, some 4-, 5-, and 6-year-olds will say that a row that received one or two more objects has more even when it is shorter after the addition and will say that a row from which one or two objects are taken has less even though it is longer than the other row after the subtraction (Siegler, 1981). It is not yet clear when children will begin to choose to use the comparison strategies over the change transformation information. Perhaps only when children begin consistently to count or to match in a static compare situation would they also do so after a change transformation of one set within the compare situation. Alternatively, such behavior may wait until children can quantify the difference in a static compare situation, for it is only then that they may become aware of the importance of the relative sizes of this difference and of the change transformation.

9.3.3.2. Transformations That Leave Cardinal Number Unchanged: Displacement Transformations. When the transformation is a displacement of the objects in one set, the original pretransformation cardinal relation between the two sets still holds for the two sets after one is displaced (see Table 9-9). In the classic conservation of number situation, the two sets are equivalent before the transformation, and the objects in the sets are arranged so that the equivalence is obvious by length, density, and matching (the objects are in optical one-to-one correspondence just opposite one another). However, the displacement of the objects in one set by stretching them out or by pushing them together makes the sets appear to be nonequivalent both by length and by density.

9.3.3.2.1. Developmental Sequence of Strategy Use. Young children typically respond to this posttransformation situation as if it were a static compare situation (see Table 9-10). They seem to go through about the same developmental sequence of use of comparison strategies here as they do when there is no displacement transformation, that is, as in the static compare situation. At ages 3 and 4, children base the postdisplacement equivalence judgment on length, density, or nonquantitative strategies (Fuson, et al., 1983; Katz & Beilin, 1976; Piaget, 1941/1965; Siegler, 1981; Starkey, 1981). At age 4 they can use count or match strategies when no conflicting perceptual information is present but will use length or density information rather than count or match information if lengths or densities are misleading and perceptually obvious (Cowan, 1984; P.H. Miller, Heldmeyer, & Miller, 1975; Piaget, 1941/ 1965; Schonfeld, 1986; Wagner & Walters, 1982) and may even seem to change their counting in order to make the count result agree with the length result (Wagner & Walters, 1982). A bit later they will spontaneously choose length or density strategies but will use count or match information if these strategies are imposed or strongly cued (Cowan, 1984; Fuson et al., 1983; Gelman, 1982a; Herscovics et al., 1986; Millar & Mackay, 1978; P.H. Miller, Heldmeyer, & Miller, 1975; Schonfeld, 1986; Whiteman & Peisach, 1970). By age 5½ or so, children can count to compare two sets (Saxe, 1979) and will spontaneously count or match to compare the two sets (Fuson et al., 1983; LaPointe & O'Donnell, 1974; Siegler, 1981). They will quantify small sets earlier than larger sets (by subitizing or by counting), and this quantification seems to be largely responsible for set size differences in correct equivalence judgments in the conservation sitation (Tollefsrud, Campbell, Starkey, & Cooper, in preparation, cited in Cooper, 1984; Young & McPherson, 1976). The developmental sequence in Table 9-10 is an outline of the indicator properties and testing actions that children use to ascertain relations in the cardinal number conservation situation (Murray, 1981; Wallach, 1969).

One important class of questions about the developmental sequence outlined in Table 9-10 for both the static compare situations and the dynamic situations concerns what contextual factors determine the strategy and the strategy information a child will use in a given situation. A second class focuses on the factors that lead a child to move from level to level. A third class that applies only to the dynamic situation is what impels children on to the further levels available in that case, to the level of conservation of numerical equivalence. Definitive data are not available for any of these questions at present. Too few studies have reported specific strategies used by children, and those that have generally have not reported within-child data that would help one understand multiple uses of strategies, conflicts between strategies, or transitions in strategy use. Studies have also rarely obtained information about what strategies or what strategy information children *can* use rather than just what children spontaneously *do* use. Rarely have techniques for measuring the relative salience of or children's preference for certain strategies (e.g., a dimensional preference task, Gelman, 1972; Miller & Heller, 1976) been used along with measures of strategy preference and strategy competence. Studies also have not usually compared strategies used in static compare situations with those used in a dynamic situation within a compare situation. Thus, our remarks at this time can only be tentative. We discuss briefly the contextual factors that affect strategy choice and then outline the major positions concerning how children move on to conservation of numerical equivalence. Discussion of factors that move children from perceptual strategies to counting or matching is in sections 9.3.4 and 9.3.5, and a discussion of Piagetian conservation of number is in 9.3.6.

9.3.3.2.2. Contextual Factors Affecting Strategy Use. As many researchers have pointed out, equivalence judgments in the equivalence conservation situation are very susceptible to attributes of that situation (e.g., Gelman, 1969; P.H. Miller, 1978; Moore & Frye, 1986b). Because many different strategies are available in this situation, manipulations that affect the relative salience of cues for a given strategy will influence the strategy or the information used. For example, Moore and Frye (1986b) compared the "naughty teddy bear" method of McGarrigle and Donaldson (1975) (in which a naughty teddy bear rather than the experimenter makes the displacing transformation) to a trick procedure of their own and concluded that the naughty teddy bear method improved equivalence performance by distracting children from the displacing transformation, that is, by making it less salient. Some contexts also may make the counted words more salient, increasing the use of the count information. Thus, for example in our experiment 2, hearing the same count words (for equivalent sets) rather than different count words (for nonequivalent sets) seemed to make children more likely to use the count information; Cowan (1987) also found that children used counting over length more when counting gave the same number word than when it gave different words. One can manipulate the salience of the length or density differences in two static compare situations or in the posttransformation situation by making the differences very large or very minimal; Fuson et al. (in press) and Melnick (1973) found better performance when the length difference was minimal than when it was large. If a given situation follows another equivalence situation, the strategy just used on the earlier situation can then affect the relative salience of strategies in the new situation, that is, the salience of the strategy just used will be increased relative to the usual salience of that strategy (P.H. Miller, 1978; P.H. Miller & Heller, 1976; Siegler, 1981).

The effort required by a given strategy, and perhaps a judgment of the accuracy with which the strategy can be accomplished, also seems to affect strategy choice. The very common finding of correct equivalence judgments with small sets but not with large sets (e.g., Baron, Lawson, & Siegel, 1975; Cowan, 1979b, 1987; Gullen, 1978; Millar & Mackay, 1978; P.H. Miller & Heller, 1976; Siegler, 1981; Smither, Smiley, & Rees, 1974; Winer, 1974, 1975) could easily stem from the considerably greater effort that must be expended to count or match the longer rows as well as to the availability of the relatively easy subitizing strategy on very small sets and of a "subitize and add" strategy on sets from four to six. Providing guidelines connecting the objects in two sets can make the matching strategy more salient and also much easier to carry out and has been found to increase the use of the matching strategy (Avesar & Dickerson, in press; Cowan, 1984). Being able to move objects also makes matching much easier to carry out, and matching will be the strategy of choice to make a set equivalent to a given set displayed with objects, even if the set is large (our experiment 1; also Comiti, Bessot, & Pariselle, 1980). In contrast, when the matching strategy is difficult to apply (Baroody, 1982), even adults may fail to use it to judge cardinal equivalence.

A final factor that has been little examined is the child's perceptions of the acceptable strategies and, more subtly, of the speed-accuracy trade-off expected in a given situation. Young children may be reluctant to count in some kinds of equivalence tasks, even when encouraged to do so (e.g., Cuneo, 1982, found this with 3- and 4-year-olds on a numerosity scaling task). Children may also assume that the experimenter wants an answer quickly, resulting in the use of the rapid perceptual strategies.

9.3.3.2.3. Learning That Displacement Transformations Do Not Affect Cardinal Number: Multiple Routes to Conservation of Cardinal Equivalence.
The difference between the static compare situation and the dynamic situation within a static compare situation is that with the latter one does not *have* to make a comparison to establish the cardinal relations in the posttransformation situation. If one knows that a displacement of one set does not affect the cardinal relation on two sets, one can simply use this information and the original cardinal relation to decide the final cardinal relation. Thus, in an equivalence conservation situation, one can immediately give a correct equivalence judgment after the displacement without comparing the final states. Children do come to be able to do this sometime around age 6 or 7. The crucial questions here are "How do children learn to give such immediate

correct judgments?" and "When do we want to call these judgments conservation of numerical equivalence?" At present several alternatives are
proposed to each of these questions, but definitive data concerning the correctness of these positions are not yet available.

The essential argument of a first set of positions is that children do learn
fairly early (by age 4) that a displacement does not affect the cardinality of a
given set (i. e., they learn identity conservation) but the misleading perceptual
information in the posttransformation equivalence conservation situation
conflicts with the invariance information from the displacement transformation, e.g., Acredolo's (1982) identity conservation proposal, Bryant's (1974)
conflict hypothesis, Elkind's (1967) transitivity argument given in 9.3.2.2.
These proposals depend on finding unambiguously that children do give immediate correct equivalence judgments in the single-set dynamic situation
without using comparison strategies before they do so in the two set equivalence conservation situation. As discussed previously, such data are not yet
available. These positions also are necessarily concerned about whether a
child actually believes that a length transformation changes the number of
objects or whether the use of "more" for the longer row is just due to linguistic confusion. This is a complicated issue and is discussed by Siegel (1978,
1982). However, in our experience with static compare and conservation
situations, some children do really seem to believe that a stretch changes the
quantity of objects. This position was articulated by a 4-year-old in our experiment 3 who refused to agree that the longer row "looked like more but
really had the same number" as the shorter row saying, "If you taked them
off and stacked them, you'd know they were the same, but for now there are
more because they are more spread out." Because few subjects are so articulate, we see this as a difficult issue to resolve. Finally, to the extent that
these proposals depend on children's using transitivity, establishing such use
may be complicated by findings that the use of transitivity and memory for
the original premise are independent (Brainerd & Kingma, 1984).

A second set of positions focuses on the use of specific numerosities in the
conservation situation. Here the argument common to all positions is that
children in the equivalence conservation situation use subitizing and/or counting to ascertain the specific numerosities of the two sets after the displacement transformation and base their equivalence judgment on these specific
numerosities. A common thread in these positions is that Piaget's account
underestimates the ability of children to use counting to make accurate equivalence judgments in the equivalence conservation situation. Klahr (Klahr,
1984; Klahr & Wallace, 1973, 1976) proposed that children first conserved
with small numbers by subitizing both sets and then produced the conservation rule by using redundancy elimination and generalization over time-line
entries. The discussions focused on identity conservation, but similar processes were suggested for equivalence conservation. The divergent paths of
data generalization and rule formation allowed for individual differences in
the kinds of conservation rules that were formed (i.e., various restricted ver-

sions of the complete rule were proposed as possible). Gelman & Gallistel (1978) argued that children first reasoned about cardinal relations only with specific numerosities, moved to a semialgebraic stage roughly corresponding to the application of identity conservation on an uncounted but specifiable numerosity, and then moved to a fully algebraic stage in which they could reason without specified numerosities. One-to-one correspondence was considered to be a relatively late occurrence, a position then modified in Gelman (1982) and in Gelman and Baillargeon (1983) to propose that 3- and 4-year-olds can use one-to-one correspondence in certain equivalence situations. It was further proposed in Gelman and Ballargeon (1983) that children may justify correct equivalence judgments by asserting the irrelevance of the transformation or the fact that nothing was added or subtracted before they justify judgments by reversibility or by compensation. This suggestion stemmed from training studies with preschoolers in which preschoolers made correct posttransformation equivalence judgments and justified them only with no addition/subtraction or the irrelevance of the transformation (e.g., Botvin & Murray, 1975).

Seigler (1981) and I (Fuson et al., 1982; Fuson & Hall, 1983) independently focused on both counting and matching as strategies that children can and do carry out to ascertain cardinal relations in the equivalence conservation situation before they move on to knowing immediately that a displacement preserves the cardinal relation and thus do not need to count or match. Siegler suggested that children move to this final rule by using processes like Klahr and Wallace's "redundancy elimination" principle. We suggested (Fuson et al., 1982) that repeated counting or matching experiences may lead to an inductive generalization that displacement transformations do not affect cardinal equivalence. Both of these positions allow inductions to be derived in the equivalence conservation situation independently of those that might be derived in the identity conservation situation; that is, correct immediate equivalence judgments in the identify conservation situations do not necessarily precede such judgments in the equivalence conservation situation.

Klahr's (1984) "time-line generalizations" seem to be specifications of reasoning by induction. However, he argues that such generalizations are first applied to subitizing experiences (i.e., children induce the rule from experiences with subitizable sets) and that children then move on to this advanced level of immediate correct equivalence judgments on smaller sets without subitizing. It does seem possible that children do carry out Klahr's object generalization and/or symbol generalization to form at least partial equivalence classes for the number 2 and possibly for the number 3 (i.e., for many situations a 2 is a 2 is a 2). However, for 3-year-olds to classify transformations and classify subitized situations and coordinate these over many equivalence conservation situations seems to be quite an assumption of complex behavior by these very young children, especially since there is some question that all 3-year-olds even subitize successfully (see 7.6.1; also Young & McPherson, 1976). Furthermore, both Cooper (1984) and Silverman and Briga

(1981) argue convincingly that children who respond correctly only on small-number conservation problems are actually quantifying the end state (e.g., when part of the end state arrays are screened, performance drops to chance). Thus, it seems more likely that children just continue to subitize in each small-number conservation situation and then later use Klahr's proposed developmental processing mechanisms on the results of counting or of matching rather than on those of subitizing.

These two routes to immediate correct equivalence judgments—(1) focusing on the invariance of the transformation and using a deductive logical conclusion based on identity conservation and transitivity and (2) using an inductive empirical conclusion reached by coordinating the results of the accurate comparison strategies matching or counting with the type of transformation—would seem to produce similar justifications related to the nature of the transformation (see Table 9-10). Each of these might be stated by directly asserting the irrelevance of a displacement transformation (e.g., "You just spread them out") or by asserting what the displacement transformation is not (e.g., "You don't add any or take any away"). Both of these are generally considered to be acceptable Piagetian concrete operational justifications. Irrelevance of the transformation justifications (the positive description) may be given earlier than the no addition or subtraction justifications (the negative description); we found kindergarteners giving the former but not the latter and first graders giving many more of the former than of the latter (Fuson, 1986c; Fuson et al., in press).

The other two generally accepted Piagetian justifications, reversibility and compensation, may be given later because they may require more advanced conceptual structures. A brief review of the changes outlined in chapter 8 in children's cardinal conceptual operations, in their conceptual unit items used for counting, and in their cardinal conceptual structures is relevant here. These conceptual structures determined how children were able to think about a given cardinal number addition and subtraction situation. The earliest of these conceptual unit items are perceptual unit items (Steffe, et al., 1983). Perceptual unit items are used by children in counting perceptually present entities. Each entity is taken as an equivalent thing-to-be-counted and is given one counting word. Perceptual unit items are sufficient for solving simple addition and subtraction problems by counting all the entities or by taking away entities, and children do this from about age 4. The counting and matching used in equivalence situations up to the level of an inductive generalization seem also to be using perceptual unit items. Children take each entity as an equivalent thing-to-be-counted or thing-to-be-matched and carry out counting or matching of these entities.

The next more advanced conceptual unit used in addition and subtraction situations is a perceptual unit item that can simultaneously represent an addend within a sum. With these unit items, children can think about an addend and the sum at the same time and can relate the addend to the sum. With these simultaneous representational perceptual unit items, it would seem that children could make a major advance in dynamic equivalence situations. It would seem that a child could now "see" a matching between two sets before the displacement transformation and also follow that matching and the individual unit items while one set is transformed to its final state. The simultaneous unit items here would permit a child to represent the unit items both before and after the transformation and see that the matching that existed before the transformation is maintained during and after the transformation, using what Saxe (1979) called "dynamic correspondences." The child who does this might then give a "reversibility" justification such as, "They're the same because you could just move them back again." The difference here is that the child is not just referring to an empirical return, what Piaget (1967) called "renversabilité." Instead, the simultaneous perceptual unit items gave this reasoning a general deductive character: it is *logically necessary* that the set have the same amount, not just empirically true, and thus is operational reversibility. With simultaneous representational unit items, a child could also deduce the logically necessary conservation of the cardinal order or equivalence relation by "seeing" how a transformation did not change the counting words that would be attached to the perceptual unit items before and after the transformation. Reversibility also would be given as the justification for this logical inference based on thinking about counting. This view of logical inferences using simultaneous perceptual unit items in matching or in counting seems to be consistent with Piaget's later emphasis (1979) on correspondences and transformations in conservation and his view that empirical correspondences may prepare the way for logically necessary correspondences drawn deductively from the system. The difference between the earlier inductive generalization and this later deductive generalization using simultaneous perceptual unit items reflects Piaget's distinction between *empirical* generalization and *reflective* generalization (Piaget, 1978, cited and discussed in Kamii, 1985, p. 21).

The simultaneous representational perceptual unit items may come from considerable practice with counting in addition and subtraction situations or they may signal a more general representational change: the ability to consider and compare two aspects of a given situation simultaneously. To the extent that the latter is true, another view of the conservation situation may occur at roughly the same time as this reasoning. This aspect is coordinating the conflicting information given by the length strategy and by the density strategy in the typical conservation situation. The length strategy says there are "extras" out at the ends of the row, and the density strategy says there are "extras" in the middle of the row. The general relationship between the coordination of this conflict by compensation and the conservation of various quantities including number is still an unsettled issue (Silverman & Rose, 1982). There have been suggestions by several writers (e.g., Wallach, 1969) that the conserving child cannot really adequately quantify the conflicting length and density information in order to determine equivalence, and recent evidence supports this position (Pringle & Hennessey, 1987). However, we clearly have had children give compensation justifications in numerical equivalence tasks (e.g., "This has some out here but this one has these in the middle"). We suggest that the notion of density may be fairly closely linked for young children with the idea of a transformation. Most of the descriptions of density given in experiment 3 by children aged 4 to 5½ referred to the entities being spread out or pushed together, even though that task was a static compare situation. Children's concept of the visual state of "being crowded together" may carry strong motion components of "crowding together," an experience children have in certain games (and in certain carpools). If this is so, then a child wrestling with the conflict between length and density information might well also think of reversibility and use the reasoning previously outlined. If the concern with the length-density conflict is still paramount, the child might still give a compensation justification. However, this justification will merely *articulate the perceived conflict* and not describe the reasoning by which the child deduces equivalence (or, in general, deduces the maintenance of the cardinal relation over a displacement transformation). This position then suggests that the compensation justification will be closely linked to the ability to give a reversibility justification.

There thus may be multiple routes to conservation, via the left- and right-hand sides of Table 9-10 (see also Brainerd, 1979a). There may also be individual differences within a given route. For example, some children may move on to the deductions via simultaneous perceptual unit items used in counting or matching without really ever making an inductive generalization. To pursue the issues raised by this proposal, we will need new experimental tasks. We will need to know what kinds of justifications children can give and can understand rather than just what they spontaneously give, we will have to do within-children analyses of strategy data, and we will have to report strategy data separately rather than pooling it across children and across strategies, as is usually done presently. This research may also in some cases need to include brief teaching and learning episodes in order to control for previous learning experiences that might mask conceptions children have but are not readily available or conceptions that they do not yet have but are very easy for them to construct (i.e., for which they already possess the prerequisites).

We also suggest that there is a later postconservation stage in which children make a further advance in their thinking about cardinal number. First, we discuss some issues in children's use of counting and matching in equivalence and order situations, and then we return to a discussion of this later stage in 9.3.6: Piaget, conservation, and cardinal number.

9.3.4. Counting in Equivalence Situations

A developmental sequence of the use of counting in equivalence situations is outlined in Table 9-11 in a bit more detail than previously discussed. This outline serves to identify several areas about which we do not presently have much information. The use of counting in equivalence situations obviously must begin with the how-many question rule, that is, knowing that the last word said in counting a set is the answer to the question, "How many are there?" (see chapter 7 for discussion of how children learn this first connection between counting and cardinality). To judge two sets equivalent, children also need to learn a "same count number implies cardinal equivalence" rule, as suggested by Fuson and Hall (1983). It is not clear whether such a count-equivalence rule also requires that children be able to make count-to-cardinal transitions from the count meaning (attached to the last object counted) to the cardinal meaning of that word (as referring to the set as a whole and to the numerosity of the set); see chapters 7 and 8 for discussions of this transition. Because the count words are attached to the last objects in a set (and therefore each count word is attached to a different set), it seems possible that a child could answer an equivalence question without really understanding that the count word referred to the cardinality of the set. The count words for equivalent sets are, after all, "the same numbers." It may even be that some wordings of equivalence questions require a count-to-cardinal transition, while others do not. Alternatively, it may be that this transition is only required when children begin to use count information instead of length or density information as a basis for equivalence judgments. Relinquishing the perceptually salient length or density "extra" in favor of counted specified numerosities would seem to require at least a notion that the obtained count words refer to the set as a whole and not just to the last objects in the set (as do count words). Because of the ambiguity of where the count-cardinal transition occurs developmentally, it is placed in parentheses in Table 9-11.

To use counting to judge one set to have more than or less than another set, a child must be able to establish cardinal relations on the specific numerosities they obtained by counting the two sets. It is at present not clear how children learn these cardinal relations on specific counted numerosities. We reviewed the evidence concerning this issue in Fuson and Hall (1983). The two major alternatives are (1) children may use count-to-cardinal transitions to change the count words into cardinal words and then use cardinal relations on these cardinal words (e.g., they may know that five things are more things than are four things) or (2) they may consider the count words as sequence words (words in the number-word sequence) and derive a relation on the sequence words (by using the location within the sequence), which is then translated into a cardinal relation (by a rule such as: later in the sequence implies more objects). For numbers less than 10, the first method may be quite possible. One might have enough direct experiences with sets of objects of these sizes to learn order relations on them directly. However, results of K. Miller and Gelman (1983) suggest that kindergarten children may use the second method for numbers below ten. For numbers above 10, most people simply do not have experiences with comparing cardinal sets, so the second method is necessary. Fuson and Hall (1983) discuss some data supporting this position. For very large numbers, base-ten numbers and base-ten conceptual knowl-

Table 9-11. The Development of Counting in Equivalence Situations

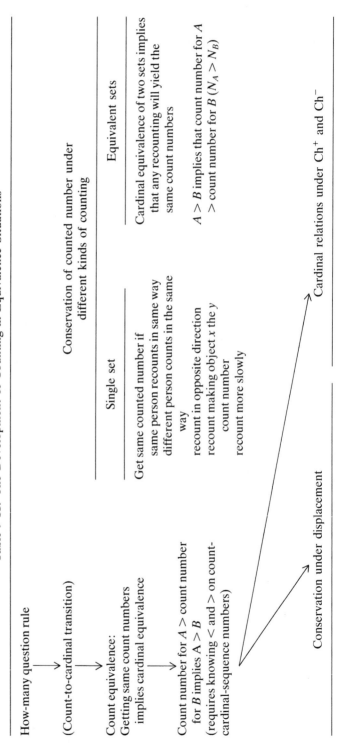

Conservation of counted number under different kinds of counting

Single set

Equivalent sets

How-many question rule →

(Count-to-cardinal transition) →

Count equivalence:
Getting same count numbers implies cardinal equivalence →

Count number for A > count number for B implies $A > B$ (requires knowing < and > on count-cardinal-sequence numbers)

Get same counted number if
same person recounts in same way
different person counts in the same way
recount in opposite direction
recount making object x the y count number
recount more slowly

Cardinal equivalence of two sets implies that any recounting will yield the same count numbers

$A > B$ implies that count number for A > count number for B ($N_A > N_B$)

Cardinal relations under Ch^+ and Ch^-

Conservation under displacement

If $A > B$ and Ch^+ (B) or Ch^- (A) then count to find cardinal relations:
1. Count both posttransformation sets
2. Count original "extra" ($[A - B]$) and count the change in Ch^+ or Ch^-

Specific numerosity

Single set	Two initially equivalent sets
Count number of a displaced set = count number before displacement: $N_{Dsp(A)} = N_A$	Count number of A = count number of B implies count number of Dsp (A) = count number of B: $N_A = N_B$ implies $N_{Dsp(A)} = N_B$

No specific numerosity

Single set	Two initially equivalent sets
Inductive generalization that Dsp $(A) \cong A$	Inductive generalization that if $A \cong B$, then Dsp $(A) \cong B$
Deductive generalization via simultaneous perceptual unit items that Dsp $(A) \cong A$	Deductive generalization via simultaneous perceptual unit items that if $A \cong B$, then Dsp $(A) \cong B$

Note. Ch^+ is a Change-Get-More transformation and Ch^- is a Change-Get-Less transformation; Dsp (A), the displaced new set A; $\cong$ is equivalent to.

edge (see 8.7) are used to decide the cardinal relation between numbers such as 8,397 and 8,541. It is not at present clear for what size of numbers children move from using sequence relations to using relations derived from base-ten knowledge in order to decide cardinal order relations. We represent in Table 9-11 our present lack of knowledge about how children derive the cardinal relation between two counted words by specifying that children must know a > or < relation on count-cardinal-sequence number words.

We have not yet addressed the major issues of how children might ordinarily learn the count-equivalence rule (learn that getting the same count numbers for two sets implies that the sets contain the same amount) or begin to count to obtain count numbers instead of just using length information that is already available. Because it is difficult to differentiate "the same counted number words" from cardinal equivalence (the same number of things, the same amount), children's initial use of count-equivalence when there are no misleading perceptual cues may simply stem from a generalization over (a confusion of) these two meanings. When there are misleading perceptual cues, the reticence of children to use count information instead of length information may be related initially to a lack of confidence in the accuracy of their counting. That is, faced with a conflict between length and count information, they conclude that the counting was in error and use the length information. The finding of Cowan (1987) that children make fewer length consistent judgments when the count information is provided by the experimenter than when it is obtained by themselves suggests this.

Others, more confident of their counting or more intrigued by the conflict, may count again. If they obtain the same count result, they may continue to count again. Some children in our experiments 2 and 3 behaved in just this fashion, counting both sets for a given trial as many as six times. Such counting and recounting may be accompanied by expressions of surprise and amazement at the counting result, as by one child in task 3 in experiment 3 who on every trial said the longer row had more, then spontaneously counted and said, "Oh my God! I'm wrong again. They're the same." Such conflict between a counting result and the length or density result would seem to lead a child to make the distinction we found in experiment 3 that most of them could make when asked: the distinction between a row that looks like more than another row (using length or density) and one that is really more than the other row (using counting or matching). When this distinction was made, most of the 4- and 5-year-olds spontaneously counted or matched the rows to decide if they really were the same. Thus, children seem predisposed to trust counting or matching and to think spontaneously of using these strategies if the perceptual strategies are called into question. Children of this age also quite readily used feedback that counting was more reliable than length; such feedback increased the spontaneous use of counting in equivalence situations (Michie, 1984b). Such feedback from parents, preschool teachers, siblings, and other sources would seem to be readily available in the environment of young children and would seem to increase both their willingness to use count information over length or density information and their spontaneous tendency to count in equivalence situations. The tendency to count would also seem to be strengthened by a home or school environment in which counting is supported and encouraged. Frequent experience in counting sets of objects may lead children to approach such situations with a predisposition to count; such experiences may account for the few children aged 3½ to 5½ who counted to judge cardinal equivalence in experiment 1. The stress in school on counting may have some considerable effect on this tendency to count in equivalence situations.

We have already discussed the fact that children's use of counting in equivalence situations eventually gives way to conservation under Displacement transformations, that is, to the immediate knowledge that equivalence is preserved under the displacement, and therefore there is no need to count in order to ascertain equivalence. Such conservation can occur when a single set is displaced or when one of two equivalent sets is displaced (i.e., identity or equivalence conservation) and can occur when specific numerosities are known or when they are not known (a distinction between quotité and quantité, Gréco, 1962). This leads to the four situations listed at the bottom left in Table 9-11. Although some evidence seems to indicate that identity conservation precedes equivalence conservation (see 9.3.2.2) and that quotité conservation precedes quantité conservation (see Gréco, 1962), other evidence seems to find developmental independence even between identity quotité conservation and equivalence quantité conservation (Herscovics et al., 1986). Therefore, at present the developmental relationships among these four conservation situations are not really clear.

There are two equivalence situations in which children must continue to use some quantitative means to ascertain the cardinal relation between two sets: when one set is initially greater than another and either some amount is taken from that set (a Ch^- transformation) or some amount is added to the other set (a Ch^+ transformation). In these cases no logical rule can generate the cardinal relation, because it depends on both the size of the change and the size of the initial difference in the two sets. Cardinal relations can be established in such situations by either of the two methods listed in Table 9-11, which are (1) count the two sets after the change transformation has been made or (2) compare the original difference between the two sets and the amount of the change. At present we do not know much about when children can use or do spontaneously use either of these methods, especially when the "extra" or "change" is large.

Finally, with counting one further kind of conservation needs to be learned. This is conservation of counted number: that the same count number (and therefore an equivalent set) results when a set is counted in a different way as long as the counting is accurate. This kind of conservation again has been little studied, and one can think of many manifestations of it. Some of these are listed in Table 9-11. Several of these can be considered as a situation in which the displacement transformation is carried out on the counting itself rather than on the objects in the set. Others may have to do with how the counting itself is carried out. For example, some of Wagner and Walter's (1982) children seemed to believe that one would get a different count number if one counted more slowly. One of these aspects of conservation of counted number is related to Gelman's order irrelevance principle and has been examined in several studies (Baroody, 1984; Gelman & Gallistel, 1978; Gelman et al., 1986). This principle asserts that a child can make any object the *n*th counting word (e.g., "Make this object the 4"). There seems to be little question that children as young as age four can count in various specified ways (i.e., can make almost any object the *n*th object, with small sets at least), but at the moment it is less clear that children know that such different counting will produce the same last count word (Baroody, 1984; Frye et al., 1986). Even counting a row from opposite directions seems to be problematic for some children. Herscovics et al. (1986) reported that only 5 of 22 kindergarten children predicted after counting a row that they would find the same number if they counted in the opposite direction, though 9 additional children on a second trial predicted they would find the same number (after having counted in the opposite direction on the first trial).

Ginsburg (1977) has observed that children often get a different number when they count a set a second time and they seem unperturbed by this outcome; this is certainly consistent with a lack of conservation of counted number under different counting. However, in a small study Briars and Fuson (1980) found that when 4- and 5-year-old children were confronted with the fact that they had gotten different answers on two different counts, they usually said that they were right the second (most recent) time and did not count again. High school students, when similarly confronted (they were doing a very difficult counting task), invariably counted a third time in order to decide when they were correct. Thus, failure to recount a third time after a different second count ought not to be taken as evidence of lack of conservation of counted number under different counting. Again, at the moment we know little about the developmental relationships among various aspects of conservation of counted number under different counting or about relationships between these aspects and conservation of numerical equivalence under displacement. Clements (1984) found that instructing children on various counting tasks improved performance on Piagetian tasks including conservation and that instruction was not equally effective in the opposite direction; instructional studies then might help explore these relationships.

9.3.5. Matching in Equivalence Situations

Very little information is presently available concerning the developmental course of matching in equivalence situations. Most research has underestimated children's ability to use matching and their knowledge that matching implies cardinal equivalence because the particular equivalence situations studied have been ones in which matching is difficult to carry out. Russac

(1978), for example, used a single linear matching situation in which objects alternated; thus, the pairs from the matched sets were not clear, so children often had one more in one set than in the other. When objects cannot be moved and the objects are identical, close together, and small (for example as in the stimuli used by Brainerd, 1973), matching is difficult to carry out even for adults (see Baroody, 1982). In contrast, a combination of color (because it is so salient to young children) and movable objects may be particularly powerful in inducing matching: my daughter, before she was three, spent much time totally engrossed in spontaneously putting colored wooden dolls into (and then out of and then into) their proper color-coded seats in a toy bus. The use of matching may also be underestimated in the literature because children evidently find it more difficult to verbalize their use of matching than their use of counting (Fuson et al., 1983).

Issues similar to those in Table 9-11 also arise for matching. Children need to learn rules relating the results of matching to cardinal equivalence. Experiences of particular children with matching may lead to individual predispositions to use matching even when it is not easy to do so, such as with identical objects arranged in rows. Such experiences may account for the tendency of a few children to match in experiment 1 and in Fuson et al. (1983). The tendency for most children to match may be brought about by their awareness of the conflict between the "extras" isolated by the length strategy and the "extras" isolated by the density strategy. This conflict leads to a necessity to compare the length "extras" with the density "extras" in order to decide which row has more. If this is difficult to do because of the arrangement of objects, the child may then turn to an alternative method of isolating extras, that is, to matching. A conflict between the length "extras" and the density "extras" might also lead to increased awareness that one must be thorough in one's search for extras and use every entity in any comparison. Such awareness also would lead to the use of matching.

Children also need to learn that cardinal equivalence (or inequivalence) is conserved under different matching procedures. Knowledge of such conservation under different matches would seem to be quite helpful in the eventual formation of the notion of a cardinal number as an equivalence class, that is, as the class of all sets that can be put into one-to-one correspondence and in understanding the relationship between cardinal equivalence obtained by counting and by matching. In counting each set one forms a one-to-one correspondence between the counting words and the objects in the set, and transitivity across the same count words used for both sets creates a one-to-one correspondence between the objects in the two counted sets. Both of these would seem to be quite late understandings.

9.3.6. Piaget, Conservation, and Cardinal Number

Piaget (1941/1965) proposed a fourth stage following the familiar stage 3 concrete operational conservation of quantity, that of a

...correspondence between the objects and the numerals used to count them. This last type of correspondence, which is characteristic of a fourth stage, in which practical correspondence is replaced by the ability to use numeration correctly, does not concern us here, since the object of this volume is the study of the genesis of number, and it is only when operations are logically established on the practical plane that counting becomes truly numerical. (p. 74)

Central also to Piaget's concept of number are the relationships of number to class inclusion and seriation:

Number is at the same time a class and an asymmetical relation, the units of which it is composed being simultaneously added because they are equivalent, and seriated because they are different from one another.... Since each number is a whole, born of the union of equivalent and distinct terms, it cannot be constituted without inclusion and seriation....It is, in fact, when the child's intuitive evaluations have become mobile and he has therefore reached the level of the reversible operation, that he becomes capable of inclusions, seriation and counting. (p. 184)

The evidence is quite clear, however, that children do count correctly and do use count information to decide correct cardinal relations on two sets before they reach Piaget's stage 3, operational conservation. We suggest that the solution to this seeming contradiction, and the heart of Piaget's meaning of cardinal "number" and counting becoming "truly numerical" as in the preceding quotes, is in an advanced conceptual structure children use in carrying out addition and subtraction operations on cardinal number (all of these conceptual structures are discussed in chapter 8). This conceptual structure occurs later than the simultaneous perceptual unit items discussed in 9.3.3.2.3. For this more advanced conceptual structure, the basic conceptual unit is not a single-unit item but a cardinal number itself. Now children no longer have to deal with cardinal situations by thinking about sets of unit items that represent those situations. They now can think of a single cardinal number as a single conceptual unit. When necessary, cardinal numbers can be decomposed into ideal unit items, but these ideal unit items are extremely abstract and flexible. Each ideal unit item has been stripped of its perceptual attributes and is a single "one" that is interchangable with every other ideal unit item. Cardinal numbers are constituted by these ideal interchangable commutable "ones" (see Piaget, 1977, for a discussion of the importance of commutability).

When children can think of a cardinal number as a single entity, they can then conceptualize the inclusion of one cardinal number within another. "Six" can now be included in "eight" directly without generating perceptual unit items with which to think about the inclusion. "Eight" can be seen to be "seven and one" and also "six and two" and also "five and three" and also "four and four." Cardinal numbers can now also be seriated via the use of ideal units items, for the smallest difference between any two numbers (one) now consists of an ideal unit item "one" that is interchangable and identical for all numbers with this smallest difference. The sequence of number words thus now can be considered as involving the systematic seriation of all cardinal numbers, separated by identical ideal unit items of "one," and simultaneously as involving the inclusion of each cardinal number within the next. The use of such an embedded number-word sequence in which cardinal numbers can be conceptualized as seriated and included within each other then constitutes "truly numerical counting." Counting is no longer a procedure in which sequence number words are used on perceptually present entity representations of cardinal numbers; counting now is carried out by sequence number words which themselves constitute representations of cardinal numbers. Cardinal numbers now are embedded within this sequence and are at this level even difficult to disentangle conceptually from the sequence. The sequence, count, and cardinal meanings have collapsed together for each number word. The conceptual integration of these meanings was begun at the preceding level, that of sequence unit items in which the sequence words represent addends and sums in addition and subtraction (see 8.5).

This cardinalized number-word sequence and the ideal unit items of which it is composed also make possible another relationship viewed by Piaget as central to the notion of number: the relationship between cardinal and ordinal number. In Piaget's staircase experiments (1941/1965), the child eventually comes to realize that there are n stairs before the $n + 1$th stair. That is, any ordinal number refers to the particular entity within a linear ordering that is preceded by a cardinal number one less than it. Even phrasing this relationship requires an understanding of some conceptual link between cardinal and ordinal numbers. We believe that this link ordinarily arises from counting: children count and then make a count-to-cardinal transition in a cardinal situation and make a count-to-ordinal transition in an ordinal situation.[11] In the former case the cardinal reference is to the whole set of counted entities (and tells how many there are), and in the latter case the ordinal reference is to the last counted entity (and tells in which relative position that entity is in relation to the other entities). Counting, and the perceptual unit items or ideal unit items with which it is carried out, then forms the link between cardinal and ordinal numbers. When children have the conceptual structure of a cardinal number, counting can then be carried out by ideal unit items. This permits a child to establish the relationship between an ordinal number and the cardinal number that precedes it, and the ideal unit items permit the child to see this relationship as logically necessary rather than just as empirically true.

We then would like to reserve the term "cardinal number" for this later stage in which a child can consider a cardinal number itself as a unit, can decompose the cardinal number into ideal unit items if necessary, can compare

---

[11] Whenever the ordinal object is not the last object in the ordering, this count-to-cardinal transition is a subset transition in which the uncounted entities (those past the ordinal object in the ordering) are ignored (see 8.3). Any counting of the cardinal set which precedes the ordinal object also requires a subset transition, for the ordinal object and any other objects past it must be ignored.

and relate cardinal numbers, and has cardinal numbers embedded within the number-word sequence so that they are seriated and included within each other. Counting with such a number-word sequence then is truly numerical counting. When children are still counting only with perceptual unit items, cardinal situations are able to be conceptualized only as *specific numerosities that are closely tied to the set of counted entities*. This restriction does not imply that preoperational children possess little knowledge about numerosities or about cardinal situations. Perceptual unit items are sufficient for children to establish relations of cardinal equivalence and inequivalence and to carry out addition and subtraction operations in a considerable range of addition and subtraction contexts (see chapter 8). Furthermore, the move to the use of perceptual unit items to ascertain cardinal equivalence in the face of misleading perceptual arrangement of objects is an important advance, for it means that children have begun to use the correct kind of units in this discrete quantity situation. What this distinction between specific numerosities and number does remind us of, however, is the limitations in the conceptions that underlie even young children's rather sophisticated behavior.

9.4. Summary

Three experiments examined the strategies children aged 3½ to 6 used to generate a set equivalent to another and to decide the cardinal relation ($\cong$, $<$, $>$) on two sets. Major results are summarized here; for a longer summary see 9.2.4. In experiment 1 children predominantly used matching to make a set equivalent to a display of objects in a row, predominantly counted to make a set of a given numerosity, and predominantly used length to decide which of two sets of objects arranged in parallel rows had more (even though density also varied and length was always a wrong cue for cardinal number). In experiment 2 children were asked to count in the task from experiment 1 with 7, 8, or 9 objects in parallel rows. Only a few of the children aged 3½ to 4 improved their equivalence judgments, the majority of the children aged 4 to 5½ improved but only on about half the trials, and all of the children aged 5½ to 6 improved on a majority of the trials. The counting information was used more on the trials with equal sets than with unequal sets. For the children below age 4, remembering the counts of both sets was considerably more difficult than counting both sets accurately, 20% versus 52% accuracy. For all other half-year age groups, counting and remembering seemed to be equally difficult, with accuracy ranging between 67% and 83%. The youngest children were able to coordinate counting and remembering accurately on the same trial (and thus provide themselves with adequate count information) on 18% of the trials. This figure ranged from 53% to 69% for the half-year age groups from age 4 to age 6. Thus, many of the 4- and 5-year-old children could frequently provide themselves with accurate counting information, remember both count words, coordinate these two sources of information on the same trial, and use the count information to judge cardinal relations.

In experiment 3 presence of misleading length cues had a very strong effect on the strategies used by 4- and 5-year-old children. When length was a misleading cue (i.e., when one of the two equal rows was longer than the other), children predominantly used perceptual strategies (mostly length) to make their final cardinal equivalence judgment, doing so on 65% of the trials while using counting on 32% of the trials and matching on 10% of the trials (some children used both counting and matching on the same trial). In sharp contrast, when length was not a misleading cue and objects could be moved, children based 75% of their final equivalence judgments on counting (or number) and based 34% of their judgments on matching while basing only 12% of their final judgments on perceptual strategies (again some children both counted and matched). When then told that entities can sometimes be arranged so that they look like more but are really the same,[12] most (80%) of the 4-year-olds and all of the 5-year-olds given a task like their first task did make a distinction between two meanings of "more," choosing the longer row as the row that "looks like more" and then spontaneously counting (on 62% of the trials) or matching (on 35% of the trials) to decide that the rows "really are the same."

Three different classes of cardinal relational situations were described: the static comparison of two cardinal situations, the dynamic transformation of a single cardinal situation, and the dynamic transformation of a cardinal situation within a static compare situation (see Table 9-9). The strategies by which the appropriate cardinal relation can be determined for each class of situations were outlined, and a developmental progression in children's use of these strategies was outlined (see Table 9-10). The discussion, as does the literature, concentrates on cardinal situations derived from Piaget's conservation of numerical equivalence task in which two sets of entities are arranged in parallel rows with length being a misleading cue (e.g., the row with more objects is shorter).

In the static compare situation in which an order or equivalence relation must be established on two cardinal situations, 3-year-olds can use length and density to make this judgment. However, they use only one of these (usually length) and ignore the other, leading frequently to erroneous judgments of cardinal relations. They also use nonquantitative strategies such as color of objects, alternating choices, and guessing. Four-year-olds begin to use length or density more consistently, but still use only one of these and thus make incorrect judgments. If 4-year-olds are asked to count or match to make equivalence judgments, many of them can carry out these strategies correctly and can use the count information or the match information to make an

---

[12] Children were told that they would see some cases in which one row would look like more but the rows would really be the same and some cases in which one row would look like more and really be more.

accurate equivalence judgment. For counting, the ability to do so with equal sets may precede the ability to do so with unequal sets (i.e., to judge > or <). However, some 4-year-olds will ignore the count or match information and use the length or density information. By age 5½ many children will spontaneously count or match to establish an order or equivalence relation on two cardinal situations. By age 7 children begin to be able to quantify length and density information that conflict (i.e., when one row is longer but the other is denser), although this ability may improve for a considerable period of time for large arrays.

Within the dynamic situations transformations were classified as those that change cardinality (the Change-Get-More and Change-Get-Less addition and subtraction cardinal operations discussed in chapter 8) and those that merely displace the elements of a cardinal situation. Children seem to understand the change meanings of "get more" and of "get less" very early (perhaps before age 1), but do connect these change meanings to the cardinal relational meanings of "have more" and "have less" by age 2. However, in a dynamic change transformation within a compare situation, these children ignore the initial states and make the cardinal relational judgment just on the basis of the change transformation (so that a set that gets another one has more even if it had several fewer in the beginning). Some 3-year-olds then use the initial state information as well as the change information, but they do not accurately quantify and relate these differences, so are only correct if the original difference was one. By age 5 and 6, many children can coordinate differences of two and three (e.g., answering correctly that a set that received two successive additions but had been three less than the other set was still less than the other set).

For displacement transformations of one set within a compare situation (the classic Piagetian task), two different kinds of developmental progressions are suggested in the literature. One is that children understand the invariance of a cardinal situation under a displacement transformation and gradually become able to maintain this invariance in the face of misleading length information; children then use this invariance of a single set under a displacement transformation and transitivity to deduce that the cardinal relation on the pretransformation sets pertains to the posttransformation sets. Another set of positions emphasizes that children can ignore the transformation and use the strategies from the static compare situation to establish cardinal relations on the posttransformation end state. This position was extended here to suggest that children who count and match to determine equivalence in the conservation situation may then relate their count or match results to the displacement transformation and make an inductive generalization that displacements do not affect the equivalence relation. Both these children and any children who might have followed the route of deduction of invariance of displacements from identity conservation and transitivity will make immediate equivalence judgments in the conservation situation and justify these judgments by two Piagetian justifications: the irrelevance of the transformation (e.g., "You just spreaded them") and nothing added or subtracted (e.g., "You didn't take any away").

I further suggested that when children have available the conceptual simultaneous perceptual unit items described in chapter 8, they might use these unit items in counting or matching in cardinal equivalence situations. With these unit items children can think of a single entity as being in two different cardinal situations (in chapter 8 these are in an addend and simultaneously in the sum). Thus, children could represent both the pretransformation and posttransformation sets by the same simultaneous perceptual unit items and follow the unit items for the transformed set as they are moved by the transformation. Thus, the child could see that the matching that existed before the transformation (or the counting that was carried out) is maintained during and after the transformation. The child who does this might then give a "reversibility" justification, such as, "They're the same because you could just move them back again." The difference here is that the child is not just referring to an empirical return, what Piaget (1967) called "renversabilité." The simultaneous perceptual unit items instead give this reasoning a general deductive character. It is *logically necessary* that the set have the same amount, not just empirically true, and thus is operational reversibility. The ability to use simultaneous perceptual unit items might also be related to the ability to consider two aspects of the conservation situation simultaneously, that is to articulate in a compensation justification the conflict between the information given by the length strategy and by the density strategy in the typical conservation situation (the length strategy says there are "extras" out at the ends of the row, and the density strategy says there are "extras" in the middle of the row).

Piaget (1941/1965) proposed a fourth stage following the familiar stage 3 concrete operational conservation of quantity. I hypothesized here that this stage occurs when children reach the advanced conceptual level discussed in chapter 8, that of considering a cardinal number to be itself a single conceptual unit. Such a cardinal number can be decomposed when necessary into ideal unit items, each of which has been stripped of its perceptual attributes and is a single "one" that is interchangable with every other ideal unit item. These ideal unit items permit the sequence number words to become cardinal numbers. The sequence of number words now can be considered as involving the systematic seriation of all cardinal numbers, separated by identical ideal unit items of "one" and simultaneously as involving the inclusion of each cardinal number within the next. Use of such a cardinalized number-word sequence in which cardinal numbers can be conceptualized as seriated and included within each other then constitutes the "truly numerical counting" described by Piaget as stage 4. It is only at this stage of a unified, embedded, cardinalized number-word sequence that we would wish to say that children understand *cardinal number*. Before that, children show much competence in cardinal situations. But as long as they count only with perceptual unit items, they are limited to conceptualization of cardinal situations only as *specific numerosities that are closely tied to the set of counted entities.* It is the integration of counting, sequence, and cardinal meanings within a unitized number-word sequence that moves the child from specific numerosities to cardinal number.

This review and discussion found counting and matching to play central roles in children's ability to establish equivalence and order relations in cardinal situations. This is primarily because children initially cannot think about cardinal situations without representing these situations with perceptual unit items. Children's cardinal and counting conceptual structures become more abstract and flexible through their very considerable practice in school with counting in addition and subtraction situations. The development of these structures are described in chapter 8, and some of these structures are related in this chapter to children's thinking in equivalence situations.

Part IV   Number Words, Counting, and Cardinality: The Increasing Integration of Sequence, Count, and Cardinal Meanings

10. Early Relationships Among Sequence Number Words, Counting Correspondence, and Cardinality

10.1. Introduction

Earlier chapters have focused on young children's ability to produce the number-word sequence (chapter 2), make accurate correspondences when counting (chapters 3, 4, 5, and 6), and relate counting to developing concepts of cardinality (chapters 7, 8, and 9). In this chapter data are provided that indicate how these various aspects of counting in a cardinal situation fit together for children of varying ages, that is, how relatively difficult these aspects of counting are. The focus here is only on the earliest relationship between counting and cardinality, the ability to answer a how-many question with the last counted word.

From the earlier chapters, we know the effect of set size on each of these aspects of counting. Most children aged 3 years and older can accurately produce the initial part of the number-word sequence but not the later part. Thus, as set size is increased, most children will reach a part of the sequence that they cannot yet produce accurately. Children make more correspondence errors as set size increases, both because the opportunity to make such errors increases and because the rate of errors per object increases with set size for some kinds of correspondence errors. Set size does not affect children's ability to give the last counted word as the answer to the how-many question. What these statements do not give us, however, is how these increases in errors with set size for sequences and correspondence relate to each other or relate to the steady rate of last-word responding or how these three aspects are related within individual children. The first part of this chapter addresses these questions. Because one answer to this set of questions has been provided by Gelman and Gallistel (1978), our results are compared to theirs. We pursued the question of the relationships among these aspects of counting because our own unsystematic observations of children's counting revealed what we thought were substantial variations from the pattern reported by Gelman and Gallistel.

The second part of the chapter focuses on issues of what children understand about these aspects of counting while the first part concentrates on what children actually do when counting. This discussion is framed within the influential position of Gelman and colleagues (described following) that preschool children's counting is based on five counting "principles" (e.g., Gelman & Gallistel, 1978; Gelman & Meck, 1986). We use the recent distinctions among conceptual, procedural, and utilization competence made by Greeno, Riley, and Gelman (1984) in this discussion. We conclude that these five principles involve quite different kinds of conceptual understanding and relate to procedural competence in different ways; they thus vary in the extent to which the term "principle" seems appropriate. It therefore would be helpful if future discussions of what children do when counting and what children understand about counting abandoned the use of the term "principle" and instead used the later distinctions among conceptual, procedural, and utilization competence. This step would increase the clarity of future discussion and would permit such discussions to address the whole range of children's early competence in counting rather than remaining focused on continuing debate about whether children do or do not "have" these five original counting principles.

10.2. Developmental Relationships Among Sequence, Correspondence, and Cardinal Aspects of Counting

This section provides data concerning the effects of age and set size on relationships among three aspects of counting: children's ability to produce accurate sequences, their ability to make accurate correspondences, and their knowledge that the last word said in counting tells how many entities were counted. These three general aspects of counting were discussed by Gelman and Gallistel (1978), who proposed that the counting of young children adheres to three how-to-count principles: the stable-order, the one-one, and the cardinality principles.[1] The first two of these principles pertain to two components of accurate counting: "the tags used must be drawn from a stably ordered list" (the stable-order principle) and "every item in a set must be assigned a unique tag" (the one-one principle). The third principle (the cardinality principle[2]) concerns an aspect of counting in cardinal situations, namely. "the last tag used in a count has a special status; it represents the cardinal value of the set" (all definitions from a recent statement of the principles in Gelman and Meck, 1986, p. 30). Gelman and Gallistel (1978) concluded that for preschool children the relationship among these three principles is as follows:

> (1) At small set sizes (2-3) children adhere to all three principles; (2) as set size increases they begin to have trouble with the one-one principle, and they stop using the cardinal principle; and (3) in enumerating the largest sets they try to adhere to the one-one principle but fail, while continuing to adhere with fair success to the stable-order principle. This pattern is true regardless of age, although, not surprisingly, the younger the child the smaller the set sizes at which he begins to falter. (p. 130)

Judging from their graph on p. 124, the decrease with set size in the use of the cardinality principle reported by Gelman and Gallistel (1978) was large. The cardinality principle was applied by 80% of 4-year-olds for set size 2, by 50% for set sizes 7 to 11, and by only 25% for sets of 19 objects. For 3-year-

---

[1] This discussion contains some unavoidable redundancy with some points in chapter 7 concerning the development of early relationships between counting and cardinality. However, this chapter extends the focus there to the three-way relationship among the sequence and correspondence aspects of counting and the cardinality principle.

[2] As in chapter 7, we use the recent label "cardinality principle" (Greeno et al., 1984) rather than the original Gelman and Gallistel (1978) term "cardinal principle" to avoid the possible interpretation of "cardinal principle" as "the most important principle."

olds, the percentage of children using the cardinality principle declined from 76% to 30% to 23% to 10% use for set sizes 2, 7, 11, and 19, respectively. Gelman and Gallistel (1978, p. 127) suggested that this decline might reflect a child's decision to refrain from using counting outcomes to describe the cardinality of a set once the set size exceeded the child's counting accuracy limit. More recently, Gelman (1982b) and Gelman and Baillargeon (1983) suggested that the declining use of the cardinality principle with larger sets might be due to the increased attentional demands of counting the larger sets (where counting is less automatized) such that insufficient attention is left over for using the cardinality principle.

Gelman and Meck (1983) suggested that the child's failure to exhibit overtly the cardinality principle with large sets should not be taken to mean that the child lacks understanding of the cardinality principle. They provided evidence that, when watching a puppet count large as well as small sets, children can recognize errors in the number-word sequence, identify some violations of the one-one principle, and identify violations of the cardinality principle. However, these subsequent reports provided no new data concerning empiri-played all three of the principles showed a large decrement with set size, although no separate data concerning the children's own use of the cardinality principle with large set sizes were included. Gelman and Meck concluded that performance demands can mask the young child's knowledge of the counting principles. This argument was expanded in Greeno et al. (1984), where three separate aspects of counting were differentiated: conceptual, procedural, and utilizational competence. The principles fall within conceptual competence, actual counting behavior within procedural competence, and use of counting in various situations within utilizational competence. However, these subsequent reports provided no new data concerning empirical relationships among the principles, and the original Gelman and Gallistel relationship was still asserted.

Some aspects of the names and definitions of these principles seem problematic. However, discussion of these concerns is postponed until after the data have been presented. Therefore, in the reports of the following experiments, the names and operationalizations of these principles are those used in Gelman and Gallistel (1978) and in more recent work. In particular we use the term "cardinality principle" rather than the more neutral term "last-word response" that was discussed and used in chapter 7. This distinction is discussed again after the presentation of the data (in 10.3.3).

Four experiments were undertaken in which the relationships among children's use of the three how-to-count principles were examined over a wide range of set sizes (2 to 26). Because each experiment was also designed to provide data on other aspects of children's counting behavior, each experiment could provide data only on some parts of these relationships.[3] It is much

---

[3] Other aspects of the data from these studies have been discussed in Fuson, Pergament, Lyons, and Hall (1985), Fuson, Pergament, and Lyons (1985), and chapters 5 and 7.

easier to assimilate the results of these experiments if the results of all of them are presented together in a combined table. Therefore, rather than the usual serial presentation of the methods and results of each experiment, the methods of all experiments are described first and then the results of all of them are presented and discussed together.

10.2.1. Methods of Experiments 1, 2, 3, and 4

10.2.1.1. Experiment 1 Method. Forty-eight middle-class children ranging in age from 3-2 (3 years 2 months) to 4-7 (mean age 4-0) attending preschool in a northern suburb of Chicago served as subjects.

Each child received six rows of a small number of objects (two rows each of 4, 5, and 6 objects) and, 7 to 10 days later, six rows of a larger number of objects (two rows each of 9, 12, and 14 objects). Within each set size the objects in one row were heterogeneous in appearance and in the other were homogeneous. Size was not counterbalanced because we did not want to discourage children by giving the larger arrays first and because Gelman and Gallistel (1978) had given their objects in increasing set sizes. The three homogeneous sets of objects were small free-standing dolls, small toy soldiers, and 1-inch wooden blocks, all colored the same. The heterogeneous sets were different small toy animals, heterogeneously sized and/or colored toy pigs, and 1-inch wooden blocks of different solid colors. Objects were glued to a board in a single row. The homogeneous and heterogeneous sets were alternated, with half the children receiving a homogeneous trial first and half receiving a heterogeneous trial first. The same types of toys were used for both sizes of arrays.

Each board was placed on the table in front of the child. The child was told to count the Xs, where X was the type of object. As the child counted, the experimenter recorded on a prepared array the number words said by the child; each word was recorded at the location to which the child's finger was directed when the word was said. Points without words were also recorded, and words said with no accompanying point were marked with a dot. Violations of one-to-one correspondence could be determined from this record. Children were then asked, "How many Xs are there?"

10.2.1.2. Experiment 2 Method. Forty-eight middle to upper-middle-class children attending two preschools in a northern suburb of Chicago served as subjects. Ages ranged from 2-8 (2 years 8 months) to 4-11 (4 years 11 months) with a mean age of 3-10. There were 7 two-year-olds, 19 three-year-olds, and 22 four-year-olds.

Four trials were given, using sets of four, five (twice), and six objects. A row of small toys was placed in front of the child. The child was asked, "How many Xs are there?", where X was the type of toy presented. If a child did not do anything, the child was directed, "Count the Xs and tell me how many there are." If a child counted but did not give an answer to the how-many question, the child was asked again, "How many Xs are there?" The experimenter recorded the number words said by the child, the objects to which the child was pointing while each word was said, and the child's response to the how-many question.

If the cardinality principle was used, use of the other principles was assessed for that count. If no cardinality principle was used and the child counted more than once for a trial, use of the other principles was assessed for the first counting trial.[4]

10.2.1.3. Experiment 3 Method. The subjects were 45 middle- to upper-middle class children attending a preschool in Madison, Wisconsin. There were 19 two-year-olds, 23 three-year-olds and 3 four-year-olds; ages ranged from 2-4 to 4-3 (mean age was 3-1).

All children were given six trials on linearly arranged objects with set sizes of 2 through 7. Sets of size 2, 3, and 4 (very small sets) were alternated with the sets of 5, 6, and 7 (small sets). Half of the sample received a very small set first, and half, a small set first. Children turned their backs as the experimenter arranged a row of objects. After they turned back around, they were told to "Count the Xs" and were then asked, "How many Xs are there?" The number words said by the child were recorded at the object to which the child was pointing when each word was said. The response to the how-many question was also recorded.

All 23 children who used the cardinality principle on two or more trials were given nine additional trials, three each on three different sizes of sets: very small (2, 3, and 4), small (5, 6, and 7), and very large (19, 23, and 26). These children formed the sample labeled 3a in Table 10-1. Each consecutive set of three trials contained one set of each size, and the order of sets within each set of three was counterbalanced. Stimuli consisted of rows of stickers such as stars, animals, and smiling faces. To determine whether a failure to use the cardinality principle on the very large sets resulted from a child's forgetting that the how-many question had been asked rather than from the child's not being able to use the cardinality principle for very large sets, children who failed to use the cardinality principle on the very large sets were directed to "Count the Xs and tell me how many Xs there are."

10.2.1.4. Experiment 4 Method. The subjects were 48 middle- to upper-middle-class children between the ages of 3-6 and 5-5 who attended a preschool in a northern suburb of Chicago. For the analyses the children were divided into two groups of 24 each, one with ages from 3-6 through 4-5 (mean age 4-0) and one with ages from 4-6 through 5-5 (mean age 5-1).

The counting stimuli were irregularly spaced red or blue dots affixed in a row on a white strip of cardboard. One strip was made to contain each of the

---

[4] The repeated counts were in response to the directions or questions of the experimenter, not self-corrections of errors, so this choice did not result in lower accuracy scores.

following number of dots: 7, 8, 9, 16, 18, and 19. Each successive pair of strips contained one larger and one smaller number. Half of the children within each half-year age group had a smaller number (7, 8, and 9) first, and half had a larger number (16, 18, and 19) first.

A strip was placed in front of the child, and the child was told to "Count the dots." The number words said by the child and the dots pointed to while saying each word were recorded by the experimenter. When the child was finished counting, the child was asked "How many [blue, red] dots are there?" The interviews were audiotaped so that the number-word sequences for the longer rows could be checked if the experimenter did not record all of the words.

10.2.1.5. Experiments 1, 2, 3, and 4 Scoring. For experiment 1, children were scored as satisfying the stable-order principle for a given set of *n* objects if their first *n* words were the same over both trials of that set size, whether or not the sequence was correct (following Gelman & Gallistel, 1978). For example, if on the two arrays of set size 6 a child responded, "One, two, three, five, six, eight," the child was given credit for a stable sequence on set size 6. For experiments 2 through 4, repeated trials of the same set size were not given. Therefore, the three (or for experiment 2, four) trials at each set size were grouped together, and the stability of the sequences produced over those trials was assessed. For each set of *n* objects, only the first *n* words said were scored. For a stable sequence to be credited, the first *n* words said for the larger sets within a set size grouping had to contain the same first *n* words said for the smaller sets within that grouping. Thus, a child saying "One, two, four, five", "One, two, four, five, eight", and "One, two, four, five, eight, ten" was given credit for a stable sequence for the sets 4, 5, and 6, but a child who said "One, two, three, four" and then the other two sequences was not so credited. All the sequences of a given set size grouping had to meet this criterion to be judged as stable (S) sequences. For an accurate (Acc) sequence on a trial of *n* objects, the first *n* words had to be correct; this criterion thus also had a similar embedded nature.

Again following Gelman and Gallistel (1978), one criterion for the one-one principle was that the same number (N) of words was produced as there were objects in the set (pp. 87, 109). Note that this criterion does not ensure that one and only one count word was paired with each object, because a child could skip a count word for one object and give two words for another. Gelman and Gallistel in another analysis (p. 113) credited the one-one principle only if the child gave each object exactly one word, that is, used an accurate correspondence (Acc). Therefore, correspondence was also scored in this way.

Children were credited with using the cardinality principle if they answered the how-many question with the last word they had said in counting. This word did not have to be the correct cardinality of the set.

Counting satisfied the S/N criterion on a given that if it satisfied the stable-

Table 10-1. Percentage of Trials That Demonstrated the Three How-to-Count Principles and Accurate Sequences, Correspondence, and Counting

Set size		Experiment 1		Experiment 2				Experiment 3				Experiment 3a		Experiment 4			
		3-2 to 4-7[a] Mean 4-0 (n = 48)		2-8 to 3-11 Mean 3-4 (n = 26)		4-0 to 4-11 Mean 4-6 (n = 22)		2-4 to 2-11 Mean 2-8 (n = 19)		3-0 to 4-3 Mean 3-6 (n = 26)		2-4 to 4-3 Mean 3-4 (n = 23)		3-6 to 4-5 Mean 4-0 (n = 24)		4-6 to 5-5 Mean 5-1 (n = 24)	
		S/N[b]	Acc[c]	S/N	Acc	S/N	Acc	S/N	Acc	S/N	Acc	S/N	Acc	S/N	Acc	S/N	Acc
2, 3, 4	Sequence	98	98					88	77	99	99	97	94				
	Correspondence	77	76					56	54	94	94	84	81				
	Cardinality	71						18		62		83					
	Counting	76	75					49	49	92	92	81	78				
4, 5, 6	Sequence			86	84	98	98										
	Correspondence			61	57	84	82										
	Cardinality			44		73											
	Counting			57	53	83	81										
5, 6, 7	Sequence							67	56	92	85	87	74				
	Correspondence							42	35	83	82	64	58				
	Cardinality							18		59		93					
	Counting							25	21	76	69	61	54				

7, 8, 9	Sequence	100	100	100	100
	Correspondence	78	78	86	86
	Cardinality	91	91	86	100
	Counting	78	78	85	85
9, 12, 14	Sequence	89	86		
	Correspondence	46	45		
	Cardinality	67			
	Counting	45	44		
16, 18, 19	Sequence	79	42	96	79
	Correspondence	36	36	69	69
	Cardinality	91	91	69	100
	Counting	35	19	69	64
19, 23, 26	Sequence	32	4		
	Correspondence	14	14		
	Cardinality	93			
	Counting	12	4		

Note. Experiment 3a subjects ($n = 23$) are those subjects from experiment 3 who used the cardinality principle on two or more trials in experiment 3.

[a] Age 3-2 to 4-7 represents 3 years 2 months through 4 years 7 months; mean 4-0 is a mean age of 4 years 0 months.

[b] The S/N criterion for sequences was that the *same* sequence to *n* was produced over repeated trials, for correspondence was that the same *number* of words was produced as there were objects, and for counting was that these criteria for sequence and correspondence were met.

[c] The Acc (accuracy) criterion for sequences on a trial of *n* objects was that an accurate sequence up to *n* was produced, for correspondence was that exactly one word was given to each object, and for counting was that these accuracy criteria for sequence and correspondence were met.

order (S) principle criterion and the same number (N) one-one criterion. Counting was accurate (Acc) if both the sequence and one-one correspondence satisfied the accuracy criteria on that trial.

10.2.2. Results and Discussion

10.2.2.1. Differences Between the Criteria. The percentage of trials that demonstrated the three how-to-count principles and accurate sequence, correspondence, and counting are given in Table 10-1. For the stable-order principle, the difference between the trials fitting the S/N and the Acc criteria indicate those cases in which children consistently used their own incorrect number-word sequence when counting, as reported by Gelman and Gallistel (1978) and by Fuson et al. (1982) and summarized in chapter 2. These cases appear in two-thirds of the cells in the table. These percentage differences (the percentage of trials on which children exhibited stable but inaccurate sequences) range between 2% and 37%. These differences were small for most cells but did rise to as much as a third of the trials for sets of 16, 18, and 19 for 3½- to 4½-year-olds, experiment 4. Children of all ages produced such sequences. The youngest children (the 2-year-olds) produced some such sequences even on the smallest sets (on sets of 2, 3, and 4, experiment 3), and the oldest children (the 4½- to 5½-year-olds) produced such sequences for large sets (16, 18, and 19, experiment 4). As reported by Fuson et al. (1982), most of these incorrect but stable sequences consisted of an accurate portion of the number-word sequence followed by a stable portion of number words produced in the correct order with no repetitions but with one or more number words omitted.

The difference between the two criteria for the one-one principle (the correspondence percent in the S/N column and that in the Acc column) was small or nonexistent in most cases. Only for the youngest children did it rise even to 4% to 7% (for sets of 4, 5, and 6 for 2- and 3-year-olds in experiment 2 and for sets of 5, 6, and 7 for 2-year-olds in experiment 3).

Counting scores varied relatively little between the S/N and Acc column criteria because counting performance was primarily determined by the correspondence performance (which showed little difference between the S/N and Acc criteria) rather than by the sequence performance. The exception was for the very large sets (16, 18, 19 for the 3½- to 4½-year-olds in experiment 4), where 16% of the trials had consistent incorrect sequences with correct correspondences (i.e., showed principled S/N counting but not accurate counting).

10.2.2.2. Effects of Set Size on the Principles. The effect of set size on the percentage of trials that satisfied a principle varied by the principle. Set size affected use of the stable-order principle in only a few cases. The stable-order principle was used on a very high proportion of trials (above 85%) in all cases except three: for trials of 5, 6, and 7 objects for the 2-year-olds in experiment

3, for trials for 16, 18, and 19 objects for 3½ to 4½ year-olds in experiment 4, and for trials of 19, 23, and 26 for 2- and 3-year-olds in experiment 3a. In contrast, the number of trials on which the one-one principle was used (by either criterion) showed large drop-offs with set size. For example, in experiment 3a, use of the one-one principle fell from 84% to 64% to 14% for sets of size 2 to 4, 5 to 7, and 19 to 26. Finally, the number of trials which satisfied the cardinality principle showed with increasing set size either no change or a very small decrease (4% at most). However, with very young children and very large sets, there was some evidence that children may need more than one chance to demonstrate use of the cardinality principle. In experiment 3a on the sets of 19, 23, 26, children used the cardinality principle on 80% of the first trials given but on 93% of the trials when the second chance on a failed trial was included. The similar nature of the number words for these large sets may contribute to this initial difficulty. On the wrong first efforts, half of the answers were in the late teens and 20s and were the word just before or just after the last counted word. However, even though a repeated trial led to more uses of the cardinality principle, the use on the initial trial of the very large sets (80%) was equivalent to the use with the very small sets (83%).

10.2.2.3. The Relationship Between the Stable-Order and One-One Principles. At every age group and at every set size, more trials fit the stable-order principle than fit the one-one principle. In most cases this difference was large, ranging up to 43% (for the 3½- to 4½-year-olds on sets of 16 to 19, experiment 4). This relationship also held for these two aspects of counting when the accurate criterion was used. The single exception was for the very largest sets (19 to 26 in experiment 3a), where there were a few more trials (10%) with accurate correspondence than with correct sequences. The S/N counting entries in Table 10-1 reveal the within-child relationship between use of the sequence and the one-one principles: The amount by which the counting percentage is less than the correspondence percentage is the percentage of trials on which the one-one principle was used but the stable-order principle was not used. These differences are very small (7% or less) in all but one case (17% for the 2-year-olds in experiment 3 on sets of 5 to 7). Thus, except for this one case, practically no child used the one-one principle without also using the stable-order principle. The same analysis using the percentages in the Acc column yields the relationship between production of accurate sequences and of accurate correspondences. For the accurate criteria, all but four cells show a difference of 5% or less. In these four cells from 10% to 17% of the trials on sets of 5 to 7, 16 to 18, and 19 to 26 in experiments 3, 3a, and 4 are by children demonstrating accurate correspondences but not accurate sequences. Thus, the precedence of accurate sequences over accurate correspondences may occasionally be violated, especially on sets so large that children have not yet learned the number-word sequence.

Analysis of principle use by individual children (rather than trial data pooled across children) indicated a similar relationship. For most ages and for most set sizes, counting did adhere to the stable-order principle before it adhered to the one-one principle. For these cases either there were no children whose counting consistently (at criterion levels of 50% and above) showed the one-one but not the stable-order principle, or McNemar's tests indicated that the small number of such children was significantly less than the number of children showing the stable-order principle but not the one-one principle. This was also true for the relationship between the use of accurate correspondences and accurate sequences. However, there was one exception for the principles and two exceptions for the accurate criteria in which McNemar's tests indicated that the relationship was independent. In experiment 3 on set sizes of 5 to 7, five children produced one-one correspondences without stable sequences on 67% of their trials while 10 children used stable sequences but not one-one correspondences. For the accurate criteria these figures were 5 and 12. On experiment 4 on sets of 16 to 19, on 67% of the trials four of the 3½- to 4½-year-olds counted with accurate correspondence without using an accurate sequence, while six used an accurate sequence without using accurate correspondence. Thus, within individual children correspondence ability may occasionally outstrip the knowledge of a stable sequence or of the conventional correct sequence, but for most sets and for most ages sequence performance exceeds correspondence performance.

10.2.2.4. The Relationship Between the Stable-Order and Cardinality Principles. For most set sizes and most ages, counting adhered to the stable-order principle on more trials than it adhered to the cardinality principle. The exception was for the children aged 3½ to 4½ on sets of 16 to 19 in experiment 4, where the cardinality principle was used on 91% of the trials and stable sequences were produced on only 79% of the trials. In this case, McNemar's tests on within-child use of these principles indicated that the number of children using the cardinality principle and not the stable-order principle was significantly greater than the number of children using the stable-sequence principle and not the cardinality principle at the 67% criterion of use, $\chi^2 = 8.33, p < .05$. With the exception of the large sets of 16 to 19 in experiment 4 for both ages of children, accurate sequences were produced more frequently than the cardinality principle was used. In that one case, the cardinality principle was used on more trials than were accurate sequences produced: 91% versus 42% for the younger and 100% versus 79% for the older children. Here, McNemar's tests on within-child data indicated that significantly more children in both age groups used the cardinality principle and did not produce accurate sequences than vice versa (at both 100% and 67% criterion levels), χ^2 ranged between 4.0 and 19.0, $p < .05$. Thus, because use of the cardinality principle does not seem to drop with set size but the production of stable sequences (and even more so, of accurate sequences) does so drop, the relationship between the stable-order principle and the cardinality principle may be reversed for very large sets: Some children may demonstrate the cardinality principle and not stable sequences or accurate sequences.

10.2.2.5. The Relationship Between the One-One and Cardinality Principles. The relationship between the one-one principle and the cardinality principle depended on both set size and age. Because for most set sizes and ages adherence to the one-one principle was almost the same as carrying out accurate counting, this relationship is similar to that between accurate counting and the cardinality principle (see chapter 7 and Fuson, Pergament, Lyons, and Hall, 1985, for more details).

For the very small sets (2 to 4 in experiment 3), the one-one principle was adhered to on many more trials than was the cardinality principle. Within-child analyses pooled across age indicated that significantly more children (16) used the one-one principle without using the cardinality principle than used the cardinality principle without using the one-one principle (1 child), McNemar's $\chi^2(1, 17) = 13.24$, $p < .01$.

For sets just larger than this (4 to 6 in experiments 1 and 2 and 5 to 7 in experiment 3), examination of principle use by individual children revealed that use of these principles was actually independent. For experiment 1 and for both age groups in experiments 2 and 3, McNemar's tests indicated that there was no significant difference between the number of children demonstrating the one-one and not the cardinality principle and the number of children demonstrating the cardinality and not the one-one principle. To illustrate this result, Table 10-2 displays children in experiment 1 classified by principle use at four different criterion levels. On the sets of 4 to 6 between about a half

Table 10-2. Number of Children Demonstrating the One-One Principle and the Cardinality Principle by Set Size at Four Criterion Levels (Experiment 1)

Cardinality principle	One-one principle							
	100%		88%		67%		50%	
	N 1-1[a]	1-1[b]	N 1-1	1-1	N 1-1	1-1	N 1-1	1-1
	Sets of 4, 5, 6							
Not CP[c]	10	7	5	10	4	10	3	10
CP[d]	13	18	12	21	8	26	7	28
	Sets of 9, 12, 14							
Not CP[c]	18	2	15	2	12	3	11	4
CP[d]	20	8	17	14	16	17	15	18

[a] N 1-1: The child did not display the one-one principle at the criterion level.
[b] 1-1: The child did display the one-one principle (said one word for each object).
[c] Not CP: The child did not display the cardinality principle at the criterion level (e.g., on 100% of the trials for the 100% columns).
[d] CP: The child did display the cardinality principle at the criterion level (e.g., on 100% of the trials for the 100% columns).

and a third of the children used one principle without using the other, and the children who used only one principle were about equally split in which principle they used. Different criterion levels were used for the different experiments because they contained different numbers of trials. The McNemar's tests indicated independence of principle use at one or more criterion levels at or above 50% for each age cell for the sets of 4 to 6 and 5 to 7 in Table 10-1. Thus, for sets between 4 and 7, the results of three experiments indicated that use of the one-one and cardinality principles was independent: equal (nonsignificantly different) numbers of children used each principle without using the other.

For sets of 7 to 9 and larger, counting satisfied the cardinality principle on considerably more trials than it satisfied the one-one principle. The number of trials by which demonstration of the cardinality principle exceeded that of the one-one principle ranged up to 55% for 3½- to 4½-year-olds for sets of 16, 18, and 19 in experiment 4. Within-child analyses supported these findings. McNemar's tests indicated that significantly more children used the cardinality principle and not the one-one principle than vice versa for sets of 7 to 9 in experiment 4, for sets of 9 to 14 in experiment 1, and for sets of 16 to 19 for both age groups in experiment 4, χ^2 ranged from 5.0 to 14.73, $p < .05$. The comparison between the correspondence and cardinality percentages for sets of 19 to 26 in experiment 3a (14% versus 93%) does not represent the percentages for children of that age range because the children in experiment 3a were those children from experiment 3 who demonstrated the cardinality principle on the smaller sets. These figures do demonstrate, however, that children will still use the cardinality principle when their correspondence is poor.

Thus, the relationship between these two principles is considerably more complicated than that reported by Gelman and Gallistel (1978). For very small sets (2, 3, and 4), use of the one-one principle precedes use of the cardinality principle. For sets between 4 and 7, use of these principles is independent (some children use each without using the other). For sets larger than 7, many more children use the cardinality principle without using the one-one principle than vice versa.

10.2.3. Summary of Experiments 1, 2, 3, and 4

These experiments indicate that the relationships among children's adherence to Gelman and Gallistel's (1978) three how-to-count principles vary considerably by set size.

For very small sets (2, 3, and 4). Counting does adhere to the stable-order and one-one principles before it adheres to the cardinality principle.

For slightly larger sets (4 through 7). Some children display the stable-order and one-one but not the cardinality principle, but just as many children display a different combination of principles: the stable-order and the cardinality principle but not the one-one principle. That is, within this set size range, adherence to the one-one and to the cardinality principle are independent.

For sets between about 7 and 16. The principles seem to be ordered (from most to least frequently displayed): stable-order, cardinality, and one-one. That is, some children display the stable-order principle and not the other two, and some children display the stable-order and the cardinality principles but not the one-one principle.

For sets above 16. Adherence to the principles seems to be ordered: cardinality, stable-order, and one-one. There are children who demonstrate only the cardinality principle and there are those who demonstrate the cardinality and stable-order but not the one-one principle.

The result for small sets is consistent with that of Wilkinson (1984), and the results for the large sets indicate that the performance demands of very large sets may interfere with the use of the cardinality principle on the first but not with a second attempt on a very large set. There are also certain age and set size combinations in which use of the one-one principle exceeds use of the stable-order principle. Of course, these set sizes are approximate, and performance depends on age as well as on set size. These relationships also only concern linear arrays. The data on counting correspondence errors in chapter 4 indicate that counting conforming to the one-one principle would drop considerably for objects arranged in random arrays, and thus this principle might be the last to be demonstrated for even smaller set sizes than above when the counting is of objects in random arrays.

The reasons for the difference between our results and those of Gelman and Gallistel (1978) may be mainly procedural.[5] The fact that our procedure was similar to that of Wilkinson (1984) and that his results are similar to ours with respect to the cardinality principle support this notion. Our procedure and that of Wilkinson involved separate directions for the measures of counting and of the cardinality principle. Children first were asked to count and then were asked how many objects there were. In the Gelman and Gallistel procedure, only one instruction was given; this was sometimes "How many?" and sometimes "Count them" or "Go ahead." The latter two instructions would seem to measure the child's volunteering of the cardinality result rather than the ability to give this result when asked for it. It seems possible that as their experiment continued (the larger set sizes were given later), some children decided that the required task was primarily focused on counting accuracy and such children then just counted and stopped telling the experimenter the results of their count on each trial (i.e., stopped demonstrating the cardinality principle). This tendency might have also been reinforced by the repeated counting given within each set size—each size was given six times.

---

[5] Some of these same arguments are advanced in 7.6.2.2 but are repeated here so that this chapter is self-contained.

The Gelman and Gallistel procedure might than have underestimated the ability of children to use the cardinality principle on the larger sets. Furthermore, as noted by Gelman and Gallistel, repeated questioning on the same set may have convinced children that their counting was in error, and a child therefore might stop giving the counted result, that is, might stop using the cardinality principle. In this case it is not that children usually monitor their counting sufficiently well to know when their counting is in error and thus stop using the cardinality principle (witness the large number of trials in our study and in the Wilkinson study in which children counted inaccurately and still used the cardinality principle). Rather, it may be that when something makes children believe that their counting is wrong (such as having an adult ask them to count the same array over and over), they may then not use the cardinality principle.[6] Finally, even when a how-many question was asked, it was asked only before counting began. This procedure would seem to increase the likelihood that a child might forget that a how-many question had been asked, especially when counting the larger sets. Frye et al. (1986) recently reported that this procedure did result in a signfiicant drop with set size in the use of the cardinality principle, whereas our procedure (asking the question after the counting) showed no effect of set size. This finding and the consistency of our set size data across several studies suggest that the Gelman and Gallistel data and procedure considerably underestimated the ability of their sample to give last-word responses.

10.3. Children's Understandings About Sequence, Correspondence, and Cardinality Aspects of Counting

10.3.1. Understanding Sequence Aspects of Counting

Our results clearly indicate that many children do produce a stable sequence before they produce a correct sequence, or all least, that they produce a stable portion (two or more words) that follows an accurate portion of a sequence. This is consistent with evidence from Gelman and Gallistel (1978) and from Fuson et al. (1982). Furthermore, our data were scored by the strong criterion described by Wagner and Walters (1982). The incorrect stable words had to be the same for smaller sets as for the larger sets (e.g., within the set sizes 16, 18, and 19, the first 16 words said for the row of 16 and the first 18 words said for the row of 18 had to agree with the first 16 and 18 words of the sequence said for 19). Our data reported earlier in this chapter did suffer from the related issue of being gathered in a single session and on a single task, circumstances that one might expect to maximize such stability.

---

[6] We are indebted to Peter Pufall for pointing out this distinction to us in a letter responding to a paper by G. Pergament reporting some of the data in experiment 1.

However, Baroody and Price (1983) and Fuson et al. (1982) reported that the stable portions from some children remained stable over periods ranging up to 10 weeks and 5 months, respectively. More data clearly are needed about the time course of stable portions and about how the stable portions move to becoming accurate. However, the data at this time do clearly indicate that the number-word sequences produced by children have stable incorrect portions that follow the correct portion of the sequence and that these portions are stable for some children across periods of time ranging up to 5 months.

What can one conclude about children's understanding of the sequence aspect of counting from this knowledge of the kinds of sequences children actually produce? Several kinds of evidence indicate that, at least by age 3 and earlier for some children, children understand that when counting they must use *the special list of counting words*, that is, the accurate conventional sequence. This conclusion differs from the interpretation of the stable-order principle as indicating knowing that counting must use *any* stably ordered list. First, Saxe, Sadeghpour, and Sicilian (in press) reported that many 3-year-olds and some 4- and 6-year-olds do not accept counting with the alphabet as correct even for a puppet who lives in a country where "people use letters to count" and even after having demonstrated this kind of counting themselves. Thus, children first seem to view the sequence aspect of counting as requiring *the special conventional number-word sequence* and only later do they expand this notion to include other stably ordered lists such as the alphabet.

Second, evidence such as that provided in Gelman and Meck (1983) that children identify errors in the sequence produced by a puppet as counting errors implies that the child understands counting to require the special conventional number-word sequence, not that the child understands that any stably ordered list will do. Children in that study were not given repeated trials of the same unconventional but stably ordered list used over trials. They were given single trials that violated the accurate number-word sequence. Similarly, the evidence in Gelman and Gallistel (1978) and in Gelman and Meck (1983) that children will count objects in nonstandard orders but still use the standard order of number words is evidence that the child will use the correct conventional list in counting, not that they believe that any stably ordered list will do. Furthermore, it is not clear that children consistently even identify errors in the conventional sequence produced by a puppet as counting errors. Saxe et al. (1987) reported that the majority of 4-year-olds and a fourth of the 6-year-olds failed to identify a puppet's counting three objects as "one one two" or as "one three four" as wrong, in contrast to the identification of sequence errors as errors reported by Gelman and Meck (1983).

Third, the nature of the incorrect sequences produced by children suggest that they are trying to produce the special conventional list of counting words but that they have not yet learned to do so. Virtually all of the sequences produced by children aged 3 and older in all of the studies reported in this book, and most of the sequences produced by 2-year-olds, began with an accurate portion from the conventional sequence of number-words. That is, children produced a list that was accurate up to some point. The sequence of English number words is rote up through twelve and at best is irregular between thirteen and twenty. Regardless of whether children learn only the first twelve words by rote and then learn a pattern and exceptions to this pattern up to twenty or learn the first twenty words by rote, this is a difficult learning task. A conceptual "principle" that one is learning the special list of counting words (or even a stably ordered list) offers little specific guidance for the details of this learning. Learning the conventional sequence is a prolonged task, and it is a serial learning task. One might expect imperfectly learned sequences to exhibit exactly the features they do exhibit, that is, a first accurate "learned" portion followed by an imperfectly learned relatively stable portion with omissions that later are filled in with the correct missing words. Why almost all children continue to produce numbers words beyond these stable portions rather than simply saying, "That's all I know" is discussed below.

The evidence that children produce stable incorrect portions is taken by Greeno et al., (1984) and Gelman and Meck (1986) as evidence that a child understands that a sequence must be stably ordered but that the sequence does not have to be correct, i.e., that any stably ordered list will do. But how does this view of a child's understanding (that any stably ordered list will do) apply over the long time during which a child is learning the accurate sequence? First, what is the impetus for a child ever to change his or her sequence? If any stably ordered sequence will do, why do virtually all children continue to learn the standard conventional sequence rather than stick to their stably ordered incorrect sequences? The longitudinal data reported in Fuson et al. (1982) indicate that a stable incorrect portion is filled in over time and that a new stable incorrect portion is formed at the end of the accurate portion of the sequence. Thus, over the course of learning the whole sequence to twenty, a given child produces several different stably ordered sequences. Does the child think at each point that each stably ordered sequence is as good as another? What then would make a given child abandon the old stable sequence for a new one? This pattern seems rather to fit the notion that the child is operating under the long-term goal of learning the conventional sequence, and each stably ordered sequence represents the child's best effort toward that goal at that time.

Fourth, to say that children understand that the counting words *must* be produced in the same stable order over repeated counts (as opposed to saying that they understand that one conventionally does so produce words) and to focus particularly on examples of stable nonstandard sequences as evidence of this understanding seems to us to require children to understand something of cardinality, for it is the cardinal *use* of counting[7] that requires a stable order

---

[7] The ordinal and measure uses of counting also, of course, require a stable order of the list.

of the counting list. But how can children understand, even implicitly, anything about cardinality when they do not even know that the last counted word tells the cardinality of a set? The evidence is quite clear that children produce limited stable sequences long before they can demonstrate the cardinality principle.

These four arguments support the position that children understand at a very young age (by age 2 or 3) that the sequence aspect of counting requires the use of *the special list of counting words*. This list is composed of all the separate number words in the list, and children do come to learn all of these number words. Much of this learning is rote learning (who could predict that the sound "eight" follows the sound "seven"?) and is accomplished according to the laws that govern such learning. However, the list also has certain features that involve conceptual understanding. These features then might be the focus of conceptual competence about this list. What features does this special list possess, and at what ages do children understand each feature? We suggest that up to one hundred this list has several important features and that children come to understand these at varying times. These features are the following:

1. The list is composed of number words.
2. The list is a list (the words are said in one standard order that is stable over repeated productions of the list).
3. Each word in the list is unique (it appears only once in the list).
4. The list has a decade structure between twenty and one hundred.

Above one hundred, the higher level structural features of the list (anticipated by the decade structure) dictate the production of words from the list: the production at this level is certainly determined by these structural features rather than being a rote production of a serial list. However, learning of this later part of the conventional list typically occurs at the school age and is related to the learning of the base-ten place-value system of numeration rather than to counting, that is, number words above one hundred are primarily used to say (read) number symbols rather than to count. We therefore concentrate on the features of the portion of the list only up to one hundred.

Children very early come to understand the first feature, that only number words are used to count, and they are able to make the required differentiation of number from nonnumber words. Very young children who are just beginning to learn the number words and the alphabet may confuse these at first (see the examples for one of my daughters at age 1 year 8 months in Table 1-2). However, this differentiation seems to be made quite early, probably by age 2½ for most children. In all the counting done by the several hundred children aged 2½ to 6 reported in this book, we almost never had children use anything except number words to count, and these few exceptions often occurred when children were "playing around" rather than concentrating. Gelman and Gallistel (1978), Saxe et al. (in press), and Baroody (1986b) also reported very few uses of words other than number words in counting. Thus, children learn very early to separate number words from other words and to use only number words in counting.

As discussed previously here and in chapter 2, the counting of almost all 3-year-olds and of many 2-year-olds exhibits the stable order of the accurate conventional sequence up to a certain length. Because children cannot learn the whole list in one trial, this would seem to be evidence that children understand the second feature: The counting words are a list. There is anecdotal evidence (Baroody, 1987a; Greeno et al., 1984; my own conversations with parents of young children) of some 2-year-olds using consistently a stable portion without a preceding accurate portion, that is, words from the conventional sequence with omissions but not starting with one, e.g., "two, six" or "eight, nine, ten" or "two, seven." Thus, children may show evidence of this second feature before they have learned the initial words in the list. The particular words learned first by a particular child would seem to be a function of serial learning laws (e.g., primacy, recency), the salience and appeal of particular words for a given child, and other factors (e.g., which numbers the child hears on "Sesame Street"). Once a very young child has learned a particular stable portion, refusal to change this list to the conventional list may reflect the more general 2-year-old "declaration of independence" rather than a conviction that their list is as good as the conventional list (i.e., that any stably ordered list will do). The fact that almost all such stable portions of which I have heard consist of words ordered as in the correct conventional sequence (although with omitted words) suggests that these children are trying to learn the conventional sequence rather than trying to produce "any stably ordered list." The explicitness with which children understand that the list is ordered is another matter and is not at all clear.

These conclusions concerning the early understanding of children that they are learning a list are contradicted by a striking aspect of the number-word sequences produced by most children: the frequently large nonstable incorrect final portion that follows the accurate and stable incorrect portions. In this portion, which may consist of more than twenty words (and even more for children whose nonstable portions are in the decades), the words are not produced in a stable order over repeated trials. We have sometimes called these portions a "spew" to characterize this lack of repeated order.[8] Does a child who produces such nonstable final portions lack understanding of the second feature, that the list is a list? One might argue that a child who really understood that the number-words were a list would simply stop counting after reaching the end of his or her stable portion, thus refusing to produce words that were not stably ordered. Although we have very occasionally had such refusals ("I don't know the next words so I can't count those") and Baroody and Price (1983) note such a case in their sample, the willingness of children both when counting objects and when just asked to "count as high as you

---

[8] These portions do have some structure; it is described in chapter 2.

can" to continue counting on and on far past their stable portions has been striking. When children have reached the limits of their current knowledge of the conventional list and are faced with the alternative of stopping or of violating the list feature of counting, most children seem to prefer to continue counting only with the first feature (using number words) rather than to conform to the second feature but stop counting. Thus, for many children up to at least age 5, the understanding of the feature that the counting words are produced in a list governs the production of words early in the list but is readily violated for the production of words later in the list. At what age one wants to judge that a child understands the list feature thus seems doomed to be a source of controversy, at least until other kinds of evidence concerning children's understanding is obtained. Baroody (1986a) also argues that spews violate the stable-order principle only if a child remembers previous spews. However, this is a difficult criterion to satisfy, for if a child remembers previous spews (words beyond the stable portion), one would think that the child would have the capacity to extend the stable portion that much further (i.e., the end of the stable portion is in some ways a measure of the present limits of a child's memory and it is therefore unlikely that the child can remember any spew). For all these reasons, it seems desirable to develop some more direct measure of what part of a sequence produced by a child is thought by the child to be accurate.

The third feature, that each word in the list must be a *unique* word, matters only when the number-word sequence is used for cardinal, ordinal, or measure purposes. That is, it is only the requirement that a given count word not be able to refer to sets with different numbers of objects (or to different positions in an ordering or to different numbers of units of measure) that dictates that each word in the list be unique. Baroody and Price (1983) discussed this requirement of uniqueness and pointed out that one must be sure that a child remembers saying a given number word earlier in the sequence before concluding that a later repetition violates this feature. The analysis of uniqueness is also complicated by the fact that the English number-word sequence does contain some patterns of repeated words, although these repeated words do have additional syllables attached in order to make them unique. For this reason, the repetition later in the sequence of words said earlier might reflect a child's awareness of the repeated pattern but a failure to notice or to have learned the additional differentiating syllables.

The main kind of evidence to date concerning the uniqueness feature comes from analysis of the unstable inaccurate portion of children's number-word sequences, although the error-detection method used by Gelman and Meck (1983) and Briars and Siegler (1984) could be used.[9] Baroody and Price

---

[9] Saxe et al. (1987) used the error-detection method with counts of "one, one, two" and "one, three, four" and reported that about two thirds of their 4-year-olds and one third of their 6-year-olds did not identify both of these as errors, but they did not report data separately for the "one, one, two" (uniqueness) trials.

(1983) concluded from the number-word sequences produced by their sample that some children did not yet appreciate uniqueness. Words were repeated very close to their first occurrence so that memory was unlikely to be a problem. In the number-word sequences we analyzed in Fuson et al. (1982), one fourth of the nonstable incorrect final portions contained repetitions of a word from early in the accurate portion, and one-half contained words from later in the accurate sequence or stable portions. Many of these latter repetitions met the memory criterion used by Baroody and Price because they occurred quite close to their first occurrence. Therefore, it may be that the feature of uniqueness is not understood until age 5 or even later.[10] Finally, of course, the judgment of understanding of the feature of uniqueness based only on the number-word sequences that children produce is subject to the same difficulties discussed previously with respect to the second feature: Children may have some understanding of uniqueness but be willing to violate it quite readily rather than stop counting. Due to all of these difficulties in interpreting the sequences children do produce, direct evidence concerning this feature would certainly be useful. Understanding *why* the words *need* to be unique (as opposed merely to understanding that each word in the number-word sequence *is* unique) would seem to be an even later understanding, for it requires understanding of relations between counting and cardinality.

The sequences children produce begin to show evidence of understanding the fourth feature, the decade structure, sometime between age 4½ and 6 (Fuson et al., 1982; Siegler & Robinson, 1982). The sequences for most children show an x-ty, x-ty one, x-ty two....x-ty nine repeated pattern during this age range. It does then take children a long time to solve the decade problem, that is, to learn to generate all of the correct x-ty to x-ty-nine chunks, and the sequences produced by most children while they are learning the correct sequence of decades do violate the list and the uniqueness features. Children will continue counting on and on, producing x-ty to x-ty-nine chunks in different orders over repeated trials and repeating such chunks within a given trial. However, these repetitions clearly show evidence of understanding the repetitive x-ty to x-ty-nine pattern of the English number-word sequence between twenty and one hundred.

10.3.2. Understanding Correspondence Aspects of Counting

The activity of counting a group of simultaneously present objects is more complex than is implied by the definition of the one-one principle ("every item in a set must be assigned a unique tag" Gelman and Meck, 1986, p. 30).

---

[10] As with many aspects of number, this uniqueness feature may be appreciated earlier for very small numbers. An example is in Table 1-2 for my daughter at age 3 years 6 months: You were counting pictures [and] got to twenty. I said, "Twenty-one, twenty two." You said, "No this one [pointing to the second picture] was two." This example also displays a confusion between words with and without differentiating syllables (two and twenty-two).

The one-one principle focuses on the one-to-one correspondence between words and counted objects. The focus on this correspondence ignores the fact that words exist in time and objects exist in space. Consequently, some act having both temporal and spatial components is required to create the word–object correspondence. We have termed such acts "indicating acts" and have discussed several different indicating acts in chapters 3 through 6 (e.g., pointing with a finger, eye fixation, moving objects). Counting therefore needs to be considered as not just involving a correspondence between words and objects but rather as involving two correspondences: the temporal correspondence between an indicating act and a spoken number word and the spatial correspondence between an object and an indicating act.

Within the temporal and the spatial correspondences, several different kinds of errors are made by children. The evidence from chapters 3 through 6 is quite clear that these different errors show different patterns of decrease with age. Consequently, there is not really a single "one-one" principle but rather many different aspects of creating one-to-one correspondence that must be learned and practiced. These different kinds of correspondence errors would seem to constitute the features of the correspondence aspect of counting that children must come to understand. Even if this assumption of many different kinds of knowledge is implicit in the term "the one-one principle," the term itself is misleading with respect to this assumption as well as to the nature of the two (temporal and spatial) correspondences that must be established in counting. Research concerning conceptual understanding of correspondence needs to differentiate children's knowledge about different kinds of correspondence errors rather than pooling all understanding into a single measure of "understanding of correspondence."

Such differentiation of specific kinds of correspondence errors is especially important because there is some evidence that the relationship between conceptual knowledge and procedural knowledge (i.e., between what children know about various aspects of one-to-one correspondence and the extent to which children's counting displays these aspects of one-to-one correspondence) may vary with the type of correspondence error. Some attempts have been made to measure directly what children understand about one-to-one correspondence rather than merely inferring conceptual knowledge from observations of use of one-to-one correspondence in counting (Briars & Seigler, 1984; Frye et al., 1986; Gelman & Meck, 1983). The results of these studies combined with our studies on children's correspondence errors in counting reported in chapters 3 through 6 indicate that, for some kinds of counting errors, conceptual and procedural knowledge seem to develop differently. For example, children know that skipping objects is an error at ages when they continue to make such errors, but their own number of errors of omission (such as pointing without saying a word) decreases at an age at which they say that such behavior is not a counting error (our studies in chapters 3 through 6; Briars & Seigler, 1984; Frye et al., 1986; and personal communication about these last data, Frye, January 21, 1987). Thus, counting behavior (procedural knowledge) seems sometimes to reflect conceptual knowledge and sometimes not to do so (see Baroody and Ginsburg, 1986, for a similar conclusion about aspects of young children's arithmetic). Therefore, there may not exist a single relationship between principles and skill (between conceptual competence and procedural competence) that applies to all types of correspondence errors. Of course, generalizing across different studies in this way may be problematic. It therefore seems important that research concerned with children's conceptual understanding include separate measures of conceptual and of procedural knowledge for each aspect of one-to-one correspondence that is of interest.[11]

There may also be limitations of error-detection tasks in measuring children's conceptual competence about correspondence. Error detection tasks measure the ability to detect and remember errors as well as measuring underlying knowledge about whether or not detected errors are actually errors. Variables such as set size and location of the error thus would seem to affect performance. For example, Briars and Siegler (1984) found that children identified fewer errors at the beginning and middle than at the end of an array. Different kinds of errors may also vary in the ease with which they are detected. Furthermore, such studies require a very high level of attention, for a momentary lapse might occur just at an error. Present studies using error detection report a range of different results even for the simple cases in which an object is counted twice or is skipped over without being counted (Briars & Siegler, 1984; Frye et al., 1986; Gelman & Meck, 1983; Saxe et al., 1987). These results range from Gelman and Meck, where even 3-year-olds detected such errors on 75% of the trials for sets of 6 and 12 objects to Saxe et al., where two thirds of the 4-year-olds and a fifth of the 6-year-olds did not identify all such counts as errors for sets of 3 items (the double-count occurred on a set of 2 and the object skipped on a set of 4). Difficulties of memory or of detection seem to be ruled out by the very small sets used in the Saxe et al. study, suggesting that there may even be other variables that affect results in these studies.

An adaptation of the error detection task that might be more involving to children and might produce more verbalizations and observable behavior about correspondences is to ask children to teach the experimenter (or a puppet or another child) to count. Such a request might produce verbal descriptions of counting as well as demonstrations of it. Within this teaching context, the puppet might also make certain kinds of correspondence errors to see if the child will correct them. This latter step is of course subject to the problems with an ordinary error detection task, but the teaching context might produce more attention and investment by the child. A second possible

---

[11] Briars and Seigler (1984) gathered both kinds of data, but they did not compare the kinds of correspondence errors children made when counting to the children's judgments of such errors as being errors. The counting of much of their sample was fairly accurate, so such an analysis might have been limited by ceiling effects with respect to specific kinds of correspondence errors.

method to assess conceptual competence about various aspects of one-to-one correspondence stems from one of the stated functions of principles (of conceptual competence): to guide children's practice (Gelman & Meck, 1986). This suggests comparing a condition involving a considerable amount of practice with a condition using direct instruction by an experimenter about the various aspects of correspondence. If children have adequate conceptual understanding of correspondence, such practice should reduce errors. If children lack understanding of some kinds of correspondence errors, direct instruction may enable them to reduce errors. Of course it is always possible that some correspondence errors result from age-related or individual motor organizational difficulties, and neither practice alone nor instruction will reduce such errors. In doing such a study, one would have to control children's effort when counting for all error assessments, for effort has a very considerable effect on counting correspondence errors (see chapter 3).

One aspect of the one-one principle as it is defined seems to belong to the sequence aspect of counting rather than to the correspondence aspect of counting. The one-one principle is identified as requiring knowledge that each object is assigned a *distinct* or *unique* word (e.g., Gelman & Gallistel, 1978, p. 113; Gelman & Meck, 1986, p. 30). However, as discussed in 10.3.1, it is the nature of the sequence that is produced that determines whether each word is unique or whether a word is used more than once. Therefore, it seems clearer to confine knowledge about correspondence to knowledge that each object receives a *single* (rather than a unique or distinct) number word.

The "abstraction principle" (the item-indifference principle in Gelman & Meck, 1986) was identified by Gelman and Gallistel (1978) as one of the five counting principles. It has been the "step-child" principle, receiving relatively little attention compared to the other four counting principles. However, it focuses on a crucial aspect of correspondence: to what kind of objects are words made to correspond? Gelman and Gallistel argued persuasively that young children count heterogeneous as well as homogeneous arrays. We found (chapter 5) that heterogeneity of color and objects affected the particular types of correspondence errors made by children but did not affect the overall accuracy level. Children also never were reluctant to count heterogeneous arrays. Thus, children seem willing to designate a range of different kinds of objects as things-to-be-counted within the same count.

The abstraction principle also relates to a crucial distinction made by Steffe et al. (1983) and adopted in this book. Counting requires a unitizing of the things-to-be-counted in which differences between things are ignored and each thing is taken as an equivalent unit. Steffe et al. specify a developmental progression in the conceptual units used by children in counting; we have described an adaptation and extension of this progression in chapter 8 for children aged 4 to 8 that extends through addition and subtraction of large numbers. The first kind of conceptual unit, and the kind used in counting a single set of entities, is a "perceptual unit item." This term is used because counting at this level requires the physical presence of entities. Thus, the abstraction principle might be stated as the willingness to take a whole range of different physical entities as the basis for perceptual unit items in counting. Correspondence thus does not actually involve correspondences among words, points, and objects; rather it involves correspondences among words, points, and perceptual unit items children construct from objects.

It is difficult to say exactly when a child is using perceptual unit items during counting; it is easier to decide when a child is not using them. Very young children, and sometimes older children who are not trying hard, count by directing some points generally at a set of entities and saying some words. The goal seems to be to "do some counting" (i.e., point and say number words) rather than to "count those entities." For very young children such "counting" may involve only a few words and points, no matter how many entities there are. Three-year-olds may rapidly direct a large number of words and points at a set of entities; we called such counting a "flurry" in chapters 3 through 6. We did not observe such flurries in children older than 3, and all 3-year-olds also counted by pointing at particular entities (i.e., used perceptual unit items) when asked to be very careful or to try really hard. Thus, children do seem to use perceptual unit items by age 3, that is, they take individual entities as separate equivalent "countable" units and direct indicating acts (usually points) at these units.

10.3.3. Understanding Cardinality Aspects of Counting

The lack of an effect of set size on use of the cardinality principle and the consistency of children's cardinality principle responses across trials clearly seems to qualify for the label "principle." Whether responding to a how-many question with the last word said in counting ought to qualify for the label "cardinality" principle is another matter discussed at some length in chapter 7. There we point out that in previous assessments of the cardinality principle, no evidence was obtained concerning whether the child understood that the last counted word refers either to the whole set or to the cardinality of that set. To the contrary, evidence of various kinds is reported in chapter 7 to indicate that, for many children, such a last-word response is in fact not a reference to cardinality. Therefore, the choice of the term "cardinality" principle does not seem wise. We much prefer the use of the potentially less misleading term "last-word responding" or "last-word rule" when there is no evidence beyond giving the last word as the response to a how-many question. When there is evidence of the cardinal reference of the last counted word, the term "cardinality principle" then does seem appropriate. We conclude from the evidence in chapter 7 that the first relationship between counting and cardinality constructed by some children may be a cardinality principle but that for many children the first such relationship is only a last-word rule in which the last word does not have a cardinal reference. However, even the latter is an important step, for it is the first indication of understanding that counting has a purpose beyond itself. It signals an important new outward orientation of the counting child, an orientation that can help the child become sensitive to the many uses of counting in constructing numerical concepts.

Some data reported in chapter 7 suggest that, for very early last-word knowledge, the activity of counting may itself interfere with the ability to demonstrate last-word knowledge. Some children were able to recall the last counted word when the experimenter counted but not when they counted, and some other children who were given brief instruction on last-word responding were able to give last-word responses (answer the how-many question with the last counted word) when the experimenter counted but not when they counted.

The fifth counting principle identified by Gelman and Gallistel (1978) is the "order irrelevance" principle: "the order in which items are tagged is irrelevant" (Gelman & Meck, 1986, p. 30). This principle only applies in cardinal or in measure situations, for the units in these situations can be counted in any order. In an ordinal situation counting must follow the linear ordering in that situation. Gelman et al. (1986) reported interesting data concerning children's ability to give a particular entity a designated count word (e.g., "Make that one the three"). However, it is not so clear why this order irrelevance relationship between counting and cardinality should be singled out. Children come to understand many different aspects of relationships between counting and cardinality. A considerable part of this book is devoted to articulating and providing data on what children must come to understand about cardinality aspects of counting. Chapter 7 focuses on early relationships between counting and cardinality, chapter 8 covers the later relationships between counting and cardinality required by the operations of addition and subtraction on whole numbers (these are summarized in Table 8-4), and chapter 9 reviews the understandings required by the use of counting in establishing equivalence and order relations on cardinal numbers (these are summarized in Table 9-11). Several of the last understandings are fairly similar to the order irrelevance principle. Many of these relationships between counting and cardinality involve inductive generalizations for which the term "principle" also seems appropriate. There therefore does not seem to be anything particular to distinguish this fifth counting principle from several other kinds of count-cardinal conceptual competence. There could well then be four or six or ten counting principles.

10.3.4. Principles About Principles

Is the term *principle* useful in considering children's growing knowledge about and skill at counting in cardinal situations? The three how-to-count principles describe very different kinds of knowledge and are related to skilled performance in different ways. The stable-order principle and the one-

one principles seem to function almost as definitions of accurate counting[12] rather than as understandings about counting. They also each require a considerable amount of detailed specific knowledge (the number-word sequence) or a considerable amount of skilled motor activity (and, depending on the situation, the ability to carry out effectively some strategy for remembering which entities have been counted—see chapters 4 and 6). Thus, these principles have two kinds of problems. They are both trivially true (impossible to invalidate) and provide impossibly high standards for actual behavior. Because these principles define crucial aspects of counting, the issue of whether children "have" these principles is trivial at some level because children *must* have *some* kind of implicit understanding of these aspects of counting in order to attempt to carry out counting activity. Because these principles define *accurate* counting, one cannot possibly expect *new* counters to satisfy these definitions. So these principles give both too little and too stringent guidance for determining whether children "have" the principles, making controversy almost inevitable. The cardinality principle is different. It clearly seems to be a principle. It refers to a relationship children make between one aspect of counting activity (the last counted word) and some other aspect of the situation (the how-many question or the whole set of entities). It is more like the principle about paints enunciated at age 3 years 10 months by my daughter (see Table 1-2): "White and yellow make light yellow. [pause] White makes any color light."

The abstraction and order irrelevance principles are still different kinds of principles; they are descriptions of what and of how children will count. In Gelman and Gallistel (1978) the term "principle" was also applied to three kinds of numerical reasoning principles: principles of relations, operations, and reversibility. These certainly are central aspects of numerical concepts that young children must and do come to understand, and the basic thesis there that young children's numerical reasoning principles operate on specific numerosities is one supported by the data and discussions here in chapters 7, 8, and 9. However, the use of the term *principles* for all of these quite various kinds of concepts and relationships among concepts does not seem helpful. The range of exemplars of a principle is too large to permit focused discussion.

These difficulties then may have led to the particular way the principles were used in the model of counting developed by Greeno et al. (1984), a model supposedly based on these principles:

> A third result involves the way in which formal principles correspond to the schemata that we have developed to represent implicit understanding of the principles. We did not formulate a schema for understanding of order, another schema for one-to-one correspondence, and so on. Instead, it seemed more reasonable to

---

[12] We are assuming here that the stable-order principle really reflects the child's understanding that the conventional list of number words is required in counting.

hypothesize schemata that represent different aspects of the various principles, and often include aspects of different principles. If our analysis is accepted, then competence for each of the principles is distributed among several schemata, rather than being located in any single structure. This emphasizes that a child should not be considered as either having or not having competence regarding any of the principles, since it clearly is possible for the child to have developed some aspects of the competence and not others. (p. 137)

Thus, Greeno et al. seem to have been unable to use each principle to generate separate nonoverlapping elements of conceptual understanding. Rather the 12 schemata of conceptual competence they use in their model relate to the original principles in compex ways. Of what use then are the principles? Why has not the effort at specifying the conceptual competence involved in counting moved to the level of the 12 model schemata or to other schemata? Do children really "have" those 12 schemata or do they "have" different schemata? If "a child should not be considered as either having or not having competence regarding any of the principles," how can we answer questions concerning whether the counting of young children adheres to these five principles, including assertions that the five original (Gelman and Gallistel, 1978) principles function as the "initial competence children bring to the task of acquiring skill at counting" (Gelman and Meck, 1986, p. 31)? And if "a child should not be considered as either having or not having competence regarding any of the principles," why should we not abandon the principles and instead move on to considering directly the separable and measurable aspects of this conceptual competence? In particular the distinction among conceptual competence, procedural competence, and utilizational competence (Greeno et al., 1984) seems to apply to the sequence, correspondence, and cardinal aspects of counting and thus might be used instead of the principles.

In the discussions of understanding within the sequence, correspondence, and cardinality aspects of counting (in 10.3.1, 10.3.2, and 10.3.3), problems were identified in concluding that the specific five counting principles originally identified by Gelman and Gallistel (1978) function as the "initial competence children bring to the task of acquiring skill at counting" (Gelman & Meck, 1986). However, we think it is fruitless to suggest any alternative set of understandings as children's initial conceptual competence and oversimplistic to adopt a general principle before skill[13] or skill before principle position (or even a modified "some-principles-first" view, Gelman and Meck, 1986, p. 40). It seems likely that there is an almost constant interaction between children's conceptual competence and their procedural competence. If this is so, choosing the moment of "initial competence" seems quite problematic. It also seems likely that there are individual differences in young children and in the experiences they have when counting that may differentially emphasize conceptual or procedural competence. For example, children may vary in the

---

[13] This distinction might also be called meaningful versus rote or conceptual versus procedural competence.

extent to which they reflect on their counting activity and perhaps in the extent they even are able to reflect on this activity if provoked to do so. Parents and siblings would seem to differ considerably in the extent to which they explain certain aspects of counting (leading to differing amounts of conceptual understanding) and also differ in the criterion for acceptable counting behavior (leading to different levels of counting proficiency). For these reasons, then, there may not even be a single relationship between conceptual and procedural competence that applies to all children.

From the discussion of the various understandings involved in each of the sequence, correspondence, and cardinality aspects of counting, it is clear that ascertaining the relationships between conceptual and procedural competence even within one of these aspects is a difficult problem and that ascertaining how these relationships relate to each other across the different aspects of counting is dauntingly complex. It may then be more useful to concentrate energies in attempting instead to understand any possible *sequences within* conceptual or within procedural competence, for these can guide attempts to provide home and preschool environments that can support children's competence in counting and in cardinality. This position is consistent with Case's developmental theory of instruction (Case, 1985a, 1985b). It is for this reason that this book focuses so much on developmental progressions in children's conceptual and procedural competence in counting.

10.4. Summary

The relationship among the sequence, correspondence, and cardinality aspects of counting is crucially affected by the fact that set size differentially affects the task difficulty of each of these aspects of counting. For both the sequence and one-to-one correspondence aspects, counting larger sets is a more difficult task. For the sequence this is because larger sets require that one knows more words and many of these words must just be learned by rote. For correspondence, it is because larger sets require a higher criterion of accuracy in order for one-to-one correspondence to be demonstrated, that is, there are more chances to make a correspondence error on large than on small sets. The cardinality principle (last-word responding) only has to be demonstrated once for each set, no matter how large, and no special new knowledge is required. Some temporary effects of very large set sizes on last-word responding may be felt on the first (but not on a second) attempt at that set size. Number-words that sound alike (like the twenties) may make it a bit more difficult to differentiate the last word actually said when counting, and it may be somewhat more difficult to remember that one is supposed to answer a how-many question after counting a large than a small set. Aside from this temporary effect, set size has no effect on last-word responding.

The relationship among these aspects (among children's adherence to the

three how-to-count principles) was found to differ considerably from that reported by Gelman and Gallistel (1978): that children adhere to the sequence,
then to the correspondence, and last to the cardinality aspects of counting.
We found that for very small sets (2, 3, and 4), counting does adhere to the
stable-order and one-one principles before it adheres to the cardinality principle. For slightly larger sets (4 through 7), this order of principles remains
true for some children. For these sets children display the stable-order and
one-one but not the cardinality principle. However, just as many children
display the stable-order and the cardinality principle but not the one-one
principle. That is, within this set size range, adherence to the one-one and to
the cardinality principle are independent. For sets between about 7 and 16,
the principles seem to be ordered (from most to least frequently displayed):
stable-order, cardinality, and one-one. For sets above 16 adherence to the
principles seem to be ordered: cardinality, stable-order, and one-one. Of
course, these set sizes are approximate, and performance depends on age as
well as on set size. These relationships also only concern linear arrays. The
data on counting correspondence errors in chapter 4 indicate that counting
conforming to the one-one principle would drop considerably for objects
arranged in random arrays, and thus, this principle might be the last to be
demonstrated for even smaller set sizes on such arrays. An analysis of the
procedure followed by Gelman and Gallistel and recent data reported by Frye
et al. (1986) indicate that the Gelman and Gallistel procedure underestimated
the ability of children to use the cardinality principle and therefore produced
an inaccurate account of the developmental relationships among these aspects
of counting.

Within the sequence, correspondence, and cardinal parts of counting,
several aspects of conceptual understanding were identified in this chapter.
Children come quite early to understand that counting requires the use of the
special list of counting words. Features of this list (up to one hundred) that
children come to identify and conform to are that the list is composed of
number words, that it is a list (has a standard order), that each word in the list
is unique, and that the list has a decade structure between twenty and one
hundred. The two basic correspondences in counting (word-point and point-
object) create many different kinds of correspondence errors (see chapter 3),
and children can have conceptual as well as procedural competence about
these various kinds of errors. Some evidence suggests that the relationship
between conceptual and procedural competence may vary with the type of
correspondence error. Possible difficulties with error detection as a method
of measuring conceptual competence about correspondence were identified,
and two other possibilities were described. The importance of the focus of the
Gelman and Gallistel abstraction principle, what it is that a child will take as a
countable item, was discussed and related to the use of perceptual unit items
(Steffe et al., 1983). By age 3, most children do seem to be able to take many
different kinds of entities as separate equivalent "countable" units. The consistency of last-word responding seems to qualify for the term "principle" but

the use of the term "cardinality" principle was questioned. As discussed in chapter 7, there is considerable evidence to indicate that last-word responding for many children does not imply understanding of the reference of the last counted word to the set as a whole or to the cardinality of the set. Nevertheless, even last-word responding without this understanding of cardinality is a noteworthy advance, for it indicates awareness that counting has a use beyond itself. The order irrelevance principle (Gelman & Gallistel, 1978; Gelman & Meck, 1983; Gelman et al., 1986) is one of several understandings about relationships between counting and cardinality[14] that young children must come to understand; other related understandings pertaining to the conservation of the counting result under different forms of counting are discussed in chapter 9 (see especially Table 9-11).

The broad range of cases to which the term "principle" has been applied was pointed out, and the usefulness of this term was questioned. It was concluded that the later distinction (Greeno et al., 1984) among conceptual, procedural, and utilizational competence is a more fruitful one. The possibility of individual differences in abilities and experiences that would affect relationships between conceptual and procedural competence was discussed, and it was suggested that a single relationship between conceptual and procedural competence may not exist for all children, even within one aspect of counting.

It seems appropriate to close this chapter on children's sequence, correspondence, and cardinality aspects of counting with the observation that the single most striking attribute of the data about children's counting and concepts of number reported in this book is the really amazing level of competence young children display. Counting is a very complex activity, but most children by age 4½ can count quite long rows of objects quite accurately if they are trying hard (see chapter 6). Children age 4½ also begin to use counting to carry out operations and to establish relations on cardinal situations. There is still much to learn after this age concerning the uses of counting in cardinal, ordinal, and measure situations, but counting activity itself shows a quite high level of mastery by age 4½. Our conclusion then is similar to the position presented in Gelman and Gallistel (1978) and defended vigorously since then: The counting of preschool children demonstrates considerable competence.

---

[14] The order-irrelevance principle does not apply in ordinal situations, for the counting there must follow the established linear ordering on the situation.

11. An Overview of Changes in Children's Number Word Concepts From Age 2 Through 8

Young children's early experiences with number words occur in many different specific situations. These situations fall into seven mathematically different kinds of situations: cardinal, measure, ordinal, counting, sequence, symbolic (numeral), and nonnumerical situations. These uses are described in chapter 1. In English the same number words are used for six of these kinds of situations. For ordinal situations, special ordinal modifications of these number words are used; most of these ordinal number words sound quite similar to the standard numbers words (having *th* on the end). Because the words are identical for most situations, and similar even in ordinal situations, it is fairly easy to relate uses of the same number word across these mathematically different situations. However, very young children show little understanding of any such relationships. Their initial uses of number words are confined to use within a given kind of situation. A major aspect of the learning that occurs throughout the period from age 2 through 8 concerns the increasingly complex relationships between different kinds of situations.

The separate situations and some relationships between various pairs of situations are sketched in Figure 11-1. Each kind of situation has very many specific entries, which are probably organized into semantic networks of various kinds. The situations in Figure 11-1 contain only a few suggestive entries (some taken from the diary entries in Tables 1-2 and 1-3). Addition and subtraction operations can be carried out in cardinal, measure, and sequence situations; these are placed in an inverted triangle within each of these situations. Equivalence and order relations can be established on cardinal, measure, sequence, and ordinal situations; these are placed in a square

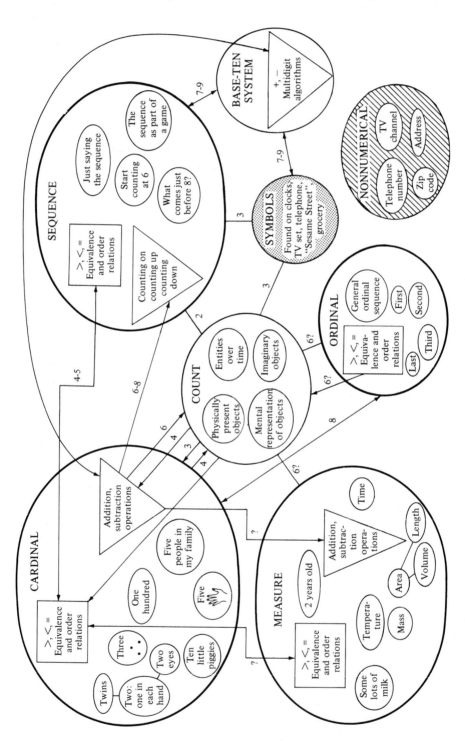

Figure 11-1. A partial mental map of a young child's early experiences with number words.

within each situation. Arrows connect various situations. Approximate ages in years have been entered for these relationships, but these ages of course depend very heavily on the size of the numbers involved. The ages entered are for the more general cases of number words larger than five (but not necessarily larger than ten). There is considerable variability in the amount of data to support each entry. Those for which there are practically no data have a question mark placed after them. The relationships between counting and cardinal situations were discussed in chapters 7 through 9, between cardinal and sequence situations in chapters 8 and 9, and those between cardinal and ordinal situations are briefly discussed in this chapter.

Figure 11-1 captures one major aspect of learning in the period from age 2 through 8: the increasing number of relationships between different kinds of situations. Another major aspect of learning during this period that is not reflected in the figure is the very considerable increase in knowledge about different specific situations within each kind of situation. Portraying this would require successive versions of Figure 11-1 over different ages. These versions would show increasing numbers of entries within each kind of situation and changing networks of relationships within each kind of situation. These versions of Figure 11-1 would also seem to vary quite considerably for different children. The entries would be determined by the specific experiences of individual children, which could be quite different. For example, some children might live in an environment containing many different number symbols that would be labeled for the child. An older sibling might teach a given child addition at a young age. One preschool might have the children doing a lot of counting and saying the number-word sequence, while another might do practically nothing in these areas. Thus, it does not seem likely that one could develop a single series of figures like Figure 11-1 that would apply to all children.

A second major aspect of learning over the age span 2 through 8 that is not reflected in general in Figure 11-1 is that larger and larger number words are learned over this age span. This learning is discussed in chapters 2 and 10. One ultimate outcome of this learning that is reflected in Figure 11-1 is a new later mathematical situation: the base-ten system of numeration. This system has obvious links to symbol, sequence, and cardinal situations and is discussed in chapter 8. Some research indicates that addition and subtraction of multidigit numbers and some concepts of place-value and of base-ten numeration are within the understanding of second graders of all ability levels if they are taught the multidigit algorithms with materials that physically embody the base-ten system (Fuson, 1986a, 1987). Other more advanced concepts within this base-ten domain are the English names for very large numbers, exponents, and scientific notation.

Figure 11-1 includes only uses of whole numbers. Other numerical domains—decimals less than one, integers, rational numbers—also come to be learned in the middle and later elementary school years. However, learning about these different kinds of numbers may suffer from a problem that is the opposite of the young child's problem of nonexistent or inadequate connections among different number-word situations. These domains seem to suffer from being too closely connected to the cardinal numbers, that is, from inadequate differentiation from the cardinal numbers. Thus, for example, many children think that ⅙ is smaller than ⅐ because 6 is smaller than 7 or that .2 × 3 should be bigger than 3 because 2 × 3 is bigger than 3. This problem probably stems from at least two sources: simple interference from the very well-learned relations and operations on cardinal numbers and an inadequate experiential basis for the decimal, integer, and rational number domains. Certain aspects of the measure number domain may also suffer from the latter deficiency. School mathematics instruction in this country for these domains typically involves verbal instruction about the correct manipulation of symbols for the domain. This poverty of concrete experiences that could provide meaning to the basic numerical constructs and to the order/equivalence relations and operations on these numbers is in sharp contrast to the richness of the experiences young children have with cardinal numbers.

A third major aspect of learning over the age span from 2 through 8 years that is not reflected adequately in Figure 11-1 is the nature of the changes in children's conceptual structures over this period. These changes underlie many of the relationships given by arrows in Figure 11-1. This book concentrates on such changes in three situations: the cardinal, counting and sequence situations. These conceptual changes are summarized in Table 11-1. The changes in conceptual structures for the sequence are discussed in chapters 2 and 8 and those for counting and cardinal situations in chapters 7 through 9 (see those chapters for any clarification required for this necessarily brief overview).

The sequence moves from an initial *string* state, in which number words may not even be differentiated into separate words (no word units may exist), to an *unbreakable list* of number words, in which words are differentiated but the sequence must always be said beginning with *one*. The counting situation[1] moves from some number words and points being directed vaguely at entities to one in which the counter "sees" a counting situation as consisting of equivalent "countable" entities, of perceptual unit items (Steffe et al., 1983). At this time it is possible to establish a one-to-one correspondence between the perceptual unit items and the sequence words. This is done by the use of an indicating act (such as pointing) that simultaneously creates a temporal word-point correspondence and a spatial point-entity correspondence (see chapters 3 through 6).

At first, counting situations are only counting situations; counting is done only for itself. However, sometime during age 3 (for most children) children

---

[1] Because there are so few data concerning children's counting of entities distributed over time, this book concerns only counting of entities distributed in space and all existing at the same time.

answer the question "How many entities are there?" with the last counted word (see chapter 7 for a discussion of how and why this occurs). Some children at this time also seem to be able to make a cardinal integration of the counted entities and make a count-to-cardinal transition in which the last counted word takes on a cardinal meaning as the manyness of the cardinal set of entities. For others, this step seems to take some further time. Once a child has reached this level, however, counting can be used for cardinal addition and subtraction operations.

The next conceptual level within the sequence is that of a *breakable chain* in which a child can begin saying the sequence at any word. In counting and cardinal situations, perceptual unit items become capable of simultaneously representing a sum and an addend embedded within that sum. The cardinal conceptual operation of embedded integration allows a child to integrate these simultaneous perceptual unit items into the embedded sum situations shown in Table 11-1. This sequence ability combined with the simultaneous perceptual unit items allows children to carry out new, more efficient solution procedures in addition and subtraction situations: counting on, counting up, and counting down with entities. To count on for 8 + 6, for example, one would represent the 6 by some entities, begin the counting with 8, and continue counting the representation of 6 (thus counting on six more words: "eight, nine, ten, eleven, twelve, thirteen, fourteen").

At the next level the sequence, counting, and cardinal situations become more closely related. The sequence becomes a *numerable chain* in which the number words themselves form the cardinal addition and subtraction situations. The number words can be used as sequence unit items in counting and can simultaneously represent the sum and the addends embedded within the sum. Sequence versions of counting on, counting up, and counting down become possible in which some method of keeping track of the second addend is used instead of the second addend being represented by entities. These keeping-track methods usually involve matching or double counting the sequence units items for the second addend. This requires a paired integration of the sequence second addend words and the representation of the second addend by the keeping-track method. The sequence unit items provide a very flexible means of representing and solving many different kinds of addition and subtraction situations. Children first learn forward-sequence counting solution procedures and then learn backward-counting situation procedures (the counting down procedures: see chapter 8).

Finally, the sequence becomes a *bidirectional chain* in which the forward- and backward-counting solution procedures are related to each other. Over the previous levels the unit items required to represent a cardinal situation have become increasingly abstract and decreasingly have required physically present entities. At this new level no entities are required for a cardinal situation. A given specific cardinal number has now itself become "concrete" to a child. The child can conceptually operate on and relate specific cardinal numbers. When necessary, cardinal situations can be represented by ideal

Table 11-1. Developmental Levels in Sequence, Counting, and Cardinal Conceptual Structures

Sequence structure	Counting and cardinal conceptual units	Cardinal conceptual structures	Cardinal conceptual operation	Cardinal relations
String No units				
Unbreakable list Separate words; start from one	Perceptual unit items Single representation addend *or* sum			
Unbreakable list Separate words; start from one	Perceptual unit items Single representation addend *or* sum		Cardinal integration	
Breakable chain Separate words; start anywhere	Perceptual unit items Simultaneous representation addend *within* sum		Embedded integration	Count equivalence ⇒ Cardinal equivalence Count >, < ⇒ Cardinal >, <

Numerable chain Sequence unit items			
Sequence unit items Simultaneous representation addend *within* sum		Embedded integration	Inductive generalization about displacement transformations Deductive generalization about displacement transformations
Bidirectional chain Cardinal numbers Can be decomposed into ideal unit items[a]		Numerical equivalence	Truly numerical counting

[a] At this level a child may still solve a problem using an object or sequence procedure, but the procedure will not necessarily directly model the problem representation.

Note. In the cardinal conceptual structures, a dotted line represents the unknown set and a solid line represents a known set. PI is paired integrations: the pairing of the embedded integration of the second addend with the integration of the keeping-track method for that addend.

unit items, that is, by abstract identical iterable *ones*. However, cardinal addition and subtraction situations can now be represented by a triplet of three cardinal numbers (e.g., 8, 6, 14) related to each other by cardinal equivalence (Table 11-1). This triplet relationship entails both an addition (addend + addend = sum) and a subtraction (sum − addend = addend). Thus, at this level a child first has a representation of, a meaning for, a cardinal number without having to represent it by a set of perceptually apprehendable entities.

Children's understanding of equivalence and order relations on cardinal situations also goes through a developmental sequence that is described in chapter 9. Evidence is fairly clear about the first part of this sequence, but the later parts of it are much more tentative. This developmental sequence is given in the right-hand column of Table 11-1. Children come to understand a "count equivalence imples cardinal equivalence" rule, namely: if two cardinal situations yield the same count word, then they have the same number of entities. A bit later children become able to use counting to establish an order relation on two cardinal situations.[2] With numbers below ten, children may know order relations directly for pairs of cardinal words. For larger number words, the order relations on the cardinal situation are derived from the sequence order relations (if a word is later in the sequence, it represents the larger cardinal situation). Children also use matching in cardinal equivalence situations. Considerable experience with counting or matching in cardinal equivalence situations may then lead to the inductive generalization that a displacement transformation (one in which entities are merely moved around in space) on one cardinal situation does not affect any cardinal equivalence or order relation on that situation. Children in the Piagetian conservation of number task may then immediately respond correctly and give justifications that refer to the irrelevance of the transformation or to the type of transformation (one not involving addition or subtraction). Later, considerable experience with simultaneous perceptual unit items in addition and subtraction situations may allow a child to deduce (rather than induce) conservation by mentally "following" matched or counted perceptual unit items through the transformation and "seeing" that the end state is composed of the identical unit items that constituted the initial state; this deduction would be justified by a logically necessary operational reversibility. A related ability to represent two aspects of the situation would lead to the use of the compensation justification. Finally, a fourth postconservation stage of truly numerical counting occurs in which a child's number-word sequence is unitized, embedded, seriated, and cardinalized (see following).

The developmental levels within the sequence are quite clear and fairly well supported by data (see chapter 2). Most of the levels for the count and

---

[2] Knowledge of these equivalence and order rules is displayed considerably later in situations in which length of an array is misleading than in those in which length cues are consistent with number.

cardinal situations and for the relationships between the count and cardinal situations are also fairly clear and well supported (see chapters 7 and 8). However, the relationship between the two sequences of levels is not so clear. In general the sequence conceptual levels are required by the counting and cardinal levels, and so they occur earlier than the counting or cardinal levels in which they are used. The relationships between children's understanding of cardinal equivalence and order relations (the right-most column in Table 11-1) and their understanding of cardinal addition and subtraction operations are not at all clear at present. One possibility is the way in which these levels relate to each other in Table 11-1. However, the deduction using simultaneous perceptual unit items may occur earlier than the sequence unit item level, and some aspects of truly numerical counting may occur with sequence unit items (see the following discussion).

Table 11-1 provides some sense of the changes that occur in children's conceptualizations of sequence, counting, and cardinal situations. However, it does not demonstrate one major aspect of these changes: that the representation of the sequence changes over this period so that sequence, counting, and cardinal meanings become integrated within the sequence itself. Figure 11-2 displays major aspects of this increasing integration. At the string level the sequence is not related to any other situation. At the unbreakable list level, the sequence is used in counting, and one-to-one correspondences can be established with perceptual unit items "seen" by the counter in the counting situation. Later in the unbreakable list level, the conceptual operation of cardinal integration enables a counter to make a count-to-cardinal transition from the count meaning of the last counted word as paired with the last counted entity to the cardinal meaning of the word as describing the many-ness of all the entities.[3] At the breakable chain level a cardinal-to-count transition for the first addend enables a child to count on by moving from the cardinal meaning of the first addend (*eight* in Figure 11-2) to the count meaning as paired with the last entity in the first addend and then continuing to count the entities representing the second addend. A count-to-cardinal transition at the end of the sum count up to thirteen enables the thirteen to refer to the cardinality of all of the entities (that is, to the sum). At the numerable chain level no entities need to be present. The same transitions occur, but now the cardinal situations are represented not by sets of entities but by sets of number words.

The evidence supports the developmental progression up to this level. We propose in chapter 9 a fourth postconservation stage of truly numerical counting (see the discussion there with respect to Piaget's statements) and also

---

[3] Resnick's characterization of the preschooler's representation of number as a mental number line (1983, p. 110) is roughly similar to the unbreakable list level. However, what is described by the term mental number *line* is actually a mental number-word *sequence* such as discussed here. A number *line* is a measure model in which numbers are represented by *lengths* on the line, such as by Cuisenaire rods. Number words are discrete entities, not lengths.

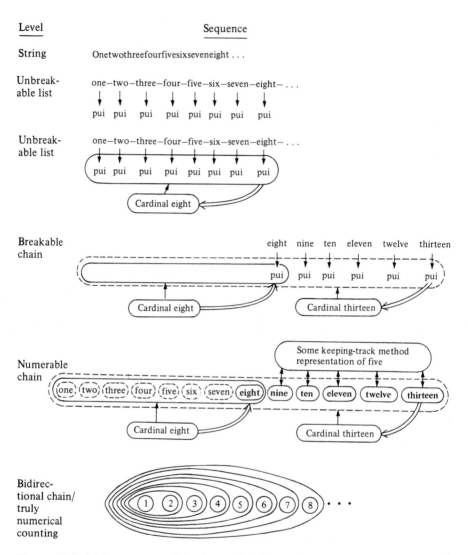

Figure 11-2. Major aspects of the increasing integration of sequence, count, and cardinal meanings.

suggest that there is a bidirectional chain level in the sequence (chapter 2; also Fuson et al., 1982). There are several aspects of relationships among sequence, counting, and cardinal situations and of relationships between cardinal and ordinal situations that do occur relatively late. We place these all within Figure 11-2 at a single *bidirectional chain-truly numerical counting* level. Research is clearly needed at this level, and such research may find sublevels in which certain aspects in the table occur before others. Ways in which various thinking strategies children use for addition and subtraction

Bidirectional chain/truly numerical counting (*cont.*)

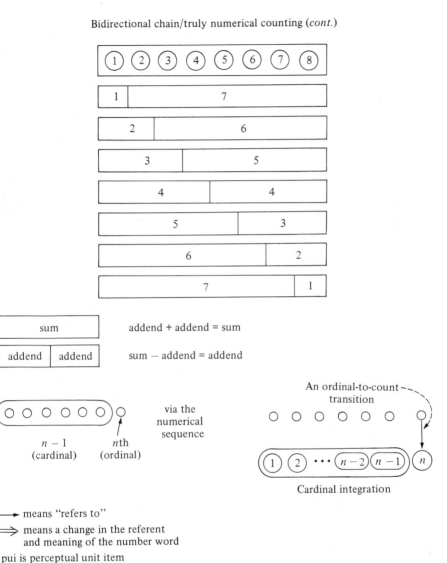

→ means "refers to"

⟹ means a change in the referent
and meaning of the number word

pui is perceptual unit item

Figure 11-2. *Continued*

(see chapter 8) relate to aspects of this level are also of interest and might well be a focus of future research.

One aspect of this truly numerical counting level is that the sequence is both seriated and embedded. Because each word of the sequence is now an ideal identical iterable *one*, and because each word is now both a sequence word and a cardinal word (that is, it can refer to all of the words up to and including itself), each next word represents a cardinal number that is one larger than (using the cardinal as well as the sequence meaning) the earlier word. This cardinalized sequence thus displays both class inclusion (the embeddedness of each cardinal number within the next) and seriation. These were the requirements of a truly operational cardinal number for Piaget (1941/1965). The child at this level then is capable of the progressive summation of sequence-counting-cardinal words.[4] The conceptual operation of numerical equivalence also enables any given cardinal number to be seen as composed of all possible combinations of smaller numbers and as decomposable into all such possible combinations. The sum of two numbers is now also related to its two addends within a triplet addend-addend-sum structure such that knowing any two of the numbers will yield the third, either via addition (addend + addend = sum) or via subtraction (sum − addend = addend). Finally, cardinal and ordinal situations are related via the embedded numerical sequence so that a child knows that there are $n - 1$ entities in the cardinal set preceding the nth ordinal entity. This is first accomplished by an ordinal-to-count transition from the nth ordinal entity to the sequence n, which is now a cardinal as well as a sequence n for the child and is known to have $n - 1$ entities before the n. For example in Piaget's staircase problem, for a doll standing on the eighth stair a child could make a cardinal integration of the stairs preceding the nth stair and use the backward chain to know that the cardinality of those stairs would be the sequence word before n, that is, would be $n - 1$.

Brainerd (1973, 1979b) presented a theory of children's understanding of number in which ordination preceded cardination. Ordination was the internal representation of transitive asymmetric relations, while cardination required the use of correspondences to establish numerical equivalence. Tasks measuring ordination were found to be much easier than those measuring cardination, and an argument was made that axiomatizations of set theory in which cardinal number was primary were problematic, whereas those in which ordinal number was primary were not problematic. It was concluded that ordinal number rather than cardinal number was the child's earliest notion of number. This theory did provide a useful focus on the importance of linear orderings (transitive asymmetric relations), but both bases of its conclusions are actually problematic. Evidence from Baroody (1982) indicates that the cardination task was so difficult that even some adults have trouble with it; Kingma and Roelinga (1984) demonstrated that one can change the order among seriation, ordinal correspondence, and cardination by varying the processing load of the different tasks; and Michie (1985) used tasks equated on other dimensions to measure understanding of cardinal number and ordinal number situations and found that children

---

[4] The term progressive summation is taken from Saxe (1982). He defined counting as *the progressive summation of correspondences*. However, a progressive summation that involves representing the correspondences involved in the activity of counting seems to us to be an even more abstract notion than the progressive summation of sequence-count-cardinal words and therefore would occur even later than this.

understood cardinal number first. With respect to set theory, the various axiomatizations of set theory actually all permit the construction of the natural numbers and all permit cardinal and ordinal numbers to be derived.[5] Many aspects of Brainerd's arguments actually apply to sequence and counting situations, as we have discussed them here. In that sense understanding of certain aspects of these situations does seem to precede understanding of related aspects of cardinal situations. Sequence and counting play especially key roles in addition and subtraction cardinal operations.

We have sketched developmental sequences within sequence, counting, and cardinal situations and indicated how these become increasingly integrated over the age span 2 through 8. Many specific questions remain unanswered about these developmental sequences, and especially about their relationships to each other. One of the major unanswered kinds of questions concerns the extent to which progression along these developmental sequences is due to experience and practice with sequence, counting, and cardinal situations versus simple maturation. As in most areas, the answer is undoubtedly that a mixture of these is involved. However, the work of Case indicates that experience and practice are crucially important and can change children's level of performing quite considerably. The basic argument is that practice leads to increased automatization, which leaves more processing space for noncounting aspects of a task. Results of Case et al. (1979) indicate that the automaticity of the number-word sequence can affect the difficulty of the counting task in which it is used, and that considerable practice in counting can increase the performance of 4-year-olds so that it is like that of the 6-year-olds. Likewise, developmentally appropriate training in quantification seems to increase the performance of lower-class 4½-year-olds on tests of scientific and practical reasoning tasks to the level of normal 6-year-olds (Case & Sandieson, 1986, 1987).

The kind of conceptual analysis carried out in chapters 7 through 9 may seem quite abstract and have clearer implications for the cognitive development than for the education of young children. However, this approach has already yielded a highly effective instructional method for the addition and subtraction of single-digit cardinal numbers. An initial conceptual analysis of what young children must come to understand in order to count on (Fuson, 1982a, 1982b) was followed by assessing whether these understandings differentiated children who could count on from those who still counted all and whether teaching counting-all children these understandings would lead to counting on (Secada, et al., 1983). This was followed by classroom level

---

[5] In particular even in Russell's system (Russell, 1903; 1919; Whitehead & Russell, 1910–13) the Peano axioms are derivable, and thus in Brainerd's (1979b) terms the ordinals can be derived from the cardinals. Furthermore, Peano's axioms do not define the ordinal numbers; they define a structure that can be satisfied by the ordinal numbers or by the cardinals. Finally, the paradoxes discussed by Brainerd apply to any naive set theoretical development of the ordinals or cardinals but not to formal set theories.

studies in which teachers did the teaching based on an instructional unit (Fuson & Secada, 1986) and by an extension of counting on for addition to counting up for subtraction (Fuson, 1984; Fuson, 1986b, Fuson & Willis, in press). The instructional units followed the normal developmental sequence of understandings except that a more efficient one-handed method of keeping track was taught for sequence counting on and counting up. This method of adding and subtracting single-digit numbers was then efficient enough to be used in the multidigit addition and subtraction algorithms, which could be taught to second graders of all ability levels and to high ability first graders because one did not have to wait until they had memorized their facts (Fuson, 1986a; 1987). These instructional units were demonstrated to be effective when used by classroom teachers with a range of student ability and to accelerate the learning of addition and subtraction by 2 to 3 years (cf. Fuson, Stigler, & Bartsch, in press). Thus, the conceptual analysis of children's understandings can have important educational results. A second obvious result of the developmental sequences in children's representational abilities presented here is that young children who can represent cardinal situations only with perceptual unit items will need to be provided with entities for cardinal addition and subtraction. They simply cannot represent or understand cardinal addition and subtraction without such representations.

We have been struck in all of our number work by how wide the age span is for correct performance on any task. There is frequently a span of as much as 1½ or 2 years in the age at which children respond correctly to some number task. This means that there is a very considerable span at school entry in the experiences and abilities of children. More use of "Sesame Street" by parents in all homes might help to close this gap. The program provides experiences of direct teaching of the number-word sequence, the symbol–number-word connection, and the meaning of addition and subtraction. Learning the first two requires considerable and repeated input; television is ideal for this, especially for parents who are very busy or under stress or for other reasons are less likely to provide such experience to their young child. Meanings of addition and subtraction can also be conveyed well on television, both by visual experiences over time and in the interactions among people on the ("Sesame") street. "Sesame Street" also provides certain gamelike formats, which children then carry into their own activities (see the diary entries in Tables 1-2 and 1-3 concerning "Sesame Street" activities). Such child-initiated activities then may elicit interaction from parents who ordinarily would not provide number-word experiences for their children. Progression through the levels in Table 11-1 takes several years and requires a very considerable amount of practice counting in cardinal situations, experiences that must be provided in the home and in schools and preschools.

In summary, over the age span from age 2 through 8, children come to understand increasingly complex relationships among the mathematically different situations in which number words are used. They gain a considerable amount of knowledge concerning different specific situations within each kind of situation. Larger and larger number words are learned. Important changes occur in children's conceptualizations of the sequence, counting, and cardinal situations. Increasingly abstract and complex conceptual units are used in these situations. The relationships among sequence, counting, and cardinal situations become closer and more automatic until finally these become integrated within the number-word sequence itself. At this level the number-word sequence is a seriated, embedded, unitized cardinalized, truly numerical sequence.

References

Acredolo, C. (1982). Conservation-nonconservation: Alternative explanations. In C.J. Brainerd (Ed.), *Progress in cognitive development research: Vol. 1. Children's logical and mathematical cognition* (pp. 1–31). New York: Springer-Verlag.

Ashcraft, M. H., & Fierman, B. A. (1982). Mental addition in third, fourth, and sixth graders. *Journal of Experimental Child Psychology, 33*, 216–234.

Ashcraft, M. H., & Stazyk, E. H. (1981). Mental addition: A test of three verification models. *Memory & Cognition, 9*, 185–196.

Avesar, C., & Dickerson, D. J. (in press). Children's judgments of relative number by one to one correspondence: A planning perspective. *Journal of Experimental Child Psychology.*

Baron, J., Lawson, G., & Siegel, L. S. (1975). Effects of training and set size on children's judgments of number and length. *Developmental Psychology, 11*, 583–588.

Baroody, A. J. (1982). Evaluating the validity of Brainerd's cardinality task. *Child Study Journal, 12*, 79–87.

Baroody, A. J. (1983). The development of procedural knowledge: An alternative explanation for chronometric trends of mental arithmetic. *Developmental Review, 3*, 225–230.

Baroody, A. J. (1984). Children's difficulties in subtraction: Some causes and questions. *Journal for Research in Mathematics Education, 15*, 203–213.

Baroody, A. J. (1986a). Basic counting principles used by mentally retarded children. *Journal for Research in Mathematics Education, 17*, 382–389.

Baroody, A. J. (1986b). Counting ability of moderately and mildly handicapped children. *Education and Training of the Mentally Retarded, 21*, 289–300.

Baroody, A. J. (1987a) *Children's mathematical thinking: A developmental framework for preschool, primary, and special education teachers.* New York: Teachers

College Press.

Baroody, A. J. (1987b). The development of counting strategies for single-digit addition. *Journal for Research in Mathematics Education, 18*, 141–157.

Baroody, A. J., & Ginsburg, H. P. (1983). The effects of instruction on children's understanding of the "equals" sign. *The Elementary School Journal, 84*, 199–212.

Baroody, A. J., & Ginsburg, H. P. (1984, April). *TMR and EMR children's ability to learn counting skills and principles.* Paper presented at the annual meeting of the American Educational Research Association, New Orleans.

Baroody, A. J., & Ginsburg, H. P. (1986). The relationship between initial meaningful and mechanical knowledge of arithmetic. In J. Hiebert (Ed.), *Conceptual and procedural knowledge: The case of mathematics* (pp. 75–112). Hillsdale, NJ: Lawrence Erlbaum.

Baroody, A. J., Ginsburg, H. P., & Waxman, B. (1983). Children's use of mathematical structure. *Journal of Research in Mathematics Education, 14*, 156–168.

Baroody, A. J., & Price, J. (1983). The development of the number-word sequence in the counting of three-year-olds. *Journal for Research in Mathematics Education, 14*, 361–368.

Bebout, H. C. (1986). First-graders' levels of verbal problem performance. In *Proceedings of the Tenth International Conference on the Psychology of Mathematics Education* (pp. 1–6). London: University of London Institute of Education.

Beckwith, M., & Restle, F. (1966). Processes of enumeration. *Psychological Review, 73*, 437–444.

Behr, M., Erlwanger, S., & Nichols, E. (1980). How children view the equals sign. *Mathematics Teaching, 92*, 13–15.

Beilin, H. (1969). Stimulus and cognitive transformation in conservation. In D. Elkind & J. H. Flavell (Eds.), *Studies in cognitive development: Essays in honor of Jean Piaget* (pp. 409–438). New York: Oxford University Press.

Beilin, H. (1975). *The child psychology series: Experimental and theoretical analyses of child behavior. Studies in the cognitive basis of language development.* New York: Academic Press.

Bell, M. S., & Burns, J. (1981a). *Counting, numeration, and arithmetic capabilities of primary school children.* Proposal submitted to National Science Foundation.

Bell, M. S., & Burns, J. (1981b). [Primary school children's performance on counting, numeration, and arithmetic tasks.] Unpublished raw data.

Bell, M. S., Fuson, K. C., & Lesh, R. A. (1976). *Algebraic and arithmetic structures: A concrete approach for elementary school teachers.* New York: The Free Press.

Blevins, B., Mace, P. G., Cooper, R. G., Starkey, P., & Leitner, E. (1981, April). *What do children know about addition and subtraction?* Paper presented at the biennial meeting of the Society for Research in Child Development, Boston.

Blevins-Knabe, B., Cooper, R. G., Starkey, P., Mace, P. G., & Leitner, E. (1987). Preschoolers sometimes know less than we think: The use of quantifiers to solve addition and subtraction tasks. *Bulletin of the Psychonomic Society, 25*, 31–34.

Botvin, G. J., & Murray, F. B. (1975). The efficacy of peer modelling and social conflict in the acquisition of conservation. *Child Development, 46*, 796–799.

Brainerd, C. J. (1973). Mathematical and behavioral foundations of number. *Journal of General Psychology, 88*, 221–281.

Brainerd, C. J. (1977). Feedback, rule knowledge, and conservation learning. *Child Development, 48*, 404–411.

Brainerd, C. J. (1979a). Markovian interpretations of conservation learning. *Psychological Review, 86,* 181–213.

Brainerd, C. J. (1979b). *The origins of the number concept.* New York: Praeger.

Brainerd, C. J., & Hooper, F. H. (1975). A methodological analysis of developmental studies of identity conservation and equivalence conservation. *Psycyhological Bulletin, 82,* 725–737.

Brainerd, C. J., & Hooper, F. H. (1978). More on the identity-equivalence sequences: An update and some replies to Miller. *Psychological Bulletin, 85,* 70–75.

Brainerd, C. J. & Kingma, J. (1984). Do children have to remember to reason? A fuzzy-trace theory of transitivity development. *Developmental Review, 4,* 311–377.

Briars, D. J., & Fuson, K. C. (1979). [Developmental changes in spatial strategies for remembering already counted objects.] Unpublished raw data.

Briars, D. J., & Fuson, K. C. (1980). [Developmental changes in the interpretation of getting two different count words for the same set of objects.] Unpublished raw data.

Briars, D. J., & Larkin, J. H. (1984). An integrated model of skills in solving elementary word problems. *Cognition and Instruction, 1,* 245–296.

Briars, D. J., & Siegler, R. S. (1984). A featural analysis of preschooler's counting knowledge. *Developmental Psychology, 20,* 607–618.

Bruner, J. S., Olver, R.R., & Greenfield, P. M. (1966). *Studies in cognitive growth.* New York: John Wiley & Sons.

Brush, L. R. (1978). Preschool children's knowledge of addition and subtraction. *Journal for Research in Mathematics Education, 9,* 44–54.

Bryant, P. E. (1974). *Perception and understanding of young children: An experimental approach.* New York: Basic Books.

Carpenter, T. P. (1975). Measurement concepts of first- and second-grade students. *Journal for Research in Mathematics Education, 6,* 3–14.

Carpenter, T. P., Bebout, H. C., & Moser, J. M. (1985, March). *The representation of basic addition and subtraction word problems.* Paper presented at the annual meeting of the American Educational Research Association, Chicago, IL.

Carpenter, T. P., & Moser, J. M. (1983a). The acquisition of addition and subtraction concepts. In R. Lesh & M. Landau (Eds.), *Acquisition of Mathematics: Concepts and Processes* (pp. 7–44). New York: Academic Press.

Carpenter, T. P., & Moser, J. M. (1983b). *Addition and subtraction questions: How they develop* (project paper). Madison: Wisconsin Center for Education Research.

Carpenter, T. P., & Moser, J. M. (1984). The acquisition of addition and subtraction concepts in grades one through three. *Journal for Research in Mathematics Education, 15,* 179–202.

Case, R. (1985a). A developmentally based approach to the problem of instructional design. In S. F. Chipman, J. W. Segal, & R. Glaser (Eds.), *Thinking and learning skills: Vol. 2. Research and open questions* (pp. 545–562). Hillsdale, NJ: Lawrence Erlbaum Associates.

Case, R. (1985b). *Intellectual development: Birth to adulthood.* Orlando, FL: Academic Press, Inc.

Case, R., Kurland, M., & Daneman, M. (1979, March). *Operational efficiency and the growth of M-space.* Paper presented at the biennial meeting of the Society for Research in Child Development, San Francisco.

Case, R., & Sandieson, R. (1986). *Horizontal and vertical enrichment: A developmental approach to the teaching of central conceptual skills* (First Year Report).

Ontario Institute for Studies in Education.

Case, R., & Sandieson, R. (1987, May). *A developmental approach to the isolation and teaching of central conceptual skills in middle school mathematics and science.* Paper presented at the National Science Foundation conference on middle grade mathematics, Dekalb, IL.

Chi, M.T.H., & Klahr, D. (1975). Span and rate of apprehension in children and adults. *Journal of Experimental Child Psychology, 19,* 434–439.

Clements, D. H. (1984). Training effects on the development and generalization of Piagetian logical operations and knowledge of number. *Journal of Educational Psychology, 76,* 766–776.

Cobb, P. (1985, April). *Children's concepts of addition and subtraction: From number to part-whole.* Paper presented at the annual meeting of the American Educational Research Association, Chicago.

Cobb, P. (1986, April). *Counting types and word problems.* Paper presented at the annual meeting of the American Educational Research Association, San Francisco.

Cobb, P. (1987). An analysis of three models of early number development. *Journal of Research in Mathematics Education, 18,* 163–179.

Comiti, C., Bessot, A., & Pariselle, C. (1980). Analyse de comportements d'élèves du cours préparatoire confrontés à une tâche de construction d'un ensemble équipotent à un ensemble donné. *Recherches en didactique des mathématiques. 1,* 171–217.

Cooper, R. G. (1984). Early number development: Discovering number space with addition and subtraction. In C. Sophian (Ed.), *Origins of cognitive skills* (pp. 157–192). Hillsdale, NJ: Lawrence Erlbaum.

Cowan, R. (1979a). Performance in number conservation tasks as a function of the number of items. *British Journal of Psychology, 70,* 77–81.

Cowan, R. (1979b). A reappraisal of the relation between performances of quantitative identity and quantitative equivalence conservation tasks. *Journal of Experimental Child Psychology, 28,* 68–80.

Cowan, R. (1984). Children's relative number judgments: One-to-one correspondence, recognition of noncorrespondence, and the influence of cue conflict. *Journal of Experimental Child Psychology, 38,* 515–532.

Cowan, R. (1987). When do children trust counting as a basis for relative number judgments? *Journal of Experimental Child Psychology, 43,* 328–345.

Cuneo, D. O. (1982). Children's judgments of numerical quantity: A new view of early quantification. *Cognitive Psychology, 14,* 13–44.

Davis, H., & Bradford, S. A. (1986). Counting behavior by rats in a simulated natural environment. *Ethology, 73,* 265–280.

Davis, H. & Memmott, J. (1982). Counting behavior in animals: A critical evaluation. *Psychological Bulletin, 92,* 547–571.

Davis, H., & Perusse, R. (1987). *Numerical competence in animals: Definitional issues, current evidence and a new research agenda.* Unpublished manuscript, University of Guelph, Ontario.

Davydov, V. V., & Andronov, V. P. (1981). *Psychological conditions of the origination of ideal actions* (Project Paper 81-2), (English translation), Madison: Wisconsin Research and Development Center for Individualized Schooling, The University of Wisconsin.

De Corte, E., & Verschaffel, L. (1985a). Beginning first graders' initial representation of arithmetic word problems. *Journal of Mathematical Behavior, 1,* 3–21.

De Corte, E., & Verschaffel, L. (1985b, April). *An empirical validation of computer models of children's word problem solving.* Paper presented at the annual meeting of the American Educational Research Association, Chicago.

De Corte, E., & Verschaffel, L. (1985c) Working with simple word problems in early mathematics instruction. In L. Streefland (Ed.), *Proceedings of the Ninth International Conference for the Psychology of Mathematics Education* (pp. 304–309). Utrecht, The Netherlands: State University of Utrecht.

De Corte, E., & Verschaffel, L, & De Win, L. (1985) Influence of rewording verbal problems on children's problem representations and solutions. *Journal of Educational Psychology, 77,* 460–470.

Dienes, Z. P. (1960). *Building up mathematics (4th ed.)* London: Hutchinson Educational, Ltd.

Durkin, K., Shire, B., Riem, R., Crowther, R. D., & Rutter, D. R. (1986). The social and linguistic context of early number word use. *British Journal of Developmental Psychology, 4,* 269–288.

Elkind, D. (1967). Piaget's conservation problems. *Child Development, 38,* 15–27.

Elkind, D., & Schoenfeld, E. (1972). Identity and equivalence conservation at two age levels. *Developmental Psychology, 6,* 529–533.

Frye, D., Braisby, N., Lowe, J., Maroudas, C., & Nicholls, J. (1986). *Young children's understanding of counting and cardinality.* Manuscript submitted for publication.

Fuson, K. C. (1979a, November). *Counting solution procedures in addition and subtraction.* Paper presented at the Wisconsin Wingspread Conference on the Initial Learning of Addition and Subtraction Skills, Racine, WI.

Fuson, K. C. (1979b). The development of self-regulating aspects of speech: A review. In G. Zivin (Ed.), *The development of self-regulation through private speech* (pp. 135–217). New York: John Wiley & Sons.

Fuson, K. C. (1982a). An analysis of the counting-on solution procedure in addition. In T. P. Carpenter, J. M. Moser, & T. A. Romberg (Eds.), *Addition and subtraction: A cognitive perspective* (pp. 67–81). Hillsdale, NJ: Lawrence Erlbaum.

Fuson, K. C. (1982b). *The counting-on solution procedure: Analysis and empirical results.* Unpublished manuscript. Northwestern University.

Fuson, K. C. (1984). More complexities in subtraction. *Journal for Research in Mathematics Education, 15,* 214–225.

Fuson, K. C. (1986a). Roles of representation and verbalization in the teaching of multi-digit addition and subtraction. *European Journal of Psychology of Education, 1,* 35–56.

Fuson, K. C. (1986b). Teaching children to subtract by counting up. *Journal for Research in Mathematics Education, 17,* 172–189.

Fuson, K. C. (1986c, November). Effects of collection terms on class inclusion and on number tasks. Paper presented at the annual meeting of the Psychonomics Society, New Orleans.

Fuson, K. C. (1987, April). *Teaching the general multi-digit addition and subtraction algorithms to first and second graders.* Paper presented at the biennial meeting of the Society for Research in Child Development, Baltimore, Maryland.

Fuson, K. C., & Darling, C. L. (1984). *A study of the effectiveness of the graphics tablet and an Apple lle microcomputer in recording errors in children's counting.* Unpublished manuscript.

Fuson, K. C., & Hall, J. W. (1983). The acquisition of early number word meanings.

In H. Ginsburg (Ed.), *The development of children's mathematical thinking* (pp. 49–107). New York: Academic Press.

Fuson, K. C., Lyons, B. G., Pergament, G. G., Hall, J. W., & Kwon, Y. (in press). Effects of collection terms on class inclusion and on number tasks. *Cognitive Psychology*.

Fuson, K. C., & Mierkiewicz, D. (1980, April). *A detailed analysis of the act of counting*. Paper presented at the annual meeting of the American Educational Research Association, Boston.

Fuson, K. C., Pergament, G. G., & Lyons, B. G. (1985). Collection terms and preschoolers' use of the cardinality rule. *Cognitive Psychology, 17*, 315–323.

Fuson, K. C., Pergament, G. G., Lyons, B. G., & Hall, J. W. (1985). Children's conformity to the cardinality rule as a function of set size and counting accuracy. *Child Development, 56*, 1429–1439.

Fuson, K. C., & Richards, J. (1980, April). *Children's construction of the counting numbers: From a spew to a directional chain*. Paper presented at the annual meeting of the American Educational Research Association, Boston.

Fuson, K. C., Richards, J., & Briars, D. J. (1982). The acquisition and elaboration of the number word sequence. In C. Brainerd (Ed.), *Progress in cognitive development research: Vol 1. Children's logical and mathematical cognition* (pp. 33–92). New York: Springer-Verlag.

Fuson, K. C., & Secada, W. G. (1983). The development of number word sequence skills. In J. Bergeron & N. Herscovics (Eds.), *Proceedings of the Fifth Annual Meeting of the International Group for the Psychology of Mathematics Education* (Vol. 1, pp. 266–274). Montreal: University of Montreal.

Fuson, K. C., & Secada, W. G. (1986). Teaching children to add by counting on with finger patterns. *Cognition and Instruction, 3*, 229–260.

Fuson, K. C., Secada, W. G., & Hall, J. W. (1983). Matching, counting, and conservation of numerical equivalence. *Child Development, 54*, 91–97.

Fuson, K. C., Stigler, J. W., & Bartsch, K. (in press). Grade placement of addition and subtraction topics in China, Japan, the Soviet Union, Taiwan, and the United States. *Journal of Research in Mathematics Education*.

Fuson, K. C., & Willis, G. B. (1986). First and second graders' performance on compare and equalize word problems. In *Proceedings of the Tenth International Conference on the Psychology of Mathematics Education* (pp. 19–24). London: University of London Institute of Education.

Fuson, K. C., & Willis, G. B. (1987). [Teaching addition and subtraction word problems via schematic drawings]. Unpublished raw data.

Fuson, K. C., & Willis, G. B. (in press). Subtracting by counting up: More evidence. *Journal for Research in Mathematics Education*.

Gelman, R. (1969). Conservation acquisition: A problem of learning to attend to relevant attributes. *Journal of Experimental Child Psychology, 7*, 167–187.

Gelman, R. (1972). The nature and development of early number concepts. In H. W. Reese (Ed.), *Advances in child development and behavior* (Vol. 7, pp. 115–167). New York: Academic Press.

Gelman, R. (1982a). Accessing one-to-one correspondence: Still another paper about conservation. *Journal of Psychology, 73*, 209–220.

Gelman, R. (1982b). Basic numerical abilities. In R. J. Sternberg (Ed.), *Advances in the psychology of intelligence* (Vol. 1 pp. 181–205). Hillsdale, N. J.: Lawrence Erlbaum.

Gelman, R., & Baillargeon, R. (1983). A review of some Piagetian concepts. In P. H. Mussen (Ed.), *Handbook of child psychology: Vol. 3. Cognitive Development* (pp. 167–230). New York: John Wiley & Sons, Inc.

Gelman, R., & Gallistel, C. R. (1978). *The child's understanding of number.* Cambridge, MA: Harvard University Press.

Gelman, R., & Meck, E. (1983). Preschoolers' counting: Principles before skill. *Cognition, 13,* 343–359.

Gelman, R., & Meck, E. (1986). The notion of principle: The case of counting. In J. Hiebert (Ed.), *Conceptual and procedural knowledge: The case of mathematics* (pp. 29–57). Hillsdale, NJ: Lawrence Erlbaum.

Gelman, R., Meck, E., & Merkin, S. (1986). Young children's numerical competence. *Cognitive Development, 1,* 1–29.

Ginsburg, H. P. (1977). *Children's arithmetic: The learning process.* New York: D. Van Nostrand.

Ginsburg, H. P., & Russell, R. L. (1981). Social class and racial influences on early mathematical thinking. *Monographs of the Society for Research in Child Development, 46,* (6, Serial No. 193).

Gréco, P. (1962). Quantité et quotité. In P. Gréco & A. Morf (Eds.), *Structures numériques élémentaires: Etudes d'épistémologic génétique* (Vol. 13, pp. 1–70). Paris: Presses Universitaires de France.

Greeno, J. G., Riley, M. S., & Gelman, R. (1984). Conceptual competence and children's counting. *Cognitive Psychology, 16,* 94–143.

Groen, G. J., & Parkman, J. M. (1972). A chronometric analysis of simple addition. *Psychological Review, 79,* 329–343.

Gullen, G. E. (1978). Set comparison tactics and strategies of children in kindergarten, first grade, and second grade. *Journal for Research in Mathematics Education, 9,* 349–360.

Hamann, M. S., & Ashcraft, M. H. (1985). Simple and complex mental addition across development. *Journal of Experimental Child Psychology, 40,* 49–72.

Hatano, G. (1982). Learning to add and subtract: A Japanese perspective. In T. P. Carpenter, J. M. Moser, & T. A. Romberg (Eds.), *Addition and subtraction: A cognitive perspective* (pp. 211–223). Hillsdale, NJ: Lawrence Erlbaum.

Herscovics, N., Bergeron, J. C., & Bergeron, A. (1986). The kindergartner's perception of the invariance of number under various transformations. In G. Lappan & R. Evan (Eds.), *Proceedings of the eighth annual meeting of the North American chapter of the International Group for the Psychology of Mathematics Education* (pp. 28–34). East Lansing, MI.

Hiebert, J. (1981, April). *Young children's solution processes for verbal addition and subtraction problems: The effect of the position of the unknown set.* Paper presented at the 59th annual meeting of the National Council of the Teachers of Mathematics, St. Louis.

Hodges, R., & French, L. (1987, April). *Classes and collections: Their influence on class-inclusion, cardinality, and number conservation.* Paper presented at the annual meeting of the American Educational Research Association, Washington, DC.

Houlihan, D. M., & Ginsburg, H. P. (1981). The addition methods of first- and second-grade children. *Journal for Research in Mathematics Education, 12,* 95–106.

Hudson, T. (1983). Correspondences and numerical differences between joint sets.

Child Development, 54, 84–90.

Hudson, M., Guthrie, K. H., & Santilli, N. R. (1982). The use of linguistic and non-linguistic strategies in kindergarteners' interpretations of 'more' and 'less.' *Journal of Child Language, 9*, 125–138.

Jensen, E. M., Reese, E. P., & Reese, T. W. (1950). The subitizing and counting of visually presented fields of dots. *The Journal of Psychology, 30*, 363–392.

Kamii, C. K. (1985). *Young children reinvent arithmetic: Implications of Piaget's theory.* New York: Teachers College Press.

Katz, H., & Beilin, H. (1976). A test of Bryant's claims concerning the young child's understanding of quantitative invariance. *Child Development, 47*, 877–880.

Kaufman, E. L., Lord, M. W., Reese, T. W., & Volkmann, J. (1949). The discrimination of visual number. *American Journal of Psychology, 62*, 498–525.

Kaye, D. B., Post, T. A., Hall, Y. C., & Dineen, J. T. (1986). Emergence of information-retrieval strategies in numerical cognition: A developmental study. *Cognition and Instruction, 3*, 127–150.

Kingma, J., & Roelinga, U. (1984). Task sensitivity and the sequence of development in seriation, ordinal correspondence, and cardination. *Genetic Psychology Monographs, 110*, 181–205.

Kintsch, W., & Greeno, J. G. (1985). Understanding and solving word arithmetic problems. *Psychological Review, 92*, 109–129.

Klahr, D. (1984). Transition processes in quantitative development. In R. J. Sternberg (Ed.), *Mechanisms of cognitive development* (pp. 101–139). New York: W. H. Freeman.

Klahr, D., & Wallace, J. G. (1973). The role of quantification operators in the development of conservation of quantity. *Cognitive Psychology, 4*, 301–327.

Klahr, D., & Wallace, J. G. (1976). *Cognitive development: An information processing view.* Hillsdale, NJ: Lawrence Erlbaum.

Kwon, Y. (1986). *Correspondence errors in children's counting.* Unpublished manuscript, Northwestern University.

LaPointe, K., & O'Donnell, J. P. (1974). Number conservation in children below age six: Its relationship to age, perceptual dimensions, and language comprehension. *Developmental Psychology, 10*, 422–428.

Lawson, G., Baron, J., & Siegel, L. (1974). The role of number and length cues in children's quantitative judgments. *Child Development, 45*, 731–736.

Lieberthal, E. M. (1979). *Complete book of fingermath.* New York: McGraw-Hill.

Luria, A. R. (1959). The directive function of speech in development and dissolution. Part 1: Development of the directive function of speech in early childhood. *Word, 15*, 341–351.

Luria, A. R. (1961). *The role of speech in the regulation of normal and abnormal behaviour* (J. Tizard, Ed.), Oxford: Pergamon.

Mandler, G., & Shebo, B. J. (1982). Subitizing: An analysis of its component processes. *Journal of Experimental Psychology: General, 111*, 1–22.

Markman, E. M. (1979). Classes and collections: Conceptual organization and numerical abilities. *Cognitive Psychology, 1*, 395–411.

Matsuzawa, T. (1985). Use of numbers by a chimpanzee. *Nature, 315*, 57–59.

McCloskey, M., Sokol, S. M., & Goodman, R. A. (1986). Cognitive processes in verbal-number production: Inferences from the performance of brain-damaged subjects. *Journal of Experimental Psychology: General, 115*, 307–330.

McGarrigle, J., & Donaldson, M. (1975). Conservation accidents. *Cognition, 3*, 314–350.

McLaughlin, J. A. (1981). Development of children's ability to judge relative numerosity. *Journal of Experimental Child Psychology, 31*, 103–114.

Melnick, G. I. (1973). A mechanism for transition of concrete to abstract cognitive processes. *Child Development, 44*, 599–605.

Michie, S. (1984a). Number understanding in preschool children. *British Journal of Educational Psychology, 54*, 245–253.

Michie, S. (1984b). Why preschoolers are reluctant to count spontaneously. *British Journal of Developmental Psychology, 2*, 347–358.

Michie, S. (1985). Development of absolute and relative concepts of number in pre-school children. *Developmental Psychology, 21*, 247–252.

Millar, C., & Mackay, C. K. (1978). Conflict between cues in number conservation tasks. *British Journal of Educational Psychology, 50*, 188–191.

Miller, K. (1984). Child as the measurer of all things: Measurement procedures and the development of quantitative concepts. In C. Sophian (Ed.), *Origins of cognitive skills* (pp. 193–288). Hillsdale, NJ: Lawrence Erlbaum.

Miller, K., & Gelman, R. (1983). The child's representation of number: A multi-dimensional scaling analysis. *Child Development, 54*, 1470–1479.

Miller, K., & Stigler, J. W. (1987). Counting in Chinese: Cultural variation in a basic cognitive skill. *Cognitive Development, 2*, 279–305.

Miller, P. H. (1978). Stimulus variables in conservation: An alternative approach to assessment. *Merrill-Palmer Quarterly, 24*, 141–160.

Miller, P. H., Heldmeyer, K. H., & Miller, S. A. (1975). Facilitation of conservation of number in young children. *Developmental Psychology, 11*, 253.

Miller, P. H., & Heller, K. A. (1976). Facilitation of attention to number and con-servation of number. *Journal of Experimental Child Psychology, 22*, 454–467.

Miller, S. A. (1977). A disconfirmation of the quantitive identity-quantitative equiv-alence sequence. *Journal of Experimental Child Psychology, 24*, 180–189.

Miura, I. T. (1987). Mathematics achievement as a function of language. *Journal of Educational Psychology, 79*, 79–82.

Modgil, S., & Modgil, C. (1976). *Piagetian research: Compilation and commentary* (Vols. 2, 4, 7, 8, 12). London: NEFR Publishing.

Moore, C., & Frye, D. (1986a). Context, conservation and the meanings of 'more.' *British Journal of Developmental Psychology, 4*, 169–178.

Moore, C., & Frye, D. (1986b). The effect of experimenter's intention on the child's understanding of conservation. *Cognition, 22*, 283–298.

Murray, F. B. (1981). The conservation paradigm: The conservation of conservation research. In I. E. Sigel, D. M. Brodzinsky, & R. M. Golinkoff (Eds.), *New directions in Piagetian theory and practice*. Hillsdale, NJ: Lawrence Erlbaum.

Nesher, P. (1980). The stereotyped nature of school word problems. *For the Learning of Mathematics, 1*, 41–48.

Pepperberg, J. (1987). Evidence for conceptual quantitative abilities in the African Grey Parrot: Labelling of cardinal sets. *Ethology, 75*, 37–61.

Pergament, G. G., & Fuson, K. C. (1982). Effects of size of set, homogeneity of objects, and collection nouns on children's accurate counting and use of the car-dinality rule. In S. Wagner (Ed.), *Proceedings of the Sixth Annual Conference for the Psychology of Mathematics Education—North America* (pp. 78–84). Athens, GA: University of Georgia.

Piaget, J. (1965). *The child's conception of number*. New York: W. W. Norton. (Original work published 1941).

Piaget, J. (1967). Cognitions and conservations: Two views. *Contemporary Psychol-*

ogy, 12, 532–533.

Piaget, J. (1968a). *On the development of memory and identity*, Barre, MA: Clark University Press.

Piaget, J. (1968b). Quantification, conservation, and nativism. *Science, 162*, 976–979.

Piaget, J. (1977). Some recent research and its link with a new theory of groupings and conservations based on commutability. In R. W. Rieber & K. Salzinger (Eds.), *The roots of American psychology: Historical influence and implications for the future. Annals of the New York Academy of Sciences, 291*, 350–357.

Piaget, J. (1978). *Recherches sur la généralisation* (Etudes d'épistémologie génétique, XXXVI). Paris, Presses Universitaires de France.

Piaget, J. (1979). Correspondences and transformations. In Frank B. Murray (Ed.), *The impact of Piagetian theory* (pp. 17–28). Baltimore: University Park Press.

Pollio, H. R., & Whitacre, J. D. (1970). Some observations on the use of natural numbers by preschool children. *Perceptual and Motor Skills, 30*, 167–174.

Potter, M. C., & Levy, E. I. (1968). Spatial enumeration without counting. *Child Development, 39*, 265–273.

Pringle, R., & Hennessey, A. (1987). *The role of size and density in number equivalence judgment: Chronometric and developmental analyses.* Manuscript submitted for publication.

Pufall, P. B., & Shaw, R. E. (1972). Precocious thoughts on number: The long and the short of it. *Developmental Psychology, 7*, 62–69.

Rathmell, E. C. (1978). Using thinking strategies to teach the basic facts. In M. Suydam & R. Reys (Eds.), *Developing computational skills: 1978 Yearbook of the National Council of Teachers of Mathematics* (pp. 13–38). Reston, VA: NCTM.

Rathmell, E. C. (1986). Helping children learn to solve story problems. In A. Zollman, W. Speer, & J. Meyer (Eds.), *The Fifth Mathematics Methods Conference Papers* (pp. 101–109). Bowling Green, OH: Bowling Green State University.

Resnick, L. B. (1983). A developmental theory of number understanding. In H. P. Ginsburg (Ed.), *The development of mathematical thinking* (pp. 109–151). New York: Academic Press.

Resnick, L. B., & Neches, R. (1984). Factors affecting individual differences in learning ability. In R. Sternberg (Ed.), *Advances in the psychology of human intelligence* (Vol. 2, pp. 275–323). Hillsdale, NJ: Lawrence Erlbaum.

Riley, M. S., Greeno, J. G., & Heller, J. I. (1983). Development of children's problem-solving ability in arithmetic. In H. Ginsburg (Ed.), *The development of mathematical thinking* (pp. 153–196). New York: Academic Press.

Rogoff, B., & Wertsch, J. V. (1984). *Children's learning in the zone of proximal development: New directions for child development.* San Francisco: Jossey-Bass.

Russac, R. J. (1978). The relation between two strategies of cardinal number: Correspondence and counting. *Child Development, 49*, 728–735.

Russell, B. (1903). *The principles of mathematics.* Cambridge, England: Cambridge University Press.

Russell, B. (1919). *Introduction to mathematical philosophy.* London: Allen and Unwin.

Saxe, G. B. (1977). A developmental analysis of notational counting. *Child Development, 48*, 1512–1520.

Saxe, G. B. (1979). Developmental relations between notational counting and number conservation. *Child Development, 50*, 180–187.

Saxe, G. B. (1982). Culture and the development of numerical cognition: Studies among the Oksapmin of Papua New Guinea. In C. J. Brainerd (Ed.), *Progress in cognitive development research: Vol. 1. Children's logical and mathematical cognition* (pp. 157–176). New York: Springer-Verlag.

Saxe, G. B., Guberman, S. R., & Gearhart, M. (in press). Social and developmental processes in children's understanding of number. *Monographs of the Society for Research in Child Development.*

Saxe, G. B., & Kaplan, R. (1981). Gesture in early counting: A developmental analysis. *Perceptual and Motor Skills, 53*, 851–854.

Saxe, G. B., Sadeghpour, M., & Sicilian, S. (in press). Developmental differences in children's understanding of number word conventions. *Journal for Research in Mathematics Education.*

Schaeffer, B., Eggleston, V. H., & Scott, J. L. (1974). Number development in young children. *Cognitive Psychology, 6*, 357–379.

Schonfeld, I. S. (1986). The Genevan and Cattell-Horn conceptions of intelligence compared: Early implementation of numerical solution aids: *Developmental Psychology, 22*, 204–212.

Secada, W. G. (1982, March). *The use of counting for subtraction.* Paper presented at the annual meeting of the American Educational Research Association, New York.

Secada, W. G. (1984). *Counting in sign: The number string, accuracy and use.* Unpublished doctoral dissertation, Northwestern University.

Secada, W. G., Fuson, K. C., & Hall, J. W. (1983). The transition from counting-all to counting-on in addition. *Journal for Research in Mathematics Education, 14*, 47–57.

Siegel, A. W., Goldsmith, L. T., & Madson, C. R. (1982). Skill in estimation problems of extent and numerosity. *Journal for Research in Mathematics Education, 13*, 211–232.

Siegel, L. S. (1977). The cognitive basis of the comprehension and production of relational terminology. *Journal of Experimental Child Psychology, 24*, 40–52.

Siegel, L. S. (1978). The relationship of langauge and thought in the preoperational child: A reconsideration of nonverbal alternatives to Piagetian Tasks. In L. S. Siegel & C. J. Brainerd (Eds.), *Alternatives to Piaget: Critical essays on the theory* (pp. 43–63). New York: Academic Press.

Siegel, L. S. (1982). The development of quantity concepts: Perceptual and linguistic factors. In C. J. Brainerd (Ed.), *Progress in cognitive development research: Vol. 1. Children's logical and mathematical cognition* (pp. 123–155). New York: Springer-Verlag.

Siegel, L. S., & Brainerd, C. J. (1978). *Alternatives to Piaget: Critical essays on the theory.* New York: Academic Press.

Siegel, L. S., & Goldstein, A. G. (1969). Conservation of number in young children: Recency versus relational response strategies. *Developmental Psychology, 2*, 128–130.

Siegler, R. S. (1981). Developmental sequences within and between concepts. *Monographs of the Society for Research in Child Development, 46* (2, Serial No. 189).

Siegler, R. S. (in press). The perils of averaging data over strategies: An example from children's addition. *Journal of Experimental Psychology.*

Siegler, R. S., & Campbell, J. (in press). Diagnosing individual differences in strategy choice procedures. In N. Frederiksen (Ed.), *Diagnostic monitoring of knowledge and skill acquisition.* Hillsdale, N.J.: Lawrence Erlbaum.

Siegler, R. S., & Robinson, M. (1982). The development of numerical understandings. In H. W. Reese & L. P. Lipsitt (Eds.), *Advances in child development and behavior* (Vol. 16, pp. 242–312). New York: Academic Press.

Siegler, R. S., & Shrager, J. (1984). Strategy choices in addition and subtraction. How do children know what to do. In C. Sophian (Ed.), *Origins of cognitive skills* (pp. 229–293). Hillsdale, NJ: Lawrence Erlbaum.

Silverman, I. W., & Briga, J. (1981). By what processes do young children solve small number conservation problems? *Journal of Experimental Child Psychology, 32*, 115–126.

Silverman, I. W., & Rose, A. P. (1982). Compensation and conservation. *Psychological Bulletin, 91*, 80–101.

Smither, S. J., Smiley, S. S., & Rees, R. (1974). The use of perceptual cues for number judgment by young children. *Child Development, 45*, 693–699.

Starkey, P. (1981). Young children's performance in number conservation tasks: Evidence for a hierarchy of strategies. *Journal of Genetic Psychology, 138*, 103–110.

Starkey, P. (1987, April). *Early arithmetic competencies.* Paper presented at the biennial meeting of the Society for Research in Child Development, Baltimore, MD.

Starkey, P., & Cooper, R. G. (1980). Perception of numbers by human infants. *Science, 210*, 1033–1035.

Starkey, P., & Gelman, R. (1982). The development of addition and subtraction abilities prior to formal schooling in arithmetic. In T. P. Carpenter, J. M. Moser, & T. A. Romberg (Eds.), *Addition and subtraction: A cognitive perspective.* (pp. 99–116). Hillsdale, NJ: Lawrence Erlbaum.

Starkey, P., Spelke, E., & Gelman, R. (1983). Detection of intermodel numerical correspondences by human infants. *Science, 222*, 179.

Steffe, L. P., Cobb, P., & von Glasersfeld, E. (in press). *Construction of arithmetical meanings and strategies.* New York: Springer-Verlag.

Steffe, L. P., von Glasersfeld, E., Richards, J., & Cobb, P. (1983). *Children's counting types: Philosophy, theory, and application.* New York: Praeger Scientific.

Steinberg, R. M. (1984). A teaching experiment of the learning of addition and subtraction facts (Doctoral dissertation. University of Wisconsin-Madison, 1983). *Dissertation Abstracts International, 44*, 3313A.

Steinberg, R. M., (1985). Instruction on derived facts strategies in addition and subtraction. *Journal for Research in Mathematics Education, 16*, 337–355.

Stigler, J. W., Fuson, K. C., Ham, M., & Kim, M. S. (1986). An analysis of addition and subtraction word problems in American and Soviet elementary mathematics textbooks. *Cognition and Instruction, 3*, 153–171.

Strauss, M. S., & Curtis, L. E. (1984). Development of numerical concepts in infancy. In C. Sophian (Ed.), *Origins of cognitive skills* (pp. 131–155). Hillsdale, NJ: Lawrence Erlbaum.

Tamburino, J. L. (1980). *An analysis of the modelling processes used by kindergarten children in solving simple addition and subtraction story problems.* Unpublished master's thesis, University of Pittsburgh.

Thomas, R. K., Fowlkes, D., & Vickery, J. D. (1980). Conceptual numerousness judgments by squirrel monkeys. *American Journal of Psychology, 93*, 247–257.

Thornton, C. A. (1978). Emphasizing thinking strategies in basic fact instruction. *Journal for Research in Mathematics Education, 9*, 214–227.

Underhill, R. (1984). External retention and transfer effects of special place value curriculum activities. *Focus on Learning Problems in Mathematics*, *1 & 2*, 108–130.

Van Oeffelen, M. P., & Vos, P. G. (1982). Configuration effects on the enumeration of dots: Counting by groups. *Memory and Cognition*, *10*, 396–404.

von Glasersfeld, E. (1982). Subitizing: The role of figural patterns in the development of numerical concepts. *Archives de Psychologie*, *50*, 191–218.

Vygotsky, L. S. (1962). *Thought and language*. E. Hanfmann, & G. Vakar (Eds. and Trans.) Cambridge, MA: MIT Press.

Vygotsky, L. S. (1978). *Mind in society: The development of higher psychological processes*. M. Cole, V. John-Steiner, S. Scribner, & E. Souberman (Eds.). Cambridge, MA: Harvard University Press.

Vygotsky, L. S. (1986). *Thought and language*. A. Kozulin (Ed.). Cambridge, MA: MIT Press.

Wagner, S., & Walters, J. A. (1982). A longitudinal analysis of early number concepts: From numbers to number. In G. Forman (Ed.), *Action and thought* (pp. 137–161). New York: Academic Press.

Wallach, L. (1969). On the bases of conservation. In D. Elkind & J. H. Flavell (Eds.). *Studies in cognitive development: Essays in honor of Jean Piaget* (pp. 191–219). New York: Oxford University Press.

Walters, J. A., & Wagner, S. (1981, April). *The earliest numbers*. Paper presented at the biennial meeting of the Society for Research in Child Development, Boston.

Weiner, S. L. (1974). On the development of more and less. *Journal of Experimental Child Psychology*, *17*, 271–287.

Whitehead, A. N., & Russell, B. (1910–13). *Principia mathematica. Vols. 1–3*. Cambridge, England: Cambridge University Press.

Whiteman, M., & Peisach, E. (1970). Perceptual and sensorimotor supports for conservation tasks. *Developmental Psychology*, *2*, 247–256.

Wilkinson, A. C. (1984). Children's partial knowledge of the cognitive skills of counting. *Cognitive Psychology*, *16*, 28–64.

Willis, G. B., & Fuson, K. C. (1985). Teaching representational schemes for the more difficult addition and subtraction verbal problems. In S. K. Damarin & M. Shelton (Eds.), *Proceedings of the North American Chapter of the International Group for the Psychology of Mathematics Education* (pp. 288–293). Columbus, Ohio.

Willis, G. B., & Fuson, K. C. (1986). *Teaching schematic drawings for the solution of addition and subtraction word problems*. Unpublished manuscript, Northwestern University.

Winer, G. A. (1974). Conservation of different quantities among preschool children. *Child Development*, *45*, 839–842.

Winer, G. A. (1975). Analysis of the relation between conservation of large and small quantities. *Psychological Reports*, *36*, 379–382.

Woods, S. S., Resnick, L. B., & Groen, G. J. (1975). An experimental test of five process models for subtraction. *Journal of Educational Psychology*, *67*, 17–21.

Young, A. W., & McPherson, J. (1976). Ways of making number judgments and children's understanding of quantity relations. *British Journal of Educational Psychology*, *46*, 328–332.

Zivin, G. (1979). *The development of self-regulation through private speech*. New York: John Wiley & Sons, Inc.

Author Index

Subject Index